1st Air Region

2nd Air Region

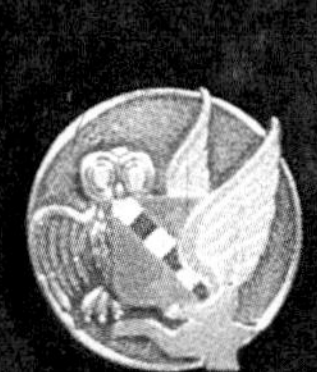

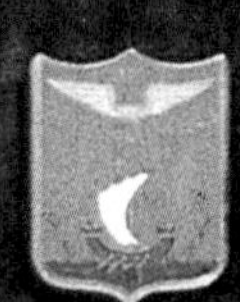

3rd Air Region

4th Air Region

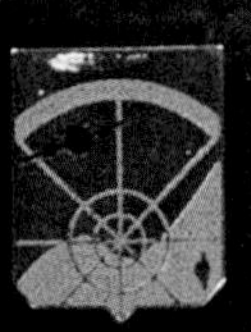

A History of

French Military Aviation

A History of

French Military Aviation

Charles Christienne and Pierre Lissarague
Translated by Francis Kianka

Smithsonian Institution Press *Washington D.C.* *1986*

Originally published as Histoire de l'Aviation Militaire Française

Translated with permission of Charles-Lavauzelle
First printing in English in the United States of America

Library of Congress Cataloging in Publication Data

Christienne, Charles.
A history of French military aviation.

Translation of: Histoire de l'aviation militaire française.
Includes index.
Supt. of Docs. no.: SI 1.2:H62
1. Aeronautics, Military—France—History.
I. Lissarrague, Pierre. II. Title.
UG635.F8C4813 1985 358.4'00944 85-600032
ISBN 0-87474-310-9

The paper in this book meets the guidelines for permanence and durability of the Committee on Production Guidelines for Book Longevity of the Council on Library Resources.

Photo credit: PASM = Air and Space Museum, Paris.

CONTENTS

PART 3 : Between the Wars

PART 4 : The Test of War

PART 5 : Toward Revival

PREFACE

A number of books, articles, and documents have dealt with certain aspects of the French air forces, and there have been some excellent works recounting the evolution of aeronautics around the world. Up to the present, however, there has been no book relating the history of French military aviation. This book is intended to fill that gap.

It was clearly the responsibility of two specialized, official services of the French government, the Musée de l'Air (Air Museum) and the Service Historique de l'Armée de l'Air (Air Force Historical Service), to promote this undertaking. To achieve this goal a number of obstacles had to be avoided beginning with the desire to define an official history. In making use of the public archives kept by the two services or provided by others—the archives of the French National Assembly proved especially valuable for the period between the two world wars—the authors have attempted to treat in a completely independent spirit the problems that often arose and remained unanswered.

It was also necessary to guard against devoting too much space to anecdotal history. This is not intended as contempt for "small-scale history." Based as it is on the aviators' unending reminiscences, such material at times does more than the study of written reports to throw light on the various facets of a particularly complex society. But there was so much to tell, from the Fleurus balloon in 1794 to the Mirage 2000, that it was imperative to go straight to the essentials.

Finally, it was necessary to avoid tiring readers out with too dry a publication. For this reason the authors have abstained from including the mass of footnotes without which a book cannot claim to have scholarly value. (For readers interested in this documentation, all bibliographic data for this history is now available at the Air Force Historical Service.) The intention of the authors has been to reach the largest possible audience. We hope that military aviation buffs will find something in both the text and the illustrations to satisfy their curiosity. It is also our hope that this work will recall to the younger members of the Air Force the heroic deeds of their predecessors. Finally, we believe that as it is presented this book will be an accurate—and necessary—point of departure for all researchers who wish to examine more thoroughly the many points that still remain obscure.

Although we believe that on the whole we have produced a useful work, we are fully conscious of its shortcomings. These are attributable, for the most part, to archival problems. In some cases the records are missing, destroyed in the course of the war or turned over to other services and subsequently lost; in other cases the records are not accessible to the public because of their proximity to us in time. For this reason we have dealt schematically with contemporary Air Force history, limiting ourselves to strictly public sources.

We have put into this book, the result of a joint labor extending over several years, all our knowledge and, above all, the attachment that we have for the Air Force.

PART 1

From the Beginnings to the First World War

Introduction

It is difficult to establish the date of birth of French military aeronautics since its existence has taken such various forms. The first unit of military aeronauts, officially created on April 2, 1794, by a decree of the Revolutionary government, the French National Convention, existed for only a few years. It was followed by the creation of the aeronauts of the Loire during the Franco-Prussian War (1870–1871), an aeronautical corps just as official as that of 1794 but much shorter-lived.

It was not until October 16, 1874, that a Communications Commission was established, a section of which was entrusted with the study of military balloons. From that date to the present there has been a definite continuity in the study and use of, first, balloon corps and, later, aviation units in the French armed services.

It might seem arbitrary, therefore, even incorrect, to begin a history of French military aeronautics as far back as 1794. There is some justification for this decision, however. It would be unfortunate to omit the exploits of the first aeronauts, not only because of their picturesque nature but also because this first group of airmen—the nucleus, as it were —displayed a type of courage and enterprising spirit that can still serve as an example today. It would also be regrettable to pass over in silence the various difficulties that arose in the introduction of ballooning into the French army.

Another consideration in this decision to begin with such an early date was that it would be of interest, in recounting aeronautical events as far back as possible, to uncover certain attitudes of French military and political leaders toward the new branch of the service as well as to discover the distant origin of the many characteristics that make up the peculiar nature of aeronauts. Most of this first part, however, will be devoted to the definitive beginning of military ballooning after the Franco-Prussian War and to that of aviation from 1909 on.

A Grand Premiere: The Aeronauts of the Republican Era (1794–1799)

For centuries in Europe technical progress in warfare remained very slow. No doubt because they well knew the difficulty of training large numbers of troops to handle weapons, military leaders as a group did not look favorably on the introduction of new devices whose presumed advantages did not outweigh in their minds the risk of losing those concrete ones acquired through long experience. The birth of military ballooning in France was a remarkable exception to this rule and led to the appearance of a new breed of military men—balloonists, the ancestors of all aviators.

The French were the first to use balloons as aerial observation posts on the battlefield. The explanation for this fact is quite simple: these lighter-than-air craft were invented in France which, since the middle of the eighteenth century, had benefited from a combination of favorable circumstances—economic, demographic, and scientific—that directed the minds of that "age of enlightenment" toward advancements in technology. It was the Revolutionary army of the First French Republic that, thanks to a small group of scientists supported by the members of the Committee of Public Safety, was to turn to its advantage the invention of balloons, which had taken place under the ancien régime.

The Birth of Ballooning

In order to understand the story of the aeronauts of the Republican army, however, one must go back to the discovery of the balloon and to the research that accompanied it. Credit must go to the Montgolfier brothers, Joseph Michel and Jacques Etienne, sons of a paper manufacturer of Annonay, for the invention of the first hot-air balloon, or "Montgolfier," a balloon whose light envelope contained air heated by a small stove suspended beneath it.

On November 21, 1783, the scientist Pilâtre de Rozier and the Marquis d'Arlandes, an official of the crown, ascended in a Montgolfier balloon from the Porte de la Muette in Paris, climbed to approximately one thousand meters, and landed near the present-day Porte d'Italie after a twenty-five-minute flight. Ten days later, on December 1, 1783, the scientist J. A. C. Charles, accompanied by M. Robert, took off in his own balloon, inflated with hydrogen, from the Tuileries Gardens before the eyes of some three hundred thousand Parisians who had been alerted to the impending flight by notices posted about the city. The pair of aeronauts rose to over three thousand meters and after a two hours' flight landed at Nesles, a town about thirty kilometers from Paris. Their flight, which took place before a crowd that was fairly large for the time, caused quite a stir.

On March 2, 1784, Jean Pierre Blanchard took off in a hydrogen balloon from the Champs de Mars in Paris for a solo flight before a large group of spectators. He landed shortly afterward at Billancourt after flying over Meudon, a town southwest of Paris. Flying from Dover on January 7, 1785, Blanchard, with an American "passenger," John Jeffries, a doctor in the British army, successfully completed the first balloon crossing of the English Channel.

For two years popular enthusiasm for the aeronauts remained strong. Their popularity can be seen in the many objects that were decorated in the "balloon style" of the times: pottery, clocks, fans, snuffboxes, furniture, dresses, even hairdos. Balloon ascensions were a part of all festive occasions, and some men made them their profession, not only in France—in Paris and in the rest of the country—but in other lands as well. From 1783 until the beginning of the French Revolution in 1789 there were a great number of balloon ascensions, both public and private, and thus the balloon was considered, at least in France, a highly developed machine.

Nevertheless, right from the start there were several people who believed that balloons would never be truly practical until they could be steered. Many solutions to the problem of controlling the direction of balloons were proposed, most of them fantastic, calling for the use of sails, oars, and even birds as draft animals. Among all of these ideas one design, exceptional for its time, must be singled out, that of Jean Baptiste Meusnier, a lieutenant (ten years later, general) in the French Corps of Engineers. As early as 1785 he proposed an elliptical gasbag that was extremely well designed and included a number of features that would be put into practice at a much later stage of development.

Cutting cloth for balloons.
At the right is a wooden pattern used for cutting.

Making varnish.

Applying the varnish.

A balloon being prepared for flight.

Joseph Montgolfier (1740–1810); drawing by E. Pehet, 1838 (PASM Collection).

François Pilâtre de Rozier (1754–1785); drawing by A. Pujos, engraved by H. Legrand, 1783 (PASM Coll.).

Jean Pierre Blanchard (1753–1808); etching by I. Sewel Cornhill, 1785.

Man's first flight: November 21, 1783. Pilâtre de Rozier and the Marquis d'Arlandes take off in a hot-air balloon from the Porte de la Muette, Paris; 18th-century engraving.

Marquis François Laurent d'Arlandes (1742–1809), as captain and assistant medical officer of the Bourbenois Regiment; oil on canvas, artist unknown, 1772 (PASM Coll.).

Etienne Montgolfier (1745–1799); drawing by A. Pujos, engraved by H. Legrand, 1783 (PASM Coll.).

J. A. C. Charles (1746–1823); etching by S. C. Miger (PASM Coll.).

Sword with balloon ornamentation; 18th century (PASM Coll.).

Propulsion of the Meusnier steering balloon, or dirigible, was to be by means of aerial propellers (at a time when water propellers did not yet exist) turned by handcranks, for lack of any other motor available at the time. His projected dirigible was never constructed, however, because of a lack of funds.

Meusnier was ahead of his time; a century would go by before another French military engineer, Colonel Charles Renard (1847–1905), established his reputation with the invention of the first truly navigable balloon.

From the very beginning, however, the balloon's potential for military use was not overlooked by aerial experimenters. For example, before his historic free flight from Paris on November 21, 1783, Pilâtre de Rozier had experimented with tethered, or captive, balloon ascensions. His passenger on October 17, 1783, Giroud de Villette, had easily recognized all the surroundings of Paris as far as the suburb of Corbeil and remarked: "This fairly inexpensive machine would be very useful to an army for discovering the enemy's position, maneuvers, movements, and supplies and for reporting them by signals." And after his flight with De Rozier, the Marquis d'Arlandes had noted in his report the military value of the balloon and had recommended that its observation instruments be perfected. Prints and engravings circulating at that time throughout Europe adopted these ideas and depicted, often in a very exaggerated manner, armies aboard balloons engaging in aerial combat.

The First Balloon Companies (1794)

From its creation in April 1793 the Committee of Public Safety, a major arm of the Revolutionary government, was concerned with enlisting scientific discoveries in the service of the state. Thus, shortly after the death of General Meusnier, on June 13, 1793, near Cassel, the Committee sought out the plans for his dirigible balloon. These were located at Cherbourg, but on examination were found to be too ambitious to implement at that time. A simpler alternative to the construction of the innovative Meusnier dirigible was then chosen. The Committee of Public Safety entrusted a scientist, Louis Bernard Guyton de Morveau, with a balloon that had been seized among the possessions of an émigré, Lallement de Saint-Croix, and instructed him to determine its best use in the interests of the Republic. After studying the balloon, Guyton de Morveau asked that experiments be carried out to perfect a new method for producing hydrogen. He also recommended that the tests be done with the balloon tethered, since using a free balloon seemed dangerous to him. Working with fellow scientists Laurent Lavoisier and Jean Marie Joseph Coutelle, Guyton de Morveau succeeded in generating hydrogen by running water over iron filings that had been heated red hot in a brick furnace. On July 30, 1793, the balloon was entrusted to Captain Lhomond of the Republican army, and, after being repaired and inflated with hydrogen at the Tuileries, it was presented in October to the members of the Committee of Public Safety. Convinced of its usefulness, on November 24 they decided on the construction of a new balloon capable of carrying two observers. Nicolas Jacques Conté, who had helped Coutelle, was given this new task at the Petit Château of Meudon, in a wing of the building that has since disappeared.

On April 2, 1794, Conté's work had progressed so much that the Republican government, in the National Convention, officially established a balloon company under the command of Coutelle, who was appointed a captain. Coutelle thus had the honor of being the very first officer of an aeronautics unit anywhere. The balloon company consisted of a lieutenant, a sergeant major who functioned as quartermaster, two corporals, and twenty enlisted men. Their number would eventually increase to a total of about fifty men. The same decree of the National Convention also specified the uniform to be worn by the aeronauts. It was inspired by that of the Corps of Engineers: blue breeches, jacket, and coat, red piping on the collar, the black facings and buttons of the infantry, and blue jacket and trousers for work. For their weapons the balloonists could carry a short saber and two pistols.

On May 3, 1794, the company, after just one month of training, joined the Army of the Sambre-et-Meuse commanded by General Jean Baptiste Jourdan, who had been notified as early as August 28, 1793, by the Committee of Public Safety that he would be sent a balloon "for the observation of the enemy's troop movements." Captain Coutelle left for Jourdan's army first in order to make all the preparations necessary for the balloon and for the construction of the furnace needed for generating hydrogen. The balloon itself and the company's supplies were to arrive later with Captain Lhomond. The Committee also gave Jourdan some firm advice and instructions in its letter to him: "Preparations [for the balloon] must be made in a safe, enclosed place behind the lines; the hydrogen will not last longer than twenty-four to thirty hours. It is best to launch the balloon when the weather is expected to be neither rainy nor windy. It will be prudent, for the first ascension, to let out a moderate amount of rope, and if the balloon ascends to two hundred fathoms, that will be quite the limit." The letter indicated that the balloon might well have another advantage even more important than its use as an observation post: it would in itself be an element of psychological warfare, since "its appearance will inspire fear [in the enemy]." The observer in the balloon would communicate with the ground through a system of signals, colored flags and flames that could form twenty-one different combinations. "If [the observer] has a message that cannot be communicated by the signals, he can write it down and throw the message overboard attached to a ball with a streamer. Finally, the general can have signals displayed beneath the balloon which he wants to have repeated immediately and which will be visible to commanders who have been alerted to their meaning. Two men must ascend in the balloon no matter what purpose [the general] has in mind: a soldier for observing and making judgments on [the enemy's] positions and maneuvers and a scientist with an up-to-date knowledge of ballooning, who is to be in charge of the conduct of the balloon and to direct the handling of the cords [by the ground crew] while in the air according to the signals agreed upon, for the safety of the ascension and for coordination with the army's movements."

The Committee of Public Safety took great pains to develop military ballooning, as evidenced by the printed instructions on the duties assigned to the balloon company, which were distributed to general officers. In these instructions the object of the company was "to put at the disposal of the general all the services that can be furnished by the art of aeronautics: (1) to clarify the enemy's marches, movements, and plans; (2) to transport quickly signals previously agreed upon with the major generals and commanding officers in the field; (3) finally, as circumstances required, to distribute public notices in territory occupied by the despots' henchmen."

The First Military Operations

After arriving at the front the balloon company began first by constructing a brick furnace in order to generate the hydrogen needed to inflate their balloon, the *Entreprenant* (*Enterprise*), which had been built at Meudon.

The first military ascension of the balloon took place on June 2, 1794, from the town of Maubeuge, which was being held by the French army in the face of Austrian artillery fire that aimed at the balloon but failed to hit it. Captain Coutelle and Adjutant General Radet were thus the first men to use a captive balloon in military operations. On June 21, 1794, the *Entreprenant*, fully inflated, left Maubeuge safely and was transported by tow lines during a difficult night march to the vicinity of the town of Charleroi, which was occupied by the Austrian army. On June 23 Coutelle, whose spirit seemed immune to all discouragement, began his ascensions once again. Won over by his enthusiasm for the balloon, Generals Maison, Morlot, and Olivier agreed to climb aboard the craft. Thanks to their observations all the enemy's maneuvers were

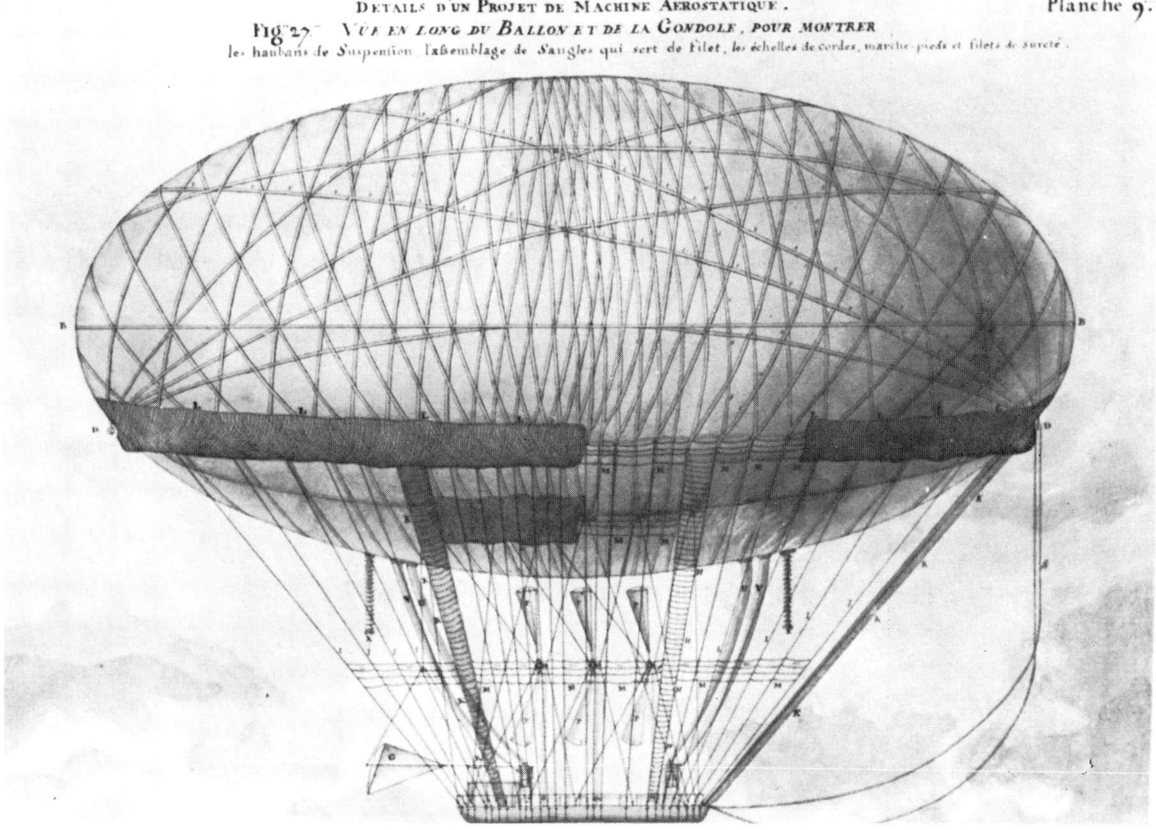

General Meusnier's design for a dirigible balloon, 1785: Details of a Design for an Aerostatic Machine, Longitudinal View of the Balloon and the Cupola, showing the suspension shrouds, netting, rope ladders, walkways, and safety nets; watercolor (PASM Coll.).

Louis Bernard Guyton de Morveau (1737–1816).

Nicolas Jacques Conté (1755–1805).

Jean Marie Joseph Coutelle (1748–1835); engraving by Mallet, 1807 (PASM Coll.).

frustrated, and the Austrian garrison, completely demoralized, surrendered on June 26 without the knowledge of their command post. This French occupation of Charleroi, revealed to the Austrians only at the last moment, at the height of the battle, would contribute to the French victory at Fleurus. During these operations at Charleroi on the twenty-sixth of June the *Entreprenant* remained in the air for the entire day, supplying information to General Jourdan and Representative Louis de Saint-Just of the Committee of Public Safety, who were quartered in the Moulin de Jumet. The enemy had been disoriented by the sight of the "diabolical contraption" which detected all its movements. In a letter to Representative Guyton de Morveau, also a member of the Committee, Adjutant General Rochefort emphasized the terror which the balloon had inspired in the enemy, referring to depositions from several Austrian and Dutch deserters: "They assured [us] that General Cobourg [the Austrian commander] had cursed the balloon copiously, that he kept saying that 'there's nothing those scoundrels don't invent; there's a spy in that thing and I can't get at him to have him hanged!'"

Baron Selle de Beauchamp, an officer of the balloon company, wrote in the same vein in his memoirs that "the sight of this magnificent tower set up in the middle of a level area where nothing obstructed its view caused discouragement among the enemy's soldiers, who hadn't any idea of such a thing." Were the French to be the only ones to use such a device for very long? The balloonists thought so and continued their ascensions in the service of the Republican army.

In view of the successes thus far achieved, the Committee of Public Safety, on June 23, 1794, established a second balloon company with a contingent of men and officers similar to that of the first. This unit was put under the command of Captain Delaunay.

No one voiced any doubts at this time about the usefulness of balloons in the army. On October 31, 1794, at Meudon, the National School for Aerostation (ballooning) was founded by government decree and put under the direction of Nicolas Conté. A number of balloons were built, with memorable names reflecting the revolutionary ideology of the times: the *Martial*, *Emule*, *Céleste*, *Industrieux*, *Intrépide*, *Précurseur*, *Svelte*, *Vétéran*, and *Agile*.

The first balloon company followed the Army of the North, ascending from Brussels and Liège. General Jourdan, however, who was protecting the flank of the Army of the Rhine, was forced to retreat, and the town of Würzburg, where the balloon company was quartered, was surrounded by the Austrians and fell on September 3, 1796. This spelled disaster for the aeronauts, who were captured along with their equipment, including their balloon, which is preserved today in the collection of the military museum of the arsenal in Vienna, Austria. The balloon company did not regain its freedom until after the preliminary stages of the Peace of Leoben in April 1797.

The first balloon unit was thus eliminated from the war because of its inability to retreat in time. In fact, military tactics had changed their style, and a war of sieges and battles against fortified places had become a war of movement. This new type of warfare brought to light the difficulties of using military balloons: in spite of the truly sporting efforts of the aeronauts, the balloon's movement was slow and complicated, while its inflation required a brick furnace which was time-consuming to construct and, of course, stationary. These drawbacks were emphasized by the French generals, who insisted that the balloon company be disbanded. Without denying the validity of their argument, it still appears to have been more a pretext for their getting rid of a device that tended to overshadow their glory as the generals of the Republic. As the balloon's contribution to victory was exalted, the role of the military commanders in that victory was diminished. It is easy to imagine General Jourdan's annoyance on hearing ill-intentioned people repeat that without the *Entreprenant* the battle of Fleurus might not have been won by the French army. This was a very human weakness and one that would be encountered later whenever anyone tended to give to aeronautics too great a

①

②

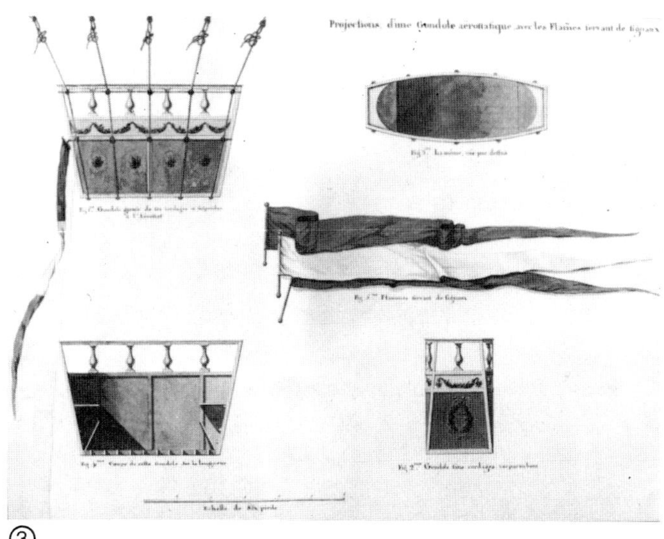

③

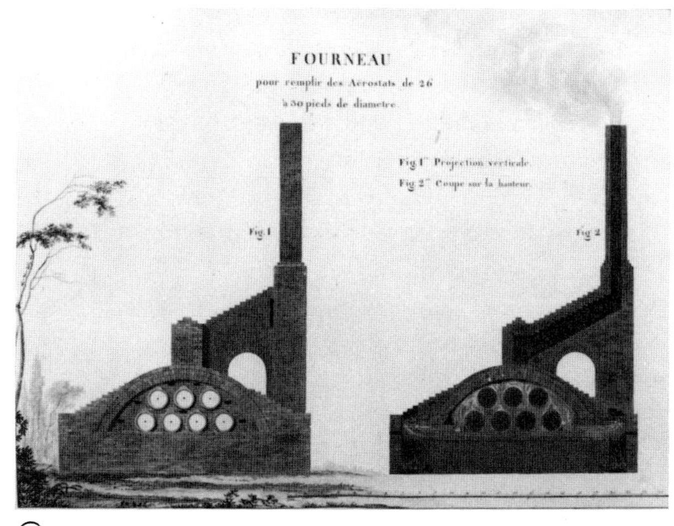

④

1 *The aeronauts of the Republic; oil painting by Edouard Detaille (PASM Coll.).*

2 *The Battle of Fleurus; engraving by Naudet and Le Beau (PASM Coll.).*

3 *A balloon basket used by the aeronauts of the Republic; drawing by Conté (PASM Coll.).*

4 *A brick furnace used for making hydrogen; drawing by Conté (PASM Coll.).*

role in the winning of the war. For this reason one must express admiration for those commanders-in-chief who could recognize the services rendered by aviation and even more admiration for those who understood its potential uses in warfare.

The Aeronauts' Decline

Although Napoleon Bonaparte used balloon equipment at the siege of Mantua, Italy, in 1796, in that very year General Lazare Hoche, Jourdan's successor as commander of the Army of the North, decided that the aeronauts were of no use to him and asked that they be disbanded. The corps, however, was not abolished by the ruling Directory, but the aeronauts did remain inactive at Strasbourg.

A letter from Representative Guyton de Morveau indicates the kind of atmosphere that reigned at that time. In his letter of June 22, 1796, he deplored the balloons' inactivity.

My opinion of the balloons as instruments of war has not changed since the battle of Fleurus, and how could it have? It's as if one were to question whether maps and field glasses are of use to a general in directing his own troop movements and in observing those of the enemy. Today the desire for fame is greater than it was in the third year [of the Revolutionary era]. Our circumstances are different now; when French territory was invaded the only thought was for the safety [of our country]. Do generals who have over and over again proven that they know how to win battles without balloons need such things? [Using them] would diminish the laurels of the victor of the tournament since they would cause it to be believed that the opponents were not fighting on an equal footing.

The balloons, nevertheless, still had their staunch supporters. For example, on the insistence of Conté and Coutelle, Bonaparte agreed to the participation of the aeronauts in his campaign in Egypt. With his consent a balloon company was formed from parts of the two earlier companies, and the remainder was disbanded. Unfortunately, the Egyptian campaign did not turn out to be the opportunity the aeronauts had been hoping for in order to prove the value of their balloons. Their equipment, packed aboard the ships *Orient* and *Patriot*, was lost when Admiral Nelson, the British naval commander, attacked the French fleet at Abukir Bay, at the mouth of the Nile, in August 1798. Conté then returned to his original vocation as a scholar and uncovered some of the riches of Egyptian culture, little known at the time. As for the balloon company's personnel, they were transferred to technical duties, manufacturing munitions, pumps, and even printing presses. The former aeronauts successfully solved all the mechanical problems that arose in their new duties since they were masons, mechanical fitters, chemists, and, above all, men who knew how to cope. In fact, it would not be hard to identify them with aviation mechanics, who are capable of adapting to all kinds of situations.

In spite of their devotion to duty, however, Bonaparte did not feel any gratitude toward the aeronauts for their efforts during his campaign. On February 18, 1799, the two balloon companies were officially disbanded, and the ballooning school at Meudon was abolished. In 1802 the unemployed aeronauts were scattered and turned once again to other professions. Their short-lived traditions were entrusted to the Engineering School at Metz, which soon forgot them. It was not until seventy years later that a balloon corps would be established again in France.

The experience of these first military balloon units was valuable, however. The engineer-aeronauts were endowed with energy and courage. It is difficult to overemphasize their spirit of determination when balloon inflations lasted from thirty-six to forty-eight hours and at times even from fifty to sixty hours, during which the aeronauts had to remain alert, hold the balloons in place, and guard against unexpected mishaps, which might include cracks in the masonry of the hydrogen-generating furnace. Nothing, it seems, could discourage these first airmen, whom Baron Selle de Beauchamp described in his memoirs as "children of Paris, dandies, notarial and legal clerks, salesmen, some with education, and then some workmen, a country curate." Nor will Coutelle's fearlessness be forgotten, as he swung in his balloon with the basket crashing into the ground at each shift of the wind. Even the enemy paid him their respects by requesting a parley so that the unfortunate victim might be allowed to descend, for "he ought not to perish through circumstances alien to warfare."

If these first balloon units were able to be put into service quickly, it was owing to new breakthroughs in technology, such as the method of generating hydrogen and the manufacturing of varnish, the credit for which belongs primarily to a team of scientists and to Coutelle and Conté. It was Coutelle, in fact, who, in the middle of the campaign, had envisioned a modification in the shape of the balloon that would improve its maneuverability in the wind. Experiments with the cylindrical balloon built from his plans at Meudon were not conclusive, but it is clear that, supported with more faith and perseverance by his military superiors, ballooning would be well on its way to great advances.

Buttons from the uniform of an aeronaut of the Republic (PASM Coll.).

The Occasional Use of Balloons in the Armed Forces (1802–1874)

Various Attempts in France and Abroad, 1802–1870

Although the balloon companies' traditions were not preserved, the memory of the balloon used at Fleurus, the *Entreprenant*, remained strong. The experience of the aeronauts of the Republican army served as a reference point on many occasions in both Europe and America. It was not until 1870, however, that military balloons were again used on a significant scale in France.

It seems that General L. N. M. Carnot tried to use a balloon while he was under siege in Anvers in 1815. In 1826 the minister of war set up a commission to study the advisability of resuming research in ballooning. The report submitted by the commission took into account the work of such eminent figures as the scientist François Arago, Jean Joseph Coutelle (former commanding officer of the aeronauts of the Republican army, who had risen to the rank of colonel), the chemist Jacques Thénard, and several general officers of the Corps of Engineers. This report had no immediate consequences but served as the basis for the first studies of the commission that would be set up later, in 1874.

In 1830 the popular civilian aeronaut Margat got a contract to take part in the Algerian expedition. He brought his balloon equipment ashore at Algiers, but there is no proof that he was able to make any ascents with it. In 1859 Eugène Godard likewise offered his services to Emperor Napoleon III during the wars in Italy and carried out several ascents in a captive hot-air balloon. These attempts, although brief, were promising. Above all, they demonstrated the necessity of using hydrogen balloons exclusively. Construction of an 800-cubic-meter balloon was begun. This was the *Impérial*, which was completed too late and was turned over to the national furniture warehouse, where it was unearthed in 1870.

Apart from the brief intervention of an American balloon in Brazil in 1866, it is incontestably in the United States, during the Civil War, that one finds military ballooning that is a direct descendant of that of 1794 in France. An organization comparable to that of the French balloon companies was put into service. President Abraham Lincoln authorized Professor T. S. C. Lowe to establish a balloon corps consisting of two companies, which would operate from 1861 to 1863. Ten balloons were used, and each company—not surprisingly—consisted of approximately fifty men under the command of a captain. The first two balloons were named the *Constitution* and the *Intrepid*. Lowe turned his attention to the problem of his predecessors and greatly advanced the state of the art: hydrogen was transported in cylinders in a compressed state aboard horse-drawn wagons, thus eliminating the need for using stationary furnaces in the field.

Lowe very quickly adopted the use of the telegraph in balloon observations. Aerial photography, invented in France in 1859 by Nadar (pseudonym of Félix Tournachon) and improved by Samuel Archer King in the United States in 1861, was also used in a practical way by Lowe. It should be noted in passing that Nadar did not produce "proper" negatives until 1868, and it was not until 1880 that real aerial photographs were produced, vertical and oblique, by an amateur named Demarest.

The American balloons used during the Civil War, mainly on the Federal side, rendered services that were appreciated until 1863 when the war became one of very rapid troop movements and interest in balloons declined once again. The Union Army Balloon Corps was disbanded at the end of the war.

In France, after the Revolutionary Wars and those of the Empire, ballooning became a sport for the wealthy and a profession for others, who earned their living by numerous, and very popular, exhibitions the advertising for which was furnished by very active associations or societies.

Many of the aeronauts of this period played a big role in the events of the Franco-Prussian War. Among the most famous were Dupuis-Delcourt, Francisque Arban, Eugène Godard, Nadar, Mme Poitevin, Camille Dartois, Gabriel Yon, and Jules Duruof.

In the case of Eugène Godard, it is really a question of an entire family, or dynasty, of aeronauts. Impelled by the successes of his first hot-air balloon ascents with passengers in 1847, Godard persuaded several members of his family to learn to pilot a balloon in order to meet the flood of requests. For more than sixty years the Godards carried out the great majority of public balloon ascensions in Europe. A sister, three brothers, several daughters, an uncle, and even his father assisted Eugène Godard in his work.

As for Nadar, sketcher, caricaturist, photographer, air enthusiast, he devoted himself unceasingly to publicizing ballooning and defending the idea of heavier-than-air craft, the sign of the future. In order to finance research on a lightweight motor for such a craft, he had constructed at his own expense a 6,000-cubic-meter balloon, the *Géant* (*Giant*), to carry several passengers and thus obtain the resources necessary to support his endeavor. The *Géant* made a number of ascensions, one of which ended in the balloon's being dragged violently along the ground for sixteen kilometers. The affair ended in financial catastrophe, but at least everyone in Europe was talking about aeronautics. Nadar and his friends founded the Society for the Promotion of Aerial Navigation and launched a journal, *L'Aéronaute*, which began publication in 1863 and contributed enormously to the development of the sport of ballooning in France.

All these men experienced in the art of ballooning, motivated by a strong sense of patriotism, offered their services to the French government when their country was in danger.

The Franco-Prussian War (1870–1871)

In July 1870, at the very beginning of the Franco-Prussian War, two well-known balloon sportsmen, Gaston Tissandier and Wilfrid de Fonvielle, proposed to the minister of war that they accompany the Army of the Rhine with a captive balloon. Their proposal was not taken up. However, in the besieged city of Metz an attempt was made to use free balloons in order to communicate with the outside world. Several small, unmanned balloons were hastily constructed and launched beyond the walls of the city. Some of these balloons accomplished their mission, others fell in Prussian-held territory. Although the results may have been a little disappointing, they nevertheless indicated a path to follow.

The Balloons of the Siege of Paris

The defeat and capitulation of Napoleon III at Sedan on September 2, 1870, marked the end of the Second Empire. The Republic was proclaimed on September 4. The final sending of dispatches by train before the encirclement of Paris by the Prussian army took place from the Gare de l'Est on September 11, the Gare du Nord and the Gare de Lyon on September 13, the Gare d'Orléans and the Gare de Saint Lazare on September 17, and finally from the Gare Montparnasse on September 18. From that point on the postal administration was forced to seek other means of maintaining communications between the capital and the provinces. Some attempts were made by land and by river but without good results. Once again balloons were thought of. An association of civilian balloonists—Nadar, Dartois, Duruof, Tissandier, and Fonvielle—had just offered the new government its services in using captive balloons in the defense of Paris. The enthusiasm of these balloonists and the goodwill of Colonel Usquin, who had been designated to preside over a commission to supervise the aeronauts, had made possible some attempts at observation from captive balloons located in three parts of Paris: Nadar was installed with the *Neptune* in the Place Saint Pierre in Montmartre, Eugène Godard with the *Ville de Florence* on the Boulevard d'Italie, and Wilfrid de Fonvielle with the *Céleste* at the Vaugirard gasworks.

The balloons were the property of the aeronauts. For the handling of the *Neptune* the army furnished a detachment of the 25th Border Regiment and the navy provided eight sailors from the corvette *Jeanne d'Arc*. Other sailors, detailed for the defense of the forts of Paris, were later placed at the disposal of the aeronauts, as were some detachments of the auxiliary engineers of the National Guard.

The observations made from these captive balloons were the subject of reports sent to General Trochu, who was in charge of the defense of Paris. By September 19, however, before Tissandier could install a fourth balloon post, Paris was completely surrounded, and the problem of ballooning was posed in different terms; the priority switched to maintaining communications with the outside world, in particular with the government, which had moved to Tours and was represented in Paris by Léon Gambetta, who had remained on the spot. The postal administration immediately concluded agreements with the aeronauts Yon, Dartois, and Godard, according to which they committed themselves to construct immediately, and in sufficient number, balloons of 2,000 cubic meters and to provide aeronauts to ascend in them. The postal administration also secured possession of the entire stock of old balloons available in Paris, including even those that were used for military observations, pledging to replace them later, with new balloons if necessary. They fitted out a repair shop for these older balloons at the Palais des Champs Elysées. The results obtained with small, unmanned balloons were disappointing; it was then decided to send up balloons piloted by aeronauts.

The first ascension was hardly edifying, however. On September 21 all arrangements had been made to send up from the Vaugirard gasworks a mail balloon furnished by the aeronaut M. Mangin, who was to make the ascent himself. This balloon was in poor condition, and the repairs had been made in such haste that at the moment of departure—with the mailbags already in the basket—the inflation could not take place, and the ascent was postponed. However, a new attempt was made on September 23 with complete success: the *Neptune* became the first balloon to leave Paris—with Duruof—carrying 103 kilograms of mail. Two days later, on September 25, Mangin went up in the balloon *Ville de Florence*, bought from Eugène Godard. He carried 104 kilograms of mail and three carrier pigeons, one of which returned to its dovecote the same day bearing the news that the balloon had arrived at the end of its journey. Airmail had been invented. The postal administration had at its disposal some old, repaired balloons and four hundred carrier pigeons, so that it was able to place several in each of the balloons and to report news from the rest of the country to Paris.

Nevertheless, in spite of all these efforts, the need for new equipment was urgent. Unfortunately, the manufacturing workshops of Yon and

The inflation of Duruof's Neptune, *the first balloon of the Siege of Paris, serving as Nadar's observation post at the Place Saint Pierre in Montmartre; photograph by Nadar.*

The construction of postal balloons at the Godard workshops installed in the old Gare d'Orléans, 1870; engraving from L'Illustration.

Dartois in Montmartre and those of Godard on the Boulevard d'Italie were insufficient to keep up with the demand. A decision had to be made quickly. The postal administration then placed the halls of the Gare du Nord and the Gare d'Orléans at the disposal of the balloon builders. A number of pilots, mostly sailors, were hurriedly trained by the professional aeronauts. Since there was no opportunity to practice in real flight conditions, the necessary motions were learned indoors in balloon baskets suspended from the beams of the station halls.

It was during the siege of Paris that René Dagron perfected a photographic microcopy process in order to reduce the weight of the dispatches being delivered by balloon. He packed up to two thousand letters or digits into a film about one-quarter the size of a playing card.

From September 23, 1870, to January 28, 1871, 66 balloons left Paris, thus averaging between three and four departures a week. Fifty-eight missions were successful, six balloons were captured by the enemy, and two were lost at sea. Besides the pilots, 102 passengers were transported. The balloons carried 9,654 kilograms of mailbags containing over 1,500,000 letters. The most illustrious passenger on a balloon during the siege of Paris was Léon Gambetta, designated as head of the provisional government. He took off in the *Armand Barbès* from the Place Saint Pierre on October 7, 1870. The voyage ended very prosaically in an oak tree near Montdidier, but Gambetta was able to return to his post.

The Balloons of the Loire

The Government of National Defense, transferred to Tours, was prepared to examine all proposals aimed at restoring a situation that was approaching disaster. In November 1870 it organized the first company of aeronauts intended for the Army of the Loire. A team rather than a company, it was made up of the first aeronauts that had left Paris: Duruof and Bertaux, and the sailors Josse, Labadie, Herve, and Guillaume. These men were sent to the Château du Colombier, four kilometers from Orleans, with a balloon built at Tours, the *Ville de Langres*. Shortly thereafter the two Tissandier brothers, Albert and Gaston, joined them with the balloon *Jean Bart*. This new balloon corps was given military status: M. David, general director of the aeronautical equipment of the Army of the Loire, had the rank of colonel; his secretary became a captain, and the aeronauts—Nadar, the Tissandier brothers, Duruof, Bertaux, Revilliod, and Mangin—were appointed second lieutenants; Petit and Labadie were assistant aeronauts, and the others, although they had piloted balloons in the siege of Paris, remained crewmen. Even a military uniform was settled on—very close to that of naval officers, with a silver stripe and an anchor tilted to the right on the visored cap—which involved little change for the quartermaster general's department and very little expense.

On December 9 the company assembled at Blois, where it engaged in practice drills. General Chanzy, of the regular army, was very favorable to the balloons, but military operations at that time did not allow the aeronauts to show what they could do. Several retreats followed. Then, at Laval, where they proceeded to inflate a balloon on January 29, 1871, they heard the news of the armistice.

Conclusion: Ballooning in 1870

The use of balloons in an improvised way during this short war and the success of the Paris postal balloons, which made quite an impression during that unhappy period, made people aware of the advantage that could have been derived from a corps of well-prepared aeronauts. The lesson seems to have been learned, and immediately after the treaty of Frankfurt, which concluded the Franco-Prussian War, an intense effort was begun to reorganize the national defense. Criticism of past mistakes was the rule at all levels; everyone's thoughts turned to reform with a view to taking speedy revenge on the Germans, who had taken three administrative regions (departments) from the French in a treaty considered grossly unjust.

Ballooning became a subject of study. A committee attached to the Commission on Communications—with telegraph and carrier-pigeon sections—was established on October 16, 1874. The balloon section, entrusted to Colonel Laussedat, had as its secretary Captain Charles Renard of the Corps of Engineers, who had attracted attention by his aeronautical works. This, in fact, was the first appearance of the man who stands at the beginning of modern aeronautics.

The Definitive Beginning of Military Ballooning and the Work of Charles Renard (1874–1914)

The subcommittee on ballooning was supplied by the postal administration with the remnants of the equipment used during the siege of Paris, including a dozen balloons and twenty-eight balloon baskets stored in the Salle Vendôme, in the attic of the Hôtel des Invalides, where the subcommittee was provisionally installed.

The Parisian premises were found to be much too small. In addition, the crash of a balloon during an ascent in the middle of Paris illustrated the inappropriateness of experimenting in the city. Renard then turned to the very place that had been the cradle of ballooning—Meudon. Unfortunately, the old Château had been burned during the Revolution, and the new one had become a victim of the recent war and was being refitted by the physicist and astronomer Jules Janssen, who had established an astronomical observatory there. Renard then chose the park of Chalais-Meudon, which was in a state of neglect. A military reservation since 1831, during the period of the Second Empire it had been used for the development and manufacture of the first machine guns. Living quarters and workshops still existed and were repaired, practically without funds. But luck came to Renard's rescue. One of his colleagues, Captain La Haye, introduced him to Léon Gambetta, who had the fondest memory of his departure from Paris in the balloon *Armand Barbès*, to which he owed a good part of his popularity. Gambetta, at that time chairman of the Budget Committee in the Chamber of Deputies, met with Renard, who then obtained a large appropriation. It was thus possible to install the laboratories needed for balloon research in the park of Chalais, which in 1877 became the Central Military Installation for Ballooning, under the Fortifications Depot, the first aeronautic laboratory in the world.

The departure of the Armand Barbès *with Léon Gambetta on board and of the* George Sand, *October 7, 1870; original picture by Nadar (PASM Coll.).*

The transport of the Jean Bart, *pulled by hand by militiamen after an accident in the vicinity of Pithiviers; drawing by Albert Tissandier (PASM Coll.).*

A Name Synonymous with Dedication: Charles Renard

Born on November 23, 1847, at Damblain, in the Vosges, Charles Renard is still one of the most attractive figures in French aerostation and aviation. After finishing his studies at the Ecole Polytechnique in 1868 he chose a military career with the engineering branch. The Franco-Prussian War gave him the chance to demonstrate his physical courage and his combat leadership qualities. He was decorated with the Legion of Honor at the age of twenty-three.

Just after the war, while stationed at Arras, he reflected on recent military events and devoted himself especially to aeronautical questions. Beginning in 1874 he experimented successfully with a small decaplane glider with a hanging stabilizer, which he launched from a height of 66 meters from a tower on Mont Saint Eloi. Like Alphonse Pénaud, with whom he worked for a short time, Charles Renard considered a heavier-than-air craft his real objective but, realizing that the indispensable lighter and more powerful motors were not yet available, he knew that he was some distance yet from his goal and that many steps would be necessary before arriving at it. The first step required of him—the only priority for his superiors—was to develop a suitable lighter-than-air craft, for war could break out again at any moment, and it was necessary to be prepared this time. He would later consider the problem of dirigibles, for which the weight of the motor was less critical. Then would come the heavier-than-air craft. For all of this research the study of motors remained his primary concern.

The task was impressive, since in 1878 the subcommittee had only two officers—Renard himself and Lieutenant Arthur Krebs—assisted by the civilian aeronaut Duté-Poitevin, one warrant officer, two corporals, and nine sappers. Fortunately, a supplementary group of fourteen engineering workmen was authorized; then, starting in 1879, there were two more officers and forty more sappers. In a few months all the balloon equipment was

Lieutenant Colonel Charles Renard (1847–1905).

determined on, and a prototype was constructed.

In the fall of 1879 the minister of war, after a visit to Chalais-Meudon that had made a favorable impression on him, ordered the establishment of eight field depots, one for each army, and three fixed balloon parks (Toul, Verdun, and Belfort). Ballooning in an organized form had finally become a part of the army. Renard energetically tackled the task of procuring the material needed to equip these new units.

Starting with the spherical balloon, the equipment adopted was perfected in all its components. Renard contrived a special suspension system which kept the observation basket vertical independent of the balloon's motion. Captain Krebs devised a steam winch that, for the first time, made use of the principle of towage on two parallel drums, which permitted winding the cable in an efficient way. Renard also perfected a continuous hydrogen generator on a horse-drawn vehicle. Captain Paul Renard came to join his brother in preparing equipment for standardized production. Thanks to a modest increase in manpower, the mission assigned by the minister was quickly accomplished.

In 1880 for the first time a field unit took part successfully in maneuvers, in spite of the fact that the personnel had had little training. Later on the same balloon equipment served in several campaigns in which the aeronauts showed their effectiveness in spite of difficult terrain—the campaigns of Tonkin (1884), Madagascar (1895), China (1900), and Morocco (1909).

The Dirigible *La France*

With the most pressing requirements of his commanding officers satisfied, Charles Renard could return to his research and concern himself with perfecting the "dirigible" formula. Several aeronauts before him had tried to solve this difficult problem. The most famous, because he was the first to get some positive results, in 1852, was Henry Giffard; after him Dupuy de Lôme and the Tissandier brothers, to mention only those best known in France, attacked the problem, but without much success. Still others, abroad, had interested themselves in this question, with more or less luck. No one, however, had given a convincing demonstration because of the inability to attain an adequate flight speed. Renard and Krebs's success was complete from the first try.

On August 9, 1884, the dirigible *La France*, the work of Renard and Krebs, lifted off from Chalais-Meudon. It passed over the wood of Meudon and headed for Villacoublay after having made a wide turn. It returned to its point of departure after covering a distance of 7.6 kilometers in 23 minutes at an average speed of 5.5 meters per second.

1

2

3

1 A moment of relaxation for the balloon officers at Chalais-Meudon. Among them is Major Hirschauer (4th from left).

2 Captive balloon of the Renard type (with Renard suspension).

3 A postcard showing balloon operations in Morocco.

The principal innovation of the dirigible consisted in its 8-horsepower electric motor, the work of Captain Krebs, and the chlorochromic batteries invented by Captain Renard. The weight of the batteries was 400 kilograms, that of the motor 100 kilograms; the operating life was as much as 1 hour and 45 minutes. The dirigible made seven demonstration flights in 1884 and 1885, five of them completely successful and two interrupted but without any serious accidents.

These flights had a considerable effect on public opinion in France. As Renard explained: "Public opinion, which had always put the problem of the steering of balloons on a par with that of perpetual motion, was completely reversed. It suddenly became as favorable to this line of research as it had formerly been opposed to it." After this success Renard felt free to proceed further with his work. By 1885 the design for a new dirigible, the *Général Meusnier*, equipped with a 100-horsepower motor to make it faster, was completed. A gasbag was quickly constructed in 1888. But Renard was not to succeed in solving the problem of the motor satisfactorily. His attempts to perfect it monopolized his efforts, but at any rate his study of a whole series of the most varied motors had value. Over twenty different types were built at Chalais according to his plans: steam, gas, and gasoline motors. Renard was led to develop new concepts which bear witness to his inventive genius and are still admired by professionals today.

He obtained a ratio of 4 to 5 kilograms per horsepower on certain motors. Even before any automotive vehicle with a gasoline motor existed, he had the first high-powered internal combustion engine (100 hp) constructed according to his plans by the Puteaux arsenal in 1886. It was intended for use on the *Général Meusnier*. Unfortunately, on this point the project turned out to be too ambitious; the perfecting of this eight-cylinder motor, which was to run on gasoline and on hydrogen alternately, could not be accomplished, in spite of several years of experiments and modifications.

The fields that Charles Renard explored varied widely, from the lightest steam boiler to the first cooling radiators, and from experimental methods with fixed-point lifting screws to helicopters and to the first aerodynamic wind tunnel, set up in France in 1890.

To make the manufacture of balloon equipment more economical Renard conceived a system of standardization used from 1885 on, called "Renard's numbers," which was used in 1921 by the Permanent Standardization Commission to establish its first plan.

In 1888, when the Central Installation at Chalais-Meudon was upgraded to the Military Ballooning Directorate, Charles Renard, now a major and full of prestige from his success with the dirigible *La France*, was appointed its director.

Official support encouraged him to push his research on the 100-horsepower dirigible *Général Meusnier* to the limit, but nothing seemed to go right for him any longer. He lost a great deal of time on the difficult development of his extraordinary internal combustion engine, then set out to explore more promising lines. In addition, in trying to improve the shape of the dirigible's hull, in a small wind tunnel built for the purpose, he discovered in 1896 the existence of a critical speed for stability in relation to the shapes of the hulls. As luck would have it, the *Général Meusnier*, which had already been constructed, would have been unstable at the intended speed of 50 kilometers per hour, which Renard judged necessary for a practical dirigible. Everything needed to be started over again, and new appropriations had to be obtained.

Renard's lack of interest in publishing his works and his dislike of journalists, who were not allowed at Chalais-Meudon, caused the great amount of scientific research conducted in his laboratory to remain unknown. It must be added that the period of antimilitarism through which France passed between 1895 and 1910 led to a reduction in the military budget, and research was the first victim.

It was at that very time that Alberto Santos-Dumont's exploits filled the press. On October 19, 1901, in his "No. 6," he succeeded in flying from St. Cloud around the Eiffel Tower and back to his point of departure. This flight represented no

The dirigible La France *flying over the balloon park of Chalais-Meudon. At left, the hangar for "Y" dirigibles; in the background, the orangery of the Château de Meudon.*

Charles Renard and Arthur Krebs' dirigible La France *at Chalais-Meudon, 1884.*

advance over those of Renard's *La France*, but the latter had been forgotten. The most serious thing was that this also applied to his military superiors, who seized on Santos-Dumont's flight as a pretext for expecting private industry to furnish the dirigibles that Renard, apparently, was incapable of turning out.

Nevertheless, Charles Renard continued his work. He was the first to establish a theory of the helicopter rotor; he had Captain Ferdinand Ferber come to Meudon to work on airplanes. His work, which was not understood by his superiors, was known abroad. In 1898 Professor Samuel P. Langley came to see him and declared, "If I had come sooner I could have saved twenty years of work." Igor Sikorsky, the aeronautical engineer, came to discuss Renard's theories with him in 1906.

But administrative harassment, to which he was subjected after 1900, fatigue, and disappointments soon got the better of Charles Renard. In 1904 he presented his candidacy to the Academy of Sciences, to which he more than deserved to be admitted as a member. The minister consulted refused his support. This humiliation was a very hard blow for Renard. Overwork had already produced a serious depression in 1898. In April 1905 he was unable to surmount a new crisis and put an end to his life on April 13.

Charles Renard had a right to a state funeral. In his address on the occasion the physicist Arsène d'Arsonval said: "The greatest sacrifice that a scientist can make to his country is not to give it his blood and his life; it is to offer it his ideas and the results of his work under the veil of anonymity. The memory of the man who displayed this self-abnegation must be doubly sacred to his fellow citizens; his name must be preserved from oblivion or, worse yet, ingratitude."

Acquisition of the First Dirigibles

Not until twenty years after the brilliant demonstration of the dirigible *La France* was the French army at last provided with a dirigible. Even then, the army did not deserve the credit for the craft. It was, in fact, the Lebaudy brothers who had one of their engineers, M. Julliot, design a 2,500-cubic-meter dirigible with a 40-horsepower Daimler motor. This craft was launched in 1903 and was immediately successful. Because of the color of its gasbag, protected with a coating of picric acid, it was nicknamed *Le Jaune* (*Yellow*). It was bought by the army in 1905 and performed very well.

In 1906 the minister of war ordered a second dirigible, the *Patrie*, from Lebaudy. This was the first government contract to furnish a military airship. It was equipped with a 60-horsepower Panhard and Levassor motor. Delivered on December 13, 1906, it made about thirty flights but was lost on November 30, 1907, after escaping from the ground crew.

In the wake of this loss M. Deutsch de la Meurthe offered the government his 3,600-cubic-meter dirigible, *Ville de Paris*, built by Surcouf and Kapferer according to Charles Renard's instructions. Delivered on January 15, 1908, at Verdun, it took part in the military maneuvers of 1910 and was later used to train army personnel.

In 1907 the ministry ordered from the Lebaudy Company a new craft similar in type to the *Patrie*. It was the *République*, which was put into service in 1908. It proved to be a good airship until September 25, 1909, when a propeller blade broke during a voyage and tore the gasbag. The resulting crash was an awful one; the enormous craft fell from the sky, swallowing up the whole crew in its fall: Captain Marchal, Lieutenant Chauré, and Sergeants Réau and Vincenot. The names of the unfortunate victims were later given to four military airships. This accident can no doubt be attributed to the intense vibrations which originated in dirigible gondolas, or nacelles, of the time because of the use of very poorly balanced motors.

The army, nevertheless, continued to procure the dirigibles. In 1909 it acquired the *Liberté* from Lebaudy and the *Colonel Renard* from Astra, which were bigger and faster than earlier models.

From 1909 on, in view of the undeniable successes achieved by airplanes, opinion began to be divided on the future of dirigibles. Only those that

The Lebaudy dirigible Le Jaune *(*Yellow*), 1903.*

The dirigible Patrie *on November 15, 1906.*

could stay in the air for long periods of time were capable of making strategic reconnaissance flights, and they were also the only ones able to lift heavy loads and thus open up the possibility of their use for bombing missions. Offsetting these advantages, dirigibles required very delicate handling on the ground, were greatly dependent on the weather, and traveled at low speeds which made them vulnerable.

The French army kept the dirigibles because it still did not understand very well the use of airplanes, because dirigibles were easy to improve, and no doubt also because an entire fleet of dirigible balloons was being assembled on the other side of the Rhine in Germany.

In the military maneuvers in Picardy in 1910 dirigibles and airplanes were pitted against each other. The latter put on a brilliant demonstration, while the former, hampered by bad weather, were too often stuck on the ground. It should be noted in passing that during these maneuvers the first air-to-ground radio communication was achieved in a dirigible that had been specially equipped for that purpose by Major Ferrié. The main conclusion from the maneuvers was that dirigibles should be used for missions of long duration which required large cubic capacity and high speeds. Military purchasing programs reflected that idea for some time.

Dirigibles from 1909 to 1914: Goliath's Strength and Weakness

In 1909 the list of dirigible balloons was increased by the *Capitaine Marchal*, which was offered to the French government by Lebaudy and Panhard after the loss of the *République*.

In 1911 the Zodiac Company's *Le Temps* was offered to the government following a public subscription opened by the newspaper *Le Temps*. For its part, the army bought the 9,000-cubic-meter *Adjudant Vincenot* from Clément-Bayard; the 9,000-cubic-meter *Adjudant Réau* and *Lieutenant Chauré* from Astra; the 8,000-cubic-meter *Selle de Beauchamp* from Lebaudy; and the 6,000-cubic-meter *Capitaine Ferber* from Zodiac. In 1912 the *Fleurus* was built at Chalais-Meudon; then the army purchased the *Conté* from Astra, the *Dupuy de Lôme* from Clément-Bayard, and the *Coutelle* from Zodiac—all of 10,000 cubic meters.

In 1913 the 6,500-cubic-meter *Montgolfier*, manufactured by Clément-Bayard, was put into service. The *Spiess*, offered to the government by its manufacturer, M. Spiess, constituted a special case. It was the first rigid French dirigible, 16,000 cubic meters, 400 horsepower, with a wooden framework, equivalent to the German Zeppelins. Too heavy, it underwent further modifications when

France entered the First World War, but no other dirigibles were built along its lines. At the beginning of 1914, when the respective fleets of the Germans and the French were compared, the Germans' advantage was obvious. When questioned in the Senate about this state of affairs, the minister of war announced immediate orders for several Spiess dirigibles and for nonrigid, 23,000-cubic-meter cruisers from the French builders, Lebaudy, Clément-Bayard, Zodiac, and Astra. These dirigibles were to have engine capacities of about 1,000 horsepower and attain 80 kilometers per hour. They did not appear until 1915.

Thus the French dirigible industry born in 1905 had delivered a total of twenty-three dirigibles to the army by 1914. Two, the *Patrie* and the *République*, had disappeared; the oldest, built before 1912, had been retired or declared obsolete; and the newest were still being tested. The French therefore had only six dirigibles in August 1914 capable of serving in military operations.

The variety of types used showed that no real series had been produced and that the rationale of their use was still undetermined. The quality of the designs, on the other hand, was very good and could bear comparison with the best airships of the time, the German ones, except in size, since the Zeppelins reached a capacity of 18,000 cubic meters in 1910. France was definitely ahead of all the other countries, which were often its customers.

Germany had a large fleet at its disposal thanks most of all to the persevering efforts of Count Ferdinand von Zeppelin, who had known how to profit from the popular infatuation with his enormous rigid dirigibles with their metal framework. On the eve of the First World War twenty-seven Zeppelins had been built, including some for tourist use within the Delag Company, founded on November 10, 1909. During the same period Germany had two other manufacturers: Schütte-Lanz, which built rigid dirigibles with a wooden framework, far superior to the Zeppelin concept but less supported by the government, and Parseval, which built very good nonrigid dirigibles.

In August 1914 Germany could put twelve dirigibles in the field, ten of them Zeppelins, three of which were requisitioned from Delag.

Captive Balloons Abandoned

The fashion for dirigibles in France beginning in 1901 put captive balloons in the background. In fact, no technical progress was made in that area after the spherical balloons and Renard's airships of 1884. Worse yet, in 1911 it was decided to disband the balloon companies and assign their personnel to the dirigibles; no more captive balloons were built or even maintained. The Germans, on the

January 17, 1914, at Saint Cyr: The new Spiess dirigible on one of its first sorties. The dirigible had by then been lengthened—note the light gray parts.

other hand, after having adopted equipment similar to that of the French, continued their balloon research. Major Parseval devised a captive balloon, the *Drachen*, or kite balloon, which was cylindrical with hemispherical ends and furnished at the tail with a pocket filled by the wind, which stabilized it in direction. Kept in a tilted position by a system of cables, the balloon was subjected to a vertical thrust that was greater when the wind was stronger, and so it was not beaten down toward the earth nor rocked by the wind. The Drachen could be used in very high winds which prevented the ascent of any spherical balloon. It would be one of the first surprises for the French after the outbreak of war in 1914.

The First Studies of Aviation in the Army (1893–1909)

An Early Genius: Clément Ader

The first Frenchman to concern himself with military aviation was unquestionably Clément Ader, who had an outstanding career. Born at Muret in 1841, Ader became interested in aeronautics at an early age; he even tried out a captive glider at Castelnaudary. But he had to make a living and got a job in the administration of roads and bridges in his native region. He soon realized that he would never be able to carry out his plans to build a flying machine unless he first succeeded in making a large enough fortune.

Les Hommes du Jour

Annales Politiques, Sociales, Littéraires et Artistiques

LA "SAUCISSE" AU-DESSUS DE TOUT

Directeur : HENRI FABRE

Cette triple illustration représente : 1° Un Zeppelin dernier modèle ; 2° Le comte de Zeppelin recevant les félicitations de Guillaume II ; 3° (dans le médaillon) : le comte de Zeppelin, inventeur des dirigeables qui portent son nom.

Hebdomadaire : le samedi 30 Janvier 1915. — N° 365
15 CENTIMES

Zeppelin et ses Monstres

ADMINISTRATION
19, rue J.-J.-Rousseau
PARIS (Tél. : Louvre 21-42)

Count Zeppelin as seen in the French press.
(Cover of the weekly Les Hommes du Jour.*)*

Mechanically talented and very inventive, he perfected a combined telephone transmitter and receiver and went to Paris to market it. He played an important role in the development of telephone technology, then just beginning in the capital, and actually made a fortune from the numerous patents he had registered. He then resumed his airplane designing, and in 1882, after a long period of research, he started to build a plane of his own invention, the *Eole*, powered by a 20-horsepower steam engine. The machine, a mechanical marvel that was very expensive to build, was ready for testing in 1890.

Thanks to his connections he was able to make use of a carriage drive in the park of the Château d'Armainvilliers, which was the property of Mme Péreire. It was there that, after getting rid of every witness in order to insure secrecy, he accomplished a successful flight of approximately fifty meters close to the ground on October 9, 1890. This was the first time in the world that man had succeeded in taking off from the ground and flying in a heavier-than-air machine with an engine.

It is worth noting that from the very first thought of his machine Ader had considered its military application; hence the choice of his original design according to which the wings could be folded to facilitate transport. The secrecy of his research was explained as necessary for the protection of an invention very useful for national defense.

This first success was followed by experiments at Satory, which ended in September 1891 with a breakdown of the craft, which was about to effect a second continuous flight of 100 meters.

Having spent a large part of his fortune, and having to repair his airplane, Ader exhibited his *Eole* in a hall in Paris in the hope of finding financial support. Charles Freycinet, the minister of war, a great scientist and a member of the French Academy, came to examine the airplane in October 1891 and promised Ader his help. On February 3, 1892, a contract was signed between Ader and the French government, represented by Freycinet, who used a part of the Giffard legacy for the purpose.

This contract is of interest since it shows to what extent the difficulties of flight were underestimated at that time. The machine was to be capable of carrying one passenger besides the pilot, rising to several hundred meters, and flying for six hours at a speed of at least 15 meters per second, or 54 kilometers per hour. (This level of performance was not attained until twenty years later.)

The government granted a subsidy of 250,000 francs to Ader, who was to pay the remaining expenses himself. If his machine passed the tests, the government committed itself to reimbursing him for the 650,000 francs he had already spent and would give him a million francs for the exclusive use of the craft, which would become the property of the French government.

Ader accepted these conditions with magnificent optimism. At the same time he sent the minister of war a military memorandum in four parts covering: 1) the establishment of a school of aviation and airplanes; 2) the creation of an arsenal for the manufacture of airplanes; 3) aerial strategy and tactics; and 4) the creation of an air force.

The construction of the new machine, called "Airplane No. 3," took a long time and cost more than had been expected. This entailed distressing squabbles with the six ministers of war who succeeded Freycinet.

Finally, on July 21, 1897, it was ready. "Airplane No. 3" was taken to Satory, and construction of a 1,500-meter experimental track was undertaken by Lieutenant Binet. The airplane was of the same type as the *Eole*: a tailless airplane with foldable wings shaped like those of a bat. With its 16-meter wingspan and 56 square meters of surface, "Airplane No. 3" was loaded to less than 10 kilograms per square meter; the empty weight was 260 kilograms. A steam generator fed two 20-horsepower motors, each driving one propeller; this power pack with its accessories weighed 3 kilograms per horsepower, which should be compared to the 80 kilograms per horsepower of standard motors of that time.

Tests were performed at Satory on October 12, 1897. A test flight officially judged by Generals

Self-portrait of Clément Ader at about age thirty (PASM Coll.).

The construction of Clément Ader's "Airplane No. 3" in the shop on the Rue Jasmin, Paris.

Mensier and Grillon took place on October 14, in spite of unfavorable weather, and ended, after a flight of about 300 meters close to the ground and off the track, in a landing that broke the machine apart. Mensier's report described the test run without using the word "flight," but concluded very favorably by proposing continuation of the experiments.

But, as noted earlier, it was a difficult time for military appropriations, which were the subject of many debates in the Chamber of Deputies. Like his predecessors, General Billot, the minister of war, was tired of the continual requests for subsidies and of the delays in executing his contracts by Ader, who underestimated the difficulties. Finally, on February 8, 1898, General Billot definitively stopped the flow of government funds, although he authorized Ader to pursue his experiments at his own expense. All the government offices were favorable to the pursuit of his research, however, which indicates that the trouble was not purely technical.

Ader did not succeed in finding other financial support. Discouraged by the minister of war's decision, which remained without official explanation, and no longer having enough resources at his disposal, he had to abandon the entire project. Thus, in 1898, at the age of fifty-seven, Ader ended his career in airplane construction but continued to write books on the military aviation that was yet to be. His dreams bordered on a strange foreknowledge of what military flying would later become. He died on May 3, 1925, rehabilitated in the public mind and covered with honors.

Although it is true that his experiments had no follow-up, the fact remains that Clément Ader was really the first man in the world to succeed in wrenching himself off the ground—in 1890, thirteen years before the Wright brothers. The books that he wrote between 1907 and 1912 on military aviation certainly influenced the ideas of military aviators and military and civilian authorities from the very beginning of military aeronautics in France.

Captain Ferdinand Ferber (1862–1909): The First French Pioneer

Captain Ferdinand Ferber is one of the great names of French military aeronautics, reminding one somewhat of Colonel Charles Renard.

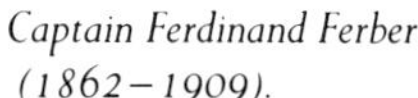

Captain Ferdinand Ferber (1862–1909).

Captain Ferber's experiment at Nice on board the "No. 5 Bis," December 1902.

In 1898 Captain Ferber, a graduate of the Ecole Polytechnique in Paris and an artillery officer, was a thirty-year-old instructor at the School of Instruction at Fontainebleau when by chance in his reading in the library there he came across a series of old articles in a German periodical dealing with Otto Lilienthal's experiments. He immediately became enthusiastic about heavier-than-air craft and considered the progressive experimental method adopted by Lilienthal to be an excellent one; indeed, he became its most zealous supporter in France. He at once felt that success was near, and he wanted France to be the first to benefit from that invention for its national defense.

At some danger to the garrisons, he built four gliders and did not hesitate to experiment with them. His "No. 4," which was very much inspired by Lilienthal's models, was the only one that seemed to him to perform satisfactorily.

Experiments with "No. 4" in 1901 at Nice demonstrated that the coefficients assumed up to then for air resistance were wrong and that the lifting power was ten times as high as had been assumed up to that time on the basis of an old theory of Sir Isaac Newton. From then on he was convinced of the "feasibility" of an airplane. He then pursued his experiments at Nice, where he had a big merry-go-round constructed, consisting of a 30-meter beam pivoting at its center at the top of an 18-meter pylon. It was thus possible to test a full-size airplane.

In 1902 the American aircraft experimenter Octave Chanute came to Paris to give a lecture, which Ferber attended. They had been corresponding since 1901, and from their correspondence there had developed a very loyal collaboration between them and the Wright brothers, whom Chanute had made acquainted with Ferber.

Ferber immediately adopted the biplane design, which has the advantage of a greater surface for the same weight. His "No. 5" is reminiscent of the Wright brothers' and Chanute's tailless model, with a horizontal control plane in front. He tested this glider for a long time at Beuil, in the Alps, and then at Nice, where he equipped it with a 6-horsepower Buchet motor driving two coaxial, counter-rotatory screws.

Since these experiments had caused a considerable stir, Colonel Renard, who had been in contact with Ferber since February 1903, succeeded in getting him assigned to Chalais-Meudon, where he arrived in April 1904 with his equipment from

Nice, purchased entirely at his own expense, and his mechanic, Burdin, hired by the army at such a low salary that in order to keep him Ferber did not hesitate to pay him extra.

At Chalais he perfected a new launching technique for gliders and airplanes, which used a long inclined cable supported in the air by three wooden pylons. The apparatus to be tested was hooked to this cable by a system that released automatically at the end of the run. This very ingenious system enabled him to develop quickly a motorized glider of an entirely new design, the "No. 6 *bis*" and to establish the stability rules for airplanes (the rule of the three V's) which were later taught at the Advanced Aeronautical School. With this glider, on May 27, 1905, he achieved a perfectly controlled motorized glide of about a hundred meters, the first European performance that could be compared with the Wright brothers' accomplishment in December 1903. As had been expected, the power was not sufficient to maintain horizontal flight with a craft weighing some 250 kilograms, but the flight angle changed from 1/5 in a glide to 1/7 with the motor.

From this test run it was easy to deduce the power needed for flight, and on the afternoon of the same day Ferber asked Levavasseur to make him a 25-horsepower engine and bought it on the basis of the plans, entirely at his own expense for lack of government appropriations.

The year 1906 passed in continual financial difficulties since the government was giving Ferber almost no aid for his experiments and he was no longer supported by Colonel Renard, who had died in April 1905. In order to continue his work with more independence, Ferber, who had been offered a position by Levavasseur (who had decided to build airplanes in addition to his motors), asked for a leave of absence, which was granted in July 1906. He was allowed to make use of the facilities at Chalais to continue his experiments. His "No. 8," with a 25-horsepower motor, was to

Ferber's flight on May 27, 1905, at Chalais-Meudon—the first motorized glide in Europe.

be completed in December 1906, but the balloonists, advised in November of the arrival of the dirigible *Patrie*, refused him space in the hangar for his craft's frame, which was being assembled, and had the launching pylons taken down, since they were considered dangerous to the gasbag of the dirigible.

On the night of November 19, 1906, the airplane, left outdoors, was destroyed during a storm. On November 12, 1906, Santos-Dumont's "XIV *bis*" had made its historic flight of 220 meters, in the presence of Ferber, president of the Aero Club of France.

Ferber, in Levavasseur's employ, immediately found his time taken up with urgent management tasks. The company was particularly in a hurry to construct planes of its own design, one of which was the *Antoinette*, to which Ferber had contributed. He did, however, have the satisfaction of being able to reconstruct a Ferber "No. 9," very close to the "No. 8" in design, which flew perfectly the first time at Issy-les-Moulineaux on July 25, 1908, showing what he could have accomplished two years earlier.

Owing to a misunderstanding with the minister of war, however, Ferber was recalled to the army and transferred to Brest. Fortunately his superiors, who had a high regard for him, gave him all the authorizations necessary to attend meetings under the pseudonym of F. de Rue. Thanks to the protection of some influential friends, Ferber was able to get out of the dead-end he had been put into. At the beginning of 1909 he was detailed by the minister of war to the National Air League, which assigned him the job of installing an airfield, "Port-Aviation," at Juvisy (not far from Orly) and establishing the second Civilian Pilots' School after the one created by the Wright brothers.

Ferber was killed, stupidly, in a plane crash on September 25, 1909, at Boulogne, while rolling along on the ground in a Voisin plane on a poorly maintained airstrip crisscrossed with unmarked gullies. He was the second airplane victim in France, Lefebvre having been killed in a Wright plane two weeks before.

It is very unfortunate that the French government did not understand the value of Ferber's experiments earlier. The political situation at that time partly explains the meager resources allotted to them, but it was most of all the lack of belief in the future of heavier-than-air craft among the military leaders which accounts for his neglect. They were not really interested in aviation until 1909, the year of Ferber's untimely death.

As Ferber himself said, his principal role was not that of an inventor but that of a propagandist. It was his goal to give France the first place in aviation and not to win undying glory for himself. The proof of this is that from 1905 on, keeping in touch with the results obtained by the Wright brothers through letters from them and from being in a position to judge the authenticity of the reported facts by a comparison with his own experience, he did not hesitate to recommend officially buying the Wrights' license in order to gain time. He finally persuaded the government to send a mission to the United States in 1906, but it returned without concluding a contract with the American inventors.

From 1902 on, having acquired invaluable experience which was at that time unique in France, Ferber published articles and gave numerous lectures advocating the experimental method, beginning with learning piloting skills with the glider. Thanks to him, beginning in 1903 the movement was launched in France. His disinterestedness was very different from the Wright brothers' attitude of secrecy, and it is certain that his personal activity contributed much to the development of aviation in France.

Aviation Research at Chalais-Meudon

We have seen the part played by Colonel Renard and then by Captain Ferber at Chalais-Meudon up to July 1906, when Ferber left the installation. After his departure the research laboratory continued to function there, the subjects studied being somewhat scattered, depending on the initiatives and tastes of the officers assigned to it.

Beginning in 1907 Captain Lucas Girardville

studied the application of gyroscopes to the stabilization of airplanes; he was among the first officers assigned in 1909 to take pilot training courses in civilian schools. In 1910, at Vincennes, where the Artillery Aviation Establishment had just been set up, he designed an enormous airplane, which was soon destroyed in a crash.

Captains Brianchon, Tarron, and Lelarge studied stabilizers and the feeding of carburetors, and also tested out various types of gliders, but with no great results.

Captain Jacques Saconney, assigned to Versailles at the head of a company of balloonists, devoted himself enthusiastically from 1904 to 1907 to the study of kites and their use in aerial photography. He went to Chalais-Meudon twice before the First World War in order to get the Aerology and Telephotography Laboratory started. While there he designed a prototype windlass-truck for kites and an automobile photographic section. This equipment was first used at the front in 1915.

Captain Albert Etévé was trained in aerostation in Morocco. He received his pilot's license early and participated in the flights of the *République*, on which he objected to the excessive vibrations. In 1909 he was assigned to Chalais-Meudon and given the task of testing the first Wright brothers planes bought by the French army. He equipped one of these with the automatic stabilization system that he had tried with success on dirigibles. But when his Wright craft, modified by his efforts, became a steady, practical machine thanks to the wheels he had added to it, that type of plane was outclassed by newer models built in France. Etévé became famous chiefly for his speed indicator, which, universally adopted in 1911, greatly facilitated piloting and increased safety. Later, detailed to the Aeronautical Technical Service (S.T.Aé.) during the war, Etévé was to play an important role in the improvement of flight technology.

Captain Dorand was assigned to Chalais-Meudon in 1894 and stayed for a long time. He became head of the Aeronautical Laboratory before 1914, then the first director of the S.T.Aé., established in 1916. Beginning in 1906 he experimented with a kite-airplane and various screw propellers and established certain theories relating to airplanes and helicopters. In 1911 he constructed a laboratory airplane that made it possible to take measurements in flight that could be compared with those of the completely new Eiffel wind tunnel. In 1912 he built a two-seated, 70-horsepower observation airplane, from which was later derived, in 1916, the AR airplane with which many squadrons at the front were equipped. In 1913 he built a twin-engined, armored plane under orders from his superiors. He is the only experimenter to have researched at the official laboratory machines directly competitive with those offered by private manufacturers. Because of its position as official judge of all prototypes, however, the laboratory was soon forbidden to continue along this line.

Thus a whole series of studies in connection with aviation was pursued at Chalais-Meudon without the production of the expected military prototype, such as Renard had successfully produced for balloons in 1880. The problem to be solved in this case was incomparably more difficult, and those who could have succeeded in doing so—Ferber, for example—were not supported at the critical moment.

The studies carried on at Meudon were principally valuable in the intellectual training of a whole generation of officers who were to play a big role in military aviation in the future. In technical development the real progress was to come from the private sector. It was most especially Henry Farman's exploit of a 1-kilometer round trip that would definitively open the age of practical aviation, a necessary stage before going on to military applications.

The Real Beginning of Practical Aviation in France

On January 13, 1908, Henry Farman won the Deutsch-Archdeacon Prize at Issy-les-Moulineaux by flying the first kilometer in a closed circuit officially observed. When one recalls that the Wright brothers achieved the same result back in

Captain Jacques Saconney (1874–1935).

Trains of Saconney-type kites, 1910.

An Etévé speed indicator.

Captain Albert Etévé (1880–1976) on his Wright biplane equipped with his stabilizer, April 28, 1910.

Henry Farman flies the world's first 1-kilometer closed circuit at Issy-les-Moulineaux on January 13, 1908, in a Voisin biplane with a 50-horsepower Antoinette engine.

1904, Farman's deed seems trivial. The reality is quite different.

In 1904 the Wrights were using an assisted launching system (a car on rails and towing by cable). Previously they had been unable to take off from their 30-meter rail if the wind was stronger than 30 kilometers per hour, that is, almost equal to their flight speed, so that when the machine left the ground it was already at the normal speed of flight. The same was true for Ferber, whose machine left the platform at its normal flight speed. Thus the difficulties of piloting for acceleration and of stability at very low speeds were eliminated.

All aviation pioneers who tried to fly their planes first taxied on the ground in order to take off with the joystick against the body. If the takeoff was successful, the plane left the ground tail down (Blériot, R. Esnault-Pelterie, Vuia) and began losing speed; or else it crawled along, tail down, in second gear, with the sense of control of depth inverted (Voisin, Delagrange, Santos-Dumont). The low power of the engines did not permit flight under those conditions, and the "hops" or "flights" were measured in tens of meters.

Santos-Dumont himself, after his achievement on November 12, 1906, could never subsequently exceed the 220 meters flown that day, in spite of attempts extending over several months.

Henry Farman was the first to understand that to reach takeoff speed it was necessary to *push* the joystick and then pull it back gradually. Once this "secret" was divulged in 1908 all the airplanes really began to fly in France and, soon afterwards, all over the world.

On October 30, 1908, Farman was the first aviator in the world to do something nobody had attempted before him, not even the Wright brothers: a 27-kilometer cross-country flight, from Bouy to Rheims.

It is thus from January 13, 1908, when Farman flew his first kilometer, that the start of practical aviation must be dated. After that nothing could stop it.

Feeling that the time for commercialization was approaching in this infant industry, a financial group came together in the United States in the spring of 1908 and advised the Wright brothers that they should lose no time in going to France to sell their airplane, through an intermediary, of course. Wilbur Wright came to France in August 1908 and established himself at Le Mans with the aid of the automobile manufacturer Léon Bollée, first at Hunaudières and then, with the army's authorization, in the larger and more open Camp d'Auvours.

In September 1908 he recommenced his flights after a three-year interruption, at first timidly, and then improving little by little to the point of breaking all records standing at that time, December 1908—altitude, distance, and duration—with a flight of 2 hours and 18 minutes.

French public opinion, which had been convinced up to then that the Wrights were "bluffing," was completely reversed. However, this was not to be the success the Wrights had been expecting for three years: the efforts of the French designers were beginning to bear fruit, as the year 1909 would demonstrate.

On July 25, 1909, the aviator Louis Blériot crossed the English Channel. The big international aeronautics meet at Rheims took place in August; all the first prizes were won by Frenchmen. The Gordon Bennett speed cup was won by Glenn Curtiss, the great American pioneer, in a machine of his own design, very much inspired by the Voisin planes of the time. Of the thirty-four aviators competing in the air meet, Curtiss, one Belgian, and one Spaniard were the only foreigners.

Three Wright planes, piloted by Frenchmen trained by Wilbur Wright, were unable to outclass their competitors: the Wrights' head start was a thing of the past. The Wrights then went to Italy and Germany to show their machines and were able to sell some there. In France the Wrights had established, at Pau in 1909, the first pilot training school in the world, where it was possible to get the civilian pilot's license that the Aero Club of France had just introduced. Several other schools were established at almost the same time by French manufacturers. In France the Wrights sold only a few machines to their student pilots and a few to the army for comparison with the French-built airplanes. Finally, in the fall, at the Grand Palais in the middle of Paris the first Aerial Locomotion Exhibit took place and was very successful.

The Birth of Military Aviation (1909–1914)

First Airplane Purchases by the Army. First Pilots

Thanks to the exploits of the first pioneers who competed for the prizes offered at races or air meets, often organized with the cooperation of the press, aviation had become very popular. The cross-

General Roques (1856–1920).

An Antoinette airplane at Rheims, 1909.

Lieutenant Colonel Estienne (1860–1936) with officers of the Vincennes Establishment, including Camerman (at right).

country flights, initiated by Farman and Blériot in 1908, made people think that aviation was going to become a common practice. The military command could not remain unaware of this publicity move, nor could they wait for the Chalais laboratory to furnish the necessary equipment on its own, as Charles Renard had done for ballooning.

General Roques, director of engineering in the Ministry of War, concerned himself with aeronautics through the facility at Chalais-Meudon. He had the Rheims air meet followed up by a commission entrusted with designing the best machines for him, which he proposed to buy on research appropriations in order to evaluate their military potential. In this way, in September 1909, two Farman biplanes with a 50-horsepower Gnome engine, two Wright biplanes with the 30-horsepower Wright-Bariquand engine, and a Blériot with a 25-horsepower La Manche-type Anzani engine were bought. They were to be used by the Corps of Engineers.

At the same time, however, some artillery officers had also followed the events at the Rheims meet and considered that two-seater airplanes could be used for adjusting artillery fire. Since they had no appropriation, it was necessary to ask the French Parliament for one. Parliament did, in fact, allocate 200,000 francs for the purchase of artillery planes, in Article "29 *bis*" of the finance act. Major Estienne, head of the brand-new Aviation Establishment created a month earlier at Vincennes, chose three Farman biplanes, two Wright planes, and two Antoinettes.

The Artillery-Engineering Corps Rivalry

Thus from the very birth of military aviation a rivalry set in between the artillery, which at first saw in the airplane the true successor of the captive balloon for artillery spotting, and the Corps of Engineers, which wished to study aerial navigation more generally in order to determine the various possible uses of it.

To these differences of opinion were added

personal considerations; Major Estienne of the Artillery Aviation Establishment at Vincennes did not want to be dependent on Major Bouttieaux, materiel director of the Corps of Engineers.

Parliament itself took up the question, and certain members attempted to settle the quarrel. The Senate urged the minister of war—General Brun, of the Artillery—to resolve the question. It would take four years.

A solution was imposed by General Brun, taking the form of a decree dated October 22, 1910: all aerostation and aviation services were placed under the authority of a general officer designated as Permanent Inspector of Military Aeronautics. The first one to fill the position was General Roques, whose first concern was to organize the nascent aviation forces. Aviation could at last function. The next two years were essentially a period of experimentation with both machines and ideas. It was not until 1912 that General Roques felt sufficiently sure of himself to propose a law definitively organizing aeronautics.

The Vincennes Military Aviation Laboratory under Major Estienne, now assured of being maintained, worked in a very different direction from that of Chalais-Meudon.

For the artillery officers the airplane was fully developed; it sufficed to choose among the civilian models available at the time those best adapted to their needs. In their eyes all that remained was to experiment with the tactics of its employment. Vincennes was to Chalais-Meudon what the Military Experimentation Center is today to the Flight Testing Center.

The artillerymen were the first to try out bombardment with shells and aerial darts, the use of incendiary grenades that could be dropped on top of a dirigible (the improvised materiel was to be an obstacle), and also signal codes for use in artillery ranging. Vincennes tried to demonstrate that observation and ranging could be carried out by the pilot alone, a thing that Chalais-Meudon, believing in the two-seater, did not admit.

The Artillery's fascination with the single-seater was justified by the low price of the planes and the ease with which they could be transported, which, it seemed, justified the systematic assignment of one airplane per battery. The artillerymen also encouraged studies of defensive armament for airplanes, but without arriving at a good solution.

During this time Chalais-Meudon concerned itself more with technical problems affecting the performance of the planes as well as their equipment.

This Artillery-Engineering rivalry, often pushed to an extreme later, at least had the merit of stimulating competition and contributed not a little to inducing reflection on the problems of utilization that were to arise from 1914 on, in wartime.

The Year 1910: First Airplane Maneuvers

While the new military pilots were being trained on the recently acquired planes it was possible to get a better idea of the machines and their capabilities.

The Wright plane soon proved to be dangerous because of the delicacy of its piloting. Major Etévé, one of the first ten licensed pilots and a military engineer who was soon to play an important technical role, managed to modify the Wrights. The Astra Company, the licensed French manufacturer of the planes, fitted one of them with wheels and a rear stabilizer; the other was fitted by Major Etévé with an automatic depth stabilizer. But it was still a very slow plane.

The Antoinette was fragile, and its engine was often in disrepair. In the end it was the Farmans that did most of the work. Frequent damage to the airplanes made new purchases of them necessary during the year.

During the last half of 1910 two military aviation schools were opened, one under Camerman at Châlons, the other at Vincennes directed by Féquant, with the first men who passed the course serving as instructors. By the end of the year fifty-two army pilots and six navy pilots had been trained.

Flight instruction in these schools was at first

based on what was taught in the civilian schools. The tests for the pilot's license were the same as for the license issued by the Aero Club of France, limited to three 5-kilometer closed circuit flights and precision landing.

The methods of instruction varied with the type of plane. The Farman two-seater permitted flight with dual controls, while for the Blériot single-seater it was necessary to begin with long sessions of rolling on the ground in a machine with clipped wings and a worn-out engine, incapable of taking off, called the "penguin" because of its swinging gait on the runway. Then, after many explanations on the ground, came the takeoff, full of unforeseen incidents.

The duration of instruction in the flight schools varied widely, from a few weeks to several months, depending on the weather and the availability of aircraft and supplies. From the start, in the military schools, cross-country flights were encouraged as well as the participation of the officers, after leaving the school, in the races and meets so fashionable at the time, in which they cut a very fine figure.

In September 1910 large-scale military maneuvers took place in Picardy. For the first time airplanes were used in them, at the same time as dirigibles. Two army corps took part, the 2nd and the 9th. The 2nd Army Corps had 2 Farmans, 1 Sommer, and 1 Blériot for its use; the 9th had 2 Farmans, 1 Wright, and 1 Blériot. These planes were piloted by regular officers or trained reservists, such as Paulhan, Latham, Louis Breguet, and Robillard.

The region chosen for the maneuvers was not a favorable one for the use of aircraft: constant winds, deep valleys, and apple orchards, which reduced the possibilities for landing and hampered the observation of troops on the ground who took refuge there.

Colonel Hirschauer's report noted that the meteorological conditions were particularly unfavorable to the dirigibles: winds were blowing almost continuously at velocities higher than 10 meters per second and sometimes attained 15 to 18 meters per second. This grounded them almost completely. As for the aviators, the colonel reported that they "went beyond what was demanded of

Military maneuvers in Picardy, 1910: the Liberté *making an ascent above the troops.*

A Breguet plane piloted by Louis Breguet in the Picardy maneuvers of 1910.

them, beyond any hopes that could have been conceived." Indeed, the airplanes had successfully carried out most of their assigned reconnaissance and liaison missions. Nevertheless, it appeared necessary to give the observers a more thorough training.

The airplane proved itself to be an indispensable military instrument which only needed to be perfected. The earlier experiments in photography, done at Châlons, and in radio, done at Buc, then revealed their full significance.

When these maneuvers were over, some of the pilots expressed surprise that no one had thought of arming their craft; they proposed doing so in preparation for a future military conflict. General Roques's conclusion was that, "Airplanes are as indispensable to armies as cannon and rifles. That is a truth that we must freely admit under pain of having to feel the force of it." Soon after the maneuvers the army ordered 20 Blériots and 20 Farmans.

After the accidental death of Captain Ferber in 1909, the year 1910 soon, unfortunately, also had its first losses: Captain Madiot was killed on October 25, 1910, in a Breguet plane, and Lieutenant de Caumont crashed in a Nieuport on December 30.

1911: The Military Airplane Competition

The year 1911 was dominated by the specter of a coming war which could be predicted from the new claims being made by Germany. The sending of the German gunboat *Panther* to Agadir on July 2, 1911, raised emotion in France to a fever pitch. In order to avoid risking war the president of France, Joseph Caillaux, ceded half of the Congo to the Germans. It would not be returned to the French until 1919. This episode, which shed little glory on France, highlighted its military weakness and led patriots to demand that the nation rearm more quickly. In this way it was beneficial to the development of aviation.

It was also in 1911 that airplanes engaged in military operations for the first time. First, the Italians, during their war against the Turks, used the Blériots they had bought from the French to make reconnaissance flights in Libya from Tripoli in October 1911. Then Lieutenant Barès lent the support of French aircraft to the Serbs at Ioannina during the Balkan War of 1912. It was also during that war that the Turks, Bulgarians, Serbs, and Rumanians in 1912 and 1913 hastily put together air forces (9 to 15 planes per country), for the most part with French planes, although some Austrian ones (Etrichs) were also used. Some French civilian pilots offered their services to one side or the other, and a number of officers were officially placed at the Serbs' disposal.

Attention was drawn to the role that could be played by airplanes in the overseas territories of France. In 1911 an airfield was established at Biskra, Algeria, for the use of Farman planes, and Lieutenant Sido was sent to French West Africa to set up an aviation unit there.

The great aviation event of the year, however, was the competition for military airplanes, the tests of which were carried out at Montcornet, near Rheims, from October 8 to November 28, 1911.

The goal was to provide a three-seater plane—one pilot, one observer, and one copilot—capable of traveling 300 kilometers and landing on short airstrips with varied surfaces, including a cultivated field. After eliminations, which insured that the planes had passed these tests and satisfied minimum conditions of vertical and horizontal speeds, the ranking of the aircraft was done as a function of their flying speeds.

The prizes were very large, and success in the competition promised government orders. Forty-three manufacturers enrolled with 140 machines; only 31 machines actually showed up for the competition, of which only 9 passed the elimination tests. The results were:

First place: the Nieuport 100-horsepower Gnome, piloted by Weymann (119 km/h); the winning plane was purchased by the government, and an order was placed for ten more (at 40,000 francs each).

Second place: the Breguet 140-horsepower Gnome, piloted by Moineau (95 km/h); six airplanes of this type were ordered.

Third place: the Deperdussin 100-horsepower Gnome, piloted by Prévost (92 km/h); four airplanes of this type were ordered.

The competition established the supremacy of the Gnome rotary engines, with which the first five planes in the competition were equipped, and the qualities of the Renault 70-horsepower air-turbine-cooled V-8.

No other orders for these aircraft were placed after this competition, since those ordered ab-

A Farman airplane in Biskra, Algeria, 1911.

sorbed a large part of the aeronautics appropriations, already eaten into by the expense of restoring aircraft already on hand, which was necessary three times during 1911 because of crashes.

The principal objective of the 1911 competition was to prod the manufacturers into designing sturdier planes capable of carrying heavier loads than the usual sporting planes. To emphasize this difference and to honor the memory of Clément Ader, on November 29, 1911, General Roques ordered that from then on any airplane accepted by the army would be called "Avion" (now the usual French word for "airplane").

But 1911 had seen other innovations as well. First of all, there was the inauguration of the military pilot's license requiring three 100-kilometer flights at an altitude greater than 300 meters. A mechanic's license was also instituted, as well as courses of instruction for observers.

All of the licensed civilian pilots had to undergo new tests. Of the fifty-two licensed before 1911, only thirty-one passed the new license test. Six others had been killed or retired after serious injuries; the rest had been returned to their original units or had given up aviation. One was flunked for refusing to take the oral examination on matters that the candidate considered "mechanic's business."

It should be noted that the order in which the military licenses were issued was not the same as that in which the first officers passed their civil license. This explains certain possible confusions: the No. 1 of the "military" licensees was Lieutenant de Rose, future inventor of the fighter plane, while the first military man who passed his "civilian" pilot's license, a year before, and made a solo flight on a military plane was Lieutenant Camerman.

Accidents, unfortunately, became more numerous: in 1911 there were eleven killed. These accidents were often caused by poor adjustment of the airframe (the Wright plane, in particular, was very subject to tailspin) or to lack of knowledge of certain aerodynamic phenomena. Several suctions of control surfaces took place on Farmans, as happened to Captain Tarron, who went into a nose dive, turned over, and was ejected.

Assembling a Breguet airplane beside a repair truck during the 1911 maneuvers.

The winning airplanes of the 1911 military competition; left to right: Nieuport, Deperdussin, Breguet.

The engineer Gustave Eiffel had built the first French wind tunnel in 1909, and the first results had just been published in 1911, which served to improve airplane design. Furthermore, for lack of an adequate instrument, pilots easily experienced a loss of speed; this type of accident became less common as the Etévé speed indicator came into general use. It was also in 1911 that the seat belt was declared obligatory in order to prevent ejections in flight, which had occurred several times.

Finally, in the course of the fall maneuvers, which were very satisfactory insofar as air missions were concerned, the disadvantage of equipping units with mixed types of aircraft was discovered, since it complicated the task of providing supplies. The idea then emerged of creating units equipped with machines of only one type; 1912 saw the official creation of the "flight," or "escadrille" (squadron).

On November 21, 1911, Military Aeronautics was authorized to place insignias on the wings of its planes, but the order was not given until 1912.

Although military aviation was just coming into existence, civilian activity was already quite considerable. In 1911 the aviation industry produced 1,350 airplanes, 1,400 engines, and 8,000 propellers. A good part of this equipment was exported, France being then the principal world aeronautical center. During the year the Aero Club of France issued 350 civilian pilot licenses.

1912: Creation of the "Flight" and of the Insignia

Two innovations were introduced on January 1, 1912: the regulation flight record and flight pay.

Also, five flights of six planes each with homogeneous equipment were set up during the early months of the year: the Henry Farman Flight, HF 1, at Châlons; the Maurice Farman Flight, MF 2, at the de Buc school; the Blériot Flight, BL 3, at Pau; the Deperdussin Flight, D 4, at Saint Cyr; and the Maurice Farman Flight, MF 5, at Saint Cyr.

But 1912 is primarily important for the fact that, under the pressure of public opinion which demanded further development of aviation, the law that organized the Aeronautics forces was passed on March 29, 1912. The law created flying personnel and troops; seven aeronautical companies (balloons and dirigibles); ten aeronautical sections (airplanes); and one company of engineers.

On July 14, 1912, the new Aeronautics flag was presented to the Aeronautics troops at Longchamp by M. Fallières, President of France. In fact, from 1912 on everyone wanted the creation of a Directorate of Aeronautics in the Ministry of War. This was not done all at once, but by a more complex process not begun until 1914.

For the moment, the new Permanent Inspector of Aeronautics (pro tempore), Colonel Hirschauer, was occupied with organizing the units. A decree of August 22 divided them into three groups: the first, at Versailles, under the command of Lieutenant Colonel Bouttieaux; the second, at Rheims, entrusted to Lieutenant Colonel Breton; and the third, at Lyons, with Lieutenant Colonel Estienne in command. These appointments became effective on October 1, 1912.

The autumn maneuvers, under the direction of General Joseph Joffre, took place in the region of Parthenay-Saumur-Tours-Châtellerault-Poitiers. Each of the two armies participating was supplied with one of the two dirigibles, the *Dupuy de Lôme* and the *Adjudant Réau*.

In addition to the five flights just formed, there were a flight of six Borel-Blériot single-seaters, another of four Hanriot single-seaters, and finally one equipped with prize-winning three-seaters from the military competition of 1911 (Nieuport, Breguet, Deperdussin). The artillery fielded a flight of Blériot single-seaters and the cavalry, two flights of three Blériots of the same type. Altogether, sixty planes participated in the maneuvers; forty-nine of them were piloted by officers or noncommissioned officers on active duty and eleven by reservists.

It was the first time that such a large group of air forces had been assembled. For the first time, too, these formations were linked in each army to supply and repair units that insured their autonomy. The magazine *L'Aérophile* for October 1, 1912, wrote: "We find that the improvisation of last year, certainly interesting in itself, has given way to a completely systematic and truly military regulation. . . . As it is now officially recognized that aviation plays a predominant part in the reconnaissance service, the orders and reports are given in military style. The commanding officer of a group, upon receiving the order to have such and such a sector reconnoitered, designates the flights or units that are necessary and has precise orders issued by the flight commanders at set hours, regardless of the weather."

The result of the reconnaissance operations was greatly appreciated, but two criticisms enable us to understand the turn soon taken by materiel procurement programs. General Joffre noted that while airplanes were incomparable for going in search of a large column on the road at a great distance, their contribution was more dubious in battlefield reconnaissance. At altitudes greater than

The Eiffel Auteuil Laboratory in 1910; in foreground, Gustave Eiffel.

Military maneuvers, 1912: Lieutenant Noé taking off in a Maurice Farman plane.

1912 maneuvers: Borel airplanes; note the tricolor emblems on the wings.

1912 maneuvers: a radio post.

700 to 800 meters observation became hesitant in detecting or estimating the numbers of troops not traveling on the roads. At distances usual in close combat, close and continuous contact was provided better by cavalry than by airplanes since the latter's speed of movement did not compensate for the brevity of their observation.

Lieutenant Colonel Estienne, commanding officer of the "Red" army's air units in the maneuvers, gave an opinion that accompanied General Joffre's. The reconnaissances were made at low altitude—1,000 meters or less—because of the necessity of seeing through the mist in the morning and evening. In these conditions it appeared that an unarmored plane would be greatly exposed. "As soon as the enemy is convinced that the airplane is a serious adversary," he wrote, "he will try to find means of combating it, not only in its own element by means of armed airplanes but also by using special devices mounted on automotive vehicles. . . . The conclusion is that airplanes, except those of the artillery, should be armored." This question of armor for airplanes was debated from 1913 on.

The foreign attachés, for their part, took a lively interest in the three-seater planes, and from certain indications a suspicion arose that espionage was being used to obtain information in foreign countries.

The new aviators' uniform was defined in an order of 1912: dark blue (almost black) tunic with close-fitting collar. The collar insignia consisted of a star with one wing for the aviators, while it remained a toothed wheel for the balloonists. In nondress uniform the aviators wore an armband with a toothed wheel, which exempted them, in town and until six o'clock in the evening, from wearing the saber, "wearing which was judged dangerous in flight." A special compensation—the first "flight pay"—was established in May 1912, as well as a per diem compensation for aeronautical service for unlicensed personnel making a flight under orders.

The year 1912 was especially remarkable for a press campaign prompted by the number of aviation accidents. It was not to be the last outburst from the press. Two men were killed in 1910, eleven in 1911, and twelve in 1912, from already reduced numbers of air personnel. There was an uproar in the Chamber of Deputies about it. Colonel Hirschauer was then appointed government investigator and instructed to make an inquiry, on which he reported in June 1912 in the Chamber. The explanations he gave seemed satis-

From September 26 to October 19, 1912, antiaircraft firing tests were done with a rifle, Saint Etienne machine gun, and 75-millimeter cannon. The tests were done from the ground against gliders towed by the destroyer Fourche.

factory. It is amusing to recall that, in order to give the impression that all safety measures had been taken, the colonel stated that with a view to reducing the frequency of losses of speed by using the Etévé indicator, he had given orders to add a second speed indicator on all airplanes.

The storm had passed, but the minister of war still asked that a more thorough investigation be made. This led to improvements in flight instruction in the schools and modifications of the airplanes in service. Systematic investigations after each accident became the rule.

In July 1912 Colonel Hirschauer decided that from then on military airplanes would bear two tricolor roundels under the wings. The year 1912 ended with the ordering of 400 new planes. The colonel was promoted to general on December 12 and received the title of Permanent Inspector of Aeronautics, the functions of which he had performed only in an acting capacity until then.

During the entire year the French aviation industry had manufactured: 1,425 airplanes, 2,217 engines, and 8,000 propellers. The Aero Club had issued 469 civilian pilot's licenses.

1913: The Artillerymen Take the Helm

In the autumn of 1912 a massive campaign supported by the major newspapers of the day—*Le Temps* and *Le Matin*—resulted in the creation of a National Aviation Committee with Georges Clemenceau as chairman. A national subscription was opened for contributions, which by February 1913 had collected nearly four million gold francs (fifteen million francs in 1980 currency).

Four hundred new airplanes were ordered during the first half of 1913, making it possible to furnish the equipment of the flights and to equip one with the new Caudron G 2. Nine types of aircraft were then in service: Blériot single-seater, Breguet, Caudron, Deperdussin, Henry Farman (with a Gnome engine), Maurice Farman (with a Renault engine), Nieuport, REP, and Voisin. Although the types of missions were always the same, no agreement had been reached on the most appropriate model, each pilot having his own ideas.

On April 16, 1913, a decree was issued that modified the organization of Aeronautics. Nothing had changed in the structure of the air forces (groups, establishments, "aviation centers," that is, bases), but the units were placed under the direct authority of the army corps commanders or the local administrators on whose territory they were stationed. The powers of the Inspector of Aeronautics were correspondingly diminished.

This decree may be viewed as the outcome of a long dispute between the partisans of an air force with a certain autonomy and those who wanted to see in the "flights" nothing more than a tool at the disposal of the ground units, such as the artillery batteries or the baggage trains. This debate will recur throughout the history of French military aeronautics, with more sharpness than in any other nation's armed forces.

The most unexpected thing, however, occurred late in August 1913. The minister of war, alerted, it seems, by the artillerymen, instructed General Bernard, an artillery officer entirely unacquainted with aviation, to make an inquiry into the state of the air forces. General Hirschauer could do nothing but ask to be relieved of his command, which was granted. General Bernard was appointed Chief of Aeronautical Services in September 1913 and surrounded himself with artillery officers who had had aeronautical experience.

On November 1 a new series of steps was taken: complete separation of aerostation (ballooning) from aviation, the three mixed groups being transformed into two aviation groups and one aerostation group; militarization of the repair services; and training of pilots exclusively in military camps (until then a certain number of pilots were trained by the manufacturers). Many important posts in the air services or the units were turned over to higher-ranking officers who were not aviators. In fact, on January 1, 1914, there was only one higher-ranking officer who was a pilot—Major Barès—stationed in the Balkans.

General Bernard favored an equipment program in which all planes would be armored. Several

Military maneuvers, 1913: the Blériot flight at Agen.

The dirigible Commandant Coutelle *in the 1913 maneuvers.*

The dirigible Fleurus *flies above the troops, 1913 maneuvers.*

June 6, 1914: General Bernard shows General Joffre the armored airplanes at Villacoublay. They are examining a Dorand plane.

machines were offered, but the low power of the engines meant that these heavily loaded craft were slow. Only the old two-seaters, converted into armored single-seaters, could perform creditably. Few planes were manufactured on the basis of these prototypes, and this radical change of approach introduced a hesitation that was to be felt until the beginning of the First World War.

1914: Creation of the Directorate of Aeronautics. A Narrow, Rigid Policy

Everyone was mentally prepared for the publication of a decree on February 12, 1914, that suppressed the Permanent Inspectorate of Aeronautics. A technical inspectorate was established for each branch—aerostation and aviation—the higher officers being directly responsible to the minister of war.

A decree of February 21, 1914, suppressed the Directorate of Aeronautic Materiel. The services subordinate to it became autonomous and were changed to: the Central Aerostation Materiel Establishment, which incorporated the former Laboratory of Aerology and Telephotography (Major Labadie); the Aviation Manufacture Service, handling aviation purchases and engine repair (Major Stammler); the Aeronautical Laboratory at Chalais (Major Dorand); and the Aviation Laboratory at Vincennes (Major Raibaud). To these services were added a military aviation engineering section and an aviation materiel inspectorate.

Finally, a decree of April 21, 1914, established, under the Ministry of War, the long-awaited Directorate of Military Aeronautics, entrusted, quite naturally, to General Bernard, who had inspired the reform. The separation between the aviation and aerostation services was completed. Another decree defined the fields of study of the two laboratories at Chalais and Vincennes, the latter getting the lion's share.

It is unfortunate that the high command showed little enthusiasm for the studies conducted here and there toward arming airplanes and equipping them with cameras and radios. There were a great many initiatives that deserved to be better supported.

The Michelin brothers, for example, struck by the bombing possibilities offered by the airplane, started in 1912 a heavily financed competition called the "Aéro-cible Michelin" (Michelin Air Target). The contestants were to drop 7-kilogram spherical bombs on a target 20 meters in diameter from a minimum altitude of 200 meters. There was another prize for the inventor of the best system of sighting and launching bombs. The winners—Gaubert and Scott—put 12 out of 15 bombs on the target in tests made at the camp of Châlons. The same competition was held in 1913 and 1914. It confirmed the Michelin brothers in their conviction of the importance of aerial bombing and led them a little later to perfect on their own the bombing method known as *tir en trainée*, which became regulation in 1917.

As for aerial bombs, in spite of the successful trials in combat in Morocco during the capture of Taza in May 1914, no special type of bombs for use by airplanes was being manufactured. Only "Bon" darts were ordered in 1913.

Similarly, the idea of forward firing with a weapon fixed in the axis of the airplane arose as early as 1911 and was tried out early in 1912 on a special Blériot plane with a 37-millimeter revolver cannon set in front of the propeller. In this case Colonel Estienne had allowed himself to be persuaded by Lieutenant Bellenger; the results were disastrous for the too-light structure of the plane. Tests were resumed by Bellenger and Blériot at Buc with a Hotchkiss machine gun, which was

Captain Bellenger (1878–1977).

Villacoublay, February 9, 1914: a machine gun mounted on a Deperdussin two-seater.

Captain Jean Faure testing a 37-millimeter cannon on a Voisin.

better tolerated by the airframe. Six airplanes of this type were used by Rumania in 1913, but the pilots did not have to make use of their weapons.

Still others—Deperdussin and Voisin—persisted along this line, the latter with a movable weapon, first a 37-millimeter cannon, then a machine gun (in August 1914). These were semi-official trials which made possible Frantz and Quénault's first aerial victory on October 5, 1914.

The armored airplane prototypes were presented on June 6, 1914, to General Joffre. Voisin unveiled a new plane with a 100-horsepower Canton-Unné engine and a 37-millimeter gun. Several other models, which were too heavy, remained at the prototype stage. When the war began only three models survived from this program: the parasol-wing Morane-Saulnier, the Blériot-Gouin, and the Voisin were added to those ordered in 1912 and 1913 and still fit for service.

In 1914 the recruitment of pilots was continued, and the training speeded up: from 1909 to August 1914 the army trained 657 pilots, 220 of whom were in service in 1914. Of about 1,250 airplanes purchased, 126 were in service at the beginning of the war, and a similar number were in the general reserves; over 50 were being used in the flight training schools.

Military purchase orders played a big role in the aviation industry from 1913 on. Certain companies went out of business for lack of orders, such as Sommer, Antoinette, the C.G.N.A. (making Wright planes under license), and a part of REP (Robert Esnault-Pelterie). Certain others, in 1914, had to agree to manufacture planes of another brand, such as Breguet, Nieuport, and REP, which made Voisins, or Blériot and Deperdussin, which manufactured Caudrons.

The only engines still in use in 1914 were the 80-horsepower Gnome rotary, the 70-horsepower Renault, and the 85-horsepower Canton-Unné.

From 1911 on the army standardized its manufacturing orders, with planes having a control column and rudder-bar as at present and a throttle lever the opposite from what is used today. One had to pull the throttle lever to open it fully. In fact, France did not change the direction of the throttle's movement until after the Second World War, in order to fall in line with the Anglo-Saxon system. This action must have pleased the horsemen of 1911, who had recommended the latter arrangement by analogy with their habit of pulling on the reins to slow down their mounts.

In 1914 Roland Garros, a test pilot with Morane-Saulnier, which was then producing the fastest plane of its time, was invited by Captain de Rose to visit the Vincennes air base. Saulnier studied machine gun synchronization, but firing toward the ground proved catastrophic: one ball out of ten hit the propeller; the very design of the machine gun then in use made synchronization of the weapon impossible. An attempt was then made to protect the propeller blades with steel; the idea seems to have been Colonel Estienne's. But war broke out before this system could be perfected; the attempts started over again a few months after the beginning of the war.

It is remarkable that all of these experiments were carried on with practically no official support. For the high command only the role of scout belonged to the airplane, and there was a fear that the presence of any armament would divert the crew from its primary mission. This is demonstrated by the reaction, on July 2, 1914, to Captain Jean Faure, who had just reported on his tests of the 37-millimeter cannon on the Voisin plane: "Very interesting work which shows that the officer that conceived it has a spirit of research that deserves to be encouraged, but one that smacks much more of Jules Verne than of reality."

Still less interest was shown in studies of aerial photography and radio. The first experiment with a radio on board a plane took place in 1911. In 1912 a staff note stated that the use of the radio was inconceivable on board a two-seater since the observer must not be distracted from his mission; only a three-seater might be suitable. A committee was even established, presided over by Major Ferrié, to pursue these studies. In 1913 experiments conducted at Buc and at Villacoublay, although cut short by accidents, showed that with relatively reduced sets, weighing about 50 kilograms, it was possible to get a range of 100 kilometers. These initial studies were not encouraged, and it was still necessary to improvise in this area in 1915.

For his part, Captain Saconney, head of the Telephotography Laboratory at Meudon, had perfected a complete photographic apparatus which he asked to have tested in the maneuvers of 1913. But the minister of war rejected his request, arguing that it was impossible to train observers who were specialists in photography in time for the maneuvers.

These maneuvers of 1913, the last conducted before the war, confirmed the high command in its approach to military aviation. The operations took place in the south of France, between Agen and Toulouse. General Joffre, who was still in charge, asked for three flights to be put at the disposal of each side. They were made up of six airplanes of the same type in homogeneous units, consisting solely of the personnel ordinarily assigned to them and not of requisitions from different formations, as had been the case in 1912. There was thus a closer approximation to the conditions under which the aviators would have to operate in wartime. The pilots took with them observers who, this time, had received some instruction. On the ground, before takeoff, notebooks containing silhouettes were handed out to aid in recognizing the enemy. The men were thus trained to avoid any possible confusion in future combat. The results received comment in the speech made by General Pau to the aviators: "Thanks to you, hour by hour, starting in the morning, we have known what the enemy was doing. The reports were numerous and prompt; better yet, they were exact."

War began in earnest before the experiments with arms and equipment could be completed, and it was on the battlefield that the needed adjust-

An armored Blériot 43 in 1914.

ments and improvisations were made.

Mobilization, in principle, had been well prepared for, but the results were disappointing; it took some time to straighten out the disorder of the first assignments. Nevertheless, there were 21 flights available: biplanes: 5 Maurice Farmans, 4 Henry Farmans, 2 Voisins, 1 Breguet, and 1 Caudron; monoplanes: 4 Blériots, 2 Deperdussins, 1 Nieuport, 1 REP, and 2 Blériot cavalry single-seaters.

What is most surprising is that because of the delays of 1913 and 1914 the artillery, which held the reins of power, no longer had a single flight at its disposal that specialized in firing control. The old equipment had been revised, and the "Couade" prototype, on which Lieutenant Colonel Estienne rested his hopes, was not ready in time. Since balloons had been abandoned three years earlier, at the beginning of the war the French found themselves in a critical situation in this respect.

As a result of program changes and indecision, from June 1913 to August 1914 only 350 planes were bought. This enabled the Germans, who had been far behind the French in aviation, to catch up with them.

Nevertheless, some good came out of General Bernard's administration; the standardization of aircraft equipment, aimed at reducing the number of types, was a good thing. But the idea of armor-plating planes was premature, since the engines produced less than 100 horsepower. It is undoubtedly there that the lack of direct experience displayed by the commanders appointed, who worked out aeronautical problems in a fashion too exclusively logical, without giving engineering the weight that it has always had in aviation, did the most damage.

One month after France's entry into the war, in the face of the first results, General Hirschauer was recalled to head the Directorate of Aeronautics.

Conclusion: The Creation of Military Aviation before 1914

The first five years of French military aviation, in spite of the inevitable errors that encumber every creative work and the policy disputes, which come so naturally to the French, were nevertheless positive. This was due for the most part to the previous existence of an already well-developed industry.

It must be remembered that in England the first company to manufacture airplanes, in 1909, was Short, which specialized in balloons. It was still a matter of manufacturing under the Wright license. Bristol made the Breguet under license in 1912; other companies made the Blériot. In fact, the first English military airplanes were just beginning to appear at the start of the war.

The United States was still further behind. The first plane bought by the United States Army—and just one plane—was a Wright, in 1908; it was two years before a second was ordered. In fact, the United States Army (much reduced in size compared to contemporary European armies) was hesitating among several equally faulty planes in search of, preferably, an American-made craft. Burgess was the firm that supplied the first planes in numbers greater than one, and then Curtiss, which had distinguished itself at the Rheims air meet. (Glenn Curtiss held license No. 2 of the Aero Club of France, issued early in 1910.) In August 1914 the American army marshaled a total of twenty-eight airplanes.

Only Germany, for a long time cautious because it was very confident in its Zeppelins, was able to catch up with French aeronautics, although its industry did not start up until 1910, and then it was on the basis of the models of the Austrian Etrich. The French delays of 1913 and 1914, even though France had had the best start, enabled Germany to be at least on a par with it in August 1914. Since it surpassed the French with its Zeppelins and especially since it had maintained—and perfected—its kite balloons, it actually enjoyed a very distinct qualitative superiority in the aerial field.

But aviation was to be further perfected on the battlefield, and the gap was not so great. Fortunately for the French, thanks to the incomparable development of sport aviation in France for nearly ten years, France had a lead in the industrial field and large reserves of high-quality civilian pilots and engineers. These two factors were to save the French from the worst in the early days of the war and give them the advantage a little later on.

PART 2

The Great War in the Sky
The 1914-1918 Air War

Introduction

The First World War was to see the development of military aviation beyond all expectations. The novelty of battles in the sky brought forward a new class of combatants—the aviators. It also made it possible for certain exceptional men to give the full measure of their courage, intelligence, and daring, thus helping to maintain the image of the individual hero, which was otherwise so blurred in that war of masses. It was on this that French aviation would found its traditions.

But the First World War was also the occasion of great technical and industrial progress brought on by the war effort. Of all the branches of the armed forces it was undoubtedly military aeronautics that developed most rapidly in the course of the conflict, and of all the belligerents it was France that devoted the greatest effort to aviation. At the time of the armistice in 1918 France possessed one of the two leading aeronautical industries in the world, sharing that distinction with that of Great Britain, after having held the first place until 1917. France had at its disposal the most powerful military aviation in the world.

But to arrive at that position, which helped bring about the final victory, great efforts had to be made, painful revisions of prejudices were needed, and great courage had to be displayed. For, at the beginning of the war, the ideas that generally prevailed, in both France and Germany, were that the conflict would be of brief duration and would assume the form of a war of movement, since everyone thought that only offensive action would be effective.

On the French side all the logical conclusions were drawn from those beliefs, and so it was that at the beginning of hostilities General Bernard, Director of Aeronautics, had all the flight training schools closed and all those awaiting instruction sent back to the corps from which they had come. As it was also conceded that in a war of movement captive balloons were difficult to use, in 1911 the companies of field balloonists had been disbanded, leaving only the four stationary centers intact. However, even for those, from 1913 on, it was acknowledged that their equipment would not be replaced.

Reconnaissance and artillery ranging had to rely on the use of dirigibles and airplanes. It was very surprising to discover, right at the start, the vulnerability of the dirigibles, which very quickly made it necessary to confine their use to nighttime (this was true of both French and German dirigibles). It was also surprising to find that the Germans had retained balloons and were using an improved type, the Drachen, or kite balloon, and that the supply train of their aeronauts, being entirely motorized, gave them good mobility.

The airplane soon proved effective, especially for observation, but not being equipped with the means of quick communication with the batteries on the ground, it was not the equal of the balloons, which were connected directly by telephone with the artillery command posts.

In the heat of the first battles of 1914 it became necessary to modify all the prevailing notions, to create and perfect equipment adapted to war. The advance of Germany's troops posed such a threat to Paris that the aeronautical engineering services had to be evacuated to Lyons. During the first hours of the war the first efforts at rectifying the situation rested on a handful of high-quality fighters.

We shall study here the evolution during the war of the two principal branches of aeronautics—aerostation and aviation. For the former, which comprises dirigibles and balloons, the story is relatively simple, for from 1916 on the evolution of the equipment and its use was practically at a standstill. On the other hand, the history of aviation is much more complex, keeping pace with the potential of the materiel, which was replaced time after time in accordance with a technical progress which did not stop at the end of the war.

For greater clarity, then, this part will be divided into three main chapters: dirigibles, balloons, and airplanes. It must be remembered, however, that this classification does not correspond to the military value of the means employed—the part played by balloons was considerable throughout the war, as we shall demonstrate—nor, even more emphatically, to the value of the crews. The courage and the exploits of the balloonists, although they have remained little known, were in no way inferior to those of the aviators, who had a more popular public image.

After following the major conflicts on the battlefield, we shall look into the part played by the home front, or the rear, which was of decisive importance in supplying weapons and in training personnel.

French Aeronautics at the Beginning of the War

The better acquainted we are with the general situation of aeronautics at the beginning, the better we shall be able to measure its evolution during the fifty-two months of the war.

The aviation section comprised 21 flights of 6 airplanes each in peacetime, to which were added 2 BLC (Blériot cavalry) flights of 4 airplanes each. Of these 23 flights, 11 "covering" flights could be mobilized immediately. In addition, 297 airplanes were on order, and 65 had been delivered on August 1.

Immediately after mobilization new flights were created from airplanes delivered or salvaged behind the lines, and certain airplanes manufactured to fill foreign orders were also requisitioned. On August 3 the DO 22 was activated (with airplanes made at Chalais-Meudon). On August 6 the flights MS 23 and V 24 were created, as well as BLC 5. On August 12 the C 25 single-seater flight was created, which became MF 25 on August 15. The 1st Aviation Artillery Section of the Vincennes Laboratory was attached a little later to the 22nd Artillery Regiment; it became the HF 32.

Aviation personnel numbered about 3,500, including 240 officers and 240 noncommissioned officers for 21 flights and 2 BLC's, as well as: 4 airports and "first reserves" for replacements (Rheims, Belfort, Verdun, and Camp Châlons); 2 companies of workmen at Saint Cyr and Lyons; 2 depot companies at Lyons and Rheims; and 2 "second reserves" for replacements at Lyons and Saint Cyr. Each flight was made up of only about 50 men.

CHAPTER I

Dirigibles in the First World War

At the beginning of the war all the belligerents had the intention of using dirigibles for reconnaissance of enemy ground forces and possibly for bombardment; only the Germans and the British envisaged their use at sea, and they assigned very few dirigibles to that mission. The British were the only ones to concern themselves solely with their use at sea, but still they had only four units at their disposal: a French Astra-Torrès, a German Parseval bought in 1913, and two English balloons (the *Beta* and the *Delta*, of rather mediocre performance).

The state of the air forces existing in August 1914 may be summarized as follows. Germany could marshal 232 airplanes and 12 dirigibles (9 of them Zeppelins) and numerous Drachen kite balloons in the armies. France put into service 162 airplanes and 6 dirigibles; it had no balloons in its armies, but only four stationary bases equipped with a few spherical balloons. Austria-Hungary had 56 airplanes. Great Britain could muster 84 airplanes and 4 dirigibles attached to the navy, but no balloons. Russia put into service about 190 airplanes, many of them of French design, but no dirigibles or balloons.

In fact, the role of aeronautics, limited to observation, the often poorly understood real possibilities of the craft, and the very limited numbers of machines, always delicate to use, did not give aeronautics a very great weight in combat in 1914. The imbalance of the air forces in Western Europe, apparently in favor of the Germans, was not really of such a nature as to tilt the balance to one side rather than to the other.

It was only little by little during the war that aeronautics came to assert itself and play an increasingly important role. The balance of forces in November 1918 was much more telling in this regard.

In France mobilization of the aeronautics units—aerostation and aviation—was effected according to Plan XVII of February 14, 1914, modified in July 1914.

The aerostation section was made up of: 4 stationary companies (the 21st to the 24th) at Toul, Epinal, Belfort, and Verdun; 8 companies (the 1st to the 8th) manning 8 ports of registry for dirigibles: Toul, Epinal, Belfort, Verdun, Maubeuge, Versailles (2 companies), and Langres; 1 company of workmen at Châlons; and 1 depot company at Versailles. Personnel after mobilization numbered about 4,000, including 70 officers and 220 noncommissioned officers.

The Adjudant Vincenot.

The Dupuy de Lôme.

The Montgolfier.

The Conté.

Germany marshaled: 9 Zeppelins (3 of them requisitioned from the Delag Company); 1 Schütte-Lanz (rigid, with a wooden framework); 1 Gross-Bassenach flexible airship; 1 small training Parseval; and 1 Zeppelin L 3, belonging to the navy, which had lost two other Zeppelins in 1913. It should be noted that the German Zeppelins were identified by a letter followed by a number assigned in order: Z for the Zeppelins built before the war; LZ for army Zeppelins manufactured during the war; and L for the navy's Zeppelins.

France had six dirigibles at its disposal: 3 Clément Bayards—the *Adjudant Vincenot*, the *Dupuy de Lôme*, and the *Montgolfier*; 1 Astra—the *Conté*; 1

Zodiac—the *Commandant Coutelle*; and 1 Chalais-Meudon—the *Fleurus*. The navy had no dirigibles assigned to it.

Russia, which before 1914 had bought a Lebaudy, an Astra, and a Parseval, had no dirigibles in service in August 1914.

As we shall see further on, the use of dirigibles on land was soon found to be disappointing and practically ceased in 1916–1917. In contrast, because of the development of the war at sea and under the sea, the dirigible proved to be a remarkable means of reconnaissance and surveillance of the seacoasts. Since the naval war—blockade and then unremitting submarine warfare—developed in 1916 and more intensely in 1917, it was at that time that large appropriations for the navies came about. It should be recalled that the record tonnage sunk by the Germans was 900,000 tons and occurred in April 1917.

On land the German army used a total of 34 dirigibles in the eastern, western, and southern parts of its territory. It stopped using dirigibles in the east at the beginning of 1917. The navy used a total of 78 dirigibles, of which 64 were Zeppelins, 9 Schütte-Lanzes, 3 Parsevals, and 1 Gross-Bassenach. Six of these machines were used for training.

At the beginning France used the 6 dirigibles in service at the start of the war, to which were added in 1915 several Zodiac and Astra-Torrès dirigibles. In 1917 three of these craft still in serviceable condition—the *Fleurus*, *Lorraine*, and *CMT*—were turned over to the navy with their crews, the army having definitively abandoned the use of dirigibles. In July 1918 the navy had 37 dirigibles, 10 of which were in reserve.

It was in Great Britain, which had hesitated for a long time in adopting dirigibles and was behind in their manufacture at the beginning, that these machines were manufactured in the largest numbers for the navy's needs. At the time of the armistice Great Britain had 103 of them, after having manufactured over 200. It gave a certain number of small dirigibles of the SS type to its allies, including France.

Using Dirigibles in Land Operations

The role played by French dirigibles in the war cannot be discussed without recalling that played by German and Allied dirigibles as well.

After the first bombardment of the war, on August 3, by a German airplane on Lunéville, the first bombardment by a dirigible was undertaken by the Germans on August 6, on the square of Liège, with the Zeppelin *Z VI*, which was hit by cannon and returned damaged. The *Z VII*, on a reconnaissance mission over French installations in Alsace, was also hit. The *Z VIII*, more unfortunate, was downed by French artillery. Sorties became less frequent, for the Germans still had only a few of the machines, and the damage suffered had to be repaired. The *LZ 38* bombarded Yarmouth in January 1915 and London, which was a target for a long time, on May 1. Paris, attacked for the first time by a "Taube" on August 30, 1914, was again attacked by the *Z 10* and the *LZ 38* on March 12, 1915. It was not to be bombed thereafter except on January 29, 1916, by the *LZ 79*, which was damaged on the return trip.

At the beginning of the war the dirigibles were vulnerable only to land weapons; antiaircraft weapons existed only in an embryonic state. But because of the low ceiling of the dirigibles of that time—less than 2,000 meters—as well as their low speed and the enormous size of the target they offered, dirigibles were very vulnerable. The heavy German losses are explained by the fact that their dirigibles came out only in the daytime.

On August 14 two French planes piloted by Césari and Prudhommeaux carried out the first bombardment of a dirigible hangar, at the Metz-Frescaty field. On June 7, 1915, in Belgium, Lieutenant Warneford of the Royal Navy Air Service, in a Morane single-seater, succeeded in bombing and destroying the *LZ 37*. This is the first instance of "counter-bombardment," of which we shall see several examples up to 1945.

On the Eastern Front, where there was little antiaircraft to be feared and still less pursuit, the Germans used their Zeppelins for a long time, even in daylight. There were maritime surveillance missions in the Baltic and in the Black Sea, long-range reconnaissances, and bombing missions. Taking off from bases in Lithuania, Poland, Hungary, or Bulgaria, the Zeppelins bombed Warsaw, Sebastopol, Odessa, Bucharest, the Rumanian oil installations, and later the Italian ports of the Adriatic. The entrenched Allied camp of Salonika was thus attacked by the *LZ 85*, which, after being damaged, had to be set down in the marshes of the Vardar, where its commanding officer had it burned.

The German Zeppelins flew a total of 136 missions in the west, 103 in the east, and 37 in the Balkans. A total of 50 dirigibles were used; 25 were destroyed, 17 of them by enemy action.

The Germans, unlike the French, built dirigibles at a great pace until 1917 with the idea of using them for terror bombings of the Allies' cities. By synchronizing the air attacks with a massive ground operation the Germans were hoping to produce such a psychological effect as to cause their enemies to give up political power in the event of a successful ground attack. It is no doubt for that reason that London was attacked much more often than Paris, in the hope of getting a separate treaty with the British. But in spite of the great Zeppelin production during the war, the Germans were never able to put more than a third of their strength on the line at any given time.

To put them out of range of cannon and especially of pursuit planes, from 1916 on the Germans concentrated on increasing the tonnage of their dirigibles—the only means capable, in spite of the weight of the bombs, of raising the flight ceiling and at the same time increasing the speed and the radius of action. In 1914 the Zeppelins had a volume of 22,000 cubic meters. In 1915 they went up to 32,000 cubic meters, in 1916 to 55,000, and in 1918 to 68,000 cubic meters. At the same time, and with several years' delay at Schütte-Lanz, the original cylindrical shapes of the Zeppelins gave way to better, streamlined bodies, starting in 1916 with the *L 30*. The power increased from 600 to 1,600 horsepower, the speed from 75 to 120 kilometers per hour; the maximum weight of the bombs carried reached about 4 tons and the altitude 7,500 meters for the best machines. From 1915 to 1918 there were ten different types of Zeppelins, from Type O to Type X.

The Germans were slow to make night flights for lack of navigating and locating equipment. For this purpose, starting in 1916, they used radiogoniometry (radio direction-finding equipment).

But the German dirigibles suffered throughout the war from a severe handicap: the difficulty of predicting the weather. Thus the famous raid of October 19, 1917, turned into a catastrophe because of an unforeseen storm: of 11 navy Zeppelins launched against England only 7 were able to return to Germany, the others having drifted to France. The *L 49* was able to land intact at Bourbonne-les-Bains, the *L 45* was destroyed on the ground near Sisteron, the *L 44* was shot down by cannon in the Meuse, and the *L 50* was lost in the Mediterranean. Beginning in 1917 bombardments on land became more and more the work of the multi-engined G airplanes on the Western Front and of the giant R airplanes, chiefly used on the Eastern Front.

On the French side the dirigibles revealed the same weakness when used in land operations.

The *Fleurus* was the first Allied airship to penetrate into Germany; on August 19, 1914, it flew over the Saar and went on as far as Treves on a night reconnaissance mission.

From the beginning the dirigible missions were often carried out at night, since in 1914 the blackout was still unknown and navigation was done with the enemy in full view. Moreover, all the bivouacs were lighted, and observation was quite rewarding; all that was needed was good weather.

But mistakes were soon made. In 1914 there were such press campaigns bemoaning the French inferiority in dirigibles that the troops on the ground who saw such a craft could not fail to take it for a Zeppelin. No particular orders were given (free corridor for crossing the line, for example), and the reconnaissance flares dropped by the balloons were mistaken for enemy fire.

On August 9 the French airship *Conté* was

The Zodiac dirigible Marquis d'Arlandes *at Saint Cyr, 1915.*

subjected to friendly fire for ten minutes near Lunéville; seriously damaged, it had difficulty returning to its base at Epinal. On August 24 another incident occurred. Forced to withdraw before the German advance, the *Dupuy de Lôme* was riddled with French bullets upon its arrival at night, although it had notified the commanding officer at Rheims of its approach. A pilot was killed, and the balloon had to be rebuilt. The enemy was, in fact, less dangerous to the French dirigibles than their own troops. This led the high command to forbid their flights after the *Dupuy de Lôme* affair; they were not resumed until April 1915.

The balloonists took advantage of this order to discontinue the flights and worked to perfect their equipment and methods. A large-faced compass and a drift indicator were adopted for compass navigation; Salmson designed the fin assemblies of the 90-millimeter shells used as bombs, and bombsights were installed. Recognition signal projectors were also installed as well as other improvements.

Behind the lines, in the rear, after the disappointing trials of the first prototypes of the 22,000-cubic-meter flexible dirigibles, these were transformed into smaller balloons. Thus the first Astra, the *Pilâtre de Rozier*, was cut in two and gave birth in September 1915 to two balloons—the *Pilâtre de Rozier* and the *Alsace*.

Finally, the military command modified its concept of the use of dirigibles. Since the fronts had been stabilized, strategic and tactical reconnaissance lost some of its importance; moreover, the troops on the ground had adopted the habit of extinguishing their fires at the sound of the engines. Also, the enemy learned to adjust its firing better, and it became more accurate at each sortie. It was thus necessary for the dirigibles to fly at higher altitudes. Priority was therefore given to aerial bombardments.

From April to September 1915 it was the *Adjudant Vincenot* that carried out the greatest number of bombing missions against the railroad stations and troop concentrations at Valenciennes, Aulnoye, Douai, Cambrai, and Tournai. Positive results were obtained, but the airship, commanded by the famous Captain Joux, received over one hundred bullets in its vital systems. It is remarkable to note that in six months this airship, which held the world record for sorties, carried out only thirty-one missions; the Germans did no better. This gives an idea of the fragility of the balloons and of the restrictions on their use.

Beginning in September 1915 the first 15,000-cubic-meter dirigibles began to appear: the *Alsace*, the *Champagne*, the *D'Arlandes*, and the *Pilâtre de Rozier*. The last three, at the request of Captain Joux, were equipped with an upper platform armed with an antiaircraft machine gun, which the Zeppelins adopted in turn. These balloons carried 1,300 kilograms of bombs and had a ceiling of 2,800 meters loaded and 4,000 meters after dropping their bombs. They were still inferior to the Zeppelins of the time because of the limitation on their volume imposed by the flexible envelope design.

Bombing missions were no longer carried out except on dark nights. The *Alsace*, which continued to fly low and on bright nights in order to improve its accuracy, was destroyed on October 2, 1915, and the whole crew was taken prisoner (the commanding officer was Lieutenant Cohen). It is true that on September 2 the *Commandant Coutelle* had also been destroyed in the forest of Bouchet, although it was navigating with greater prudence.

During the battle of Verdun the *Adjudant Vincenot* and the *Champagne* were used in that sector in spite of very intense antiaircraft fire which eventually destroyed them. The *Adjudant Vincenot* was hit on June 2, 1916, and landed south of the Calonne trench, where its crew was gathered in by French troops. On May 21, on its way back from bombing the railroad station of Brieulles-sur-Meuse, the *Champagne* had also been hit by two shells. Its crew was able to land within French lines, and it was possible to repair the balloon (the commanding officer was Captain Joux).

From June to September 1916 there was only one dirigible left, the *D'Arlandes*.

In June 1916 the commander in chief thought it necessary to improve the employment of the dirigibles, which until then had been largely left to the initiative of their commanding officers. He appointed Captain Joux inspector of dirigibles with the assignment to improve their operating methods.

But at the same time submarine warfare was developing, and the needs of the French navy came into conflict with those of the army, which could content itself with the use of airplanes in its operations. Starting in 1915 Chalais-Meudon had perfected a remarkable airship for the navy—the *CM-T*, with a very streamlined shape, designed by Captain Letourneur. Eight other airships, intended for the army, were under construction by civilian manufacturers, such as the *Lorraine*, the *Fleurus II*, the *Corfou*, the *Capitaine Caussin*, the *Flandre*, and others.

On February 25, 1917, it was finally decided to withdraw the army dirigibles from the land fronts and turn them over to the navy.

In all, the French dirigibles carried out 63 missions on the land fronts in the west. Land missions totaled 28 in 1914, 19 in 1915, 14 in 1916, and 2 in 1917.

The rate of French dirigible losses (6 out of 10) was comparable to that of the Germans (25 out of 50). The total number of combat missions—61 French and 276 German—compared to the number of dirigibles in use—10 French and 50 German—gives an average number of missions per dirigible of 6.1 for the French and 5.5 for the Germans. It may be concluded that the use of dirigibles was fairly similar on the two sides. The very low rate of use, however, clearly demonstrates that they were not suited very well for use on the land fronts.

On the other hand, dirigibles proved extremely useful for missions at sea.

Using Dirigibles in the War at Sea

The dirigible's characteristics—long autonomy of flight, long range of action, higher payload than that of the airplanes—were precious for its use in the empty areas where there was little reason to fear antiaircraft fire and pursuit. It was natural that the navies of both sides thought of using their services for surveillance at sea.

The mission entrusted to the dirigibles by the German navy was twofold: on the one hand, to assume responsibility for conducting the strategic bombings undertaken by the army from 1914 on; on the other, to carry out reconnaissance missions at sea for the benefit of the navy and the protection of minesweepers near the coast. The German navy had dirigibles of its own from the beginning of the war; when the army stopped using them in the west at the end of 1916 its resources went to reinforce the navy's.

In all, the German navy made use of 78 dirigibles; it carried out 200 bombing missions, 53 of them over England, and 1,145 reconnaissance flights. It was Captain Schutze's *L 11* that first spotted Jellicoe's English fleet on the occasion of the Battle of Jutland (May 30–31, 1916).

The British, who were particularly vulnerable to Zeppelins approaching by way of the North Sea, organized various systems of protecting themselves. Night pursuit squadrons and antiaircraft guns were developed. Then the British navy used twin-engined seaplanes and land-based pursuit planes taking off from pontoons towed out to sea. Thus antiaircraft fire destroyed 3 Zeppelins, and airplanes and seaplanes accounted for 14 others; 6 Zeppelins were destroyed on the ground by bombing; and 30 were lost because of weather or mechanical failure. In all, the German sailors lost three-quarters of their dirigibles in operations.

In spite of these terrible losses, the Germans pushed firmly ahead with the use of dirigibles, which were the only means of compensating for the numerical inferiority of their fleet. In 1917 it took only six weeks to build a Zeppelin.

On the Allied side it was the British that first understood the part that dirigibles could play in the surveillance of coasts infested with floating mines and submarines. From the beginning of August 1914 they used a craft hastily constructed from an old Willows airbag with a *BE 2C* airplane fuselage as nacelle. This little 1,800-cubic-meter balloon was the forerunner of the "blimps" ordered from the beginning of 1915 from Armstrong-Witworth and Airships. Fifty little blimps called *SS* (Sea Scouts) were quickly constructed. They were followed by machines of the same class—*SS P*, *SS Zero*, *SS Twin*—of from 2,000 to 3,000 cubic meters, 100 to 200 horsepower, cruising at 65 kilometers per hour for over twelve hours. One hundred and fifty *SS* craft of varying specifications were delivered.

To increase the range of action and carry out reconnaissance missions, beginning in 1916 the English also turned out type C (Coastal Patroller) dirigibles, 5,000-cubic-meter Astra-Torrès trilobal airships with a firing position above the hull; then some NS's (Northern Sea), 10,000-cubic-meter Astra-Torrès craft of 500 horsepower, the most successful of the British dirigibles.

The English also made several rigid airships.

The German Zeppelin dirigible L 49 *after a forced landing at Bourbonne-les-Bains, October 20, 1917.*

Navy dirigible balloons at Rochefort-sur-Mer, 1918: at left, Zodiac blimp VZ 4; *in the hangar, Astra-Torrès* AT 4.

The Navy dirigible AT 3 *at Bizerte, Algeria, April 1, 1918.*

After the unfortunate *Mayfly* of 1911, which broke in two on its first flight, the *R 9* was used at the end of 1916. Then, inspired by the Zeppelin technology learned from the wreckage of the dirigibles shot down, but poorly adapting it, they produced the *R 23*, *24*, *25*, and *26*, which, however, were greatly inferior to the Zeppelins of the time.

The British manufactured a total of 226 dirigibles of all types and gave several to their allies, in particular several *SSZ*'s and a *C* to the French navy while the latter was waiting for airships belatedly ordered by it in France. Their losses due to enemy action were only two *C*'s attacked by German pursuit seaplanes.

At the beginning the British used their blimps somewhat like balloons, touching down along the coast at open-air encampment points. Then they built nineteen centers equipped with mooring masts; twelve camps were then added. The total number of flight hours gives an idea of the activity of these dirigibles: 340 hours in 1915, 7,000 hours in 1916, 22,400 hours in 1917, and 53,300 hours in 1918, for a total of 83,040 hours of flight time.

In France the navy was first equipped in March 1915 with two *SSZ*'s and a *C* acquired in England. In 1916 it installed bases all along the Channel and the Atlantic coastline and equipped itself with Zodiac, Astra, and Chalais-Meudon dirigibles. In 1917 it received the army's airships and extended its installations to the Mediterranean, as well as to Salonika, Oran, Algiers, Bizerte, and Corfu. All of the dirigibles were twin-engined. The 10,000-cubic-meter AT (Astra-Torrès) "cruisers" were equipped with machine guns and 75-millimeter guns. The armament of the smaller blimps was more modest (47-mm cannon). An airship school had been established at Rochefort-sur-Mer.

In 1917 the annual production capacity had risen to 4 CM's, 10 AT's, and 12 Zodiacs. The navy had 5 dirigibles in 1916, 8 on January 1, 1917, 25 on July 1, 1917, and 36 a year later. Total hours of flight time were 4,150 in 1917 and 12,150 in 1918. The losses were slight: one CM-T lost off Sardinia, one *SS*, which hit a cliff in the fog, and two AT's, which were victims of breakdowns or of the weather in the Mediterranean.

The effectiveness of the dirigible missions is indisputable: no ship convoy accompanied by a dirigible was ever attacked by submarine. Although there is no absolute proof of the destruction of a submarine by a dirigible—by gunfire or more often by bombing—there are strong reasons to believe that at least four German submarines were destroyed by French airships. Sixty submarines were spotted, and over one hundred mines were destroyed during the war. The resources allocated to these missions were always small, however, on the order of 4,000 men. The crews of the French dirigibles had become very skillful. They navigated by reckoning with wind speeds that the aerostation personnel calculated from observations made at posts up to 1,000 kilometers apart and mostly situated east of the bases. This meteorological network belonged to the aerostation branch itself; navigation was facilitated by direction-finder readings made on board from transmitting posts on the ground. Astronomical sighting was sometimes used at night or above the clouds.

After their capture in France in October 1917 the German *L 45* and *L 49* were studied by Chalais-Meudon, which set up a rigid aircraft project, the realization of which was begun by Le Creusot in May 1918. On January 1, 1918, an ambitious program provided for the construction of ten rigid airships deliverable from within eighteen months to two years. At the same time two gigantic dirigible hangars were built at Orly to shelter them. After the armistice everything was canceled, and only the hangars were completed, although they never housed any dirigibles.

Among the other belligerents, only Italy followed the example of the French and English allies and constructed about ten semi-rigid dirigibles of the Forlanini type peculiar to that country. Its army used them for bombardments and missions at sea. In all, these Italian dirigibles carried out 258 bombings and totaled up 1,400 hours of flight time.

Thus the dirigibles proved too vulnerable on the defended fronts and too fragile to be thrown into combat against a powerful enemy. On the other hand, they rendered the greatest services in the protection of convoys and in coastal surveillance, especially since the German submarines of the time had no snorkels and so could hardly leave the coastline and traveled most often on the surface.

Naval Aviation

The dirigibles' success in operations at sea should not, however, make us forget the important part played by airplanes and especially by seaplanes in the patrolling of the coasts.

At the beginning of hostilities the navy aeronautic service had a total of 8 seaplanes and not a single dirigible. On January 1, 1917, it still had only 159 seaplanes and 4 dirigibles, while the protection of convoys and the security of the ports were becoming more essential as the length of the war increased and France's industrial potential was based more and more on replenishment of the raw materials necessary for the manufacture of arms, not to mention the demands to be satisfied in

An F.B.A. seaplane Type H at Saint Raphaël, 1917.

A Donnet-Denhaut seaplane at Saint Raphaël, 1917.

foodstuffs for both the civilian and the military population.

Implementation of the new programs was entrusted to the Technical and Industrial Service of Maritime Aeronautics created in 1917 and placed directly under the authority of the Undersecretary of State for Aeronautics, in this case representing the Ministry of the Navy. On November 11, 1918, the Maritime Aeronautical Service had 1,264 seaplanes, 40 dirigibles, and 200 captive balloons at its disposal.

The role of the seaplanes was in antisubmarine operations in coastal areas. Their missions were divided between escort and scouting of ship convoys. Their patrols detected lurking submarines, attacked them, and destroyed them. They also spent long hours exploring the sea to detect mines laid by the enemy. They also had the duty of correcting the fire of ships of war, conducting bombardments (by bombs or torpedoes), and engaging enemy squadrons in combat.

The seaplanes were assigned to centers (8 to 42 aircraft) and combat posts (4 or 6 seaplanes subordinate to a nearby center); there were also ports of call. These formations were scattered along all the French coasts, including the coast of Corsica. This arrangement was supplemented by centers situated in Portugal and in the eastern Mediterranean, as well as in Africa—Algeria, Tunisia, Morocco, and Senegal. The division into areas of responsibility derived from agreements with the British.

To increase the effectiveness of coastal patrolling the minister of war put several coastal flights of airplanes at the disposal of the navy. These squadrons, made up of land-based bombers or gunplanes, were organized like the army squadrons.

The seaplanes were practically all equipped with hulls—in general, biplanes of 200 to 300 horsepower (F.B.A., DD, Lévy-Besson, Coutant, and Tellier armed with a 75-mm gun)—for bombing or with floats for pursuit (Sopwith, Spad, and Hanriot). To reconnoiter the flotilla the F.B.A. flying boats were used on the *Campinas*, the French navy's first aircraft carrier (the seaplane was catapulted and landed on the water, where a crane picked it up and put it back on board; there was no flight deck). Conclusive experiments repeating those of the British were done with a Hanriot pursuit plane with wheels taking off from a wooden platform resting on a gun turret; the plane landed on the ground. But the range of all these airplanes was less than forty nautical miles, and the dirigible was still irreplaceable for long patrols, the planes taking off only upon alert.

In principle the personnel for maritime aviation was recruited from the navy crews, who were trained in maritime operations. But as far as the flying personnel was concerned the navy had to allow some exceptions to the rule because of the shortage of personnel fit to perform these functions. The maritime aviation schools consisted of the Berre School for training navy pilots who had obtained their military license in the army schools; the Hourtin School, which trained all of the observers; the Saint Raphaël School, which served several purposes—an applied training school for pilots and observers from Berre and Hourtin; an advanced training school; a school for shop personnel (mechanics, carpenters, stevedores, armorers); and a school for section heads.

CHAPTER II

Captive Balloons

Since 1911 France had completely discontinued the use of captive observation balloons in favor of airplanes. The appearance of the German Drachen balloons in August 1914, and especially the excellent results that they enabled the artillery to obtain, demonstrated the mistake made by the French.

It took all the competence and faith of several exceptional men to redress a situation so seriously compromised; this must be recalled before recounting the use of balloons, which, having been established in 1915, varied little up to the conclusion of the war.

Captain Saconney, who before the war had had the opportunity to work at Versailles in the aerology laboratory on various observation devices, undertook the first initiatives in this direction. Using balloons found in the stationary balloon parks, improvising winches from requisitioned vehicles, training a few observers, and himself making the first trials at the front, Saconney succeeded in persuading the Army of the East and then the commanding general of the XVIIth Army Corps.

The G.H.Q. followed very quickly, and thanks to competent measures taken without delay 10 companies of 3 sections, each putting 30 balloons into service, were at the front by October 1914 and 10 others at the beginning of 1915. At the end of 1915 the number was up to 36, and a few months later the 75 companies judged necessary for all of the armies had been activated.

Parallel to this a corresponding effort was being made behind the lines to develop and manufacture new materiel. By first copying the German Drachen, the defects of which were soon brought to light, its design was improved; but most especially, thanks to Captain Albert Caquot, a greatly improved balloon was sent to the front at the beginning of 1916. This very successful balloon was later adopted by the navy and by the Allies. What was most surprising—and unfortunate for the French—was that even the Germans adopted it, after capturing several balloons of the new type that had been sent up within French lines and had been torn from their cables by a bad storm on May 15, 1916. Thus by the end of the war the "Caquot" balloon had been universally adopted.

In fact, tremendous effort had been put into technical development and manufacturing in France, which resulted in the production of almost perfect equipment turned out in abundance. By the time of the armistice the total number of balloons manufactured had risen to more than 1,100, over 200 of which had been turned over to the Allies. From 1916 on it had been possible to give parachutes to the French balloonists, the first

A French spherical captive balloon photographed by a Caudron G 3 observation plane, on the Somme, April 1915.

A horse-drawn steam winch for captive balloons, 1915.

A Caquot "M" captive balloon, May 15, 1916.

A Navy 760-cubic-meter balloon.

to be so equipped; and a new and still further perfected type of balloon was being developed for manufacture, thanks to Captain Letourneur. Improvements in both the methods and the training of observers, added to the quality of the equipment, enabled French ballooning to play an important part in the war, which the development of aviation should not cause one to forget.

Balloon Operations

It is hardly possible here to follow in detail all the operations in which balloons were used since this would amount to recounting all the battles of the war. Recalling the most striking episodes will no doubt suffice to show the importance of balloons in the course of that war.

At the early stages the leading role went to Captain Saconney, an able and enthusiastic man, an innovator and propagandist. At the head of the 30th Company, which he had just activated, he immediately worked with the first heavy artillery pieces (115 and 120 mm) put into service in late August of 1914, then with the first group of 105-mm guns turned out by Le Creusot, which reached the front on September 28, 1914. He very quickly cleared the way for the missions proper to the balloon: observation, artillery ranging, verification of demolitions, sector reconnaissance. Since the balloon was connected directly to the battery by telephone, reaction time was reduced to a minimum. Thanks to his talents as an observer and the judicious use of simple equipment and effective methods, he very quickly obtained exceptional results, which were sufficient to convince artillerymen and staff officers of the balloon's military value.

In a few months he perfected the general rules for the employment of balloons: distance of the point of ascension (about 5 km from the lines); altitude of observation, continuing observation to increase the yield (the balloonists spent entire days in their nacelles); point of encampment to the rear of the point of ascension and out of sight; and installation of telephones.

At the end of December 1914 Saconney was made battalion commander and given command of three companies, on which he imposed his rules for balloon use. Thus, from September 27, 1914, to February 10, 1915, in spite of the winter, the 20th Company put in 172 hours of ascensions (124 in a spherical balloon and 48 in kites), for a total of 80 sightings for batteries and 67 ranging operations. It was with Saconney's aid that the G.H.Q. issued its first instructions on the employment of aerostation (October 6 and December 1, 1914).

But in addition to Saconney a number of other observers particularly distinguished themselves at that time: Warrant Officers Arondel and Mathieu and Sergeants Tourtay, de Laujardière, and Forest. Lieutenant Weyl produced the first photographic panorama on October 20.

In May 1915, during the operations in Artois, aerostation was employed on a large scale for the first time. Tourtay reported some convoys, which were destroyed by the artillery; Arondel accomplished 25 rangings on June 19 between noon and 1730 hours, an uncommon feat in the course of the war.

In Champagne in September 1915 occurred the first use of what has become an institution: the "army balloon," or "command balloon," as well as the "army corps balloon," reporting directly to the army or army corps command post without delay, especially on the progress of friendly forces, which is always a difficult thing to follow.

When launching the Verdun offensive the Germans, greatly concerned with reducing the effectiveness of enemy artillery, tried to neutralize the French observation efforts. We shall see later what their tactics were for eliminating the airplanes. To deal with the balloons they devised the plan of aiming two long-range guns at each of them; the first fired time-fused shells at the balloon, and the second fired percussion shells at the winch. The balloonists were trained in the classical evasive movement called the "cartesian diver"—seeing the shots fired and counting on a lead time of about 45 seconds, they telephoned to the winch for a rapid rise or descent (5 meters per second) of 100

An observer in a captive balloon; the parachute is packed in its bag at the side of the basket.

meters; if the order was judiciously given and executed, the shell burst too high or too low. But in this case the maneuver was rendered ineffectual since in a short time the telephone lines were cut and the maneuver became impossible. For several days the French batteries were totally blinded, and this benefited the Germans so much that they were able to maintain the air superiority that they had acquired the first day.

It took a month for Major de Rose, the creator of pursuit tactics, to repulse the German airplanes and enable the balloons to resume their observation. Once again they proved very useful, as appears in Joseph Bédier's report on Tourtay:

A few days after 2 April, new attack. Second Lieutenant Tourtay sees the Germans rapidly descending the slopes and indicates their successive positions during their advance. That day the situation before Verdun was grave, and the precariousness of our communications was such that only the balloon could report the facts. General Nudant knows Second Lieutenant Tourtay and has a high opinion of him; but is he sure of having recognized the Germans? He could have made a mistake, and only the general's staff and the general himself are inclined to believe that he took for enemy infantry our own light infantry who are holding that line. Second Lieutenant Tourtay swears on his honor as an officer, and our fire is set off. In the night the 74th Infantry Regiment counterattacks and partially retakes the trenches of the wood of la Caillette; the prisoners that they take declare that our barrage of the day before littered the railroad track with German cadavers. Thus by the work of a balloonist the route to Fleury and Souville was blocked.

During the Battle of the Somme (July 1916) French air superiority was assured, and the balloons were able to ascend very close to the front. Attacks by airplanes were rare, but the artillery frequently fired at the French balloons, several of which were damaged. It was also on that occasion that for the first time balloons were equipped with radio transmitters to fill in when the telephones broke down or even to simplify communications, which sometimes extended 100 kilometers through several telephone links.

The German pull-back of March 1917 (done voluntarily to shorten the lines) was the occasion for a pursuit by French troops in which the balloons had to demonstrate their ability to maintain their communications in spite of the movement. The operation was difficult, the balloons being moved sometimes with winches and sometimes by hand, and the balloonists widening the gaps in the barbed wire entanglements, clearing obstacles, improving the bridges, etc. Nevertheless, it was possible to maintain observation and communications.

Everything had been carefully prepared for Nivelle's offensive at the Chemin-des-Dames (April 1917) in order to gain the great success expected. The number of balloons per section was increased, but only one of every two balloons was inflated so as not to give the alarm; the encampments and access routes were prepared. The distance of ascension had been limited to 7 or 10 kilometers from the front; it was planned to move one balloon while the other was ascending in order to insure continuity. In fact, the balloons were very active; for the 5th Army alone, from April 9 to 20, 1917, we can compare the activity of the balloons and of the airplanes.

	By Balloon	*By Airplane*
Demolition rounds	405	109
Counter-battery rounds	165	209
Encounters or verifications	235	74
Batteries spotted	1,059	315
	1,864	707

In August 1917, during the action to relieve Verdun, the balloon companies were equipped with a radio receiver which enabled them to listen in on the airplanes flying over the sector. It was thus possible for the pilots to call the balloonist observers' attention to such and such a particular point; at the end of 1917 equipping the companies with receivers became the rule.

In July 1918 the third German offensive was executed against the 4th and 5th Armies. For the 4th Army General Gouraud, warned since May 1918 of the German preparations thanks to the detailed and methodical study of aerial photographs of the sector, had prepared a remarkable defensive arrangement which proved very effective. He had organized two lines, the first of which, lightly held, was to be evacuated to the second, which was powerfully organized and out of range of the attacking artillery.

It was thus necessary for the balloons, while maintaining continuity of observation, to fall back several kilometers. The terrain was organized accordingly, the encampments predetermined, the roads ready, and the telephone lines installed. Moreover, to forestall any surprise, extra balloons kept watch at night. Uninflated balloons were also in place on the second line.

The enemy launched its attack during the night of July 14-15; the command post was immediately informed of this and at the same time of the precise limits of the artillery fire supporting the offensive. Throughout the fighting the balloons, stationed in depth, were able to accomplish their mission to everyone's satisfaction.

In the final stage of the war, which corresponds to Foch's offensives from July 18, 1918, on, movement was resumed, and the balloons had an opportunity to prove their ability to follow the troops very closely. Since the enemy had to shift its batteries and its flying fields, and French air superiority was maintained, the balloons grew bolder and ascended at only 4 or 5 kilometers from the lines, moving forward by rushes. The French airplanes were also shifted from field to field and sometimes had difficulty in getting back in contact with the batteries, which were constantly on the move. This allowed the balloons to play a very active part in this phase, sometimes carrying out twice as many battery ranging and spotting missions as the airplanes. To get the most out of the balloons, it was often the artillerymen themselves that pulled their cables.

During the Champagne offensive of September 26, 1918, the 21 balloons of the 4th Army, though greatly hampered by the bad weather, nevertheless carried out 500 battery spotting and 400 ranging missions. In a general way the balloon observations of explosions, fires, marches of convoys, and so on, kept the military command informed on the enemy's withdrawal movements.

The balloon companies' radio did wonders in this phase when telephone communications were easily broken. It even reached the point where the French command could follow the advance of its troops on the ground only through the balloons' reports. Thus the feverish improvisation of the early phase of the war was followed by a fruitful period of organization.

In all, the balloonists numbered a little less than 2,000 officers and observers and a grand total of about 10,000 persons. They lost only 128 killed, about half of them observers. It is the observers

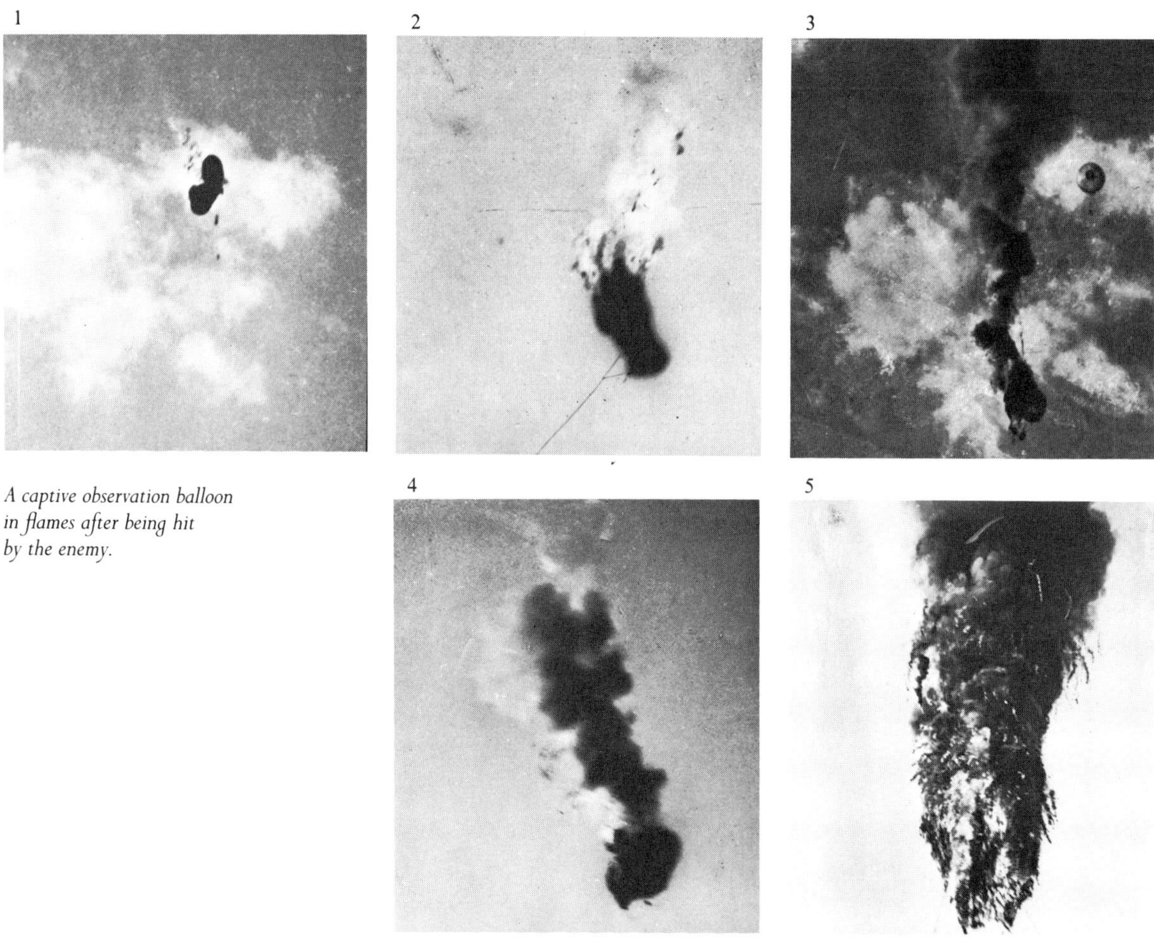

A captive observation balloon in flames after being hit by the enemy.

A Caquot winch with two motors, on a Latil four-wheel drive tractor, 1915.

that deserve the most credit for the effectiveness of the balloons' work, which demanded a great deal of responsibility and endurance. It was an obscure and unrecognized job, perhaps because the rate of casualty losses was lower than in most of the other branches of the service. However, the balloonists' acts of bravery and the adventures survived by a good number of them were by no means ordinary. Numerous balloons were destroyed by fire; at least five balloons had their cords cut by a shell explosion or an airplane wing and drifted away. On May 5, 1916, 24 balloons surprised by a storm were torn from their winches, and 18 observers jumped by parachute; of these, 11 landed in French-held territory, 2 among the enemy, 2 were seriously wounded, 2 were killed by being dragged along the ground, and the last landed in free fall. But none let the documents he had with him fall into the hands of the enemy.

The services rendered by the balloonists are beyond dispute, but they could not have been performed if the balloonists had not had the protection of the French fighter planes, as we have seen at Verdun. In fact, balloons and airplanes were complementary, the former insuring a continuity that could not be expected from the airplanes, and the latter extending the range of observation.

The useful range of the cannon and other weapons of the time permitted the balloons to ascend at 5 to 7 kilometers from the lines and to be able to observe up to 4 or 5 kilometers beyond the lines. It was clear that an increase in the range of the enemy's heavy weapons would prohibit all use of balloons. This is exactly what we shall soon see, after 1918.

CHAPTER III

Aviation during the First World War

At the beginning of the war the airplane was considered and used only for observation. Since the prevailing view was that the airplane crews could not see anything if they flew higher than 1,000 meters, little thought was given to adapting airplane engines for altitude or even to get good rates of climb. Taking nearly fifteen minutes to climb to 800 meters—the usual performance of planes at that time—worried no one. On the other hand, since this low altitude exposed the craft to the fire of light guns, a great deal of time and energy was spent trying to armor-plate the airplane, a project that could not succeed because of the low power of the engines available. These efforts were finally abandoned, and very soon, beginning in the spring of 1915, designers were working to achieve greater altitude. Finally, in order to improve observation, the two-seater design with push motor was often adopted, which made it possible to place the observer on a veritable balcony; this arrangement proved disastrous when pursuit planes, with axial fire attacking from the rear, began to be used. These simple examples show the importance of the technical factor in the use of the airplane; this will also be demonstrated below by the study of aerial operations in the various phases of the war.

In following the operations four phases will be distinguished:

1) Beginning with Verdun (March 1916) the fleets were more numerous, and pursuit began to play an important part; the military command concerned itself with utilization and with principles; there was a desire to employ aircraft en masse, but the industry could not keep up—there was the "aeronautical crisis" aggravated by French reverses in early 1917.

2) In the course of 1917 production was greatly increased, and ambitious plans were drawn up. The British, for their part, made an enormous manufacturing effort. That year saw aviation, now come of age, employed en masse.

3) Finally, 1918, thanks in large part to the definitive establishment of air superiority, turned out to be the year of victory.

The First Months: The Test of Battle (August–October 1914)

As mentioned earlier, at the time of mobilization there were 23 French flights, to which 4 others were added during August 1914; even with the low production of the very first months of the war, a few more units were mustered, so that in October 1914 the French had 31 flights at their disposal, each consisting of 6 planes, except for 3 BLC flights consisting of 4 single-seater airplanes.

All of the flights were attached to the five armies on the line. Their essential mission was daytime reconnaissance to the enemy's rear, while the dirigibles were relied on for night reconnaissance and for bombing. But the dirigibles, which were decidedly too fragile and vulnerable, were a disappointment. As for the airplanes, they flew numerous missions, and the information reported caused astonishment in the army staff officers, who showed skepticism and sometimes irritation. But more and more, faced with the evidence of the facts, they had to concede the accuracy of the information transmitted to them. This was particularly the case with the Battle of the Marne.

The air unit of the entrenched camp of Paris had been activated on August 30 when the enemy was marching on the capital. This Paris air unit, under the orders of the artillery squadron commander, Charet, had the mission of making reconnaissance flights, but also, because of the German advance, of flying patrols over Paris to attack any enemy planes that might be encountered.

Luckily the governor of Paris was General Gallieni, who was well disposed toward aviation, as reported by Captain Bellenger: "During the large-scale maneuvers of 1910 Gallieni questioned me at length on aviation–its potential, its difficulties, the services it could render. He is one of the rare generals that believe in aviation; he is a man of decision and is not afraid of responsibilities."

On September 2 Corporal Louis Breguet, who had offered his services to General Gallieni, carried out a reconnaissance mission with his observer, Watteau, flying one of his own prototypes. The information brought back indicated a change of orientation of the German army under General von Klück, whose orders were to go around Paris on the north in order to encircle it according to the Schlieffen plan. But here was von Klück advancing obliquely toward the southeast, east of Paris, thus positioning himself in such a way as to present his poorly protected flank to the French troops! It was a daring maneuver aimed at eliminating the British corps and surprising the French in retreat. At the same time Captain Bellenger, commanding the air section of Maunoury's 6th Army, who had at his disposal the two perfectly trained flights REP 15 and MF 16, reported the same change of direction of von Klück's army. Unfortunately, the commanding officer of the Second Bureau of the 6th Army, Commander Dutilleul, who, thanks to the intelligence services, had had in his possession since August 27 the directives

The departure of a Morane-Parasol in September 1914.

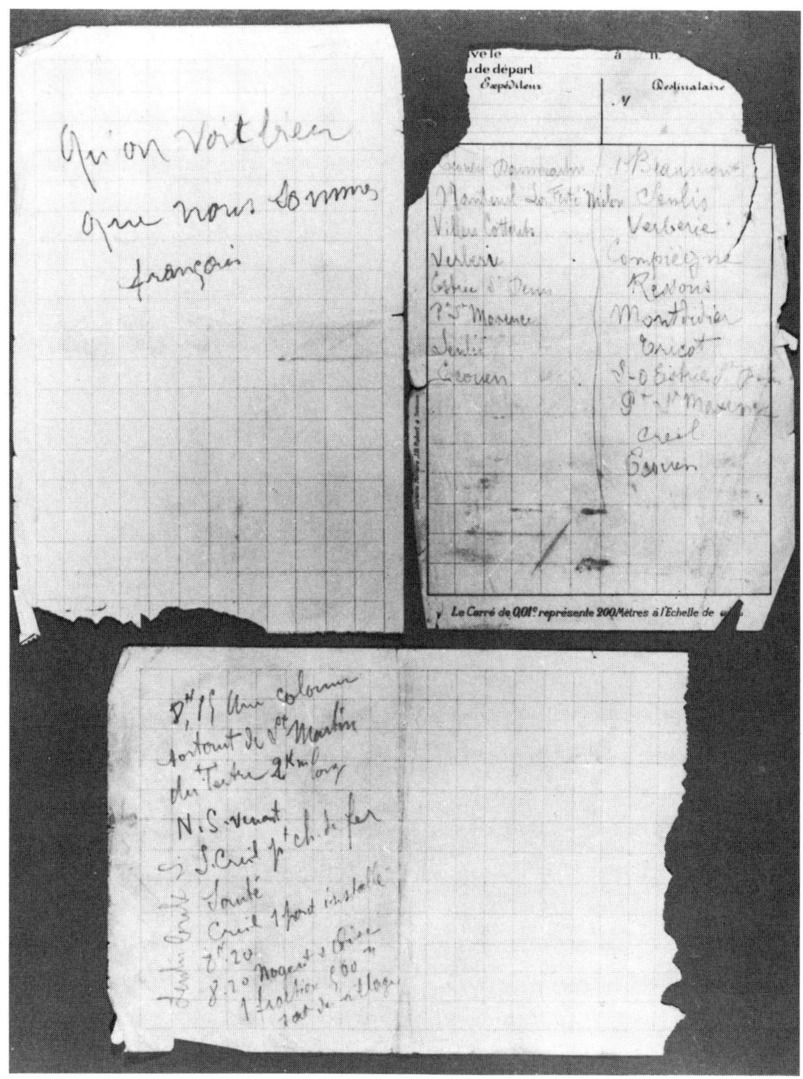

Notes written in flight by the observer Reusser of the Sixth Army, during the reconnaissances of September 1 and 2, 1914 (PASM, Bellenger Coll.).

given to von Klück, could not be brought to believe the reports sent by the aviators. The next day, September 3, Lieutenants Prot and Hugel confirmed the report: the German columns had turned up at Douy-la-Ramée, Nanteuil-le-Haudouin, and Betz. There was no doubt about it; von Klück was avoiding Paris and advancing obliquely to the southeast!

Giving up the attempt to convince the commanding officer of the Second Bureau or the chief of staff of the 6th Army, Bellenger went to the liaison officers of General Gallieni and the British general, French. They both gave the word to their respective commanding officers (which explains the fact that the origin of the intelligence is sometimes attributed to the British).

Gallieni lost no time admitting a fact that had been cross-checked by the observations of his own air unit of the entrenched camp. He urged Joffre to profit by this unexpected opportunity to "go for" von Klück, in the words of General Clergerie, his chief of staff, which was done. The victory won on the Marne shed light on the services that aviation could render in keeping the command informed.

This case was the most remarkable of the war, but it was not unique. The use that was made of the aerial observations depended essentially on the army commanding officers and their staffs, who were more or less well disposed toward the aviators, who were sometimes thought of as "undisciplined acrobats not worth wasting time on."

Thus the use made of the thirty or so flights varied widely and often left them with time on their hands, which the flight commanders used to practice various experiments. So it was with bombarding enemy troops with steel darts launched in packets of 500, or with 90-mm shells (the 75-mm's were too much in demand with the artillery to be diverted from the supplies) or 155-mm shells, or with the Aasen bombs (with a hydrocarbon base) made before 1914 for Morocco. These missions were authorized only on the way back from reconnaissance missions.

This was also the way that certain crews perfected artillery ranging, by local understandings with division batteries and the use of special codes. In September 1914 some pilots succeeded in spotting the artillery of a German army corps that was being shifted, and directed French fire on it, at Thiaucourt; half the artillery of the army corps was destroyed. This exceptional feat of arms was cited in a communiqué by General Joffre.

Others, no doubt in order to overcome the skepticism of staff officers, carried cameras on board (often on shoulder straps), and thus demonstrated the value of the aerial photograph.

It is true that during this period of several months the French and German planes, all devoted to the same reconnaissance tasks, sometimes passed each other in the air; and it is possible that some of these saluted each other, as the story goes. But it was natural for crews that were in a position to recognize the advantage of aerial observation to want to prevent the enemy from enjoying that advantage. Hence the idea arose of taking a hand firearm—rifle or revolver—along on a mission to attack an enemy accidentally encountered. Only the two-seaters, of course, permitted this sort of exercise.

The first duels proved disappointing because nobody had studied the theory of aerial fire, and the crews fired too far away to do any damage. It is thus understandable that higher staff officers were skeptical about the very possibility of aerial pursuit. A directive of the German high command of October 2 forbade its crews to seek combat; on the

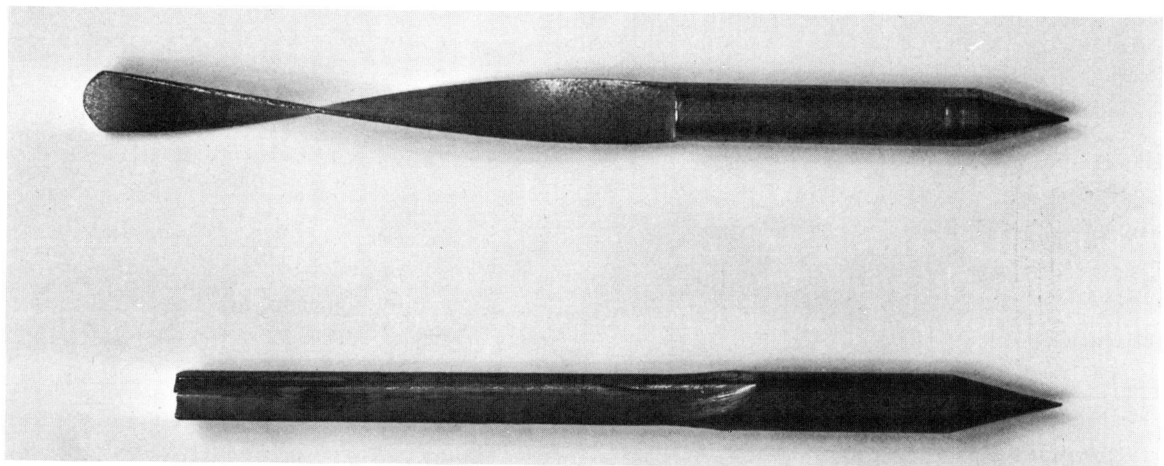

"Bon" darts.

French side, carrying arms on board was allowed only for the purpose of self-defense in case of a forced landing behind enemy lines.

But on October 5, 1914, the pilot Joseph Frantz and his observer, Quénault, succeeded for the first time in destroying a German two-seater in aerial combat. Their Voisin airplane had been equipped with a machine gun mounted on a pivoting fork according to an arrangement invented by Gabriel Voisin. Pursuit appeared realizable.

As for bombing by airplane, that possibility had been demonstrated on August 3, only six hours after the declaration of war, by a German Taube which dropped three small bombs on Lunéville. The French did not respond to that raid until August 14, when Lieutenant Césari and Corporal Prudhommeaux attacked the dirigible hangar at Metz-Frescaty. The next day Lieutenant Finck, renewing the attack, succeeded in damaging a Zeppelin.

But at the beginning of the war it was particularly the Germans that resorted to bombing: 3 bombs on the railroad station at Vesoul and 2 on that at Lure on August 14; 3 on Lunéville again on August 19. Ten days later two airplanes attacked Belfort, and on August 30 a Taube started the bombardment of Paris by dropping 2 bombs and a message saying: "The German army is at the gates of Paris; you have nothing left but to surrender. —Lieutenant Hindelsen." Paris received 17 more bombs in four raids in September and 26 in three raids in October. Altogether the 50 shells dropped killed 11 and wounded 50.

In fact, the bombing devices used were not very effective and produced little physical effect; the aim pursued by the bombers was psychological in nature. Throughout the war, and particularly in conjunction with the big offensives launched by the Germans, the latter tried to use bombardments to demoralize the rear, although they did not succeed in doing so.

The French G.H.Q., which considered these bombings of cities rather ineffectual, while their own raids on Metz had had a certain success, was led to promote the bombing of military objectives immediately to the rear of the front in support of maneuvers on the ground.

Pilot Frantz and mechanic Quénault on October 5, 1914, at the time of the first aerial victory in the world.

Thus General Joffre, foreseeing the part that aviation could play, summoned the only higher officer who was a pilot, Major Barès, on September 25 and instructed him to organize aeronautics in the armies.

On September 27 the first Bomber Group, GB 1, was created, made up of three flights of Voisin LA 5's. It was immediately understood that, like artillery, aerial bombing could achieve results only if it was concentrated. In a few days Barès understood the lessons learned from the first two months of the war.

It also appeared that if the armies were to be

able to count on an air force for reconnaissance and for pursuit, it was also necessary to place at the army corps's disposal the means of observation and of artillery ranging. The cavalry, for its part, should have available its own reconnaissance units, attached to the cavalry divisions. Finally, aerial bombing should be strongly developed. It was thus necessary to have reconnaissance, observation, bombing, and pursuit planes available.

The test of battle also revealed the disadvantages presented by too great a diversity in the types of planes. Among the twelve types of craft used, most had shown their fragility or poor performance. Therefore, only the four best were chosen: the Voisin LA 5 for reconnaissance and bombing, the Maurice Farman VII for reconnaissance, the Caudron G 3 for observation and artillery ranging, and the Morane Parasol—the fastest—which seemed best adapted to pursuit.

First Plan and Launching of Aerial Armaments

The G.H.Q.'s first plan of October 8, 1914, led to a big increase in numbers. In three months the 31 flights of October 1914 were to be increased to 65 flights, distributed as follows: 16 bomber flights (in 4 groups); 16 army reconnaissance and pursuit flights; 3 cavalry flights; and 30 army corps observation flights. All of these flights were of six airplanes each, except those of the cavalry, which had only four each.

To make sure that all of these 384 airplanes were in flying condition it was also necessary to replace them constantly (half the stock every month), create a reserve in advance, and set up schools to train the necessary personnel. Taking everything into account, this plan led to the manufacture of 2,300 airplanes and 3,400 engines.

But in October 1914 the French were turning out only about a hundred planes a month of all types, and the flight schools had been closed. The effort needed to remedy this situation was considerable.

Fortunately, on October 25 General Bernard, Director of Aeronautics, whose mistakes were obvious, was replaced by General Hirschauer, former Permanent Inspector of Aeronautics (in 1912).

Production rose from 100 airplanes a month in October to 137 in November, 192 in December, 262 in January, and peaked at 431 in March 1915. Unfortunately, that rate could not be maintained and fell off a little in the course of the year for lack of funds, which Hirschauer could not get. This was the occasion for the first organizational crisis that French aeronautics experienced in the rear, and it led in September 1915 to the creation of an Undersecretariat of State for Aeronautics.

Nevertheless, as of March 30, 1915, the G.H.Q. had at its disposal at the front 53 first-line flights, including two called the Serbia flight and the Orient flight; 11 repair and replacement units; 9 first reserves; 1 second reserve; and 1 general reserve of pilots and airplanes. These formations employed a total of 130 line officers, 500 pilots (officers and men), 240 observers, and 4,650 enlisted men (mechanics, drivers, etc.).

It should be added that the designers had been able to perfect new types of planes, thanks to the more powerful engines available at that time. For example, the G 4 twin-engined plane replaced the G 3, the Voisin LA 5 S increased to 140 horsepower, the Farman XI replaced the VII, and the Morane Parasol gained in power.

Most of the operations of 1915 were carried out with these machines. The French also committed themselves to furnishing airplanes to their British and Russian allies. In January the proportion of materiel to turn over to the Allied armies had been fixed at 15% of the total production of each factory, 7.5% for England and 7.5% for Russia. The Russian military attaché indicated that this percentage was not equitable, since Great Britain had a greater industrial capacity than Russia.

Operations in 1915

It is through operations that we shall see the first flight tactics and the programs of future prototypes worked out.

Major Barès (1872–1954).

Bombing

The Voisins, which had the greatest carrying capacity, specialized in bombing. The first flight was the V 14, which took the name of VB 1 (Voisin Bombing Flight No. 1); it was later renamed VB 101. The 90-mm shells equipped with fin assemblies by Salmson soon took the place of the Aasen bombs used by the dirigibles. Bomb racks were installed in record time with the support of the designer, Gabriel Voisin, who did not hesitate to go to the airfields near the front to confer with the crews. Bombsights were soon adopted to replace the nails driven into the side of the fuselage in the "heroic" days. Bombing was done in the daytime and in the eye of the wind, which surpressed the drift and further reduced the ground speed resulting from the airplane's own speed, which did not exceed 90 kilometers per hour. At an altitude of 1,500 or 2,000 meters there was little to fear from machine guns on the ground, while antiaircraft fire and pursuit were still nonexistent. Bombing could thus be done without great risk, apart from engine failure, which unfortunately was common at that time.

There were no bombing tactics until 1915. Once the objective had been designated by the flight commander on a list drawn up by the G.H.Q., the weather determining the choice, all the planes available flew individually to that objective to drop their bombs and kept starting over until it was decided to stop the attack.

The credit goes to Major de Goÿs for initiating organized bombing, the effectiveness of which was perceived very quickly as depending on its massive employment. The three flights of GB 1 (Bomber Group 1) were combined with a supply center and installed near Nancy on the plateau of Malzéville, now famous in French history.

The training of the crews was improved, and bomb racks were perfected for 155-mm artillery shells weighing 40 kilograms, which could not be manipulated for throwing overboard.

By May 1915 flight GB 1 was ready. It was necessary to wait until May 27 for favorable weather, since the strength and direction of the wind were of some importance—the objective chosen was at a distance, and it was necessary to insure the planes' return. That objective was at Ludwigshafen and consisted of the Badische Anilin factories, which were making explosives and mustard gas. On May 27 at 3:00 A.M. 18 planes of flight GB 1 took off at fifteen-second intervals; the first to return were back at 8:50. All returned except one, that of Major de Goÿs and Lieutenant Bunau-Varilla, who had engine trouble and were taken prisoner. De Goÿs, after several attempts, succeeded in escaping, but not until 1918.

This raid had important material effects, which the enemy did not try to conceal as it did on later occasions, but most especially it had considerable repercussions. The raids were multiplied under the command of Lieutenant Commander Cayla, de Goÿs's successor, who was later in charge of armaments in the S.T.Aé.

On June 15, 1915, 23 airplanes attacked Karlsruhe in reprisal for the raids of German airplanes and Zeppelins on French and English cities; on Ausust 25 of the same year 62 airplanes dropped their bombs on the blast furnaces at Dillingen, causing terrible damage there. The same happened at Saarbrücken, Treves, and other German sites. Germany was learning about the war on its own soil.

All this led the Germans to mobilize a dense antiaircraft defense around their vulnerable points

A Caudron G 3 two-seater with a Rhône 80-horsepower engine.

A Maurice Farman Type VII with screw propeller and a Renault 80-horsepower engine.

1915: General Joffre, during inspection of a flight, examining a captured German airplane.

A pilot preparing to leave on a mission in a Voisin.

A Maurice Farman 11 flying over a friendly convoy.

A twin-engined G 4 taking off from the Belfort airfield. Note the twin-boom fuselage serving as a landing skid, characteristic of the Caudron G 3 and G 4.

and to devote some flights of Aviatik pursuit planes to defense. French losses then increased since the Voisins, being too slow, were vulnerable.

The results of these bombings were systematically underestimated by the German communiqués and in the reports that French ambassadors in "neutral" countries sent back on them, which came in a roundabout way through persons who favored the Germans. The true results, nevertheless, became known to the G.H.Q. through its agents. They were appreciated to the point that in July 1915 it requested the creation of 50 bombing flights, increased by that time to 10 planes each. At the same time it advertised for a more powerful airplane to bomb the city of Essen; hence the name of "Essen airplane," or "SN." This type of airplane gave rise to several programs for "powerful airplanes," for which a technical commission was created.

Major de Goÿs (1876–1933).

It is proper to mention here the essential part played in this affair by the Michelin brothers, André and Edouard. Even before the war, as we have seen, they believed in the effectiveness of aerial bombing; it will be recalled that they established a prize bearing their name which was to reward the military crew that was most adroit in bombing a target on the ground.

In their mind this bombing should be done *en traînée*—in a series of bombs dropped at regular intervals by means of a mechanical device. It was possible in that way to cut the railroad lines, which at that time constituted the essential means of military logistics.

On August 20, 1914, in a spirit of patriotism, they made the government an offer to manufacture in their plants at Clermont-Ferrand 100 airframes of a type to be specified to them, adequate engines for which would be furnished by the government. They also offered to furnish at cost any aircraft requested by the government. This offer was accepted late in 1914. Breguet was entrusted with working out a prototype.

When the G.H.Q. advertised in July 1915 for the Essen airplane, the Michelins proposed to participate in the "powerful airplane" competition with the Breguet-Michelin prototype "SN 3," with a 200-horsepower engine, a Michelin sight, a mechanical intervalometer, and bomb-throwers under the wings for about thirty 8-kilometer bombs.

This plane, whose general concept was reminiscent of the Voisin, but which was better equipped and heavier, was judged good but a little slow (130 km/h maximum) and lacking in range. Rated first in the competition, it was modified a little and manufactured in quantity under the type number BM IV, which did not appear at the front until the beginning of 1916. The whole of 1915 and the first part of 1916 were needed for perfecting it and getting production under way.

The Michelin brothers realized that for the best possible utilization of their materiel—planes, bombs, bomb-throwers, sights—a bombing school was necessary. But a field had to be found. That was the only condition set by the minister of war,

Major de Goÿs's group which bombed Ludwigshafen on May 27, 1915.

General Gallieni. It was found in January 1916 near Aulnat. Because the ground was too sticky, a concrete runway 400 meters by 20 meters was constructed, the first of its kind in the world.

André de Bailliencourt, a Breguet test pilot, tells how the trainees were instructed in sighting before the flight.

They were trained in bombing with the "moving carpet." Inside a hangar a sort of tower was set up, and the trainee took his place on top of it. He had all the apparatus before him: sights, computation tables, regulator, bomb release. Below him, close to the ground, was a moving carpet, which could be run at varying speeds and on which were painted various landscapes, forests, roads, villages, and, of course, the objective to be hit. The trainee was thus in the same situation as if he were in a plane seeing the ground go past below him. Taking account of a given altitude, he did sightings, determined his relative speed, and when the moment came released his bomb, represented in this case by little lead bombs with a sharp point at the front end, which would thus stick in the moving carpet. The instructor could correct the errors committed and have the operation started over until a normal result was obtained. Little by little the trainee became a bombardier.

The Michelin brothers also established at Malintrat, early in 1916, the first testing ground for real bombs. Actual experiments were done to study the effect of the bombs on railroad tracks, railroad cars, and masonry structures. Official commissions visited the site several times and reported very favorably on the methods used.

It is no exaggeration to say that it is to the initiatives taken by the Michelin brothers that we owe the first rational study of bombing aimed at causing destruction for purely military purposes. These studies were repeated later all over the world.

But in 1915 bombing operations were done only by the Voisins and Maurice Farmans assigned, in addition to the GB 1, to flight MF 29 of Captain Personne, based in Argonne, and MF 25 of Captain Maurice Happe, based farther east at Belfort. Gradually, from June to August 1915, at Malzéville, three other GB's of four flights of Voisins, created several months earlier, were added to the GB 1.

In this early stage of aerial bombing a special place is occupied by Captain Happe and his famous flight MF 25 of Farman XI's. A graduate of Saint Cyr, at first an infantryman and then an artil-

Projectiles dropped by the French in late October 1915. The bombs were simple shells varying in caliber from 75 to 220 millimeters, fitted with tail assemblies. The antipersonnel projectiles, shown at left, ranged from the hand grenade to the box of 500 darts.

leryman, after a special training course he quickly became fascinated with aviation. He was authorized to take the course at the Advanced Aeronautics School and obtained his pilot's license in 1912. This solid technical training before the war led him to play an important part in the perfecting of bombing.

But he was also a man of exceptional courage who took every risk necessary, a man with a strong sense of duty who did everything to accomplish the missions entrusted to him and increase their effectiveness. Thus on bombing missions he did not hesitate to stay for a long time at the objective in order to observe the effect of his crew's bombs, passing over the objective last, in defiance of the antiaircraft fire which was becoming more dangerous every day. This enabled him to detect anomalies in the functioning of the 155-mm shells and then suggest the necessary modifications.

Beginning in July 1915 he was the first to observe errors of navigation on the part of certain crews, and, understanding the importance of concentrating the bombs in time, he invented group flying and, after training, adopted the "V" formation. He recognized the disadvantage of thus offering an easier target to antiaircraft fire, but this was largely compensated for by the defense against Aviatik two-seaters due to the cross-fire of the formation. He thus proved himself a tactician well before the Germans had invented the patrol for pursuit.

The introduction of the Fokker E in the autumn of 1915 confirmed his belief in the importance of formation flying, but he added to it defense by maneuver, which he taught to his crews, setting the example himself. Thus on September 25 Happe took off with two teammates to attack the Rothweil gunpowder factory. On the way to the objective the formation was engaged by the German ace Böhme in an Aviatik two-seater, who attacked Happe's plane. The latter, although heavily loaded, succeeded in extricating himself by maneuvering. Böhme then attacked the two teammates, whom he shot down in succession. Happe went on alone and set fire to the gunpowder factory. On the way back he was again attacked by two patrols in the Black Forest and at Lörrach; he succeeded in getting past them and landed at Belfort. The plane was riddled with bullets, but he and his machine-gunner got out of it miraculously unharmed.

Happe's army exploits led the Germans to put a price on his head, to which he responded by painting the wheels and part of the wings of his airplane red, asking in a weighted message dropped on the Habsheim airfield that they attack his plane and spare his companions. The Germans nicknamed him "the Red Devil."

However, the bombings, by either the MF 25, the MF 29, or the GB's of Malzéville, did not go on without losses from antiaircraft fire or engine failures. To these were soon added the losses caused by German fighter planes, which became more dangerous with the Fokker E, although its performance was not very good—but the French planes were very slow (about 95 to 100 km/hr) and vulnerable.

Then, beginning in July 1915, night flights were tried, but it was discovered that while this improved safety from enemy defenses, it complicated the navigation and reduced the accuracy of the bombing. Only bright nights were useful, and the intensity of the attacks declined a great deal.

For this reason daytime flights were never abandoned, but an attempt was made to protect the bombardiers by means of the new fighter that had just appeared, the Nieuport XI "Bébé." But its range was short, and most of the raids were made without escort. The idea then arose of creating an escort fighter, which appeared first in the form of a bombing plane with no bombs and with a gun on a turret—the Voisin gun-plane, which had its successors.

The French high command, which strongly supported bombing for strategic purposes and was the first of all the belligerents to engage in it, realized that the bombings being ordered were costing very dear in both airplanes and human lives. Because of the low tonnages carried, the destructive effects were quickly repaired; it was decidedly not in this way and by these means that the war would be shortened.

It thus modified its policy, and from September 1915 on it used the means at its disposal almost exclusively in the immediate rear of the battlefield

Maurice Happe (1882–1930).

Marieux Airfield, June 1915: a Voisin landing upon returning from a mission.

on such military objectives as appeared suitable: railroad stations and tracks, bivouacs, disembarkation zones, supply depots, etc. Flying shorter distances, the planes benefited more from the element of surprise and were loaded to capacity with bombs. Night flying was practiced a great deal; navigation was facilitated by the use of gasoline fires arranged in triangles pointed in a known direction toward the enemy. In this way the effect was better insured, and safety was also insured by the installation of the first on-board electric searchlights, which were very useful in case of a landing in the fields, which was always a possibility.

The GB 3 was placed at the disposal of the attacking army for the Artois campaign (September, December 1915) and installed at Humières, in the department of Pas-de-Calais. GB's 1, 2, and 4 were sent into Champagne to support the offensive of October 1915; they were then based at Aulnay. Their most important mission was the attack on the Vouziers railroad station; 62 airplanes took part in it. Attacked by Fokkers and Aviatiks, the expedition lost only three planes. The GB's returned to Malzéville in December for training in night flying.

The G.H.Q.'s plan presented on November 25 called for only 31 flights of 10 bombers each instead of the 500 bombers envisaged in July. At the height of the enthusiasm—especially in the rear—there had even been suggestions during the summer to mount fleets of 600 and even 750 bombers with no thought of the industrial effort implied by such projects, which would have been beyond the capacity of the French aeronautics industry at the time.

In the latter part of 1915 expeditions continued to be launched over the Saar—increasingly costly missions, for antiaircraft fire was increasing, and the Fokker E's, reserved primarily for the defense of the ground occupied by the Germans, were beginning to be more numerous. Against this plane, which attacked from the rear and from above, the French Voisins and Farmans had no defense except maneuver, and the G.H.Q. advertised for new types of planes so as to be able to continue to operate in the daytime.

Thus the missions were continued, but the GB's were more and more often taken away from Malzéville in connection with the fighting in Artois or in Champagne. One complete flight, the V 113, was transformed into Voisin gun-planes and devoted to the attack against the Drachens or against railroad stations, tracks, and trains near the front.

Little by little the GB's were transformed into groups of night bombers between November 1915 and March 1916. The latter year promised to be a difficult one for bombing.

The Aircraft of the Army Corps

For observation the airplanes adopted in the G.H.Q.'s plan of late 1914 were usable up to the fall of 1915. The observation planes used during 1915 were essentially the Caudron G 4 twin-engined plane with front turret and the Maurice Farman XI with propulsion engine. They were reliable aircraft and easy to pilot (which is important for reducing crashes); the observer had excellent visibility. German fighter planes did not really show up until 1916, and few Fokkers were seen near the French lines, so that the French observation planes were not harassed very much.

Their performance was mediocre, however. Having little engine power at their disposal, they had a ceiling of 3,000 meters and could carry only a small load. The first encounters with enemy fighter planes showed them to be definitely obsolete. By the end of 1915 several prototypes were in the testing stage, but replacements were slow in coming, and 1916 was a difficult year for observation too.

Nevertheless, the use of airplanes for observation, reconnaissance, and artillery spotting was being perfected; it was practically codified after the Battle of Artois. Radio began to appear, transmitter only and in Morse code. Here again, the Germans had gotten ahead of the French, although as early as 1912 French dirigibles had begun to experiment with radio transmission during maneuvers. Girardeau, of the S.F.R., hurriedly improvised a series of

A Farman 11 equipped with a camera of 1.20 meters focal length.

sets having a pivoted magnet (developed for automobile magnetos), which were used until 1915. It was not until 1916 and, more especially, 1917 that more advanced sets were available. Aerial photography was used very early, starting in late 1914.

Apart from the development of equipment, the use of observation aircraft changed rather little from 1915 to 1917. At the very beginning air-to-ground liaison was achieved by reports made after the flight, then very soon by radio transmission from the plane and strips of cloth spread out on the ground. Sometimes the plane dropped a weighted message, and more rarely it landed in a field near the unit it was supporting.

However, with the introduction of new equipment—cameras, plate photographs, and field laboratories—the effectiveness of this branch of the service improved dramatically. By the end of 1915 no one anywhere disputed the importance of observation. The last serious incident, that of the "Tranchée des Tentes" (Tent Trench) in September 1915, was the last in which skepticism was shown toward the aviators.

During an episode in the French offensive in Artois a company succeeded in taking a German trench, the Tent Trench. A German counterattack forced the French troops to withdraw, but the forward unit, which had no warning, held on. The French command, which was unaware of its presence at the place, ordered a general artillery fire on the German troops, thus including the Tent Trench. French planes, flying over the sector several times and recognizing the area marked out with ground signals by French soldiers, signaled to the army corps command post, which would not believe them. For three days the bombardment continued, until an officer succeeded in getting out of the trench and informed the French command, which was finally convinced.

The services rendered by observation at that time were such that the number of flights on the line continually increased. There were 50 army corps flights on October 1, 1915, and there were 80 in the spring of 1916.

The Beginnings of Combat in the Air

It has already been noted that in the very first months of the war many aviation crews took arms on board with them—carbine or revolver—to attack the enemy if encountered. Frantz and Quénault's exploit in 1914 opened a new era by offering proof of the possibility of effective aerial fire.

Immediately the question was who would "bring down a Boche." Victories were won in the Morane L, the fastest plane of the time, the firing being done with a carbine by the observer. Such were the victories of Gilbert and Puechredon on January 15, 1915, and those of Navarre and Robert, Pelletier-Doisy and Chambe, and Bernis and Jacottet in April. Guynemer won his first victory with Guerder on July 19.

There were three flights in particular that distinguished themselves: the MS 23 (Vergnette and Garros), the MS 12 (de Rose), and the MS 3 (Brocard). But the real revolution that marks the origin of what became the classical pursuit was brought about by the machine gun fixed in the plane's axis firing through the propeller and pointed by maneuvering the single-seater plane.

Roland Garros of flight MS 23, a Morane test pilot before the war, was acquainted with the fruitless efforts at synchronization made by the engineer Saulnier in 1914. With the consent of his flight commander, Captain Vergnette, he located Saulnier and resumed with him the study of a sturdier device permitting the pilot to fire through the arc swept by the propeller; a steel deflector attached to each blade of the propeller deflected the bullets that might hit it. The experiments were quickly carried out. Assisted by his mechanic, Jules Hue, Garros perfected the bullet deflector. The improved device was mounted on a Morane-Saulnier monocoque Type N.

Garros joined flight MS 26 on the Northern Front at Dunkirk. When a storm destroyed his airplane he remounted the device on a Morane-Saulnier Parasol Type L. With this plane he was able to demonstrate definitively the validity of axial firing. From April 1 to 18, 1915, he shot down three enemy planes. After that remarkable exploit it was decided to equip other planes with the deflector. Unfortunately, on the afternoon of April 18 during a mission over enemy lines Garros's plane was hit by antiaircraft fire, and the captured plane gave the secret away to the enemy.

The Germans then asked Anthony Fokker, a Dutch engineer in their service, to copy the Garros system as quickly as possible. But Fokker did better. He succeeded in synchronizing the firing with the passing of the propeller blades in front of the machine gun.

In fact, in July 1914 Saulnier had taken out a patent covering synchronization of the machine gun with the engine, and the device had even been tested. But he had only the Hotchkiss machine gun to work with, and its moving parts were too heavy for their movement to be stopped instantly in the course of firing. The tests made in 1914 ended in failure. It should be added that the same idea existed at practically the same moment in England and in Germany, but no tests were done in those two countries before the war.

Fokker had the advantage of having two German machine guns to work with—the Parabellum and the Spandau—both of which could be synchronized. His study was conducted rapidly, and the equipment was produced and mounted within a few months on a Fokker M 5 K (closely copied from the Morane N) with an Oberursel engine, an exact copy of the 80-horsepower Gnome engine. The result was called the Fokker E 1. From July 1915 on the plane was tried out at the front by the pilot Boelke with success. The production series, immediately started, supplied the first airplanes with the device in the fall. To prevent the secret of this weapon from falling into the hands of the Allies, the German command decided not to use the Fokker E 1 beyond the front lines. It was not until October 1916 that a Fokker lost in the fog landed by mistake at a French airfield, Plessis-Belleville; another Fokker had been captured in April 1916 by the English.

Thus for a long time the only planes that the Germans used over the French lines were single-engined or twin-engined Aviatik two-seaters used for pursuit.

The French, for their part, were flying Morane

A Voisin LA 5 S, 140-horsepower, equipped with searchlights for night bombing: at left, the observer (M. Bonon); at right, the mechanic (M. Malvilan). Photograph taken in September 1916.

Preparing for an observation mission: map reading.

Preparing for a photographic mission on board a Caudron G 4 (army reconnaissance), with a camera of 1.20 meters focal length and boxes of photographic plates.

Machine gun and "Garros"-type bullet-deflecting propeller on a Morane N.

Roland Garros, by Carrier Belleuse (PASM Coll.).

N's, then in the fall of 1915 a single-seater derived from the Nieuport 10 two-seater observation plane, meant to replace the Farmans and G 4's. The two-seater 10 and a somewhat more powerful version, Type 12, were used as fighter planes in 1915 and 1916. The single-seater version, armed with a Lewis light machine gun placed above the upper wing to fire over the propeller, was a success. This was the Nieuport XI, with a wing surface of 13 square meters, and was called the "Bébé" (Baby) because of its small size. Greatly superior to the Fokker in speed and maneuverability, it was inferior to it only in armament; the loader held only 25 cartridges, and reloading required an inconvenient maneuver. The Bébé was bought immediately by the Royal Navy Air Service and soon after by the French army. In spite of its flying qualities, which could be appreciated only by a pilot, this plane did not arouse great enthusiasm in 1915 in the G.H.Q., which, in its plan of November 25, did ask for fighter flights but wanted two-seater, twin-engined planes for that purpose, thinking mostly of escort for the bombers, which at that time were facing the few German fighter planes practically unaided. Fortunately for the French, about a hundred Bébés were available at the time of Verdun when the real birth of aerial pursuit took place.

The Outflanking of Verdun: Fighter Planes Obliged to Create Tactics

Although aerial combat was a creation of 1915, one cannot speak of a fighter air force, that is, its employment, tactics, and doctrines, until the moment when fighter planes were present in sufficient numbers on both sides to permit an aerial maneuver.

It was not until the fall and winter of 1915 that the bombers, in the course of their missions in the Saar, encountered aerial defense fighter planes, and they were still very few. Bombing tactics would be greatly influenced by them. On the other hand, over the rest of the front, which extended for nearly 600 kilometers, the density of fighter planes was so low (there were not more than one hundred Fokkers on the line altogether) that they hardly bothered the French army corps planes. Both sides contented themselves at the beginning with distributing a few defensive fighter planes to protect the observation planes from the rare incursions of enemy fighters into their own lines. All that was to change at Verdun.

Verdun and the Struggle for Air Superiority (February 1916)

Falkenhayn, the German chief of staff, had decided to launch a big offensive in the spring of 1916 in the Verdun sector, which the French could not abandon. Convinced of the important part played by aviation when it was used en masse, he succeeded in getting together a fighter reserve by assembling most of the Fokker E's and Pfalz E's—180 in all—but without getting political agreement to create a single command for the whole air force.

It was his intention from the beginning of the offensive to blind the French artillery by depriving it of its balloons and army corps airplanes. He devised an original tactic to achieve this: he had heavy guns, carefully camouflaged, moved by night as close as possible to the lines. These guns were used in pairs, one firing time-fused shells at a balloon already aloft and the other firing percussion shells at the winch on the ground; the fire was evidently ranged by planes. This thwarted the balloon's traditional maneuvers to avoid the shots fired at it. These tactics succeeded perfectly.

At the same time, in order to neutralize the observation planes Falkenhayn had the sky constantly occupied by his fighters concentrated in a reduced sector. French planes could not take off, nor could the few defensive fighters in the area engage the German patrols, the three or four planes of which were always superior in number to the one or two escort fighters the French continued to use. Thus from the first day—February 21, 1916—the Germans gained local air superiority for the first time in the war.

The advantage on the aerial level alone was slight, for the Germans did not yet have day or night bombers. They had only a few wings (Geschwader) of 6 flights consisting of 6 single-engined, general-purpose planes—pursuit, defense, light bombing—of various types. The bombings that they carried out were not very effective. But air superiority was important to the fighting on the ground since the effectiveness of the French artillery was reduced to direct sighting. No counter-battery firing was possible, and in this artillery war that was a very severe handicap.

It is easy to understand the reaction of Joffre, who called Major de Rose of the MS 12 to his G.H.Q. and gave him carte blanche to rectify the situation. De Rose assembled in the Bar-le-Duc–Verdun sector all the available Moranes and

A captured Fokker E III.

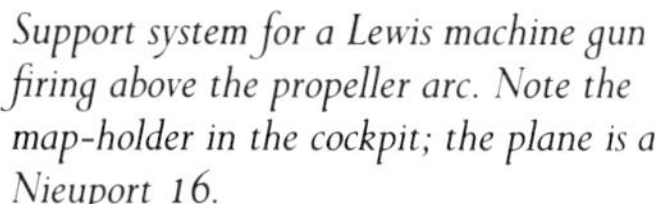

Support system for a Lewis machine gun firing above the propeller arc. Note the map-holder in the cockpit; the plane is a Nieuport 16.

A Nieuport XI Bébé.

Nieuport XI's and drew from all the flights of the front the best pilots, who had distinguished themselves by their combative spirit. He thus formed 15 elite flights with the mission of "sweeping the sky" and driving the Germans out of it, operating in strong patrols of four or five planes taking their turn in the air to insure continuity. The French flights regained air superiority, and the army corps planes were able to resume their work and get rid of the heavy guns too near the front. The Caquots made ascents again. Farmans or Nieuports equipped with special Le Prieur rockets succeeded in setting all the German balloons afire, except one, in a single day (May 22, 1916). By April 1916 the situation was rectified, and in May the retaking of the fort of Douaumont ended the German advance. The offensive had failed, but the battle continued with the unparalleled bitterness that has become legendary.

Aerial pursuit was really born at Verdun. Navarre, who won most of his victories there, became the most popular hero of the moment; he was nicknamed "the sentinel of Verdun."

All the pilots mentioned below were at Verdun: Guynemer, Nungesser, Chaput, Brocard, Deullin, Lufbery, Boillot, and others. Many of the French pilots were wounded or killed; de Rose was killed accidentally in a demonstration and was replaced by Captain Le Révérend, an unquestioned master.

From the month of April 1916 the French had ascendancy over the enemy, who no longer dared to penetrate the French lines. The fighting was still bitter, but now it was in enemy-held territory. The victory of Verdun was complete, both in the air and on the ground.

It was on the occasion of Verdun that the famous Lafayette Escadrille of American volunteers appeared; in May 1916 it won the first victory of American volunteers by destroying a German two-seater near Mulhouse.

To try to regain the advantage in the air the Germans attempted to mitigate by tactics the manifest inferiority of the Fokker E, whose merits were sometimes overestimated by the German high command. The German pilot Immelmann, the ace of the Fokkers, invented the acrobatic figure that bears his name; he was killed in June 1916. Boelke, the greatest German tactician thought up the "Jagdstaffel," or double patrol with six planes in two stages. With this tactic, for example, on September 16, 1916, Boelke's six planes destroyed six British planes during the same combat, on the front entrusted to the English.

Many lessons in the employment of air forces were learned from this climactic phase of the war. Until then a very narrow view had prevailed: priority was given to observation or to bombing; fighter aircraft were thought of only in the role of immediate protection—each observation plane was flanked by one or two fighters, and all of the fighter planes were distributed by units along the whole land front. This led to a great consumption of materiel without, however, giving the possibility of defense against an attack in force. There was no close protection that could hold its own against Boelke's Jagdstaffel. Moreover, since operations on the ground were being carried out in small areas, as at Verdun, it was always possible for the enemy to concentrate sufficient forces to gain air superiority in such a localized area. Similarly, daytime bombing on the front or in the immediate rear in support of ground operations was conceivable only with air superiority.

These findings gave rise to the idea of establishing a reserve fleet of combat aircraft—the term used from 1915 on to describe pursuit planes—that might be capable of attacking objectives on the ground with its onboard weapons. This fleet was at the disposal of the G.H.Q., which sent it into the area of its choice.

But while it was relatively easy to concentrate forces in view of a planned action, it was much more difficult to protect French forces against all enemy attacks, and everywhere at once. Also, the ground troops did not feel well protected unless they saw friendly planes above them continuously.

This was to be the story of the employment of airplanes during 1916 and 1917 and until the summer of 1918, when French air superiority became so absolute that the problem was definitively solved. Meanwhile the war would go through phases in which the mastery of the air

Major de Rose (1876–1916).

The fall of a Voisin biplane set on fire west of Verdun in April 1916 by the German pilot Boelke, whose black Fokker accompanies the plane, which is diving toward its own lines. Photograph taken at a distance of 800 to 900 meters by the observer of a French biplane.

passed from one side to the other, most often on the occasion of a change in materiel.

Several protective tactics were tried out in turn for defense against fighter planes on patrol. After the close protection system, the system of "continuity" by sector was established. The Verdun area of operations was divided into air sectors; each sector was continuously assigned to the same observers, who thus changed flights with each shift. This enabled the observation officers to have a perfect knowledge of the sector, which was essential in this tumultuous region. Similarly, the fighter flights were assigned to a specific sector, with which they very quickly became familiar. Their role was to provide continuity in the air of one or more patrols in their sector; when their fuel ran out, the planes returned to the field, where they were relieved without delay.

It was in the course of these "continuous" patrols that the French pilots outlined their first tactics. As the Germans quickly learned to be on the lookout for French patrols, the idea was conceived of authorizing certain aces to make free "pursuit rounds," either singly or in groups of two or three planes. They took up positions high in the sky, ready to swoop down on an enemy hypnotized by the continuous patrol and unaware of this other threat.

The Somme—July 1916

After Falkenhayn's hopes for a quick victory at Verdun were dashed by the French reaction, it was a surprise to him to see the Allies launch an offensive on the Somme on July 1, while the battle was still going on at Verdun.

During the winter of 1915–1916 the French had agreed with their Russian allies to launch simultaneous offensives in the east and in the west in order to prevent the game of seesaw played by the Germans attempting to counter the uncoordinated offensives of the Allies in 1915. The month of July had been chosen for these 1916 attacks, and there had been plenty of leisure to prepare things well since the French had the choice of sector. The Somme was chosen so as to engage the bulk of the British forces, which had seen little action until then. Twenty-six English and fourteen French divisions were to make the main effort.

The aerial equipment had been prepared carefully. Thus the balloon companies had received double the usual number of balloons, the second one placed far forward to be inflated at the desired time. All the telephone lines had been strung in advance as well. Continuity of observation could be achieved in spite of the advance of the troops on the ground.

Similarly, the aviation units had been strongly reinforced. The pursuit planes were Nieuport 17's, more powerful and equipped with a Lewis machine gun and loaders holding 47 cartridges, greatly superior to the Fokkers. Having learned the lessons of Verdun and being equipped with these new aircraft, the French fighters completely dominated the sky.

The British, for their part, also had a pursuit plane that was superior to the Fokkers—the DH 2 with pusher propeller and fixed machine gun. The German successes in the British sector were due solely to the inexperience of the young DH 2 pilots and to the very superior tactics inaugurated by Boelke. One should add that the British army corps airplanes—BE 2 C's, for the most part, or FE 2 B's—with their engines in the rear, were distinctly outdated and were easy prey.

The Battle of the Somme was a glorious epoch for the Allies as well as for French aviation and, in particular, its pursuit element.

An assembly of several fighter flights was arranged at Cachy; the carefully camouflaged hangars and barracks did not give the alarm to the enemy. The fighter command was given to Captain Brocard of flight N 3, whose famous emblem was the stork. From the beginning of the attack the Drachen balloons were eliminated by Le Prieur rockets, and the planes of the sector by French fighter planes. The Germans were put in the situation they had put the French in at Verdun in February. The Germans responded only with a staggered dispatching of squadrons, which the French had no trouble in neutralizing. The French mastery of the air was complete in July, August, and up to the middle of September 1916. Cachy became a high point of fighter aircraft, where the storks of Brocard, Guynemer, Heurtaux, Deullin, and Dorme became famous, as well as some other remarkable flights, such as the N 65 of Nungesser and Féquant. It is astonishing that at that moment the Germans maintained a purely defensive stance, contenting themselves with wheeling in big formations of ten or twenty planes to provide a protective barrage for their observation planes.

It was not until September, when General Erich von Ludendorff replaced Falkenhayn, who had been beaten at Verdun, that things changed. The new commander took up the idea of a separate air force again and obtained what his predecessor had been unable to—creation of the Kogenluft, ancestor of the Luftwaffe, to which the aviation and antiaircraft units were directly responsible. Ludendorff placed General von Hoeppner at the head of it.

In fact, the German pilots bitterly complained of not having a high-quality pursuit plane. Their designers had not succeeded in turning out the expected prototype, to the point where in desperation the German high command ordered them to copy the Nieuport, recognized as the best pursuit plane of the day.

Finally, in the fall appeared the Albatross D I, a highly successful single-seater biplane that was to cause the Allies a great deal of trouble. Just as maneuverable but a little faster and better armed than the Nieuport—it was the first aircraft with synchronized twin machine guns—the Albatross dominated the Nieuport in combat and, of course, also dominated the inferior British planes. When it arrived at the front in quantity, early in 1917, the German pursuit became formidable.

From the time of its appearance the French aces complained of their Nieuports. Learning that the Spad VII with a Hispano engine was undergoing testing behind the lines, they insisted that it be turned over to them without delay, and there was no way to refuse them. But the synchronization of the new Vickers machine gun had not been perfected, and, more important, the engine was prone to seizing. Many aces, such as Nungesser, then preferred to go back to a Nieuport 17, the last models of which had a synchronized machine gun and one hundred cartridges.

In September 1916 the English put into service the Sopwith Pup single-seater with a synchronized machine gun and an 80-horsepower Rhône engine. It was perfected more rapidly than the

Before the attack on Douaumont, May 22, 1916; the team of pilots that were to attack the enemy observation balloons with Le Prieur rockets: Le Prieur, de Beauchamp, de Germes, Nungesser, Chaput, Barrault, Guigner, Réservat.

Spad, but was not available in large numbers until 1917. A little slower than the Spad VII, it was nevertheless superior in altitude to its German rival of 1917, the 160-horsepower Albatross D III, because of its light weight.

Everyone had realized by then that acquiring air superiority with a successful new airplane could only be a temporary achievement. The performance race was on, accompanied by a production race the goal of which was to profit by numerical advantage. Finally, an attempt was made to improve the organization of the units in order to facilitate engaging the planes in larger formations.

In October 1916 the "combat groups" were created, also called "pursuit groups"; groups 2, 12, and 13 were placed respectively under the orders of Majors Le Révérend, Brocard, and Féquant. At this time it was decided, in making flight designations, to reserve two-digit numbers (11 to 99) for fighters and three-digit numbers for bombers (101 to 199) and other planes (201 to 299). But this was not carried out in a completely systematic way.

Bombing in 1916

At the beginning of 1916 aerial bombing was in a crisis. The planes available—Voisin LA 5's, Maurice Farmans, and from February on the first Breguet-Michelin BM IV's—had more and more trouble defending themselves against the Fokker E's and Aviatiks. Gradually the crews were trained in night flying. The GB 3 officially became a night group on March 11, 1916, and remained stationed at Malzéville.

The GB 1 experienced many vicissitudes. On February 3 it lost three of its flights, which were sent to the rear for training on Nieuports. The fourth flight, the VB 101, was sent on March 14 to Lemmes near Verdun, where it played an active part. Later, in April, the GB 1 got two new flights of Voisins and one of Caudron G 4's. In February the GB 2 lost its three flights, which became Caudron army corps flights. Practically nonexistent, the GB 1 was reconstituted in March with a flight of 20 Capronis, to which it added a second flight much later. The GB 4, under Happe's command, was made up of heterogeneous flights of Farmans and Breguet-Michelins, to which the first Sopwith single-seat bombers were added in October. The GB 5, made up of Breguet-Michelins, was created in February 1916.

The Verdun offensive manifestly surprised bombing in mid-evolution. In anticipation of the plane of the day given priority by the G.H.Q., which did not have much confidence in the effectiveness of night bombing, the size of the bomber fleet was reduced, and temporary solutions were sought, such as that involving the Sopwith, whose speed and rear defense were attractive and which

Navarre, the "sentinel of Verdun."

Aerial view of the fort of Douaumont, December 31, 1916.

A British airplane destroyed on the Somme near Estrées, 1916.

was ordered in large numbers, but turned out to be a disappointment because of the small load it carried (60 kg of bombs). Nevertheless, bombing activity was far from negligible at Verdun.

At the beginning only the MF 25 based at Vadelaincourt was on the spot and could carry out a few daytime missions while continuing its night training; it became operational by night in April. The newly created GB 5 with its BM IV's was sent to the sector, but it was greatly hampered by the shortcomings of the 220-horsepower Renault engine with which the planes were equipped. It took the GB 5 a long time to overcome its difficulties; it quickly left the Verdun sector. Then the C 66 and the V 110 of the GB 2 and the independent VB 101 arrived in Verdun. Other flights came to lend their assistance as needed.

Bombings were done by day until May 1916,

The aces of the Stork flight, drawn by J. Moulignon at the request of Captain Brocard, 1916.
Left to right, with their signatures: Brocard, Guynemer, Dorme, Heurtaux, Deullin, and De La Tour.

when that practice was given up. The objectives chosen were almost always the same—the railroad system behind the front lines, which supplied the German offensive. It was noted that in preparation for their attack the Germans had fitted out fourteen rail lines, the one with the heaviest traffic being that which followed the valley of the Meuse. There was thus nothing surprising about the fact that the objectives aimed at by the French bombardiers were Brieulles-sur-Meuse, Dun, Damvillers, Etain, Longuyon, Montmédy, and the nearby cantonments.

It is remarkable that, in spite of their mastery of the air at the beginning, the Germans were never able to prevent daytime bombings by the French; but these did not take place without losses. Safety was better insured at night in spite of the increasing number of searchlights and antiaircraft guns. The French bomber crews learned to overcome the hazards of night flying at a time when the equipment was still very primitive.

The effectiveness of these missions is not in dispute, but the mass of objectives to be hit in proportion to the meager means of bombardment at the time—night raids were then being made by 6 or 12 planes dropping 200 kg of bombs each)—explains the fact that the bombing activity alone could not stop the flow of attackers. The effect on morale was certainly important, although it was not decisive either. It was necessary to alter the scale before the bomber plane could make a difference in the battle.

Other aviators covered themselves with glory. After Captain Bouchet, the theoretician of night flying who commanded the GB 1 in 1917, there was Captain Laurens, nicknamed "Laurens the owl" because he was so much at ease in the dark of night, and Captain Vuillemin, who distinguished himself by the precision of his bombing in a G 4 of the Audun-le-Roman railroad station in March 1916. On June 1 the MF 5 C.A. flight, escorted by 3 Nieuports, dropped 28 bombs of 120 kilograms each on a German headquarters in Woëvre in the daytime.

In September the bombers were shifted to the Somme, and the MF 25 carried out the missions

A Spad VII. A mechanic is spinning the propeller before the engine is started. This plane bears the famous "Stork" of Guynemer's Flight SPA 3. During the First World War his unit had a total of 171 confirmed enemy planes shot down and 160 probables.

The Battle of the Somme, October 10, 1916, altitude 200 meters: attack on Bois Hart, with the first wave of the attack taking off. At the top, a group of German planes in flight.

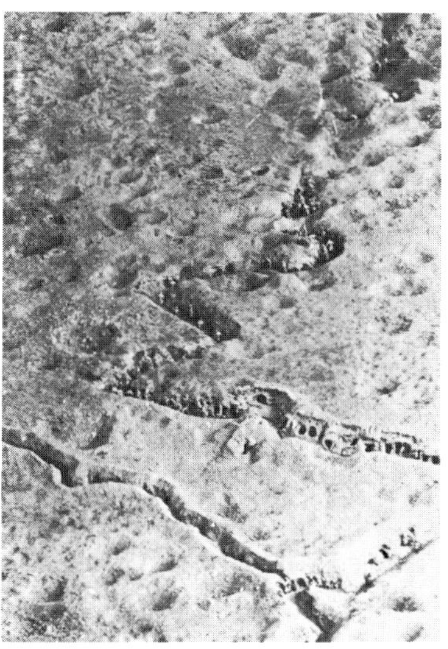

An oblique aerial photograph: the Battle of the Somme, Vermandovilliers attack, September 17, 1916.

of the last phase of the fighting at Verdun practically alone.

The forces engaged on the Somme were greater and the action more coherent. As of April 1916 the GB 3 was put in place at Esquennoy to familiarize the crews with the sector. The VB 101 came in at the end of June from Sacy. On July 1 the arrival of BM 117 followed on the heels of that of the GB 5; to these were later added a flight of G 4's and two of Maurice Farmans.

In contrast to what was done at Verdun, the units were largely dispersed, and the planes went to their objectives by different routes, a practice that insured fuller information reported by the crews, for it had been noted that on the way back from a mission the aviators could do very useful night reconnaissances, especially since reference points were numerous and the information all the more precise on that account. The importance of knowledge of a sector was one of the major lessons learned from Verdun.

The bombardiers that had gun-planes at their disposal hit upon the idea of using them to attack the antiaircraft searchlights which were increasing in number. A preliminary attack by three or four specialized planes became the rule. Another innovation of the Somme operations was that the German airfields were systematically attacked for the first time. In particular, the VB 101 attacked the Grisolles field north of Ham several times. The last attack, on November 23, 1916, made in the daytime and with no losses, dropped 171 bombs weighing 120 kilograms each on that field, which the Germans then abandoned.

Otherwise, the objectives were, as usual, the railroad stations and tracks and then the bivouacs and cantonments. The bombing units acted logically and effectively without seeking personal exploits and glory.

Besides these major campaigns of Verdun and the Somme, bombing was done in Alsace—the work of the MF 29 and of the new GB 4, reconstituted with new flights and entrusted to Happe. These formations carried out many attacks on railroad stations, factories, and airfields, but often had heavy losses.

For example, the famous "Battle of Habsheim" was engaged on March 18, 1916, by a formation of

A Breguet-Michelin BM IV.

23 planes of the GB 4 (13 Farman 80 hp's, 4 Farman 130 hp's, 3 G 4's, and 3 BM's with 37-mm guns). Attacked by a formation of 10 German fighters (1 LVG and 9 Fokkers or Aviatiks), the French formation lost four planes and the Germans a similar number, two of which were dragged into their fall by two French bombers that they had set afire and that had thrown themselves on the victors. The rest of the formation reached the objective, the Habsheim airfield, and dropped 57 bombs on it and 15 on the Mulhouse station.

Later, on June 22, in the course of a ten-plane mission, Happe succeeded in shooting down a Fokker with his old Farman.

While the French command was pushing training in night flying, Happe prepared for a big daytime raid which took place on October 12 and was the last big battle before bombing was restricted to night flying. The expedition was aimed at the Mauser rifle factory at Oberndorf, located far behind enemy lines. Participating in the mission were the MF 29 with 6 Farmans, the MF 123 with 5 planes, and the BM 120 with 14 planes, 8 of which were bombers and 6 fighters. Escort was provided by 18 Sopwiths, 12 of them French and 6 English. Some Nieuports accompanied the formation as far as possible and, after turning back and refueling, took off again to insure that all the planes

A flight of Voisin gun-planes; the sailors in the photo were assigned to the 37-millimeter guns.

of the formation were found upon their return. Finally, a flight of G 4's created a diversion. The operation was well staged, but it was difficult, for the expedition had to face antiaircraft fire and pass within the proximity of four German airfields.

Of the 23 bombers that started out, 14 arrived at the objective, 4 turned back because of mechanical difficulties, and 5 were shot down. In addition, the escort units lost in combat 3 BM IV gun-planes and 1 Sopwith, and the English lost 3 of their 6 Sopwiths.

The conclusion was evident: in spite of all their tactics and in spite of the bravery of the crews, the French airplanes were too outclassed by those of the enemy to fight in the daytime. The Sopwith, which was maneuverable, fast, and able to defend itself, appeared to be a good pursuit plane in its two-seater version and a possible daytime bomber as a single-seater thanks to its good range of action.

The Sopwith had already distinguished itself in the raid of September 24 executed in two single-seaters by Captains Beauchamp and Daucourt, who, taking off from Vadelaincourt, dropped their bombs on Essen and returned without having been challenged after having flown 800 kilometers over enemy territory.

On November 16 Captain de Beauchamp did still better with his specially equipped Sopwith, taking off from Luxeuil to fly to Munich, where he bombed the railroad station. He crossed the Alps and landed in Italy after eight hours of solo flying. Many other bombing missions took place in 1916.

Between February 3 and May 22 the Germans had carried out several bombardments of French cities, in particular Bar-le-Duc several times and Paris itself on May 11 and 22. The G.H.Q., with the consent of the government, decided to carry out in reprisal a raid on a German city far within enemy lines. Karlsruhe was chosen, and the mission was entrusted to Captain de Kerillis's flight C 66. The formation took off in the middle of the day on June 22 to take advantage of the sun, which would be shining in the eyes of any fighter pilots that came to meet them or pursued them on the way back, according to the tactics adopted by de Kerillis. The planes reached Karlsruhe and at an altitude of 300 meters dropped 38 "Gros" bombs, which caused considerable devastation in the city, which had not been alerted; there were 800 casualties. On the way back, attacked by 20 fighter planes, de Kerillis lost a third of his planes. This reprisal, which was terrible for the time, stopped German bombings of French cities for six months. It was not until January 1917 that the German pilots, furnished with new twin-engined planes, resumed their bombings of cities in order to demoralize the civilian population.

We should also mention the activity carried on

Captain de Beauchamp.

A Sopwith 1 ½ Strutter single-seater used as a bomber. This machine bears the name "General Rapid Transport Service Company."

by the British from French airfields in Lorraine. Having suffered attacks by Zeppelins and German airplanes on London and other cities, the British wanted to attack cities in Germany. They obtained permission to take off from the French airfields at Luxeuil and Ochey. The English Sopwiths used by the Royal Naval Air Service—they had nothing else at the time—carried out several successful missions against factories in the Saar region. But the Germans reacted by attacking Nancy, which caused the French to ask that their allies go back to their own sector.

Observation and Reconnaissance Aviation

The types of missions flown by the army corps flights changed no more than the long-range reconnaissance missions entrusted to the army flights.

The installation of a camera on an AR airplane.

Methods were improved, however, and this greatly improved their effectiveness. From 1916 on blanket photographs were used, which were assembled and reproduced by printing and widely distributed. Because of the intensity of the artillery bombardments, the ground was so cut up as to make ordinary maps unusable. The photographic sections were increased, and the equipment was much improved. New cameras of longer focal length enabled even G 4's and Farmans to operate at high altitude without much fear of antiaircraft weapons or pursuit.

The radios used were also perfected. Communications with the ground were better maintained, and the confidence now placed in the aviators facilitated reports.

The most serious problem was that posed by the increasing number of German combat aircraft. The French planes with pusher engines could not defend themselves, and the others were decidedly too slow.

As of April 21 General Joffre asked that the series of Farmans (for which there were orders for another six months) be cut off and called for a faster plane with a tractor engine, equipped with a rear defense.

The Technical Service for Aeronautics, created on February 28, 1916, had not heeded that request and had set itself three priorities responding to the wishes of the G.H.Q.: to launch the C.A. airplane with engine in front; to perfect the synchronization of the Vickers machine gun; and to get a share in the three-seater, twin-engined plane, which seemed to be an aircraft of the future.

Fortunately the problem of defense in the rear had already been solved in 1915 with the Etévé turret.

But, paradoxically, no manufacturer was willing to study the C.A. airplane, which was to be equipped with the 160-horsepower Renault engines already on order for the Farman 40's. The Technical Service assigned Captain Lepère to design this plane; it turned out to be the AR inspired by the Dorand of 1914. The prototype was first flown in September 1916; although its speed was still moderate, 750 units were ordered and delivered to the front in flights in April 1917. The test of fire revealed its vulnerability, and it was to remedy that that the AR 2 with a 190-horsepower engine was produced in July 1917.

At the same time the Technical Service was studying a twin-seater with turrets front and rear, the plans for which were completed in June 1916. Its construction was entrusted to the firm of Letord, of Meudon; it was at the front from April 1917 on.

Caudron, for its part, having already presented the undermotorized twin-engined R 4 at the end of 1915, with two 80-horsepower Gnome engines, produced a derivative in 1916, the G 6, equipped with two 110-horsepower Rhône engines. It turned out to be an excellent army reconnaissance plane, with which 38 flights were equipped beginning in spring 1917.

Another airplane was proposed: the Salmson-Moineau equipped with a Canton-Unné engine mounted transversely, whose crankshaft with double driveshaft powered a propeller on each side of the fuselage. This machine, first equipped with a 160-horsepower, and later a 240-horsepower, engine, could also defend itself with turrets front and rear and still was single-engined.

The idea was ingenious and convinced the authorities. An order was issued, although the plane was not very fast (they were relying on its fire power rather than its maneuverability and speed) and although a new factory had to be built to manufacture the series. The plane was not delivered at the front until the late summer of 1917, when the German pursuit was very strong; it had to be withdrawn from the front after five months of service.

Nothing in these plans and experiments in the spring of 1916 made it possible to count on a new C.A. plane before 1917. For this reason it was decided to bridge the gap by temporarily adopting the Sopwith 1 1/2 strutter with a 130-horsepower Clerget engine, which the British had been using in France since May 1916. But here again the manufacturing delays were underestimated, and the Sopwith was not put into service before December 1916. Once it was at the front its fragility and its low payload were realized, but since it was fast and had a turret, it was used for a little bit of everything: observation, bomber escort, and even as a single-seated bomber, but with limited success.

Of all the prototypes produced toward the end of 1916 two soon became successes: the Salmson 2 A 2 with the 270-horsepower Salmson 9 Z engine, whose payload made it possible to carry the armament and equipment that had become necessary by 1917, and the Breguet XIV A 2, whose prototype got off the ground on November 26, 1916.

From the existing evidence 1916 was a hard year for observation aircraft. But it became worse in the winter of 1916–1917 and up to the fall of 1917, a period during which German pursuit enjoyed a manifest superiority because of the quality of its planes. Fortunately for the French, 1917 was to see the German offensives take place mainly in Flanders, where most of the burden was borne by the British.

1917: The Employment of Aviation En Masse

Both sides had acquired enough aerial experience by 1916 so as to make it possible to establish armament policies and theories of employment. All of the belligerents made efforts to correct their mistakes in the choice of equipment, and all of them had made mistakes. How could they have avoided doing so? The lessons learned were very nearly the same everywhere.

The need for aviation was no longer in dispute; it was even felt that the materiel needed to be increased. In 1916 a sudden increase in the size of the programs was observed, as well as an increase in production efforts, especially in Great Britain.

The supreme commands were interested at first in observation and reconnaissance aviation, and more than half of the equipment was devoted to these missions everywhere. But to insure freedom of action in the sky it is also necessary to have a

An oblique aerial view of the Chemin-des-Dames taken on September 30, 1917.

force of fighter planes that can outclass the enemy's. Whereas in France this necessity was apparent at a very early date (by October 1914), it came more slowly for the other Allies, whose lag in this field was made up only later and with difficulty. As for the Germans, after their invention of synchronization they believed too readily that they had a definitive superiority and neglected to pursue the perfecting of their pursuit planes. By reserving the Fokker E for aerial defense against French bombers for too long they slowed down the perfecting of tactics and lost most of their advantage. The French regained the upper hand at Verdun and on the Somme. Once again, with the Albatross, they committed a similar error in not bringing out a new prototype soon enough. When they woke up in January 1918 and launched the Fokker D VII, it was too late; the Allied armament had become formidable in quantity, and the Kogenluft was definitively dominated, although to the end it inflicted heavy losses on the enemy.

Ideas differed most in regard to the employment of bombing. The French were the first and, for a long time, the only ones to practice strategic bombing and indirect support at the enemy's immediate rear. Fairly soon the equipment at their disposal proved poorly adapted, and they reduced that effort to a minimum, using it almost solely at night while awaiting airplanes suitable for daytime use, which did not arrive until the beginning of 1918, and for night bombing of strategic objectives, which did not occur until the summer of 1918. French leaders were convinced that bombing was not effective unless employed en masse, for they were primarily concerned with getting material results that had a directly perceptible effect on the fighting on the ground. The ideas of France's allies and enemies, however, differed considerably from theirs.

As for the enemy, because of the weakness of the bombers of the time in comparison to the fire power of the artillery—a branch that the Germans favored to the end, even at the expense of the tanks—aerial bombing had no value except the psychological one of affecting the morale of the civilian populations. This explains the attacks on cities from August 3, 1914, on, and very soon on Paris and London, in spite of the ridiculously low tonnage of bombs dropped. It is also the reason for the development of the Zeppelins, which were alone in being able to reach London with a less ridiculous tonnage—a policy maintained for a long time in spite of the heavy losses and the slight results obtained.

In 1915 the Germans became acquainted on the Eastern Front with the Russian four-engined Sikorskys used against them in indirect action with no decisive results, but that spurred them on to construct heavy airplanes to replace the Zeppelins. The first of these planes was used in the east at the beginning of 1917.

These planes were used mainly in strategic actions; it was not until 1918 that they made their appearance in battle for lack of planes better adapted to that purpose. Curiously enough, the

Germans neglected daytime bombing. The attack units formed in 1916 had a capacity for dropping shells or bombs, but they were used more for support missions involving gunfire, attacking the trenches or accompanying the infantry directly in combat. The numerous CL prototypes started in 1916 were not used until 1917.

For the British, the indirect action made possible by distant bombing was immediately attractive. The idea was consonant with a plan that counted more on a maritime blockade and roundabout action in the Dardanelles than on costly direct confrontation to win the war. Unfortunately, the first Short bombers engaged in 1916 were a technical setback, and it was not until 1918 that the advanced Handley Pages could be sent to France; and only a moderate number—a few hundred—of them were manufactured before the armistice. No decisive result could be expected from the action of the few flights activated. While eager to take part in daytime bombing, the British did not have the first units of a suitable type, consisting of DH 4's, until the middle of 1917.

The intervening period was taken care of, after a fashion, by a variety of planes, often poorly adapted fighters, such as the escort fighter plane Bristol Fighter, which proved to be a good assault plane, or the light Sopwith used in its single-seater version as a bomber. The RAF did not have time to improve this mediocre situation, which resulted from the priority given from 1916 on to mass production before making sure of the quality and suitability of the products. The effort undertaken in all fields by Great Britain did not bear fruit until late in 1918; the RAF would have been formidable in 1919. Fortunately the British, who had experienced many disappointments with their observation planes, succeeded better toward the end of 1917 with combat planes. In the fall of 1917 they had the Camel and, at the very beginning of 1918, the SE 5 A at their disposal, both effective and mass produced.

We shall follow here the general development of

Before the offensive of April 1917, General Lyautey, minister of war, makes a visit to the aviators (behind him, a Moineau plane).

operations in 1917 and 1918, years of a massive employment of aviation in the war. The very large numbers of aircraft put into service necessitated a reexamination of the problems of organization.

Situation of the Forces in 1917

In the fall of 1916 the G.H.Q. issued a new plan calling for 187 flights (in general, of 10 planes each), or about 1,950 planes in action. But the parliamentary committee on aviation criticized that plan, which neglected night bombing and lacked ambition. Politicians' reports denounced the inadequacy of the air forces. All this led, as we shall see further on, to a political crisis in early March 1917 having to do with the organization of the rear. The Undersecretariat for Aeronautics was reestablished under Daniel Vincent, and production was immediately stepped up.

On March 15 the G.H.Q. presented a new plan for 189 flights, but this time the flights had been enlarged to 15 planes, which brought the number desired up to 2,665 planes.

On June 1, 1917, the French had effectively 2,665 airplanes on the line, out of a total of 5,806 (2,172 for the armies of the north and east, 209 for the entrenched camp of Paris, 284 for the foreign theaters of operations). This result may seem satisfactory if we compare it to the resources of the Kogenluft during the same period—2,360 planes—and especially if we take the British resources into consideration—a little less than 1,000 planes.

Unfortunately, the quality of the French airplanes on the line left something to be desired: while the Spad VII appeared in the summer of 1917 and was soon produced in great numbers, there were still too many Farmans, Salmson-Moineaus, and other AR's for observation, and the French were still awaiting the twin-engined bombers and, in particular, "the" daytime bomber. This situation did not really improve until the beginning of 1918.

Moreover, the year 1916 cost heavily in human lives. General Nivelle, who became commander in chief at the beginning of 1917, crowned with glory won at Verdun, affirmed that he was going to effect in April 1917 the long-awaited breakthrough that would lead to victory.

The offensive that he launched in April at the Chemin-des-Dames ended up with slight gains of ground and led to a total disillusionment that had serious consequences for the army's morale. The French were led to ask their British allies to take the responsibility in 1917 for carrying out most of the operations on the ground.

For their part, the Germans, who entrusted the conduct of the war to Ludendorff in September 1916, decided to finish with the Russians on the east. They therefore executed a strategic withdrawal in the west intended to shorten the front line so as to release fifteen divisions to reinforce their forces in the east. They then adopted a defensive attitude in the west.

The entry of the United States into the war in April 1917 brought no immediate relief, for the American army had to be created from scratch. It did, however, encourage the French to slow down their military operations to save the blood of their soldiers and prepare for 1918, which everyone believed would be the decisive year.

All this resulted in a slowing down of the war in the air, while efforts were pushed to the limit to produce the materiel needed to insure victory. Nevertheless, France was obliged to make an unexpected effort to give aid to its ally Italy after the defeat of Caporetto. During the last days of October, 7 flights were sent, along with some balloon units. They were reinforced during 1917 and 1918.

General Duval was called upon on August 2, 1917, by General Pétain to take command of Aeronautics at the G.H.Q., replacing Major du Peuty, who had been appointed in February 1917 by General Nivelle as successor to Major Barès.

The Operations of 1917

The beginning of the year was very calm. The Allies were preparing for the offensives planned for

April. The Germans had decided on their withdrawal and began to move out the civilian population starting on February 9. Their plan was to abandon to the Allies only an unusable countryside. They methodically destroyed 264 villages, 38,000 houses; they sawed the trees down at the base, clogged the wells; the airfields were plowed up and blown up with mines. All these operations were carried out with the greatest discretion from February 9 to 24, with the forced assistance of the civilian population. Aerial reconnaissances reported a great deal of information, but no one could envisage a German retreat.

On February 24 and 25 the Germans disengaged from the English 5th Army; on the night of March 12–13 came their disengagement from the French 3rd Army. The whole operation was completed in several successive stages by April 8, when they reached the Siegfried Line, a strong position prepared in advance.

From the end of February the French troops occupied the evacuated area, but the advance was very slow because of the destruction that had been done. Taken totally unawares, the Allies could not exploit the German retreat. The VB 101 was alone in throwing all its available planes upon the retreating troops on March 17. During the night of March 17–18 it attacked the railroad stations of the sector; in April it made very great efforts, dropping a total of 24 tons of bombs. But these missions could interfere very little with an operation in which three German armies were engaged.

None of General Nivelle's plans were changed. On April 9 the British attacked in Artois after an intense artillery preparation; the weather was very poor. This offensive was stopped on April 14, 8 kilometers from the bases from which it was launched. The French 3rd Army, which was operating at the right wing of the English, got only meager results. Nothing decisive was gained.

Finally, on April 16 came the launching of Nivelle's long-awaited offensive in the Aisne, at the Chemin-des-Dames. Massive forces had been accumulated: 5,000 guns bombarded the German lines for two days. But the enemy knew how to take advantage of the terrain, which lent itself admirably to the defensive with its caves or grottos, which offered excellent shelter against bombardments.

The weather was extremely poor from April 6 on, and it was practically impossible for the observation planes to do artillery ranging or to observe the results. When the troops threw themselves into an attack, they fell upon nearly intact defenses. In spite of the furious determination that was put into the fighting, the advance was minimal in comparison to the big losses. The tanks of Colonel Bossut, who was killed in the action, were used for the first time by the French at Berry-au-Bac. They were very quickly destroyed by artillery; their employment still needed to be perfected. All the operations stopped on May 8. It was necessary to concede failure, which brought on a new crisis in the country and in the army.

Thanks to the superiority that their modernized fighter planes gave them, the Germans won considerable victories, of which Baron von Richtofen got the lion's share, mostly at the expense of the English.

The month of April, nicknamed "Bloody April" by the British, cost them 139 planes—73 with pusher engines, 25 Sopwith 1 1/2 Strutters, 24 Nieuport Bébés, and even 13 two-seaters of the quite new Bristol Fighter type and 4 Spad VII's. From April 4 to 9 alone 75 airplanes were lost in Artois.

The tactics and experience of the Germans were far superior to those of the English, too many of whose fighter planes, moreover, were completely obsolete. These included the BE 2's, FE 2 B's (which were reclassified as night bombers), and the RE 8's, which were a little better but whose first appearance in service had been disappointing.

The year 1917 was very difficult for English aviation, which had no quantity of suitable fighter planes until the arrival of the Sopwith Pup in the summer and, more especially, the Camel in the fall. In addition, organization of the air forces was behind the times, and aircraft were being used in dispersed fashion. All this would change with the creation of the Royal Air Force on April 1, 1918.

All these factors explain the somewhat excessive admiration of the British for von Richtofen and his "circus" and the prevailing opinion among them that the Germans had absolute air superiority over all the Allies put together.

Things were not so gloomy on the French side. Thus at the time of the action at the Chemin-des-Dames the balance of air operations, from April 6 to 25, was as follows in the table below.

French Losses in Combat, in Numbers of Planes

	Within Allied Lines	*Behind Enemy Lines*
Army corps airplanes	10	6
Fighter planes	7	10

German Losses in Combat, in Numbers of Planes

	Within French Lines	*Behind Enemy Lines*
Army corps airplanes	1	8
Fighter planes	43	20

Total for the two sides: 33 French and 72 German planes lost.

This table shows the keenness of French pursuit: the majority of the combats between fighters came out to its advantage. Certainly there could be no question of an absolute superiority of the Germans facing the French flights.

But it is true that the forces concentrated by the Germans greatly hampered the army corps planes and the balloons. In addition, the very bad weather that prevailed in that sector during April greatly reduced the effectiveness of the observation planes—Sopwiths, G 6's, AR's—that had recently been put into service and were still somewhat confusing to their crews. The winds were so violent at times that several observers were thrown from their posts.

Perhaps the notion of German air superiority found a favorable echo among the combatants on the ground in search of an explanation for the defeat at the Chemin-des-Dames. If so, it would not be the last time that an attempt would be made to cast aviation in the role of the scapegoat. But it is no doubt true that the French fighter planes sought combat too exclusively and somewhat neglected to protect observation planes as the Germans did.

These tactics were modified for the offensives in Champagne and at Moronvillers with Major Ménard's combat group, GC 15. By placing patrols at intervals in the sector where the army corps planes were to operate a sufficient freedom of action was obtained.

During April and May the GC 15, flying Nieuport 17's, made 3,000 sorties and engaged in 700 combats, two-thirds of them within the German lines. It destroyed 52 enemy planes and lost 21 pilots. For example, on May 27 on the occasion of a local offensive the Germans maintained an exceptional continuity in flight of 45 planes in order to insure air superiority. The GC 15 succeeded in stopping and then turning back the German planes, causing the enemy 7 losses without suffering a single one itself.

Aviation cut a good figure in the offensives with limited objectives launched by General Pétain during the rest of the year in order to allow the troops to regain confidence: Flanders, July 31; Verdun, August 20; Malmaison, October 23. The work to be done was of the same style as that achieved on the Somme in 1916, where there was complete success. Moreover, from the summer of 1917 on the French had the Spad VII, which had finally been perfected.

The Battle of Flanders (June 7–November 6, 1917)

It was mainly to relieve the French army, perhaps with the secret hope of finishing the war by a British breakthrough, and no doubt also to come to the aid of the British Admiralty, which was greatly disturbed by the losses suffered in the Atlantic from German submarines based on the Belgian coast, that General Haig undertook the Battle of Flanders. It was the biggest operation of 1917,

A Nieuport above the lines on August 9, 1917. Photo taken from the observation plane that it is protecting.

bringing into play 12 divisions of General Plumer's British 2nd Army, 20 divisions of General Gough's 5th Army, and 6 divisions of General Anthoine's French 1st Army.

After a brilliant success at Messines on June 7 the offensive was pursued to the east of Ypres. The fighting continued for a long time, with a thoroughly British obstinacy. The English were now seasoned and fought quite well, but the ground, completely waterlogged by the rains, made all operations bog down. The memory of the mud of Flanders was left engraved on the combatants' minds. After a big ground gain of 5 to 10 kilometers in depth on a front of some 50 kilometers, the offensive, carried on in a terrain where the men sank in to their knees, stopped on November 6 at Passchendaele.

On November 20 General Haig launched an offensive in Artois with the participation for the first time[1] of an armored mass of 75 Mark IV tanks of the Royal Tank Corps entrusted with insuring the breakthrough. Poorly sustained in depth and without liaison with the aerial fleet (150 fighter planes and an equal number of single-engined bombers) engaged in the operation, this offensive did not go far.

Thus the Battle of Flanders did not result in any strategic decision. Nevertheless, it had the great importance of forcing the Germans to keep large forces in the west and to give up the entire offensive against the French forces.

British losses were considerable in 1917: 790,000 men, including 36,000 officers (killed, wounded, or prisoners), against 820,000 Germans and 470,000 French.

For the British the Battle of Flanders remains, along with that of the Somme, the theater of their greatest exploits in the First World War. The participation of French aviation in the battle was far from negligible, and many French aviators died in Flanders, including Guynemer, who disappeared on September 11, 1917, at Poelcapelle on Belgian soil.

At the beginning of 1917 the MF 36 was practically alone in engaging in bombing in that region. Then, in the course of the first six months, formations of the Royal Naval Air Service (RNAS), then of the Belgian air force, of French seaplanes, and finally in May the VC 116 were installed there. The VC 116 attacked the objectives of the sector by gunfire until September, when the flight resumed bombing.

[1]The English were the first to use a few tanks, on the Somme in 1916, but that premature engagement of not yet perfected prototypes played no part in the battle.

Beginning in February the British attacked the port of Zeebrugge and the objectives of the region. The Belgians lent their assistance to these actions.

On the eve of the Battle of Flanders the G.H.Q. sent flight V 109 of the GB 3 in support. The flight leader was Lieutenant Mahieu, whose name has become famous in the history of bombing. The G.H.Q. then sent in S 108, which had replaced its old Voisins with Sopwiths.

The Germans brought in practically the whole of their bomber force for the battle: 21 flights out of 22 (of 6 twin-engined G's each). They were used mainly for psychological raids of demoralizing effect on cities such as Dunkirk, Harwich, London, or Paris. This explains the mediocrity of results they obtained on the field of battle. They deployed a big fighter force in the region, no doubt anticipating a very powerful offensive.

The objectives that the French chose were essentially the immediate rear of the enemy lines and the airfields. The activity of the French flights of Voisins by night and of Sopwiths by day was very great and French losses considerable, but it is astonishing that the Germans did not attack the airfields from which these flights took off.

The British had only DH 4's and Sopwiths at their disposal in Flanders. The first three Handley Page 0/100 twin-engined planes were indeed convoyed to France in December 1916 for evaluation. Unfortunately, the third plane landed by mistake in Laon, which was in German hands. It was not until October 30, 1917, that the English put a first group of heavy bombers in place at Ochey to carry out reprisal raids in Germany. Their direct contribution to this battle was thus negligible.

Bombing in 1917

The bombing crisis continued into 1917 for lack of materiel suited to the missions. In the course of the year a number of planes that were disappointing and were kept only, for lack of better ones, on an interim basis engaged in the operations.

After the Sopwith, which had already appeared in 1916, came the Paul Schmitt, which had rated second in the competition for powerful airplanes held in 1915. Ordered in quantity, its manufacture was slow in getting under way, and it was not delivered until 1917. The first two flights—PS 125

A German airplane shot down by Jean Chaput.

A Voisin 8. This plane came into service late in 1916. Because of its 220-horsepower Peugeot engine it could carry 180 kilograms of bombs.

and PS 126—were created on April 8, 1917, the third—PS 127—on April 14, and the last—PS 128—on May 13.

But the plane was very disappointing. It was too slow for a daytime bomber, its immense wingspread interfered with group flying and maneuvering, and it carried only 100 kilograms of bombs. The Paul Schmitts were soon withdrawn from the front.

The PS 125 switched to Voisin 8 Peugeots on January 24, 1918, the PS 126 adopted the Breguet XIV B 2 in November 1917, the PS 127 also got Breguets in December, and the PS 128 was switched to Sopwiths on July 31, 1917.

It was not until late in 1917 that the Breguet XIV B 2 appeared, making it possible to resume daytime bombing. The improvement represented by this plane came essentially from the construction of the fuselage of duralumin, adopted for the first time in mass production, and from the 300-horsepower Renault engine, very reliable and powerful enough to lift the plane off the ground at 185 kilometers per hour and propel it at 145 kilometers per hour at an altitude of 5,900 meters.

At the time it was put into service it was nearly the equal in speed and maneuverability of the German pursuit planes, to the point that certain crews dismounted their rear defense turret to carry more bombs. That did not last long, however.

The Breguet possessed a system for automatically releasing at regular intervals the 32 eight-kilogram bombs that it carried. In 1918 a system of releasing bombs in imitation of the flight leader was adopted, which insured a good density of strikes and freed the crews from concern with sighting, allowing them to devote themselves better to their own defense.

But the Breguet was to be primarily the airplane of 1918. For the time being it was necessary to fight with the planes available: Farman 40's, Breguet-Michelins, which had at last been perfected, Voisins, of which the new Type 8 with a more powerful Peugeot engine carried more bombs, Voisin gun-planes, and Caproni three-engined planes. The groups that flew at night were equipped with these planes. Only the Sopwiths and Paul Schmitts were used in the daytime with fighter plane protection. Thus the bulk of the bombing was done at night.

In spite of its difficulties, the bombing section

remained very active throughout the year and greatly improved its methods. The objectives were essentially the same: attack in the enemy rear, with preference for railroads, supply depots, and cantonments spotted in the daytime by reconnaissance planes, and airfields. The units also constantly supported operations under way.

It should be noted that the bombing action was generally continued well after Allied offensives had stopped, since the reinforcements brought up by the enemy were still on the spot or were engaged in big movements that increased their vulnerability. Thus the Champagne offensive that was stopped late in May was followed by bombings as late as August, at which time French units were shifted to the Argonne in preparation for the next offensive, so that there was no rest for the air force, whose mobility was its strongest suit.

One interesting aspect of the aerial war was the "airfield war" that was undertaken systematically from August 18 on in the Verdun region. It was engaged in by flight MF 25 and by the GB 1 with two flights of Voisins. Up to then and after the middle of 1916 the French had certainly already had occasion to attack the German airfields, but counterstrokes were rare for lack of bomber planes at the enemy's disposal.

But 1917 was precisely the year of the creation of that branch in the German army. On February 25 the First Bomber Squadron (Kampfgeschwader) was created with 3 flights of 6 planes. Of the 18 planes of its complement 15 were twin-engined G's of the three types AEG, Rumpler, and Gotha.

On April 1 there were three squadrons equipped with G airplanes, and eight in July 1917, or nearly 100 planes. These machines were all twin-engined biplanes (two 260-horsepower Mercedes engines). They flew at 140 kilometers per hour and could carry 400–600 kilograms of bombs 250 kilometers. They were intended only for night bombing.

The crews had first to be trained and to perfect their methods of navigation. By late spring the Gothas had grown bold and attacked the south of England by day on May 26 and June 5; 17 planes bombed London on June 13, and 22 on July 7; Harwich was attacked by 16 planes on July 16. But on July 12, 18, and 22 during attacks on London 5 Gothas were shot down. The Germans definitively ended their daytime flights in favor of night flights, which they mastered little by little. Saint Denis was thus attacked by night on July 27.

But although these raids were being carried out successfully for the moment, it was clear that strong bomber units could be maintained only at the expense of the fighter forces. In August the bomber force was reduced to 4 squadrons of 6 flights of 6 planes each, which economized on personnel while keeping the same number of planes.

It was at that moment that the MF 25 inaugurated the "airfield war," attacking the Remonville airfield on August 18. On the 20th, when 9 planes of the flight had left to attack new airfields, their base—Vadelaincourt—was bombed. Seven airplanes were lost, and a mechanic was wounded. The MF 25 struck back on the 22nd; its airfield was again attacked. On the night of the 25th fires were started on the German base of Laix. In August and September the German bombers attacked the MF 25 almost every night without succeeding in destroying it, since the planes of the flight took off before nightfall and landed at Bellefontaine, making it, in effect, their new base.

At Vadelaincourt all precautions were taken: eight antiaircraft machine guns were in place, the lookouts were on the watch, shelters were constructed. Damage to the planes was greatly reduced, but other fields in the vicinity were also attacked.

In September the two groups of the GB 1 came to reinforce French attacks on the objectives of the region and sometimes lent their support to the MF 25's action concentrated on the airfields. Great damage was done to the enemy. The Germans, however, carefully prepared for their counterstroke. For several days they photographed all the French airfields they had been able to spot.

On the night of September 26 the Crown Prince's bomber squadron simultaneously attacked Vadelaincourt, Sénard, Lemmes, and Osche. In contrast to the earlier raids, the Germans showed

The Warhorse of Bombers: The Breguet XIV

In June 1916 Louis Breguet had begun on his own the research and development of a plane entirely new in its conception. Abandoning the formula in favor at the time, that of the pusher engine, he returned to his prewar planes with the engine in front. Using his formula of aircraft range of action, he aimed at getting a minimum deadweight, drag, and fuel consumption. He persuaded the Renault Company to boost its 220-horsepower engine to 275 and even 300 horsepower.

Breguet had to keep insisting in order to get the necessary materials, especially since he wanted to use for the first time the new metal duralumin, an aluminum-based alloy containing copper, magnesium, and manganese. The parts were put together by a process involving sulfur. The engineer Vuillierme did all the strength calculations needed.

The prototype was ready for flight testing on November 21, 1916. The tests were satisfactory, but because of the new technology that Breguet had used the government was not entirely convinced of its airworthiness and demanded long static tests. In order to remove the last remaining doubts pilots were recalled from the front to test the plane as well. In addition, one of the first planes produced was taken to Aulnat, where the pilot André de Bailliencourt, assisted by the chief pilot of the school there, Sergeant Roux, had to make at least 150 landings, some with the plane loaded, in order to test the landing gear. The first machine was received at Villacoublay on May 4, 1917. It was reserved for observation (Type A2). In May the Michelin plant also turned out a Breguet XIV bomber (Type B2), which became the archetype of all bomber planes until 1945. It was provided with all the modern equipment perfected by Michelin, such as the intervalometer and the sight used for dropping bombs at regular intervals.

In March 1918 a Rateau compressor was tried out on a Breguet XIV. It consisted of a turbine driven by the exhaust gases and rotating at high speed (30,000 rpm). The results were conclusive: the time required to climb to 5,000 meters was 27 minutes instead of 47, and the speed at that altitude was 193 kilometers per hour instead of 147. The turbo-compressor was not mass produced until after the armistice, however.

A Breguet XIV B 2 of Flight BR III, with a 300-horsepower Renault engine. Armament: a dorsal rear turret TO-3 or TO-4 armed with twin Lewis 7.62-millimeter guns; a Vickers 7.62-millimeter machine gun on the left side of the fuselage, permitting fire in pursuit and controlled by the pilot; a Lewis machine gun firing through a trap-door fitted under the fuselage, which came into use during 1918 (fired by the rear bombardier-gunner); and two Michelin bomb-release systems for dropping 32 eight-kilogram bombs at regular intervals.

The cockpit of a Breguet XIV B 2.

Bombs under the wings of a Breguet XIV B 2.

up this time in formation; they dropped flares to illuminate the objective, and the attack proved very effective. The airfield at Sénard was hit the hardest. Less serious damage was done at the other fields, but, all in all, the Germans wreaked more destruction than they had in the earlier raids.

The morale of the French crews was not affected. During the day on the 27th as many airplanes as possible were brought up quickly from the reserves of the front and put in the air, hit or miss, by the evening of the 27th in order to conceal from the Germans the extent of their success: 11 Voisins in the GB 1 and 4 Farmans in the MF 25 (no more had been found) attacked the Marville and Mars-la-Tour airfields. The next day a few planes were hastily repaired, and 8 planes of the MF 25 attacked the Puxieux fields and some barracks. They started over again on the 29th.

The GB 1 was then sent to Champagne. Only the MF 25 continued to attack the German airfields, until winter set in and the operations were discontinued.

Although the French succeeded in forcing the Germans to abandon the Remonville and Mars-la-Tour airfields, this "airfield war" ended in an indisputable victory for the Germans, who had more powerful means available to them. It is remarkable that in spite of this exchange of bombs neither of the protagonists was really able to put the other out of action. This was because the reserves enabled losses to be quickly made up for, and also because it was impossible to neutralize for very long a meadow without a runway, especially with the low tonnages of the time and with bombs poorly suited to the purpose.

Throughout 1917 night bombing of the industrial centers of the east was carried on, often with the aid of English units (Sopwiths, DH 4's, sometimes a few Handley Pages, whose first bombing by an isolated plane dates from March 16 in the Metz region). The Voisins, Breguet-Michelins, Capronis, and Farmans did what they could, often at the cost of heavy losses but without ever getting discouraged. But it became clearer and clearer that the employment of these means could not be expected to be decisive.

In September the GB 5, which had been using Breguet-Michelins, was reequipped with Breguet XIV's. Two flights, the BR 117 and the BR 120, carried out daytime raids with an astonishing

An antiaircraft gun, April 1917.

A Salmson A 2 observation plane.

facility that augured well for the part that the reemerging daytime bombing would soon play.

The Plans of the G.H.Q. at the End of 1917

On October 18 Colonel Duval, head of the Aeronautical Service at the G.H.Q., set up a new plan that was approved by Commander in Chief Pétain. The G.H.Q. asked that the units be increased to 238 flights with 2,870 planes, including 30 flights of 15 bombers.

Sopwiths were no longer wanted, and the twin-engined Letord three-seater was recommended. It was to be able to do reconnaissances while taking care of its own defense, but it was late in coming into service.

In September a new Undersecretary for Aeronautics was named, Jacques Louis Dumesnil. Barely thirty years of age, having served for some time in the C 13 in 1917, he knew the needs of the front and hammered away at increasing production from the time of his arrival. He was on excellent terms with the G.H.Q., and soon the difficulties began to fade away. Dumesnil suggested to Duval that the latter present more ambitious plans, which the former undertook to carry through if he was given the means.

Thus on December 7, 1917, a new plan was proposed, raising the number of airplanes on hand to 4,000 by July 1, 1918: 1,500 army corps planes, 1,500 fighter planes, and 1,000 bombers. From then on, all efforts—industrial as well as those connected with personnel training—were to focus on implementing that plan.

Most of all, good prototypes were now available, thanks to the efforts of the Technical Service's designers. The Breguet XIV A 2 and the Salmson 2 A 2 of the army corps had come into service in the fall of 1917. They were completely satisfactory, and all that was necessary was to push forward their production. The twin-engined Letord plane was in the testing stage.

The Spad VII had been fully in service since the summer; the Spad XIII was ready, but it fell victim during the winter to problems that were not definitively solved until the spring of 1918.

At the request of the G.H.Q. a program of two-seater fighters had been launched, the prototypes of which were under construction by the end of 1917: the Hanriot-Dupont 3 C 2 and the SEA 4 C 2.

The bomber was further behind. While the Breguet XIV B 2, in service since September 1917, corresponded exactly to the G.H.Q.'s wishes for the daytime bomber, this was not true of the twin-engined night bombers.

The Voisin X BN 2 with Renault engine finished its testing. A little slow, it served in 1918 as an interim plane in anticipation of the Farman F 50 with twin 240-horsepower Lorraine engines, equivalent to the German Gothas, and the Caudron C 23 with twin 230-horsepower Canton-Unné engines, which was to threaten Berlin.

Robert Esnault-Pelterie manufactured the Caproni three-engined plane with three 170-horsepower Isotta engines under license; late in 1917 an improved twin-engined version was prepared. Finally, a Caudron twin-engined R XI was to be tested for reconnaissance and escort missions.

The manufacturing plans having been launched for 1918, the G.H.Q. got down to questions of organization in the light of the experience of 1917.

A Spad XIII

The Spad XIII's two synchronized Vickers machine guns.

The Voisin Renault bomber, painted black for night sorties, returning home in the morning, December 1917. Watercolor by Alfred Daguet, January 1918 (PASM Coll.).

The synchronization system of the Vickers machine gun and the engine (from L'Aéronautique pendant la Guerre Mondiale / Aeronautics during the World War, *ed. Maurice de Brunoff, 1919).*

A. Cooling sleeve of the machine gun
B. Breech casing
C. Rear support
D. Directional synchronization mechanism
E. Collimator support
F. Oscillating synchronization rod
G. Cartridge case
H. Ejection duct of the left machine gun
I. Link ejection duct of the right machine gun
L. Cover of the cartridge feed duct
M. Springs to prevent cartridge belt from flapping
N. Box to receive links from the right machine gun
O. Fire control
P. Pull to regulate position of the cartridge case

THE AIRPLANE OF THE ACES: THE SPAD XIII

The Spad XIII, designed by the engineer Louis Béchereau, was incontestably the best fighter plane of the First World War. Béchereau had designed a remarkable airplane in 1913, the Deperdussin monocoque, which, flown by Maurice Prévost, exceeded 200 kilometers per hour. In the fall of 1915, on the advice of the G.H.Q., he designed a fighter plane based on the Swiss engineer Marc Birkigt's Hispano-Suiza engine.

The prototype Spad V, equipped with a 140-horsepower 8 A engine, was flown for the first time in May 1916, by the pilot Béquet. In the summer of 1916 it was supplied to the Air Force in its definitive form, the Spad VII, which had a 150-horsepower engine. It was armed with a synchronized Vickers machine gun.

Unfortunately, when the Spad VII was put into service defects showed up that delayed its use at the front. It was not until the summer of 1917 that it was perfected; the engine had been increased to 180 horsepower. The more powerful Spad XIII, equipped with a 200-horsepower Hispano-Suiza engine and better armed (two synchronized Vickers machine guns), was under study during the same period of time. Its prototype, the S 392, was flown for the first time in April 1917 at the Buc airfield. Again, engine defects postponed its use at the front until January 1918. The correction of these defects made the Spad XIII a very reliable airplane. In the final stage of its development the engine was brought up to 220 horsepower with reducer, which made the installation of a 37-millimeter gun possible. The Spad XIII was maneuverable and fast (215 km/hr) and had a strength that enabled it to dive without breaking. It was the easiest plane to mass produce and the most manufactured craft of all the belligerents.

The Winning of Air Superiority by the Allies

Finally, starting in the summer of 1917 the Allies produced airplanes that performed at least as well as those used by the Germans. First of all, the French had the Spad VII with a 180-horsepower Hispano-Suiza engine and a synchronized Vickers machine gun; then in the fall the English had the Sopwith Camel with a 130-horsepower Clerget engine and two synchronized machine guns, followed soon (January 1918) by the SE 5 A with a 180-horsepower Hispano-Suiza engine. These machines remained in service until the armistice and were produced in very large numbers. It was an SE 5 that shot down Schaffer, a Camel that downed von Richtofen. The Spad XIII with a 200-horsepower Hispano-Suiza engine and two machine guns appeared in January 1918 and was soon the best fighter of the day.

A new generation of pilots took over from the old ones—Fonck, Chaput, Boyau, and others—who had disappeared. There were still aces, but now they were primarily patrol leaders.

The Germans tried to produce new planes to outclass those of the Allies. In imitation of the Sopwith triplane of 1916, of which only a small number were manufactured, and of the Nieuport triplanes and quadriplanes, which did not really go into production, the Germans put Fokker and Pfalz triplanes in service in the fall of 1917 with the idea that that formula made it possible to produce a very light plane with equal surface. But in spite of their excellent rate of climb, these planes had the defect of not diving well, and their speed was somewhat low. Moreover, they came apart in the air, and only 400 were manufactured. Von Richtofen was killed in a triplane.

In March 1918 the Fokker D VII with a 180–200-horsepower Benz engine appeared. It used a wing profile that was thick for the time and gave it a rate of climb almost equal to that of the Camel. It was also more maneuverable than its two formidable adversaries. The Fokker D VII caused the Allies a great deal of trouble beginning in May 1918, when it became available in quantity along with another new fighter, the Pfalz XII, which performed equally well.

But although Germany could still develop and manufacture quality airplanes, it was handicapped by the naval blockade, and its production was becoming harder and harder to develop further. In

The R XI (left) was put into service at the beginning of April 1918. Twin-engined, with a crew of three, powerfully armed with five machine guns, and very maneuverable, it was used for protection on the massive daytime bombing raids carried out by the Breguet XIV B 2's. These machines of the same speed as the bombers provided close protection, while Spad formations at different altitudes were responsible for cover at a distance. In 1918 the bombing formations thus protected were formidable to the German Fokker D VII and Pfalz XII fighters, which suffered heavy losses. The R XI may be considered as the first escort fighter especially adapted to this type of mission.

1918 it reached the ceiling of its potential. On the other hand, the Allies, who knew how to make airplanes just as good and had now overcome their organizational problems, were able to double their production every year. The race for air superiority, a function of quality and quantity, was lost by Germany. From the spring of 1918 on the Allies had absolute mastery of the air and retained it to the end of the war.

Preparation for the Resurgence. The Winter of 1917–1918

During the fall and winter of 1917–1918, a season unfavorable for large-scale operations, the G.H.Q. prepared for the fighting of 1918, which everyone supposed would be of unprecedented magnitude. It was clear that, since Russia had been eliminated from the conflict, the Germans would try to snatch victory before the American army arrived in France in force.

The winter respite was used to codify the employment of fighter aircraft, whose first drill regulations came out on March 2, 1918, in the form of a "Note on the Employment of Flights and Combat Groups in Battle." A school was established for advanced training in pursuit and bombing, the C.I.A.C.B. (Centre d'Instruction de l'Aviation de Chasse et de Bombardement/Fighter and Bomber Instruction Center), directly under the G.H.Q., where crews were employed that had been trained in the schools behind the lines and had already been transferred to the forward G.D.E. (Group de Division d'Entraînement/Training Division Group). From then on, therefore, the flights at the front no longer had any training duties, since the personnel assigned to them had already received long training in combat skills.

The whole of the fighter, or pursuit, air forces was split into two parts. First, protection for the army command's observation planes was to be provided by "independent" combat groups placed at their disposal; second, the offensive actions reserved to the G.H.Q. were to be the work of "combat squadrons" formed of three groups trained in flying in large formations. The combat squadrons were created on February 4, 1918.

"Offensive actions" included seeking out and attacking enemy air units, attacking the Drachen balloons, and attacking troops on the ground. The combat squadron comprised 12 flights and a supply depot with means of transportation, since the mobility of the squadron was fundamental. In addition, the squadrons and the groups had staffs, each flight comprising about 150 men and 15 planes; in all, the squadron had nearly 200 planes and 2,000 men.

It was also in the fall of 1917 that the long-awaited daytime bomber finally appeared, the Breguet XIV B 2 two-seater. It carried 250 kilograms of bombs, could stay in the air four and a half hours, and had a ceiling of 6,500 meters. Armed with a synchronized axial machine gun and twin Lewis guns in a turret, it was big enough to defend itself against pursuit, at least when flying in formation. Its Renault engine was the most reliable of the time.

In the summer of 1918 the Caudron R XI three-seaters with 220-horsepower Hispano engines were put into service, well armed for the time (five machine guns) and with a long range. Almost as maneuverable as fighter planes, they provided close protection for the Breguets; they were the first real escort fighters accompanying bombers for the entire duration of their missions.

On February 13, 1918, the Breguet XIV units were similarly organized in daytime bombing squadrons of three groups of three flights of 15 planes. The squadron was thus provided with nearly 150 planes and a complement of 1,700 men. The first daytime squadron activated was No. 12, under the command of Vuillemin.

Finally, the G.H.Q. combined a fighter flight with a bomber flight to form what were called "groupings," which were given the name of their commanding officers. Thus in March 1918 the Ménard grouping and the Féquant grouping were created. These two officers, among the first to be licensed as pilots in 1911, had not ceased to participate in aerial combats throughout the war. The two groupings together were headed by Major Le Révérend.

The organization of these large numbers of planes, intended to be shifted as a unit in the course of operations, was not simple. Each combat group needed a suitably prepared field of about 20 hectares (50 acres), whose installations had to be linked by telephone to various command posts. Hangars had to be available to shelter the planes, equipment, and supplies, and there had to be roads to serve the various installations.

General Duval, aeronautics aide to the commander in chief, had the task of providing for all these needs. The workmen and hangar builders, precursors of the air force engineers, numbered in the thousands.

The fighter squadrons' mission was no longer to provide an impossible continuous presence in the air but to intervene en masse to gain air superiority locally in support of an offensive or in order to retrieve a locally compromised position. They were also to make it dangerous for the enemy to use French air space—several free-pursuit patrols aided by well-developed antiaircraft artillery were sufficient. They were also sometimes asked to attack ground troops by machine gun and also, on occasion, to protect bombing raids and reconnaissance missions.

Battlefield objectives were more specifically designated for the bombers: reserves and supply dumps, convoys on the march, artillery batteries that had been spotted, etc. Consideration was being given to resumption of long-range bombardment of industrial targets even before the big

A Breguet XIV B 2 of Flight BR 66.

carriers under study became available, such as the Farman F 50, which was not ready until three months after the armistice.

The improvement in materiel also affected observation forces, which in 1918 finally were supplied with a remarkable airplane: the Salmson Sal 2 A 2, a two-seater with a 260-horsepower Salmson engine, almost as fast as a fighter and as well armed as the Breguet XIV, which in its A 2 version was also used for such missions. Radios were being installed on a large scale and had come into regular use.

The use of aerial photography had greatly increased. Each group had its own photo section. Results of missions were exploited and distributed within a few hours to the advance units. The progress achieved can be seen from the following figures: 48,000 photos taken in 1914 and 1915, 293,000 in 1916, 474,000 in 1917, and 675,000 in 1918.

Thanks to the great production of aircraft in 1917 and 1918 and to technical progress, the high-quality French planes were now numerous and provided with abundant reserves. Everything was ready for the operations of 1918.

1918: The Year of Victory

The First Half of 1918

At the moment when the Germans launched their March 21 offensive in Picardy at the junction point between the British and French armies the Féquant grouping was stationed in the Soissons region and Ménard's in Champagne. The fog greatly hampered air operations until March 24. Only light patrols were flown, chiefly to reconnoiter the enemy's movements. On March 23 Paris was bombarded, and the French command, supposing that it was a matter of air raids, sent pursuit planes out on the presumed return route of the enemy planes. This was in vain, however, since the bombardment was being done by Big Berthas (giant cannon firing a 120-kilogram shell every fifteen minutes). The planes finally found the location of the Big Berthas, which were then silent.

As soon as the weather cleared, the French air force, in order to gain air superiority, was engaged by half-groups and by groups of four flights in the critical zone between the Somme and the Oise. An enemy observation plane, therefore, was able to see the breach opened between the British and the French armies. On the other hand, the French commanders were always perfectly informed. The German planes were eliminated in two days, and the French planes then turned their weapons toward the ground. The bombers dropped their projectiles unceasingly on all the crossings of the Somme and of the Crozat Canal as far as the Oise, while British planes were also engaged in the sector.

On March 27 the Champagne grouping, which had moved, was in readiness, the attacks redoubled; the planes were launched eighty at a time against enemy troop concentrations. The results of these attacks carried out from March 24 to 30 were confirmed by prisoners and by the destruction visible to French troops on the ground. The impetus of the offensive was slowed down enough to allow for the arrival of reinforcements. For the first time the air force had demonstrated the effectiveness of its direct participation in the battle.

On April 4 Ludendorff suspended his offensive and organized new positions. But the battle in the air continued.

The Féquant grouping was sent to Beauvaisis and the Ménard grouping to the rear of Amiens. Enemy troops on the ground had had time to camouflage and protect themselves, and German aviation remained in force. It was therefore necessary to resume the fight for air superiority. On May 16 two hundred bombers were sent to attack the German airfields. Fighter planes took off in whole groups, escorting bombers or acting individually. But German fighters often refused battle with such formations; they had lost many of their best pilots, they were short on supplies, and their planes were inferior to the Spad XIII until the appearance of the Fokker D VII in May 1918. Von Richtofen, after having been shot down in April 1918, wrote:

Major Vuillemin (1883–1963).

General Duval.

Victor Ménard (1881–1954), left, in conversation with the engineer Béchereau, designer of the Spad VII and Spad XIII.

Philippe Féquant (1883–1938).

"If German industry does not soon supply us with a considerable number of single-seater planes of much better quality than our present ones, it will soon be impossible to fly on the Western Front." The Fokker D VII explains the furious battles of May 1918 in which Chaput was killed.

It was on May 14 that the First Air Division was created, composed of the Ménard and Féquant groupings for pursuit and daytime bombing and the Chabert and Villomé groupings for night bombing. It was put under the command of General Duval, who remained in charge of aeronautics at the G.H.Q. This reform made the coordination of attack orders with the receiving of reports still more effective. The mobility of the units was further improved, and the effectiveness achieved was soon discernible.

At the time of the launching of the German offensive of the Chemin-des-Dames (May 27, 1918) Duval gave orders at 6:00 A.M. to the Ménard grouping to go to Tardenois, which was particularly threatened. The first units took off three hours later. Patrolling along the lines, even attacking columns on the march by machine gun, the crews went to their new stations. On the evening of the same day the entire grouping was in place.

But in the face of the German drive it was necessary to change airfields every day and beat a retreat even while continuing to carry out missions. The night squadrons, poorly supplied with bombs because of the crowding on the roads, participated in the battle in the daytime, machine-gunning convoys and bivouacs. It was under conditions of considerable difficulty that the French air force succeeded in two days in again overpowering the enemy air force. The second grouping was rushed from Amiens on May 31; from May 31 to June 2 the French air force shot down 56 planes, damaged 46, set 10 Drachen balloons afire, and dropped 200 tons of explosives.

Mass Attack on Ground Troops

From that time on the massive use of air forces against troops on the ground became more and more frequent. Beginning in the summer of 1918

The mechanics of Flight BR 117 preparing their Breguet XIV B 2's for a bombing mission in July 1918. Insignia: silhouette of a rooster in profile atop a bomb, painted in blue on a white circle.

every Allied offensive was supported by an air force of 300 to 500 planes. Thus the offensive of the Fayolle army group launched on July 15 enjoyed the support of 69 flights, or 1,000 planes. On August 8 Rawlinson's British 4th Army had 400 airplanes at its disposal, and General Debeney's French 1st Army, which was operating at the same time, had 600.

Air action was often very effective in attacking ground forces. Thus on June 4 a strong German troop concentration was reported to the east of the forest of Villers-Cotterets, in the ravine of La Savière, which sheltered them from artillery fire. In an attempt to block the attack thus being prepared for, at the request of the commanding general of the army General Duval sent 120 bomber planes under Major Vuillemin. The Breguet XIV's passed the objective at an altitude of 600 meters and renewed their attack, dropping 7,000 bombs. The German assault did not take place.

The same kind of action took place on June 11 in support of the Mangin counteroffensive that stopped von Hutier. A cloud of French fighters held the sky while the bombers attacked the German artillery batteries, which were helpless.

A report of the Undersecretary of State noted:

About 400 French bomber planes operated constantly over the battle zone or in its immediate vicinity from March 29 to June 12, 1918.

Nearly 1,200 tons of explosives were dropped in eighty-two days. Thus in less than three months more projectiles were thrown at the enemy than during the two years 1916 and 1917, during which a total of 987 tons were dropped.

In the same period the French airplanes engaged in nearly 2,000 combats, and 59 enemy balloons were shot down. (During 1916 and 1917, 54 were destroyed.)

715 German airplanes were set on fire, captured, or destroyed.

French losses were appreciable: 115 French planes were lost, and 91 were damaged. (These totals include accidents, as is not the case with the German figures.)

Nevertheless, the Fokker D VII's did not hesitate to attack the Breguets in spite of the protection of the Spads. Losses were heavy and were of the same order on both sides. In this game the German air force was very quickly exhausted. It could no longer deter bombings, and it became definitively impotent toward the end of 1918 when Caudron R XI's joined the Spads to oppose the Fokker D VII's.

A slight modification in air force organization on June 15 should be noted. The terms "Ménard grouping" and "Féquant grouping," which gave a provisional sound to this experiment, now ratified by success, were abandoned in favor of the term "brigade." From then on the First Air Division comprised the First Brigade, which was turned over to Major de Goÿs, who had just escaped from the enemy, and the Second Brigade, which was under Féquant.

The last German offensive, in July 1918, was again the occasion for a brilliant aerial feat of arms. The Germans had thrown a number of bridges across the Marne at a point out of artillery range. Two bombing squadrons attacked these objectives without respite for several days, turning them, according to German reports, into a "real hell"; 45 tons of 10-kilogram and 20-kilogram bombs were dropped on July 15 alone.

Allied Offensives in July 1918 and After

Thus far the Air Division had shown its effectiveness in helping to remedy difficult situations. Now that Foch was taking the initiative it became easier to get even better results.

The First Division moved continually, depending on the rhythm of the battle and the point of attack chosen by Foch, from Picardy to Lassigny, then from the Oise to the Somme.On September 8 General Duval turned the command of the Air Division over to Colonel (later, General) de Vaulgrenant. After having supported Mangin's and Humbert's armies in forcing the Hindenburg Line in September the Division moved 200 kilometers from there, into Lorraine, to participate in the first big operation entrusted to General Pershing's Americans—the reduction of the Saint Mihiel salient. Command of the air forces was given to General Mitchell.

The Allies assembled 1,500 planes for this operation, including 900 French and 160 English planes. The battles in the air were furious, especially on September 14, when, during an expedition over the railroad station of Conflans-Jarny, the GB 4 and the supporting crews of the R 46, equipped with Caudron R XI's, were heavily attacked over their objective and fought a terrible battle to get through. Seven of the crews were shot down, but eight enemy planes were destroyed, and finally the objective was reached and bombed.

On September 16, 1918, General Pershing sent a letter of thanks to Colonel de Vaulgrenant: "Having begun with the attack on 12 September 1918 and having continued to the end of the operation, your airplanes, both fighters and bombers, not only showed the highest qualities of organization and teamwork, but also penetrated to great distances within enemy lines and showed qualities of bravery beyond all praise. The use of an air unit like yours in close liaison with ground troops contributed heavily to the victory." It was the end for the Germans; they became more and more powerless and were never able to launch massive raids.

General von Hoeppner, commander in chief of the German air forces, says of 1918: "The enemy was attacking simultaneously along practically the entire front. We could no longer, as in 1917, concentrate all our forces at a given point to gain air superiority. We were numerically inferior everywhere" (*L'Allemagne et la guerre de l'air / Germany and the Air War*, 1923).

Beginning in the fall of 1918 bombing sorties were flown by 150 to 200 airplanes at a time. A bomber squadron was closely escorted by a group of R XI's for close cover and, at greater altitude, by one or sometimes two groups of Spads for more distant protection.

On September 28, 1918, Colonel de Vaulgrenant congratulated himself on the liaison that existed between bomber units and escort units.

The flights of R XI's had been given to the Air Division for the organization of an airplane lookout service. But in the meantime the imperious necessity had arisen of giving the daytime bombers close-in protection. This mission could hardly have devolved on any but the R XI's. This organization answered the desires of the bombardiers and those of the men of the R XI flights as well. The proof of this may be seen in the fact that the squadron commanders always try to associate the same R XI crews with the same bomber group and that a real moral bond has been established between them; the R XI crews stake their honor on most particularly protecting their bomber group, and the bombardiers have confidence in the R XI crews that they know and have been in a position to appreciate.

As for the fighters, the individual combats of the beginning of the war were a thing of the past. Major de Goÿs, commanding the First Brigade, wrote on October 25, 1918:

Protection at a distance, provided today by pursuit planes (single-seaters) will probably be provided tomorrow by fighter planes (two-seaters) with greater effectiveness. It consists in keeping the enemy's attack aircraft away from the bombing operation. For this, "shooting down the Boche" should be subordinate, barring exceptional circumstances. The essential thing is to permit our bombers to carry out under the best possible conditions their mission of destruction of the objectives set for them.

Just as for the R XI three-seaters, this mission is purely one of sacrifice. The fighter aircraft accompanying bombers must therefore be imbued to the highest degree with the "mission spirit" and eliminate individual success from their program to devote themselves solely to their task of protection.

There was no longer anything that could resist the action of the Air Division, the results of which were all the more important since the war had developed into a war of movement, and the troops, no longer sheltered by trenches, were extremely vulnerable. In October 1918 in the Seraincourt region a fresh German division that was to relieve another could not do so because it was destroyed in its bivouacs by an aerial bombing. In November 1918 in the Chesne region in the course of an advance the French troops found a battlefield strewn with cadavers of soldiers and horses and with artillery pieces; it was a battery on the move that had been surprised by the bombers.

The Division had just arrived in Lorraine, near

Nancy, at the beginning of November and was preparing to participate in Mangin's final offensive when the armistice put an end to the fighting.

The Division had a chance before the armistice to attack Marienburg, 150 kilometers behind the lines, in force (November 10). Since its creation in May 1918 the Division alone had shot down an official total of 637 airplanes and 125 Drachen balloons and had dropped 1,360 tons of bombs.

Statistics

Personnel and Materiel as of November 11, 1918

When the Allied troops entered Germany after the armistice and could inventory the remaining air material they were astonished to see the state of attrition of the German air force, which had only 1,800 warplanes fit for service, including fewer than 200 bombers on the Eastern Front.

German industry had not reached the point of producing planes as fast as they were used up. As soon as they left the factory the planes were sent to the flights; there was no reserve. This explains the lack of massive German actions during the last months of the war.

In contrast, the organization of the Allies' production had made surprising progress since 1917. At the time of the armistice, on the Western Front alone the French had 3,437 first-line airplanes (for a theoretical complement of 3,600) in 258 flights—126 observation flights, 80 fighter flights, and 52 bomber flights.

The 16 flights of the interior (antiaircraft and coastal flights) comprised 148 airplanes. There were 3,886 planes in reserve or stockpiled in the arsenals of the interior. The schools had 3,000 planes at their disposal and the domestic service 400 others. There were also some 300 first-line airplanes in the 30 overseas flights. In all, French military aviation had 11,836 airplanes.

The British had 1,800 planes on the Western Front and a total of 2,690 on all fronts, with a grand total of nearly 20,000 airplanes in various locations.

The Americans had 740 airplanes in France on the front lines. The Italians put into service at the front about 1,200 airplanes, including about 100 in France.

All in all the allies had a little over 6,000 first-line airplanes in the west opposing the 2,700 (theoretically fit for service) at the disposal of the Germans in the summer of 1918.

Since the quality of the Allies' equipment was at least equal to that of the Germans and their methods of employment were equally good, the Allied superiority was dazzling.

The distribution of the 90,000 men of the French air force was approximately as follows:

On line at the front	30,000
In the forward reserve	10,000
In the schools	25,000
In service at the rear	25,500

To these must be added the naval aviation forces: 11,000 men serving the 400 first-line, coastal defense seaplanes and the 800 others in reserve or under repair.

The losses in flying personnel killed or missing during the war, in combat or by accident, came to 5,533 men, for a total of 16,458 pilots and 2,000 observers trained in five years; three-quarters of these losses occurred in the last two years. The losses were most severe in fighter and bomber forces; the observation planes, protected and employed on the lines, suffered relatively fewer losses.

It must be noted again that these totals include the losses due to accidents in training or in service at the front; these accidents were very numerous and often fatal. Thus the French lost in combat only about 3,000 planes out of 40,000 manufactured for their use; nearly 300 pilots were killed in school or in training. But it was especially in accidents at the front that numerous losses occurred, which may be estimated at about 35 percent of the total losses. This percentage was increasing toward the end of the war, approaching 45 percent during the last six months. (See the detailed table of losses for the months from May to October 1918.)

A Breguet XIV B 2 of Flight BR 131 during a bombing mission.

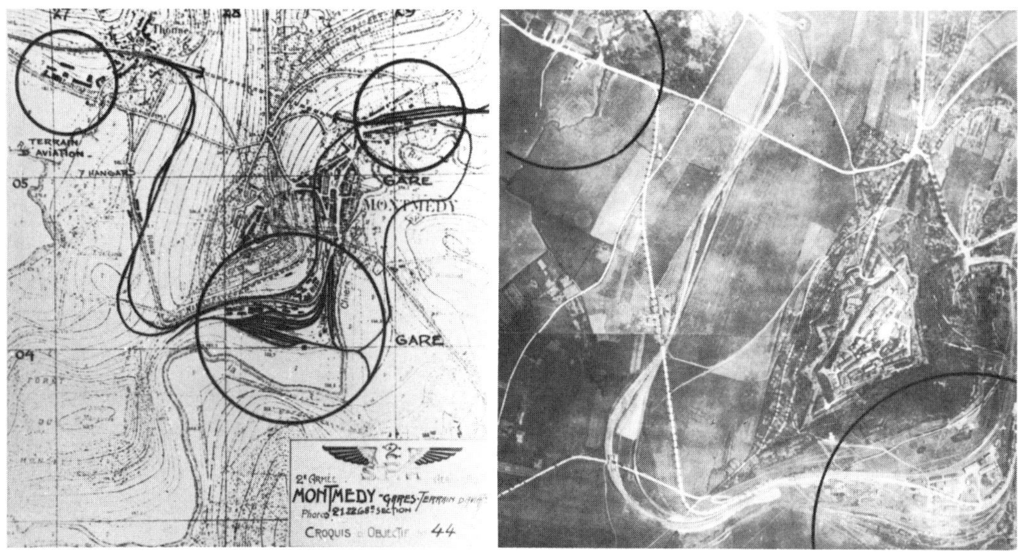

An objective slip for the bombing of the Montmédy station and airfield, 1918.

Bombing of a German cantonment north of Vouziers, October 10, 1918.

Bombing of objectives at Vouziers by Flight BR 131, October 10, 1918. The bombs dropped over the city are visible in the photo.

Finally, losses due to antiaircraft fire may be estimated at about 15 percent of the total. Thus the distribution of losses by cause comes to 50 percent in aerial combat, 15 percent from antiaircraft fire, and 35 percent from accidents.

The Losses of the Other Belligerents

The losses suffered by the other belligerents were distinctly greater than those of the French.

The British lost about 8,200 men killed or missing and 4,000 airplanes in combat.

The Germans, according to the work by von Hoeppner mentioned above, counted 7,780 killed or missing in combat or in accidents. Von Hoeppner admitted only 3,128 airplanes lost, which seems low in relation to the casualty figures. Since the German archives have been lost, no better or more detailed figures are available.

One may conjecture, however, that the figure for human losses is closer to reality than that for planes lost in combat, if only because more care is devoted to establishing the status of the victims.

On the other hand, the number of victories reported on one side and the other displays a certain discrepancy. France officially recognized 2,049 victories in the air, of which 307 were within French lines and 1,742 behind enemy lines, and 357 Drachen balloons set on fire (which were counted as victories). In addition, 1,901 victories were regarded as certain though unconfirmed. By counting only a third of these into the totals one arrives at the figure generally accepted in France of 2,700 victories and 357 Drachens. (Cf. Major Orthlieb's *L'Aéronautique hier et demain/Aeronautics Yesterday and Tomorrow*, 1920.)

This figure in itself is very close to the 3,128 airplanes "conceded" by von Hoeppner. Yet the British claim a number of victories even higher than that of the French.

Von Hoeppner asserted that the German aviators shot down 4,865 airplanes and 614 Drachens in the west, to which antiaircraft fire added 1,588 airplanes, for a total of 6,453 planes shot down.

It is very hard to take a firm position on this question because of the lack of irrefutable documents on the German side and because of the methods used by the British to confirm aerial victories until well into 1916. It seems, however, that French victories and losses were fairly balanced; this is explained by good organization in advance. The overall numerical superiority that the French air forces almost always enjoyed permitted very soon, from 1916 on, the employment of planes en masse, which made the German patrols falter. And the quality of the French materiel, especially in regard to fighter planes, enabled their forces to fight the Germans on at least equal terms.

What is most striking is the case of the British, who probably suffered more losses than they won victories. There were several reasons for this: the general and long-lasting—until the middle of 1917—inferiority of English fighter planes, the obstinacy in keeping observation planes as obsolete as the BE 2 C in service well into 1917, and no doubt also the poor organization and the engagement of bombers without regard to losses and when the planes had not been sufficiently perfected. Finally, it must be noted that the Germans always attacked the British armies in force, more often than they attacked the other Allies, in the hope of winning a victory of political consequence.

As for the Germans, it is probable that they really did have more victories than defeats, since their organization was centralized very early and their materiel was always of good quality, except during certain periods. It must be emphasized, however, that the systematic engagement of powerful German formations occurred mainly on the front held by the British, where victories were easier, at least until 1918. One must also note that the famous "Von Richtofen Circus" served chiefly in that zone, as if the German high command had tried to make von Richtofen the first ace of all the belligerents for psychological reasons.

But German losses were enormous during 1918 when, completely outclassed in numbers and performance, the German fighter force, accused of cowardice by a command that had not foreseen the outcome, was engaged to the limit under heroic

French Losses in Personnel in the Last Six Months of the War (May–October 1918)

	May	June	July	August	September	October
IN COMBAT (aerial combat and antiaircraft fire)						
Killed	43	63	51	65	47	41
Wounded	63	114	114	68	59	58
Missing	105	119	70	85	103	56
	211	296	235	218	209	155
ACCIDENTS AT THE FRONT						
Killed	58	35	41	58	48	38
Injured	74	86	67	38	41	48
	132	121	108	96	89	86
ACCIDENTS (in the interior)						
Killed	25	26	36	34	37	14
Injured	32	27	36	33	37	32
Missing			2			
	57	53	74	67	74	46
Grand Total	400	470	417	381	372	287

A Farman F 50, a twin-engined night bomber. Ordered in large quantities, it was put into service at the front in August 1918. By the time of the armistice 170 of them had been delivered and three flights already existed. By October 1918 they were being manufactured at the rate of 50 a month. This plane, weighing 3,116 kilograms and equipped with two 260-horsepower Lorraine engines, could carry 500 kilograms of bombs and reach a speed of 151 kilometers per hour in flight. It was intended to replace the Voisin X BN's still in service in 1918.

conditions. For this reason, completely disheartened by the campaign of disparagement launched against them in spite of their sacrifice, many German aviators gave up, abandoned their flights, and went home once the armistice was proclaimed. This fact, shamelessly pointed out by von Hoeppner in his book, was attributed to the lack of discipline of the aviators, who, according to him, did not have the traditions of the army and the navy.

Conclusion

Some remarks may be made on the part played by aviation in the overall course of the operations.

Today the fleets of planes engaged in 1914–1918 may seem very large. It must be emphasized that those fleets consisted solely of planes of rather low individual output. The slowness of the observation planes and their simple radio and photographic equipment (1 camera with 12 plates) enabled them to gather only a small amount of information on a single sortie. The situation was similar in regard to attacks on ground troops; the Spad had only two 7.65-millimeter machine guns firing a limited number of nonexplosive balls at a slow rate.

The Breguet XIV with its three machine guns was a little better armed, but it could drop only about thirty 10-kilogram bombs. Although this type of bomb was very effective against exposed personnel, it quickly became useless as soon as even slight protection was used.

Furthermore, in a war of masses of infantry and artillery such as the First World War, the part played by the air forces, while its usefulness is not to be denied, cannot be considered decisive. In 1918, however, it did succeed in demonstrating the necessity of a massive action and showing the importance of a "clogging" role, slowing down enemy action and facilitating counterattacks.

After the war everyone tried to "draw the lessons" from the recent conflict. A debate arose between the champions of "cooperation," that is, those who saw no use for aviation except in reconnoitering for the troops on the ground (the reader will have noted that in 1918 half the airplanes engaged were devoted to observation and a good part of the fighters to their protection) or supporting them directly, and the champions of mass action by an air force kept in reserve, as foreshadowed by the First Air Division (which then represented only a quarter of the total number of planes).

In France, where effective aerial bombing did not appear until very late and then almost exclusively in direct support of the ground fighting, it was hard to imagine an independent role for aviation at the strategic level. Nevertheless, from 1915 on there were bombings of explosives factories; in 1918 thought was being given to the possibility of resuming that action soon, thanks to the Farman F 50, which did not appear in quantity soon enough. (There were three flights of F 50's and two of Capronis at the time of the armistice. The first flight of Caudron C 23's was just being formed then.) The fact that France won the war without that, added to the failure of the German bombings by Zeppelins or Gothas, had grave consequences later on, since it caused France to neglect the study of strategic bombing for a long time.

The second observation necessary here is to emphasize that from the fall of 1916 until the summer of 1917 French planes were outclassed by the German fighter planes. Furthermore, until the Battle of the Somme they were the ones that took the initiative in perfecting the tactics and the employment of air forces.

This is explained by the poor understanding of technical problems on the part of the French officers of the time. In the rear those responsible for Aeronautics were very often artillerymen who were poorly informed on the special problems of aviation and who tried to favor numbers at the expense of quality. Even when they took account of the French technical inferiority they underestimated the time necessary to remedy the situation. At the front the combatants did not understand the importance of matters of technical and industrial organization either, thinking they were doing the right thing in giving first priority to rapid delivery of materiel to the front and believing it was possible to make improvements while carrying out missions. These attitudes, understandable in some respects but condemned by the facts, led to serious crises of confidence between the front and the services in the rear. It was not until the beginning of 1917 and the arrival of Daniel Vincent in the Undersecretariat for Aeronautics that the situation finally changed and that the good results to be obtained by thorough planning were at last demonstrated.

The first Farman F 50 at the front, July 1918, intended for the first tests in the combat zone. Mechanics from the Farman Company, recognizable by their caps, lend assistance to the test crew.

A Caudron C 23 twin-engined bomber, put into service just before the armistice. This plane, weighing 4,130 kilograms and equipped with two 260-horsepower Canton-Unné engines, could carry 1,000 kilograms of bombs and fly for 5 hours at 130 kilometers per hour. It compared well with the German Type G twin-engined planes such as the Friedrichshafen.

CHAPTER IV

Organization in the Rear

While the G.H.Q. was trying to solve with the means at its disposal the many problems facing it at the front, the services behind the lines had to provide both the personnel and the materiel that were urgently needed. Little or nothing had been done before 1914 to sustain a conflict of such duration and magnitude. No one had foreseen the development that aviation was to have. It was thus necessary, first, to improvise, to manage with the small funds allocated to the aeronautical services, and then, finally—and very late—to organize a real war industry.

The present chapter deals with the problem of the general organization in the rear, then with that of the Aeronautical services, and finally with the organization of the schools.

The Directorate of Aeronautics (12th Directorate): August 1914–September 1915

It has already been noted that at the beginning of the war the destiny of Aeronautics was in the hands of General Bernard, director of Aeronautics. One of his first decisions, in August 1914, was to close the schools and send all the mechanics from the depots of the aviation groups back to their original corps, so convinced was he, along with everyone else, that the war would be of short duration. It did not even occur to him to ask the G.H.Q. what its needs were. The month of August toppled all the preconceived ideas, and in the face of the deficiencies in Aeronautics (in particular, the disappearance of aerostation) General Bernard was replaced on October 25, 1914, by General Hirschauer, the former permanent inspector of Aeronautics. Immediately following his arrival General Hirschauer and his assistant, Colonel Bouttieaux, tried to remedy the situation. By the fall Hirschauer had already ordered 2,300 airplanes, 3,400 engines, and 1,000 automobiles for the units at the front. The rate of production, which was 1.5 planes a day in August 1914, rose to 4.5 in November, 10 in February 1915, and 14 in March. In November the schools at Pau and Avord were reopened; during the winter the school at Chartres was established, and the schools at Etampes, Buc, and Le Crotoy were militarized. Dijon and Ambérieu had just started in the summer of 1915.

But the critical situation of August 1914 and the part played by aviation had persuaded Joffre to invest heavily in it. He decided to appoint an aviator, Major Barès, to the post of Director of the Aeronautic Service at the G.H.Q., replacing Colonel Voyer, who favored dirigibles too exclusively. Barès wasted no time. Finding that there was no plan at all in the Ministry of War, he undertook to draw one up. He had as assistants, among others, Captain de Goÿs and Captain Jaillet, the latter in charge of aerostation. On October 5 Barès submitted to Joffre a plan raising the number of flights from 31 to 65 and limiting the types of planes used to four: Morane for pursuit, Maurice Farman for reconnaissance, Caudron for artillery ranging, and Voisin for bombing.

This program for 390 airplanes had almost been realized in March 1915. On March 30 the air force comprised 51 flights, 11 airfields, and 9 reserve flights. The personnel rose to 130 officers, 500 pilots, 240 observers, and 4,350 men. Barès then issued a new plan for 78 flights, followed by another for 119. During the summer of 1915 the complement of the flights rose from 6 planes to 10. The program of September 7, 1915, for 119 flights corresponded to 1,190 planes, 400 officers, 1,400 pilots and observers, and 10,000 men. From the mobilization to July 1, 1915, France had turned 391 planes over to its allies (including 264 to Great Britain and 53 to Russia). These allies had also been authorized to buy directly from the manufacturers 389 airplanes (Great Britain 127 and Russia 181). Under these conditions the new plan was difficult to carry out.

Still, in order to reduce deficiencies in the rear Barès had to create a supply reserve at Mortemets, near Versailles, which centralized all replacements except automotive vehicles, and a general reserve of flight personnel and rolling stock at Bourget-Dugny. These reserves functioned from the end of 1914 on. The planes were delivered to Dugny, where the pilots took them over and flew them to their flight's airfield. Thanks to this simple organization the French units gained ascendancy over the enemy in the spring of 1915, and the bombing sections covered themselves with glory. But all this did not occur without a certain disorder, as is the case with any improvised undertaking, and consequently not without clashes.

General Hirschauer had certainly done what he could, but he was in charge of only the 12th Directorate of the Ministry of War and did not get the means indispensable for developing the air services properly. Moreover, the services were staffed with officers (the military engineering corps did not yet exist) who were sometimes incompetent but most especially were too often lacking in enthusiasm. It is also true that in a number of cases the G.H.Q. had exceeded its powers in negotiating with the manufacturers; the services profited by this to absolve themselves of responsibility. Misunderstandings between the front and the rear increased.

Creation of an Undersecretariat of Aeronautics (September 13, 1915–February 8, 1916)

It became clear very quickly, in 1915, that the organization was defective. Aviation was a single entity and should be directed by a single head whose authority extended to both the front and the rear. Parliament—both the Chamber of Deputies and the Senate—was persuaded that the success of Aeronautics depended on a better organization which would insure the development of production.

On September 13, 1915, it was decided to create an Undersecretariat of State for Aeronautics, entrusted to René Besnard, deputy and chairman of the War Budget Committee.

The first undersecretary of state immediately took the necessary measures to put things back in order. He created a bureau of statistics to find out the numbers produced and the deliveries made. Until then great efforts had been devoted to forming units, but little had been done to keep the inventory of materiel up to date, and disorder and waste prevailed. The undersecretary obtained from Major Barès the creation of an Inspectorate General for air materiel turned over to officers at the front, while he himself set up an Inspectorate of

Aeronautical Materiel. Then, to put himself in a position to increase production, he reorganized the three essential services: the Technical Service, Production Service, and Repair Workshops. He detached from the S.F.A. (the Aeronautical Manufactures Service) at Chalais-Meudon the Industrial Service, which he located near him, in Paris on the Boulevard Saint Germain, so that he could concern himself with matters of supply, labor, construction of new factories, etc.—the bases of an industrial policy.

Within the S.F.A. he created an Inspectorate of Aviation Manufactures, entrusted with following up with the manufacturers questions of manufacture, control, price, acceptance, etc. This bureau was subdivided into territorial subinspectorates.

All of these innovations, which have become customary today under more highly developed forms, caused René Besnard to make many enemies for himself. In order for these very sound reforms to succeed they should have been carried out by new officers, coming if possible from the front, but Major Barès opposed this.

In the fall of 1915 the G.H.Q., aware of the mediocre quality of its airplanes compared to the enemy's, inaugurated an extremely daring plan for renovation. It involved increasing the power of the planes, which the G.H.Q. wanted to be twin-engined three-seaters (to provide their own defense). This program appeared very realizable to the G.H.Q., which in May 1915 had discovered the Hispano-Suiza engine, developed by the Swiss engineer Birkigt in Barcelona, Spain. Once the purchase of two engines was decided upon, the tests were carried out at Chalais-Meudon in July 1915.

Testing was begun immediately and showed that with a few modifications in details this engine would make it possible to give the planes a power source combining the safety of a fixed engine with the relative lightness that had until then been the attribute of rotary engines. Its capacity was 150 horsepower. At the time it was the only engine to pass a confirmation test of fifty hours, which was conclusive. All that remained was to manufacture it in quantity, and to the G.H.Q. it appeared that the program of 1,890 planes of October 1915 would be realized in the spring of 1916. The figure was reduced to 1,726 planes by René Besnard, and the quantity to be expected by April 1 was set at 450 airplanes, or 18 a day, which seemed the largest possible number.

It was obviously an industrial revolution, but Besnard had done everything to put himself in a position to succeed at it, and he approved the G.H.Q.'s plan despite its difficulties and its cost.

Besnard was then attacked very vigorously by members of Parliament, who, like Pierre Etienne Flandin in December 1915, proposed a plan different from the G.H.Q.'s which would have kept the Maurice Farman and the 100-horsepower Renault and Canton-Unné engines. The later course of the war would show that in the long run it was Barès and Besnard who saw the matter correctly.

Unfortunately Besnard, severely criticized on all sides, was not supported by Barès, who still had an unfavorable opinion of the rear.

It was then that Besnard had to notify the Salmson Company about serious defects in its Canton-Unné engines, then being manufactured. The company sought the support of Senator Charles Humbert, who spearheaded a press campaign seeking to discredit the undersecretary of state. Finally, disheartened by the procedures resorted to against him, Besnard submitted his resignation, which was accepted (it was his third offer) on February 8, 1916. René Besnard, paid homage by the Chamber of Deputies in private session some months later, was a victim of two evils that poisoned France throughout the war: industrial interests and political intrigues. Inadequately supported by the officers of his services, who allowed themselves to be influenced too much by these political attacks, he was unable to get the results that he had a right to expect from his reforms.

The Directorate of Aeronautics Reinstated (February 1916–March 1917)

The minister of war, General Gallieni, was not a warm partisan of the undersecretariat; he made use of René Besnard's departure to restore the 12th Directorate of his ministry and chose as director Colonel Régnier, again an artillery officer, a very hard worker but one who knew nothing about aviation. To a certain extent he represented the revenge of the military on the civilians, and it was no doubt for that reason that, better sheltered from political attacks, he was able to stay in that position until March 1917.

The year 1916 was a very difficult one for aviation. For one thing, contrary to expectations, no harmonious relationship arose between Colonel Régnier and Major Barès. The former attempted to take charge of the Mortemets and Dugny reserves created by the G.H.Q. late in 1914. This attempt, vigorously opposed by Barès, together with Régnier's ideas of reorganizing the services in the image of those of the artillery, definitively widened the chasm between the Directorate and the G.H.Q.

The Battle of Verdun, starting in February, displayed the weakness of the French air forces, which the commander in chief did not succeed in making up for by a successful organizational effort. The Battle of the Somme, in which the French had the advantage, was a bit deceptive. By September 1916 French technology, compared with that of the German Albatross D 1, was undeniably lagging behind. Unexpectedly, the Hispano engine was not yet perfected.

As of March 1, 1916, fifteen hundred 150-horsepower engines had been ordered to equip the Spad VII. Everything seemed to be going quite well until, as the first engines began to be produced, breaks in the crankshafts were found, breaks that had not occurred during testing. From February 1916 the production of airplanes other than the Spad was almost at a standstill and, what is more, involved only outmoded planes such as the Maurice Farman (which continued to be delivered until April 1917) for lack of satisfactory new prototypes.

By May 1916 everyone was talking about the aeronautical crisis. During the last six months of 1916 secret committees and parliamentary commissions of inquiry multiplied. In December 1916 Daniel Vincent, chairman of the Aeronautics budget committee, made a report on the air forces that had great repercussions. In that document he questioned the number of airplanes on the line and their quality. Thus, for example, from the 2,023 planes officially "in line" on November 1, 1916, Vincent deducted 196 in the G.H.Q.'s training group and 409 in the general reserve. There thus remained at the front only 1,418 planes, including 328 pursuit planes, 837 reconnaissance planes, and 253 bombers. Of the 328 pursuit planes there were only 25 Spad VII's; 80 other planes were obsolete. Of the 837 observation planes 802 were of an outdated type (Maurice Farmans and Caudron G 4's). The Sopwith was the only good, up-to-date plane, and there were only 7 of them on the line. All of the bombers were outmoded.

There was once again the dramatic clash of two commands—front and rear—that could not come to an understanding, as well as the incapacity of the Directorate in the rear to promote production. The industrial structures had remained almost what they were in 1915 since no manufacturer was willing to make the investments and the efforts at rationalization that would have improved productivity. To justify their attitude they pointed to the G.H.Q.'s continual change of programs; the Directorate of Aeronautics fell into step with them instead of imposing its leadership on them.

The Directorate General of Aeronautics (February 10–March 20, 1917)

In January 1917 General Lyautey, the minister of war, gave General Guillemin the task of conducting an inquiry into the air force with the aim of improving its organization. He concluded that it was necessary to create a Directorate General of Aeronautics over both the front and the rear and also concerning itself with the navy and the Allies. On February 10 this office was created, and General Guillemin was, quite naturally, named to head it.

The G.H.Q. reacted strongly, trying to limit the power of the new bureau.

On February 15, 1917, at the request of the

minister of war, Barès had to leave his post, he too being the victim of a spiteful campaign. He was accused, among other things, of retaining the Maurice Farman and even suspected of having linked his interests to the manufacturer's (when in fact he had never ceased to advocate the replacement of that particular plane).

Major du Peuty succeeded Barès in General Nivelle's G.H.Q. Full of enthusiasm and ability, he had the sole defect of being an aviator full of eagerness for action but with little inclination for organizational questions. Thus he too had to learn his job, like General Guillemin—for other reasons—at the head of the Directorate General of Aeronautics.

Contrary to the government's programs, the production of recent-model planes was still lagging behind that of the older types, which were being turned out in satisfactory numbers. Thus from July 1916 to April 1917 instead of the planned 800 Spads only 268 had been received.

In March 1917 a member of the Chamber of Deputies, Raoul Anglès, a captain and pilot, delivered a solidly based indictment against the Directorate General and General Guillemin, judged not for his moral character, which was not at issue, but for his lack of technical competence. Anglès emphasized that on March 1, 1917, instead of the 1,850 airplanes asked for by the G.H.Q. there were only 1,586, of which only 411 were newer models; large orders were still being placed for outmoded AR planes instead of Sopwiths. He also objected to the disproportion between the Aeronautics personnel assigned to the front—15,534 and 1,550 pilots—and to the rear—19,350 and 729 pilots, not counting trainees.

A cabinet crisis brought about by the resignation of the minister of war, General Lyautey, caused the fall of Prime Minister Aristide Briand. In the new government headed by Alexandre Ribot the Undersecretariat of Aeronautics was reestablished and entrusted to Daniel Vincent.

The fighter ace René Fonck greeting Jacques Louis Dumesnil, undersecretary of state for aeronautics, on a visit to the front.

The Administration of Daniel Vincent (March 20–September 12, 1917)

When he began his post in the Undersecretariat Daniel Vincent held a number of winning cards. An observer second lieutenant in flight V 116, he had a clear idea of life in an aeronautics unit; longtime chairman of the Aeronautics budget committee, he was also well acquainted with the problems of the rear. Unfortunately, this competent man, who was to have a remarkable influence on his department, in short order also fell victim to political intrigues.

During the six months that he remained in his post Vincent succeeded in reorganizing his services and in obtaining manufacturers who speeded up their production and who, at the same time, busily studied new models. Thanks to the direct consultation with the manufacturers, Vincent strove to assist them as much as possible by guaranteeing them raw materials and labor. He also forced them to accept orders for planes other than their own brands. He fully utilized the capacities of every existing factory (Renault had 30% of its machinery idle) and made a special effort in the production of engines.

During the summer and fall of 1917 production increased remarkably; monthly production of engines doubled. The manufacturing of outmoded planes was finally stopped in order to put the effort into the production of Breguets and Renault and Hispano-Suiza engines.

Within the 12th Directorate, placed under his responsibility, Vincent avoided creating a break; he even succeeded in improving the general atmosphere. Then he made an effort to replace less enthusiastic officers with aviators returning from the front, and he revised the functions of each service. In particular, he reformed the Technical Service (S.T.Aé.), directed since 1916 by Colonel Dorand, a pioneer in aviation and himself the designer of several airplanes. Under Dorand's direction the Technical Service had gradually taken on the habit, on the basis of the G.H.Q. programs, of doing the development and testing itself for planes whose construction was then entrusted to the private sector. This was typically the case for the AR plane or the Letord three-seater. Daniel Vincent confined the Technical Service to judging the plans of the designers and to providing technical assistance.

Because of the increase in deliveries to the front relations between the front and the rear improved distinctly. Finally, on August 2, 1917, General Pétain placed the air forces under Colonel Duval, appointed aide to the commander in chief and chief of the Aeronautical Service to the armies.

This officer of very high quality, who would very soon be promoted to the rank of general, was the real organizer of the large air force that General Pétain wanted to perfect. Immediately there was complete understanding between Vincent and the G.H.Q. For the very first time the latter's plans were almost realized: on August 1, 1917, from a program of 2,665 planes set up on March 2, 1917, 2,335 planes had been put into service, including 63 R 4's, 302 G 6's, 469 Nieuports (110 horsepower), 27 Breguet XIV's, 521 Spads, 32 Salmsons, and 697 Sopwiths. The improvement in quality was considerable. General Nivelle, author of the plan of March 2, had insisted on giving priority to the quality of the planes rather than to their numbers. On the same date the British mustered 1,200 planes and the Germans, according to the intelligence services, 1,980.

Relations between Colonel Duval and Daniel Vincent were very cordial from the beginning; frequent meetings took place, which produced excellent results. On September 6 the two agreed to raise the production program to 2,870 airplanes.

But soon everything soured for Vincent. For negotiations on aeronautical affairs with the Allies he had a delegate to the interallied service, Pierre Etienne Flandin. Although relations between these two men had been entirely normal, Vincent decided, after a few months, to suppress this delegation and turn its functions over to a bureau of the 12th Directorate that was directly under his control.

M. Painlevé, the minister of war at the time, held this against him, and a paper war began

Raymond Poincaré at Villacoublay in 1918. He is accompanied by M. Loucheur, minister of armaments (on his right, in a derby hat) and J. L. Dumesnil (behind him). At left (in light-colored uniform), Colonel Dhé.

between the minister's military staff and the undersecretary. On September 12, 1917, when Painlevé replaced Ribot as prime minister, he took advantage of the reshuffling of the cabinet to promote Vincent to minister of public instruction, despite the opposition of the G.H.Q., some of the deputies, and public opinion. It appeared that everything would have to be done over, but fortunately Vincent got Painlevé to appoint as his successor Jacques Louis Dumesnil, previously undersecretary of state for the navy and in charge of the Aeronautics budget.

One may say that the French are indebted to Daniel Vincent for having undertaken a serious restoration of the aeronautics situation, which it was up to his successor to continue. These figures illustrate the results already obtained at the time of his departure: plane production, which in February 1917 was 820 a month, had risen to 1,204 in September, and engine production from 1,263 to 1,838. The armies' total stocks, fixed at 2,363 in January, reached 3,556 in August (including 2,312 first-line planes). Three-quarters of the September production represented new types of planes.

The Last Undersecretary for Aeronautics: Jacques Louis Dumesnil (September 12, 1917–November 8, 1918)

Dumesnil had youth in his favor—he was thirty years old—and a good deal of enthusiasm. Having spent a short time in flight C 13 from April to June 1917, he had a good idea of the needs of the front. He was also a hard worker. All these qualities, however, did not save him from criticism, which was more intense because at that time Paris was suffering from the raids of the German Gotha bombers.

Moreover, at the moment when everyone had finally agreed to give an absolute priority to airplane production (War Committee decision, October 8, 1917), which implied priority in allotment of manpower and in freight reservations for imported raw materials, the undersecretary should have been given broader powers, perhaps to the extent of making him a minister. This would have enabled him, for example, to determine the recall of personnel from the front, which the G.H.Q. had refused to grant him.

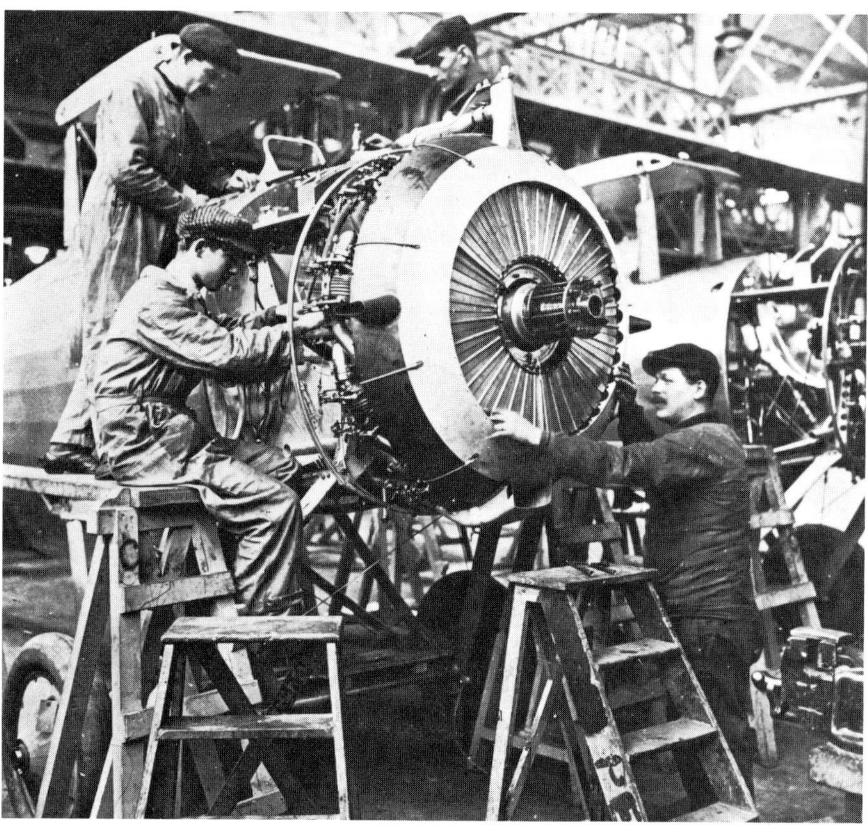

The installation of a Canton-Unné star-shaped engine in a Salmson 2A2 plane at the Salmson plant.

Instead, Painlevé issued two decrees in November 1917 that subordinated the Undersecretary for Aeronautics to the minister of armaments, M. Loucheur; and, as far as airplane production was concerned, the Aeronautical Manufactures Service was placed directly under the orders of the minister of armaments. In other matters, however, Dumesnil was under the minister of war.

General Pétain reacted immediately, pointing out the danger of this division of responsibilities; but he got no satisfaction from Georges Clemenceau, the incumbent prime minister after November 23, 1917. On December 1 Pétain tried again, pointing out that during November the front had received only 15 Breguets instead of 155, 39 Salmsons instead of 120, and none of the planned 15 R 11's that had been expected. The situation was the same with regard to the delivery of new engines. But the prime minister refused to nullify the decrees.

Finally, faced with the ambiguous situation created by these decrees, Minister of Armaments Loucheur and Undersecretary of State Dumesnil devised an exceptional solution. Colonel Dhé, a former cabinet officer under Prime Minister Painlevé, had been named Director of Aeronautics upon Clemenceau's coming into power. He had thus succeeded Colonel Guiffart, whose ability and zeal were well known. Colonel Dhé was not an aviator, and so had to learn on the job, but the knowledge he had of the ministries, combined with his brilliant qualities as a man and as an officer, enabled him to make an unorthodox organization work. Loucheur and Dumesnil delegated to him the right to sign for them on whatever matters overlapped in their spheres of authority.

With that system in place, thanks to the goodwill and zeal of all concerned and especially to the personal efforts of Dumesnil, who had a perfect understanding with the G.H.Q., it was possible to achieve surprising production levels, to which we shall return later. The wartime record was set for planes in August 1918 with a production of 2,853 and for engines in July 1918 with 4,490.

The improvement in production made it possible to carry out the G.H.Q.'s plans, increased from the plan for 2,665 planes, already mentioned, to that for 2,870, requested by General Pétain on

The paint shop of the Levasseur Company, where the Spad was made, 1917.

Finishing a wing frame.

September 6, 1917 (100 army corps flights of 10 planes; 40 artillery flights of 10 planes; 8 A.L.G.P. [heavy, long-range artillery] flights of 15 planes; and 30 bomber flights).

It turned out to be more difficult to realize the plan for 4,000 planes that Dumesnil judged possible in 1919 and that he proposed to the War Committee on October 8, 1917. That plan was approved "with the figure of 4,000 not considered as limiting, but as a step toward an unlimited production."

Those 4,000 planes were to be on the line in

Manufacturing captive balloons at Chalais-Meudon, January 1918.

Static tests of an airframe at the Caudron plant.

July 1918. The plan provided, among other things, for two air divisions. Because of various delays it was postponed first to October 1, 1918, and then to January 1, 1919.

Unfortunately, the promises of priority in support of aviation made in the War Committee were not entirely kept, and the objective was not completely attained. In November 1918 France had only 3,600 planes on the front line (and 3,400 existing), part of which were obsolete models.

Two months before the armistice the G.H.Q. was working on a plan for 4,200 planes to be carried out by the end of the first quarter of 1919. At the same time Dumesnil was beginning to lay the foundations for a later and more ambitious plan for 6,000 planes, which time would not allow to be put to the test.

The Manufacture of Airplanes

The Aeronautical Manufactures Service (S.F.A.)

The Aeronautical Manufactures Service (S.F.A.), subordinate to the Directorate of Aeronautics, was installed in 1914 at Chalais-Meudon. In the face of the German advance of September 1914 the S.F.A. was exiled to Lyons, where it established a subsidiary that remained active throughout the war. It returned to Paris in December 1914.

At the beginning of 1914 the section of the S.F.A. that was concerned with the research and development of materiel was detached from it to become the Technical Section of Military Aviation. At the same time the Industrial Service was created, attached directly to the Directorate of Aeronautics. In March 1916 Colonel Stammler was appointed head of the S.F.A.

In March 1917 the S.F.A., which had now gained in importance, left Chalais-Meudon and was installed at Nanterre. Colonel Stammler, victim of an intrigue cooked up by an industrialist, was replaced by Colonel Guiffart on the order of the minister. At that time the service had 150 officers, 1,150 enlisted men, and 400 civilians. On August 1, 1917, Colonel Guiffard gave way in turn to Major Guignard, who had to oversee the expansion of the service's activity.

As we have seen, from November 1917 on the S.F.A. was subordinate to both the Ministry of Armaments and the Undersecretariat by way of a "Central Manufactures Service," the head of which was Colonel Dhé, the director of Aeronautics.

The board of directors of the S.F.A. took up quarters in Paris, on the Rue Scheffer, in December 1917, with the services staying at Nanterre.

In January 1918 it was given responsibility for the aerial photography service and most of the functions of the industrial service. Its personnel increased to 370 officers, 1,800 enlisted men, and 475 civilians.

In May and June 1918, faced with the threat of German offensives, the S.F.A. prepared for decentralization into the provinces. Without changing the manufacturing in progress, it established subsidiaries in Bordeaux, Tours, Marseilles, Montauban, and other cities. It was felt that even if no move was necessary, these shops would not be useless, since they made it possible to increase production. But the impending victory made this extension unnecessary.

In 1918 the S.F.A., still under the orders of Major Guignard, was subdivided into 17 services and 140 subservices; it comprised 400 officers, 3,000 enlisted men, and 700 civilians.

Its role was not to manufacture planes itself or even to conceive of new models but to provide general direction for the manufactures entrusted to private industry. Three thousand factories of all sizes were thus monitored by the service, including 37 main factories for the manufacture of planes and 23 for the manufacture of engines. It played a considerable part during the war and especially in 1918, when nearly half of the planes delivered to the army were built.

The two tables give an idea of the volume of work accomplished by this service: 48,426 planes manufactured up to November 11, 1918, including 8,500 training planes and 9,460 turned over to the Allies.

Monthly Production of Engines

	1914	1915	1916	1917	1918
January		307	1,001	1,579	2,567
February		370	965	1,204	3,117
March		696	1,178	1,552	3,139
April		584	1,249	1,721	4,029
May		652	1,262	1,986	3,847
June		603	1,295	1,885	4,274
July		538	1,552	1,960	4,490
August	40	571	1,561	1,965	4,320
September	100	533	1,579	1,899	3,934
October	137	648	1,727	2,089	4,196
November	209	687	1,624	2,537	3,502
December	374	897	1,792	2,715	3,148
	860	7,086	16,785	23,092	44,563

Monthly Production of Planes (including Seaplanes)

	1914	1915	1916	1917	1918
January		262	501	846	1,714
February		280	422	832	1,668
March		431	505	1,225	1,647
April		421	526	1,107	2,100
May		355	603	1,258	2,071
June		378	541	1,143	2,459
July		340	664	1,330	2,622
August	50	383	745	1,302	2,912
September	62	454	814	1,276	2,322
October	100	402	731	1,470	2,362
November	137	367	752	1,550	1,392
December	192	416	745	1,576	1,383
	541	4,489	7,549	14,915	24,652

A very great effort toward standardization was made in 1918, so that at that time there were only 13 types of warplanes being manufactured. This undoubtedly explains the fact that the planes produced in the largest numbers by any belligerents were the Spad XIII (7,300 planes) and the Nieuport Bébé (7,200); next in France came the Sopwith (4,200), the Breguet XIV (3,500), the Spad VII (3,500), and the Salmson A 2 (3,200).

These figures may be compared with those of Great Britain: Sopwith Camel (5,500), SE 5 A (5,200), RE 8 (4,077), BE 2's of all types (3,600), and DH 9 (3,200).

As for Germany, the plane produced in the greatest numbers, the Albatross C V two-seater observation plane, reached only 2,800 units, and the fighter plane manufactured the most, the Pfalz D III, not more than 2,100, as well as the best German fighter plane, the Fokker D VII.

But it was in the manufacturing of engines that France succeeded best, with a production of 86,936 new engines produced up to November 11, 1918, which permitted plenty of replacements and even enabled France to supply 24,550 engines to its allies (12,800 to Great Britain). Those manufactured in the largest numbers were the 200–220-horsepower Hispano (20,300, to which may be added those manufactured under license), the 110-horsepower Rhône rotary (9,650), the 80-horsepower Gnome (8,700), and the 130-horsepower Clerget (6,300). These figures may be compared with those of Great Britain, France's principal competitor at the time. The British engine manufactured in the largest numbers was the 250-horsepower B.H.P. (4,332), while the Rolls-Royce 190–220-horsepower Falcon—undoubtedly the best British engine—did not exceed 1,632 units.

There was similar industrial progress in the area of arms and equipment. For example, the monthly output of on-board machine-gun turrets rose from 100 in 1916 to 5,000 in October 1918. The production of on-board equipment such as watches, altimeters, tachometers, oxygen inhalers, and many small items of equipment made necessary by technical development was counted in the tens of thousands.

The Technical Section

The Technical Section was detached from the S.F.A. in 1916 and was directed by Colonel Dorand and later, beginning in January 1918, by Major Caquot. Its function was to promote the research and development of materiel.

At the beginning of the war the entire responsibility for research belonged to the manufacturers, who had no contract with the government for the development of their prototypes. They had almost no guidance, even on what materiel to produce, and based their work on the desiderata expressed by certain aviators at the front who made them aware of their personal ideas. The Technical Section was engaged only in judging the quality of the planes with the aid of pilots detached for that purpose from the front.

Little by little things improved. Programs were proposed, technical specifications were established, and methods of inspection and testing were perfected. But it was only from 1917 on that France had the benefit of an effective organization.

The Technical Section was divided into several services, and each of them was responsible for a category of materiel: airplanes, engines, armament, equipment, rolling stock, components, etc.

The means for on-the-ground testing were very meager. Throughout the war the French had only a single wind tunnel at their disposal, the one that Gustave Eiffel had installed at Auteuil in 1910, one of the most modern in the world at the time. Thanks to that great scientist they thus had the benefit of a remarkable tool and were able to profit from his extraordinary competence. The wind tunnel made possible studies of the shapes of bombs and dirigible hulls, the streamlining of airplane wings, and the shape of radiators and propellers, which brought about real advances. But the French lacked such equipment in sufficient quantity, and the wind tunnel studies remained sketchy, the manufacturers preferring to follow their own ideas and then do flight tests. The result was that during the war 264 different prototypes were produced (new prototypes or versions of the same prototype with different engines) for the 38 that were actually put into service. It was the same, of course, with the other belligerents. The English tried out 309 different versions for the 73 types put into service and the Germans 610 for the 72 types adopted. Many of these prototypes proved unusable upon their first flight, but enough of them were left to feed the Technical Section.

By 1917 the Technical Section, thanks to Captain Toussaint, had perfected the methods of static tests on the ground and of flight tests that were used at Villacoublay and that were adopted by the Allies in 1918.

Gradually the laws of aerodynamics became clear, and the structures were perfected. New concepts took shape, and if the end of the war had not interrupted the work, the French could have put some quite remarkable planes into service in 1919, such as the Nieuport 29 fighter, the S.E.A. two-seater pursuit and reconnaissance plane, the

Blériot four-engined plane, and perhaps a Moineau with thick wing and retractable landing gear, which was in the planning stage at the time of the armistice.

At that time the research and development of a prototype took six months. It took almost another six months for tests and perfecting, and another three months to equip the factories and start the series. But the combatants at the front, seeing a prototype undergoing tests, could not understand not getting the new plane immediately. This has always been a cause of misunderstanding between the front and the rear.

It was undoubtedly in the area of engines that France was most successful, not only in production but more especially in performance. This was due to Captain Martinot-Lagarde, who was able to put the criteria of power and lightness above every other consideration and who subjected the engines to long tests on the ground (10 hours of endurance tests in 1914, 50 in 1916, and 100 in 1917).

France completely dominated the field of rotary engines—the Gnome, Rhône, and Clerget—whose power was pushed to the practical limit of 200 horsepower imposed by the stresses due to centrifugal force. These highly reliable engines were very light for their time and made it possible to produce very fine single-seaters such as the Nieuport Bébé or, in 1917, the British Sopwith Camel. The Germans even copied the Rhône engine in a version called the Oberursel, from the name of the place where it was manufactured. Among other planes, the Fokker E was equipped with it.

The best engines in use in 1918 were the 300-horsepower Renault, the 200-horsepower Hispano-Suiza, and the 260-horsepower Salmson, which was a 9-cylinder, water-cooled, star-shaped engine. All of these weighed between 1.35 and 1.65 kilograms per horsepower, counting the accessories, the radiator, and the cooling liquid. The 300-horsepower Renault was particularly noted for its sturdiness; it was credited with an average of only one breakdown per 200 hours of flight, which was an enviable record for the time.

In 1918 there were eight engines in the testing stage with capacities ranging from 160-horsepower rotary to 600-horsepower stationary double star, and in the research stage there were many engines between 300 and 800 horsepower. It was not until 1919 that the first engine with a Rateau turbo-compressor was produced in quantity—the 300-horsepower Renault, which would have made higher ceilings possible for the fighter planes. The Breguet XIV, because of this engine, reached 50 kilometers per hour at an altitude of 5,000 meters. Only three flights had been organized at the time of the armistice, and the finishing touches were not put on until a little later.

In Germany, apart from the 80-horsepower Oberursel and the 130–160-horsepower Siemens rotary engines, only straight 6-cylinder, water-cooled engines were used, which were derived directly from racing cars (Mercedes, Benz, and Maybach). These engines were a little more powerful than those of the French in 1914, but were also heavier. Their development consisted in increasing their dimensions, and hence their weight, so that in 1918 the German engines in service ranging from 175 to 280 horsepower weighed 1.85 to 2.18 kilograms per horsepower under the same conditions as the French engines. This increase in weight, which was due to the priority given to guaranteed performance, led to planes that were heavier and slower than those of the French. This wiped out the advantage the Germans had in aerodynamic design—often better than French design thanks to their excellent aerodynamic laboratory at Göttingen. As for production, the Germans never succeeded in manufacturing enough engines, and their air units complained of a lack of spares.

The British started last in the aeronautics industry and never caught up. The Royal Aircraft Factory developed several types of engines, but they were not powerful enough. A large number of manufacturers tried their hand at this difficult task. Only Rolls-Royce turned out good engines, and it did not produce them in sufficient numbers. Other manufacturers produced attractive prototypes, which were hastily ordered in quantity but were incapable of holding up in service. Their specific gravity ran from 1.63 kilograms per horsepower (Sunbeam) to 1.85 kilograms per horsepower (Rolls-Royce). The Siddeley Puma, a modified B.H.P., ran for only a few hours, as did the A.B.C. engine "Dragonfly." Great Britain ordered many engines from France to mitigate these deficiencies, especially Rhônes and Hispanos. Its last fighter planes, produced in the largest numbers in 1918, were equipped with French engines. However, in 1916 Britain decided to develop a very powerful

Colonel Girod, inspector general of the aeronautics schools from 1915 on, reviews the trainees of the Etampes school, February 27, 1917.

Stationary training at the Pau school.

Aerial view of the Châteauroux Military Aviation School: at the center of the circle, the control tower; around the circle, names of the towns situated in the indicated direction. Note the "T" indicating the direction of the runway.

aeronautics industry, and in 1918 it was already producing more planes than the French industry.

As for the United States, from its entry into the war in April 1917 it concerned itself with the aeronautics industry and tried to do its own manufacturing. In 1917 it decided to send a team of engineers to Europe, who toured the factories there in order to study production methods. This team was responsible for the 400-horsepower V-12 Liberty engine designed for easy mass production; its weight per horsepower was not more than 1.45 kilograms. Unfortunately, this engine, first manufactured in 1918, was difficult to perfect. It did not work really well until after 1919.

In Italy Fiat turned out a 300-horsepower straight six engine, styled like the Mercedes but lighter (1.84 kg/hp). By using two rows of cylinders in a V arrangement Fiat produced a 600-horsepower engine, the most powerful one in 1918, but it was not put into service. Italy also manufactured the 160-horsepower Isotta-Fraschini and the 200–220-horsepower S.P.A. But its production levels were not sufficient, and it bought Rhônes and Hispanos.

The French aeronautics industry was undeniably the world leader until 1917, when Great Britain surpassed it in planes but not in engines. At the end of 1918, 190,000 persons were working for the aeronautics industry in France, including 70,000 in the area of engine production.

Personnel Training: The Schools

In 1914 the army had in operation an aviation school established at Pau in 1911, which had 50 airplanes, and a second school established at Avord, with 40 airplanes. At the beginning of the war 321 licensed military pilots were in service.

We have seen that General Bernard had the unfortunate idea of closing the schools at the beginning of the war, an error corrected by his successor, General Hirschauer, who reopened Avord in November and Pau in December 1914. The obvious need for pilots brought about the establishment of new schools: Chartres in January 1915, Etampes in February, Le Crotoy and Buc in March, Ambérieu in August, and Châteauroux, Bron, and Tours in October 1915. Later, in May 1917, the schools at Istres and Dijon were established.

In 1917 Buc, Etampes, and Dijon were closed, and Pau, Avord, Le Crotoy, and Chartres were made into schools for advanced training. Finally, Tours, Orly, and Juvisy were turned over late in 1917 to France's Belgian and American allies.

The schools for advanced training received pilots newly licensed on Voisins, Caudron G 3's, and Nieuport 80 horsepowers to retrain them in their specialties—fighter, bomber, or observation planes, or twin-engined planes.

For example, at Pau, which specialized in advanced training for the fighters, four basic figures were taught: tailspin, lifting the nose of the plane, gliding, and steep banking. First there was a demonstration on the ground, in which an instructor explained the figures that were being executed in flight by another instructor at the same time; then the motions were rehearsed in a cockpit still on the ground; and finally the trainee attempted the figure in a solo flight in a Nieuport Bébé (13 m^2).

There were other schools, such as Cazaux, which beginning in 1915 trained machine gunners and bombardiers and then fighter pilots.

Mechanics were recruited from among civilian auto mechanics. A school was established at Bordeaux to give them the rudiments of aeronautical technology, which is fortunately simple.

What level of training was given to the pilots? At the beginning a license was granted after twenty-five hours of flight, which took forty days to three months, depending on the season. Then the pilot was sent to a flight, where he got practical experience. Generally he was assigned to the type of plane that he had flown when qualifying for his license (Farman, Caudron, or Voisin). The inadequacy of this training, even when completed in the flight, was soon realized.

Pilot training became more serious after 1916. The same initial phase of twenty-five hours of flying time was retained. The tests for a license

A Breguet XIV A 2 of Flight BR 35, belonging to the 20th Army Corps. Called the "Armistice Breguet," this plane flew the white pennant of the German parliamentarian, Major Von Geyer, who brought the armistice conditions. The pilot who flew him to Spa, Belgium, was Lieutenant Minier.

René Fonck carrying the air force colors in the Victory Parade in Paris, July 14, 1919.

consisted of a spiral descent of 500 meters, two 60-kilometer round trips, two 200-kilometer triangles in two days, one hour at 2,000 meters, and 50 landings. After passing these tests the pilots were sent for advanced training according to the following scheme: army corps or fighter pilots to Avord for training in a Sopwith or Nieuport (25 hours); fighter pilots to Pau for acrobatics, then to Cazaux for gunnery (45 hours); reconnaissance to Chartres (25 hours); bombing to Le Crotoy, where the bombardiers' school was located (40 hours).

After these various training periods, which lasted from three to six months depending on the season, the pilots were sent to the division training groups (G.D.E.) under the G.H.Q., which had replaced the Bourget-Dugny general pilot reserve in February 1916. The head of the Aeronautic Service of the G.H.Q. drew on the G.D.E.'s to keep the flights at the front up to strength.

At the end of 1917 the C.I.A.C.B. (Fighter and Bomber Instruction Center) was established at Cazaux, making it possible to abolish the G.D.E.'s. Late in 1918 the combat pilot training cycle lasted about a year. Participation in pilot training was meant to be on a voluntary basis, but in 1914 and 1915 it was difficult to get personnel that the commanding officers of the corps did not want to release. A good number of wounded, "unfit for infantry duty," were received for flight training. It was only gradually that the G.H.Q. could get the personnel it needed.

The medical examination for flight personnel was fairly simple at the beginning, but became more serious later on. The maximum weight for a pilot was 75 kilograms (165 lbs.), the candidate had to be physically sound and to have a good sense of smell, the test being to distinguish blindfolded a glass of gasoline from a glass of ether.

Finally, in December 1917 preliminary technical instruction on the ground was introduced for pilots, consisting of about two weeks at the Technical School at Dijon.

It might be amusing to recall the originality of the earliest pilot training in the various flight centers. The method used in 1915 at Pau for Blériot pilots was to learn first to taxi on the ground in a "penguin" with clipped wings, then to fly in a normal airplane. This method produced good results but caused quite a few crashes. It took about eighty days to get a license using this method.

At Buc, after taxiing in a "penguin" the trainee was given a few lessons in a G 3 two-seater and then came back to take off in a Blériot.

In the course of the war a mixed method was adopted inspired by the procedure used at Buc, the takeoff being made in either a G 3 (which took a total of fifty days for the license), a Maurice Farman (forty days), or a Nieuport (sixty days).

Beginning in 1917 the progression was in the order: Maurice Farman, Voisin, G 3, Nieuport. In this way the licensed pilot could later adapt himself more readily to any type of plane in the various advanced training centers.

In 1918 the cost per pilot graduated from the schools' cycle was: fighter—45,250 francs; bomber—42,250 francs; army corps—32,500 francs.

The numbers immobilized in the pilots' schools, although distinctly smaller than those of the other Allies, were very large. In October 1918 they reached 18,370 persons, of whom 250 were officers, 12,000 enlisted men, and 6,120 civilians, to whom must be added 4,760 pilots undergoing training. There were 2,000 planes in service, 400 in reserve, and 1,600 under repair. The accident rate in the beginners' schools was 1 person killed for every 250 trainees licensed.

The number of licensed pilots turned out by the schools during the war was: 134 in 1914; 1,848 in 1915; 2,698 in 1916; 5,609 in 1917; and 6,900 in 1918. The total number was 16,825 licensed pilots. At the end of 1918 the intention was to raise the number of licensed pilots produced to 1,000 per month in 1919.

In 1918 the flight schools registered 360,000 hours of flying time in 3,000 airplanes each worth about 30,000 francs.

CONCLUSION

The Air Force in the First World War

After coming into the war with no well-defined plan and with very meager resources the air force became, in all of the nations at war, a branch that was given special attention.

The effort invested in aeronautics was considerable in all the belligerent countries, especially in France. Of a total plane production estimated at 200,000 planes for all the participants in the war, France manufactured one-fourth; of the 225,000 engines, it produced two-fifths, a good part of them for its allies (28,500 out of 90,000). The costs were proportionate to the effort: of the 60 billion 1918 francs spent by the belligerents for aeronautics, France spent 23 billion[1]—0.1 in 1914, 1.16 in 1915, 3.25 in 1916, 5.0 in 1917, and 13.5 in 1918. The warplane manufactured more than any other in 1914–1918 was the Spad XIII, at 7,300 units. French factories turned out nearly 7,200 Nieuports and 3,500 Breguet XIV's. The English plane manufactured the most, the Sopwith Camel, ran to only 5,500 units. No German plane reached 3,000 units.

The French aeronautics industry employed 190,000 persons and turned out almost as much materiel in 1918 as Great Britain's, which had 347,000 persons employed.

Remarkable progress was made in just four years. The 65 to 80 kilometers per hour of the first Blériots and Deperdussins had risen to 180 kilometers per hour for the Breguet XIV and 220 kilometers per hour for the Spad XIII. The 1,000-meter ceiling had become 7,000, and the climbing times had been divided by five. Aerial armament had come into being, as had radio and aerial photography. Equipment lacking on the first aircraft came into use and was improved continually. Oxygen and electrically heated suits were also used.

This remarkable progress was a general phenomenon, and France had an active part in it. In the field of engines French supremacy was recognized by all. At the time of the armistice France was ready to produce the world's first engine with a turbo-compressor, which would have put its bombers out of range of enemy pursuit and anti-aircraft fire.

The employment of the various branches—

1. France's total war costs were 850 billion paper francs (one 1914 gold franc = five 1918 paper francs). The price index of 100 in 1914 rose to 191 in 1916 and 340 in 1918.

pursuit, observation and reconnaissance, bombing, and aerostation—was highly perfected; the effectiveness of the air force was universally recognized. Direct participation in ground fighting, introduced in 1918 with brilliant success at the moment when tanks, also employed en masse, were proving their usefulness in making the long-sought breakthrough, prefigured the use that would be made of these weapons later.

Only strategic bombing had not produced the expected results; great advances were yet to be made in that field.

Not yet able to claim to play a major part in the mode of waging war, aviation nevertheless demonstrated that its use increased the effectiveness of the forces on the ground—the infantry and the artillery. Aviation was no longer merely a sport; it had become an indispensable auxiliary on which everyone wanted to be able to rely.

It was also learned that, apart from its scouting role, the air force, in order to be effective, had to be employed en masse. The importance of acquiring air superiority escaped no one, and special attention was given to having the best pursuit planes and to training pilots in a proper way. Nevertheless, France did not go so far as to judge it indispensable to unite all its air forces (including antiaircraft) in a single service, as the English did and before them the Germans.

It may be that the French feared an "independence" that would remove the air force from the battlefield when it was really needed. It may also be that too big a part of the glory went to the aviators—as after Fleurus—at a time when the infantryman's contribution was judged still greater. In the victory parade in Paris in 1919 the air force was represented on the Champs Elysées only by its flag, carried by René Fonck marching on foot alone, lost in the midst of detachments from all the regiments. It was to make up for that "affront" that the aviator Godeffroy flew a plane under the Arc de Triomphe a short time later. The interservice rivalry, which has done so much damage to the country since then, was already springing up in France.

With the intent of confining aviation to its admittedly indispensable role of auxiliary to the artillery and the infantry, the other deeds of the aviators in 1918 were forgotten—attacks on the ground, bombings, long-range reconnaissances. However, the future was already foreshadowed in actions in which airplanes flew over tanks.

Because the First World War was characterized by the immense suffering of the greatest number—the infantrymen in the trenches—the spirit of sacrifice was exalted, and there was an unwillingness to attribute the victory to anything other than the big battalions. But that meant forgetting that while the war did employ great numbers of obscure combatants, it also became a war of materiel, thus differing fundamentally from earlier wars. In 1914 the infantry represented 67% of army personnel, in 1918 not more than 45%. The "skilled" branches had partly replaced it. The artillery had grown from 16% to 26%, the engineers from 3% to 7%, the supply services from 4% to 7.5%, and the air force, practically nonexistent in 1914, represented 3.5% in 1918, and the tanks 0.5%. Army leaders did not accept this development easily.

If the French air force has become a defense tool, it is due to a few exceptional men. It is hard to say whether the intelligence, dedication, faith, or courage of these men should be admired most. For it was not easy to create a balloon service in two years starting from almost nothing, or to form flights of planes when the pilot training schools were closed.

One must not forget the role played by such men as Barès, Joux, Tortay, du Peuty, and Duval at the G.H.Q., nor those who were able to galvanize energies and invent rules of employment, for example, de Goÿs, Happe, de Rose, Féquant, Ménard, and Le Révérend. Nor must one forget what is owed to the combatants—whether they were aces like Fonck, Guynemer, Brocard, Nungesser, and Dorme, or less renowned heroes like Beauchamp, Beaumont, and Védrines, or simple pilots whose names are not remembered because they were too numerous—for having sacrificed themselves for the success of French arms.

One must also express esteem for those in the rear, the chief demands on whom were organizational talent, competence, and dedication. More often disparaged than praised, sometimes unjustly attacked, they nevertheless have the merit of having succeeded, in spite of all difficulties, in making France one of the very first aeronautic producers when it was far from being the first industrial country in the world and very far from being the most populous.

There has been no hesitation here to show the quarrels that stirred the various services nor even the political intrigues and the industrial interests at play. It would be unfair to forget that that was—and still is—the common lot of all countries when it comes to creating organizations in an entirely new field, as the field of aviation was at that time.

Thus in England the role of the Royal Aircraft Factory, held in as low esteem by the English combatants as the French Technical Service for

Production of Airplanes in France and Great Britain, 1914–1918

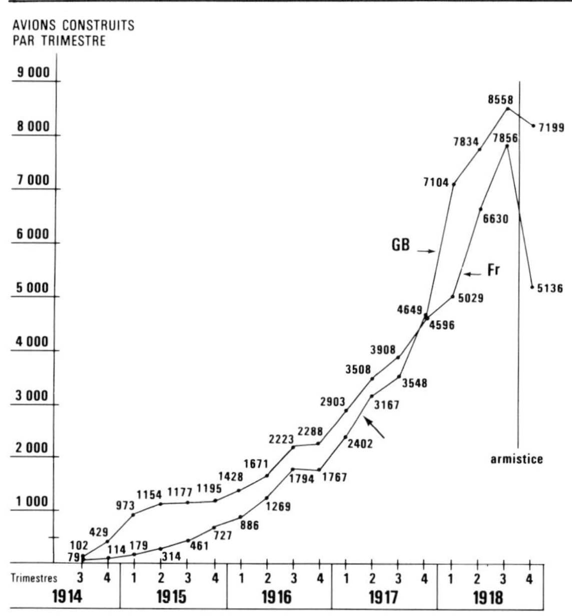

France

Airplanes produced of which 9,480 were supplied to the Allies.	51,700

Great Britain

Up to December 1918		
Airplanes produced:	52,027	54,789
Airplanes bought: (2,000 in France)	2,762	
Seaplanes produced:	3,065	3,355
Seaplanes bought:	289	
		58,144
Planes actually produced:		55,092

From the point marked by an arrow, the figures are for planes inspected, not for planes delivered to the armies.

Production of Engines in France and Great Britain, 1914–1918

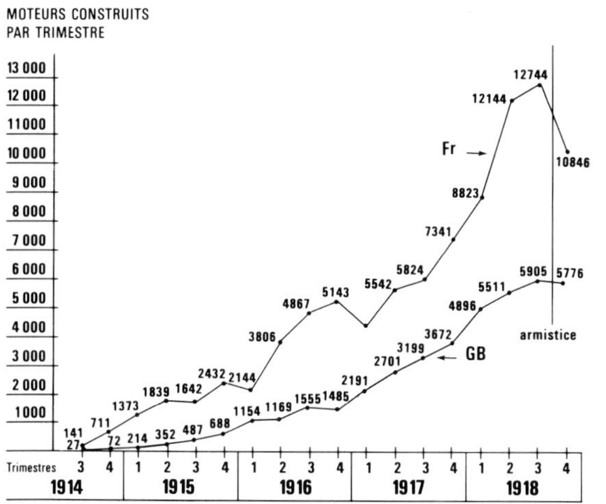

France

Engines produced	92,386
Engines sold	24,550
Total available for the air forces	67,836

Great Britain

Engines produced	41,034
Engines bought	16,897
Total available for the air forces	57,931

Aeronautics and the S.F.A., seems to have been rather pernicious in retaining outmoded airplanes for too long because it reserved for itself the task of research for all the prototypes. The fact that aeronautic production came under a minister of armaments in that country instead of an under-secretary of state for aeronautics does not seem to have been more advantageous in regard to quantities produced, at least until 1918. On the other hand, that fact may explain the emphasis on quantity rather than on quality.

In Germany the more centralized organization that was arrived at earlier could have produced better fruits, but the frantic striving for the best airplane of the moment in order to gain air superiority more quickly resulted in an incredible sprouting

Forces in Service at the Time of the Armistice

	Total No. of Planes in Service on All Fronts	Total No. of Flights in Service on All Fronts	On the Western Front—France		Other Fronts and Overseas		Number of Planes in the Home Country			
			Flights	Planes	Flights	Planes	In Schools	Air Defense	First Reserve	Naval Air
France	3,737	288	258	3,437	30	300	3,000	150	3,000	400
Great Britain	2,690	199	106	1,799	50	700	6,000 + 29 SqOTU	(14 Sq) 200 planes	?	1,000
U.S.A.	740	45	45	740	0	0	5,000	0	?	?
Germany	2,940 (theoretical)	275 (theoretical)	180 (actual) 251 (theoretical)	1,800 (actual) 2,700 (theoretical)	24	220	?	?	= 0	?

Note: The German figures are uncertain. The only almost sure estimate is: 1,800 planes in service in France and reserves nonexistent at the time of the armistice. Only the underlined figures are known with certainty.

Aeronautical Production during the First World War up to December 31, 1918

	Planes			Engines		
	Total (Including Seaplanes)	Including Planes Supplied to the Allies	Plus Planes Bought from the Allies	Total	Including Engines Supplied to the Allies	Plus Engines Bought from the Allies
France	51,700	9,460*	100	92,386	24,550	0
Great Britain	55,092	1,500	3,051	41,034	?	16,897
U.S.A.	11,000 incl. 8,000 trainers	0	4,800	32,000	?	?
Germany	38,000	3,000		41,000	?	?

Note: Only the underlined figures are known with certainty.

*U.S.A.	3,205	Italy	1,300
Great Britain	2,175	Belgium	400
Russia	2,000	Rumania	300

of different prototypes and versions (610) and dispersion of the production efforts, which had repercussions on the number of airplanes produced.

We have also seen the failure of the United States to get an aircraft industry under way in less than two years.

One must not forget what men such as Hirschauer, Vincent, Dumesnil, and Dhé accomplished in administrative posts, what Dorand, Stammler, Etévé, Caquot, Martinot-Lagarde, Cayla, and others did in technical positions, and what Gustave Eiffel did in the field of research. Many of their assistants, in more obscure but equally necessary positions, contributed to the success of the programs.

The prestige of the French army and of its air force, the first in the world, was immense in other countries. We shall see examples of this in the period between the wars, when many nations came to ask France for help in shaping their armies after the French model.

The same was true in aeronautics. French supremacy in engine design and production was unquestioned, and even the most successful of the Allies' planes were often equipped with French Hispano and Clerget engines. As for airframes, the later planes were considered very good, although other countries—Britain and soon the United States as well—also turned out very good aircraft.

But the war ended, and there was thought of turning again toward sport and commercial aviation. Would the French know how to profit from the good position that they occupied?

In fact, the country had been bled white; the economy was very seriously affected, and three-quarters of French capital wealth had evaporated. Inflation appeared along with the treasury debts. The country, in the consciousness that it had fought "the war to end all wars," wanted only to be at peace and to bind its wounds. Politics, in the bad sense of the word, resumed its claims, and Clemenceau, "Father Victory," fell from power at the next elections.

For aviation, which lives and develops only on faith, the future would be difficult, and everyone felt it, especially the technicians, who had suffered their misunderstandings with the combatants at the front and with the politicians. Aeronautical engineering is difficult, and maintaining it at a high level is possible only as the result of a delicate balance of which few are aware. Without the military appropriations that had insured its progress before, how could it be carried on?

J. L. Dumesnil, ill, handed in his resignation in November 1918 and was not replaced. Military aviation was put back under the control of the Directorate of Aeronautics of the Ministry of War, which was also in charge of the nascent civil aviation sector. Colonel Dhé was replaced on April 20, 1919, by General Duval. Lieutenant Colonel Leclerc was his assistant for civil aviation; Saconney succeeded him in May.

The future did not look very bright for French aeronautics in spite of the eminent position that it occupied at the time of the armistice, November 11, 1918.

Special Topics, 1914–1918

THE FIRST FLIGHTS OF THE WAR

First Army (Dôle)

Flight No. 5, MF, at Epinal
Flight No. 9, BL, at Epinal
Flight No. 17, Br, at Dijon
Flight No. 18, BL, at Dijon
Flight No. 3, BL, at Belfort
Flight No. 10, BL, at Belfort

Second Army (Dijon)

Flight No. 1, HF, at Toul
Flight No. 8, MF, at Nancy
Flight No. 19, HF, at Lyons
Flight No. 20, MF, at Lyons

Third Army (Châlons)

Flight No. 2, MF, at Verdun
Flight No. 7, HF, at Verdun
Flight No. 13, HF, at Châlons
Flight No. 16, MF, at Châlons

Fourth Army (Fontainebleau)

Flight No. 14, V, Camp Châlons
Flight No. 21, V, Camp Châlons

Fifth Army (Paris)

Flight No. 4, Dep, Maubeuge
Flight No. 6, Dep, Rheims
Flight No. 11, C, Douai
Flight No. 12, N, Rheims
Flight No. 15, REP, Rheims

Light Cavalry Flights

BLC 2 at Nancy, attached to the 2nd Cavalry Division
BLC 4 at Rheims, attached to the 4th Cavalry Division

Abbreviations

BL: Blériot, 80-hp Gnome
BLC: Blériot (cavalry), single-seater, 60 hp
Br: Breguet, 120-hp Canton-Unné
C: Caudron single-seater, 60-hp Gnome
(or two-seater, 80-hp Gnome)
Dep: Deperdussin, 80-hp Gnome
HF: Henry Farman, 80-hp Rhône
MF: Maurice Farman, 70-hp Renault
N: Nieuport, 80-hp Gnome
REP: Robert Esnault-Pelterie, 80-hp Rhône
V: Voisin, 80-hp Rhône
After August 3, 1914:
Do: Dorand, 90-hp Anzani
MS: Morane-Saulnier, 80-hp Gnome
V: Voisin, 120-hp Canton-Unné

THE ACES

The aerial victories won by the fighter planes were sometimes cited in the official daily communiqué accompanied by the name of the pilot.

It frequently happened that the recurrence of the same names emphasized the existence of exceptional pilots. They soon came to be designated by an expression very widely used at the time to describe men who stood out from the rest—"aces."

The expression was widely used by journalists, who knew how to make themselves understood by the public at large. It was later given a precise meaning: an ace was a fighter pilot cited five times in the official communiqué for the confirmed victories he had won in the air. Historically this custom began in France.

In order to be confirmed a victory had to entail the certain destruction of an enemy plane. The confirmation had to be either by friendly troops on the ground or by the testimony of two other pilots. If the enemy plane hit was in a desperate situation, but its having crashed could not be confirmed—it may have disappeared into a cloud or fallen behind enemy lines, with no witnesses other than the pilot—the victory was only probable and did not count for the aces' prize list.

In 1916, and especially from 1917 on, aerial combat was transformed from the duel that it had been to a combat of patrols, then of formations, and only certain aces were authorized to carry out missions alone or in a patrol of two planes.

An attack on a Drachen staunchly defended by antiaircraft machine guns was considered as at least as dangerous as an attack on a plane, and a success was counted as a victory.

Most of the aces were not credited with the total number of their victories, especially in 1917. Very often, taking advantage of their right to add free pursuit missions, either solo or in pairs, to their normal missions in heavy formations, a good number of the French aces went in search of the enemy behind the German lines and won victories that could not be officially checked and thus confirmed.

Of course, certain aces profited by this situation and claimed to have won more victories than they actually had, but in the small units that the flights were at that time each pilot's character was well known. For example, no faith was put in the declarations of Charles Nungesser, whose confirmed victories alone are indisputable—still, he had 43 of them—but no one doubted the 127 victories claimed by René Fonck. It is true that he was exceptionally accurate in his firing, sure and quick in judging a situation, and extraordinarily dexterous, for in three years and several hundred combats he received only a single bullet in his fuselage! His case was unique in the annals of the two world wars. Moreover, his rectitude was legendary.

The same is true of René Dorme, who is credited with only 23 victories, while he won over 50 others within enemy lines beyond any possible doubt.

As for Georges Guynemer, the second ace on the official list with 53 victories, it is probable that his real score was also higher. But what especially struck his contemporaries and distinguished Guynemer from all the other aces among his comrades in arms was his self-abnegation and his supreme sacrifice on September 11, 1917. For it took an astonishing energy to keep going into combat in spite of having been brought down himself in the course of unbelievable attacks that he, nevertheless, made and in which he was wounded twice.

1
2
5
6
MADO
7
8
9
10
11
12
13
14

1. *Captain René Fonck (1894–1953)*	*127 probable victories and 75 confirmed victories*
2. *Captain Georges Guynemer (1894–1917)*	*53 confirmed victories*
3. *Lieutenant Charles Nungesser (1892–1927)*	*43 confirmed victories*
4. *Captain Georges Madon (1892–1924)*	*41 confirmed victories*
5. *Lieutenant Maurice Boyau (1888–1918)*	*35 confirmed victories*
6. *2nd Lieutenant Michel Coiffard (1892–1918)*	*34 confirmed victories*
7. *Lieutenant Jean Bourjade (1889–1924)*	*28 confirmed victories*
8. *Captain Armand Pinsard (1887–1953)*	*27 confirmed victories*
9. *2nd Lieutenant René Dorme (1894–1917)*	*23 confirmed victories*
10. *Lieutenant Gabriel Guérin (1892–1918)*	*23 confirmed victories*
11. *2nd Lieutenant Marcel Haegelen (1896–1950)*	*22 confirmed victories*
12. *2nd Lieutenant Pierre Marinovitch (1898–1919)*	*22 confirmed victories*
13. *Captain Alfred Heurtaux (1893–)*	*21 confirmed victories*
14. *Captain Albert Deullin (1890–1923)*	*20 confirmed victories*
15. *Captain Henri Hay de Slade (1893–1980)*	*19 confirmed victories*
16. *Lieutenant Jacques Ehrlich (1893–1953)*	*19 confirmed victories*
17. *Lieutenant Bernard Barny de Romanet (1894–1921)*	*18 confirmed victories*
18. *Lieutenant Jean Chaput (1893–1918)*	*16 confirmed victories*
19. *Captain Armand de Turenne (1891–)*	*15 confirmed victories*
20. *Captain Paul d'Argueff (1887–1922)*	*15 confirmed victories*
21. *Lieutenant Gilbert Sardier (1897–1976)*	*15 confirmed victories*

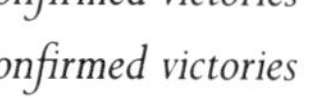
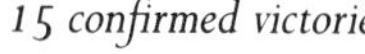

The statistics show that fifty percent of the victories confirmed in France were the work of only about four percent of the pilots—the aces. This fact, which is true for the other belligerents as well and was to be repeated during the Second World War, but was discovered for the first time in 1914–1918, naturally inclined public opinion to consider them as supermen. The accounts of their extraordinary exploits could only reinforce that idea.

The British rules for the confirmation of victories were less strict than those of the French, at least at the beginning of the war. They contented themselves with the English pilot's simple declaration, for, as the Supreme Command said, "The word of an officer is not to be doubted," and all the pilots were officers. But it was soon observed that adding up all the victories declared gave a total greater than the effective strength of the German air force. Beginning in 1916 rules similar to those used by the French were applied.

The Germans followed the same practice as the French, but the total number of victories for each pilot was closer to the number of his confirmed victories, for several reasons having to do with the employment of fighter aircraft by the Germans. The use of large formations earlier than the French used them, the command's dislike of free pursuit in solo flights, and the fact that the combats of German fighter aircraft most often took place within their lines (the proportion of aerial combats within the German lines may be estimated at not less than two out of three for most of the war) had the effect that victories were almost always confirmed. Thus the number one German ace, Manfred von Richtofen, claimed only about 10 "probables" in addition to the more than 80 victories credited to him by the German command.

In all the countries concerned the aces enjoyed very special consideration from the military command as well as the unreserved admiration of their compatriots.

THE INSIGNIAS OF THE FLIGHTS

Unit insignias that were added to the distinctive official, regulation markings began in the French Aeronautical Service and spread from there to all branches of the armed forces.

The French Aeronautical Service entered the war with the tricolor emblem, while the Germans displayed the Maltese cross.

Soon, between the emblem of nationality and the special marking of the airplane—initials of the manufacturer, type, and serial number (first regulation marks, still in force)—it was found necessary to indicate in addition the formation to which the machine was assigned as well as that formation's serial number. Soon each flight possessed an insignia—a fetish or symbol—the origin of which was sometimes comical. As early as 1913 during the large-scale maneuvers insignias were affixed in order to distinguish the flights while in the air, but it was the First World War that was to generalize their use. At the beginning they were simple geometric motifs, but soon they also included allegorical animals, birds, famous characters from the illustrated papers of the day, insects, or plants. An insignia often recalled a unit's specialty, perpetuated the memory of one of its actions, or even represented a pun. Most often the intention was humorous.

The design was completely free since no regulation provided for their use. The choice of an insignia was a de facto privilege of the commanding officer first appointed upon the creation of a new unit, but the design was suggested by one or another of the pilots, and the drawing was the work of the most skillful pilot or mechanic of the unit.

The flight insignia thus appeared as if created by the very founders of the unit, who from then on would devote themselves to bringing glory to it. In thus founding a tradition the members of the flight considered their insignia as a sacred emblem almost on a par with the flag.

When planes began to fly in formation in 1916 the custom arose of painting on the fuselage, beside the insignia, a serial number internal to the flight and associated with each pilot who habitually flew in the same plane.

This serial number was inscribed either in Arabic numbers or in Roman numerals. It was sometimes inscribed on a colored background to make it stand out more, red being reserved for the flight leader. Certain pilots also adopted the habit of attributing a name or a device to their planes and sometimes painting a personal insignia on it. Thus, for example, Major de Rose took a rose as his emblem, and Charles Nungesser adopted a strange emblem on a black background representing a skull and crossbones beneath a coffin flanked by lighted candles. This macabre insignia really represented a simple pun. At the beginning of the war Nungesser was assigned to a unit of hussars. He made himself famous by capturing single-handed a German "Mors" vehicle carrying some officers, so that to his comrades he became "the hussar of the Mors," and he took for himself the famous skull and crossbones insignia of the Prussian hussars.

Guynemer called his plane *Vieux Charles (Old Charley)* and chose a red stork. Fonck had a big red star painted on the underside of his wing. Nungesser, attacked by mistake by a British pilot in spite of his French tricolor emblem, decorated his wings with a broad tricolor band.

Insignia of the SPA 103. This insignia, authenticated by the signature of René Fonck, is that of a plane assigned to this ace of aces.

Personal insignia of Charles Nungesser (original insignia painted on the cloth of his plane).

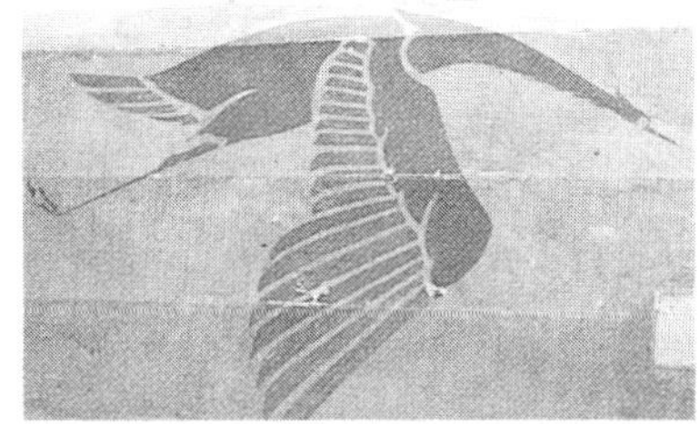

Insignia of the SPA 3, as shown on Georges Guynemer's Spad VII, Le Vieux Charles (Old Charley) (PASM Coll.).

← Flight 11 (observation). The red hen (a paper-folding design), insignia of this flight, was also the personal insignia of Major Vuillemin, who kept it throughout his career (a printed cloth of 1918 representing the insignia).

Personal insignia → of Captain de Rose (a printed cloth of 1918 representing the insignia).

SPA 48 (fighter).

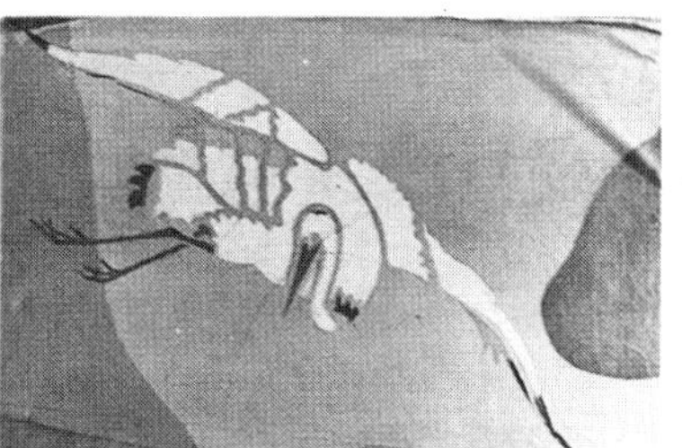

SPA 73 (fighter).

SPA 94 (fighter): death using a scythe.

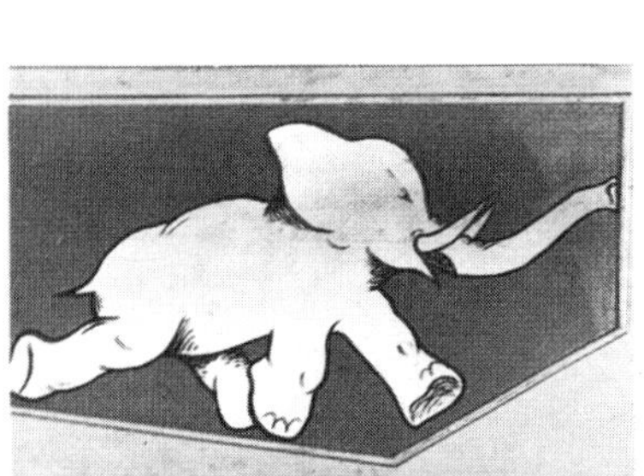

SAL 28 (observation).

BR 221 (observation).

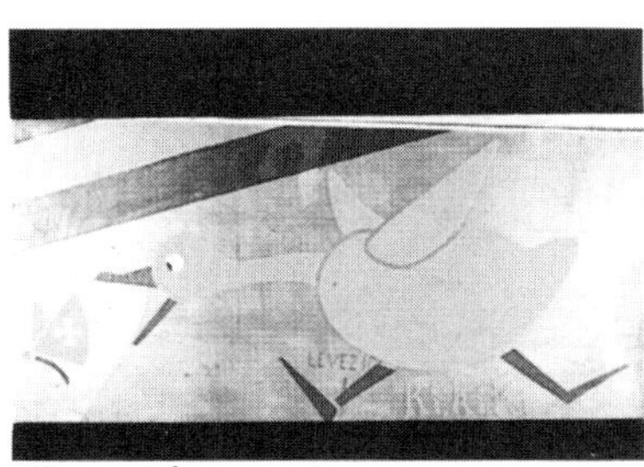

BR 224 (observation).

VB 101 (bombing).

MF 25 (bombing).

MF 29 (bombing).

Except as otherwise indicated, these insignias were cut from the cloth of the fuselages by the pilots themselves as souvenirs (PASM Coll.).

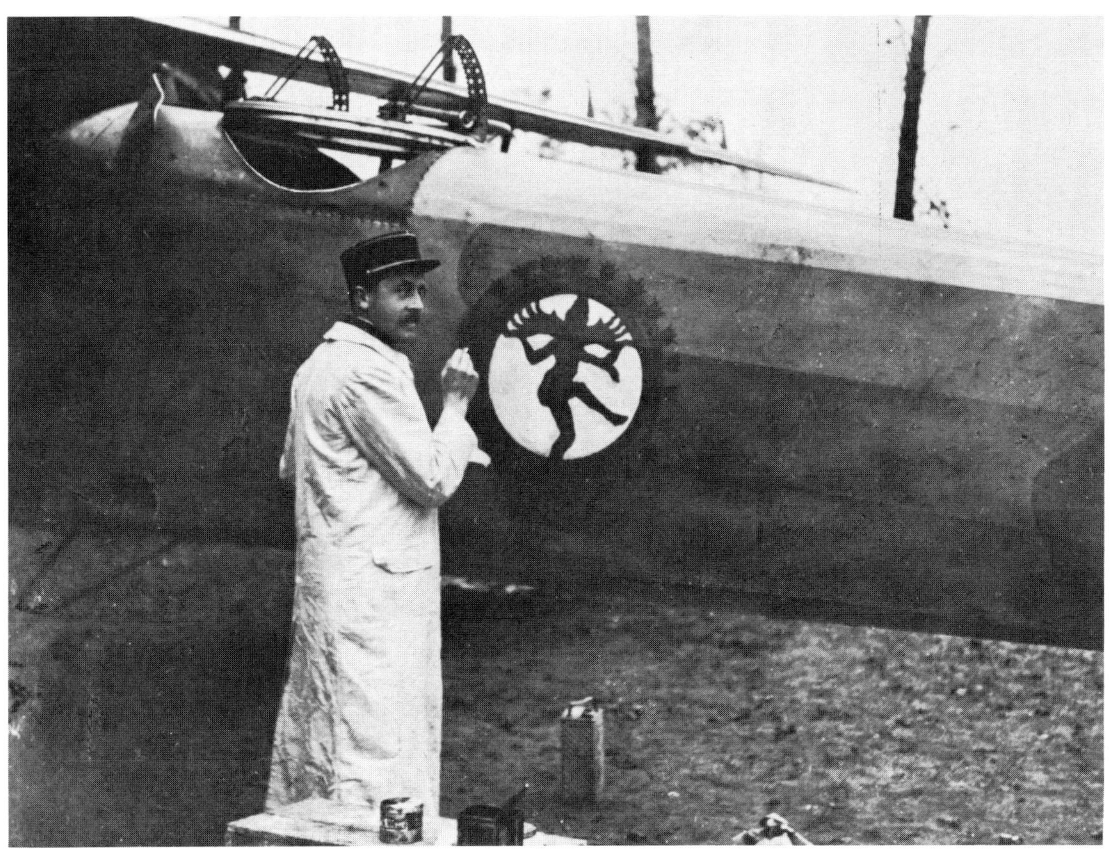

A mechanic from Flight BR 243 painting the insignia of the unit, the god Siva (copper color on a white background).

SPA 3 (fighter).

SPA 31 (fighter).

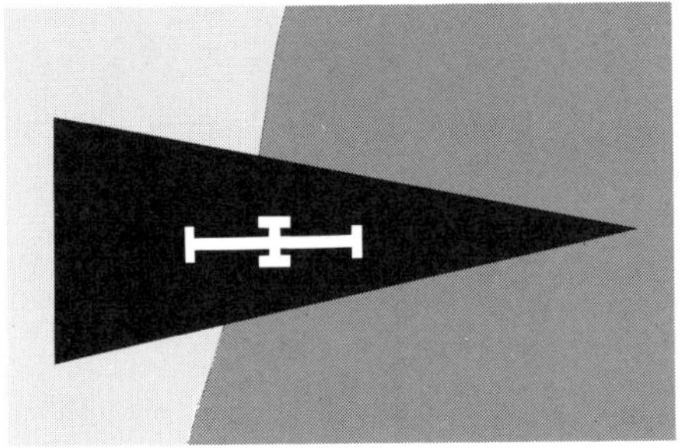

SPA 77 (fighter).

SPA 83 (fighter).

SPA 92 (fighter).

SPA 96 (fighter).

SPA 102 (fighter).

SPA 150 (fighter).

Representations on cloth of fuselage insignias done by a sketching department of the Military Aeronautical Service quartered in the Hôtel des Invalides, Paris, in 1918 (PASM Coll.).

STRATEGIC BOMBING

The first attempts at strategic bombing took place during the First World War.

After the first experimental missions carried out successfully in 1914 against the Ludwigshafen poison gas and explosives factories, the French G.H.Q. asked for the creation of a strategic bombing force. It was first made up of specialized flights of Voisin L.A. 5's or Farman XI's, but very soon, by the end of 1915, it was necessary to accept the facts: these planes, taken into combat with great courage by skilled crews, carried too few bombs and their engines broke down too often. This was not the way in which the French could hope to dry up the source of enemy arms.

The Caproni 33 three-engined plane was tried in turn but did no better. The G.H.Q. abandoned strategic bombing and turned to using its planes to fire directly on the battlefields.

The British tried their luck with strategic bombing in 1916 with the Short Bomber and the Handley Page 0/100, but with no greater success because of the technical defects of these machines. But they were more persevering, and finally in July 1917 they produced a successful bomber, the Handley Page 0/400, 84 of which were maintained in service, used chiefly on German cities in reprisal for the bombings suffered in England, mostly in London, the work of the Zeppelins and the first Gothas, which appeared in the spring of 1917. But this force was still too weak to influence the outcome of the war; it served mostly to train the crews and to work out a doctrine of employment.

An insular country, England was more inclined to take indirect action than to face the enemy on the ground, which did not take on the same character of necessity for England as it did for France, whose territory was invaded. For this reason the British concentrated their efforts on producing a four-engined plane, the Handley Page V/500, which could carry 500 kilograms of bombs to Berlin. But the first plane put into service, on November 8, 1918, could not carry out the planned raid.

In the entire course of the war English bombers made 1,850 attacks on Germany in 5,600 sorties and dropped 800 tons of bombs, the largest of which reached 675 kilograms in 1918.

The Germans were first in this area, carrying out big raids over London and Paris with their Zeppelins. Confronted with the problems raised by the use of such fragile craft, they tried to substitute airplanes for dirigibles with bombing missions.

The first Gotha II planes were delivered in the fall of 1916, and Captain Brandeburg was assigned to create the special bombing service, which was a long time in getting under way. The first raids on Dover and Folkestone took place in May 1917 in the daytime and were followed by a few others as late as September, when the British defense got organized and bombing missions were flown only at night.

Several types of planes were used in succession, the most successful and the ones manufactured in the largest numbers being the Friedrichshafen G. IV and the Gotha G. V. The Germans also made several giant airplanes, the "Riesenflugzeuge" R, equipped with three to five 260-horsepower engines and with a wingspread of up to 45 meters! But these monstrous planes never had much success. In spite of all their efforts (nearly 1,500 G and R planes were manufactured), the

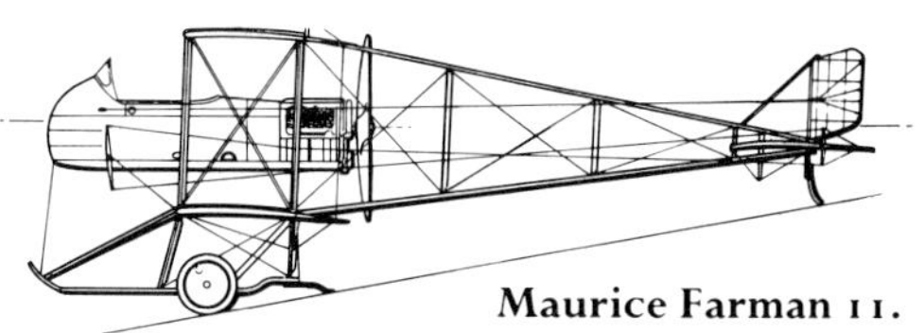

Maurice Farman 11.

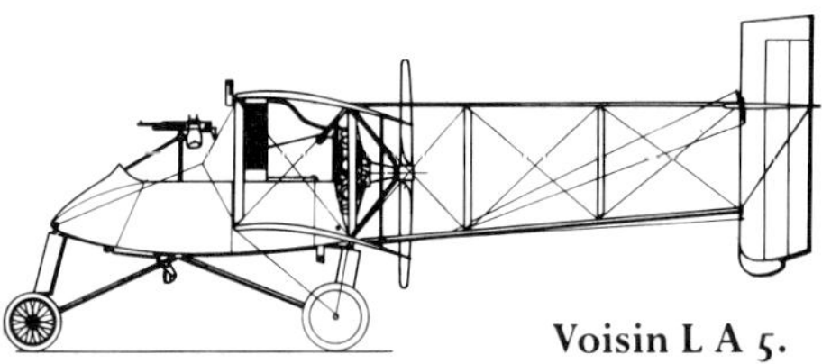

Voisin L A 5.

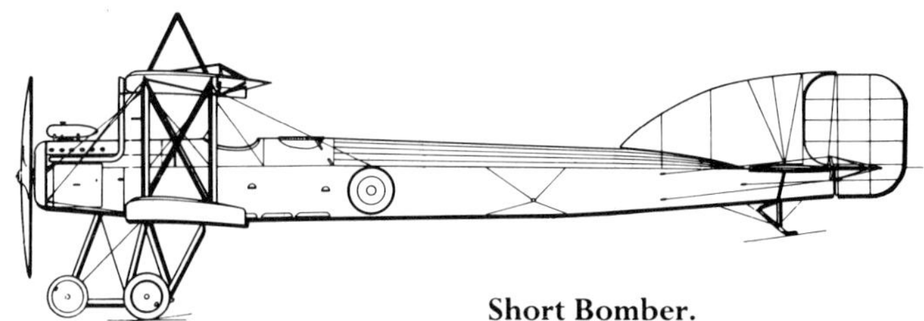

Short Bomber.

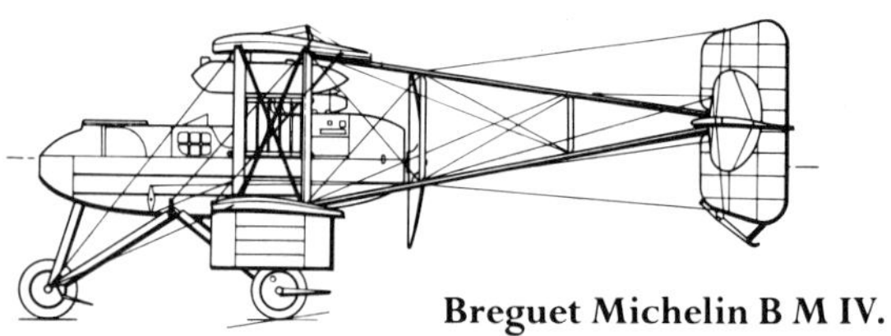

Breguet Michelin B M IV.

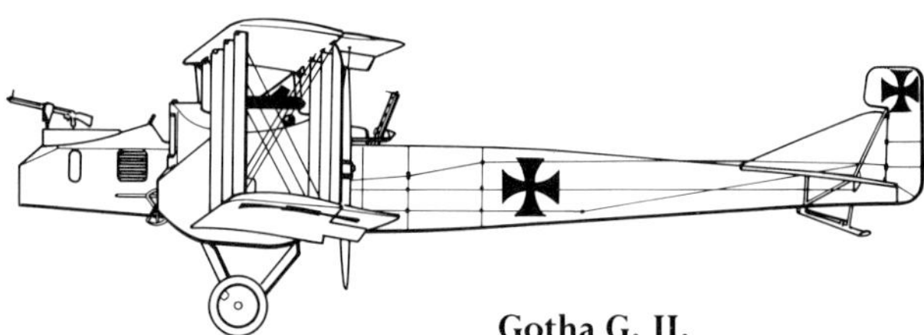

Gotha G. II.

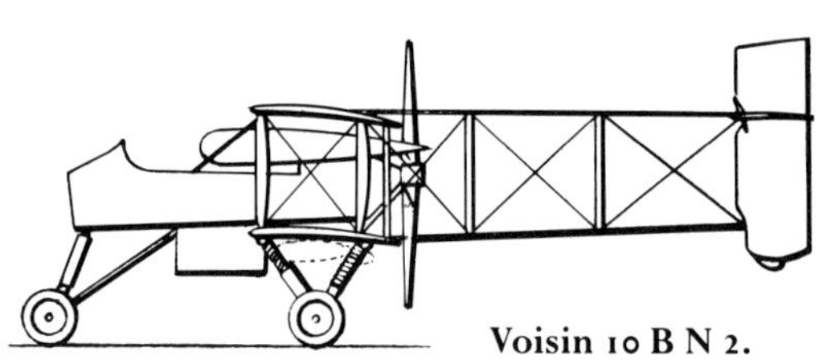

Voisin 10 B N 2.

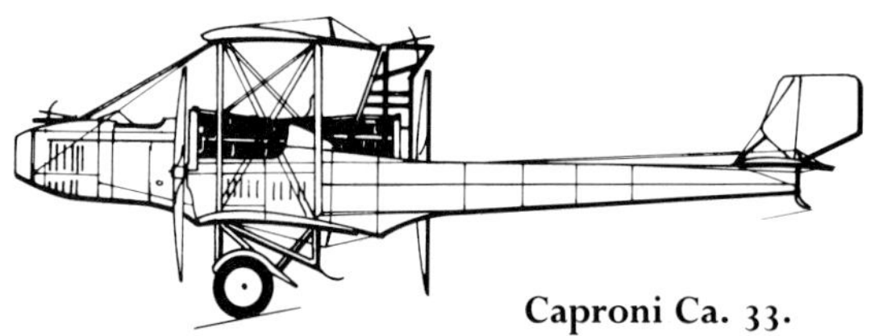

Caproni Ca. 33.

1915 **Maurice Farman 11**
Endurance: 3 h 45 min
Bomb load: 130 kg
Speed: 106 km/h
Weight at takeoff: 928 kg

Voisin L A 5
Endurance: 3 h 30 min
Bomb load: 60 kg
Speed: 105 km/hr
Weight at takeoff: 1,140 kg

Short Bomber
Endurance: 6 h
Bomb load: 410 kg
Speed: 125 km/h
Weight at takeoff: 3,084 kg

1916 **Breguet Michelin B M IV**
Endurance: 400 km
Bomb load: 377 kg
Speed: 130 km/h
Weight at takeoff: 1,580 kg

Gotha G. II
Endurance: —
Bomb load: 480 kg
Speed: 145 km/h
Weight at takeoff: 3,190 kg

1917 **Voisin 10 B N 2**
Endurance: 3 h
Bomb load: 340 kg
Speed: 125 km/h
Weight at takeoff: 1,313 kg

Caproni Ca. 33
Endurance: 3 h 30 min
Bomb load: 450 kg
Max. speed: 136.8 km/h
Weight at takeoff: 3,810 kg

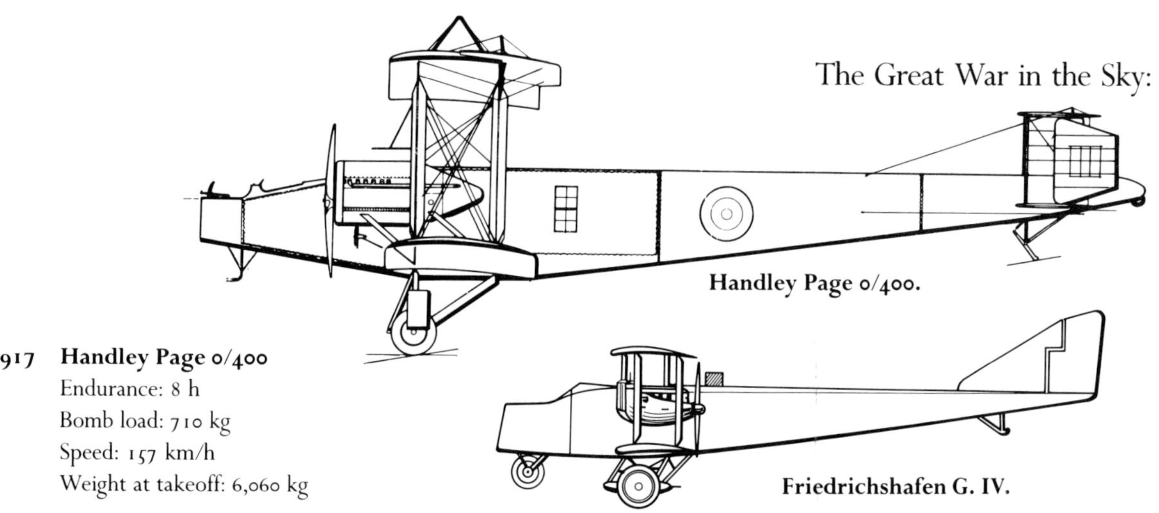

Handley Page 0/400.

1917 **Handley Page 0/400**
Endurance: 8 h
Bomb load: 710 kg
Speed: 157 km/h
Weight at takeoff: 6,060 kg

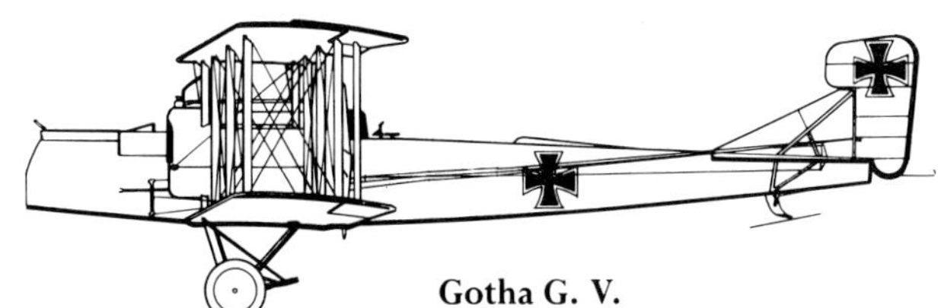

Friedrichshafen G. IV.

1918 **Friedrichshafen G. IV**
Endurance: — Bomb load: —
Speed: 142 km/h
Weight at takeoff: 1,235 kg

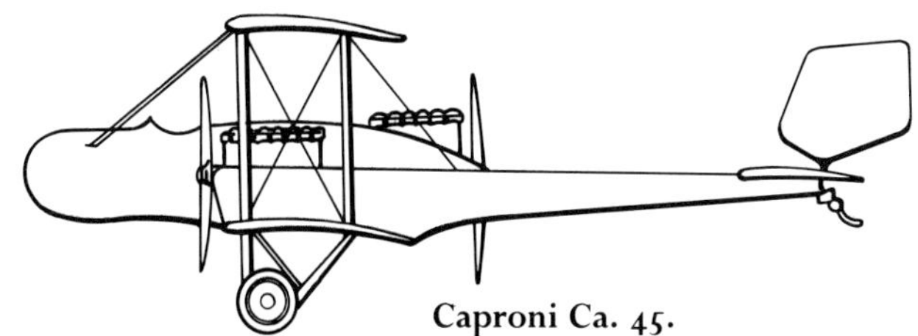

Gotha G. V.

Gotha G.V.
Endurance: 7 h 30 min
Bomb load: 350/600 kg
Speed: 140 km/h
Weight at takeoff: 3,890 kg

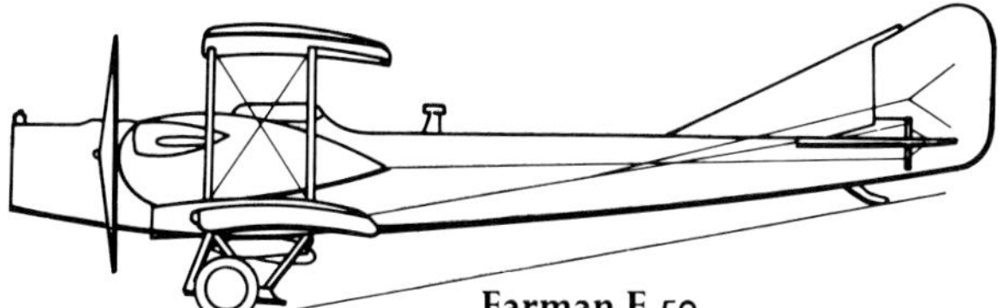

Caproni Ca. 45.

Caproni Ca. 45
Endurance: 4 h Bomb load: —
Speed: 140 km/h
Weight at takeoff: 3,300 kg

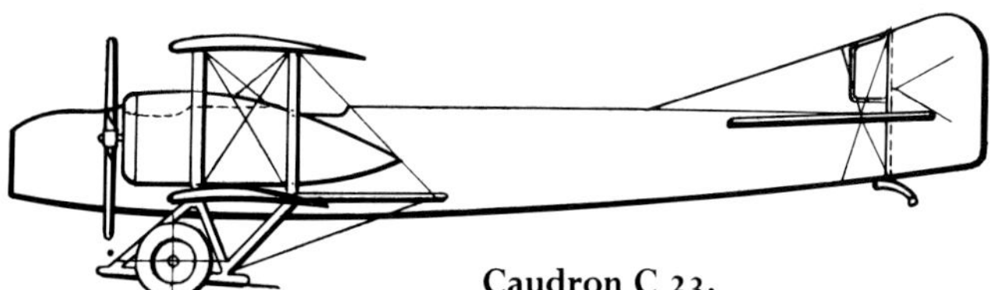

Farman F 50.

Farman F 50
Endurance: 600 km
Bomb load: 500 kg
Speed: 151 km/h
Weight at takeoff: 1,816 kg

Caudron C 23.

Caudron C 23
Endurance: 5 h
Bomb load: 720 kg
Speed: 140 km/h
Weight at takeoff: 1,830 kg

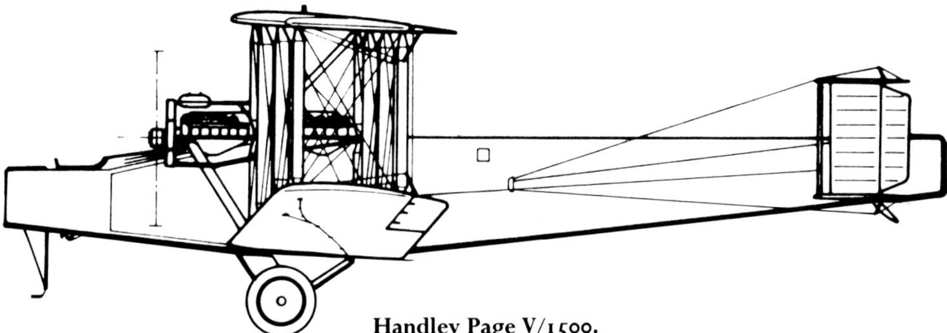

Handley Page V/1500.

Handley Page V/1500
Endurance: 6 h
Bomb load: 3,390 kg
Speed: 145.6 km/h
Weight at takeoff: 13,608 kg

Germans were never able to maintain more than 220 in service. On a single occasion they succeeded in getting 43 in the air for the same mission, but most often the raids were carried out by 10 to 15 planes and, in exceptional cases, 25. During the entire war the Gothas did not drop more than 100 tons of bombs on England and not more than 30 on Paris.

It is no exaggeration to say that this bombing, used chiefly for psychological reasons, was a failure, and that the Germans realized it. They then tried to use their bombers in direct support of the fighting on the ground, choosing the same types of objectives that the French assigned to their planes. They succeeded in some operations against munitions dumps or against airfields. But these bombers were not very effective since they were used at night and were consequently greatly restricted by the weather—sighting was possible only on moonlit nights—and they were hard to maneuver because of their size.

On July 16, 1918, they were engaged in the daytime at low altitude over the bridges of the Marne, then being used by French troops who were going on the offensive, to avert an onset of panic among German troops surprised by the French attack and with no friendly aircraft in the sky to protect them.

Then, beginning in March 1918, pushed by the British and strong in their confirmed air superiority, the French G.H.Q. decided to resume a strategic action aimed at preventing the shipment of iron ore from the Briey basin. For three months the combined efforts of the French daytime Breguet XIV's, relieved at night by French and Italian Capronis and British Handley Pages, were directed against the rail system of the region. One hundred tons of bombs were dropped with practically no effect. It is only now realized that in order to have achieved the result desired it would have been necessary to use at least one hundred times that tonnage even to begin to see effects produced. In 1918 the French were very far from being able to put on such "performances."

It thus appears that all the attempts at strategic bombings made during the First World War were failures. Studies of the bombing operations carried out in all of the countries after the armistice did not lead everyone to the same conclusions, except on the effectiveness of bombing in direct support of troops on the ground.

As concerns strategic operations against cities, transport infrastructures, or factories, the ineffectiveness of aviation was clearly recognized by 1918. But some drew the conclusion that it was almost definitively inept and fought for keeping the air forces primarily tied to the fate of the land forces. Others, on the other hand, predicted that a natural technical evolution would enable air forces to succeed in such missions as were planned for it in 1916. The debate went on throughout the twenty years that separate the armistice from the Second World War.

The preeminence of the technical factor in aviation is demonstrated particularly in regard to the effectiveness of aerial bombing. But there were only a few people who felt that to improve that effectiveness it would be necessary to seek solutions to problems that had hardly been glimpsed in 1918, namely: P.S.V. (navigation without sight of the ground), flight at very high altitudes, precision bombsights, etc. It took many years for all these problems to be solved, making bombing a formidable weapon.

THE WARRIORS OF THE SKY

The use of the airplane in warfare brought forth a new type of warrior—the aviator, whose glory the press would soon celebrate and whose originality, compared to the other combatants, it would soon point out. The public, which knew only what it was told about these men, wasted no time in making idols of them, and by a well-known mechanism the aviators strove to pattern their behavior after the image that had been drawn of them. Thus a myth was born that had a gift for irritating the military leaders, evoking the jealousy of the other branches—of more obscure destiny—but also for stirring up the enthusiasm of many combatants and the admiration of an entire group of people.

For many military leaders these aviators, engaged in warfare as individuals, did not inspire unlimited confidence. They believed in the virtues of discipline and felt that discipline could only be acquired within a framework of time-honored traditions. There was nothing of the kind among the aviators, at least to all appearances. Everything that exalts individualism appeared suspect to them, as, for example, the name "ace" invented by journalists, which would never be officially recognized. Since experience showed that confirmation of aerial victories created an emulation very favorable to the success of operations, the principle was finally accepted but with very strict conditions set to limit abuses. It was the same a priori distrust that caused reconnaissance reports to be doubted. Couldn't the aviators invent extraordinary situations in order to push themselves forward? Perhaps this distrust may even be the explanation for the refusal to supply the aviators with parachutes as the balloonists were. Wouldn't certain crews have bailed out rather than fight? It took time and many casualties before the aviators were admitted to be real combatants even though they did not share the fate of their comrades in the trenches.

This feeling, however, was not general among the infantrymen, who saw aerial combats take place above their heads. It was not unusual to see them applaud the victory of one of the French pilots or risk their own lives to save the crew of a plane that had fallen near the lines. There were many of them who, seeing a plane catch fire and the crew jump out into space to escape the flames, declared that they preferred the discomfort of the trenches and the presence of comrades by their side to rely on. They were not grudging in their esteem for the aviators.

But it was most of all at home, in the rear, that the sympathy for them was greatest and most widespread, for the people there were not living in filthy trenches and could more readily appreciate individual exploits. These deeds were glorified, often with the excess characteristic of the newspapers of the day, by journalists on the lookout for sensational news that the censorship would have no reason to suppress. On the contrary, the reporting of these glorious feats of arms was judged apt to raise the morale of the population, making people forget the misery of daily life at the front and the bloody massacres of mass battles.

Thus very quickly a veritable myth of the aviator was created—a man of indomitable courage and prodigious skill, but also a creative person, whimsical, a lover of life, and . . . irresistible to women. The welcome reserved at home for the aviators was always warm; everyone wanted to be the friend of these daring young men. Sometimes the admiration went so

An airfield. The "Adrian" wooden barracks may be distinguished from the "Bessonneau" tents and hangars.

Nungesser tells Captain Féquant about his latest combat.

Charles Nungesser on his return from a mission, supported by his comrades.

far as to amount to a real cult. Thus one day when Guynemer, on leave, was shopping in a Paris department store a group of rubberneckers formed on the sidewalk, having seen him go in. When he came back out loaded with packages he got into his car, smiled, and nodded to his admirers. One woman, seeing him leave, crossed herself.

No doubt he was one of the most popular aviators, but the admiration went out to all, although not all deserved it in the same measure. Such treatment accorded to very young men could not fail to lead the more frivolous among them to profit from the situation. Invited everywhere and feted like princes, they had an easy life, at least during the brief leaves that were granted them. Their behavior often left something to be desired, and they were not very careful about the regulations, especially in their dealings with officers assigned to the rear, for whom they did not conceal their contempt. Civilians couldn't help but take their part.

The reality at the front was quite different.

It is true that they were very young—twenty-two on the average—and that they had a taste for life, while their duties confronted them with death every day. Hence that frenzy to live fast and warmly while there was time, quite unlike the soldier who passively waits for the shell that is meant for him. One man accepts his destiny, the other thinks he can change it—soldiers of equal merit but of quite different temperaments.

For risk dominated the life of the aviators—the hazard of combats that often ended in a horrible death, but also the chance of accidents, so frequent in that time of fragile, unreliable machines. Risk of death, certainly, but also the risk of serious wounds that sometimes condemned the victims to a crippled life. It is impossible to say enough about the courage of a man like Nungesser, who was very seriously wounded several times so that he could have been invalided out, but who refused the return to civilian life that was offered to him. He continued to fight in defiance of all regulations, risking, if taken prisoner, being shot by the Germans as a sniper.

Nor should others be forgotten, for example, Chaput, who, buzzing his adversary's plane, pulled the joystick in such a way as to cut his enemy's fuselage with his propeller; nor those bombardiers set on fire by German fighters, who, seeing themselves lost, maneuvered to throw themselves upon their victorious enemies and go down with them; nor Maquart de Terline, who gave his life on July 27, 1916, by deliberately throwing himself upon his adversary because his machine gun was jammed and he had no other way of bringing him down.

While these heroic acts are bound to have been exceptional, self-abnegation was an everyday phenomenon. Flight at high altitude for long periods without oxygen and with intense cold, against which the exposed fuselages offered no protection, set a harsh test for the crews who knew that the men on the ground needed their help. They flew almost all the time; they threw themselves into night flight when no equipment existed for the purpose, before Laurens and Bouchet had taken the risk of discovering that new field.

Finally, it must be emphasized that the aviators had no respite from the war. The big battles that were fought on the ground only brought about an increase in their sorties, but, before and afterwards, their battles in the sky continued.

Nervous tension and fatigue were often present, too, and sometimes nerves snapped, as in the case of Navarre, a hero of Verdun, who flew thirty-one hours in three days of combat missions and was not able to finish the war in his flight. It was sometimes worse when the determination to fight did not weaken, as in the case of Guynemer. In September 1917, in such a state of exhaustion that he returned from his missions ill and had to be helped to get back into his plane, once in it he seemed to recover his faculties by instinct. Perhaps that was the reason, never fully understood, for his disappearance on September 11, 1917, when the Battle of Flanders was under way and he had refused to go on leave. "Until you have given all, you have given nothing," he said.

Nevertheless, daily life sometimes provided a few moments of relaxation when the weather was too poor for flying or when there was a mechanical breakdown. Then it was possible to make use of the comfort reserved for those aviators whose airfields happened to be located out of range of the guns.

Certainly the luxury of the "Adrian" barracks was not great, but those barracks provided an infinitely more agreeable shelter than the mud of the trenches. Efforts were also made to increase their comfort by digging in halfway for protection against the winter cold, which the wretched stoves did not succeed in repelling. Most of all, every pilot there had a cot to himself, the supreme privilege in the misery of that war.

But it was at the flight's bar that they got together after their missions for a drink in honor of an event or to discuss the "dogfights." In the absence of the "mission room," which did not start up in the French armed forces until later, it is no exaggeration to say that it was in these bars that the young crews got from their friends their first combat lessons. It must

An accident.

Captain Alfred Heurtaux on convalescent leave and 2nd Lieutenant René Fonck, decorated at Saint-Pol-sur-Mer, November 30, 1917.

Presenting military decorations at an airfield, Pierrefonds region, August 22, 1915.

The aviator as seen by the magazine La Baïonnette, *December 16, 1915, issue.*

The bar of Flight SAL 30.
The insignia of this observation flight was a parrot's head; two may be seen above the bar.

A game of chess in the shadow of the planes.

The radio and arms shop.

be borne in mind that the flight was a very small unit in which everyone lived together. Friendships were formed there which often survived the war.

The runway was not far off, an ordinary field five hundred to six hundred meters on a side, at the edge of which hangars of green cloth, called Bessonneau hangars from the name of their designer, sheltered the airplanes.

The flight would not have existed without the mechanics, who loved their machines and were devoted heart and soul to their pilots, from whom they did not conceal their admiration, living side by side with them and sharing their troubles and successes. It was suspected that not all the mechanics were of equally high quality, and in that time of capricious machines the mechanic's quality was very important. The choice of a good companion was the undisputed privilege of the aces or of the most seasoned pilots. But all of the pilots showed their esteem for their mechanics' devotion.

It was during this war that the aviators' jargon took shape: the plane is a "zinc" or a "crate"; the "mill" (engine) "rolls" or "doesn't roll." Having a "carafe" is simply having engine trouble and having to land in a field.

This small world of the aviators had indeed already become a special world among the combatants of the First World War. It worked out a code of honor of its own, acquired undeniable titles of nobility, and forged traditions for itself on the basis of comradeship in arms. If a certain negligence about military form attached to it, that was to compensate for the stress of combat in the sky, which depended so much on technique and preparation for the mission. In courage and determination the aviators were certainly fighters.

The flight's mascots.

A little exercise and acrobatics.

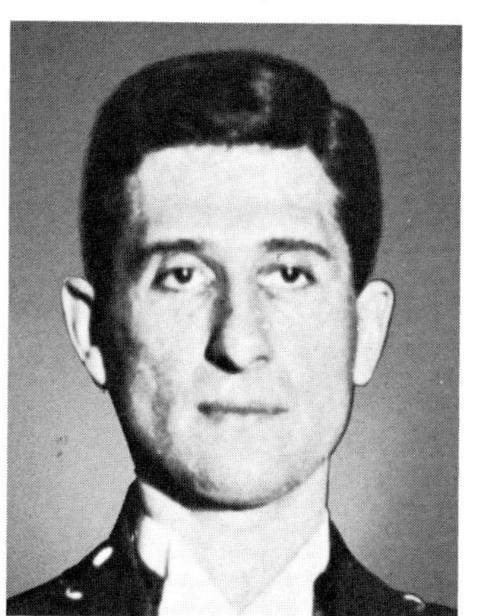

STRATEGIC RECONNAISSANCE

At the beginning of the war aviation was used mostly for observation and artillery ranging. But from 1915 on the importance of "army reconnaissance" was understood. It was entrusted to specialized flights which went as far as 30 kilometers behind the lines reconnoitering.

Many observers distinguished themselves by the accuracy of their reports or by the improvements that they introduced into the methods or the equipment, but undoubtedly the most famous, the one to whom the French owed the creation of the systematic strategic reconnaissance of the front, with no counterpart among the other belligerents, was Major Paul Louis Weiller.

A graduate of the Ecole Centrale, he was first an artillery officer, then very soon, by 1914, an observer on a plane of flight MF 22, where he took aerial photographs with an amateur "vest pocket" camera. He found great differences between the photographs he took and the maps in use by the staffs, which had not been revised for fifty years.

He worked out a method of updating maps from aerial photographs. Assigned to Captain Guichard's flight V 21, he met other officers there, engineers from major schools, with whom he worked out methods of cartography that were adopted by the Army Geographical Service.

In August 1915 he took advantage of an opportunity to pass the examination for his pilot's license and was entrusted with the command of flight C 224, an army reconnaissance flight. He quickly understood that only the photographic document could convince the military chiefs, who were always incredulous when given simple oral reports. He then perfected the cameras and had one made with a focal length of 1.5 meters in order to bring back documents that could satisfy General Mangin, his army commander, who wanted "to see some Boches" on the negatives. Taking exceptional risks—he returned from that mission wounded—Weiller was led one day to fly over the German trenches at an altitude of 150 meters in a single-engine plane to prove that the bombardment preceding an attack had left the German lines intact. The attack was then canceled.

During the entire year 1917 Weiller acquired priceless experience which showed him that by systematically flying over the enemy's rear it was possible to penetrate its intentions. He then recommended to General Foch's G.H.Q. the creation of a group of large-scale reconnaissance flights which would have the mission of photographing the rear of the whole front every day to a depth of 100 kilometers.

His recommendation was accepted, and a group of two flights of Breguet XIV's, called the Weiller Grouping, was formed in July 1918 (Br 45 and Br 220). It was later reinforced.

During 1918 Captain Weiller collaborated closely with the G.H.Q., dealing directly with General Weygand, the commander in chief's chief of staff, to whom he presented every day at Senlis a map of the enemy's rear drawn from the photographs taken during the day.

The photos were printed in a few hours at a laboratory staffed by about twenty photographers. The prints were then examined by approximately thirty draftsmen-interpreters, all from the Ecole des Beaux Arts, and each one a specialist in a certain sector. Comparison of the photos of the day with those of the preceding day brought out the changes in equipment on the ground (new roads or railroads), the shifts of depots and bivouacs, the establishment of field hospitals marked by their red cross, etc. For example, it was noticed very quickly that in

A Breguet XIV A 2 on a reconnaissance mission over the enemy lines.

Studying aerial photographs.

An aerial photograph of Sedan on September 15, 1918, taken from a Breguet XIV A 2 at an altitude of 5,400 meters. A train in the station and a number of hospitals are clearly visible. These indications made it possible to evaluate the enemy's movements and supply flow.

preparation for an attack one of the first classes of equipment set up by the Germans was the hospitals.

Thus it became possible to foretell with confidence and *one month in advance* the place where the enemy was preparing to attack or was abandoning a sector, whereas the traditional method of capture and interrogation of prisoners did not give the alert more than twenty-four hours before the attack.

General Foch, a little skeptical at first, soon realized the reliability of these predictions and used them intelligently. He launched real or simulated counterattacks on the basis of the Weiller Grouping's maps and directed the maximum effort toward the sectors being abandoned, thus harassing the enemy, who was not able to parry the blows struck with such precision.

It is not too much to say that systematizing this procedure of strategic reconnaissance—the flight tactics of which were also constantly improved, from patrols of three Breguet XIV two-seaters to flying in a single-seater at very high altitude—

An aerial photograph after interpretation.

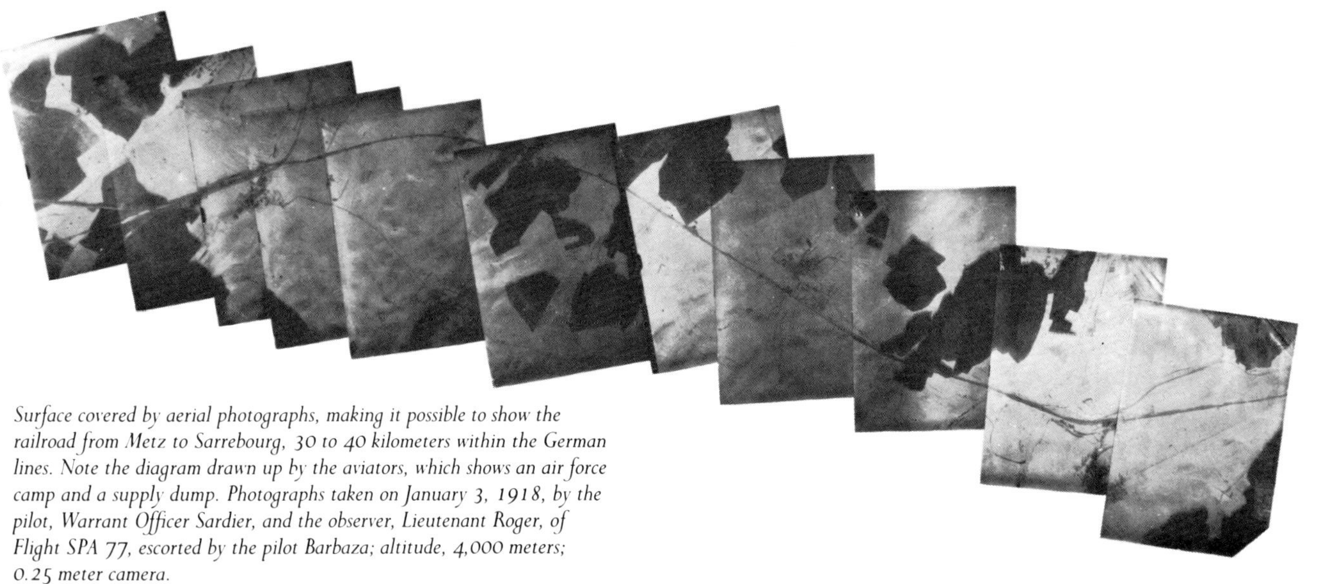

Surface covered by aerial photographs, making it possible to show the railroad from Metz to Sarrebourg, 30 to 40 kilometers within the German lines. Note the diagram drawn up by the aviators, which shows an air force camp and a supply dump. Photographs taken on January 3, 1918, by the pilot, Warrant Officer Sardier, and the observer, Lieutenant Roger, of Flight SPA 77, escorted by the pilot Barbaza; altitude, 4,000 meters; 0.25 meter camera.

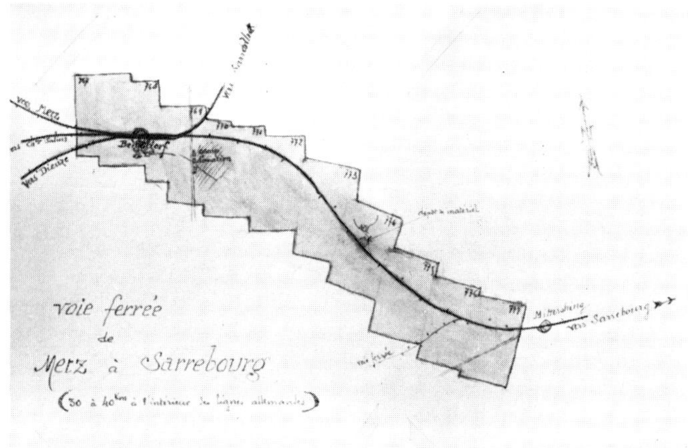

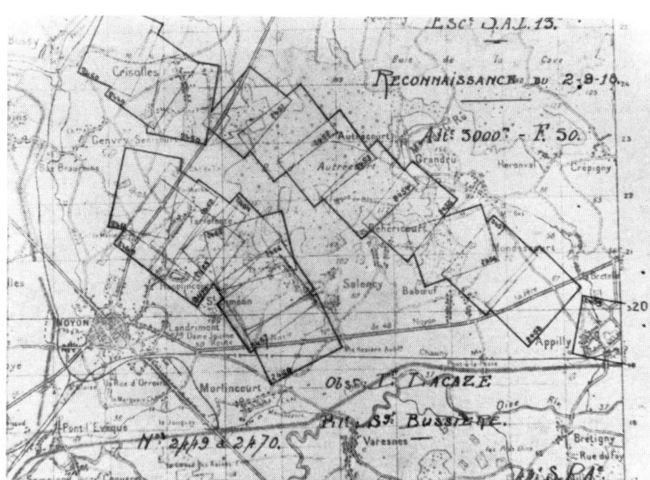

Areas covered by means of aerial photographs (reconnaissance of September 2, 1918, by Lieutenant Lacaze, the observer, and Sergeant Bussière, the pilot, of Flight SAL 13; altitude, 3,000 meters; focal length, 50 centimeters).

contributed a great deal to keeping the supreme command informed in its action.

General Foch was making no mistake when on the day of the armistice he conferred the rank of officer of the Legion of Honor on Captain Paul Louis Weiller. At the same time Foch asked him to keep this method of reconnaissance secret "to preserve for France the considerable lead it had then attained over the rest of the world in the conduct of the war."

This explains the fact that Weiller's method was long unrecognized and not distinguished from the methods of large-scale reconnaissance practiced by the Germans or by the other allies of France in the First World War.

THE AVIATORS' UNIFORMS

The goatskins used at the beginning of the war.

Very early in the war the test by fire showed the inappropriateness of the French army's uniforms, in which dark blue and bright red predominated, making the soldiers easy targets for the enemy. The creation of new uniforms was urgent.

The decisions reached in regard to the air force, a recent branch of the armed services, necessarily evoked unpredictable reactions among the aviators, which would lead to new customs and traditions.

On December 9, 1914, the aviators and balloonists, like all of the other combatants except for the colonial troops, received the horizon blue uniform. Since this new uniform was distributed very slowly during the year 1915, the aviators, who came from all the different branches, kept the uniforms of their original services, merely adding the insignia proper to aviation. This practice soon became the style for the flight personnel, and especially for the reservists, who preferred to wear the old uniforms left over from the beginning of the war, which were more becoming and less dull than the horizon blue uniform imposed by the necessity of making the troops less conspicuous to the enemy in fighting on the ground. Thus different uniforms were worn even within the same flight and in particular by the fighter pilots, whose striving for a personalized uniform at all costs led to abuses.

In the course of the war customs changed with time. The youngest, mobilized in 1917 and 1918, who had not been in any other branch before their service, showed a greater respect for regulations.

The new uniform universally adopted left nothing to

The black leather jacket, fireman type, in August 1914.

The variety in uniforms, October 4, 1915. At Le Bourget the observers came from all branches of the service.

A fur-lined jumpsuit, 1916, and a regulation helmet dating from before the war (worn in observation and bombing units; fighter pilots preferred a crash helmet).

Aviation armband (on pilot's left arm), July 1916.

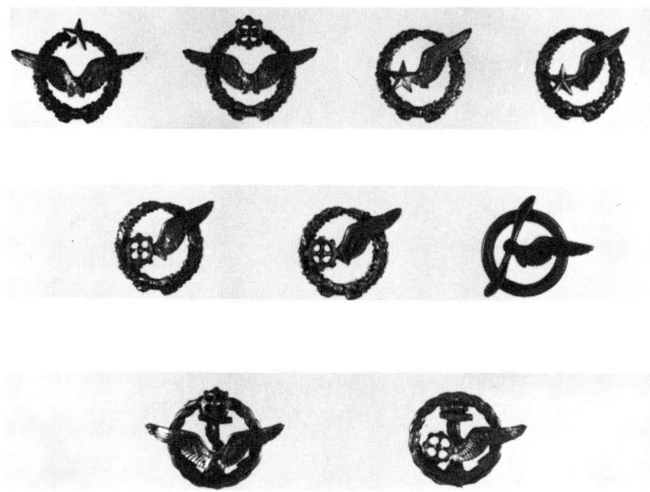

The metal insignias of the aeronautics specialties:
Top row, left to right: *Licensed airplane pilot; licensed dirigible pilot; airplane observer; student airplane pilot.*
Middle row, left to right: *Observer assigned to a dirigible, captive balloon, or kite, or a dirigible mechanic; student dirigible pilot; airplane mechanic, bombardier, gunner, machine-gunner, or photographer assigned to an airplane or a dirigible.*
Bottom row, left: *Navy dirigible pilot, 1914–1918; right: Crewman of a navy dirigible, 1914–1918.*

Silk stocking worn under the helmet for better protection against the cold.

Aviators at Breteuil, Department of the Oise, putting on warm clothing before leaving on a bombing mission, February 2, 1916.

A fighter pilot in his Spad, wearing a fur-lined jumpsuit and a close-fitting helmet, more practical than the rigid helmet.

The pilot and the observer of a Breguet XIV A 2 of Flight BR 279, using a close-fitting helmet rather than the standard one. Under this headgear a silk stocking, or whatever was handy, was worn.

The machine-gunner of a Breguet XIV B 2 wearing a face mask to protect himself from the severe weather.

distinguish the branches of the service except a few details.

In the case of aeronautics, the regulation of September 10, 1916, ended the wearing of an armband with a propeller (for aviation) or with a winged anchor (for aerostation). Specialty insignias made of metal were adopted in its place, but these were only for flight personnel. For example, the pilot received an insignia consisting of a wreath of oak leaves on which were imposed spread wings and a gold star. This insignia, nicknamed "the macaroon," is still in use today. The dirigible pilot received a similar insignia with a gold steering wheel instead of the star.

In fact, for a very long time aviators were seen wearing the armband and the insignia at the same time.

In addition to their regular uniforms, the aviators had special clothing necessitated by flying conditions. On missions they kept their fatigue jackets on or else wore a black leather jacket similar to the firemen's jacket already in service before the war. For protection against the cold they also wore a goatskin coat and soon a fur-lined jump suit as well. After 1916 electrically heated suits came into use. The helmet was still the prewar one, but the fighter pilots preferred a more practical close-fitting helmet which allowed better head movements and hence a broader field of vision in the sky.

The private soldiers in aeronautics were hardly distinguished from the other troops, unless they continued to wear the kepi, after it had been officially discarded in favor of a police cap, and the distinctive color (orange) assigned to aeronautics. Thus the tabs were orange with black braid for aviation. The colors were reversed for aerostation.

On the airfields and at the depots the mechanics mostly wore ordinary blue canvas work clothes.

All of these uniforms were worn after the war until 1922.

The Seminole Indian head painted on the fuselage of Raoul Lufbery's plane (PASM Coll.).

Harold Willis beside his plane, which also has the Seminole insignia of the Lafayette Escadrille.

THE LAFAYETTE ESCADRILLE

After the declaration of war and before the United States officially entered it there were many Americans who were eager to come and fight side by side with the French.

All these men had to join the French Foreign Legion. Late in December 1914 William Thaw and two of his friends, Hall and Bach, succeeded in getting admitted to the air force, however. On January 20, 1915, Norman Prince arrived in France with the firm intention of founding a purely American flight.

In October 1915 there were seventeen Americans in pilot training schools or in flights.

On April 18, 1916, flight 124, called the "American" flight, was finally organized at the Luxeuil-les-Bains airfield and equipped with the Nieuport Bébé. The French Captain Georges Thénault took command of it. He was assisted by Lieutenant Alfred Laage de Meux.

The first seven American pilots of the flight were Thaw, Prince, Kiffin, Rockwell, MacConnell, Cowdin, Hall, and Chapman. They were followed by Raoul Lufbery, Clyde Balsey, Johnson, Rumsey, Norman Hill, and Didier Masson.

The American flight took part in the fighting in the Verdun sector from May 1916 on. Raoul Lufbery proved to be the best pilot.

In November 1916 the flight adopted a name that became famous, the Lafayette Escadrille, which was made official on December 6, 1916.

At the suggestion of Captain Thénault the flight took as its emblem the head of a Seminole Indian, the first drawing of which was done by the mechanic Suchet and which was later modified to the head of a Sioux Indian by Sergeant Harold Willis. The pilots chose as mascots two lion cubs, a male and a female, which they named Whisky and Soda.

In November 1917 the flight got its first Spad VII's. In January 1917 it had 21 pilots for a complement of 12 airplanes. After the entry of the United States into the war in April of that year more American pilots showed up before American units were formed. They were organized into Lafayette Corps. Most of them went off for training, and the others served in the Lafayette Escadrille, whose complement was increased to 27 pilots; these were temporarily assigned to French flights.

On February 18, 1918, the heroic epic of the American volunteers ended. The flight was dissolved, and its personnel were assigned to the first American pursuit squadron, the 103rd, equipped with Nieuports. The materiel of the old 124th served to equip a French flight, which adopted the insignia of Joan of Arc.

At the time of the armistice 267 Americans had served directly in French aviation in either the Lafayette Escadrille or the Corps; 225 had been licensed as pilots, and 180 had served at the front. Of that number, 62 were killed, 51 of them in combat; 15 were taken prisoner; and 19 were wounded. The Lafayette Corps won 199 victories.

France has not forgotten the contribution of the American pilots of the Lafayette. Every year their memory is celebrated in May at Marnes-la-Coquette, near Paris, where most of them are buried.

The Lafayette Escadrille at Chaudun, Aisne, July 17, 1917:
Standing: *Soubiran, Doolittle, Campbell, Parsons, Bridgman, Dugan, MacMonagle, Lovell, Willis, Henry Jones, Peterson, Lieutenant de Maison-Rouge.*
Seated: *Hill, Masson, Thaw, Captain Thénault, Lufbery, C. C. Johnson, Bigelow, Robert Rockwell, with the mascots—the two lion cubs Whisky and Soda (Soubiran Coll.).*

The Lafayette Escadrille at the Cachy airfield, 1917.

French mechanics of the Lafayette Escadrille.

Raoul Lufbery.

Soubiran's personalized Spad VII.

A Spad VII of the Lafayette Escadrille.

THE FLIGHTS OF THE ARMY OF THE EAST

At the time when the Dardanelles expedition was suffering a defeat, marked by the loss between February and November 1915 of 145,000 men killed and wounded, the Allies decided to send help to the courageous Serbian army, which was subjected to a triple attack by Germany, Austria-Hungary, and Bulgaria.

With that objective the French and the British resolved to land an expeditionary force at Salonika in Greece, which was then neutral. General Sarrail was named to head it. He had only four divisions, made up of 35,000 French and 15,000 British troops.

In October 1915 the ships carrying Sarrail's army entered the roadstead of Salonika. It was unfortunately too late to relieve the Serbs, who had been overwhelmed by numbers. After their defeat the French government opposed the re-embarkment of the expeditionary force since the Serbian army still existed and it seemed necessary to maintain an entrenched camp, a threatening base, even over a long period of time, on the flanks of the enemy coalition.

As early as March 1915 there were two flights, called the Serbia Flight and the Eastern Flight, to cover this secondary front, which had been responsible for the outbreak of the war.

Eight flights were organized in October 1915 to take part in the Salonika expedition. Quartered before their departure at Saint Priest, near Bron, France, they consisted of three flights of Maurice Farmans, three of Voisins, one of Nieuports, and one of Caudrons.

At that time their commanding officer, Captain Denain (future minister of air) noted the inappropriateness of the planes assigned in a region where the mountain chains were often over 2,000 meters high and where the planes could not resist the faster enemy aircraft. Denain also complained of too great a disparity in the types of planes and their engines. It must be admitted that over a year later the Air Force of the East was still experiencing serious personnel and materiel problems.

In spite of the losses from combat, accidents, and disease that cruelly plagued the Allied forces, the Salonika flights always "muddled through" by themselves the best they could.

Major Denain remarked on November 10, 1916, that 15 percent of the men were to have been supplied by the intermediate depots and the Army Corps of the East. Evacuations and deaths amounted to about 60 percent of the forces sent from France (on June 17, 1916, Denain had 1,611 men, including 31 officer pilots, 43 noncommissioned and enlisted pilots, 19 officer observers, and 40 bombardier/machine gunners).

The arrival of new materiel was subject to considerable delays. At that time (November) nothing had been seen of the supplies for August. The delivery of new planes was short by 46 aircraft. To be able to hang on it was necessary to make the old planes last, to rebuild them if necessary.

The real significance of being 46 planes behind in delivery is apparent only if it is compared to the total number of planes. On November 8, 1916, the total number of planes received in the Army of the East since its formation in October 1915 was 262, less 27 planes turned over to the Serbs; 49 planes were then in service, 2 had been lost, 85 had deteriorated, 42 had

Major Denain examining a Dorand airplane at Salonika.

A Russian flight at Suesova equipped with Nieuports.

The Army of the East.
A Nieuport Bébé over a cantonment near Jassy, Rumania.

A Caquot captive balloon over the city of Jassy in Rumania.

been discarded or sent back or were in the course of being sent back, and 13 had been taken out of service and were being used for spare parts. Of the 85 deteriorated planes, 60 had been restored. The dead loss in thirteen months amounted to 25 planes, or an average of 2 planes a month.

It is easy to see that the situation of the Air Force of the East would have been extremely precarious without the constant efforts of every one of its members. And yet it was under the stimulus of this courageous army that the success was to come that would bring about the end of the war. It was in that sector that the enemy front was broken for the first time on September 15, 1918, thanks to the victory of the Dobropolye (in the Ukraine) due to the initiative of General Francher d'Esperey, who had replaced General Sarrail and General Guillaumat.

The planes then participated effectively in the exploitation of the breakthrough, intensifying their bombings and machine-gunning enemy positions.

The undisputed ace of the Army of the East was Dieudonné Costes, who had 9 confirmed victories. He engaged in 27 night bombings and 54 combats, having a total of nearly a thousand hours of flying time.

On the Eastern Front: bombing a bridge during an air raid.

An enemy plane photographed over a lake in Macedonia by a French observation plane.

Captions for illustrations in order of appearance on the following five pages:

The Entreprenant *(*Enterprise*) at the siege of Mayence, 1794.*

Portrait of Georges Guynemer, by Louise Catherine Breslau, February 1916.

A flight of Voisins bombarding the city of Karlsruhe, by Henri Farré, 1915 (PASM Coll.).

A formation of Breguet XIV's: Bombardment in 1918.

The Black Cruise. *Fort Lamy, 1933, by Albert Brenet (1976).*

1916.

PART 3

Between the Wars

Introduction

When the First World War ended, French military aviation ranked first in the world. Only British aviation could rival it, although the number of warplanes that it mustered was distinctly lower than the French total. The German air force, which had been a valiant rival, was now outlawed.

French military aviation, born a little before the start of the conflict, had begun the war in a very modest role. It had rapidly developed its efficiency in observation and in artillery ranging, then had seen the possibilities of aerial pursuit and bombing confirmed. Its fundamental doctrine was born after it had been found at Verdun that air superiority was a necessary, but not sufficient, condition to insure the winning of the war on the ground. The Duval Division later demonstrated the possibilities of independent action and proved the capability of planes to support tank operations.

The essentials of what was later developed in the field of military aviation, in both techniques and in principles, had been discovered and tested in the course of the Great War.

The prestige enjoyed by the French air forces both in France and abroad is understandable. Outside of France this prestige was due at first to the quality of French materiel. The Spad XIII and the Breguet XIV, as well as the engines produced in France, enjoyed a well-earned reputation.

It was also due to the quality of French aviation doctrine—policy and principles—the validity of which had been demonstrated in the field. There has been much talk of General Douhet's influence in this regard; there has been less talk, however, of the influence of the French aviators toward the end of the war, but it was important nonetheless.

French influence in aviation would be spread further by the sending of many missions abroad and by the exportation of French materiel. The nation's admiration for its air forces was focused primarily on the aviators because the First World War had been a war of masses. As for the infantrymen caught up in mine warfare, their endurance was exalted, and there were stories of the suffering and the horribly anonymous death in the mud of the trenches.

The aviator, on the other hand, was brilliant. If he disappeared, it was "in the open sky of glory." The myth of the air hero was created.

However, although that myth built up the prestige of the air forces in the mind of the public, it evoked less favorable feelings in the soldiers of the land forces. It was partly the press that incited jealousies and spite, which explains some of the attitudes manifested by the troops on the ground. Similarly, the idea persisted for a long time, and was expressed during the 1960s by a famous general, that the aviators were frivolous, pleasure-loving types.

One may wonder whether this partial, biased view did not sometimes have an influence on the making of decisions unfavorable to the air branch by those responsible for French defense. In fact, the air forces were soon reduced to the bare minimum, as indeed seemed logical at the time when the major problem was that of demobilization. But that was not enough. The airmen must return to the ranks and be content with what they were offered: being a secondary service of the army and the navy.

While the air forces were settling down to peacetime duties in France and in the occupation of Germany, the war was still going on in Syria and in Morocco. In the course of these colonial wars aviation played an important part, but one in which the necessity of first winning the battle in the air did not arise, and for good reasons. That experience probably had the effect of confirming the army general staff in its attitudes.

On the other hand, a conviction developed among the proponents of an "integral air force" that the air forces would play a decisive part in future wars. In order for it to be prepared for that role it was necessary for military aviation to be set up as an independent branch of the armed forces, as was being done in England, directed by an Air Ministry that would coordinate all the country's aeronautical activities.

In spite of bitter opposition, the Air Ministry came into being late in 1928 "by accident," as it were. It was gradually given the right to direct the military aviators.

The first victory was the adoption of a new uniform, but it was not until 1933 and 1934 that the basic documents appeared that created the French Air Force (the Armée de l'Air). Finally, the Air School, decided upon in 1933, saw the members of its first graduating class "integrate" in 1935. Unfortunately, at the same moment war, which had been said to be (and had been wished to be) abolished forever, again threatened the country.

The coming into power of Adolf Hitler and the relaunching of German military aviation, backed by the will of the political leaders and by considerable means, forced France to rethink the problems of its air service.

In 1934 General Denain had the first plan passed that was to renovate the Air Force. The planes provided for in that plan were to be outdated very quickly, but at the beginning of 1936 the results obtained gave the French Armée de l'Air a certain superiority over the German Luftwaffe.

The very conditions under which the respective armament plans had been carried out limited the French advantage in time, and it was easy to predict that from 1937 on German aviation would begin to be superior to that of the French.

To prevent this it would have been necessary to prohibit by arms the remilitarization of the Rhineland carried out by Hitler on March 7, 1936, in violation of the treaties. Unfortunately, in spite of Prime Minister Sarraut's bellicose speeches, Strasbourg remained under the fire of German guns. From then on everything would accelerate and lead France inevitably into war.

In the summer of 1936 it was decided to increase military appropriations considerably and to reorganize the aeronautics industry. The reorganization did not bear fruit until after 1938. Once more, however, the air appropriations were insufficient. They were even cut off in 1937 in favor of the navy.

When appropriations were finally granted to the Air Force in 1938 it was too late. The great efforts made from that time on enabled France to carry out the fastest aerial rearmament in the world but did not provide it at the desired time with all the means necessary to stand up to an enemy that had begun its preparations over three years before.

After the Munich alert, when France did not have a single modern airplane, the war began, in September 1939, when the work carried on since January 1938 was just beginning to bear fruit. Nevertheless, the French were outclassed in all fields in the number and quality of aircraft. Only the French air crews could measure up. All that remained for them when the real fighting began in May 1940 was to sacrifice themselves to save the honor of their country.

A good number of them paid with their lives for the lack of foresight of the army command in regard to the air forces and for the inconsistency of the general policy followed between the two world wars.

CHAPTER I

From War to Peace (1919–1920)

Demobilization

On November 11, 1918, French military aeronautics was at the peak of its power and prestige. Its strength in personnel, the number of its flights, the results obtained by its crews, and the quality and consistency of its operating principles classed it in the first rank worldwide. It was backed by a mass aeronautics production whose quality was universally recognized. German military aviation was prohibited, American aviation barely beginning; only British aviation could stand comparison with that of the French. The British did possess a certain advantage, which did not appear as such until later: the Royal Air Force (RAF) was an independent service.

French military aviation was far from possessing such independence, for it had to wait until 1922 to become a branch of the armed forces and until 1933 to be at last confirmed as the Armée de l'Air (Air Force).

The Problems Faced

From the time of the armistice the air forces quite naturally faced a whole series of problems connected with the transition from war to peace. The demobilization of personnel led to a decrease in the number of units. The existence of many planes meant that no more orders were being given to the aeronautics industry, which either had to convert its facilities to produce other equipment or to seek new markets.

The majority of the air units maintained were stationed in the eastern part of the country or were on occupation duty in Germany. Organized during the war, they had to invent, in spite of their reduced means, their everyday peacetime life, taking care not to allow this new arm, which had just shown itself to be revolutionary, to get bogged down in the routines of life at a military post.

Demobilization of Personnel

Two figures show the magnitude of the problem. In November 1918 the air forces had 90,000 officers and men; in October 1920 these numbered only 39,055.

This demobilization, in fact, raised few difficulties. For the nonflying personnel the end of the war, no doubt whatsoever, marked the realization of their deep desire to return to civilian life. The majority of these men were reservists who had done four years of supplementary service and wanted more than anything else to go home.

For the flying personnel the problem was sometimes different. The end of the conflict was a satisfaction to them, but at the same time it deprived them of a life that many of them had loved passionately. The flying, the close friendship within the flight, and the risk that was a part of their daily existence were all things that they would miss.

This explains the fact that some of them tried hard to pursue a career in military or civil aviation. Among those who chose the military path it is noticeable that the higher officers and a large number of the captains had come from the major schools, while most of the lieutenants had risen from the ranks.

Civil aviation offered varied prospects. Some former military pilots would take part in the development of the commercial airlines. From four companies with 27 pilots and 46 airplanes in 1919, the airlines increased to twelve companies with 72 pilots and 185 airplanes in 1920.

Other aviators were tempted by adventure with a capital "A": the flying circus, which from performance to performance offered a gaping public reenactments of aerial combats or dangerous acrobatics, or the more prestigious pioneer flights between distant cities, which often depended on obtaining financial support.

In the majority of cases the flying personnel who were not attracted to continuing an aeronautical career had little difficulty in finding civilian jobs. Many wartime fliers occupied eminent positions. The industrialists, architects, and notaries among them naturally resumed their former occupations.

Finally, there was the case of the officers who had decided to pursue their military careers but to go back to their original branches of the service, either because they felt no particular enthusiasm for aviation or in order to regain career advantages that they considered impossible to obtain in the new branch.

Absorption of Excess Planes

The reduction in personnel obviously entailed a corresponding reduction in the number of air units. In 1918 the French air forces had 258 flights; in October 1920 there were only 119. At the time of the armistice the French had 11,836 airplanes—3,886 in reserve, 400 in the interior, 300 overseas, 3,000 in the schools, and 3,437 at the front. On March 1, 1920, only 3,940 planes remained—3,050 in storage, reserved as war materiel, and 890 in the units.

Several methods had been resorted to in order

Spad XIII's lined up on an occupied airfield in Germany, June 1919.

A civilian Caudron G 3. Because of the simplicity of its handling, this plane had great success after the First World War as a touring, excursion, and training plane.

to achieve such a reduction. The first, on which great hopes had been founded, was to participate in the development of civil aviation. As noted earlier, this was, in fact, getting under way. The first commercial Paris-London flight was made by the aviator Bossoutrot in 1919. A certain number of bombers and observation planes were thus sold. Many companies also bought SAL 2's and Breguet XIV's.

Fighter planes were sold to be used for racing and for record setting. Some planes that were old but still reliable were also sold to individuals who wanted to use them for aerial touring. Thus one freshly demobilized lieutenant, having resumed his civilian activities, bought a Caudron G 3 for his own pleasure. His example was followed by many pilots who wanted to continue to fly and were attracted by the G 3's easy maintenance and handling.

But it was soon realized that the general civilian market offered little in the way of long-range prospects. Quite naturally, the foreign market was resorted to.

Since French aviation enjoyed great prestige abroad, France developed military missions in many foreign countries (a topic to be discussed later), which made it possible, among other things, for it to sell its military planes. Before the Potez 25 began to break records in this field and long before the Mirage III, the Breguet XIV had an exceptional success in the export market.

Contraction of the Aeronautics Industry

The last measure resorted to was, after taking delivery of the planes already under construction, to stop placing orders with the aeronautics industry. This explains why the numbers employed by that industry went down from 183,000 in 1918 to 100,000 in June 1919, then to 5,200 in 1920, and reached its lowest level in 1921 with 3,700 workers.

In considering these figures one must be careful

not to use them to form an unqualified judgment on this phenomenon and conclude that the French aeronautics industry disappeared. It must not be forgotten that this industry included, besides manufacturers specializing in research and development and in assembly, a very large number of general machine shops which worked as subcontractors. As the orders for new planes decreased, these shops quite naturally converted to respond to different needs, which were numerous in that period of general reconstruction of the country.

To be sure, many manufacturers did go out of business. Of the fifty or so that could be counted in 1918, only about ten remained in 1920. Those that remained hoped to survive on civilian orders and most especially on foreign orders. To assist them in getting foreign markets in 1921 the General Air Office (Office Général de l'Air/O.G.A.) was created, a privately run organization whose first president was Major Brocard. It would have a brilliant future.

The manufacturers also hoped for a resumption of orders, feeling that in any case the armed forces would be compelled to that course in order not to have their aerial equipment rapidly lose its value. The future proved them right.

Still more serious than the decline in the number of people employed by the aeronautics industry was the decline in the number of employees of the various technical bureaus which, at the state level, controlled and directed that industry. Their strength actually dropped from 4,000 to 40 persons. This exceptional reduction largely explains the decline in research activity, the effects of which were soon to be felt.

The Reforms

Evolution of the Central Administration

At the same time that these demobilization phenomena were developing, a sweeping reorganization of the aeronautics branch was decided on.

In 1918 it was headed by an Undersecretariat for Aeronautics, directly subordinate to the minister of war and entrusted at that time to J. L. Dumesnil. At the time of the armistice he resigned for reasons of health, and the Undersecretariat of State for Aeronautics was abolished on January 10, 1919. Its functions were at first carried out by the Directorate of Aeronautics of the Ministry of War and entrusted to Colonel Dhé.

On April 20 it was decided to expand the responsibilities of the Directorate and turn it over to General Duval. To the already existing services was added an aerial navigation service, which was to concern itself particularly with commercial aviation; it was entrusted to Colonel Saconney.

During the same period of time, and "spontaneously," special services concerned with aeronautics were established in several ministries. This was notably the case with the colonial, transport, and postal ministries.

Of course the solution that many wished for, but that it seemed impossible to get at the time, was the creation of an Air Ministry covering all aeronautical activities. In the absence of such a ministry the coordination of all such activities was entrusted to an agency, the Office of General Coordination of Aeronautics (O.C.G.Aé.), created by a decree of June 6, 1919. It was to assemble all the technical services scattered in various ministries, leaving those ministries retaining only the use of their facilities. General Duval undertook the direction of this new office.

The major difficulty would have to do with the budgets, for which the ministers were responsible. The affair was further complicated on January 20, 1920, by the reestablishment of an Undersecretariat of State for Aeronautics and Air Transport, assigned to Pierre Etienne Flandin. The immediate consequence was that on January 30, 1920, the O.C.G.Aé. was moved from the Ministry of War to the Ministry of Transport and placed under the direction of that Undersecretariat of State.

It included the technical, manufactures, and aerial navigation services, to which was later added the meteorological service. Directed by Inspector

General Fortant, the O.C.G.Aé. was to be the purveyor of materiel to all military or civilian users.

This solution, acceptable as a lesser evil if civil aviation had to become the principal customer of the aeronautics industry, nevertheless had serious drawbacks. For the army the most obvious consequence of the Undersecretariat of State for Aeronautics was that the Directorate of Aeronautics, the 12th Directorate of the Ministry of War, retained as its only functions those having to do with the Air Force proper, thus losing its role in civil aviation, which was logical, but also its authority over the industry, which turned out to be harmful.

It may seem improper to speak of the Air Force in 1920 since this official status was not conferred on it until passage of the law of December 8, 1922. In fact, Aeronautics did function as a branch of the armed forces, made up of three subdivisions: aviation, aerostation, and antiaircraft defense.

The Director of Aeronautics at the time was General H. A. Dumesnil. The Directorate comprised the office of the director and the personnel section; the antiaircraft bureau; the first bureau, aerostation; the second bureau, aviation materiel; the third bureau, budgets and legal matters; the fourth bureau, aviation organization and personnel; and the fifth bureau, general organization and information.

The New Structures

After the armistice the essential function of military aeronautics was to provide protection for mobilization and for the first ground operations in the event of new hostilities. This explains the importance attached to maintaining the air division, whose units, all in the regular army, were capable in peacetime of launching operations without recourse to mobilized reinforcements.

In 1919 that air division had a complement of 1

The Breguet XIV T was first used in 1919 in the form of a limousine fitted out for four passengers. In 1920 it was in regular service on the Paris-London, Paris-Brussels, and Paris-Cabourg routes.

pursuit brigade divided into 2 groupings each consisting of 2 pursuit groups of three flights; and 1 bomber brigade comprising 1 daytime grouping of 3 three-flight groups and 1 night grouping of 4 three-flight groups.

The observation units maintained on active duty would in turn comprise 29 two-flight groups. To this were added 13 flights in French North Africa, 2 flights in the Near East, and 3 colonial flights. There were thus a total of 115 flights: 18 pursuit flights, 21 bomber flights, and 76 observation flights.

At the end of 1920 the order of battle for military aeronautics was as follows.

Under the orders of the air division at Metz were:

1 pursuit brigade: the 1st Air Pursuit Regiment, at Thionville (3 groups of 3 flights) and the 2nd, at Strasbourg (3 groups of 3 flights);

1 daytime bombing brigade: the 11th Aerial Bombing Regiment (daytime), at Metz (2 groups of 4 flights) and the 12th, at Neustadt (3 groups of 4 flights);

1 night bombing brigade: the 21st Aerial Bombing Regiment (night), at Malzéville (2 groups of 3 flights) and the 22nd (night), at Luxeuil (2 groups of 3 flights);

1 mixed brigade—initially planned to have one pursuit regiment and one bombing regiment—comprising only the 3rd Pursuit Regiment, at Châteauroux (3 groups of 3 flights).

The 7 observation regiments were as follows:

The 31st Aerial Observation Regiment, at Tours (1 group of 3 flights—2 at Tours and 1 at Pau); the 32nd, at Dijon (2 groups of 2 flights at Dijon, 1 group of 2 flights at Avord); the 33rd, at Mayence (4 groups of 2 flights); the 34th, at Bourget (4 groups of 2 flights); the 35th, at Lyons-Bron (3 groups of 2 flights); the 36th, at Hussein-Dey, Algeria (8 flights); the 37th, at Rabat, Morocco (10 flights).

The air forces in the Near East consisted of 8 flights.

In addition to these there were 3 colonial flights: 2 in Indochina and 1 in French West Africa.

Altogether there were 119 flights: 27 pursuit, 32 bomber, 57 observation, and 3 colonial flights.

To serve these aviation units there were important services and establishments that should be mentioned:

The Aeronautical Technical Inspection Service, with the double mission of inspection of materiel and technical aeronautics instruction; the Directorate General of Aviation Materiel Supply (D.G.R.M.A.), which in March 1920 replaced the Aviation Depot and Supply Service (S.E.R.A.). The functions that it performed for all aviation units stationed in France proper, in the T.O.E. (Theater of Foreign Operations), or in the colonies are perfectly described by its name.

Directly subordinate to the D.G.R.M.A. were the special aviation depots (E.S.A.), which stored the new materiel arriving from the factories to constitute the reserve for wartime. There were four of these depots: E.S.A. No. 1, at Dugny (airplanes); No. 2, at Nanterre (spare parts for flying materiel, including engines, common materiel, and ammunition); No. 3, at Saint Cyr (automotive rolling stock and spare parts); and No. 4, at Dugny (collapsible hangars and tents, and machinery for setting them up and taking them down).

Also subordinate to the D.G.R.M.A. were the following:

The general aviation storehouses (M.G.A.), responsible for directly supplying the units stationed in their areas of jurisdiction with materiel of all kinds: M.G.A. No. 1, at Romilly-sur-Seine; No. 2, at Lonvic-lès-Dijon; No. 3, at Romorantin; and No. 4, at Versailles-Mortemets;

The aeronautical maritime transit sections (S.T.M.Aé.), responsible for shipments abroad: S.T.M.Aé. No. 1, at Marseilles; and No. 2, at Bordeaux;

The establishment for the sale of aviation materiel (E.L.M.A.), at Nanterre. This agency took care of the selling off of materiel not held in reserve. Because of its function, linked to the circumstances, it was a temporary agency.

In 1920 there were three schools: the aviation school at Istres responsible for pilot training; the gunnery and bombing school at Cazaux, which

General Duval presiding at a ceremonial parade in honor of Georges Guynemer.

trained bombardiers, machine-gunners, and observers; and the advanced training school for aviation specialists at Bordeaux, charged with the advanced training of aviation specialists as well as the technical training of pilots.

It should be noted that by 1920 in addition to this instruction provided by the military schools there was instruction given by civilian schools. This was the case with the student pilots who received a pilot training scholarship the year before being drafted. This system, although interesting, was found to fall short of giving the results expected.

In addition to these aviation units and services there were the aerostation units and services and those of antiaircraft defense.

The aerostation units comprised:

The 1st Regiment of Observation Balloonists, at Versailles, which consisted of the 1st Battalion, at Epinal; the 2nd, at Compiègne; the 3rd, at Saint Cyr; and the 4th, at Angers;

The 2nd Regiment of Observation Balloonists, at Toulouse, which consisted of the 1st Battalion, at Nevers; the 2nd, at Toulouse; and the 3rd, at Privas.

Each battalion was made up of three companies, each company handling one balloon.

The aerostation establishments comprised:

The central aerostation materiel establishment, at Chalais-Meudon, responsible for supplying the units with materiel of all kinds, and the center for aerostation instruction at Cosne.

Antiaircraft Defense (D.C.A.), for its part, had in operation 5 regiments, 2 establishments, and a school: the 1st D.C.A. Regiment, at the fort of Aubervillers; the 2nd, at Sedan; the 3rd, at Toul; the 4th, at Lure; and the 5th, at Sathonay.

The central D.C.A. establishment at Chartres was responsible not only for supplying and managing the technical materiel of the regiments but also for research on improvements to be made in the D.C.A. materiel and methods of using it.

The D.C.A. technical section at Arnouville-lès-Gonesse was concerned with the research, development, and testing of fire-control apparatus.

The D.C.A. school at Montargis gave an advanced training course for officers and a professional course for noncommissioned officers.

It is quite apparent that in this system the essential subdivision was aviation.

The Action Cadre of the Air Force

Stationing

The stationing of the units was indicative of the use that was expected to be made of them.

Of the 119 flights that made up the French air forces in the middle of 1920, 49 flights, or 41%, were stationed outside France proper, 20 (17%) being on occupation duty in Germany and 18 (15%) in operations in the Near East and in Morocco.

Of the 70 flights stationed in France proper, 38 flights, or 32% of the total, were in the eastern part of the country.

If one considers as favored those units stationed in France proper (although at the time Avord did not have a reputation for being an enjoyable garrison) as well as those in Algeria, Tunisia, Indochina, and French West Africa (41%), it is easy to see that in the years following the armistice the air force was not wallowing in luxury.

The Airfields and the Units

These units lived on a "field." The airfields, of course, remained identical to those of the war. The grass runway was in the center of the installation. Bessonneau hangars sheltered the planes, while the personnel lived and worked in collapsible barracks, usually of the type known as "Adrian."

The unit stationed at the airfield was the regiment, consisting of a staff, a headquarters section, a depot, a section of workmen, the groups and flights, and a photographic section.

The regiment was essentially an administrative unit, the head of which in 1920 was not always an aviator. A unit-forming corps in the sense of the law of 1882, the basic administrative law of the army, it had a relatively large staff which covered the various activities of the airfield.

A headquarters section administered the personnel, with the exception of the depot run by a section of workmen who, contrary to what might be thought from its name, had no technical responsibilities. The latter were a prerogative of the depot charged with the maintenance and repair of all the materiel of the regiment.

The group directed the flights and centralized the various training activities. For bombing it was also a tactical unit.

The flight was still the unit par excellence. It was within that unit that air training developed, traditions were cultivated, missions were organized. Very often the flight was called upon to operate on airfields other than the base airfield of the regiment or of the group. This was especially the case in French North Africa or in the Near East, where the flights possessed their operational autonomy.

The Personnel

About a thousand persons lived and worked at each airfield, or aerodrome: 15 to 20 officers of the regimental staff; 10 to 15 pilots and 35 to 50 nonflying personnel for each flight; and about 400 persons in the depot, which constituted the largest unit in numbers of personnel at the field.

But the officer complement remained weak—about 50—beyond all comparison with the present rates. In 1920 this quantitative weakness was accompanied by a certain qualitative weakness. To be convinced of this it suffices to recall that while 67% of the higher officers came from the major schools, and while only 30% of the captains were promoted from the ranks, 75% of the lieutenants came from the ranks. It was predictable that this situation would quickly lead to difficulties in command and leadership.

The Planes

The other essential element of the air unit, of course, was the airplane. Each flight operated 10 planes for pursuit and bombing and 8 for heavy bombing and observation.

During the period under discussion these machines were the planes used during the war or

A Hanriot HD 362 two-seated pursuit plane in 1918, originally intended for the massive reequipment of 1919.

Described as a "protected single-seater," the Spad XX was, in fact, a two-seater, the rear machine-gunner firing a machine gun on a pivot. A version called the C 2, with twin Lewis machine guns, was tried out but did not go into production.

those being delivered at the end of the war.

The pursuit, or fighter, planes were: the Spad XIII, the Spad XX, the Nieuport 29, and the Gourdou-Leseurre.

Another plane that might be classed among the fighters was the Caudron R XI three-seater, with which the escort flights of the 11th and the 12th Aerial Bombing Regiments (R.A.B.'s) were equipped until 1922. In that year those two flights were transformed into daytime bombing flights.

For daytime bombing the standard plane was, of course, the Breguet XIV B 2, which had a great career both in France and abroad.

For night bombing, while awaiting the Farman 60 Goliath, which came into use in 1923, the Breguet XVI Bn 2, which came into use early in 1921, the formations used the Voisin XBN, the Caproni, the Caudron 253 Bn 3, which was quickly retired from the formations, and the Farman 50 Bn 2.

During this period the observation flights saw the retirement of the Spad XV's and XVI's, as well as that of the Salmson 2 A 2's. In 1920 they were supplied with Salmson 7 A 2's and especially with Breguet XIV A 2's, with which, notably, French overseas formations were equipped.

This Breguet XIV A 2 was undeniably an excellent airplane suitable for all missions. It was found to be inadequate, however, in the Near East and especially in Morocco since its bombing capability was inferior to that of the B 2. In particular, it could not carry the 50-kilogram bombs wanted by the crews for attacking rebel redoubts.

The War in the Middle East and in Morocco

In 1919 and 1920 troubles developed in the Middle East and in Morocco which led to a considerable increase in the air force strength originally intended for those territories.

In the Middle East by the end of the First World War France had come to grips with the bands in Cilicia supported by Atatürk's regulars, while in Syria the French were subjected to sporadic attacks by Emir Faisal's desert tribes, behind whom loomed the shadow of Lawrence of Arabia. In that war, sometimes open, sometimes masked, the airplane was an essential element of security for the friendly columns advancing into a naturally difficult terrain which, because of its variations, offered many possibilities for ambushes. The airplane was also used to inspire fear in the natives sufficient to prevent them from continuing the rebellion. In fact, General Gouraud, commanding the troops in the Middle East, said that the bombings done initially with insufficient means had produced an effect exactly opposite to that desired by the French. Little by little the natives had gotten used to the raids, and the airplane lost its psychological effect. Nevertheless, he asked not for fewer planes but for more of them in order to insure the success of his military actions.

In Morocco, where instability persisted and later spread, the flights supported the ground actions directed by Marshal Lyautey. The air force contributed its fire and its sight and photographic reconnaissance. It provided communications between the different posts, dropping money, medicines, mail, and tobacco and evacuating the wounded and ill wherever the terrain permitted. It proved to be an exceptional instrument, which, as the rebellion became more active, saw its prestige increase among the combatants and its role develop even further.

Aviation Activity

Apart from the foreign theaters of operations, aviation activity was reduced during the years of transition from war to peace. Beginning in 1919, however, a series of experiments was tried in an attempt to maintain in the air force the high morale that it had in 1918.

The Military Airlines

There was, first of all, the operation of the airlines, which answered a real need—to mitigate the disorganization of the country's road network—and which opened the way to civil aviation:

Paris-Lille, from February 8 to 28, 1919, a line later taken over by the Messageries Aériennes Company

Paris-Brussels, from February 21 to June 17, 1919

Paris-Maubeuge-Valenciennes, from April 2 to June 20, 1919

Nancy-Bricy-Longwy, from April 1 to 25, 1919.

Studies of the cost prices and operating conditions of other airlines were also done. These lines were:

Paris-Bordeaux, from March 23 to June 15, 1919
Paris-London, from March 16 to June 20, 1919
Paris-Strasbourg, from April 7 to June 22, 1919
Paris-Mulhouse, from May 8 to June 18, 1919.

On this last run, Paris-Mulhouse, probably for the first time in the world, there was an attempt at operating at night. In twenty days a total of fourteen trips were made without incident.

The balance sheet of these operations was telling: 700 trips, 250,000 kilometers flown, 11,500 kilograms of mail and 15 passengers transported (or nearly 15 kilograms per trip). There were 47 engine failures and 12 plane crashes.

Pioneer Flights

During the same period the Directorate of Aeronautics encouraged aerial activities of all kinds. Military personnel participated in air meets, races, and competitions, broke records, and accomplished pioneer flights between distant cities. It was undoubtedly in these pioneer runs that the military aviators expressed themselves best.

From June 18 to 28, in a Breguet XIV B 2, Lieutenant Lemaître, accompanied by a mechanic, linked Paris to Port Etienne in Mauritania, then part of French West Africa.

From August 7 to September 9, 1919, Major Vuillemin and Lieutenant Dagnaux, each in his own plane, attempted the pioneer run from Paris to Cairo and back. Only Vuillemin succeeded; Dagnaux had engine trouble and crashed at Beirut, on the return trip.

In 1920 the most remarkable pioneer flight was accomplished by Major Vuillemin, who from January 24 to March 31 linked Paris to Dakar via Algiers and Timbuktu. His success must not be allowed to conceal the difficulties of the adventure.

The flight was really a concerted effort organized very meticulously by General Nivelle. A year

Two Breguet XVI BN 2's. In this type of plane Major Vuillemin succeeded in making the pioneer run Paris-Algiers-Timbuktu-Dakar, from January 24 to March 31, 1920.

of preparations had been devoted to shipping gasoline and essential spare parts (spark plugs, wheels) by rail, on light trucks, and finally on the backs of camels. There were also four mechanics on the ground who had to be kept supplied with water and food.

With the preparations completed, the pioneer flight was to be done in two parts. A section of five planes under the direction of Major Rolland was to make the run from Algiers to Ahaggar and back, while the Vuillemin-Dagnaux section (Captain Mézergues, pilot of the third plane, fell ill and abandoned the expedition at Istres) was to link Algiers to Dakar.

Three of the planes of the Rolland section reached Tamanrasset in Algeria; only one returned to Algiers. One crashed on the return trip, and the other, with General Laperrine on board, was lost in the desert. When his plane was found, the general had already died of exhaustion.

In Major Vuillemin's section, Dagnaux crashed near Tamanrasset, later renamed Fort Laperrine. In spite of the difficulties, Vuillemin reached Dakar with his passenger, Lieutenant Challus, but when he arrived his plane, a Breguet XVI Bn 2, was ready for the scrap heap.

This pioneer flight demonstrated the qualities of the French crews, but also the difficulties of all kinds that would have to be overcome before flights could be safely accomplished over the central Sahara.

Pioneer Flights of Foreign Aviators

This military and sporting activity served to consolidate the prestige of French aviation, although this was not the aim sought after. However, exploits accomplished abroad and foreign "propaganda" were already making the French realize that in some domains they had serious competitors.

From May 16 to 29, 1919, Lieutenant Commander Read and his crew of four on board a United States Navy Curtiss NC-4 four-engined flying boat flew from Newfoundland to Lisbon with a stop in the Azores. On June 14 and 15, 1919, the English aviators Alcock and Brown made the first nonstop crossing of the Atlantic, flying from Newfoundland to Clifden, Ireland, in a twin-engined Vickers Vimy, but capsized upon landing. Finally, from November 12 to December 10, 1919, again on board a Vickers Vimy, Captain Ross Smith flew from London to Port Darwin, Australia.

These successes of foreign military pilots did not impair the influence of French aviation. During these two years, its years of transition and also its lean years, French military aviation retained its operational efficiency. It enjoyed the confidence of certain important military leaders and could have faith in its future.

The maintenance of the air division, the effort undertaken to improve the quality of officers in the units, and the good technical capability of the French fliers enabled France to develop an air force able to take the outstanding part in the nation's defense that the lessons of war had given a glimpse of. At the end of the year 1920 anything was possible. Proud of its work in the First World War, military aeronautics, like the rest of the French armed forces for that matter, settled down into peace.

CHAPTER II

The Battle for the Creation of the Air Ministry (1920–1928)

Once the problems of demobilization and installation on peacetime airfields were settled, the air force experienced a period, from 1920 to 1928, marked by great stability in its organization.

With the passage of the law of December 8, 1922, the air force officially acquired the status of a completely independent branch of the armed forces. This made no change in its existing situation, which had anticipated the promulgation of the document, except that antiaircraft defense became a subdivision of the artillery but continued to be subordinate to the air force in its employment.

The Organization

At the peak of the pyramid was the Inspectorate General of Aeronautics, created in 1921, headed by Marshal Fayolle, who was succeeded by General Hergault. This department was to play an important part in working out the regulations and establishing materiel programs.

The 12th Directorate was still functioning. It was under General Dumesnil until 1925 and then, until its dissolution, under General Pujo.

From 1920 to 1928 the organization of the 12th Directorate underwent slight modifications, which would be tedious to enumerate, since they produced no major change in the 1920 organization depicted in the preceding chapter.

A series of measures also modified the structure of the air forces that has already been described. The reorganization was put through in 1923, prompted by General Buat, army chief of staff, who truly believed in the future of military aviation (order of October 9, 1923).

The air forces were divided into two categories: general reserve formations and ground support formations.

The First Air Division grouped together the general reserve formations. It comprised two brigades, one for pursuit and one for bombing. Within its pursuit brigade it had a few reconnaissance flights at its disposal. This division was an active service division capable of acting instantly in case of need.

The Second Air Division, on the other hand, which was established in Paris, was to comprise motorized elements. Its mission was one of cooperation with the ground forces. To carry out this mission it had two brigades consisting of 1 mixed air regiment (R.A.M.), 1 air bombing regiment (R.A.B.), 1 air observation regiment (R.A.O.), 1 air pursuit regiment (R.A.C.), and 1 observation group (G.O.). It was a novelty to see mixed regiments composed of observation flights and pursuit flights charged with protecting them. Another innovation was the creation of three mixed air brigades not incorporated in any division. There were 104 flights in all—30 for pursuit, 32 for bombing, and 42 for observation or reconnaissance. (See the table for details).

To all this, of course, were added the aerostation and antiaircraft defense sections organically attached to the big air units.

This organization proved satisfactory in practice. It remained practically unchanged from 1924 to 1928.

Certainly the part consisting of ground support aviation might seem too large, but the materiel allotted to the various air brigades would make it possible to redistribute forces between the big air units without difficulty. It was possible, if the need arose, to greatly increase the strength of the First Air Division. This idea, supported by the aviators of General Buat's entourage, was interesting, for one finds it developed throughout this period, more or less openly, by the air staffs. To a certain extent it is to be found at the base of the definition of the B.C.R. (bombing, combat, and reconnaissance plane). The Denain plan was greatly influenced by it. Unfortunately, General Buat's successors, starting with General Debeney, who succeeded him in 1923, did not have the same breadth of vision.

Just as the organization evolved only slightly, the aircraft of the period differed only very little from those of the war years. This was due in part to the state of the French aeronautics industry.

As late as 1924 the situation of the industry might have appeared good. France was exporting to twenty-eight countries, and in 1925 it held the majority of world aviation records. These brilliant achievements concealed the reality, and things were to deteriorate very soon.

Changes in the aeronautics organization had produced an extreme complication of the administrative circuits and, in particular, the separation in practice of the users from the supply services. This introduced unacceptable delays in execution. Thus a military plane deriving from a 1924 program was not defined until 1925, produced in 1927, tested in 1928, and put into service in 1930, when it took less than a year to manufacture it. Planes were

General Dumesnil, director of aeronautics from February 1920 to August 1926, with General Niessel and M. Laurent-Eynac, at Le Bourget, July 14, 1924, greeting Lieutenant Smith, the American aviator who made the first round-the-world flight, in a Douglas BT-2 World Cruiser.

Organization of Military Aviation as of July 1, 1924

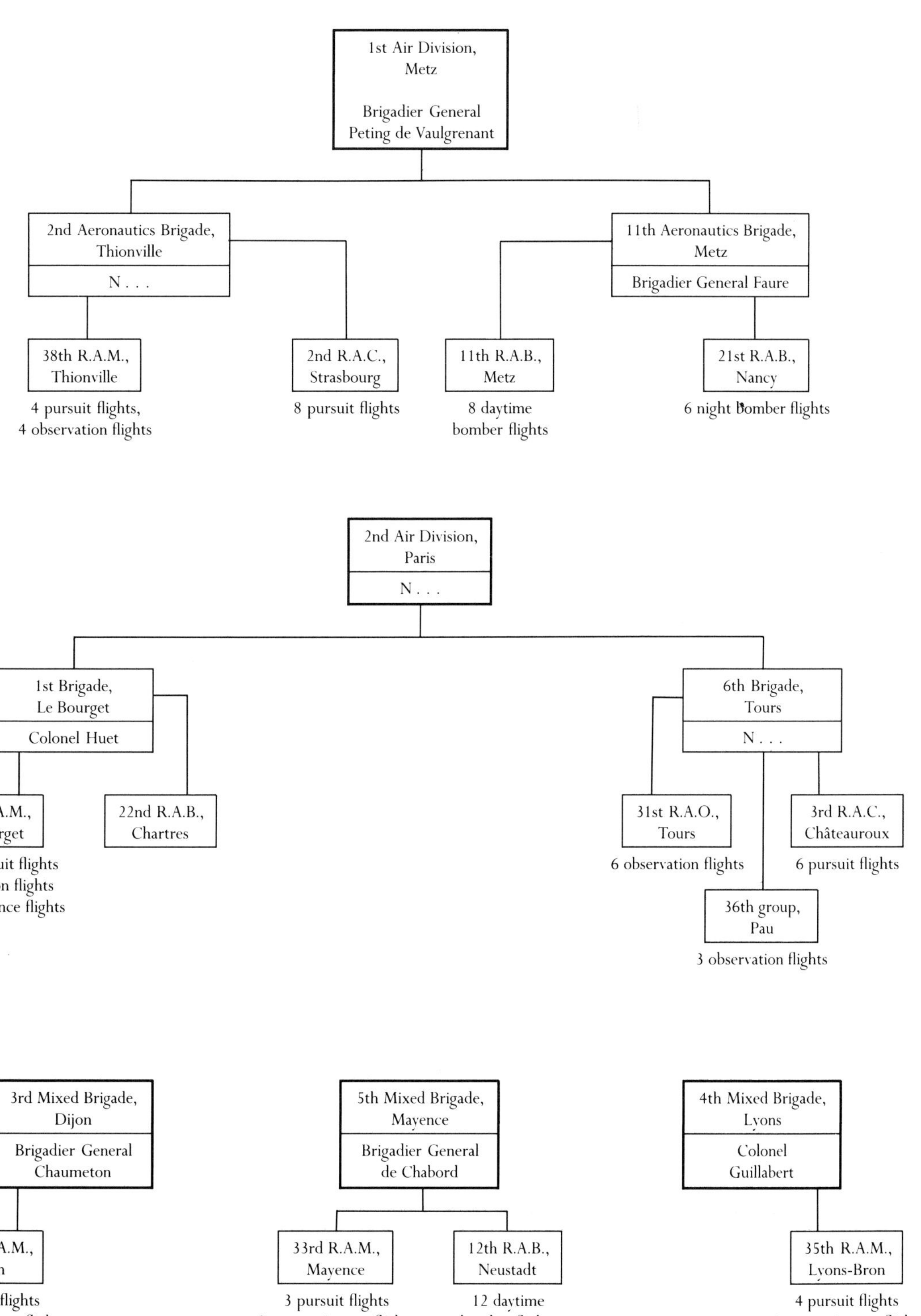

manufactured that were out of date when they arrived at the units.

Furthermore, that organization placed the S.T.Aé. at the very center of everything. It issued the orders and paid the bills. Soon it took up the practice of making all the decisions itself. It let the manufacturers assume the responsibilities but was not sparing in its criticism of them. Naturally the manufacturers had a tendency to take shelter behind the S.T.Aé. and abandon any innovation deemed too bold.

For these reasons aeronautical manufacturing remained at the handicraft stage and had to have government aid to survive. That aid manifested itself in the very conditions in which production contracts were carried out.

When the S.T.Aé. adopted a prototype the minister placed an order, usually for a small production run. That order was not given to the manufacturer responsible for the prototype but divided among several aircraft manufacturers. It is understandable that under these conditions unit prices remained high. In a total order for 200 planes, for example, four companies participated, one making 30 planes, the second, 80, the third, 50, and the last, 40.

Although such a manufacturing procedure made it impossible to reduce costs, the manufacturers were satisfied with it since the S.T.Aé. asked them to set their price per plane and gave them a 10 percent profit calculated on that price. It was thus in the interest of the aircraft companies to operate in complicated, expensive ways.

The result of these successive small production runs for military aeronautics was an increase in the types of planes in service.

Thus the 1,858 planes in service or on order in February 1926 were divided among sixteen different types:

Pursuit (fighter) planes: 350 Nieuport 29's (300-horsepower Hispano engine), 70 Spad 81's (500-horsepower Hispano engine), 40 Dewoitines (300-horsepower Hispano engine).

Bombers: 400 Breguet 19's (400-horsepower Lorraine engine) and 340 Breguet 19's (480-horsepower Renault engine).

Night bombers: 50 Lioré-Oliviers (Jupiter engine), 60 Breguet XVI Bn 2's, 40 Farman 60's (Salmson engine), 60 Farman 60's (CUZ 9 engine), 15 Farman 60's (CM 9 engine), and 2 Farman 60's (Jupiter engine).

Observation planes: 196 Breguet XIV A 2's (300-horsepower Renault engine), 135 Potez 15's (400-horsepower Lorraine engine), 40 Potez 25's (450-horsepower Lorraine engine), 40 Potez 25's (Jupiter engine), and 20 Potez 25's (Salmson engine).

In 1927, on the eve of the establishment of the Air Ministry, there were on order 22 types of new planes (3 for observation, 2 for daytime bombing, 3 for night bombing, 7 for pursuit, plus 2 multi-seater planes—the Amiot 140 and the Aviméta) and 5 for the schools and for training (Morane 130, 132, and 138, Caudron 59, and Hanriot 32). None of these airplanes, except the Wibault 7 and the Aviméta, both of metal, had extra-lift wingflaps or variable-speed propellers.

The increase in the different types of planes in service in the units posed difficult maintenance problems. The mechanics of the unit had not had enough training to adapt themselves to all these models of engines and airframes. The stocking of spare parts was particularly complicated. Many planes stayed immobilized on the runway. The situation in 1926 was such that the very mobility of military aviation was compromised. General H. Dumesnil, director of Aeronautics, wrote to the minister of war in February 1926: "If the errors of the present continue, in two years military aviation will have lost all capability of movement, all possibility of instant action, that is, immediate effective action at the beginning of a campaign. Far from being an offensive element, it will even be deprived of the mobility indispensable to combating the incursions of enemy bombers."

Personnel

Shortages of personnel on active duty were strongly felt within the formations. While awaiting

A Nieuport-Delage 29 of the 3rd Flight (SPA 103) of the 2nd Pursuit Regiment in a hangar at Strasbourg in 1923.

The Nieuport-Delage 29, designed in 1918, was a remarkable fighter plane. It was chosen to reequip French fighter units in 1919. Here, a Nieuport-Delage 29 of the 7th Flight (SPA 93) of the 33rd Mixed Regiment at Mayence about 1924.

A LeO 20 BN 3.

The prototype of the Dewoitine D 12. Derived from the D 1, this plane, although rated third in the 1923 competition, was not ordered.

A Potez 25, the most manufactured and most exported French plane from 1919 to 1939, with 2,400 supplied to French military aviation starting in 1926 and 1,500 exported to a score of countries. It was also manufactured under license. It had the peculiarity of being equipped with several different engines: the 450-horsepower Lorraine, the 520-horsepower Salmson, the Renault, the Hispano-Suiza, etc. Here, a Potez 25 with a Lorraine engine photographed at Neustadt in 1928.

the development of a more dynamic recruiting policy, the 12th Directorate decided to rely on draftees and the reserve, while maintaining a certain level of enlistments. In the case of flying personnel, these enlistees, student pilots, were recruited after finishing secondary school. After a brief examination on general knowledge and a medical exam they signed up for four or five years and received an enlistment bonus of 1,000 or 2,000 francs. After a period of military training in the regiment they were licensed as pilots at the Ecole Pratique for aviation at Istres. Upon completing this training session they were assigned directly to a unit. Since the number recruited was clearly insufficient, it was necessary to train pilots from among those drafted. To get a certain amount of work from these pilots during their military service the 12th Directorate set up a system of pilot training scholarships to train future draftees before they were called up.

The applicant for a pilot training scholarship had to pass a general education examination midway between the elementary and secondary school levels as well as a medical exam and commit himself to doing his military service as a military pilot.

He then learned to fly in a civilian pilot training center. In 1922 there were six of these: Buc, Orly, Le Crotoy, Mourmelon, Angers, and Nîmes. During his training periods he received room and board and accident insurance at government expense. When he entered the service, after basic training he was immediately employed in a flying unit. Later the recipients of these scholarships were required to receive supplementary training at Istres.

In 1920, 200 pilots were trained by these centers. The cost of training per pilot came to 26,400 francs. These pilots were intended to continue their training in the reserves, but the results depended heavily on their diligence and still more on the grants allocated for this program which were never enough.

In spite of its importance, the system of pilot training scholarships did not make it possible to recruit the desired number of personnel. This was due in part to the strictness of the medical screening and in part to the low esteem for aviation, which was reputed to be dangerous, among the general public.

As for the reserves, their training was still weak. A total of 800 pilots were enrolled in those centers, but their average flying time in 1925 was only between 7 and 30 hours a year.

There were very few civilian pilots. Whereas before 1914 the Aero Club of France had issued 350 pilot's licenses a year, in the 1920s the number of licenses issued had dropped to about 20.

Furthermore, in spite of numerous discussions in Parliament, the status of the flying personnel had not been clearly defined. It was not until the decree of 1925 that there was a precise definition of the licenses that granted the status of pilot, the conditions to be met in order to continue to enjoy it, and the rights and privileges pertaining to it. Even so, not all of these problems were resolved, and they were not resolved until the passage of the act of 1928.

The same type of difficulties was encountered in recruiting mechanics. There was a school for specialized mechanics in Bordeaux, but it was not large enough to train the 350 mechanics a year that were thought necessary. Occupational training was provided in civilian institutions.

These centers, three in 1922—the Hanriot School in Courbevoie, the School of the Lyonnaise Union of Air Combatants in Lyons, and the Military Mechanics' School in Nîmes—gave a one-year course providing the technical training and preparation needed to pass the examination for a mechanic's license. Young men who wanted to take the courses at these schools had to sign up for an enlistment period of four or five years as military airmen. On signing up they were given a bonus of 1,000 or 2,000 francs, depending on the length of their enlistment. Once they received their license they were entitled to the pay of a licensed mechanic. In order to have them reenlist much was made of the possibility of enjoying retirement after fifteen years' service and of the fact that they would have no difficulty in finding a job in the aeronautics or automotive industry in view of the value of the training they would have received and the experience that they would have gained in the service.

To satisfy the demand, these civilian schools were increased to five in 1923. It was only at the urging of a member of Parliament, M. Riché, that the Mechanics' School at Rochefort was established in 1926.

But the basic problem of recruitment was that of pay. In spite of the restrictions that were placed on him, the military mechanic found that less qualified civilian employees under his orders received higher pay. It would be a long time before an equitable solution was found for this problem.

The officer corps also experienced recruiting problems. The bad reputation of military aviation, a "daredevil" service where the risks were great, the poor prospects of advancement faced by young officers entering the corps because of the very large number of lieutenants that rose from the ranks during the war, and the difficulties encountered in passing the medical exam all help to explain the relative lack of enthusiasm manifested for the new service by students graduating from the major schools. Nevertheless, after 1921 traditional recruiting was resumed.

From 1921 to 1928 the majority of the second lieutenants commissioned came from the major military schools (64% of the total), naturally with a marked predominance of graduates of Saint Cyr (46% of the total). Officers who came from noncommissioned officers' schools represented 21%, and those who rose from the ranks, 13%. It will be noted that the latter were in the minority. Starting in 1925 some were recruited from the major civilian schools, but this recruitment remained very small until 1929.

The aeronautical instruction of the officers coming from the major schools was provided by the Ecole Militaire et d'Application de l'Aéronautique in Versailles (the School of Military and Applied Aeronautics), the new name given after 1925 to the Center for Aeronautic Studies created in 1921. This specialized instruction was confirmed by the observer's certificate issued at Villacoublay.

Upon completing the training period in Versailles the air officers were licensed as pilots at Avord. The school at Versailles also provided the training for noncommissioned officers passing the examination for officer trainees.

In spite of the recruiting policy adopted, the officer corps developed slowly and hence aged very rapidly. This phenomenon was particularly noticeable until 1936, and its effects made themselves felt as late as the beginning of the Second World War.

Aerial Activity

The aerial activity on which the military high command had insisted from 1919 on continued to develop under conditions close to those of 1919 and 1920.

To be sure, the airlines were turned over to civilians, but the Directorate of Aeronautics encouraged distance flights, often group flights, for those in the regiments. Certain exceptional trips made by individual crews became pioneer flights followed with great interest by the general public.

To these were added the inevitable maneuvers, much closer in character to military operations. Many trophies offered by private patrons and often restricted to the military maintained the spirit of competition. Finally, yielding to the taste for aviation meets, which were very much in style from 1925 to 1938, the military command organized air shows at Vincennes, Villacoublay, or Le Bourget. Large-scale flybys, in which several regiments took part, aroused popular enthusiasm.

In 1923 the minister of war regulated the participation of the military in air meets organized by civilian authorities. For the military events at such meetings the aviators were considered as being on duty, flew in their own service airplane, and were in uniform; for the other events they were on leave, flew at their own risk, and wore civilian clothes.

In fact, all the aviators of the time who took part in these shows were military men, either on active duty or in the reserves.

Pioneer Flights

Unquestionably the greatest success was enjoyed by the pioneer flights. They were very numerous, and it is difficult to mention all of them.

1922–1924

Lieutenant Pelletier-Doisy and his mechanic, Corporal Buffart, flew from Tunis to Paris. This flight was merely a preparation for the big flight that was to make Pelletier-Doisy, nicknamed "Pivolo," and his mechanic, Besin, famous in 1924. Using a Breguet XIX with a 400-horsepower Lorraine engine he flew from Paris to Tokyo between April 24 and June 9, 1924. On the way, as luck would have it, he wrecked his plane at Shanghai, and it was on a Chinese Breguet XIV that he completed his trip.

A little off the beaten path, Warrant Officer Bonnet distinguished himself by setting the world speed record on December 11, 1924, at 448 kilometers per hour in a Bernard-Ferbois plane. That record held until it was beaten by the American aviator James H. Doolittle eight years later in 1932.

1925

Colonel de Goÿs, bombing ace of 1914–1918, with Vuillemin, Pelletier-Doisy, and Dagnaux, flew from Paris to Niamey in French West Africa in two Blériot 115 four-engined planes. In the course of this exploit, taking off from Niamey Lieutenant Colonel Vuillemin suffered a serious accident in which he was severely injured.

February 3, 1925

Captain Lemaître and Captain Arrachart established the first officially confirmed distance record between Paris and Villa Cisneros in Spanish Western Sahara (3,166 kilometers in 24 hours 30 minutes) in a Breguet XIX. They went on to Dakar and returned via Timbuktu to Paris on March 24.

Captain Arrachart and the engineer Carol accomplished a Paris-Constantinople-Moscow-Paris flight in three days in a Potez 25.

1926

Pelletier-Doisy and Carol went from Paris to Peking (10,155 kilometers) via Siberia in 63 hours in a Breguet XIX.

Then came a real battle among French aviators for the world distance record.

A Breguet XIX A 2. This remarkable airplane was used in French military aviation beginning in 1923. A total of 1,000 A 2's and B 2's were ordered. Many of the planes were also exported, and they were manufactured under license in five countries. Here, Breguet XIX's on maneuvers at Chartres.

Lieutenant Colonel Vuillemin and Captain Dagnaux at the controls of the four-engined Blériot 115 Jean Casale, *which they flew from Paris to Niamey, French West Africa (Niger), from January 18 to February 7, 1925. The flight was made together with another Blériot 115, the* Roland Garros, *flown by Colonel de Goÿs, the commander of the expedition, and Captain Pelletier-Doisy. The* Jean Casale *crashed as it took off from Niamey, and Lieutenant Colonel Vuillemin was seriously injured. The radioman, Vandelle, was killed. The mechanic, Knecht, was unharmed, and Captain Dagnaux suffered a broken artificial leg as his worst injury.*

Colonel de Goÿs in front of the Roland Garros *between Warrant Officer Besin, the mechanic, and Captain Pelletier-Doisy.*

June 26–27, 1926

The Arrachart brothers covered 4,305 kilometers between Paris and Basra, Iraq, in a Potez 25 with a 550-horsepower Renault engine.

July 14–15

Captain Girier and Lieutenant Dordilly raised the record to 4,716 kilometers, Paris-Omsk, with a Breguet XIX.

The record was raised to 5,174 kilometers by Captain Weiser and Lieutenant Challe from Paris to Bandar Abbas, Iran, in a Breguet XIX.

Late in 1926 came the flight from Marseilles to Tananarive, Madagascar, by Lieutenant Commander Bernard and de Bougault. About the same time Dagnaux linked Paris to Tananarive in a Breguet XIX.

Dieudonné Costes and Captain Rignot in turn pushed the distance record up to 5,396 kilometers from Paris to Jask, on the Persian coast, again in a Breguet XIX, with a 500-horsepower engine. They continued on to Calcutta and returned by way of Delhi.

Unfortunately, two dramas unfolded in close succession in the midst of this brilliant series of successes. On May 5, 1927, Captain Saint-Roman, Mouneyres, and Petit disappeared while crossing the South Atlantic in a Farman Goliath with twin 450-horsepower Lorraine engines. On May 8 Charles Nungesser, the great ace of 1918, and his navigator, Coli, disappeared while attempting to cross the North Atlantic in a Levasseur with a 450-horsepower Lorraine engine.

On October 10 Costes and Lieutenant Commander Joseph Le Brix, his navigator, landed at Saint Louis in Senegal in their Breguet XIX called *Nungesser-Coli*. On October 14 they went on to Natal, Brazil, completing the first nonstop crossing of the South Atlantic. They then made a goodwill tour, flying all around South America, then on to New York and San Francisco, where their plane was loaded on a ship and carried by sea to Tokyo. They completed their round-the-world trip in Paris, where they were given a triumphal welcome on April 14, 1928.

October 11–21, 1927

Challe and Rapin in a Potez 25 linked Paris to Tananarive in ten days and made the return trip.

These long-distance pioneer flights made big headlines in the newspapers of the day, but they should not cause us to forget the many trips made in the various regiments. In 1922 over 60 flights of more than 1,000 kilometers were made; in 1923, 28 flights exceeded 1,500 kilometers; and from 1925 to 1928 there were over 50 flights of over 3,000 kilometers. In one regiment alone—the 34th of Le Bourget under Colonel Weiss—eight flights of over 3,000 kilometers were made in 1926, and the distance record was broken twice.

These exploits demonstrated the abilities of the most gifted French air crews, but one must not forget that similar or even greater exploits were accomplished by pilots abroad. Thus in 1924 the first round-the-world flight was attempted by four special Douglas military planes and completed by two of them. The flight included crossings of the Pacific (via the Aleutians) and of the Atlantic with intermediate stops. Then there was the nonstop crossing of the Atlantic by Charles Lindberg in May 1927 in a monoplane of only 220 horsepower. The fact is that French aviation techniques were making little progress. Flight equipment (P.S.V., or blind flying) was usually lacking. Since the second member of the crew was generally a mechanic and not a navigator, everything depended on the pilot's ability. When it was necessary to accomplish long ocean crossings the crews began to include a navigator (Coli, Le Brix, Bellonte), for in military aeronautics no one knew how to use a sextant.

All these pioneer flights and aviation records, which continued after 1928, kept public opinion in France under the illusion that it ranked first in world aviation.

Maneuvers and Competitions

Nearly every year the crews also participated in military maneuvers together with the ground forces. They rarely went beyond the narrow bounds of cooperation. However, these maneuvers sometimes provided an opportunity to test new equipment or new tactics.

The trophies placed each year in competition between the crews of various regiments helped maintain a spirit of friendly rivalry. Among the best known were the Michelin Cup, the Zenith Cup, the Lamblin Cup, and the Breguet Cup. The rules for the competitions were adapted to the goal pursued: trials of speed, precision bombing, distance, etc.

To these national cups were added foreign competitions, such as the military aviators' competition in Spain in 1923 (in which a French success got the industry an order for 40 Breguet planes) or, later, the Brussels competition (where Doret won in 1930 in a Dewoitine 27) or the Zurich competition.

Air Meets

From a very early date military aviators participated in aerial festivals. These were mostly open to the public, whose favor toward aviation was a desideratum.

A big air meet took place at Buc as early as 1920. It included civilian or military races or competitions, balloon trials, and a demonstration of "aerial warfare." Until 1928 it was primarily a matter of participation in these meetings. For example, Pinsard engaged in mock combats with the Belgian aviator Van Cothem. After the creation of the Air Ministry it became usual to put on "national aviation days" at which military tests and flybys headed the bill.

Captain Girier and Lieutenant Dordilly before their departure on the Paris-Omsk flight —4,716 kilometers nonstop.

Major Dagnaux and his mechanic, Corporal Dufer, during the technical preparation of the Breguet XIX which they flew from Paris to Tananarive, Madagascar, from November 11, 1926, to January 21, 1927.

Morocco

As already noted, as early as 1919 military aeronautics very quickly became engaged in operations in Syria and in Morocco. The fighting continued in these two territories, and aviation would continue to play a very important part, which marked it for a long time.

The ʿAbd al-Karīm affair began in 1921, first in Spanish Morocco, then in the Rif, where the Spanish forces allowed themselves to be dominated.

Starting in 1923 raids launched from the Rif threatened French Morocco. Marshal Lyautey, occupied with the task of pacification in various parts of Morocco (the Berbers in the Middle Atlas region, the Tafilalt zone on the border of Algeria and Morocco), placed some surveillance posts on the Rif frontiers and asked Paris for a few troops to strengthen his forces. He was turned down.

In 1925 the rebel leader ʿAbd al-Karīm attacked the French frontier posts; it was necessary to make a response. The French government—at that time the Leftist Cartel—sent very large forces, much too large in Lyautey's opinion, since he wanted to act primarily politically and not brutally, so as not to alienate the people. The number of ground troops stationed in Morocco reached 150,000, or a fourth of the French army! A very large proportion of these were colonial troops—North Africans and blacks. The 37th Air Regiment was also established in Morocco.

The Rif affair was practically settled in 1926, and the "Taza pocket" was reduced in 1927. But the pacification of Morocco could not be completed until the reduction of the zone of dissidence constituted by the Tafilalt on the border of Morocco and Algeria. That region was largely unknown. On the "map" available in 1925 there was only one recognized route, that taken by Charles de Foucauld in 1883–1884. It was long-range aviation—with Goliath F 60 twin-engined planes—that provided photographic coverage of that area, as it did, in fact, for all of Morocco. In 1932 when, after patient political preparation, French troops entered the Tafilalt region they had for their use the excellent map that the Geographic Service had had time to prepare from aerial photographs.

The conquest of the Tafilalt in 1932 cost the French only a single army officer and a single aviation officer, Lieutenant Hennequin, who was brought down by firearms used from the ground by the enemy.

The Air Force in Morocco

At the start of its service in Morocco the 37th Air Regiment comprised some 10 flights: Breguet XIV (later, after 1928, Breguet XIX), Potez 25 T.O.E., and Farman F 50 (later, Farman F 60).

The commanding officer of the regiment was a colonel from 1925 to 1929; he was at the same time in command of the air forces in Morocco. In 1929 a general was placed at the head of the regiment, and he had the title of Air Commander in Morocco.

At that time there were 35 1/2 flights overseas: 4 1/2 in French West Africa, 8 in Algeria, 5 in Tunisia, 10 in Morocco, and 8 in Syria. These represented a fourth of the units of French military aeronautics; an eighth of the aeronautics personnel were in the field in Morocco or in Syria.

The Missions

In Morocco there was no enemy in the air; only enemy firearms on the ground presented risks, and there were no antiaircraft weapons strictly speaking. Under these conditions the air forces were used exclusively in direct support of the ground troops: photographic coverage (mentioned above), observation, support of infantry, and liaison with isolated posts.

Observation

Observation provided information about the enemy. Oblique photographs were used to prepare for the progress of the troops on the ground, and groups of photographs were often given to column leaders to supplement the still incomplete maps. The enemy's advantage in being familiar with the

The Spad 81 of the 5th Flight (SPA 65) of the 2nd RAC, photographed durng an air show.

Lieutenant Gérardot and Captain Cornillon upon their arrival at Rayak, Lebanon, on September 14, 1927, the turnaround point of a flight made in a Breguet XIX on the route Paris-Bucharest-Rayak-Bucharest-Paris to try out radio communication and navigation over long distances. The Gérardot-Cornillon crew succeeded in many pioneer flights of this type between 1925 and 1928. Lieutenant Gérardot, a group commander, was captured in September 1939 and escaped in 1940 together with Major Plou (later a general). In 1943 he was at the head of the 1st CAF (French Air Corps), and in 1946 he became the Air Force Chief of Staff. He was famous for his impassioned defense of aeronautics. He died in 1980.

A Breguet XIV A 2 of the 4th Flight of the 37th Aviation Regiment in a group flight over Meknes, Morocco

terrain was thus largely compensated for. Artillery ranging was not practiced for the sole reason that only two 145-millimeter long-range guns were available in Morocco; the artillerymen had to fire at their targets without the aid of the planes.

Support of Infantry

Infantry support provided reconnaissance for columns, which prevented surprises; the airplane went ahead to look "behind the hill." Planes sometimes participated in the action, making attacks on the ground which chiefly affected morale.

Liaison with Isolated Posts

The airplane was found to be very valuable for carrying the mail and delivering orders from the command to isolated posts, which were generally without any radio contact. If it was possible, the airplane landed nearby; otherwise, it dropped weighted messages. The post answered the communication by means of a coded system of groundstrips which made it possible to give the essentials. The planes were equipped with radio, but radio reception on the ground was available only to relatively high levels of command. Sometimes the planes used a message pick-up by an acrobatic technique that made landing unnecessary. Flying at low altitude over mountain posts involved risks. Captain Mézergues, in fact, was killed by a bullet when flying in this fashion.

The support airplane was a powerful device for sustaining morale. On the other hand, attempts at bombing with 10-kilogram bombs had little effect against a widely dispersed enemy on the ground. The F 60's, originally intended for this type of mission, were found to be much more valuable for long-range reconnaissance and photographic coverage.

The Men

The important task carried out by the air forces in Morocco showed them to be men of action. Many great military leaders of the future served in Morocco as aviators, for example, Colonel Odic, Major d'Astier de la Vigerie, and Major Armengaud.

A Breguet XIV which crashed in Morocco. The plane belonged to the 1st Flight of the Morocco Regiment in 1920, based at Fez.

Captains Mézergues and Hennequin were both killed in operations. All of these and many others were marked by this overly specialized type of aviation, in which the technical level of the planes and their use en masse were of little interest.

Their flying, however, was particularly appreciated by the troops on the ground, who forged solid bonds of friendship with their aviator friends, whose generous exploits they admired.

In Syria pacification operations very similar to those in Morocco were conducted during the same period. These took place in the Jebel Druz region and were performed by the 38th Air Regiment.

It should be mentioned that the British RAF was conducting the same type of operations in British territories with aviation principles that hardly differed at all from those of the French. This was due to Air Marshal Sir Hugh Trenchard and was known as "air control," which aimed at reducing the heavy territorial forces of the army by using aerial police actions.

Safety

From 1920 to 1928 this aerial activity—we have just seen the general conditions under which it was carried on—was reflected in a relatively high and steadily increasing number of flying hours. From a total of 163,000 hours in 1924 it reached 195,000 hours in 1927 and 234,000 in 1929. On the average this represented a little under 100 hours per pilot in 1924 and 130 in 1929.

These figures—the totals as well as the averages—tend to obscure the reality. The flying hours were distributed very unequally among the aviators. Some pilots flew a great deal, others not very much. After 1,000 hours a flier was considered extremely experienced. But some pilots, flying fanatics, ran up much larger totals. The name Vuillemin immediately comes to mind, but he was not the only one. Captain Gérardot, for example, who got into aviation in 1919, passed the 4,000-hour mark in 1930.

While the number of flying hours increased, serious accidents reached a ceiling at a level a little below 100 a year. Of course, it was a cause for rejoicing when the number of flying hours per accident increased (1 accident per 2,000 hours in 1924, as opposed to 1 accident per 2,633 hours in 1929). But, apart from the fact that the improvement was very slow in coming, the risks were still too great. They were connected with the materiel of the period but were also aggravated by human error.

Safety improvements sought by the air command, as we shall see in the next chapter, did not become significant until 1929, the date of the creation of the Central Air Safety Service, which analyzed the causes of accidents and applied remedies.

These accidents left traces, either among the victims, in case of injury, for example, or, in case of death, among their beneficiaries and dependents. It thus seemed indispensable to protect flying personnel by a special statute. The decree of February 19, 1925, made a start toward a solution by clearly defining the conditions to be met in order to be classified P.N. (*personnel navigant*/flying personnel), as well as the tests to be passed in order to retain the advantages of the statute.

In fact, it was the law passed in 1928 that was to bring a valid solution to the problem, so much so that its provisions, which remained in force until the passing of the recent personnel statute, were

A short landing of a Morane-Saulnier 138.

The crash of a Nieuport-Delage 29.

retained in the latter document. Without going into detail on the provisions of the law, intended originally to apply only to military personnel but later extended to civilian aviators, it should be noted that it created leaves of absence for flying personnel that could run from one to five years and the Aeronautic Reserve Fund, paid into like an insurance fund and intended to idemnify the victims of aerial accidents or their beneficiaries.

The Debate on Aviation Policy and Principles

The aviators' aeronautical activities also imposed on them the obligation to reflect on the employment of their service in war. That reflection very soon manifested itself in a debate on doctrine—aviation policy and principles—which became public beginning in 1924.

This debate was not new. Even during the First World War the creation of the air division, capable of carrying out individual actions, had evoked many criticisms. In the same way the theory of the necessity of acquiring air superiority before launching a ground attack did not attract universal approval. It was an old debate, then, and a universal one. All the armies of the world were engaged in it at the same time.

In Italy the major exponent of air power, Giulio Douhet, had to undergo many trials before seeing his theories taken into consideration.

In the United States William E. (Billy) Mitchell, apostle of the new ideas, fell into disgrace and was reduced from brigadier general to colonel (which was possible under the statutes) because he had demonstrated, by sinking the former German cruiser *Ostfriesland*, that a ship was vulnerable to air attack. Later, following a press campaign that he conducted in typical American style, he was discharged from the army without a pension. He died sadly in 1936, less than five years before the

A Breguet XIX on its back.

The LeO 20 BN 3 in the Hall of Aeronautics exhibition. This airplane, winner of the BN 3 competition in 1926, began to reach the units in May 1928.

correctness of his ideas on aviation was demonstrated at Pearl Harbor.

In England, too, Sir Hugh Trenchard had to engage in some hard battles in order to have the RAF made independent. He succeeded in his goal largely because the first air battle of England, fought by the Germans in 1917, had made the country understand the importance of having the power to defend itself in the air and also to destroy the enemy's offensive power on the ground.

It was undoubtedly a debate of ideas but also a defense of established privileges. Whether in Italy, England, the United States, or France, the land and sea services fought a bitter fight to keep the latest service within their own organizations. Of course, they asserted that in so doing they were working in the interest of aviation itself. Aviation would have no chance to develop if it were cut off from its reason for being—the battle on land or at sea. This was asserted forcefully in France by the ministers of war and of the navy after the death of General Buat. For them aviation was, and had to remain, a weapon at the service of the major branches of the armed forces, the infantry, cavalry, and artillery.

The essential role of the air service was observation or artillery ranging for the benefit of the ground units. Fighter planes were useful only to provide protection for the observers. As for bombers, their use could be foreseen only in close connection with ground operations, either on the battlefield or in the areas immediately to the rear.

To the aviators, on the other hand, the experience of the last war had proved the importance of the preliminary air battle. On the outcome of that initial battle might depend the outcome of the war itself. Moreover, the theory of ground fronts rendered inviolable by fortification reinforced their position. Since fighting on the ground was to be rendered practically impossible, the battle in the air assumed first place. In addition, the use of the air would enable the belligerents to deal each other decisive blows. Without realizing it, with this very logical reasoning, which was to be developed at length by Douhet, they were furnishing a major argument to their adversaries, who did not fail to raise the specter of aerochemical warfare before the public.

The impact of that argument was not negligible at a time when France, poorly recovered from the terrible slaughter that it had experienced in the First World War, was resolutely pacifist. French statesman Aristide Briand, "the apostle of peace," was its great spokesman. "Cannons to the rear, no more war ever" was his motto and his act of faith.

The very definition of bombing, characterized as an offensive weapon, was enough to discredit it. This would be exploited later at the disarmament conferences, where the chiefs of staff of the army and the navy, anxious to preserve the totality of their respective services, found themselves in agreement in conceding that a great reduction in the aerial bombing force was possible and that it would not greatly impair France's military potential.

To be sure, at the beginning of the 1920s a bomber force that was rather large for the time was allowed to develop within the air division. But that air division did not have the purpose of conducting independent actions. At the time when Germany was still feared, the division's primary role was to cover a possible mobilization and to support the first ground operations carried out by the French army of the Rhine.

One must again emphasize that it was not only aviation policy that was at issue. Propaganda during the war had led, as we have seen, to the appearance of articles in the press on the aviators and especially on the aces. Side by side with the exaltation of their warlike exploits, their aerial combats, the journalists often dwelt on their good fortune. After shooting down enemy planes they enjoyed the "high life" at Maxim's. That, of course, was the case with only a small minority. The majority of the aviators were serious, competent, disciplined soldiers. Their life in aviation exposed them to certain risks, and they were far from being in "cushy" jobs. All this did not alter the fact that there was an unfavorable bias against both aviation and the aviators.

This feeling did not lead to personal antagonisms. The infantrymen or the artillerymen who had occasion to work with the aviators appreciated them. But isn't there always a good priest, even for the most notorious anticlericals, and a good general for the antimilitarists? Within the military establishment there was often a phenomenon of rejection of the new service. This was very clear at the military academy of Saint Cyr, where the aviation volunteers were held in low esteem. General Bailly said in an interview that at the Special Military School, in his second year when he was "gradaille d'or" (the term designating second-year students, who had a fictitious grade of "noncommissioned officer"), the general who was commandant of the school reproached him for wanting to go into aviation. Similarly, he confided that one of his comrades had received the following report: "A mediocre fellow; in a pinch he could be put into aviation." Another officer cited the advice of his instructor at Saint Cyr, who told him that: "It just isn't possible! You have every qualification to make an excellent officer; you don't want to join that bunch of hoodlums."

These few examples—and they could be multiplied—show quite well the mentality with which the problem of aviation was approached in high military circles.

It is understandable that in these circumstances many aviators wished that aviation, made independent of war, would be joined with the Technical Aeronautical Services in an Air Ministry. Though this was certainly their desire, it was, nevertheless, not clearly formulated by members of the military aeronautics forces. Although they were considered undisciplined, they had too much regard for hierarchical order to express such ideas publicly.

This vaguely diffused desire for independence was probably made known to old comrades who had served in aviation units during the war. Some of them occupied important positions in industry; others were members of Parliament. They were certainly heedful of the opinions expressed by the

A Farman Goliath equipped with Jupiter engines.

military specialists, but the fight that brought about the creation of the Air Ministry was due to other causes.

The doctrine of the integral air force was, in fact, an old idea developed during the First World War in connection with the many criticisms made of the organizations of that period. The polemics on the subject developed mostly after the disappearance of the Undersecretariat of Aeronautics and the scattering of its parts over several ministries.

The arguments advanced in favor of the single Air Ministry were varied, but they always put rank and efficiency in the foreground. Rank was an important factor. It appeared abnormal that such large-scale activities as those of the air force should be entrusted to a simple directorate on a par with the "mutual insurance directorate and the stud farm directorate."

Moreover, many had been shocked at the association of aeronautical activities with various ministries in succession. One writer emphasized "the surprising effect of aeronautics coupled yesterday with public works, today with commerce, and perhaps tomorrow established as a satellite of agriculture."

The need for efficiency was also brought to the fore to justify the change in structures. If one minister directed the entire gamut of aeronautical activities in the nation he would receive constant cooperation from those responsible for technique and from those responsible for its employment. He would also be able to reform improper methods in use in the aeronautics industry. Finally, when defending his budget in the Chamber of Deputies he would be better able to get a big increase in appropriations.

These arguments, valid as they may have been, undoubtedly would not have sufficed to persuade public opinion, Parliament, or the government had there not been, in the late 1920s, a crisis in aeronautics.

That crisis was at first an industrial one due in

part to the disastrous organization of the technical and administrative networks that were mentioned earlier and in part also to the fact that the manufacturers, depending 90 percent on the government, had acquired a relief mentality that blocked initiative.

As a direct consequence of this crisis French technology regressed, and that regression became flagrant by 1927. Whereas in 1925 the majority of world aviation records was held by France, in 1927 of the 64 records confirmed by the International Aeronautical Federation 23 were held by Germany, 19 by the United States, and only 14 by France.

In his report to the finance committee concerned with examining the aeronautics budget for 1926 Deputy H. Paté said of the industry: "The situation of the French aeronautics industry, which we might have called unhealthy and precarious last year, is neither healthier nor more stable this year." He recommended a change as soon as possible to an Air Ministry, the only thing capable of avoiding delays and duplicated efforts.

In 1928 there was more and more open discussion of the crisis in French aeronautics. The author of the report on the aeronautics budget in 1928 began his report with the words, "French aeronautics is very sick."

One of the fiercest opponents of the creation of an Air Ministry was M. Bokanowski, the minister of commerce, who had under him all the research and production services and who considered that an Air Ministry had, in effect, been realized. An unforeseen incident forced the outcome: on September 2, 1928, Bokanowski was the victim of an aviation accident at the takeoff of the plane—a Spad limousine—that was to take him to Paris after a ceremony he had presided over in Lyons. The two crew members died with him. On September 14 the Air Ministry was created by decree, the personal intervention of President Raymond Poincaré having made it possible at last to reach this long-awaited decision.

CHAPTER III

The Independence and Affirmation of the French Air Force (1928–1936)

Difficult Beginnings (1928–1933)

The personality of the first minister of air, M. Laurent-Eynac, could not be called into question and never was. An aviator in the First World War, former Undersecretary of State for Aeronautics, and chairman of the Aeronautics Committee of the Chamber of Deputies, he was extremely well informed on aviation problems. On the other hand, from its creation the Air Ministry was the object of a systematic opposition on the part of the Ministry of War and the Ministry of the Navy.

At the same time, unusually violent campaigns were launched using all types of arguments, including the lowest, to denounce the crime of lèse majesté that had been committed. The most interesting document of that campaign is incontestably the article that appeared in a very serious journal, the *Revue des Deux Mondes*, from the pen of a "high personage of great competence" who did not feel that he should sign his—to say the least—extreme utterances in regard to the Air Ministry, aviation, and aviators.

Entitled "A Case of Collective Madness: The Creation of the Air Ministry," the article developed a series of operational and technical arguments opposed to the theory of an integral (or complete) air force, all of which would be forcefully contradicted by the experience of the next war. To these arguments were added certain assertions, which the deputy Etienne Riché said, in answering them in the journal *Les Ailes* (Wings), "would provoke pure, happy laughter in the flights."

The statements in the article, ridiculous as they were, were nevertheless indicative of a state of mind that was, at the very least, distressing.

According to the "anonymous" author writing in the *Revue des Deux Mondes*, the creation of "an independent Air Force" removed it from "the traditions of discipline, moderation, and political reserve of the two old armies of land and sea." Giving "independence to a professional army, an army of staff officers, an army whose taste for the risk of adventure is general, an army composed of individualists" made the Air Force "the army of coups d'etat par excellence."

This astonishing language, as noted above, revealed a state of mind. Reading it gives a better notion of the profound lack of understanding which has plagued military aviation almost from one end of its history to the other. It also makes it easier to understand the fact that the bills estab-

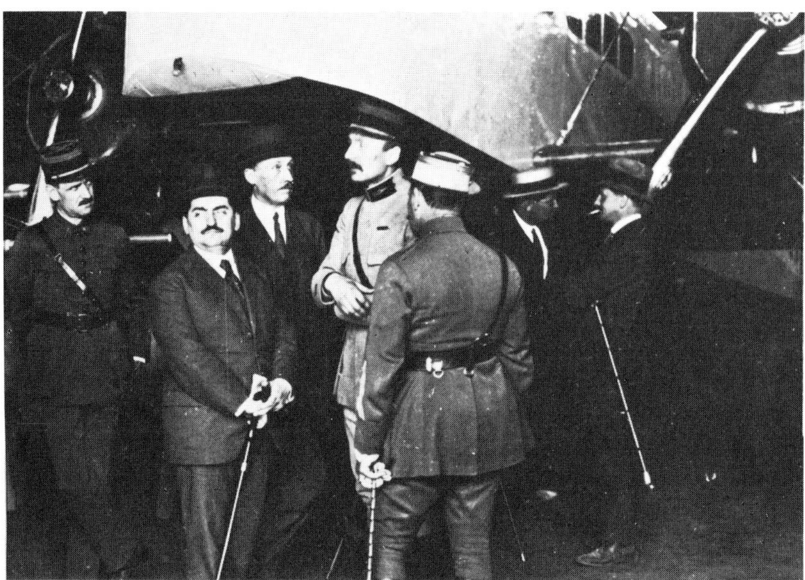

M. Laurent-Eynac, first minister of air, from September 14, 1928, to December 4, 1930. He returned to that post from March 21, 1940, until the armistice in June 1940.

lishing the Air Force,[1] drawn up at the time that Laurent-Eynac launched the new ministry, were not passed until five to seven years later.

In spite of this opposition, the new minister organized his ministry and defined his program.

The ministry, bringing together the aeronautical service of the various ministries and agencies, including the 12th Directorate of Aeronautics, comprised about one thousand persons. It was installed "temporarily" in the former Collège Lacordaire on the Rue Saint Didier in Paris. Commercial aviation remained on the Avenue Rapp and the technical services at Issy-les-Moulineaux.

After analyzing the aeronautics crisis, Laurent-Eynac made his intentions clear in a presentation before the Aeronautics Committee of the Chamber of Deputies. He stated that there was a crisis in aeronautics characterized by "the lack of technological research, the weakness of our instruction and of our doctrine, the lack of standardization, the obsolescence of our equipment, and the abundance of prototypes from the point of view of quantity, though the quality is insufficient." He remarked on the "twin defects: overabundance of military stocks and decrepitude of the commercial planes."

In the face of this crisis, the Air Ministry could not be a magical, miracle-working solution setting everything right in an instant. The new organization was only a means, but an indispensable means, of bringing the reforms that had been undertaken to a successful conclusion.

The greatest significance of the ministry was that it placed personnel and materiel under a single authority. The personnel using the equipment could request adjustments necessary to them and modifications dictated by experience. Similarly, the technicians responsible for the design of a plane, now knowing the use to which it would be put, could take that into account in working out their plans.

"In unity of purpose, in unity of means, in single

1. Bills drawn up in 1928 and mentioned by Laurent-Eynac during his hearing before the Aeronautics Committee of the Chamber of Deputies: creating an "Armée de l'Air" (Air Force), setting up its general organization, on its administration, officers and men, recruitment, and on the status of Air Force personnel.

authority and the bringing together of the scattered elements of aviation, the Air Ministry constitutes the best means of making an effort that is extremely useful but *likely to encounter many difficulties, namely—individual interests, which must give precedence to the general interest.*"

Laurent-Eynac had to deal first with the most important problem, the very one that had been behind the creation of the ministry—the crisis in the aeronautics industry.

To resolve that crisis it was necessary to carry out research and pursue a real policy of technological development and prototypes. To do this it was necessary to distribute the appropriations in a better way. From 1920 to 1928 the total expenditures for materiel and maintenance of the military, naval, and colonial flights rose to the sum of 3 billion francs, while expenditures for research and experimentation were limited to 300 million francs. It was advisable to: change this distribution—in 1929 the research appropriations were to rise from 36 million to 120 million; try to get the concentration of industry needed to provide the considerable financing necessitated by the development of tools and test equipment; and give up the disastrous policy of military stocks made up of quickly outmoded materiel, in favor of a policy of preparation for industrial mobilization (stocking of equipment and raw materials).

To obtain these results the minister relied on the Technical Directorate General, entrusted to Albert Caquot, "who, when mobilized, had directed these services with rare competence and absolute dedication." This directorate comprised a research service, a technical service whose mission was testing new materiel, and a manufacturing and industrial tooling service.

It also appeared advisable to increase the aid given to commercial aviation, which provoked no great objection.

Finally, the minister intended to organize "the national air force," which would embrace all the military, naval, and colonial air forces. It would, of course, continue to furnish forces for cooperation with the other ministries, while a new autonomous force would be developed "that would certainly be the major aeronautical force of tomorrow."

Made up of bomber and fighter flights, "this air force, depending on the government's instructions and war policy, would be able to bring its effort to bear on the enemy's nerve centers, affect the morale of its population, and take action against its railroad stations, assembly points, factories, and arsenals."

This air force for action at a distance called for airplanes of large capacity and great range. The technical solutions adopted for their manufacture were undoubtedly of importance to commercial aviation as well.

These large capacity, multi-seated, multi-engined airplanes and seaplanes were particularly suited to metal construction in accordance with what was being done abroad. In this domain, too, research was indispensable, and this provided yet another justification for the industrial policy that it was planned to pursue.

As mentioned above, Laurent-Eynac entrusted the Technical Directorate General to Albert Caquot. Caquot launched a "policy of progress," better known as the "policy of prototypes." In the minds of the minister and of his technical director this policy was aimed at two objectives: first, to promote the development of technology and avoid manufacturing too many planes that would quickly become obsolete; and, second, to encourage new talents and new ideas.

Until that time the prototypes submitted by the manufacturers on the basis of the programs proposed were examined by a Permanent Inspection Commission for New Aeronautical Materiel (Commission d'Examen Permanente des Matériels Nouveaux d'Aéronautique/C.E.P.A.N.A.), and the contracts signed with manufacturers who were to start up their plants were not paid for until the materiel had undergone testing. This system eliminated individual engineers with no financial resources, leaving the established manufacturers with a monopoly on prototypes and government contracts.

The new system permitted making new con-

Albert Caquot, one of the great French engineers, organized aeronautics production in 1916, 1928, and 1938.

tracts with large payments in advance, which could go as high as 80 percent of the price of the prototype. In return the government became the owner of the invention and had the right to have it manufactured or not. Rapidly decreasing royalties were due to the manufacturers if the machine was put through its initial test performances successfully. This system made it possible, in effect, for the number of prototypes constructed to grow along with the volume of research.

From October 1928 to March 1, 1933, 450 million francs were spent in this way, as compared to 300 million from 1920 to 1928. These appropriations made it possible to order nearly 250 airplanes and seaplanes of 180 different types, 53 of them military, and 160 engines of some 40 types. Of the total number of airplanes ordered, fewer than 50 types were kept for tests, half of these under military programs.

Violent criticism developed, perhaps inspired by the manufacturers, who looked askance at the increase in the number of their competitors. The complaints concerned the amounts "swallowed up" in the manufacture of costly toys, which cut down on the number of planes turned out in real production runs.

In addition, certain planes were ridiculed—planes that apparently did not have the slightest chance of getting off the ground, such as the Bratu three-engined commercial plane, which made history at the Villacoublay research center when its wings broke under their own weight.

Finally, it was noted that certain firms had been particularly favored, such as Farman (which, by the way, belonged to the "club" of the big manufacturers).

It is probable that there were abuses, caused by the very openness at which this policy was aimed, but on the other hand there were also some very positive results. From 1929 on over half the planes produced were made of metal, which was one of the aims sought by Laurent-Eynac and Caquot. The planes turned out were of excellent quality, and that enabled the French in 1930 to break a certain number of world records (essentially records for distance with load). In addition, this open policy revealed some talented designers, such as Bloch, Dewoitine, and Szydlowski.

It was not the development of this policy that led to the lack of high-quality planes with which France was confronted in 1938, but rather its abandonment in 1932–1933 in favor of the large production runs which deprived it in 1936 of new aircraft ready to be manufactured.

In fact, the chief criticism that can be made of the prototype policy is that it expected technical progress from private initiative instead of directing that initiative by offering it ambitious programs.

The other objectives that the minister had set himself in the matter of industrial policy were not attained. The aeronautics industry achieved neither concentration nor decentralization and did not invest enough in machinery and equipment. Moreover, the contracts continued, as in the past, to be split up among the various manufacturers, thus preventing economy in manufacture.

It was not until September 1938 and Albert Caquot's return to office that a solution was finally found for this problem. Moreover, there was no real improvement in the area of airplane prices, which until 1937 were the subject of sharp criticism in the French Parliament.

It is true that calculating the net cost of a plane was particularly difficult, for at the time no statistical data were available that could substantiate the S.T.Aé.'s cost figures. The first real study of industrial prices was done in 1937 by the engineer Thouvenot. Whether it was a lump-sum contract inflated by the industrialist to cover his risks or one that could be revised, the net costs remained practically uncheckable.

Partly in an attempt to introduce an element of comparison, it was decided in 1930 to establish an aeronautical arsenal, with a status analogous to that of the naval arsenals, entrusted to military engineers of the Air Ministry. The establishment of this arsenal, originally intended to be located at Orléans-Bricy, was postponed several times, and it was not until 1936 that it was actually established at Villacoublay.

The New Uniform

Unable to bring about the adoption of the fundamental documents creating the Air Force, the minister decided in 1928 to give the aviators a new uniform that would mark the specificity and unity of the new service. In this area, seemingly of minor importance, his critics did not mince their words. From the army's point of view, in abandoning the sacrosanct kepi the aviators were breaking with tradition; they were, so to speak, cutting the umbilical cord that had linked aviation with the ground forces since its birth.

From the navy the objection was the opposite. Because of the blue color of the uniform adopted and the cap worn with it aviators could be confused with sailors. To avoid that confusion the new uniform was given a straight cut and a row of buttons. Wearing the saber could also lead to confusion with the sailors. Appreciating this objection and the fact that an airplane's cockpit had little room for the saber, the aviators found it more practical to adopt a shorter weapon—the dagger, inspired by that worn by Polish military aviators.

The new uniform was quickly adopted by air force officers, but it took nearly five years for all the noncommissioned officers to get it. During that period it underwent slight modifications having to do mainly with the cap and the wings. As for the cap, at the beginning it was a soft type, as in the navy. The personnel were found to prefer the stiff type with a band. After some calls to order, the command gave in and decided to make regulation what had been merely whimsical.

Similarly, as for the wings on the cap or on the chest, only the flying personnel were given them. Instead of wings the nonflying personnel wore on their caps a round insignia quickly nicknamed the "washer"; it was soon abandoned, however.

As for the wings on the chest, they were meant to replace the "macaroons"—insignia of the fliers, practically abandoned until 1938.

The nonflying personnel were eager to adopt the wings for themselves, too, and the command once again decided to make them official, with the central motif indicating the specialty.

The macaroon was put back into use following a trip by General Vuillemin to Germany in August 1938. Having been given the metal pilot's insignia of the Luftwaffe, he found himself with nothing to offer in return and later decided to put the earlier metal insignia back into service.

The enlisted airmen were not equipped with their iron blue uniform until much later. Their headgear was the Basque beret until the Second World War.

Evolution of the Organization

From 1929 to 1932 various modifications were introduced into the organization of 1924. At first these were relatively minor ones, such as the creation in 1939 of a 3rd Air Division at Tours and the changes of location of the units that returned from Germany at the end of the occupation.

The first important modification took place in October 1930, when the bomber regiments were taken out of the air divisions and regrouped in a "general reserve aviation group" established at Paris, with the 11th Bomber Brigade at Nancy and the 12th Brigade at Rheims.

The most important change took place in 1932, prefiguring the definitive organization of the Air Force. On an experimental basis and in accordance with the bill introduced in 1929 but not passed, some regiments were transformed into squadrons, and air force bases were established.

Three pursuit squadrons were created, each comprising two groups of two flights: the 1st, at Le Bourget; the 3rd, at Lyons; and the 7th, at Dijon.

This left two regiments (of 3 groupings of 3 flights): the 2nd R.A.C. (Régiment Aérien de Chasse/Aerial Pursuit Regiment), at Strasbourg and the 3rd R.A.C., at Châteauroux.

The four bomber regiments were transformed into squadrons bearing the same numbers—11th, 12th, 21st, and 22nd. Three of these squadrons were each to comprise 3 heavy bomber groups of 3 flights each and 1 night fighter flight. They were the 12th, at Rheims, the 21st, at Nancy, and the 22nd, at Chartres. The 11th Squadron, at Metz, equipped with medium bombers, was to consist of 3 groups of 4 flights each (3 bomber flights and 1 flight of escort planes).

Four observation regiments were transformed into squadrons of 2 groups of 2 flights—the 32nd and 33rd, at Dijon; the 36th Squadron, at Pau, was created by adding a second group to the 36th Aviation Group at Pau.

The 31st and 38th Regiments remained the 31st, with 4 groups of 2 flights, and the 38th, with 3 groups of 2 flights.

Three reconnaissance squadrons were created, each having 2 groups of 2 flights: the 52nd, at Dijon; the 54th, at Le Bourget; and the 55th, at Lyons.

The suppression of the air regiments, together with the fact that the squadrons were not, as we shall see later, to have territorial responsibilities, led to the establishment of five air bases organized at the airfields of Dijon, Le Bourget, Lyons, Nancy, and Pau.

Each base comprised a brigade headquarters (except at Pau, where there was only half a brigade); a training center—command, general services, training squadron, mobilization center, and advanced training center for reservists; an airfield; and a depot battalion—command section, administrative services, depot companies, health service, rifle section, and volunteer section.

This experimental organization was very quickly extended to all the air forces and was made explicit in the decrees and orders issued for the purpose in 1933. According to these documents, technological progress had effects on the potential of airplanes, which required the application of new principles.

It was stated that the administrative burden imposed on regimental commanders did not leave them the time needed to provide effective training for flying formations in wartime. To remedy this

A surprising transport prototype, the Dyle and Bacalan D.B. 70.

The Potez 39 A 2.

state of affairs authority was centralized at the brigade (or half brigade) level. That authority covered mobile elements, which had a reduced administration (squadrons and groups), and fixed elements (bases), and was entrusted with providing for the needs of the squadrons. For that purpose it included ample means of training, supply, administration, mobilization, and protection.

It was later specified (in an order of November 22, 1933) that the squadron was a purely tactical formation and that the group (new type) was to be the fundamental base unit of the Air Force.

At the same time that the Air Force organization was being modified there was an apparently less logical evolution of the organization of the central administration.

There is, of course, no intention here of relating in detail the changes made in the organization originally decreed by Laurent-Eynac, either by him or by his successors, M. Painlevé (from December 13, 1930, to January 27, 1931, and from April 3, 1932, to January 31, 1933) and Jacques Louis Dumesnil (from January 27, 1931, to February 21, 1932).[1]

In spite of the desire, many times expressed, to fuse all the services in the Ministries of War, Navy, and Commerce that dealt with aeronautical matters, all that had been effected was a juxtaposition. To be convinced of this it is only necessary to realize that at the end of 1932, after four years, the Central Administration consisted of an air force staff; a directorate of the land air forces with a personnel section, an air materiel section, and a works and installations section; a directorate of the maritime air forces, which also included a personnel section, an air materiel section, and a works and installations section; a technical directorate general entrusted with the research and development of prototypes, production runs of air materiel, and servicing the bases (works and installations); a civil aeronautics directorate comprising an air materiel section and a works and installations

1. From February 21 to June 3, 1932, the Air Ministry and the Ministries of War and of the Navy were abolished by the new prime minister, André Tardieu, in favor of a different organization, with a Minister of National Defense (M. François Piétri) and two undersecretaries of state, Achille Fould and Etienne Riché. In fact, that experiment turned out to be too brief to change the existing structures. The minister of national defense had neither the time nor the means to create a central administration covering the three old ministries. He acted, in reality, as if he had been three ministers in one, going regularly to sign papers in each of the three ministries.

The instrument panel of the Blériot 127.

section; and a budget and auditing directorate.

This enumeration clearly shows the defect indicated above. It was a juxtaposition of services preserving their previous habits rather than a real fusion.

Other defects appeared. The two directorates of land air forces and maritime air forces were independent of the general staff, and the organization was complex and uneconomical.

There were an air materiel section and a works and installations section in four different directorates. The technical directorate general, contrary to what Laurent-Eynac had wanted to do, was cut off from the users, whether military or civilian. In the face of divided and sometimes opposed users, the technical directorate general saw its importance and its independence grow. It was, in fact, a veritable state within the state.

There was no doubt that problems of persons, or rather of personalities, would be engrafted upon these organizational defects.

General Denain's entourage, a little later on, was not hesitant about expressing a harsh judgment of the chief of the Air Force general staff, who at the time was General Hergault, "a general officer from the Ministry of War, largely preoccupied with problems of cooperation."

There were also complaints made that Caquot was sacrificing the production of modern planes for the units in favor of the speculative production of prototypes. In fact, these complaints were aimed not so much at the man as at the policy pursued, as was discussed earlier.

As for the chief of the general staff, it is certain that General Hergault was very careful not to "upset" the views of the staff. This does not, however, explain the delay in passage of the basic laws establishing the Air Force. Although it continued to regret the new organization, the Ministry of War had given up the demand for return of the air units to the army. It preferred to bear down on the decisions reached concerning the conditions of employment of those units. The emphasis placed in 1932 on support aviation suited the wishes of the army staff quite well.

The navy remained the implacable opponent,

A ceremonial parade in Syria about 1932. Note that the aviators are wearing the leather flying suit, and many of them are wearing boots as well. Among the army officers not accompanied by units, Major de Gaulle's tall figure is conspicuous.

Mechanics in front of a LeO 20.

Pilots in flight dress belonging to the 2nd Flight of the 11/6 in 1933 (SPA 124).

refusing to cut loose from what it considered essential—the maritime aviation to which it had paid little attention from 1920 to 1928. This attitude was such that Colonel Brocard, chairman of the Aeronautics Committee of the Chamber of Deputies, denounced it in severe terms in a letter of October 26, 1931, addressed to air minister Dumesnil. "It is a matter of public notoriety," he wrote, "that at the present time the Ministry of the Navy shows an intransigent opposition, as in the past, to the principles expressed not only in the modified reports of the Committee, but also in the very texts presented by the Government and countersigned by the Minister of the Navy."

The only solution reasonably able to free the system was to come to an understanding with the "Rue Royale" (the site of the Ministry of the Navy), even if that understanding implied the return of naval aviation to the navy itself. In any case, naval aviation was not essential to the Air Force, whatever the proponents of the "integral air force" may have thought at the time.

This was done by Painlevé, who came to an agreement with M. Leygues, the minister of the navy, in the decree of November 27, 1932. Under the terms of this agreement the Ministry of the Navy had under its authority the carrier-borne air units, the naval support air units that were not carrier-borne, and the autonomous maritime aeronautics units. The last mentioned, few in number, were nevertheless attached for employment to the Air Ministry.

There was thus no longer any obstacle to the creation of the Air Force (Armée de l'Air), and that task was carried out by those responsible for aviation from 1933 to 1936.

The Air Force from 1933 to 1936

On January 31, 1933, Pierre Cot became minister of air in the administration of Edouard Daladier. The chief of the general staff of the air forces was then General Barès, who had replaced General Hergault on January 15, 1933. General Denain, who was Barès's assistant, was assigned the functions of chief of the general staff on February 7 of that year, and became on April 1, 1933, the first

Officer and noncommissioned officer pilots at rest in 1930. In the background, Nieuport 62's.

The Nieuport-Delage 62, an improved version of the Nieuport 42, came into service in 1928.

Jacques Louis Dumesnil, minister of air from January 27, 1931, to February 16, 1932, with Dieudonné Costes on their return from a trip to Africa.

M. Painlevé, former prime minister, was minister of air from December 13, 1930, to January 22, 1931, and from June 3, 1932, to January 28, 1933.

chief of the general staff of the French Air Force. He was later to be minister of air from February 19, 1934, to January 24, 1936. It was during that period of three years that the major decisions concerning the Air Force were reached.

Definition of the Doctrine of Employment

It was logical, of course, to define first of all the doctrine of employment of the new service. The application of this logic involved some risk to the other documents, for while the problems posed by the navy had been settled by capitulation, it was obviously out of the question to return support aviation to the army. In fact, it was not so much the doctrine that raised the greatest objections. A skillful editor is capable of wording a bill in such a way that it suits all concerned. And indeed the text was approved by the high military committee in March 1933 and published as a decree. It defined the missions of the Air Force by specifying that it should be capable of participating in either support operations or in aerial combat operations and aerial defense of national territory.

The situation was not the same when it came to defining priorities and dividing available funds among the different missions. The Air Force wanted to concentrate its efforts first on bombing units, then on fighter units, by reducing if necessary the support units. This view of things was strongly opposed by the army, which declared in 1933, through its chief of staff, General Weygand, "that the views of the minister of air on aerial combat, the organization of the air forces, and the possible reductions in reconnaissance aviation call forth the most serious reservations." A little later he backed up these reservations with the threat that "if the Air Ministry took the path indicated by the armament plan . . . it would be necessary for the Ministry of War to organize the air support organically necessary to its large units."

In the face of this strong opposition, the Air Ministry, while not abandoning its doctrine, presented it in a less provocative form. It made an effort to find solutions that, while apparently giving satisfaction to the army in the matter of support forces, would make it possible, when the time came, to have units available that would be capable of participating in independent actions. In the meantime it was necessary to get the pending bills passed.

The organization law was passed first, on July 2, 1934. The organization defined in it was based on dividing the territory into air regions. The general officer commanding the air region would be directly responsible to the minister of air and "simultaneously exercise command of the troops and territorial command."

In time of war the division of the air units mobilized between the reserve air forces and the air forces placed at the disposal of the Army and the Navy is determined by the government on the basis of operations.

The reserve air forces are placed under the authority of

Organization as of March 15, 1929

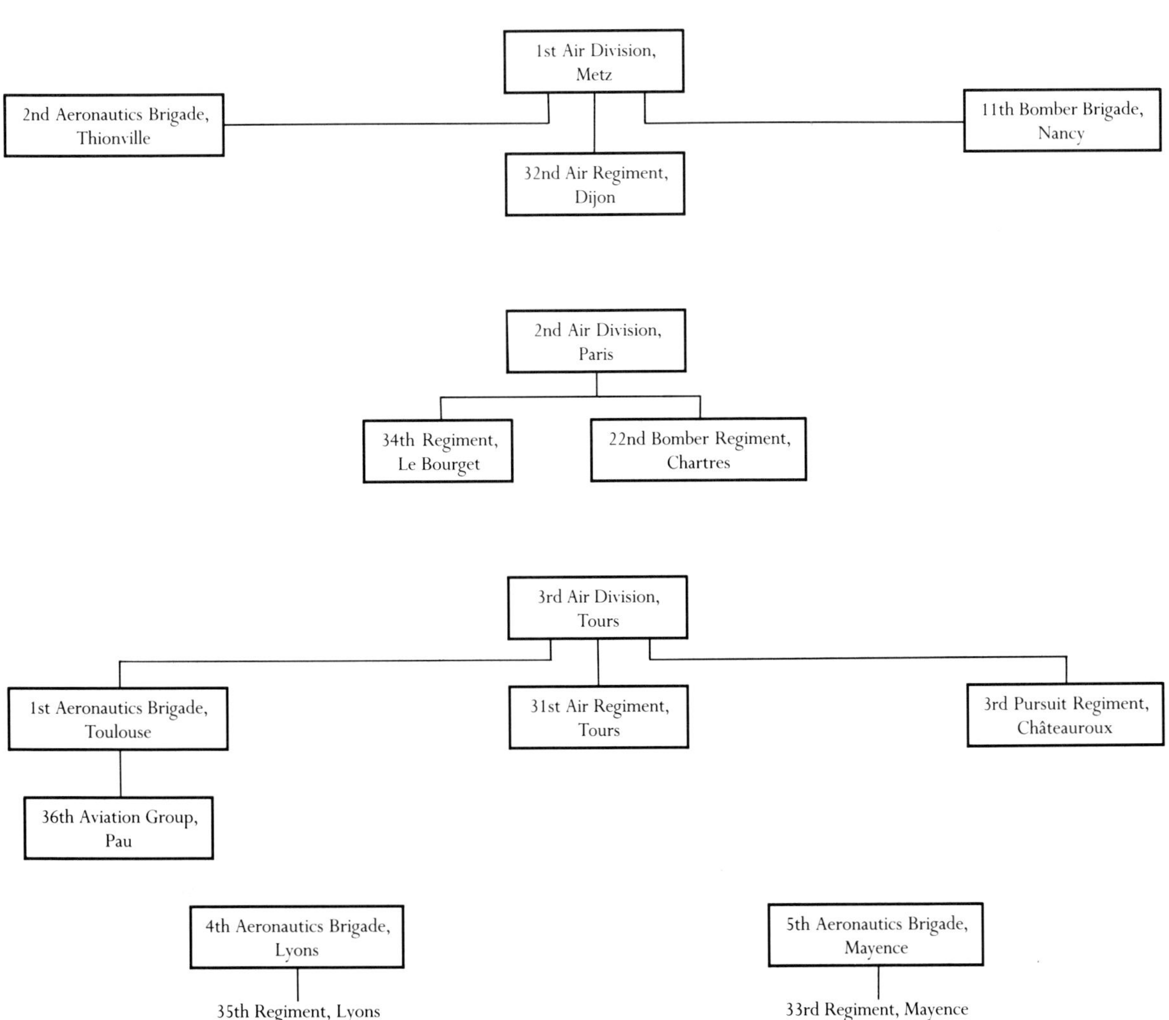

Organization as of October 1, 1930

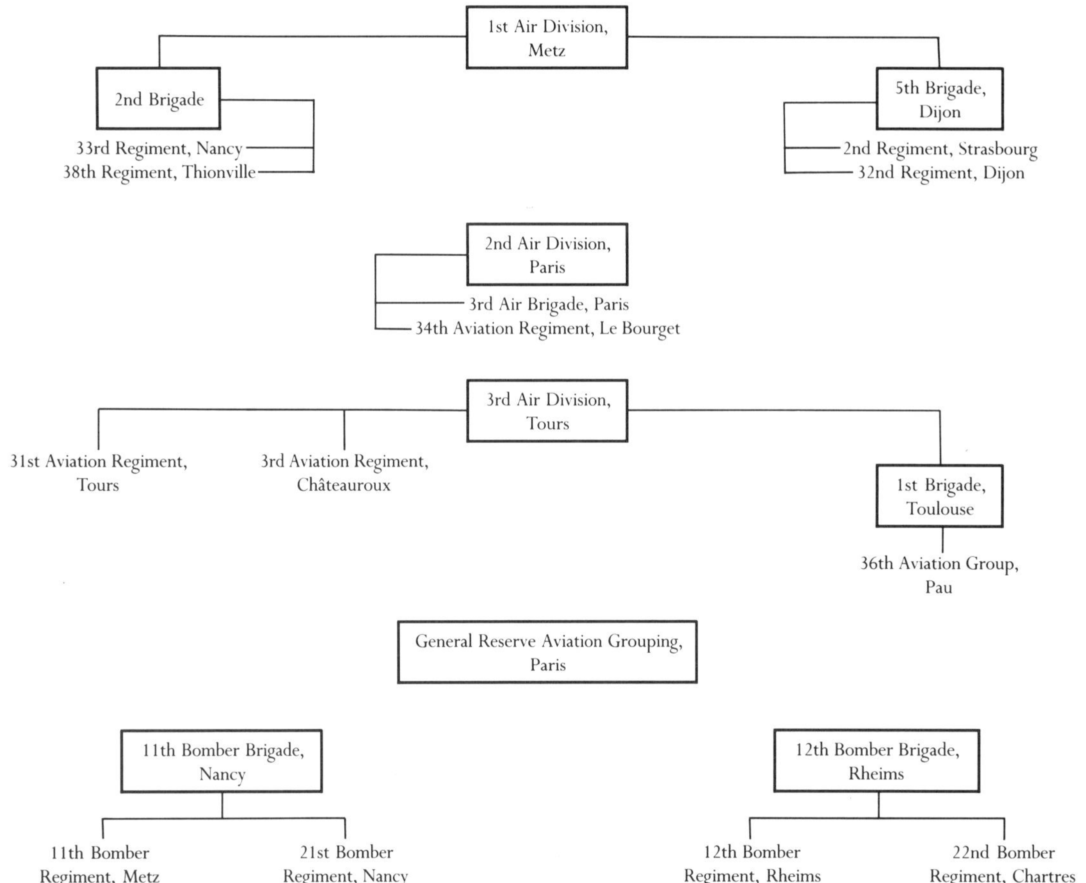

General Denain, the first to bear the title, was Chief of the Air Force General Staff from April 1, 1933, to February 8, 1934. On that date he became minister of air, a post which he held until January 24, 1936.

Pierre Cot, minister of air from January 31, 1933, to February 8, 1934, and again from June 4, 1936, to January 18, 1938.

a general officer of the Air Force, the commander in chief, who has the right of inspection over all the air forces and undertakes the direction of aerial operations, if any, that the government decides to entrust to him.

The air forces placed at the disposal of the Army are commanded by a general officer of the Air Force placed under the authority of the general officer of the Army commanding the theater of land operations in question.

The air forces placed at the disposal of the Navy are commanded by a general officer of the Air Force placed under the authority of the vice-admiral commanding the theater of naval operations in question.

This organization obviously had two major defects: 1) It contravened the principle of unity of action. No doubt the reserve forces obeyed a single head, as did the "cooperating" forces. This presupposed that these forces were distinct. The weakness of the Air Force prevented this from being the case, except for heavy aircraft. It was thus impossible for the commander in chief of the air forces to define and conduct general aerial maneuvers. 2) It violated the principle of permanence, the basis of French military organization, so well defined in the "Bouchard" report presenting the famous law of 1882.

At the opening of hostilities the Air Force changed its organization completely. The aerial units which until then were subordinated to the regions were divided among various commands which did not exist in peacetime.

In spite of the precautionary measures adopted, the Air Force was unsuited, by its very organization, to throw itself into large-scale aerial operations at the beginning of a conflict.

Before the passing of the law of 1934 the central Air administration had been reorganized. By 1933 a certain number of measures had been taken: abolition of the two directorates of land air forces and sea air forces and creation of the Directorate of

A Potez 25 TOE at Sétif, Algeria, in 1932.

Military Aerial Materiel, placed under the authority of the general staff and of the Directorate of Military Personnel; and creation of the central works and installations service.

The intention was to get greater participation of the staff in decisions concerning materiel. The result was not attained because of the powers exercised by the Directorate General for Engineering.

When he took office as minister General Denain decided to carry out a much more significant reform based on the following principles. The Air Ministry was a mixed ministry, and aeronautics policy for that reason had to be at the same time a national defense policy and a civilian policy; and it was necessary to put an end to the technicians' independence of the users of the materiel.

In consequence the decisions made were aimed at abolishing the Directorate General for Engineering and creating a directorate of aerial manufactures having among its powers everything that had to do with *the creation of military and civil aeronautics materiel, from the prototype to the production runs*; grouping within the central works and installations service everything that concerned *the creation of the infrastructure*; and making clear that the activity of the production services would from then on be directed by the users (general staff and Directorate of Civil Aviation).

These decisions were contained in the decree of March 5, 1934, defining the organization of the Air Ministry.

A decree of March 30 specified the functions and powers of the various central administrative agencies and created two important committees, the Materiel Committee and the Flight Test Commission. The Materiel Committee had the function of examining the programs submitted to it by the general staff and determining the general utilization characteristics of new airplanes. The Flight Test Commission gave the minister an opinion on the testing programs and on the reports following flight tests established by the Directorate of Aerial Manufactures.

With this organization the minister felt that he had clearly established the preeminence of the general staff over all the technical services. But although this organization certainly represented a necessary condition for obtaining that result, in itself it was not sufficient to do so.

Once the organization of 1934 had been voted into being, it was possible to establish the would-be definitive structures of the Air Force (shown here on the organizational chart). The reforms continued the organization into air bases, squadrons, and groups started late in 1932.

At the same time, in order to facilitate the training of the reserves and to meet the needs expressed by the large ground units, regional air circles were adapted to the military regions. In the mind of their creator these circles—twenty set up in 1934—were to function so that they could constitute real fighting units on the spot, almost immediately upon mobilization.

Parallel to the organization, General Denain wished to introduce far-reaching reforms in the area of personnel with the goal of developing quality and love of flying.

For quality, the decision reached in 1933 to create an Air School handling the direct recruitment of aviator officers was intended to make it possible to bring in very quickly cadet officers motivated to serve in the Air Force ranks.

The organization of advanced aviation training, the reorganization of the Center for Tactical Studies, and the long-term plan to establish an Advanced Military Aviation School were all intended to make it possible to train the future top leaders of the young service.

To reinforce an aviation mentality General Denain took measures to increase the taste for flying and to make bad-weather flying routine.

Finally, to prepare for the use of the materiel he created the Military Air Experimental Center in Rheims. It is right to emphasize the importance of this often misunderstood center, which carried out remarkable studies in the postwar period. Among them were those concerning night reconnaissance planes—the "pathfinders" of the English five years later—and the bombing tables, which later served as models for the American tables.

A squadron of 30 Potez TOE's commanded by General Vuillemin made a 24,000-kilometer round trip in Africa, called the Black Cruise, from November 6, 1933, to January 15, 1934.

The Black Cruise. Major de Turenne, commanding officer of the 4th Squadron (with blue hen insignia), with his mechanic, Sergeant Major Martinet.

Air Force Organization July 1, 1934

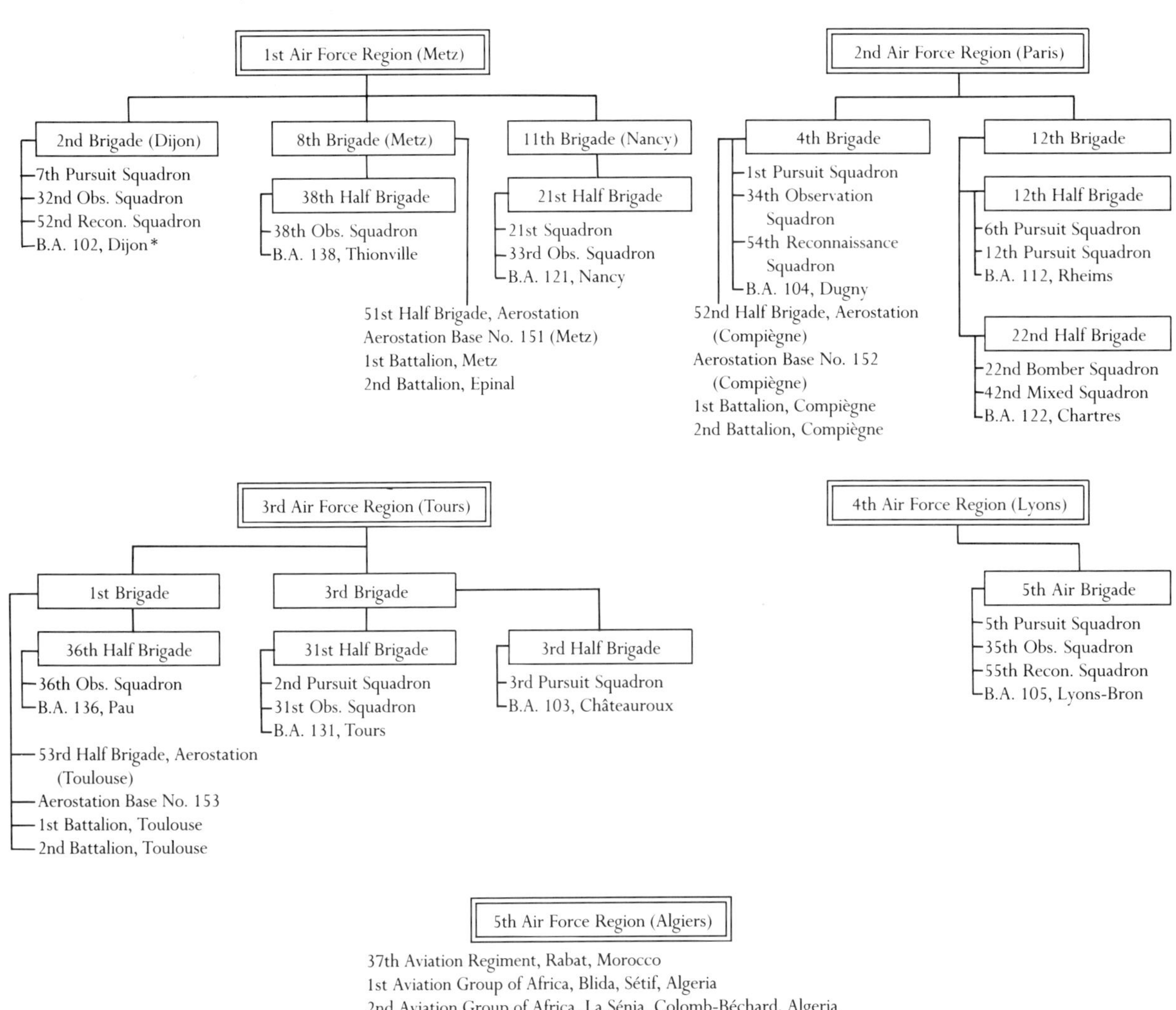

NEAR EAST

39th Aviation Regiment, Rayack, Lebanon

Colonial Aeronautics

Indochina: 4 flights. Madagascar: 1 flight. French Equatorial Africa: 1 flight. French West Africa: 3 flights. French Somali Coast: 1 half flight.

---

*For B.A. read "Air Base" throughout.

Moreover, shortly before his departure General Denain was able to witness the passage of the basic laws that endowed the Air Force with a body of legislation recognizing its identity.

To complete the whole, two specialized inspectorates were created, the Aeronautic Reconnaissance Inspectorate and the Defense Aviation Inspectorate.

The B.C.R.

One of the most violently contested ideas of that time was certainly the bombing, combat, and reconnaissance plane (B.C.R.) project.

This project may be seen as the embodiment of the theories of Giulio Douhet, which were in vogue at the time. The B.C.R. plane, carrying a heavy load of bombs, suited to reconnaissance, and having a great range, was considered capable of defending itself by fire against attacks of enemy fighters. To achieve this it had to have weapons capable of firing in all directions.

This did not correspond exactly to Douhet's theories since he also considered it necessary to endow a fighter plane, intended to carry the fire to the enemy, with the greatest possible speed. In any case, it must be emphasized that, contrary to what has sometimes been asserted, Douhet's theories as a whole were never espoused by the Air Force staff.

In fact, the B.C.R. derived partly from the conviction, based on experience, that an airplane of that type was capable of victoriously resisting fighter planes and partly from the desire to make use of it to overcome, as indicated earlier, the land army's resistance.

The experience on which it was based was that of multi-seated fighter planes of the Caudron R XI type, which in 1918 had proved effective against fighters when used to escort bombing expeditions.

The Blériot 127, which had just come into service in 1933, corresponded to this program of multi-seated fighter planes. The advances made in engines provided the possibility of giving these planes a considerable bomb-carrying capacity while maintaining their fire power.

In fact, the true reason for the B.C.R. was to be sought elsewhere. The Air Force was convinced that bombers would play a major part in the war that was being prepared for. Unable to allot all the resources that it wished to the bomber units, and obliged as it was to reserve a part of its forces for support missions, the Air Force general staff avoided the difficulty. By supplying the support forces with B.C.R. planes, it hoped to have them available to reinforce its heavy squadrons when the conflict broke out.

This was stated without ambiguity in an article on straightening out French aviation, published in *L'Aérophile* for December 1935 under the signature of General K. . . of the Air Force general staff.

> *Permitting all units designated by the term "reconnaissance aviation" to take part in aerial combat if the occasion arises by arming them with mixed materiel more appropriate to their mission—such is the origin of the first materiel program established pursuant to the decree of 1 April 1933. This program of multi-seated reconnaissance, bombing, and contact airplanes has been the subject of impassioned debates and unjustified criticisms, especially on the part of those who, improperly characterizing such planes as multi-seated combat planes, were mistaken about their role. Their role is not to go in search of aerial combat but to enable the "reconnaissance" units, the most numerous in the Air Force, to* reinforce *the heavy units if circumstances imperiously require it, while at the same time accomplishing their own missions.*

The staff's ideas concerning the B.C.R. were to give rise to a certain number of programs that were ordered under the title of Plan I. Some of these airplanes—the Bloch 200, the Amiot 143, and later the Bloch 210—met the standards for bomber planes and would have been hard to describe as "support airplanes." The ideal plane of this type was incontestably the Potez 540, which, arriving in the units in the summer of 1935, equipped the greater part of French reconnaissance units from the beginning of 1936 to the beginning of 1939.

Until 1940 bombing units were equipped with the Amiot 143, which met the standards of the B.C.R. program. It was used in the daytime, with heavy losses, against German columns in May 1940.

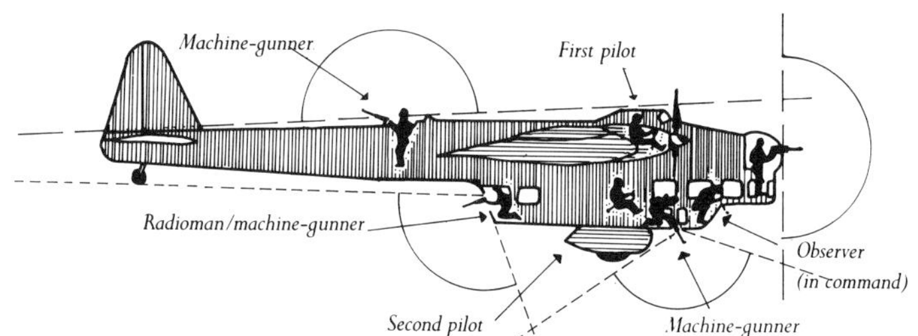

Manufactured outside the program, the Potez 540 also corresponded to the B.C.R. program. These single-seated fighters later showed their vulnerability in Spain. Here, a Potez 541.

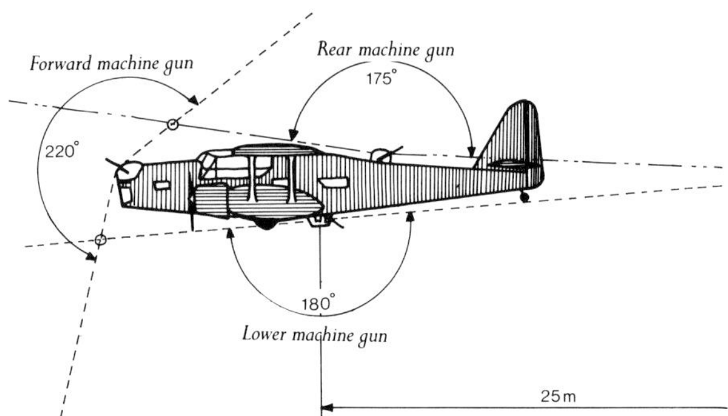

Fast for its time and crammed with machine guns, the Blériot multi-seated fighter plane met the wishes of the advocates of the multi-seater against the single-seater and inspired the B.C.R. program.

Plan I

In 1933 Pierre Cot and General Denain, finding that the Air Force was equipped with airplanes that could, in all fairness, be called outdated (for pursuit, the Nieuport 62 and 629 and the Morane 225; for reconnaissance, the Potez 25 and 39 and the Breguet 27; for bombing, the LeO 20 and 206), decided on the main outline of a plan intended to renovate the materiel in service.

This plan, called Plan I, or the "1,010 Plan," was approved by the Higher Council of the Air Ministry in June 1933 and passed by Parliament in July 1934.

The 1,010 planned airplanes were 350 bombers, 350 fighters, and 310 reconnaissance planes. These figures were later increased by 35 percent, giving a total of 1,343 planes to be manufactured. (These figures were very slightly modified in the course of carrying out the plan.)

In these figures the staff showed its willingness to restore the old priorities, which placed the main effort on aircraft used in cooperation with the other services.

The materiel adopted consisted almost exclusively of relatively old aircraft from the 1930 programs for pursuit planes and from the 1932 programs for bombing and reconnaissance planes. This would have been of no great importance if it had been a matter of a transition plan to be followed, in 1936 and later, by one of modernization, a solution adopted by the Germans.

In fact, it was no such thing. The initial plan, passed on July 6, 1934, "had as its essential object to renovate the flying materiel of our Air Force completely and to give that service, created only a year before, the means necessary for its utilization (infrastructure, communications, munitions, miscellaneous materiel, etc.). Initially planned for three years, it was to be entirely carried out by late 1936 or early 1937."

In the spring of 1935 the minister of air, finding that the realization of the plan "appears at present to be too slow in view of the latest intelligence concerning German armaments," felt it "indispensable to accelerate and intensify the realization of the three-year plan." A second installment was quickly requested to permit realization of the program of 1,010 planes by the end of 1935.

The decision to accelerate production, rejected by Parliament, was taken up by the government by virtue of the special powers that had been granted it. That decision contributed to aggravating the state of disorganization of the aeronautics industry,

The prototype of the Dewoitine 500.

which, after all, was incapable in the state it was in of turning out the planned production. It became apparent very quickly that it was necessary to spread out the planned output, if only to be able to maintain a minimum of work for the aircraft factories. In fact, the production of planes under Plan I extended over the whole of 1937 and interfered with the execution of the later plans.

As the deputy Max Hymans pointed out in his report on the draft budget for 1937:

In 1935 the intelligence received from abroad on the effort made by certain of our neighbors in the field of aerial rearmament compelled the government and Parliament to accelerate the renovation of the Air Force, which at the beginning was to have been accomplished in three years. At that time arguments were raised about the accuracy of the intelligence which the government had used to justify its requests for appropriations intended to speed up that renovation. From our present perspective it does seem that the reinforcement of German aviation was not as rapid as the government feared at the time. This supplement to Germany's military and naval rearmament was preceded by a systematic bringing together of all the means that can provide a great industrial production capability. It would probably have been more logical, before launching into very large orders that our industry was not prepared to receive, to begin by reorganizing that industry on more rational bases, which would then make it possible to turn out a larger number of airplanes each month.

This criticism, like many others made of Plan I, was no doubt justified in 1937. But what was General Denain really trying to do by attempting to carry out his plan as quickly as possible?

According to the testimony of one of his close collaborators, Denain was convinced that a conflict was possible, if not probable, by the end of 1935. On that hypothesis he wanted to have, on that date, an air force capable of outclassing the adversary.

It must be admitted that on March 7, 1936, at the moment when German troops moved into the Rhineland, the French Air Force was undoubtedly superior to the German Luftwaffe. The general quantitative superiority, 110 flights numbering over 1,000 first-line planes on the French side, against 72 flights equipped with 860 planes on the German side, was still more decisive in regard to fighter planes, where the ratio was 3 : 1.

There was also a distinct qualitative superior-

The prototype of the Breguet 420, which was first flown in 1933.

The prototype of the Dewoitine 510.

The Bloch 200, a remarkable plane for its time.

ity. While the performances of the bombers were quite close in the two services, the Dewoitine 500's and 501's with which half the fighter groups were equipped outclassed the German Heinkel 51's and Arado 68's.

Unfortunately, the government, headed by M. Sarraut—after the latter had uttered his famous words, "We will not leave Strasbourg under fire from German guns"—accepted the unanimous advice of the chiefs of staff, General Gamelin, Admiral Durand-Viel, and General Pujo, that nothing could be done without resorting to mobilization. It contented itself with verbal protests to which Hitler attached no importance.

At that moment, and only at that moment, it could be concluded that the efforts made for the Air Force to become validly operational by the beginning of 1936 had served no purpose.

A Dewoitine 500 of the 1st Flight of Fighter Group 2/4 (SPA 95).

A Bloch 120, one of the colonial trimotor airplanes adapted for use in Africa.

A Dewoitine 371. This plane was used by the Republican air force in Spain.

The Potez 540's had a bad reputation among the Spanish crews because of their extreme vulnerability.

CHAPTER IV

Preparation for War (1936–1939)

The Situation at the Beginning of Summer 1936

The elections of April 26 and May 3, 1936, resulted in a Popular Front victory. On June 5, 1936, Léon Blum formed his government and entrusted the Air Ministry to Pierre Cot.

Shortly after the announcement of the election results sit-in strikes broke out spontaneously in the nation's factories. When Blum's government was formed, employers signed the "Matignon" agreements with the unions. Not long after that, Parliament passed social legislation, collective bargaining agreements, the forty-hour work week, and paid vacations.

The economic situation grew worse. The measures adopted worried the propertied classes, and the franc was devalued in September. The political situation aroused oppositions whose virulence manifested itself in the press.

The military perceived this domestic situation in the same way as did other Frenchmen of the time. They were also sensitized to the development of a certain antimilitarism, which was sometimes shown with such violence that it led the military command to advise its personnel not to ride public transportation in uniform.

The International Situation

The international situation was even more disturbing. After the French government's evasion following the remilitarization of the Rhineland by Germany, events moved faster and always in France's disfavor, leading to an alliance between the dictators. The Rome-Berlin axis soon emerged, supplemented by a German-Japanese pact.

The Spanish Civil War

The civil war that broke out in Spain posed the greatest problems, however. Originating with the insurrection of the troops in Morocco and soon extended to numerous garrisons in Spain, that war was soon marked by the direct intervention of other powers. First Italy and then Germany lined up on the side of the insurgents. The Soviet Union intervened on the Republican side.

France was divided on the issue. The government, some of whose members were in favor of intervention—the air minister, Pierre Cot, was one of the most zealous interventionists—hesitated. After consulting with London it was decided to maintain a policy of nonintervention.

Behind the scenes, however, the minister of air furnished planes to the Republicans. Jean Moulin, the head of Cot's civilian office, organized the convoying of these airplanes, in which some military pilots took part. It should be stated here that recent studies, which were quite well done, have shown that the number of French planes furnished to Spain was very small, less than 150 in all.[1] Moreover, these planes, while suitable in 1936 for carrying out operations against a still unmodernized air force, were all old planes. The assertion sometimes made in certain circles that furnishing planes to Spain compromised the future of the French Air Force has, therefore, no serious foundation.

The Attitudes of Air Force Personnel

In the face of all these problems it is interesting to see how the Air Force personnel reacted. In fact, there was no unanimous opinion among them since the personnel did not form a homogeneous whole. There were differences in points of view between the officers and the noncommissioned officers, between the career personnel and those who had been conscripted. In the officer corps, which is undoubtedly the group that can be understood best in the present state of the studies devoted to these subjects, there was no universal understanding of what was happening and hence no identical reactions.

The differences, of course, were connected with rank. High-ranking officers—generals, colonels, lieutenant colonels—while fewer in number, were probably better informed than the others. If they did not live in Paris, they had contacts with fellow officers who were serving on the staffs of the Paris area. Stationing had a fundamental influence on the formation of opinion. At a time when audiovisual media were little developed, there was a certain gap between the France of Paris and the France of Châteauroux or of the eastern border areas.

In the Paris region and in regions of high working-class density the manifestations of antimilitarism that many saw in 1936 as directly linked to the Popular Front led to reactions of insubordination. In the provinces, on the air bases, in flying units, lack of interest in political problems was the rule. This relative lack of interest may be surprising. Reading certain authors gives an impression that the officer corps in 1936 was violently hostile to the Popular Front and was quite at home with the Cowl, which was not spoken of openly. The reality was otherwise. Adopting such an attitude was rare, if not to say extremely rare. No doubt the training of officers, and notably the military education given in the officers' schools, and particularly at Saint Cyr, was not such as to arouse in them general approval of a leftist government composed of political figures who, on the

The Breguet 470 Fulgur, one of the transport prototypes used by the Republican air force in Spain.

1. A figure of 144 (very close to the true figure) is given: 56 fighter planes—26 Dewoitine 371's and 372's, 22 Gourdon-Leseurre 32's, 5 Loire 46's, and 2 Dewoitine Turkish 510's without engines or armament; 38 bombers—17 Potez 25 A 2's, 12 Potez 540's and 542's, 4 Bloch 200's, and 3 Bloch 210's; 8 reconnaissance and liaison planes—5 Caudron *Goélands* (sea gulls) and 5 transport planes, all prototypes; and 37 trainers—18 Caudron *Aiglons*, 5 Caudron *Lucioles*, 6 Hanriot 182's, and 6 Morane-Saulnier 230's.

whole, had systematically refused military appropriations in earlier years. Moreover, that government was supported by the Communist Party, which from 1920 to 1934 had been one of the worst detractors of the military. But the officers' education possessed a stronger quality: it inculcated in those who received it an absolute respect for discipline. In 1936 this meant first of all service to their country and a complete refusal to become involved in politics. Besides, this went hand in hand with military obligations. It must be borne in mind that the military man of the 1930s, of whom everything could be demanded—things that were not demanded of other citizens, including, even in peacetime, the sacrifice of his life—did not possess the right to vote. Quite naturally, he dissociated himself from a debate in which he was forbidden to participate. He was encouraged in this attitude by the oft-repeated dogma of the obligation of neutrality owed by the army, which was and must remain the "great mute."

While little concerned with internal politics, the military aviators did, on the other hand, follow the major events that were unfolding on the world stage. They quickly saw the evidence, especially after March 7, 1936, of the inevitability of war with Germany. In the face of this eventuality, which was rapidly approaching, they wondered about the soundness of the military aviation materiel that it was their task to put into action.

The Status and Evolution of German Military Aviation

At the beginning of 1936, as we have seen, French aviation was incontestably superior to German aviation. This situation had not changed appreciably in July. Apparently the French Air Force seemed to be solid, but comparison with foreign air forces was already showing up gaps that could not be filled for a long time. A superficial examination might have made the French believe in their strength, but a more thorough examination showed them that the Luftwaffe, developing full speed ahead, was on the point of becoming the best air force in the world.

It certainly appeared to be of recent creation, and this was to have a certain significance at the beginning of the war. It would explain, up to a point, the large number of victories of the French fighters during the campaign in France in spite of the general inferiority of their materiel. But one learns fast in war, and the young German crews trained between 1936 and 1938 would become the experienced crews of the campaign in England and the beginning of the war in the east. At any rate, one should not be deceived. Although the Luftwaffe did not officially exist until 1935, aerial rearmament in Germany had begun much earlier.

The treaty of Versailles had forbidden Germany to manufacture military airplanes and had set strict limits on the size of its commercial planes. To get around the clauses of the treaty the Germans came to use several procedures, some of which were not known at the time.

At the outset, on the occasion of the signing of the Treaty of Rapallo, Germany and the U.S.S.R. had agreed on secret clauses under the terms of which the latter was to profit from the former's technical inventions in the military field. In return Germany would receive facilities in Soviet territory. One of these concessions to Germany was the free use of the base of Lipetsk, 300 kilometers south of Moscow. It was there that the prototypes of German military airplanes were tested and the officers destined for high rank in the future Luftwaffe were trained. Albert Kesselring, Stumpff, and Sperrle, who commanded the air armies in 1940, had been through Lipetsk.

To get around the provisions of the Treaty of Versailles Germany also developed sporting aviation with airplanes and gliders as well as domestic postal airlines. This made it possible to maintain aircraft factories at a minimum level.

For research on military prototypes Germany installed shops abroad, such as Flygindustri Junkers, which was in Sweden. It also ordered research and production not of military airplanes but of "military research airplanes," construction of which made it possible to keep the research bureaus busy.

In 1923 Germany obtained a relaxing of the

To get around the provisions of the Treaty of Versailles the Germans produced several types of planes officially designed for civil transport service. In fact, these planes were test models for military craft, such as the Junkers 86, which resulted in the JU-86 K bomber.

clauses concerned with transport planes and, in 1926, the suppression of those clauses altogether.

Starting in 1928 models of airplanes and engines appeared in the Berlin Aeronautical Showroom, which demonstrated the technical effort that was being made.

Lufthansa, equipped with German planes, was to play a very important part in the development of military aviation by making it possible, because of the orders that it placed, to keep an aeronautics industry in condition and to train a number of crews greater than its own needs required.

In 1933 Hitler created an Air Ministry headed by Hermann Goering, which launched many studies of military prototypes. At the same time Italy agreed to train a certain number of German pilots. General Galland went through these Italian schools and has discussed them in his memoirs. He seems not to have cherished a fond memory of them.

When the Luftwaffe was revealed in broad daylight in 1935 it had already been more than a year since German industry began its aerial rearmament.

Besides its initial head start (French rearmament did not begin until early in 1938), German military power had a superiority linked to economic, industrial, and political factors. In a comparison of the economic power of the two countries the superiority of Germany was crushing. Its industrial potential was nearly four times that of France, and its human potential (a population of 70 million) was nearly twice that of the French.

Whatever moral judgment one may make on the Nazi rulers of Germany, one is forced to recognize that they had, at least in the 1930s, perfectly understood the revolutionary part that aviation would play in a modern war. Perhaps the importance in the Nazi party of Goering, an ace in the First World War, had led Hitler to grant this new service, whose leaders were devoted to him, proportionally larger appropriations than the other services. The causes matter little; one must admit that they were granted generously to the renascent Luftwaffe at a time when the French Air Force was regularly subjected during budget debates to the greatest reductions. At the same time that Hitler was preparing to wage an air-and-ground war against France on its eastern frontier, France was devoting its meager resources to building up the most marvelous navy it would ever have—with the exception, of course, of aircraft carriers, which the navy staff felt were of no great importance.

Backed by a large budget, the German aeronautics industry had profound advantages over that of the French. At the moment of its revival it had used the funds placed at its disposal to create an industrial infrastructure that made possible the rationalization of mass production. Moreover, in 1934 when France was throwing itself with all its might into a plan intended to turn out in two years transitional airplanes hardly better than the preceding ones, Germany, after having manufactured small numbers of planes of that type, quickly put modern airplanes into production—the Dornier 17, Heinkel 111, and Messerschmitt 109. Not all of this was obvious in 1936, but French military intelligence kept the general staff well informed, and the coming into service in the early months of 1937 of the Messerschmitt 109 B 1 fighters—whose performance was similar to that of the Morane 406 that reached French units two years later—was not a surprise. The French and the German models could also be compared at the Zurich air meet in late July 1937, where the best French fighter plane of the time, the Dewoitine 510, was far outclassed in speed not only by the Messerschmitt 109, as was to be expected, but also by the Dornier 17 bomber.

It is easy to understand that to informed aviators, who were following current aeronautical events, the prospects may have appeared dismal.

The Status of French Aviation in July 1936

Those prospects were all the more dismal since the status of French aviation in July 1936 offered no hope of a rapid recovery, either in the area of materiel or in that of personnel.

The Airplanes in Service

Little by little the units saw the planes provided for in Plan I arriving. For bombing, 7 groups out of 12 were equipped with Bloch 200's and 2 groups with Amiot 143's. Three groups still had LeO 20's and 206's; these last, however, were converted to Amiot 143's, Bloch 200's, and Farman 221's on January 1, 1937, the date on which the Bloch 210's began to arrive in the units after a six-month delay.

For reconnaissance, the modernization affected 12 groups equipped with B.C.R.'s (9 with Potez 540's or 542's, 3 with Amiot 143's) and 3 groups equipped with Mureaux 117's. The other groups were flying Potez 25's (4 groups) or Breguet 27's (3 groups). The greater part of the Potez 540's were delivered in July 1937, while the Bloch 131's, with a very modern look but very modest performance, were delivered with more than two years' delay, the first in May 1938 and the last during 1939.

As for fighters, of the 16 fighter groups in France proper 10 groups had been converted to modern materiel—8 with Dewoitine 500's and 501's and 2 night fighter groups, one equipped with Mureaux 113's, the other with Mureaux 113's and Dewoitine 501's; 3 groups still had the "transition" planes, the Morane 225 and the Nieuport 629; and, finally, 3 groups continued to fly Nieuport 62's and 622's.

As one can see, the situation was not the brightest. The most "modern" airplanes with which the French units were equipped would quickly become obsolete. Their best bomber and reconnaissance planes derived from the B.C.R. formula and were incapable of being used in the daytime with a reasonable chance of success. The proof of this soon came in Spain, where the Potez 540's and 542's, remarkably safe planes, were nicknamed "flying coffins" by the Spanish crews because of the ease with which the enemy defense shot them down.

The pursuit element was a little better off, however. The planes that it possessed made it possible to give the pilots a training appropriate for flying the planes that could be called really modern, which began to reach the units late in 1938.

But these Dewoitine 500's and 501's and even the 510's, which did not reach the units until the end of the year, had performances that very quickly proved notoriously inadequate.

The Personnel Situation

If the situation of the French Air Force in regard to materiel was bad, it was equally distressing in regard to personnel.

Many problems presented themselves in this area. In July 1936 two of these predominated, that

After a fighter plane program launched in 1933 by the German Air Ministry, the first prototypes of the Messerschmitt Bf 109 were flown late in 1935. Here, one of the definitive planes of the series, the Bf 109 B.

of manpower and that of the officer corps.

After the end of World War I aviation had always had large shortages in proportion to the theoretical manpower allowed it. Until 1936 this situation, although bad, did not entail catastrophic operational consequences. The nature of the airplanes in use made it possible to mitigate the lack of technicians by the extreme resourcefulness and the very great dedication of those who were on the job. Moreover, there was relatively little flying, and it was always under relatively favorable conditions. In 1936 many things were changing. The new planes, and still more those that were on order, demanded a certain rigor for their operation. Specialized personnel, despite recruiting efforts, was always insufficient in number. It is true that the personnel training plans did not always dovetail with the manufacturing plans. Comptroller General Chossat emphasized this in one of his reports, which he prepared in December 1942 for the court of Riom.

Among the appropriations proposed for the Air Ministry, a dominant place is given to the materiel, and at first glance this seems justified. The inferiority and insufficiency of the materiel are obviously the shortcomings that affect public opinion most, and a numerous air fleet gives rise to very spectacular flybys.

We may wonder, however, whether matters of personnel, training, and schools have not been sacrificed somewhat too much to matters of materiel in the strict sense. . . .

And yet on various occasions it has been brought to light in both the Chamber [of Deputies] and in the Senate that questions of personnel are of the highest importance, and that it takes longer to train and develop pilots, navigators, mechanics, or radiomen than to manufacture materiel.

In July 1936 the peacetime needs were estimated at 39,000 and the existing manpower at about 30,000 men. The shortage was 23 percent, nearly a fourth—obviously considerable.

In addition, there were certain difficulties connected with the very advanced age of some personnel and with the officering difficulties that resulted from the very structure of the corps of flying officers. In the matter of age it is necessary to be cautious. It would no doubt seem exaggerated to assert that an aviator in his forties was already at an advanced age. Certainly in times of secure peace, when the operational necessities can coexist with a certain routine and great prudence, an aviator forty years of age is not old. But in July 1936 it was no longer a question of routine. War was at the gates, and experience proves that in wartime advanced age for aviators begins at thirty. To be sure, older comrades in arms showed their sureness and their enthusiasm in combat. These exceptions, however, must not be allowed to mask the harsh reality.

That reality was apparent from a simple reading of the Air Force list issued on July 1, 1936. Little need be said about the pyramid of ranks, except that the number of higher officers was small and that everything depended on the captains. Such a pyramid, while regrettable from the strict point of view of career advancement, was of no great importance to the conduct of operations.

It is quite another thing when, instead of concerning oneself with the pyramid, one looks at the age of the officers and their distribution in the various ranks.

A few remarks may be made concerning the higher officer cadre. The generals were relatively young compared to their counterparts in the army. This was due to the new age limits in force (still two years higher than those decreed by the 1935 law) since the promulgation of the law of April 9, 1935, fixing the status of the personnel of the active cadres of the Air Force. But the youngest major general was 53 and the youngest brigadier general 51. Half of the colonels were over 50.

Of the lieutenant colonels, 16% were over 50, 58% between 45 and 50, and only 26% below 45 years old. The youngest lieutenant colonel was 41. The youngest major was 38, about 13% were under 40, 50% were between 40 and 45, 30% between 45 and 50, and 7% were over 50 years old.

All this was worrisome, but the most serious matter had to do with the captains, who, as we have seen, represented the present and the future of the Air Force. Only 6% were under 30, 34% were between 30 and 35, 21% were between 36 and 40, and 39% were over 41 years old.

Of the 672 captains on the list, 313, or almost half, had entered the army during the First World War or earlier. Quite naturally, their seniority gave them precedence over their younger comrades, who were champing with impatience and saw their advancement blocked by the requirement to be in the top half of the seniority list in order to be promoted to major. In July 1936 only 29 of the 336 who could be recommended for promotion were under age 36.

This explains many things, particularly the difficulties that certain crews experienced in converting to airplanes equipped with modern devices (retractable landing gear, variable-speed propellers, flaps, etc.) and adapting themselves to the piloting and the instruments, since they were very strong advocates of the instinctive flying referred to in the flights as "flying by the seat of your pants."

The Organization

Poorly equipped, poorly officered, the French Air Force was also poorly organized. The principles that guided the formulation of the law of 1934 have already been discussed, and we will not return to that subject, but putting that law into practice showed up its defects and the shortcomings of French aviation doctrine. Side by side with the bomber units, on which the emphasis was rightly placed, there were insufficient fighter units and a surplus of reconnaissance units. To be sure, the underlying idea was that these last units, with their B.C.R. planes, could in case of necessity be used for missions other than those for which they were intended. The failure of the formula eliminated the possibility but left an imbalance which satisfied the land army but was simply nonsense in the aviation field.

Pierre Cot's Measures

The Reforms in the Central Administration

Upon his arrival Pierre Cot found a ministry not very different from the one he had organized in

1933 with General Denain. In the last half of 1936 he contented himself with adopting three measures concerning popular aviation, military aeronautics, and auditing.

Popular aviation, which shall be discussed later, was attached to a special section created within the minister's office.

The division of authority between the Air Ministry and the Ministry of the Navy had been regulated by the Painlevé-Leygues agreement of the end of November 1932. That agreement, which left the navy with a sizable autonomous air force, proved satisfactory in practice, with certain details remaining to be adjusted further. The decree of August 22, 1936, confirmed the division of forces and defined the conditions of airplane production. The prototypes were established by the Directorate of Aeronautical Manufactures, on its budget, in accordance with directives issued by the Ministry of the Navy. Production runs were carried out by the same directorate but on navy appropriations transferred to the Air Ministry. The navy possessed an air force of its own, but the Air Ministry retained the technical responsibilities.

Under the law of 1882 on the administration of the army, which remained applicable to the air force, the minister was to have at his disposal an agency charged with inspection and auditing of the administration in the broad sense of the term. Until 1933 these functions were performed within the new ministry by the comptrollers of the Ministries of War and of the Navy. The law of May 31, 1933, had created an aeronautics inspection and auditing corps. Beginning in 1934 the comptrollers oversaw the contracts entered into with industrialists and the subsidies for associations and works. The decree of January 20, 1936, had introduced, under the minister of air, a financial auditing committee consisting of two representatives of the Ministry of Finance and two auditors. That committee began to function in January 1937.

A decree of June 1936, internal to the Air Ministry, reinforced the order-in-council of 1935 which, to make it possible to compute the taxes on the earnings of companies working for the National Defense, set up an audit of their administrative, financial, and accounting activities. The new decree established a permanent audit of those enterprises, the commissioners being required to be present at meetings of their boards of directors and management committees.

The Framework of the Revival

The essence of Pierre Cot's action obviously did not lie in these few administrative measures concerning the Air Ministry. It concerned the revival of the air force.

This revival posed three problems: 1) a clear definition of a doctrine of employment which would be the basis for the plans to be issued; 2) the design and production of new aircraft that would quantitatively and qualitatively meet the needs which flowed logically from the practical application of the doctrine and also from French commitments and those undertaken by France's allies; and 3) the recruitment and training of the personnel needed for putting into service the planes which were planned to equip the French air forces.

In reality, although it is possible to find in the work started in July a certain policy line that was undoubtedly aimed at reinforcing the Air Ministry's independence of the Ministry of War, circumstances necessitated solutions that defy dogmatic analysis.

Measures concerning Materiel

The most important measures were undoubtedly those concerning materiel. We have seen that in 1934 and 1935 very large orders were issued to a disorganized aeronautics industry. The essential task to be undertaken was indisputably a reorganization of the production machinery. Something had to be done; there had been talk of a reorganization for five years. Upon his arrival at the Air Ministry General Denain had made a considerable effort to bring about a concentration of enterprises and a tooling up of factories with a view to industrial mobilization and geographic decentralization.

The Bloch 210.

The Farman 221 four-engined bomber.

The Bloch 131, a plane of mediocre performance despite its modern look.

Very partial results had been obtained in regard to airframes, but nothing had been done in regard to airplane engines.

The most serious point was that of industrial equipment. The aeronautics industry, particularly that which produced airframes, was still in the artisan stage. The airplane manufacturers went slow on equipment for fear that, in the absence of new orders, they could not amortize their investment costs.

The Nationalizations

In fact, the aeronautics industry had grown accustomed to being assisted by the state, which was its customer to the extent of 98 percent of its business or, in other words, its only customer. The temptation was great, for a government of socialist orientation, to nationalize the aeronautics industry. A nationalization under private charter was preferred to that extreme solution. The companies would continue to function under the law of 1867 on corporations, but the state would become the biggest shareholder.

Parliament passed on August 11, 1936, the law permitting the total or partial expropriation of any establishment manufacturing war materiel; the Air Ministry could launch its program of nationalization. Certain difficulties were encountered in carrying it out.

Those difficulties, apart from personality problems, did not come, as one might suspect, from the manufacturers, the majority of whom were accepting an advantageous solution "with a smile." They came from the budget provided, which was insufficient: 60 million francs in 1936 instead of the 150 million needed. They also came from the financial administration "by reason of the prerogatives that it still has in regard to French administration in general" and "the special prerogative that it reserves to itself in the matter of finding treasury funds."

These difficulties, however, did not prevent the factories manufacturing airplanes from being 80 percent nationalized by January 1937, the state acquiring two-thirds of the stock and indemnifying the owners. Six national manufacturing companies were created, one per region, to make it possible to accelerate the decentralization: the S.N.C.A.N. (Société Nationale de Construction Aéronautique [Nord]/National Aeronautical Manufacturing Corporation [North]), S.N.C.A.C. (Center), S.N.C.A.S.O. (Southwest), S.N.C.A.S.E. (Southeast), S.N.C.A.O. (West), and S.N.C.A.M. (South).

At the same time an old plan was carried out for the creation of an aeronautical arsenal intended to serve as a reference establishment. The Aeronautics Arsenal was created at Villacoublay with the same charter as the Naval Arsenals.

For lack of sufficient appropriations, a certain number of factories making airframes remained in the private sector: Breguet in Vélizy, Amiot-S.E.C.M. in Colombes, Morane-Saulnier in Puteaux and Vélizy, Latécoère in Toulouse, Caudron-Renault in Boulogne-Billancourt, Gourdou in Saint Maur, and Levasseur in Paris.

For the same reasons only one engine factory was nationalized, the Lorraine, which became the Société Nationale de Construction de Moteurs (S.N.C.M./National Engine Manufacturing Corporation) in Argenteuil. The others—Hispano-Suiza, Gnome and Rhône, Renault—representing 90 percent of the engine production capacity, remained in the private sector.

The Nationalization Procedures

It is important to dwell on the conditions under which the nationalizations were to be carried out in the aeronautics industry. To be sure of the success of the operation, such attractive conditions were offered to the industrialists "concerned" that they could only "congratulate themselves on having been nationalized."

For inventorying and estimating the expropriation indemnity for planes under construction, as a price basis the prices of the replacement catalogues, very advantageous to the industrialists, were adopted. The machinery and the premises were appraised very generously; in spite of this overestimation, the price at which the tools and machinery were estimated was less than 60 million francs. If one compares this figure with the annual turnover of the aeronautics industry, on the order of 1,200 million francs, one can see the extreme state of "underequipment" the industry was in at that time.

Former directors of the companies were offered posts of managing administrator, that is, "director" of the new organizations formed. M. Olive managed the S.N.C.A.O., M. Bloch the S.N.C.A.S.O., M. Potez the S.N.C.A.N., M. Outhenin-Chalandre the S.N.C.A.C., M. Arsène the S.N.C.A.S.E., and M. Dewoitine the S.N.C.A.M. The presidency of all these corporations was conferred upon a high government official, M. de L'Escaille.

Each corporation had a research office of its own, but in order not to lose the benefit of previous experience the directors were allowed to keep their research offices. They were even authorized to place them in premises close to the management, and hence within the national corporation and side by side with its research office.

Of course, these measures were sharply criticized. Besides, as the directors were the creators of the prototypes that had come out before the nationalization, it appeared normal to establish a licensing agreement remunerating the director on a private basis for each airplane of his old brand manufactured in an S.N.C.A. On that point, too, the criticism was obvious. It was natural for the directors to be suspected of favoring the manufacture of their own planes rather than those of the new corporation, and the large orders placed for Potez 63's, Bloch 151's, or LeO 45's appear to justify these suspicions. It must be remembered, however, that when they were ordered they were the most brilliant machines of their time and that they were chosen by commissions, tested by the test center, and ordered by the S.T.Aé.

The existence of collusion between civilians and military men in the Air Ministry and the directors of the companies, sometimes suggested by polemicists, does not seem probable. The fact remains that nationalization, far from robbing the manufacturers, was an exceptional financial bargain for most of them.

These financial advantages granted to the nationalized firms might seem shocking. So they undoubtedly were from a strictly moral point of view, but that was not the point at issue. What mattered was to find out whether the nationalizations would or would not make possible the development of the aeronautics industry. At the outset the answer was not clear. In January 1937 the nationalized factories saw their manufacturing stopped for inventory. It is easy to imagine the disorder introduced throughout 1937 by the reorganization of the factories. All the headquarters were in Paris; it was necessary to learn to make the factories, which until then had been independent, work on the same production series. In addition, considerable financial difficulties almost immediately arose in the S.N.C.A.

To avoid as far as possible resorting to bank loans, the interest on which was reflected in the cost price, the state would have had to back the finances of the corporations by using ad hoc budget appropriations. Since these were grossly inadequate, it was necessary to resort to "extraregulatory methods in regard to the execution of contracts, and to less strictness in establishing the costs of materials."

The measures adopted led to accounts that were very generously calculated, issuances of security money, and even an exceptional increase of 10 percent in the price of the contracts entered into with the national corporations.

In spite of these measures, payrolls were hard to meet throughout the year, and this constant search for liquid funds absorbed a considerable part of the managers' time to the detriment of the time devoted to manufactures.

The Result of the Nationalizations

At the end of 1937 in spite of everything it was justifiable to assert that the operation of the nationalizations promised well for the future. The aeronautics industry was better organized and capable at last of absorbing the appropriations made for equipment, so that the necessary machinery could be provided. If the S.N.C.A.'s had not functioned satisfactorily, that was partly due to the catastrophic situation of the industry in mid-1936 and partly to the insufficiency of the budget appropriations allocated to the Air Ministry for 1937 operations.

It fell to Pierre Cot's successor, Guy La Chambre, who had sufficient appropriations from 1938 on, to launch France's aerial rearmament at last.

The Armament Plans

The Five-Year Plan

Two weeks after passing the law on nationalizations Parliament passed a new aerial armament plan, the five-year plan, whose name was a good indication of its rationale. The task was to accomplish the complete renovation of the French air fleet in five years by annual installments amounting initially to 550 million francs. The disbursements were to be pledged from 1936 to 1940, the payments to be spread out from 1937 to 1941. The main lines of this plan had been drawn up by the general staff at the beginning of 1936.

The reasons for it were clearly set forth in a note from the general staff on June 16, 1936.

In the course of 1935 it became apparent that Germany was setting up a real military aviation, and in March the repudiation of the military clauses of the Treaty of Versailles gave that aviation a legal existence in Germany. Thanks to the Rome agreements it was possible, by shifting to the northeastern frontier the forces previously allotted to that of the southeast, to guard against the German danger, and the 1933 plan remained sufficient.

But during the early months of 1936 the situation has completely changed.

The Italo-Ethiopian conflict has forced us again to envisage certain eventualities in the southeast, making unavailable both the forces assigned to the defense of the northeast and the North African forces, whose repatriation was planned in case of mobilization.

German rearmament has continued at an accelerated pace. According to the latest information received, Germany now possesses a first-line fleet of nearly 1,500 planes, not counting reserves.

Furthermore, the reoccupation of the Rhineland on 7 March has enabled Germany to move its takeoff bases closer to our frontier. Paris is now only an hour's flight from the German airfields.

Finally, in the course of the recent London talks the air support of Great Britain, apart from its contingent character, has been revealed as practically worthless.

In the face of this situation, the French plan of 1933 becomes manifestly inadequate. At the present time France still occupies an honorable place in regard to forces in being, but is already greatly outclassed in the matter of plans and preparations for growth.

As already noted, what was needed was a plan for the modernization of the materiel. Unfortunately, modernization was not possible since the only airplanes that could be ordered were those already included in Plan I. The contracts issued in 1936 under that plan concerned: 30 pursuit planes—Dewoitine 510's (6 were later turned over to China, reducing the order to 24); 89 bombers—56 Bloch 210's, 25 Amiot 143's, and 8 Farman 222's; and 68 reconnaissance planes—Bloch 131's and 132's.

To these orders 66 Morane 405's were added in 1937 to the 247 planes ordered under the plan. Only the 66 Morane 405's could be called modern. The Bloch 131 was also often considered as modern, but actually that plane, though modern in appearance, had performance figures similar to those of the Bloch 210.

In fact, the injection of these new orders into an industry in the process of reorganization did not simplify the problems. The only positive side of the plan was its duration. To fix the main lines of a five-year plan was to assure the aeronautics industry of long-term work and thus to encourage investment. The psychological impact on the manufacturers would have been certain if the plan had come out at the beginning of 1936. Coming after the nationalizations, which had the effect of making the state the principal investor, the psychological significance was less evident.

Plan II

In any case, the five-year plan had not gone beyond the stage of the first installment when it was swallowed up in the growth plan issued in September 1936 which bears the name of Plan II.

Here again it was not a question of a new plan. In 1935 the Minister of Air had fixed the main lines of a plan for 1,500 airplanes. That plan was not followed up at the time because of financial repercussions; modified and completed, it was readopted in September 1936.

The aim of Plan II, which was approved by the cabinet in November 1936, was clearly expressed in the report of the Air Council dated November 24, 1936.

Reinforcement of our Air Force is rendered necessary by the arms buildup that is being carried out by certain powers on our borders.

Germany, which could muster only 12 flights in 1934, had 90 flights at its disposal at the beginning of 1936. It

Dewoitine 500's and 501's during maneuvers in August 1937.

A Dewoitine 510 after a crash. The plane belonged to the 3rd Flight of GC II/1 in 1936.

might strive to attain the figure of 200 flights in 1937, with 2,000 modern first-line planes. As of now it could mobilize in a month's time a number of heavy squadrons sufficient to drop 800 tons of projectiles on the Paris region in a single raid.

Italy, after having practically put its aeronautics industry on a wartime footing to meet the needs of the Ethiopian campaign, has not slowed down the tempo of its effort and is said to have 1,800 modern airplanes, of which 1,500 are in Italy proper.

The U.S.S.R., for its part, reportedly has 3,500 airplanes, the majority of which are up to date, and England has 130 flights equipped with 1,500 modern planes.

Because of the gravity of the external situation, there would thus be a risk of compromising the security of the national defense if the necessary steps were not taken now to strengthen the country's aerial defense.

These measures involve: a) development of heavy aviation up to a strength comparable to that of the German air force; b) creation of units especially prepared to carry out reconnaissance missions needed by the Army; c) development of light aviation capable of contributing to the defense of our territory in France proper and North Africa.

Plan II provided for the realization by the end of 1939 of an air force of 2,795 planes (not counting 56 seaplanes): 1,518 first-line planes and 1,277 in reserve. These planes were to be organized into 18 groups of light aircraft, 57 groups of heavy aircraft, and in regional observation or pursuit flights. In addition, it provided for 3 groups of airborne infantry equipped with 42 first-line planes.

This plan was significant on more than one score. It set forth the ideas of the Air Force general staff, which gave priority to heavy aircraft. This category was to represent 45% of the planes by the end of the plan, against 25% for pursuit and 30% for cooperation with ground forces (including 3% for the airborne infantry, which did not come under the army).

It confirmed the creation of a new service, the airborne infantry, which, transported by plane and parachuted in case of need, gave the military command the possibility of rapid maneuver on both the offensive and the defensive.

Unfortunately, the orders placed at the beginning of 1937 could only involve the same planes as those of the five-year plan. Thus the first orders involved: for pursuit, Dewoitine 510's; for bombing, Bloch 210's and Farman 222's; for reconnaissance, Potez 540's, Mureaux 115's, Bloch 131's, and C 30 Autogyros.

It was not until the latter half of the year that the Morane 406's and Potez 630's were finally ordered, thus marking the start of the Air Force's modernization. At the beginning of 1938 orders for Farman 223's and LeO 45's were also placed.

All told, the orders under Plan II, with some slight adjustments later, amounted for 1937 to 292 pursuit planes (260 of them modern), 91 heavy planes, and 149 reconnaissance planes, all of old types.

Plan IV

The last plan[1] set up under Pierre Cot's ministry, Plan IV, submitted on February 15 to the permanent committee on national defense, was important because it marked an evolution of the Air Force's thinking in comparison with the provisions of Plan II. The latter put the emphasis on increasing offensive strength. Plan IV, on the contrary, was aimed at improving aerial defense and provided for increasing the light aircraft forces by the creation of 13 new light aircraft groups. The permanent committee on national defense decided to stick to Plan II, however, and Plan IV was abandoned.

At the end of 1937 the results, in terms of aero-

1. For the record, Plan III must also be mentioned. It was to modernize the antiaircraft section. It corresponded to Cot's thesis that all means of aerial defense of the territory should belong to the Air Ministry. The permanent committee on national defense decided, later in December 1936, to keep antiaircraft within the Ministry of War. Plan III became pointless.

A French parachutist ready to jump from a Russian plane during a training session at Tushino, U.S.S.R., in April 1935.

Equipment of 1936.

Captain Veille (at left), head of the parachutist training center at Avignon-Pujaut.

Equipment of 1938–1942. The Air Force was convinced, even before the war, of the future potential of military parachuting.

A jump from a LeO 20.

nautical manufactures, were distressing. Certainly it could be hoped that the organizational reforms put into effect would finally make it possible to get the industry going again, but that was still only a faint hope. There was great concern since the materiel turned out was small in quantity and poor in quality.

At the beginning of 1938 Plan I of 1934 was practically completed (with the exception of the Bloch 131's). The five-year plan and Plan II, on the other hand, were at the very beginning of their execution. Of 771 planes, 326 of them modern—146 Morane 406's and 180 Potez 63's—ordered under the two plans by January 1, 1938, only 83 had been delivered, and all of them were old types. France still had on order 362 planes that would be outdated when they left the factories.

The sought-after modernization could not, in fact, be achieved in less than three or four years. While waiting for the French aeronautics industry to become capable of turning out in volume the modern materiel that the Air Force needed, the idea arose of resorting to foreign industry, and principally to the aeronautics industry in the United States. As we shall see later in considering the reactions of the Aeronautics Committee of the Chamber of Deputies, there was a lobby in France that rose in revolt when there was talk of purchases abroad. Such a position, while justifiable in normal times, seems indefensible when war is threatening and it is necessary to use every possible means for national defense. It was, nevertheless, often expressed from 1936 to 1939.

General Denain had been the first to think of turning to the United States. During the summer of 1937 Pierre Cot, finding out that the French aeronautics industry had no possibility of producing good quality airplane engines in quantity, sent a delegation to the United States to study the purchase of such engines. A little later Senator de La Grange, a personal friend of President Franklin D. Roosevelt, went to the U.S. to establish contact with the American manufacturers. Unfortunately, the American aeronautics industry had not yet launched its own rearmament either, and it was necessary to wait for the action of Guy La Chambre and his friend, William C. Bullitt, in conjunction with Senator de La Grange's approaches, to bring about these orders that were so necessary to France.

Personnel Problems

It is curious to note that, while plane production is often considered in judging the status of French aviation, personnel problems are rarely mentioned. However, these problems were extremely serious from 1936 on.

This lack of interest is easy to understand and was common at the very time when the difficulties arose. As a rule the successive governments naturally took little interest in the development of military manpower. The Minister of Finance has traditionally always considered it a particularly heavy load on the state budget, which should be reduced as much as possible. In addition, while supplies of materiel seem easy to justify, allotments connected with personnel are always looked upon with suspicion by the various levels of the government hierarchy. The manpower tables set up by the first section of the general staff define "theoretical needs," which are to be considered with respect but never honored. Moreover, while the idea gradually gains ground that the production of modern materiel must be preceded by a certain number of indispensable measures—creation of factories, installation of machinery, stockpiling of raw materials, etc.—only the "specialists" are perfectly aware that the "delivery" of personnel to the fighting units presupposes a stepping up of recruiting accompanied by the development of the necessary training facilities.

In July 1936 two problems were causing concern: the average age of the officers, which was too high, and the total manpower level, which was too low.

There was no magical formula available for increasing the manpower level. Even after getting adequate appropriations, it takes some time to build up the number of military personnel. And

Pierre Cot at a popular aviation festival at Vincennes.

The Luciole airplane, much used in popular aviation.

there was no increase in appropriations for this purpose in 1936 and 1937, so that there was no possibility of a radical improvement in the situation.

Nevertheless, a certain effort was made to provide the Air Force with the schools that it needed. In 1937 the Advanced Training Center received the first graduating class from the Advanced School of Aerial Warfare, and the third class from the Air School finished at Salon. However, there was still a lack of schools to provide training in various specialties, and it was still necessary to resort to the civilian schools, such as the Breguet School, which trained radiomen for the Air Force.

Popular Aviation

An interesting phenomenon of the period and one that might undoubtedly have definitively altered the basic recruitment figures was popular aviation.

The idea arose from a number of observations. The system of pilot training scholarships was very costly and had only mediocre results. In spite of the considerable amounts spent to help people learn to fly, flying time was still very expensive at

200 to 350 francs an hour (compared to the average pay of a worker in 1936, about 1,000 francs a month). Sporting aviation was thus a luxury, and the recruiting of pilots was done from only 2% to 3% of the population. It was desired to expand recruitment to the maximum in order to improve quality. Finally, it was necessary to have younger men learn to fly.

Pierre Cot wanted the reform that he proposed to be the adaptation to the Air Ministry of the unrivaled school of "gratuitousness and selection."

During an initial period aviation courses would be taught in the elementary schools. Instruction would comprise the study of aerology and the essential principles of aviation with practical work consisting in the construction of reduced-scale models. Upon completion of these courses, the pupil, if he passed the final examination, would get a certificate which would allow him to do gliding at regional centers that would be established and developed.

Then a new selective examination would allow him to engage in motorized aviation in the aero clubs. For this purpose a popular aviation section would be set up in each participating aero club, functioning under the direction of a council which had to include a representative of the Air Ministry, an instructor, and a delegate of the C.G.T. (General Confederation of Labor).

The dues were not to exceed 10 francs a month. In return the government would furnish flying materiel, workshop equipment, and fuel, as well as pilot instructors and mechanics.

It is probable that the development of this popular aviation, if it had been maintained longer, would have made it possible, once certain initial shortcomings were corrected, to establish an exceptional pool of student pilots for the Air Force. In support of this one must note that at the end of 1938 popular aviation had licensed 3,500 pilots at the first level and 1,250 at the second level. It should be observed, however, that these results, encouraging as they were, were not necessarily translated into an equally large increase in the number of military pilots.

Reforms concerning the Officer Corps

Not being able to regulate to any purpose the manpower problems of the Air Force, which required both appropriations and time, the minister set about modifying the organization of the officer corps, and first of all the officer corps of the flying personnel.

Lowering the Age Limits

The point of departure was connected with the finding that the average age of the officers of the flying personnel was too high. To lower that average age the minister had at his disposal the law of 1935 which reduced the previous age limits by five years. In fact, this law had not been completely enforced, and the age limits in force were still two years higher than they were supposed to be. As a matter of fact, the law had provided for the possibility of this slow evolution, and it seems that a majority wanted it that way.

Pierre Cot, however, felt that the process had to be speeded up. The military intelligence available, notably from the French air attaché in Berlin, placed the accomplishment of German aerial rearmament in 1938–1939. By that time it was necessary for the French to have a general staff that was very well informed and experienced. In order to achieve this it would have to be set up in 1936. The minister gave the Aeronautics Committee of Parliament the names of generals qualified to replace those who were leaving the army due to the application of the new age limits: General Féquant, who was staying on; the major generals to be appointed—Vuillemin, Mouchard, Keller, Aube, Houdemon; and the brigadier generals to be selected from among the colonels—d'Harcourt, Bouscat, Odic, Tétu.

Cot's arguments unquestionably had weight, and the names presented were those of high-ranking officers that had succeeded in winning the esteem of their subordinates. The minister himself underscored the shortage of second lieutenants, first lieutenants, and captains. The only possible solution would have been to intensify recruiting.

This could be done either by calling reserve officers to active duty or by promoting noncommissioned officers. It was, in fact, impossible to solve the immediate problem by recruiting officers coming out of the major military schools since the courses at those schools lasted two years. Perhaps a certain number of places could have been offered to officers who entered Saint Cyr in 1934. Unfortunately, although the first class was not to finish the Air School until 1937, for the first time no place was offered at the "amphi" garrison, which was held at the Special Military School in July 1936.

In fact, when the minister revealed his policy he had already chosen his method of recruiting: he would commission many of the noncommissioned officers as second lieutenants.

It is worth dwelling a bit on this decision, for it was the subject of violent criticisms and was considered as proof of the desire of the Popular Front government to politicize the Air Force.

It is probable that, at least to a certain extent, political considerations were not absent in the choice of this particular solution. It is certain that they affected the commissioning of certain noncommissioned officers. A number of scandalous commissionings were pointed out repeatedly, but, regrettable as they may have been, they were very few in number, and the greater part of the flying noncommissioned officers promoted were of high quality.

It is also interesting to note that in defending this measure Cot used arguments which, though poorly understood and not well received at a time when the recruiting of officers was expected to be done essentially by the big military schools, are today a part of the basic rules of personnel management.

"This method," he said, "will make it possible to give a well-deserved advancement to the best of our noncommissioned officers. Also, for the students from our big military schools who go into aviation, it will constitute a guarantee of advancement to higher grades.

"The young officer coming out of the [Ecole] Polytechnique knows that in aviation only a small percentage of the officers become generals; he will prefer to go into the Navy or into the Artillery. If I introduce into the corps each year a certain number of officers 30 to 35 years old, these officers will not go beyond the grades of captain or major, and consequently we shall be benefiting the others."

The proposed program was incontestably valid for achieving harmonious, long-term management of the officer corps. In any case, there was nothing shocking about taking into the officer ranks flying noncommissioned officers who by reason of necessity were going to be given the responsibility of piloting a delicate multi-seated plane or leading a fighter patrol. But at the moment when this policy was decided on, the problem to be solved was not one of long-term management. While it was true that the mass promotion of second lieutenants from the ranks made it possible to avert, for the incumbent members of the officer corps, the consequences of lowering the age limits, it had no repercussions on the overall officering of Air Force units. This measure would not place a single extra pilot in a unit. It would have been more effective to recruit at the same time a large number of reserve officers called to active duty; at the time, unfortunately, such measures were not current except in wartime.

The Results of the Officer Policy

If one tries to appraise the overall results obtained, one finds from reading the 1938 official list that there was a certain lowering of the age of the higher officers of the Air Force, but that it was clearly perceptible only at the level of the brigadier generals, the youngest of whom was 46, or five years younger than in 1936. For the other higher officer grades the lowering of the average age amounted to about two years, or to the difference between the age limits.

There was also a net lowering of the age of the captains due to the correlative improvement of the pyramid. Whereas in 1936 some 60% of the captains were over 36, this percentage had dropped to 48%. The improvement was clear but still insufficient.

Of course, one sees the inverse phenomenon in the case of first and second lieutenants. In 1938, 27% of them were over 35, compared to 17% in 1936.

It is clear from these results that personnel problems were far from being solved. But it is well to repeat that in this area nothing can be done without time and money. In 1936–1937 both were lacking.

The Organization

The final part of the minister's general action had to do with organization. In July 1936 the organization of the Air Force was defined by the law of 1934, a copy, pure and simple, of the law of 1927 on the organization of the land army. Everything was based on a regional command which commanded the units and directed the administration. Its essential task was getting the forces into condition and preparing for mobilization. This second point appeared as the main one in the 1930s. The quality of the armed forces depends on the way in which mobilization is effected. The law of 1927 also gave the army the possibility of setting up in peacetime large units capable of going into action without the necessity of resorting to mobilization. Although that possibility was offered, no one thought of making use of it, even after March 7, 1936, when Hitler's troops marched into the Rhineland. The mechanized corps recommended by General Charles de Gaulle, which corresponded to the possibility provided for in the law, was considered heretical. It had not been felt necessary to retain that clause in the law of 1934 on the Air Force. Since the peacetime general staffs did not correspond to the wartime ones, no operation could be organized rapidly.

In fact, the organization corresponded to the doctrine of employment advocated by the land army of the time, according to which the major raison d'être of aviation was to be at the service of the ground forces. To those who believed in the major role of aviation in a future conflict and who were observing foreign air forces, beginning with the German air force, the primary necessity was to do battle in the air and win. For that it was advisable to combine the active units, even in peacetime, into large air units capable of engaging instantly in independent actions. This was, in fact, a return to the concept of the air division charged with providing, by air actions, cover for mobilization and the first ground operations—a concept that had prevailed until 1933.

The Decree of October 3, 1936

This appeared very clearly in the report presenting the decree of October 3, 1936, which established the new organization.

> *By reason of its potential for instantaneous action, its strategic mobility, the Air Force is a covering force par excellence.*
>
> *The needs of air cover of the territory imperiously demand the existence, in peacetime, of an Air Force entirely suited to act without delay in case of a conflict.*
>
> *This condition can be fulfilled only by closely adapting the peacetime organization of the Command and the Units of the Air Force to their wartime organization, by the creation of large aerial combat units—homogeneous air divisions and corps.*
>
> *In addition, side by side with the large air units, it is indispensable to have available formations (regional air groups) that are more particularly designed to satisfy the Army's and the Navy's aerial observation needs.*
>
> *Finally, it has become apparent that it is necessary to strengthen the existing territorial organization, with a view to enabling it to fill completely the role that has devolved upon it in carrying out the services of the Air Ministry.*

The new organization separated the territorial command very distinctly from the operational command. The territorial command continued to be exercised by the commanding officers of the air regions, who had under them the commanding officers of air subdivisions who, in turn, had direct command over the services.

The air units were grouped in two air corps

Morane 225's of the 2nd Flight of GC I/7 (SPA 77), based at Dijon, participate in an air meet at Vichy on August 17, 1936.

A Bloch 210 that crashed at takeoff. There were many accidents of this sort in 1937, earning the Bloch 210 the nickname "flying coffin."

General Milch, German secretary of state for air, being greeted on his arrival in Paris, October 4, 1937, by M. Andraud, French secretary of state for air, and by General Fécamp, head of the Air Force general staff.

directly under the Minister of Air: a heavy air corps, organized in 3 divisions comprising a total of 8 air brigades, subdivided into squadrons; and a light air corps, organized in 3 brigades also subdivided into squadrons.

Regional air commanders were also created, adapted to each military region, under the commanding officers of air subdivisions. They served as technical advisers of the commanding officers of the military regions and exercised their authority over the regional air groups.

The wartime organization provided putting the air corps under air armies: "In peacetime as well as in wartime the large air units comprise air corps and air divisions. Air armies are established upon mobilization. . . . The air army is the unit of strategic maneuvers; it is equipped with all the means necessary to conduct such maneuvers at the tactical level. . . . The commanding officer of the air army is charged with the conduct of all air operations in the zone that is assigned to him by the Command."[1]

This new organization was the object of violent criticisms. Nevertheless, it marked an important stage on the way to a functional organization of the Air Force. It was the first attempt to release it definitively from the types of organization adopted during the first few years after the Franco-Prussian War of 1870–1871, which proved unsuited to the characteristics of employment of the new service.

Unfortunately, this attempt was inept. The air corps that were created were poorly adapted to the missions entrusted to the aviation forces, and the extremely marked division between "territorial" and "operational" deprived the latter of all control over the services. But the quality of operations—and this development was perceived clearly at the time—was more and more dependent on the satisfactory working of the different services. There was risk of a gap between the concerns of the personnel of the flying units, oriented toward the operational exploitation of the aerial equipment, and the concerns of base personnel, for whom life would be very agreeable without the planes.

Finally, the organization adopted did not, to say the least, effect economy of means. The multiplication of staffs made it necessary to place numerous officers there, notably captains. On this point, and despite other qualities that must be conceded to it, the organization in question proved to be a bad one.

The Decree of August 15, 1937

The next year the decree of August 15, 1937, was published, which organized the units according to a principle that some said had long since been condemned by experience but that was to spring up again several times later—separation of the Command and the Administration. This decree was to have only a brief effect, always excepting certain provisions concerning the air bases, which it was desired to make into real ports for the Air Force.

Status Summary

By the end of 1937, a year and a half after the Popular Front came into power, a certain effort had been made, but that effort was insufficient.

The aeronautics industry had been reorganized, but the effects of the reorganization did not appear until 1938. In the eyes of contemporaries it appeared to be in a very bad position, especially since social unrest had not spared it. There had been more strikes in the aeronautics industry than in all other industrial sectors. Even though a more thorough study may show that in relation to total production the hours lost because of strikes represented a marginal phenomenon, the impression was bad. That impression was reinforced further by the figures for airplanes produced, which dropped from an average of 43 a month in 1935 and 1936 to 25 a month throughout 1937.

No measures had been taken to overcome the latent manpower crisis.

The budgets remained insufficient, especially in

1. Order on the tactical employment of the large air units, March 31, 1937.

Guy La Chambre.

comparison to those of other countries. A third of the British defense budget was devoted to the RAF, while a sixth of the French defense budget went to the Air Force.

The date by which the renovation of the Air Force would be completed seemed to grow more and more remote, more inaccessible. This was true, but the management during the last three six-month periods was not responsible for that. An air force is not improvised; it is built up, and that takes time. But time was against them. Starting more than three years behind Germany, France had a heavy handicap. Until the end of 1937 it hoped to overcome part of its handicap by thinking that it should try for parity between the German aviation forces and the combined aviation forces of France and Great Britain. That, of course, was only a French hypothesis since the British had never agreed with them on that point. The hypothesis was reasonable, nevertheless, for the air threat was purely German.

By the end of 1937 developments in Europe no longer allowed the French to ignore the probable Italian threat and the possible Spanish one. Under those conditions it was necessary to return to the problem of enlarging the Air Force, the strength of which had to be equal to German air power, with the strength of the RAF counterbalancing the Italian and Spanish threats.

The study of an urgent enlargement of the French Air Force was launched by General Féquant in November 1937, following a trip to England by the prime minister, Camille Chautemps. This study was to result in the establishment of Plan V, which really marked a complete renovation for the Air Force. It was to be the task of Guy La Chambre, the new minister of air from January 19, 1938, on, in a second Chautemps cabinet, to perfect the plan and see to its realization.

The Administration of Guy La Chambre from January 1938 to September 1939

When Guy La Chambre was named minister of air the problems of domestic and foreign policy were very different from those of June 1936 when the Popular Front came into power.

The alliance had been broken in the Chamber of Deputies on January 15 by Prime Minister Chautemps. From then on, with the exception of the Blum cabinet (March 13 to April 17, 1938), it must be said that the Chautemps government (January 18 to March 13) and the Daladier government (April 10, 1938 to March 20, 1940) were no longer Popular Front governments.

Throughout this period economic and social problems arose in an acute form. The effort in those fields was aimed at restoring the government's finances and putting France back to work. These two objectives were soon attained. The divisions among Frenchmen derived primarily from external problems. The country had already been divided during the Spanish Civil War, interventionists against noninterventionists. After Munich it was divided into those who believed in a firm attitude toward Hitler and those who preached conciliation above all. In any case, from the beginning of 1938 the die was cast. The democracies could no longer save the peace. War was approaching, and Hitler wanted it.

It is beyond the scope of this book to enter into the often complicated details of the international events that took place during this entire prewar period. It seems worthwhile, however, to point out the principal ones, for France was to move to their rhythm for a year and a half. For the military these events were represented by alerts which followed one after another at regular intervals until the general mobilization.

On November 5, 1937, Adolf Hitler, persuaded that the democracies would let him alone, revealed his first objectives to the high military officers and diplomatic officials.

On March 12, 1938, German troops entered Austria, and on the 13th the Anschluss, or annexation, was proclaimed.

Czechoslovakia saw its military defenses in the mountains of Bohemia outflanked. Hitler coaxed the German nationals of the Sudetenland to agitation punctuated by violence and profited by it to threaten the Czech state.

From March to September 1938

The period from March to September was marked by threats of war and by negotiations. Neville Chamberlain paid a visit to Hitler at Berchtesgaden, in the face of specific threats of war. Then came the pact of Munich, in which France sacrificed its Czech ally as the price of peace.

Except for a few unyielding leftists and rightists and for the Communists, relief (a cowardly relief, Blum said later) was felt in France. Upon his arrival at Le Bourget and all along his route to the Rue Saint Dominique in Paris, Daladier was applauded by an immense crowd.

After Czechoslovakia it was the turn of Poland, linked to France by a mutual assistance pact.

Germany wanted the return to the Reich of the German city of Danzig and the abolition of the "corridor" that separated it from East Prussia. Before making his claims specific, Hitler ordered a military occupation—in violation of the Munich Agreement—of Bohemia, Moravia, and Slovakia, which became German protectorates.

On March 22, 1939, German troops occupied Memel in Lithuania. On April 6, 1939, Italian troops invaded Albania.

Throughout this period French and British representatives were negotiating a mutual assistance treaty with the Soviet Union in case of German aggression. But this did not prevent the astounding news of the signing of the German-Soviet nonaggression pact on August 23 in Moscow. From then on nothing could have stopped the war. On September 1 the German army invaded Poland. On September 3 France and Great Britain declared war on Germany.

Guy La Chambre's Action

These international events have been recalled here because French rearmament would constantly take them into account. France would try to accelerate its manufactures and recruitments at every moment, without being able to succeed in doing so. Like the hare of the fable, it had started too late.

However, at the time of his arrival in the Air Ministry on the Boulevard Victor in Paris, Guy La Chambre could normally cherish the hope of succeeding better than his predecessor, for he could benefit on the one hand from the improvements introduced into the organization of the aeronautics industry and on the other from much larger appropriations than those of the earlier years.

The Decree of February 16, 1938. The Organization of National Defense

When he took up his duties as head of the Air Ministry the decrees of February 16, 1938, had already been issued. These decrees entrusted to the minister of war the Ministry of National Defense (which already existed) and made the chief of the army general staff the chief of the National Defense general staff. Everyone had been more or less in agreement for a long time in recognizing the necessity of directing the activity of the three services through a single authority. Nevertheless, the decrees aroused the aviators' distrust.

The reactions of the Aeronautics Committee of the Chamber of Deputies to the explanations of these decrees given by the prime minister were indicative of the suspicion aroused by the new organization. The text published by the committee, which was backed by a unanimous vote of the members, said in effect: 1) It is highly desirable for the Minister of National Defense not to be simultaneously the head of another ministry; 2) it is also highly desirable that the chief of the National Defense general staff not be at the same time chief of the general staff of one of the three services, and that he have at his disposal a general staff normally composed of interservice elements; 3) the effects of the impact of land-bound thinking on the rapidly changing technology of modern aviation are to be guarded against; 4) study must be given to the means necessary to enlarge the Air Force with the least possible delay—to increase the number of planes and also the flying personnel; and 5) these decrees run counter to decisions of the committee and even of the Chamber of Deputies calling for the autonomy and completeness of the Air Ministry.

One must not be deceived. The committee's text took account not only of its anxiety but also of that of the personnel of the Air Force, whose defense the committee was undertaking. It is necessary to bear in mind that a number of members of the committee who were categorized as leftists, such as Boussoutrot, a test pilot, who was chairman, or rightists, like Robbe, a reserve officer aviator, had numerous contacts with their conrades on active duty.

La Chambre had first of all to try to reassure the parliamentarians on the committee. The decrees, he said, were much less the expression of a doctrine than the statement of an experimental finding. The old form of coordination had gaps in it that the present text was meant to fill. "It is not a matter," he stated, "as has been incorrectly said and written, of putting the Air Force under guardianship. Rather, it is a matter of effecting the synthesis of the various land, sea, and air forces, a synthesis that is necessary if we want the Command to be able to cover the hypotheses which the responsible government has the duty to include in the war plan that it turns over to the general staffs."

The new organization differed little, according to the minister, from that adopted on June 6, 1936, which made the minister of war the minister of national defense, turning over to him as a working agency the permanent secretariat of national defense. The powers remained identical: employment of armed forces, establishment and execution of armament programs, appropriations, and so on.

The difference was that earlier he was charged with coordinating, whereas now he gave final approval. He was the arbiter. But this right of arbitration left each department's right of initiative intact.

Was this a detriment done to the Air Ministry, or was it, on the contrary, a guarantee being given to it? The minister, for his part, felt that it was a guarantee since the minister of national defense, now accountable and responsible for the preparation of the three armed forces, observing the deficiencies of one or the other, would make an effort to remedy them under the best conditions.

As for the objection to giving the Ministry of National Defense to an incumbent minister of war, to do otherwise would lead to creating a minister without real power, or else, in view of the responsibilities weighing upon him, to his creating an administration for himself.

To justify the nomination of General Gamelin as chief of the general staff of national defense, La Chambre said that whoever the chief of the general staff was, he would have an origin and that examples in the past had shown that Joffre, who was from the engineers, had not, as commander in chief, neglected the infantrymen.

This last argument, it must be acknowledged, was rather specious. While the view that General Joffre had of the infantry was the same as that of other generals who came from that service, it must be recognized that the view that the leaders of the

General Vuillemin.

land forces had of aviation was very different from that of experienced aviators.

In any case, it is known today that neither Daladier nor Gamelin, in spite of appearances, had sufficient authority to direct the national defense.

The suspicion expressed by the deputies who were members of the committee and who feared "the effects of land-bound thinking on the rapidly changing technology of modern aviation" had no chance of being dissipated by the minister's fine words. He felt it hovering over his decisions on several occasions. He had to defend himself against it. When, some time later, he came to explain to the same deputies the economy of the reorganization of September 1938, he repeatedly insisted on the fact that it resulted entirely from the ideas of members of the Air Council, that the National Defense echelon had at no time meddled in its decision, and that no member from outside the Air Ministry was present at the deliberations of the Air Council on the subject.

General Vuillemin, Chief of the Air Force General Staff

To reassure the Air Force and restore its confidence the minister appointed as chief of the general staff a prestigious aviation leader, General Vuillemin. It was an excellent choice. General Vuillemin's war service was exceptional. He was an aviator in the full sense of the term, who had all his life shown his love for flying. In the 1920s he had made remarkable pioneering flights. He had proved himself to be a leader without parallel at the head of the air forces in Algeria and Morocco. To justify his choice La Chambre said later, after the war, that when he had called him to the head of the Air Ministry there was a grave crisis in the morale of the crews, who were unwilling to fly anymore. However, this is not confirmed by either the documents of the time or by evidence gathered among officers serving with units between 1936 and 1938. Besides, he himself declared to the Aeronautics Committee of the Chamber of Deputies on January 25, 1938, before Vuillemin's nomination: "As for the morale of the personnel, according to those whom I have had occasion to question about it, it is essentially dependent on the number and quality of the planes. Where they have airplanes and where the aviators fly, the morale is excellent. Where there are few or no planes there is a feeling of lassitude and profound discouragement."

Upon reading this one may qualify somewhat La Chambre's motives in calling General Vuillemin to the head of the Air Force. First of all, why did he feel the need to change the management team? The objections made—and they were made by the new minister before the Aeronautics Committee—concerned General Jauneaud,[1] the head of Pierre Cot's military office. Of course, it was within La Chambre's authority to form his military office according to his own preference, and the designation of General Bouscat as head of that office appeared to be a good choice. But the chief of the

1. It should also be mentioned that over forty years later contemporary witnesses offer judgments of this officer which are always impassioned but quite contradictory.

general staff, General Féquant, had a great deal of experience with the problems then facing the Air Force, and he had gathered around him a remarkable team composed of General Keller, chief of staff (we should now say general staff), and Colonels Tarnier and Carayon, first and second deputy chiefs respectively.

No doubt it was a matter of clearly marking the break with the "old régime," but for once the choice was relatively open. It is a frequent characteristic of the management of officers that at a given moment only two or three generals can be considered, on the basis of their age and seniority, for the highest position in the military hierarchy. This was not the case in 1938. Behind General Féquant (who died on December 24, 1938) there were three major generals promoted on October 14, 1936, and three major generals promoted during the first half of 1937. If we disregard the two generals who were born in 1882 and were to leave the service during 1939, there were still six candidates. Logically the youngest two, Generals Mouchard and Houdemon, born in 1885, or in a pinch General Aubé, born in 1884, should have been the best candidates.

General Mouchard, for example, a Saint Cyr graduate and licensed major general, combined a certain aviation experience with a profound knowledge of staff problems. He had held troop commands and had commanded a region. General Aubé, a graduate of the Ecole Polytechnique, and General Houdemon, also from Saint Cyr, while not licensed, had also had careers that would have enabled them to understand readily the formidable problems that arise at the level of the Central Administration.

However that may be, General Vuillemin's nomination was greeted with rejoicing in the air units. For the "P.N.," or flying personnel, of those units he was, it should be repeated, the P.N. type. An exceptional pilot with 5,000 hours of flying time, which at that time was considerable, an excellent fighter with 10 aerial combat victories to his credit and 17 citations, awarded the Grand Cross of the Legion of Honor as a colonel in 1934, he was the hero of the pioneer flights that penetrated the Sahara in the 1920s and the commander of the Black Cruise. Moreover, his very unassuming manner, combined with a profound knowledge of men, made him a beloved and respected leader.

War leader and marvelous aviator though he was, was he the best choice in such difficult times when, while waiting to fight the Germans, he would have to fight against the technical services, the other general staffs, the politicians, and time itself? Faced with his new duties, he quite naturally chose for his office head one of his faithful colleagues, General Mendigal. The latter, a graduate of Saint Cyr, had come into the service as a first lieutenant of the hussars, pilot in the C 11, at the beginning of 1917. Licensed by the staff college, he had taught the aeronautics course at the Advanced War College and had been chief of staff of the First Air Corps, commanded by Vuillemin. He had the reputation of being an extremely cultivated man of rare intelligence. The same reputation was also enjoyed by Colonel Bergeret, who was Mendigal's assistant at the Advanced War College. When Mendigal was named first deputy, Colonel Bergeret took over the duties of second deputy. Both were to have a considerable influence on the chief of the general staff and were considered by those in the know during that period as the real bosses of the Air Force.

Without going so far as to accept that allegation, one must say, nevertheless, that they did play a major role at the time. Did that role lead them to give an exaggerated preference to the point of view of the army general staff in the decisions made? There is nothing to prove this for certain, but their long service as teachers at the War College quite naturally predisposed them to look at problems as the land forces did. Perhaps—but this is only a hypothesis—this reproach was formulated during the period under consideration. This would explain the minister's insistence, when he presented his reorganization to the members of the Aeronautics Committee of the Chamber of Deputies, on stating that it had not been influenced by the army general staff.

Materiel: First Measures

Even before his team had been completely installed, the minister grappled with the major problem facing him, that of materiel. His point of departure was better than his predecessor's. At the beginning of 1938 the aeronautics industry had almost entirely digested the nationalizations and the upheavals born of social agitation. It was possible to inject appropriations into it rapidly and to launch the production of modern airplanes at last. La Chambre immediately realized the need for a new plan, which he estimated at the time would extend over two and a half years. He justified this time span by the consideration that "according to those who believe in graphs, 1940, by the armament curve, the classes turned out by the schools, and the rate at which our neighbors are constructing certain highways, will be the year when they are completed."

But he found that no matter what desire he might have to manufacture quickly, it was necessary to take account of the realities. And these showed that the only airplanes ready to go into production runs were the Morane 406, the Potez 63, and the LeO 45. In the case of the LeO 45 manufacture proved difficult.

Therefore, if it was absolutely desired to have airplanes quickly, the only way was to get them from abroad. At the beginning of 1938 that idea did not please the aeronautics lobby and was violently attacked. Nevertheless, La Chambre settled the details of such purchases. There was no question of manufacture in France under license. No problem would be solved by that since the limit of French manufactures was determined by the production capacity of the French industry.

It was necessary to buy ready-made, and it was necessary to see to it that the ready-made planes were not white elephants. Between the lines of the minister's statements can be read the need for diplomatic discussions to get the United States to waive the law forbidding the export of materiel less than two years after it came into service. If the U.S. held to those restrictions it would have supplied France with planes with performances similar to that of the Dewoitine 510, and that was clearly not the objective.

Finally, the French were obliged by necessity to rethink the apportionment of airplanes between fighting and bombing units. The minister asserted that if France had too few planes, priority must be given to fighters, and he added:

I am not sure that we must have an air force as offensive in character as that indicated in the regulation on the employment of the large air units. We are the country that built the Maginot Line, which is the very image of peaceful intentions. We must make sure that it cannot be said that while Geneva is deliberating we are building up an Air Force that is offensive in character. With that reservation it will be indispensable for us to have an air force capable of reprisals and some bombing planes. They cannot be Potez's, which were shot down in Spain, or our old Amiot 143's. With such airplanes we cannot claim to be able to bomb objectives at any distance within enemy lines.

Plan V

Having thus defined the main outline of his action and having, as we have seen, immediately launched large-scale tooling-up operations, the minister submitted for approval of the government a new plan called Plan V.

We have seen that this growth plan had been envisaged in November 1937. The military hypotheses used in determining needs were: a) "that the French Air Force should be capable of fighting alone against the German air forces that can normally be directly opposed to it, the British forces providing the equivalent of the effort necessary to face Italy and the possible enmity of Spain"; and b) "that the German and Italian air forces were arbitrarily stabilized in their situation of 1 January 1938."

The corresponding draft, worked out in detail at the beginning of 1938, was discussed with the Air Council on March 7–9, 1938. The main outline was decreed at the meeting of that council held on March 15, with Daladier, General Gamelin, and Admiral Darlan in attendance.

The plan had several new features. First of all, it

The Mureaux 117. Many GAO's (Aerial Observation Groups) were equipped with this plane in 1939.

was not only a plan for airplanes. For the first time a coherent set of actions was defined which would when carried out make it possible to have an Air Force capable of making use of the materiel provided.

The accent was placed on the absolute necessity "of a considerable increase in the manpower of the Air Force. Because of the uncertainties and dangers of the present international situation, this increase should be effected *immediately*. However, in view of the unavoidable delays in the recruiting and training of the personnel and in the creation of the infrastructure and the supplies indispensable to the life of the Air Force and to its mobilization and its deployment, it is essential to take all useful measures so that this increase shall be completely effected before 1 March 1941."

The selection of this date was significant. The authors of the report on Plan V, from which this passage is taken, were perfectly well aware of the irreducible delays before the effort made could bear fruit. All the speed-ups decided on later had little effect on the final date of realization, and when the armistice came in June 1940 the Air Force was still six months from being fully ready.

The second characteristic of the plan was the absolute priority given to pursuit, or fighter, aircraft. That priority was contrary to everything that had been done before (with the exception of Plan IV, which never went into effect). The Air Force was not, however, abandoning the idea that aviation was essentially an offensive service and that the essential tool of that service was bomber planes. But necessity makes its own laws, and no doctrine could prevail against the facts.

In 1938 a whole series of facts compelled the French to manufacture fighter planes first, beginning with the simple realization that in the first year of the plan only Morane 406's and Potez 63's could be manufactured. (The first Potez 63's turned out corresponded to a three-seater fighter program.) Moreover, on the basis of the evidence, it was necessary to develop at full speed an air force capable of making a defense against the German attack judged possible as early as the middle of 1939. It was thus unreasonable, even in the name of the purest doctrine, to contest the validity of the priorities set.

The plan provided for the manufacture of 4,739 planes, 2,617 for service on the line and 2,122 in reserve. The 2,617 planes were to be 1,081 pursuit planes (41%), 876 bombers (34%), 636 reconnaissance planes (24%), and 24 planes for the use of the airborne infantry.

In addition, effort was also to be applied to the quality of the materiel to be produced, for "the present state of the French Air Force's materiel is inferior to that of the German and Italian materiel of the same category. The question of as rapid a modernization as possible, which will allow us to close this gap, is thus an *essential question* that is on a par with that of quantitative needs."

In case it should be necessary to carry out the plan by stages, the following order of urgency would be adopted:

"While it is understood that there will be no delay in the updating decided upon, and already begun, of the air units charged with reconnaissance and observation missions, it seems indispensable that the effort be put: a) initially into the updating and expansion of light aviation, in accordance with the recommendations of the Permanent Committee on National Defense of 8 December 1937, and b) into the updating and then the expansion of heavy aviation."

Originally, as we have seen, the plan was to be carried out in three years. At the request of the minister of air, it was decided "that the impossible will have to be done to reduce the complete realization of the plan to two years." Two installments were planned: the first from April 1, 1938, to March 31, 1939, and the second from April 1, 1939, to March 31, 1940.

In case of difficulties General Vuillemin specified "that the number of fighter planes must not be reduced; on the other hand, replacement of the fast medium bombers with which the squadrons are equipped may be postponed to the second stage, as the existing materiel can be used at night."

Expecting the program to be realized in two years was particularly optimistic. Certainly measures had at long last been taken to enable the aeronautics industry to develop in a suitable way and to attain a high level of production. The start was much too late, however, for it to be possible to realize the objectives of the plan.

As La Chambre had indicated to the deputies, it was necessary to place orders abroad, and in May 1938 one hundred Curtiss P 36's (Hawk 75's) were ordered from the United States.

The plan would undergo various minor modifications during 1938 and at the beginning of 1939. Those discussed in the Air Council on March 27, 1939, and adopted in June 1939 seem much more important: the creation of 2 bomber brigades intended for the defense of the overseas territories (imperial division); the creation of 5 multi-seated fighter groups for bomber escort; and an increase in reserve materiel brought up to 120% for single-seaters and 200% for multi-seaters.

The real object of this last measure was to enable the industry to maintain its production rates. The new goals were set at 8,558 airplanes (3,102 in service, 5,456 in reserve); or, if we subtract the colonial air force, which had always been considered outside the plan, 8,094 airplanes (2,938 in service, 5,156 in reserve).

Decreeing the objectives of the plan, of course, was essential, but realizing them proved difficult. The modern planes which France so urgently needed had not yet been defined.

The 1936 program, which was to serve as a basis for the industrialists in producing prototypes answering these needs, had been produced by the general staff after a long delay (in September 1936), and for that reason had not been converted into a technical program until the beginning of 1937. The planes that were supposed to correspond to it still existed only on the blueprints. The only prototypes for which orders could be issued either corresponded to the 1934 program or were transition planes manufactured outside of the program.

For lack of airplanes adapted to the new programs, it was necessary to fall back on airplanes ordered on a transitional basis.

This was specified very clearly in a note from the general staff dated February 28, 1938.

a) At present: *It is possible to order only those planes deriving from the 1934 programs (Potez 63's, Lioré 45's, Morane 406's, Amiot 340's) or to place orders abroad. Either of these solutions would give us quantity but not quality, since the foreign planes that could be used (from Great Britain and the United States) are not significantly better in performance than ours. Another solution would be to run the risk of ordering, on the basis of the production plans, planes deriving from the 1936 programs on the recommendation of the Directorate of Aeronautic Manu-*

factures, which alone possesses the necessary basis for making decisions (calculations, wind tunnel tests, etc.).

b) End of 1938: *We may hope to order planes from the 1934 program whose performance could be improved (speed above 500 km/hr) by adaptation with more powerful engines.*

c) In 1939: *We may hope to order planes deriving from the 1936 program after tests of prototypes; these planes exist now only in the form of plans or mock-ups.*

The accompanying table* shows the orders issued and the planes turned out by the factories as of September 1, 1939. On that date, of the 8,094 planes planned for the last production under Plan V, 6,858 had been ordered, with the deliveries

*The words used here indicate the presence of a table in the French edition, but no such table is to be found included in the book.—Trans.

A Morane 405 exhibited at the Air Festival of July 18, 1936, at Villacoublay.

The Potez 630, the first modern plane to come into service in the units. The Potez 637 and 63-11 versions were good reconnaissance planes.

to be spread out to the end of 1940, and 1,470 had left the factories. There were considerable delays on almost all types of planes, notably the reconnaissance planes and bombers.

Manpower

It is true that at the same time difficulties at least as great as those involving production were encountered in recruiting the number of personnel needed and planned for. The priority given to fighter groups made the crisis there less serious than in the bomber units, where the shortage of radiomen limited the number of crews possible in each group.

In spite of the efforts made in 1939, the shortages existing at the time when the conflict broke out were very large—9% for flying officers, but 31% for flying noncommissioned officers, and 31% for specialist noncommissioned officers. In the latter category there were extremely serious shortages of mechanics, electricians, radiomen, maintenance men, and photographers.

Here again the effort had begun too late, and, considering the creations of new units provided for in Plan V, there was no hope, at the time when war broke out, of seeing the difficulties disappear before the beginning of 1941.

The Reorganizations

Parallel to this effort to develop the Air Force, a certain number of reorganizational measures were adopted. Some had to do with the central administration. The principal measure concerned the chief of the general staff, who combined his functions with those of inspector general. He had five inspectors general under him. These were for air defense and fighter aviation, bombing aviation, reconnaissance aviation and air force reserves, overseas forces, and the schools. This very coherent organization functioned perfectly.

The decisions concerning the general organization of the Air Force, on the other hand, were less fortunate. The organization established by the decrees of 1936 and 1937 had shown some shortcomings in practice that needed to be remedied. But its chief advantage—which, by the way, Guy La Chambre recognized—was that the transition from peacetime to wartime could be made without changing the structures.

Starting from there, it would no doubt have been possible, by retaining certain good aspects of the creation of the air corps and taking account of the defects observed, to provide the Air Force with original structures. The influence of the land army, lack of imagination, and personality problems led to rejecting all the innovations of the previous decrees en bloc and putting back in force the provisions of the law of 1934 with all its shortcomings.

The main shortcomings of this "reorganization," the subject of the decree of September 2, 1938, was that it established the unfitness of the Air Force for launching large aerial operations at the very beginning of the war. In fact, this had no effect on the course of the conflict since that "phony" war allowed ample time to establish, and indeed to break in, the structures of the Air Command.

On the whole the most serious defect, fully brought to light in May 1940, was the extreme scattering of the fighter units assigned to the different land armies. The latter had a tendency to keep them on alert on the ground in order to save them for their own needs, thus aggravating the quantitative inferiority of the French fighter forces in relation to the German ones.

Status Summary

If one attempts to make an overall judgment on La Chambre's work, it is first of all the production problems that must hold one's attention.

The problems of organization were no doubt poorly dealt with. This is due to the fact that since 1870 the authoritative text on the matter was the Bouchard report (so called from the name of the inspector who drew it up), which presented the law on the administration of the army in 1882. It defined the principles imposed on every military organization, and the Air Force was obliged for many long years to respect this dogma, which was not devised with it in mind. The organization of 1938, as we have seen, violated the major principle of continuity of the organization from peacetime to wartime. Such a way of doing things could have had grave consequences, but these did not occur, because of the length of time that the "phony" war allowed the military for getting into position.

The problems of personnel, whether concerned with the structure of the corps, with manpower, or with training, could not have been solved in such a short period of time. At the very most, since nothing adequate had been done before, it was possible to draw up the main outline of a training plan and to make a start with its realization. This was done, thanks to the clearsightedness and extreme common sense of General Vuillemin. The effects of the plan were not felt until the beginning of 1941, which we know was too late.

On the other hand, the effort made in the area of materiel was quite remarkable. France accomplished an aerial rearmament more rapidly than all other European countries and thus demonstrated what it could have done if this effort had been begun three years earlier.

The tooling-up policy adopted early in 1938 and the technical choices made enabled production in 1938 to run at a higher level than the year before and then in 1939 to attain monthly rates much higher than had been known up to then. This result, which is to be credited to the minister, was essentially due to the work of Albert Caquot, appointed in September 1938 to head all of the national corporations. He arranged for entire orders to be turned over to him by the D.T.I. (the Technical and Industrial Directorate for Aeronautics), making himself responsible for dividing them out among the corporations. By this means the new president of the corporations was able to rationalize production by giving the different factories the responsibility not of manufacturing and delivering a complete plane but of producing the whole of one of the component assemblies. The final assembly was done in a single factory. The results are shown by two figures: 40 airplanes turned out in the month of September 1938 and nearly 300 in the month of August 1939.

It should also be mentioned that half of the planes produced in September 1938 were of older models, while in August 1939 only 10 were of this type. Qualitatively, too, production was improving.

Of the single-seated fighter planes, Morane 406's were being produced at an accelerated pace, and the first production run of Bloch 151's was added. Also, the Curtisses, for which a second order for one hundred had been placed, had almost all been delivered.

For reconnaissance, the Potez 637's (roughly sixty) were to be followed by rapid production of Potez 63-11's. Only the bombing category left something to be desired. In September 1939 only 18 modern planes existed—10 LeO 45's, 6 Farman 224's, and 2 Breguet 691's.

Plans provided for following this production with that of still more modern planes—Bloch 152's and 155's, Arsenal VG 33's, and, most especially, Dewoitine 520's for pursuit, Bloch 174's for reconnaissance, and Amiot 350's for bombing.

The improvement was clear, but the shadows had not all been dissipated. The figures are revealing and explain why the directors of French aviation adopted attitudes that became the subject of discussions and criticisms after the war.

During the month of September, at the time when grave events were unfolding in Czechoslovakia, the French government convened the Defense Committee, with the three chiefs of general staffs as members, under the chairmanship of Daladier. The chiefs of general staffs were consulted on the state of their respective forces. General Gamelin and Admiral Darlan declared that their branches were ready to fight. General Vuillemin, however, stated that if war came the French air forces would not be capable of measuring up to the Luftwaffe.

The general would later be reproached for expressing that opinion. It was said that during the visit that he had made to Germany in August 1938 the German air force leaders had outrageously deceived him and that he had consequently exaggerated the adversary's strength in the air. It is certain that during his visit the Germans did their best to exaggerate their air power. Certain demonstrations, notably their showing off of the Heinkel plane, can really be attributed to pure and simple bluff. But General Vuillemin had so much aviation experience behind him and such solid common sense that it is hard to admit that he let himself be taken in. In fact, what he had seen, what he had been told by Captain Stehlin, France's deputy air attaché in Berlin, and what he already knew from the syntheses furnished by a remarkably well-informed air intelligence service enabled him to form a very accurate idea of the real strength of Nazi Germany.

The comparison was also easy to make. In September 1938 no modern airplane had yet arrived in a French unit, and in the face of the Messerschmitt 109's, Heinkel 111's, and Do 17's the French fighter force equipped with planes ranging from the Nieuport 62 to the Dewoitine 510 was practically nonexistent.

It was not the same in August 1939. At the meeting of the Defense Committee held on August 23, 1939, General Vuillemin remained silent, and the minister himself, presenting the state of the air forces, concluded that it was operationally fit. It has often been said that General Vuillemin's silence was the proof of his disagreement with Guy La Chambre. There is nothing to support this assertion. The two men have always shown great esteem for each other, and it is not likely that their opinions differed greatly in 1939. In any case, to be convinced of this it suffices to reread the terms of the letter that Vuillemin wrote to the minister on August 26, 1939. The letter shows quite well what the state of the Air Force was at the precise moment that the conflict broke out.

France's special situation permits us to note, in comparison with the situation that existed at the time of the crisis in September 1938, an enlargement and almost complete modernization of the day and night fighter forces and a beginning of modernization of the reconnaissance forces.

As for bombers, the modern airplanes manufactured in France and expected from abroad have not yet been delivered to the units. For that reason the effects of the modernization of our offensive aviation will not be felt for four or five months more.

The modernized fighter force is capable at this moment of providing protection for the working planes on active service and coverage of our territory in the daytime.

At night, because of the short range of our searchlights, we must not expect very effective action from the specialized units.

For the sake of completeness it should be noted that in the very important area of coverage of our territory the shortage of artillery will subject our fighter force to a very heavy task.

The restricted possibilities of bombing have not changed since September 1938. The poor performances of our bombers will necessitate very cautious employment tactics during the first months of war, while awaiting the delivery of modern airplanes to the units: night action at moderate range or daytime action in the vicinity of the lines under favorable atmospheric conditions, against well-known and poorly defended objectives, and, at the request of the ground command, in case of crisis, participation in the ground battle under fighter protection.

The situation of our reconnaissance forces is already greatly improved and should make rapid advances in the near future.

And at the end of this letter, after having expressed his opinion on the possibilities of the British air force and the other air forces of France's allies or friends, the general concluded:

The air power of the principal friendly or allied countries is still rather far outclassed by that of the totalitarian states, Germany and Italy.

The great aeronautical effort made during the past year by Great Britain and France has, however, enabled us to overcome in part the very pronounced lag that appeared last September in the report on forces in existence.

Great Britain and France are on the way to a still more marked recovery if we consider the high-quality materiel that is close to coming into service. In six months, provided the means of production are not weakened by enemy offensive action and the U.S.S.R. does not lend active support to the Axis, Franco-British aviation should come to counterbalance the German and Italian air forces very effectively. But this effort in the aerial field should be accompanied by a parallel effort in that of antiaircraft. This is an urgent condition required for the protection of our own armed forces, our vital production centers, and the populations of our great urban centers.

The Life and Problems of the Air Force (1936–1939)

While plans and programs were being decided on and the future of the Air Force was being prepared for, this branch of the armed forces continued to live and develop.

It is hard to grasp completely the profound upheavals that took place within it during the period from 1936 to the beginning of the Second World War. At a certain distance, one has the impression today that a gulf separated the aviation of the early 1930s from that of the 1940s. That is certainly true, but it did not always appear so clearly to those of that generation.

And yet there was a revolution in the field of technology that had considerable effects on the conditions in which missions were accomplished. The infrastructure evolved, and the personnel changed. The aerial activity was intensified. Everything was moving, but many areas remained in the shadows. Air defense, the recruiting and training of personnel, and the adoption of a coherent policy adapted to the potential of the aviation materiel—all these remained like so many black spots, with no satisfactory solution available.

The Technological Revolution

The Worldwide Technological Revolution

Around 1935 technological improvements in aviation were appearing all over the world. These had to do first of all with the airframes. All-metal construction was developed, and biplanes gradually disappeared, being replaced with low-wing monoplanes. Flaps with curved upper or lower surfaces were adopted in order to increase the lift at low speeds and thus reduce landing speeds. At the

General Vuillemin returning from his visit to Germany.

same time engine power was increased. Superchargers (with which the Breguet XIV was already equipped back in 1918) were adopted and made it possible to raise the planes' ceilings and improve their performance at high altitudes. To get the best possible effect of propellers, variable-pitch propellers were installed.

Flight instruments became more complicated; to the check-ball and the needle were added the directional gyro and then the artificial horizon. For fighter planes, collimators replaced grid sights, while the bombing planes were equipped with modern sights with stabilized aim, which were better suited to the new planes than the systems derived directly from those of the First World War.

Radio developed further, radio beacons were invented, and systems for landing under poor visibility conditions were installed. Similarly, the use of voice radio on board planes got under way.

The French Lag

Unfortunately, France lagged somewhat behind in all these fields. Of course, the French were doing research that was often remarkable on all of these subjects, but very often the research was not completed in time. This is of some importance since the adoption of new techniques was to have considerable repercussions on the functioning of military aviation.

The Problems Faced by the Crews

Really modern planes did not appear until 1938 in the fighter units and until the beginning of 1940 in the bomber units. The old pilots often had difficulties in adapting to the new techniques, which imposed reactions on them to which they unconsciously refused to accustom themselves. The best pilots, of course, succeeded without problems. General d'Harcourt said one day, during an interview, that the hardest plane he had ever piloted was certainly the Morane Parasol of 1914 and that in comparison the Dewoitine 520 was child's play to handle.

But it was not just the problems of guiding the plane that faced the pilots. The new possibilities offered should normally have made all-weather flying routine. In fact, it was undoubtedly this type of flying that appeared most difficult to the old pilots, who avoided flying into clouds. However, under the direction of Major Sassard, an advanced training course in blind flying was introduced at Avord in 1936. The trainees who had the chance to take the course recall that they flew in all weather and in all types of clouds, trying even the worst flying conditions. Back in their units they had trouble persuading the oldest pilots to fly readily without sight of the sun or the sky. Only a few pilots were capable of landing either by "ZZ" or by Q.D.M. variation (two different utilizations of the radio beams provided by a ground station on the landing field). Even pilots trained in P.S.V. (blind flying) still did not readily make landings in bad weather.

Similarly, many of the innovations adopted in aerial firing and bombing reached the units too late for full advantage to be taken of them. This was the case, for example, with the remote-controlled hydraulic turret gun of the LeO 45, the Thedenat bombsight with gyroscopic stabilizer, and the periscopic DB 30 with bubble level.

Nor was it only the pilots that were bothered by these innovations. The mechanics, who had been given general training at Rochefort adapted to the old planes, were at least puzzled by all these novelties. They needed time to learn, but there was no time, especially as there were not very many mechanics to begin with.

Complementary Technical Repercussions

Finally, the evolution of this technology had repercussions on other aspects of aviation. For example, there was the case of superchargers, which came into general use in the Air Force in 1936. Their general use led automatically to flying at higher altitudes. Other problems were then rediscovered. A research center on high-altitude flight was established, on private initiative, in 1936 at Le Bourget

The control panel of a Dewoitine 520. Note the absence of an artificial horizon.

(where a decompression chamber was installed). The center was made official six months later by the ministry, but transferred to Avord and Istres.

It was necessary to restudy inhalators, which were still in the testing stage in 1938. When the problem of oxygen was finally mastered, the planes regularly flew above 7,000 meters, and the discomfort of the poorly heated cabins was quickly noticed, as well as the poor functioning of the weapons and photographic equipment. During the winter of 1939–1940 some reconnaissance crews returned from missions in Germany, where they ran the risk of being shot down, to state that their film was unexposed, the lens having been covered with frost during the flight at high altitude.

While waiting for modifications to be made to the equipment by the technical services, the mechanics improvised solutions so that it could still function.

Transmissions

Another technique, whose importance, by the way, had not escaped the military command, had to do with transmissions. Nothing had been done before 1933, and later on the limited appropriations in the face of the immense needs to be met (since everything had to be built up from scratch) stretched out the delays beyond all reason.

Thus in 1933 there were only two radio beacons in France, essentially meeting the needs of the civilian airlines. In 1936 the Air Force began the installation of radio telephony and goniometry networks as well as a network of optical beacons.

Around 1936 the groups began to receive the first radiogoniometry (direction-finding) trucks, which made contact with airplanes in flight possible. In 1938 the first radio compasses were under study, as well as procedures for landing in poor visibility that had been developed in Germany, England, and the United States, but none of these reached the French Air Force before 1940.

Infrastructure

Many things changed at the air bases. In 1934 the airfields consisted essentially of temporary encampments. Starting in 1934 barracks-style plans were adopted, and work began in 1935 and 1936 at Toulouse, Tours, Bordeaux, Rheims, and Avord, while renovations were begun at Cazaux, Pau, Lyons, and Salon. At Salon, in 1936, buildings were started that were intended for the Air School.

The Activity of the Units

Life on the air bases changed profoundly, especially after 1936. There was little change in the atmosphere that prevailed within the air groups. The general factors affecting the life of the unit were situated essentially at the level of the group, a unit with a distinct administration, while the aerial activities depended first of all on the flights.

The group, which had become the typical air unit of this period, comprised officers who were mostly fliers, noncommissioned officer mechanics, and a few enlisted men. The strength was low —six officers per fighter group, about ten per

Apportionment and Evolution of the Air Budget from 1933 to 1939

	1933	1934	1935	1936	1937	1938	1939
Personnel							
Current francs	449	389	419	447	572	762	1,888
1935 francs	394	356	419	414	424	495	1,144
Index 1933 = 100	*100*	*90*	*106*	*105*	*107*	*126*	*290*
Materiel							
Current francs	892	1,092	1,312	1,963	2,735	4,778	33,561
1935 francs	782	1,002	1,312	1,818	2,026	3,102	20,340
Index 1933 = 100	*100*	*128*	*168*	*232*	*259*	*397*	*2,601*
Installations							
Current francs	149	152	273	252	587	963	3,250
1935 francs	131	139	273	233	435	625	1,970
Index 1933 = 100	*100*	*106*	*208*	*178*	*332*	*477*	*1,504*
Total Military							
Current francs	1,490	1,633	2,004	2,662	3,894	6,503	38,700
1935 francs	1,307	1,498	2,004	2,465	2,884	4,223	23,455
Index 1933 = 100	*100*	*115*	*153*	*189*	*221*	*323*	*1,795*
Total							
Current francs	1,898	2,070	2,451	3,145	4,529	7,381	39,798
Air Budget							
1935 francs	1,665	1,899	2,451	2,912	3,355	4,793	24,120
Index 1933 = 100	*100*	*114*	*147*	*175*	*202*	*288*	*1,449*
Price Index							
Base 1935 = 100	114	109	100	108	135	154	165

Evolution of the Military Budget of the Air Ministry in Percentage of Constant Francs
Base 100 : 1933

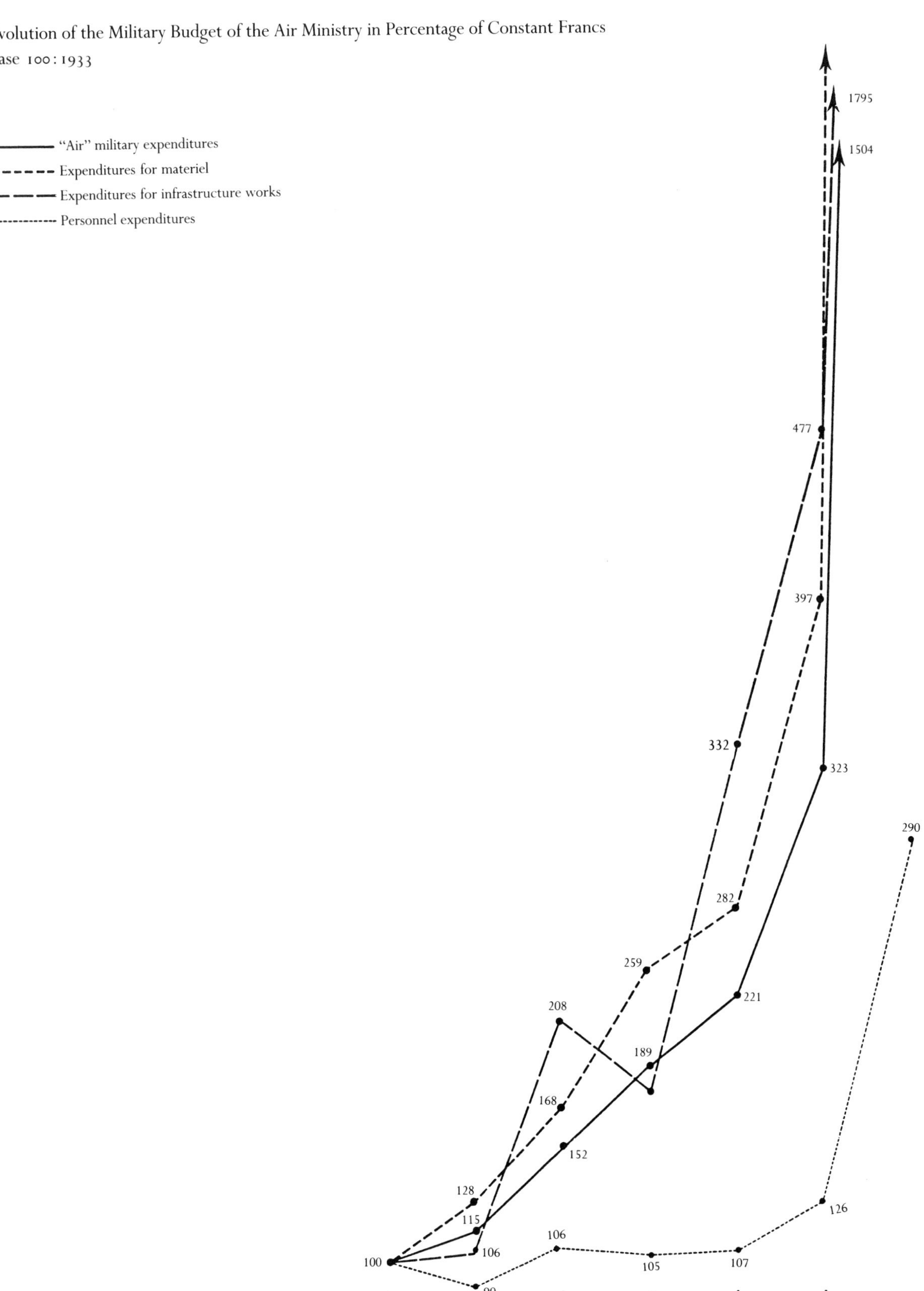

bomber group. These regulars were joined by a few reservists assigned to the unit.

Beginning in 1936 flight training was accelerated. Since it was very expensive to fly combat planes, someone hit upon the idea of providing the flights with reserve planes. Many Caudron "Simouns" were made available to the flying personnel in 1936. To encourage them to fly, they were allowed to use these planes like aero club planes and take their families on board. This arrangement for the families was soon suspended, however. Goélands were put into service in 1937 for advanced training in blind flight, with specialized instructors who in principle came from "the Sassard

The 34th Squadron leaving for maneuvers in North Africa, October 11, 1938.

Air Investment Credits

		1934	1935	1936	1937	1938	1939
Prototypes	Credits opened	127	117	248	318	347	451
	Credits used	73	69	94	152	167	241
Production Runs	Credits opened	373	369	1,280	1,263	3,452	20,805
	Credits used	293	321	1,076	1,120	2,664	14,998
Industrial Mobilization	Credits opened	7.7	10.8	181	202.2	232.1	2,198
	Credits used	2.9	6.8	65.5	97.5	185.3	494
Works and Installations	Credits opened	182.6	189.5	551	758	869	2,014
	Credits used	122.4	135	229	449	623	1,325

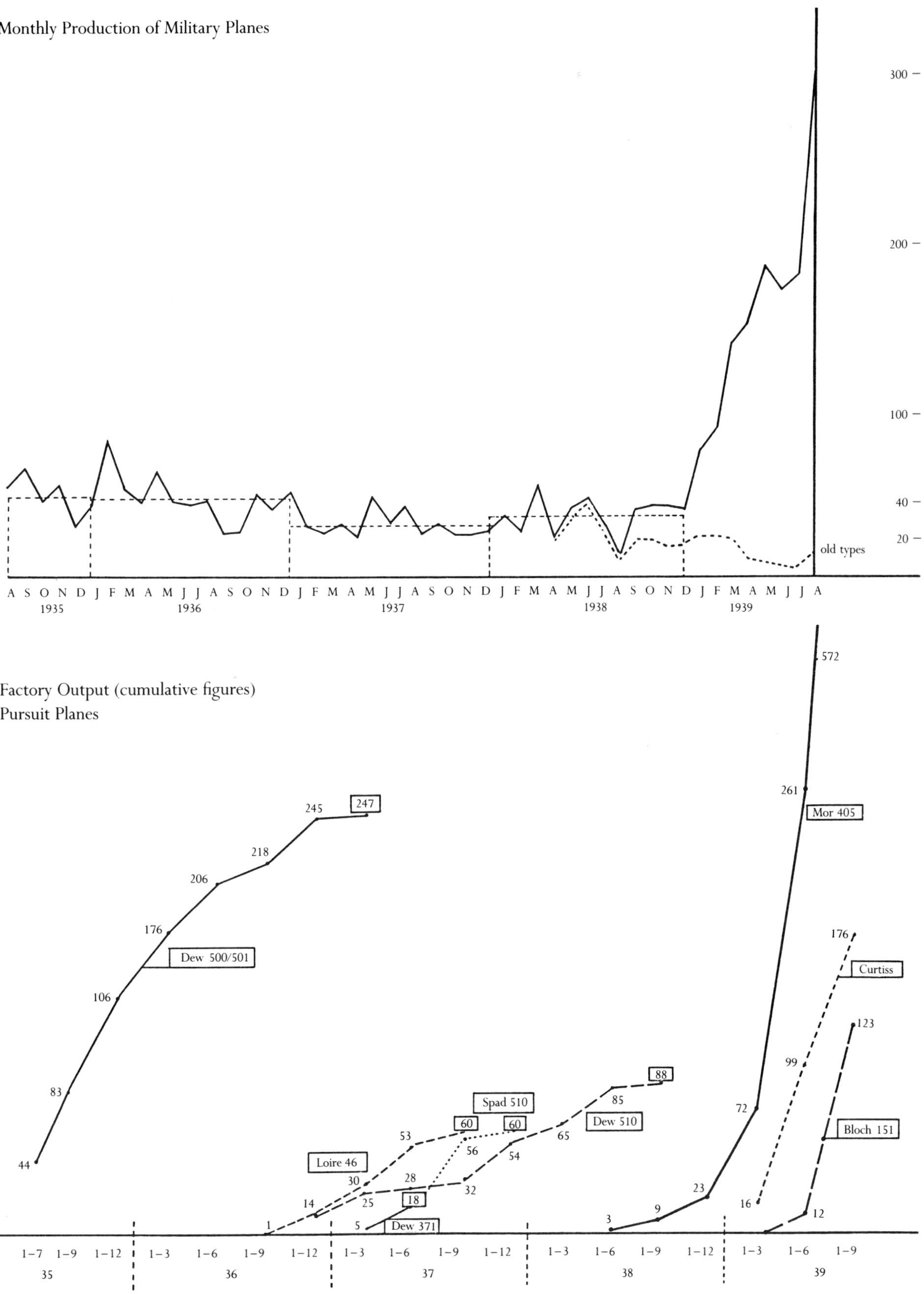
Monthly Production of Military Planes
300
200
100
40
20
old types
A S O N D J F M A M J J A S O N D J F M A M J J A S O N D J F M A M J J A S O N D J F M A M J J A
1935
1936
1937
1938
1939
Factory Output (cumulative figures)
Pursuit Planes
44
83
106
176
206
218
245
247
Dew 500/501
1
14
30
53
60
Loire 46
25
28
32
56
60
Spad 510
54
65
85
88
Dew 510
5
18
Dew 371
3
9
23
72
261
572
Mor 405
16
99
176
Curtiss
12
123
Bloch 151
1–7 1–9 1–12 1–3 1–6 1–9 1–12 1–3 1–6 1–9 1–12 1–3 1–6 1–9 1–12 1–3 1–6 1–9
35
36
37
38
39

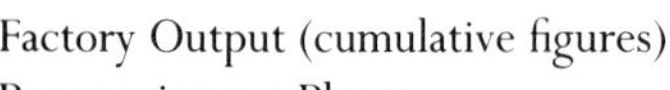

Factory Output (cumulative figures)
Reconnaissance Planes

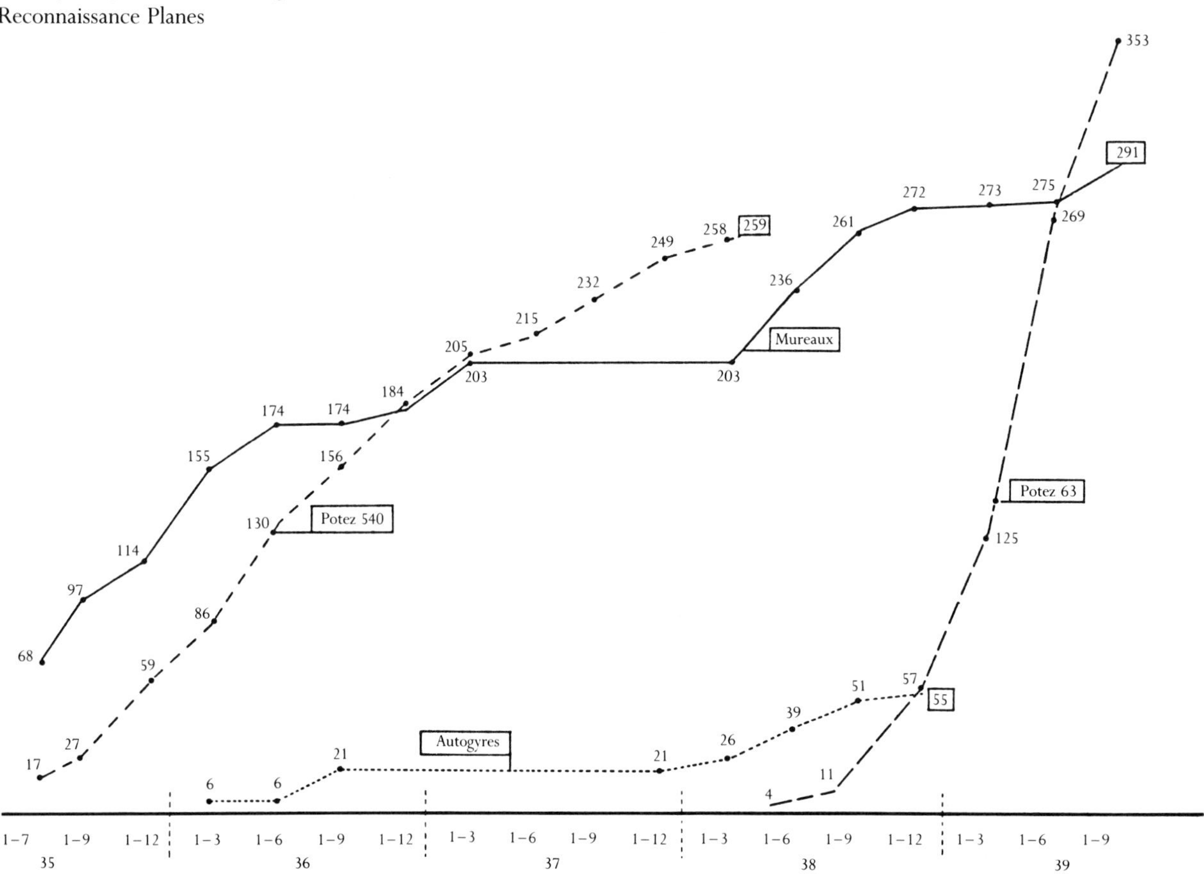

Factory Output (cumulative figures)
Bombers

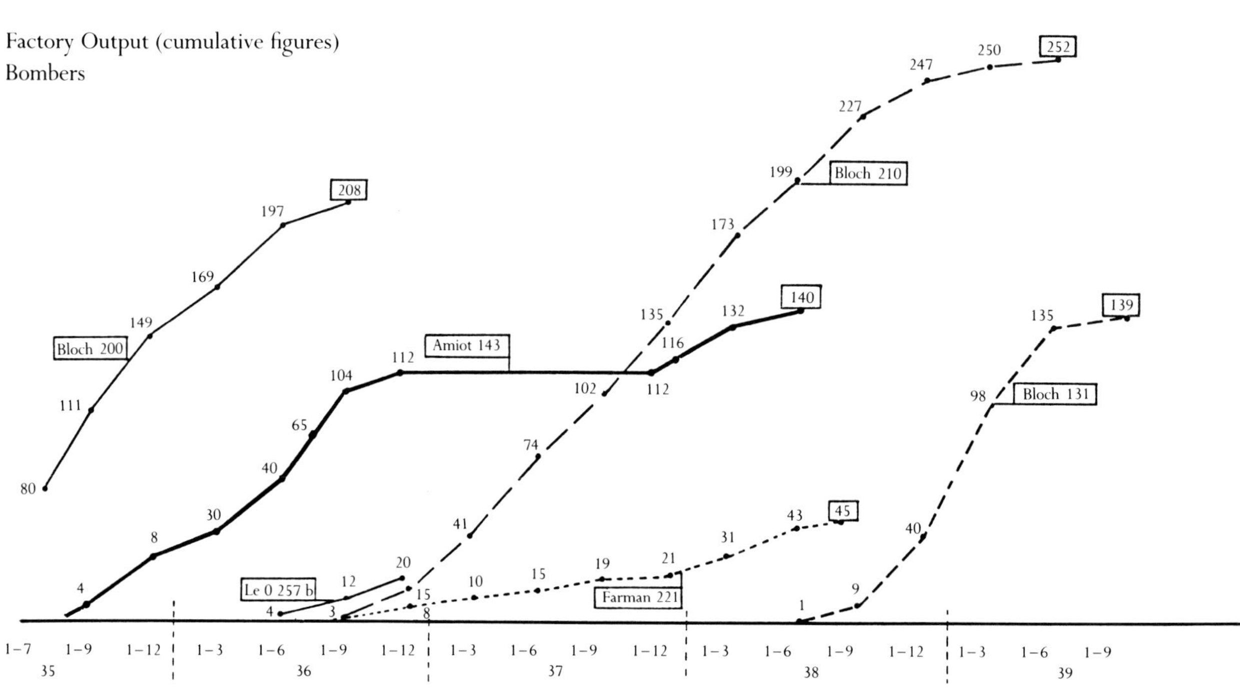

course." The first Link Trainers arrived in France in 1938, but in 1939 there was only a single one for the 450 trainees at the pilot training school at Istres. In fact, the French crews remained strongly motivated to fly and were, on the whole, well trained.

Fighter Aviation

This was particularly true of the fighter units. It is true that this branch profited from certain advantages. The planes that it used until the end of 1935, while not modern, prepared the personnel perfectly for the change to the newer planes. It was much easier for a fighter pilot to change from the Dewoitine 500 to the Morane 406 than for a bomber pilot to change from the Bloch 200 to the LeO 45.

To this advantage was added that of having been led remarkably well by two prestigious commanders, former fighter pilots of the First World War who loved combat and knew the job well: General Massenet Royer de Marancour, first inspector of the fighter force in 1932, and General d'Harcourt, who took over in 1938.

General Massenet de Marancour instituted the series of training flights and made the flight-order record book obligatory. Thanks to him systematic training developed, which placed the emphasis on formation flying, patrol work, and firing. There was a great deal of firing practice in 1938, especially at the cinematic machine gun, and the French pilots demonstrated their skillfulness. These pilots, from the most famous to the most obscure, were personally known to the last prewar inspector of the fighter force, General d'Harcourt, whose name is still venerated by all the veterans who remember him.

Finally, fighter aviation benefited from the priority given it in 1938 and had some excellent pilots transferred to it from the bomber section.

While there were thus some positive aspects to be found in the daily life of the Air Force, there were also, unfortunately, several negative aspects.

The difficulties encountered in getting the manpower needed to operate the planes provided in the plan have already been noted. The essential problem of recruiting continued to be felt constantly without a satisfactory solution being found for it.

There had never been any effort to attract mechanics into the Air Force. The pay was very low, a situation decried by the chairmen of the budget committee of the Chamber of Deputies. Thus, according to Paul Rives, a civilian warehouseman made 1,800 francs more a year than the sergeant of the service force under whose orders he was working, and a fitter mechanic made 6,000 francs a year more than the first sergeant specialist who gave him his instructions.

Moreover, the pay was not the only negative factor. Living conditions and service obligations made the military career less attractive. The only advantage, and it affected only a small number, was that of having an interesting and profitable stay overseas.

The case of the flying personnel was just as serious. It was less the recruiting that was at fault, especially from 1936 on, than the training possibilities. These were limited by the lack of training-type airplanes. It was not until 1932 that the first trainers (MS 315's) were put into service. Until then outdated warplanes were used.

In 1936 the Simoun appeared, and in 1937 the Hanriot 182. Because of the lack of time it was found necessary in 1938 to buy the license to manufacture an Italian plane, the Romano, and 20 trainers were ordered from the United States, BT 9's, which only arrived in small numbers in 1940 and were used chiefly in French North Africa.

As we have seen, while the creation of popular aviation produced interesting results, they were insufficient to enable France to overcome its lag in the numbers of trained pilots available. To do that it would have been necessary to organize the "production" of flying personnel. In fact, the first plan was not implemented until 1938, and its effects did not make themselves felt before the war broke out.

The Runways

Beginning in 1936, as already noted, a big effort

had been made in improving both technical installations and barracks. Here again, unfortunately, France started too late. Furthermore, nothing was done about the runways. The ground was simply drained to speed up drying after heavy rains. In 1940 flooding on an airfield held up for nearly three months the acceptance flights of LeO 45's just leaving the factories.

In 1939, when such things had existed nearly all over the world since 1933, there was only one concrete runway 1 kilometer long in France, called the records runway, at Istres. In 1939 construction of a hard-surface runway was begun at Bordeaux.

This delay in the adoption of modern runways led to keeping poor-performance landing gear in service: non-three-wheel landing gear, tail skids, brakes installed late, low-pressure tires.

Most of all, for lack of funds the French did not have enough airfields. This prevented any redeployment maneuver.

Air Defense

At the moment when France found itself at grips with a formidable air threat, it was suddenly discovered that the air defense of the country was, so to speak, nonexistent. To a certain extent this was the result of the insufficiency of fighter airplanes, primarily due to the manifest incapacity to organize anything serious in that area. Nevertheless, in 1931 an Inspectorate of the Air Defense of the Territory had been created, first entrusted to Marshal Pétain and then to General Duchesne. In 1935 that inspectorate had been included in the Air Force, the chief of the general staff being inspector general of Air Defense. In 1938 it was the inspector of the fighter force that assumed that responsibility. Whatever the solution adopted, the designated official could do nothing but report the lack of funds and ask the responsible ministers to provide them from their respective budgets.

While the fighter force came under the Air Ministry, the antiaircraft defense came under the Ministry of War, and passive defense was under the Ministry of the Interior. If one further observes that one of the essential means—transmissions—was based on the telephone network under the P.T.T. (the Ministry of Posts, Telephone, and Telegraph), it is easy to understand the difficulties encountered by the inspector designated to assume the task.

In fact—and it is surprising—while there had been enough agitation since 1928 over the terrifying threat of aerochemical warfare against French cities, industries, and populations to justify seeking agreements limiting aerial armaments, no serious action had been undertaken since 1933 to develop the means of resistance—airplanes and antiaircraft weapons—the means of protection, or the necessary organization.

No solution was found for this problem before the war, and while the development of the fighter forces provided for in Plan V might allow France to see its air forces grow, antiaircraft remained practically nonexistent. That is another point on which one should dwell in considering the appraisal of air defense. Although antiaircraft had proved its effectiveness in the First World War, it was sacrificed from 1920 on. Placed under the army, in contrast to Germany, where it came under the direction of the Luftwaffe, its importance was denied, and its appropriations were decreased. Unlike the situation with aircraft, France possessed a remarkable prototype dating from 1922, the 90-millimeter gun, with performance figures comparable to those of the German 88. In light antiaircraft France had the 25-millimeter and 37-millimeter guns, which were also excellent. The reason for this neglect of antiaircraft was that the army was counting on fighter aviation, while at the same time, by the budget game, it was hampering its development.

The demonstration of the effectiveness of flak, although already done in the First World War, would be a great surprise. The French troops, however, had only a small number of pieces with which to oppose the Stukas (German dive-bombers), which were very vulnerable during their dives. French cities had a still more limited number of heavy pieces to provide for their defense.

A Potez 25 TOE based at Savannakhet, Laos, in August 1919.

Debates on Doctrine

Debates on doctrine were numerous throughout the period. To simplify the matter greatly, we may say that two theses confronted each other. One emphasized the importance of the air battle at the beginning of a conflict. Getting mastery of the air was the indispensable precondition for any action on the ground, at sea, or in the air. To get that mastery it was necessary to have a large offensive air force and to concentrate air power to the maximum, as only such concentration would make possible its rational utilization in the initial air battle.

Plan II, which aimed at increasing bomber strength considerably and which led to the adoption of an organization of the air forces into air corps independent of the ground command, was the logical application of the theory supported by the majority of the "aviators."

The other thesis rejected the idea of an air battle which had its own rules. The fighting that would be launched would be general, and the role of aviation would be to participate in that fighting, in which ground forces would predominate. To perform that role the air force would have to be able to place at the land army's disposal many observation planes assigned to the large land units whose action would be protected by the fighter group assigned to each army.

This latter thesis came to prevail. There were many reasons for its adoption. The Air Force was too "young" to hope to see its ideas triumph in the face of the army and navy lobbies. If it insisted, it ran the risk of seeing its appropriations cut off, as in 1937, to the profit of another branch of the armed forces. Also, in light of the German danger, it was proper to adopt solutions that permitted increasing as quickly as possible the number of units able to oppose effectively the enemy air forces. It was thus logical to give priority to fighter planes, which, moreover, were easier to manufacture than bombers.

From September 1937 on the minister of air adopted a conciliatory attitude toward the ground-oriented ideas. He noted that "seeking aerial combat for its own sake, for systematic destruction of the opposing air forces, independent of the general fighting, would inevitably lead the Command to

Potez 56 liaison planes at Villacoublay.

General d'Harcourt.

A Breguet 27 Limousine, liaison plane of the chief of the Air Force general staff.

Potez 39's lining up to take off on a group flight during an air festival at Le Bourget, July 14, 1936.

engage practically the whole of the Air Force against uncertain objectives."

He specified that "the Supreme Command of the land forces may be sure of having at its disposal the fresh aviation units that it needs to engage in the initial battle." Finally, he gave the assurance that "the Air Force will hold itself in readiness to engage fully within the framework of the general battle."

This orientation was followed in 1938 under the authority of Guy La Chambre. It governed the actions that resulted from Plan V, which put the accent on fighter aviation. It should be emphasized that, more than doctrine alone, it was the political and industrial situation that imposed the solutions that were adopted.

Another point worth noting, since it later became the subject of numerous criticisms, is the attitude of the Air Force toward dive-bombing. Contrary to what is currently being said, this was not a real point for debate. The Air Force never denied the possibility of engaging planes on the battlefield, nor the ability of aircraft to achieve results against land forces. It simply considered that the use of such means should absolutely follow upon the winning of local or general air superiority; hence the lower priority given to "airborne artillery."

In the matter of the choice of weapons, the French Air Force, unlike the Luftwaffe and in agreement on this point with the RAF, believed more in assault aircraft than in dive-bombers, at least in regard to ground objectives. Later events—contrary to the belief of certain authors influenced by a superficial view of the action of the German Stukas in 1940—have not demonstrated that this position was bad.

In fact, if the Stukas were able to do nearly whatever they wanted in May 1940, it was because the responsible officers of the French army did not believe in the effectiveness of the airplane used as an offensive weapon and consequently, as we have already emphasized, neglected antiaircraft.

The MS 315, the basic plane of the pilot training schools.

Ministers of Air (1928–1940)

Laurent-Eynac	Sept. 14, 1928–Dec. 13, 1930
Paul Painlevé	Dec. 13, 1930–Jan. 26, 1931
J. L. Dumesnil	Jan. 27, 1931–Feb. 21, 1932
None	Feb. 22, 1932–June 2, 1932
Paul Painlevé	June 3, 1932–Jan. 31, 1933
Pierre Cot	Jan. 31, 1933–Feb. 7, 1934
Gen. Victor Denain	Feb. 9, 1934–Jan. 22, 1936
Marcel Déat	Jan. 24, 1936–June 4, 1936
Pierre Cot	Jan. 4, 1936–Jan. 18, 1938
Guy La Chambre	Jan. 18, 1938–March 21, 1940
Laurent-Eynac	March 21, 1940–June 16, 1940
Gen. Bertrand Pujo	June 16, 1940–July 12, 1940

Chiefs of Staff (1930–1940)

Gen. René Michaud	Oct. 5, 1930–Jan. 3, 1931	Chief of General Staff of Air Forces
Gen. Joseph Barès	Jan. 4, 1931–Aug. 26, 1931	Chief of General Staff of Air Forces
Gen. Emile Hergault	Aug. 27, 1931–Jan. 15, 1933	Chief of General Staff of Air Forces
Gen. Joseph Barès	Jan. 16, 1933–April 1, 1933	Chief of General Staff of Air Forces
Gen. Victor Denain	April 1, 1933–Feb. 8, 1934	Chief of General Staff of the Air Force (Armée de l'Air)
Gen. Joseph Barès	Feb. 15, 1934–Sept. 2, 1934	Chief of General Staff of the Air Force (Armée de l'Air)
Gen. Picard	Sept. 3, 1934–Dec. 25, 1935	Deputy Chief of General Staff
Gen. Bertrand Pujo	Dec. 26, 1935–Oct. 14, 1936	Chief of General Staff of the Air Force (Armeé de l'Air)
Gen. Philippe Féquant	Oct. 15, 1936–Feb. 21, 1938	—
Gen. Joseph Vuillemin	Feb. 22, 1938–Sept. 2, 1939	Commander in Chief of Air Forces
	Sept. 2, 1939–July 4, 1940	

Conclusion

On November 11, 1918, French military aviation ranked first in the world. From 1919 to 1928 it survived after a fashion without modernization. To all appearances, it remained significant, and the world believed in its power. Wasn't it part of the powerful French Army, whose prestige was at its zenith? By that period, however, aviation achievements by other nations (pioneer flights, records, development of civilian airlines) should have given France a hint of its decline. The creation of the Air Ministry and the development of the prototype policy did not succeed in relaunching the Air Force toward modernization. Appropriations were too small, and the animosity brought to bear against the young service was too great. The work of general reorganization undertaken under the direction of Pierre Cot could have borne excellent fruit, such as the promotions to the Air School which took place after 1935.

Unfortunately, the modalities of aerial rearmament adopted in 1934, perfectly justified if the French government had opposed the German reoccupation of the Rhineland by force of arms, definitively compromised the chances of the French aeronautics industry.

The airplane orders placed by the government in 1935 aggravated the situation. Production was disorganized; delays constantly increased. The reason was connected with the lack of long-term plans, which could have reassured the industrialists about their future and thus encouraged them to invest. The five-year plan and Plan II were aimed at attaining that result. Unfortunately, apart from the fact that they could only provide for old planes (the production of modern planes did not get under way until late in 1937), these two plans were launched during the period of disorganization of the industry that followed upon its nationalization and was aggravated by the social agitation of the time.

It was not until 1938 that the aeronautics industry developed its machinery and started up production on modern foundations. Airplanes did not begin to be turned out in large numbers until the start of the war. This fact made itself felt in September 1939: the number of modern airplanes that France had at its disposal was notoriously insufficient.

Moreover, the planes ordered in 1937 and 1938 belonged to the program of 1934, which was beginning to be out of date. Their performance, comparable to that of the German planes in service at the time of the declaration of war, was distinctly inferior to that of the new models with which the Luftwaffe began to be equipped in September 1939.

While the materiel problem unquestionably appeared as the major weakness of the French Air Force, there were many other factors that aggravated the state of French aviation.

The transition from a peacetime to a wartime organization, which might have been expected to prevent any action at the beginning of the conflict, had no repercussions because of the "phony" war, the prudence of those responsible for French defense having ruled out in advance any possibility of offensive actions.

On the other hand, the division of the French fighter force into small packets aggravated, as if intentionally, its quantitative inferiority to the enemy fighter force.

The manpower problems had no profound influence on the effectiveness of the French air forces, for they were masked by the insufficiency of materiel. Nevertheless, it must be pointed out that if the aeronautics industry had produced the planes planned at the beginning of the war, France would not have had enough pilots before 1941 to operate them.

The debates over theory, or doctrine, were equally important. However, they played only a negative part in the evolution of aviation during that period. The ideas on aerial combat, whose force was demonstrated during the conflict, had no chance to prevail. They only caused the "wrong-headed" Air Force to run the risk of seeing its appropriations cut.

Beginning in 1937, when the Air Force budget was cut in favor of the navy, the aviators were on the way down to a humbling position. The Air Force became an auxiliary weapon for the ground forces and was largely confined to the role of purveyor of intelligence.

In fact, in the 1936–1939 period French aviation was suffering from the fact that the ranking military leaders did not believe in it. To be convinced of this one need only recall that the big ground units were dangerously lacking in antiaircraft weapons, which would have enabled them to fight effectively against the Stukas, which were very vulnerable to light antiaircraft fire.

This lack of general conviction of the usefulness of the air forces explains both the delay in France's aerial rearmament and the mistakes made in the choice of the programs adopted.

There was one bright spot in this somewhat dark picture of the state of aviation in 1939; it had to do with the personnel. Faced with fighting in planes, some of which were outdated, the personnel of the Air Force units always showed a morale that was up to any test. Their esprit de corps and the high quality of their training brought them honorable successes against their adversaries from across the Rhine.

At the beginning of the war they had a sure confidence in the outcome of the conflict. They were finally seeing the modern airplanes that they had long dreamed of arriving in large quantities. Certainly the modernization of the units was never complete and would not have been essentially so until the beginning of 1941. But didn't the country's highest authorities affirm that it was ready, and that in the shelter of its impregnable Maginot Line France would have time to forge the weapons for victory?

Like the rest of the French, the aviators had confidence in the assurances displayed by the "great army leaders" of the time. Besides, those assurances corresponded to the exceptional climate of pacifism in which the nation basked throughout this period, even, unfortunately, after 1933.

Later, launched into the fighting, they would realize the emptiness of certain assertions. But it would be too late, and many of them would pay with their lives for the mistakes made by those very ones who, subsequently, tried to throw the responsibility for the defeat on an air force in which they had not believed and that they had kept at the lowest level from 1920 to 1938.

Captions for illustrations in order of appearance on the following four pages:

Aerial Combat in 1939–1940.

Free French Air Force Planes: The Lorraine Group.

Insignias of Algerian Aviation Units.
Light Aircraft and Support Flight (EALA) 9/72; EALA 2/72
EALA 3/71; EALA 15/72; Liaison and Observation Flight 4/45
Air Liaison Flight 53; EALA 12/72
EALA 7/72; EALA 14/72; Fighter Squadron I/20, Aurès-Nementcha
Grouping of Specialized Air Units of the Sahara; 3rd Flight of Overseas Group 86 (later, Saharan Reconnaissance and Support Group 76).

Air Force Uniforms
1. *Officer Aviator, 1912–1915: Flight Dress*
2. *1916 to 1922–1925*
3. *1925 to 1935–1937*
4. *Balloonist Company, 1794–1799: Soldier and Officer*
5. *Balloonist of the Army of the Loire, 1870–1871: Crew Chief*
6. *Flight Dress, 1938–1940–1941*
7. *Flight Dress, 1970–1980*

1
2
3
4
4
4
5
6
7

PART 4

The Test of War

CHAPTER I

Mobilization and the "Phony" War

Mobilization is not war. This reassuring formula, invented in August 1914, was to be invalidated once more by the events of the month of September 1939. Mobilization? It was not exactly peace, either.

As the plans drawn up before the outbreak of the crisis had provided, the Air Force as of August 22 formed the "A" echelons of pursuit, bombing, reconnaissance, and observation. Four days later the deployment of general cover took place, and then, on August 27, the reserve echelons of the fighter and reconnaissance groups were activated in their turn. On September 1 the bombing units did the same. Finally, at 0000 hours on September 2, the general mobilization, which began after the German aggression against Poland, removed the air force personnel's last doubts. Most of the units on active duty had already left their peacetime bases for the airfields and landing strips that had been assigned to them. On September 3, at 1700 hours, upon the expiration of the ultimatum that it had addressed to the government of the Third Reich, France entered the war.

Contrary to what its leaders had expected, the Air Force was not the victim of a sudden attack by the Luftwaffe. Occupied in the east, Germany had maintained only reduced forces facing the French and the British. The 115 groups and 17 flights of the French Air Force (23 groups and 9 regional flights of fighters, 33 bomber groups, 14 reconnaissance groups, and 47 observation groups, as well as 8 police flights or Saharan flights) deployed according to plan.

Profiting from the unexpected respite that was to be known as the "phony" war, the French air forces busied themselves with improving their situation and providing themselves with the better adapted and more modern planes that the aeronautics industry was preparing to give them. At the same time great upheavals took place in the major military commands.

Reorganization of the Major Commands

In the little town of Saint-Jean-les-Deux-Jumeaux, very close to the headquarters of the First Air Army commanded by General Mouchard, General Vuillemin, commander in chief of the air forces, established the supreme air headquarters (G.Q.G.A.) at the beginning of September 1939. At that moment the Air Force was divided into three air armies adapted to the organization of the ground command and each having air support forces at its disposal (one group of fighters and one reconnaissance group per land army, one observation group and one or two balloon companies per army corps, cavalry division, light mechanized division, or armored division) as well as reserve air forces (fighter, bomber, and reconnaissance units).

Connected with the theater of operations of the Northeast, facing Germany, General Mouchard's First Air Army comprised 15 fighter groups, 2 of which were night fighters of the Paris region, plus 4 regional flights, 15 bomber groups, 11 reconnaissance groups, and 31 observation groups. General Houdemon commanded the Third Air Army, connected with the theater of operations of the Alps and composed of 5 fighter groups and 1 fighter flight, 4 bomber groups, 1 reconnaissance group, and 5 observation groups. As for General Bouscat's Fifth Air Army, it was entrusted with covering North Africa with 3 groups and 4 regional flights of fighters, 11 bomber groups, including 2 naval support bomber groups, 1 reconnaissance group, and 9 observation groups.

In the eyes of the Air Force high command, such an organization had the defect of being at the same time heavy and excessively centralized. For this reason the creation of the land army groups became the occasion for establishing new structures. Thus the First Air Army was divided into two air operations areas adapted tactically to the two land army groups of the Northeastern Front. The air operations area North (Z.O.A.N.) was set up on October 1, 1939, under the command of General d'Astier de la Vigerie, shortly after the appearance of an air operations area East (Z.O.A.E.) commanded by General Pennès. Each of the area commanders remained subordinate to the First Air Army, an echelon which still existed, in matters involved in putting the reserve air forces into operation, but was only a technical adviser to the commanding officer of the army group in all that concerned the employment of the ground-support air forces. At the end of October the formation of an Army Group No. 3, embracing the Eighth Army and the forces along the Swiss frontier, gave rise to the establishment of an air operations area South (Z.O.A.S.), headed by General Odic and subordi-

Minister of Air Guy La Chambre and General Vuillemin at a ceremonial parade during the "phony" war. Later, La Chambre was a defendant in the court action in Riom, and Vuillemin testified as a witness.

nate to the Third Air Army under General Vasselot de Règne, soon replaced, on December 9, by General Laurens.

The experience of the first few months of the war quickly showed the uselessness of the air army echelon between the commander in chief of the air forces and the air operations areas for the employment of the reserve forces. The new organization that was set up comprised a command of ground-support air forces and of ground antiaircraft forces (F.T.A./Forces Terrestres Anti-aériennes) placed at the disposal of the commanding officer of the ground forces on the Northeastern Front, which General Vuillemin turned over to General Tétu, three air operations areas North (General d'Astier), East (General Bouscat), and South (General Odic), an air operations area on the Alpine Front (General Laurens), and a command of air forces and F.T.A. in North Africa.

Meanwhile, the Air Force organization had been reshaped in the territories of the Middle East. The creation on August 31, 1939, of a commander in chief of the French forces in the eastern Mediterranean, to which position General Weygand was appointed, led to the establishment of a command of the air forces in the eastern Mediterranean the following October, with General Jauneaud in charge. He had under him 4 flights of Potez 25 T.O.E.'s stationed on the spot and a mobile grouping which was to include one group each of bombing, reconnaissance, and observation planes.

Equally important was General Vuillemin's decision to establish within the G.Q.G.A., on October 11, 1939, a series of inspectorates (air defense to General Aube, pursuit to General d'Harcourt, bombing to General Pastier, reconnaissance to General Odic, aerostation to General Bienvenu, technical inspectorate to General Gambier) to keep the commander in chief of the air forces informed on the evolution of methods of employment and make a report on the updating of the planes in service.

Finally, on February 17, 1940, except for a few very special cases, the bomber brigades and squadrons disappeared in favor of groupings directly subordinate to the air divisions. Two months later, on April 15, General Vuillemin defined the organization of the assault bomber groupings, whose basic aircraft was to be the Breguet 693.

After being commandant of the CEAM (Military Air Experiment Center) in Rheims before the war, General Tétu became, in February 1940, commanding officer of the ground-support air forces and ground antiaircraft forces of the Northeastern Front.

During the eight months of the phony war, the structures of the Air Force had undergone profound changes. Like every undertaking, they contained a number of defects, not the least of which was the direct subordination of multiple pursuit and reconnaissance units to the ground forces. The German offensive on the Western Front was to show up many others, in both materiel and in industrial policy.

The Industrial Effort

When the war began the First Air Army, facing Germany, had only 312 single-seated fighter planes—138 Morane-Saulnier 406's and 94 Curtiss Hawk

H-75's—and 37 three-seated Potez 630's and 631's. Apart from the 39 night fighters of the same type assigned to the defense of the Paris region, the other fighters available were Dewoitine 501's and 510's, Spad 510's, and even Nieuport 622's. The rest of the fighter forces had 120 single-seaters and 35 multi-seaters at their disposal.

In the whole of the bomber forces there were only 8 modern planes (3 Potez 633's and 5 LeO 45's). All the rest were Bloch 200's or 210's, Amiot 143's, Potez 540's, and Farman 222's barely capable of being used at night. The situation of the reconnaissance forces, where the majority of the planes in operation were Bloch 131's (transition planes of Plan V) and a few Potez 637's, was equally disturbing. As for the observation units, dominated by Mureaux 115's and 117's and Potez 25's and 39's, their condition was hardly brilliant, and the first engagements with German fighters quickly revealed the decrepitude of the materiel.

This description clearly shows that as of September 3, 1939, the French Air Force was in the midst of a period of renovation and rectification and that the effort made since the setting up of Plan V had not yet borne fruit. Any intelligent policy would therefore be directed toward speeding up the entry into service of modern airplanes within the units and would also do a complete review of the goals set for the aeronautics industry.

At the time of the mobilization the plan of aviation needs was not greatly altered, but the peacetime manufacturing schedule was replaced with a wartime schedule. Whereas the peacetime schedule called for monthly outputs of 335 planes for 1940, the wartime schedule set a rate, for the seventh month of the hostilities, of 780 planes a month. This change in the manufacturing schedule led to the working out, on September 14, 1939, of a new plan—the wartime Plan V, or the 3,200 plan. In this last case the Air Ministry and the G.Q.G.A. proposed a monthly production of 1,600 planes and set the following distribution by categories: pursuit—1,314 first-line planes and 391 in reserve, or a total of 1,705; bombing—995 planes in service and 298 in reserve, or 1,293; reconnaissance—188 planes in service and 57 in reserve, or 245; and observation—707 planes in service and 218 in reserve, or 925.

With the 3,204 planes in service and 964 in reserve (4,168 in all) provided by the wartime Plan V, the officials of the Air Force, while maintaining the number of groups of fighters, horizontal bombers, reconnaissance planes, and observation planes, nevertheless increased the manpower. On the other hand, they came out in favor of definitively abandoning dive-bombing and also heavy bombers, relying instead on assault bombers, with the number of such groups doubling. The planes to be manufactured were capable of giving the air forces a definitely modern look. The fighter forces were to be equipped with Dewoitine 520's, Bloch 152's, Arsenal VG 33's, and Potez 671's (multi-seaters), reconnaissance with Amiot 351's, Bloch 174–175's, and Potez 63-11's, and bombing with Breguet 693's, Bloch 175's, LeO 45's, Amiot 352's and 354's, and even Breguet 691's. But in the month of September 1939 these provisions were at best theoretical, as they did not correspond to the industrial potential of the time. In fact, the technical and industrial directorate had been overly optimistic, and as the plan was put into practice industrial and technical difficulties of all kinds arose, entailing more and more lengthy delays.

In February 1940 the G.Q.G.A. recognized that in view of the production capacity of the French aeronautics industry the figures called for by the wartime Plan V would not be attained. General Vuillemin consequently suggested to the minister of air that the provisions of the plan be adjusted to the nation's industrial potential and to the offerings of the American market and considered it necessary to place orders abroad. Moreover, he thought that the Air Force should not count on decisive help from the Fighter Command of the RAF. These circumstances led the commander in chief of the air forces to ask for an increase in French fighter forces (1,500 single-seaters and 200 multi-seaters) and to submit to the minister to whom he was responsible a new plan, Plan V a. Besides the fighter forces, this new plan favored assault aviation

(300 planes planned) and raised the complement of observation groups from 9 planes to 12. It was published, with slight modifications, on April 25, 1940, under the name of Plan VI. At the time of completion of the plan, May 1, 1941, the Air Force was to have 3,534 first-line planes—1,314 fighters, 732 bombers, and 1,032 reconnaissance planes (9,186 counting the reserves). In fact, Plan VI, which was to start on May 1, 1940, never went into effect.

This new plan implied a radical transformation of the manufacturing schedule. To enable the air forces to maintain the potential defined in Plan VI the technical and industrial directorate proposed a monthly production of 742 airframes, to be raised in June 1940 to 1,678. Conscious of the impossibility of attaining such levels, the general staff of the Air Force preferred to reduce this figure to 823 (942 counting American planes).

In reality, industrial production was far below the stipulations of both the technical directorate and the chief officials of the Air Force. It is interesting to compare these two sets of figures for the period of the phony war.

	Provisions of the Wartime Plan V	*Planes Actually Produced*
1939		
October	422	254
November	615	296
December	710	314
1940		
January	863	358
February	1,066	279
March	1,254	364
April	1,430	330
May	1,699	434

The Air Force high command founded great hopes on the Arsenal VG 33 fighter plane with its elegant lines. However, on June 25, 1940, only five of these planes had been delivered to the French air forces.

The Curtiss H-75 was the first American plane received by the French Air Force under the policy of purchases from the United States after an initial order for 100 planes in May 1938.

It can easily be seen that real production never at any time corresponded to the plan. There was even a decline in production in October 1939 and in February 1940, the second due to the lack of preparation for industrial mobilization. The planners then found themselves obliged to reduce the planning figures to 632 for May and 715 for June.

These deficiencies pushed the Air Ministry to develop its policy of purchases from the United States. The 3,300 planes (700 single-seated and 300 multi-seated fighter planes, 1,200 three-seated assault and bombing planes, 700 four-seated bombers, and 1,200 training planes) that Guy La Chambre had asked the Jacquin-Thouvenot mission to obtain from American manufacturers are clear evidence of the hopes that the minister founded on the transatlantic aeronautics industry. These hopes were at first cruelly disappointed with the institution of the arms embargo law promulgated at the moment of the oubreak of war in Europe. It was not until the "Cash and Carry" law (November 1939) that the French mission, which had meanwhile been instructed to buy 2,200 extra trainers, could work under easier conditions. In December 1939 the incapacity of the French aeronautics industry to satisfy the needs of the Air Force led La Chambre to ask for still more materiel from the United States. The departure of René Pléven for America resulted in the establishment of a joint Franco-British plan for 4,700 planes. Most of the models selected existed only in the prototype stage, but their performances met the requirements that had been formulated by the French. Finally, during the fighting on the Meuse, the French representatives bought, by letter of engagement, the first LB-30's (B-24 Liberators) that came off Consolidated's assembly lines, some P-39 Airacobras, some Curtiss P-40's, Lockheed P-38's, and Brewster 240's. In fact, none of these planes ever arrived in France. After the signing of the armistice the British took them over on their own account.

Modernization of the Units

From the middle of September, in the face of the possibility of a German surprise attack, the Air

Force high command decided to withdraw the greater part of the bomber groups of the First Air Army from the line of fire and station them farther to the rear. Then on December 3, on the basis of the planned manufacture of new materiel that the minister of air had communicated to him, General Vuillemin established a vast program of modernization of the units placed under his orders.

At the time of mobilization the fighter forces had 23 groups, 19 of them modern (12 of Morane-Saulnier 406's, 4 of Curtiss H-75's, and 3 of Potez 631's), and 9 regional fighter flights (Dewoitine 501's and 510's, Spad 510's, and Nieuport 62's). The first confrontations with the Luftwaffe demonstrated that the Morane 406's and Curtiss H-75's were capable of holding their own against the Messerschmitt Bf 109D. But what would happen when the Germans threw in their Bf 109E's and 110's? With this in mind and after some losses in several units equipped with Morane-Saulnier 406's, the G.Q.G.A. worked out, early in November 1939, a program of expanding the fighter forces and at the same time attempting their modernization. Ten new groups were to be formed in such a way as to put into service, by the end of April 1940, 14 groups of Morane-Saulnier 406's, 10 of Bloch MB 152's, 8 of Dewoitine 520's, 4 of Curtiss H-75's, and 1 of Arsenal VG 33's. But the shortage of trained personnel was a factor in holding up the planned expansion. Furthermore, the considerable delays in the manufacture of Bloch 152's, Dewoitine 520's, and VG 33's impeded the modernization of the groups equipped with Morane 406's. Thus on the eve of the German offensive the French Air Force had only 28 fighter groups (15 with Morane 406's, 8 with Bloch 151's or 152's, 4 with Curtiss H-75's, and only one, the GC I/3, with Dewoitine 520's) and 7 flights of Potez 630–631's, 5 of them night flights, out of the 38 units that it had been planned to organize. In addition, the GC III/4, consisting of flights 571 and 573, had been formed and equipped with Dewoitine 510's.

As for bombing, as early as December 4, 1939, the groups of the First Air Army, except for a few units equipped with Farman 222's and Amiot 143's, had been regrouped along with 4 groups of Bloch 210's of the Third Air Army in the South of France, where they gave rise to the Bomber Aviation Training Grouping of the Southeast (G.I.A.B.S.E.) and began their conversion to LeO 45's, Amiot 350's, and Breguet 691's. In fact, this last plane was reserved for training, and the crews had to operate

In November 1939 the Air Force high command decided to proceed with a new modernization of the fighter forces and gradually replace the Morane-Saulnier 406's on the verge of becoming outdated.

Planes Produced and Accepted 1 September 1939–1 June 1940

Fighter Planes Monthly Production

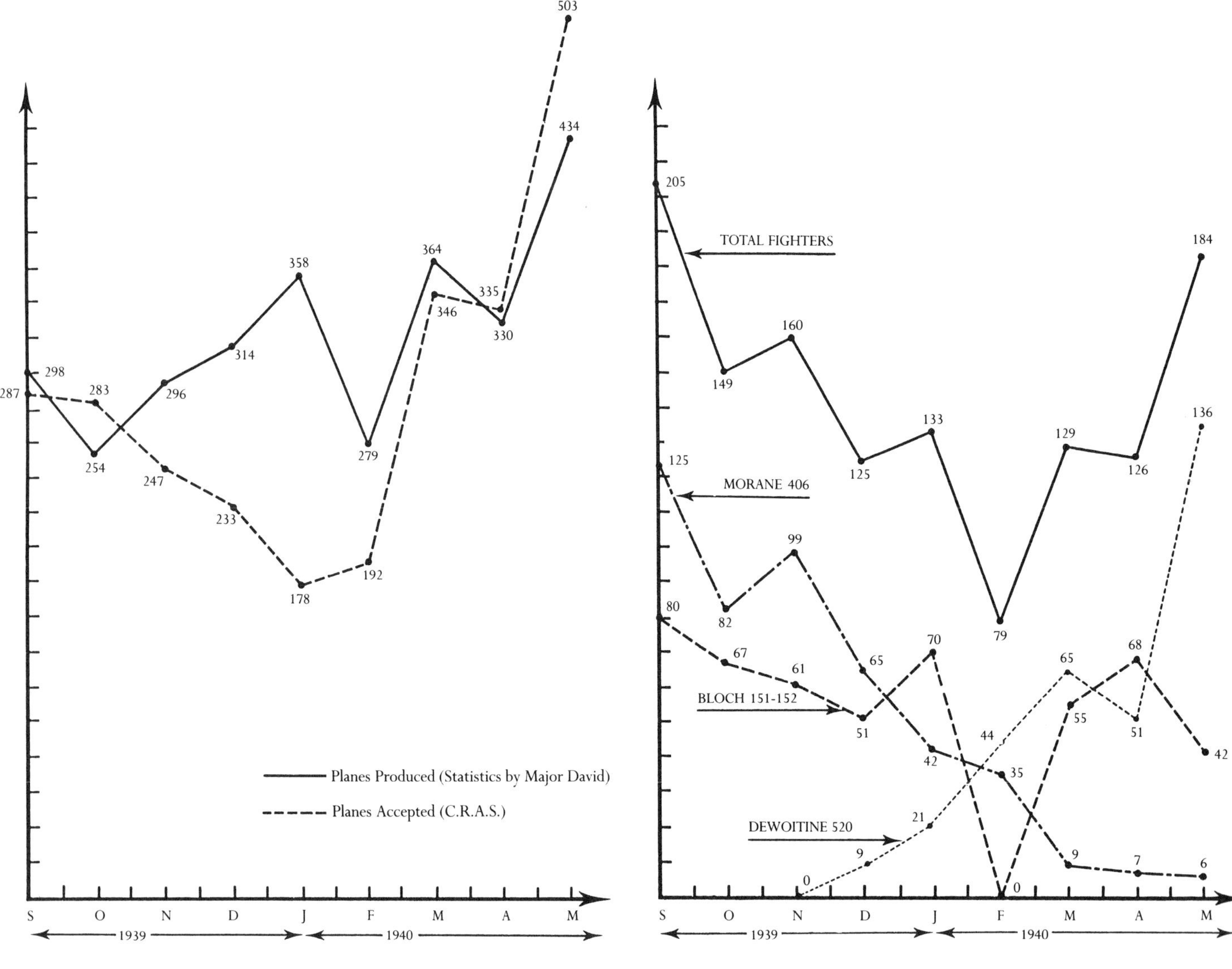

Reconnaissance Planes Monthly Production

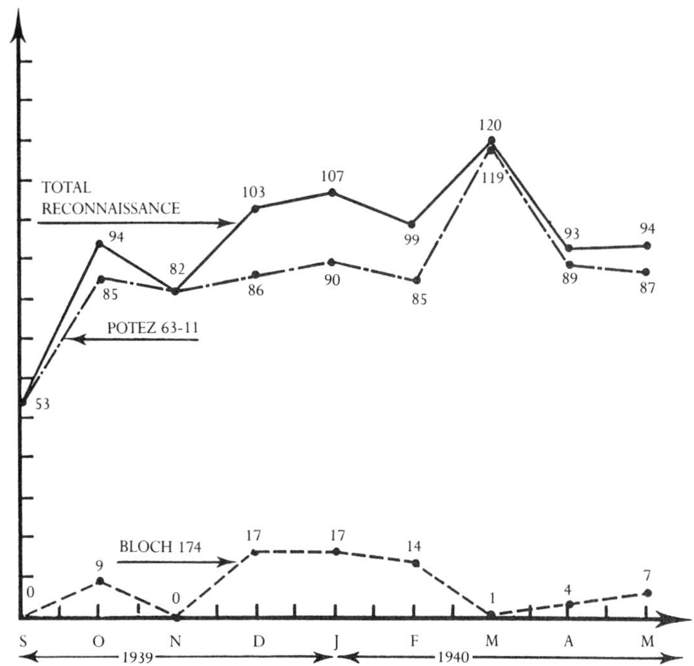

Bombers Monthly Production

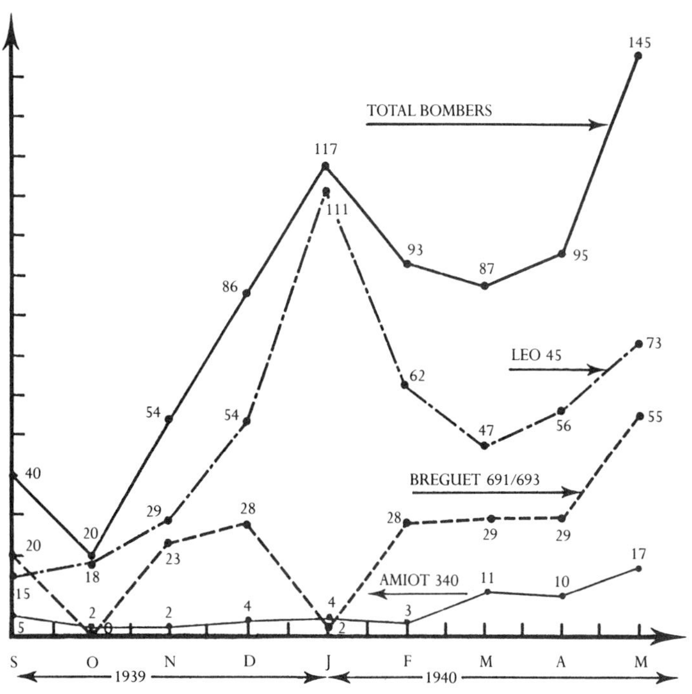

on Breguet 693's with a Gnome and Rhône engine. A grouping was also organized in North Africa, although on a smaller scale, for training the groups equipped with the American Glenn Martin 167's and Douglas DB-7's. Although great efforts were made in this area for several months, the inferiority of the French bomber forces on May 10, 1940, was crushing. It must be said that the G.Q.G.A.'s plans did not involve, until May 1940, any new forces in this field. Only the modernization of existing groups had been planned, with four of them to be equipped as assault bomber groups.

The switch to LeO 45's gave rise to many difficulties, notably because of the delicate handling of that plane. As for the Amiot 350's, problems of all kinds impeded their rolling out of the factory. The first ones did not appear in the units until March 1940, and they still had to be assigned for training, since they were not up to combat. For their part, the Breguet 691's had continual engine problems, and the fragility of their landing gear did not help. The definitive machines, the Breguet 693's, were not delivered until April 1940, compelling the crews to get their training on Potez 633 B2's, which were almost unusable as assault planes. Finally, in all the groupings the shortage of on-board radiomen reached nearly 50 percent, and airplane mechanics were not available in sufficient numbers. Thus on May 10, of 33 bomber groups only 7 possessed modern materiel (LeO 45's, Breguet 693's, and Glenn Martins), 6 were still flying old planes (4 with Amiot 143's and 2 with Farman 222's), and 20 others were in the process of conversion to LeO 45's, Amiot 354's, and Breguet 693's. The number of crews that had experience with modern airplanes was small (and most of them were not trained in night flying), and yet the bomber groups were to be thrown into battle almost immediately. To sum up, bombing aviation suffered from a shortage of materiel, placed at its disposal too late and in too small amounts, and serious shortages of adequately trained personnel.

According to the plans of December 3, 1939, by the spring of 1940 the reconnaissance forces should have had 15 groups (3 with Bloch 175's, 2 with Amiot 350's and Bloch 175's, 4 with Potez 63-11's and Bloch 175's, and 6 with Glenn Martins and Potez 63-11's). At the beginning of hostilities it numbered 14 groups, 12 of them in France proper. Four of these 12 had just received Potez 637's, which were to be used only temporarily while awaiting the delivery of new aircraft to the units. But because of the considerable production delays the decision was made to equip them temporarily with Potez 63-11's originally intended for observation. As for the newly created forces, the general staff had planned only one: a group called upon to do reconnaissance missions for the G.H.Q. In any case, the coming into service of the German Bf 109E on the Western Front at the beginning of 1940 interfered with the reconnaissance sorties of the French Potez 63-11 and forced the high command to limit their penetration into enemy lines to about 50 kilometers. Only the coming into service of the Bloch 174's and Glenn Martin 167's could have remedied the situation. But the former reached the units very late and, for a long time, only in very small quantities. It was found necessary to retire the Bloch 131's from service because of their excessive vulnerability; reconnaissance strength was thus much reduced for many months. When added to the difficulties in training specialized personnel, these circumstances placed reconnaissance aviation in a difficult situation on May 10, 1940, even though it had 14 groups out of 15 equipped with modern materiel (actually, Potez 63-11's).

At the beginning of the war the observation section, with its 47 groups, 36 of them in France proper, was certainly the most disadvantaged of all the Air Force subdivisions. For this reason it was decided to equip it as quickly as possible with Potez 63-11's. To speed up the training of the crews the G.Q.G.A. opened a center at Toulouse, supplemented in November and December by those at Romilly and Saint-Etienne-de-Saint-Geoirs, which were reserved for the First and Third Air Armies. The fact remains that the training of the crews proved to be very sketchy. Pressured by the land forces, the G.Q.G.A. had to limit the training to a minimum, and many groups were declared op-

A Potez 63-11 assembly line. In spite of the poor preparation for industrial mobilization and the departure of many specialists for the front, the French aeronautics industry manufactured 1,927 modern airplanes from September 1939 to May 1940.

A Dewoitine 520 assembly line.

erational when they had done only a few flights around the airfield or practice flights in their combat plane without any training in war missions and without practice in firing or maneuvers with fighter planes. On May 10, 1940, the observation section had 48 groups, 35 of which, engaged on the Northeastern Front, had each received 6 Potez 63-11's.

The Personnel Crisis

No less decisive than the modernization of the flying materiel were the problems connected with the training of personnel. In fact, when war came the Air Force was in the midst of a personnel crisis. Although the mobilization had increased the manpower of the air forces considerably, at the begin-

The Potez 63-11's assigned to the reconnaissance and observation groups suffered very heavy losses at the hands of the German fighter forces. They often had to operate in isolation.

In September 1939 the aerial observation groups were largely equipped with Mureaux 115's. Like the Mureaux 117's, they were unsuited to modern warfare and would be replaced by the Potez 63-11.

ning, even though certain staffs or services were overstaffed, most of the formations had big shortages. On October 5, 1939, apart from officer pilots and observers, all the other specialties, both at the officer and at the noncommissioned officer levels, showed deficits (60% among noncommissioned officer radiomen, 31% among noncommissioned officer machine-gunners, 77% among noncommissioned officer aerostation mechanics).

On September 26, 1939, a special commission was formed at Air Force headquarters for the purpose of solving, at the flight schools, the problems posed by the implementation of the wartime Plan V, or the 3,200 plan. In some fifteen months, January 1940 to April 1941, this program called for training 1,800 pilots, 3,200 observers under the Air Ministry, and 1,800 observers under the Ministry of War. All this demanded the creation of an enormous infrastructure in observation schools and in pilot training groups at 6 runways, airplane resources that the Air Force did not have (of the 3,760 planes needed, it possessed only 1,000), and a large number of instructors (1,200). In this last area, the resource inventory taken at the time of mobilization showed only 600. Nevertheless, a reorganization plan for the flight schools was worked out and presented to the minister of air on October 28, 1939. It recognized that the creation of the schools necessary to satisfy the needs of the 3,200 plan would not be completed until the end of 1940, that is, with a lag of nine months compared to the original plan (March 1940). Still, since it appeared that the estimated rate of losses for the first three months of the war was far higher than the actual losses, the planners estimated that the 3,200 plan could be carried out in the desired time, by April–May 1940, on the assumption that the winter of 1939–1940 would not be an excessively bad one for losses.

The Versailles and Bordeaux schools each gave rise to two pilot training groups of the new type and an observers' school. In addition, a pilot training school was established at Meknes and another observation school at Rabat, both in Morocco. But in April 1940 the results obtained were far from matching the theoretical calculations of the preceding October. Bottlenecks at the schools were almost the rule, and it was necessary to scale down the plan.

The situation was all the more dramatic since Plan V a, adopted in February 1940 and renamed Plan VI in April, called for still more trained personnel. Since the output of the schools was practically zero, as the Air Force general staff noted in March 1940, the Air Force had to resign itself to a shortage of officer and noncommissioned officer pilot personnel throughout 1940 and until the completion of Plan VI. There was no way, in fact, to remedy this deficiency. The situation was distressing, to say the least, for both the next few months and for the distant future. And on April 18, 1940, less than a month before the German offensive, the general commanding the Z.O.A.E. (Air Operations Area East) reported that in case of crisis his air units would be incapable of sustaining a continuous effort.

The Phony War in the Air

On September 4, 1939, the G.Q.G.A. arranged for the implementation of the reconnaissance plan that it had established in order to inform the highest authorities on the deployment of the Luftwaffe and of the German ground forces. These actions fell to the strategic reconnaissance groups I/33 and I/52 (Potez 637's), reinforced by the LeO 45's of the 31st Squadron. GR II/22, GR II/55, and GR 14 (Bloch 131's), at the same time as the Potez 637's of GR II/52, were assigned to tactical reconnaissance for the benefit of the land armies established along the German frontier. At the very beginning these units could fly quite tranquilly over the advance posts of the Siegfried Line. On the Western Front the Luftwaffe had been given orders to stay on the ground, while the Flak (German antiaircraft) batteries had been ordered not to open fire. It was not until September 8 that everything would change.

Meanwhile, from September 7 to 15 the air forces were to take part in the ground offensive

A Link trainer in a school of the 3,200 plan. In fact, the training went very slowly, and at the time of the armistice the Air Force had only 4,742 flying officers of the 5,960 whose training had been planned and 3,348 flying noncommissioned officers of the 6,040 planned.

A blimp during the "phony" war. At the time of the mobilization, 49 companies of observation balloonists were activated, one-third of which were equipped with blimps. Only 10 were modernized before the attack of May 10, 1940. The battle that followed demonstrated the vulnerability of this materiel.

On May 10, 1940, the Air Force had 47 LeO C-30A's or LeO C-40's at its disposal. The autogyros, integrated into the GAO's, could not be engaged because of the Luftwaffe's superiority.

launched in the Saar by the Third and Fourth Armies with the aim of relieving Poland. Only the air operations area created on September 6, under the command of General Pennès, was involved in this affair. It had at its disposal GC (fighter groups) II/5, I/3, II/4, and II/7, later supported by GC II/6 and III/2, equipped with Morane 406's and Curtiss H-75's. The 3rd Air Division (10th and 6th Brigades plus GR I/52), commanded by General Canone, and the 6th Air Division (9th and 15th Squadrons plus GR I/33), commanded by General Valin, also participated in it, as well as the F.A. (air force) 104 (one fighter group and one reconnaissance group), GAO (observation group) I/520, and the 81st Balloon Battalion, which were parts of the 20th Army Corps. General Pennès' essential mission was to support the ground forces whose attack was to take place during the night of September 7–8. He was also to reinforce the fighter planes of the Fourth Army on the morning of September 9 during the assault on the Auersmacher salient. Finally, if the need arose, it was planned to call upon the 3rd and 6th Air Divisions starting on September 10.

In fact, the air operations were limited to a pursuit job carried out by Grouping 22 and some reconnaissance and observation sorties done by GR 14 and GR I/52 and by GAO's 520, 505, and 507, which had come up as reinforcements in the meantime. If the bombing forces took part, it was solely within the framework of reconnaissance missions carried out behind the Siegfried Line (GB I/32 and II/35, flying Bloch 200's and Amiot 143's). On September 8 there were a few aerial combats and the machine-gunning, at the Saarbrücken airfield, of two German Bf 109's by a Morane 406 of the GC I/3. The next day fighter planes again attacked the Saarbrücken airfield. The same day two Mureaux 115's were engaged by Flak, and one of them was hit and crashed. (The day before, in the afternoon, another Mureaux 115 of the GAO 553, carrying Lieutenant Davier as observer and Master Sergeant Piaccentini as pilot had been shot down in the Saverne sector; these two men were the first members of the French Air Force to die in this war.) In this kind of sortie the pilots got acceptable results from the Mureaux 115's, while the Potez 25's and 39's of the GAO 505 proved

His 20 victories in 1939 and 1940 brought Edmond Marin la Meslée, shown here in a Curtiss H-75, the honor of being named a Chevalier of the Legion of Honor. He became commanding officer of the Champagne group and was shot down on February 4, 1945.

completely ineffective. On September 13, after the GC's I/3, II/4, II/5, and II/2 had been returned to their respective armies, the fighting on the ground gradually came to a halt. The offensive on the Saar, which was an offensive in name only, was on the point of ending. The Air Force had shown itself to be very valuable to the ground forces, but its planes had been distinctly outclassed by those of the Luftwaffe.

It was also on September 8, a really busy day, that the French fighter forces scored their first air victories (two Bf 109's shot down by the Curtisses of GC II/4). On their side, the German fighters applied themselves to sweeping the French reconnaissance planes from the sky. The numerous Bloch 131's and Potez 637's that bore the brunt of this increase in the Luftwaffe's activity were soon replaced by bombers without fighter escort, which quickly met the same fate. The first major encounters of fighter planes did not take place until the last third of September. They reached their greatest intensity toward the end of the month, with 12 Bf 109's and a Henschel Hs 126 destroyed on September 30.

The relative fury of the battle in the air hardly concealed the calm, just as relative, that prevailed on each side of the Franco-German frontier. Since the conflict seemed to be moving toward a war of positions in which neither of the adversaries appeared to want to take the responsibility for starting a major battle, General Vuillemin decided to adopt a defensive attitude and to oppose all incursions of German reconnaissance. But, by bringing a powerful fighter force into action, he also counted on continuing the reconnaissance missions over Germany. Besides, the "phony war," or the "Sitzkrieg," as the Germans called it (literally, "sit-down war"), could only help the efforts of the Air Force to modernize the units and increase their number. This whole period, nevertheless, was dominated by the desire of the commander in chief of the air forces to economize as much as possible on men and materiel. On October 1 he ordered a strict limitation on the employment of observation units after the heavy losses registered in that section. Finally, desiring to save for the decisive battle the greatest possible number of trained reconnaissance crews (the seriousness of the manpower problem is well known), General Vuillemin reduced the range of action of flights made by the Potez 637's and 63's to 11 kilometers in enemy territory (in November 1939) and decided to withdraw the too vulnerable Bloch 131 from the front.

This desire to economize resources also appeared in the declarations of the commander in chief of the French air forces at the beginning of January 1940. In the interest of the Allies he thought it was necessary not to engage in a major air battle during the coming year but rather to await the realization of the rearmament plans. For this reason he assigned only minimum forces to "external" actions (possible support of the Finns in the struggle against the Soviet Union, the scheme of bombing the Baku oil refineries, or setting up a possible expeditionary force to disembark at Salonika). Finally, it was well understood that in case of a German air attack the Air Force would not hesitate—and this entered into the views of the leaders of the RAF Bomber Command—to attack Germany's war production, iron ore reserve, and oil supplies. All that, however, was quite theoretical. It would still have been necessary for the French air forces to have the means to carry out such a program.[1]

The entire winter and the first days of spring were devoted to reconnaissance efforts. Since neither of the belligerents dared take the crushing responsibility of launching a strategic bombing campaign, the Farman 222's were used to drop leaflets on German cities. The French fighter force was used to keep French air space free of long-range German reconnaissance planes such as the Dornier Do 17. In these actions pilots like Marin La Meslée, Accart, and Le Gloan distinguished

1. In accordance with the prewar general staff agreements, the British had dispatched to the Continent an Advanced Striking Force of 160 Fairey Battles and an organic air force, the Air Component, designed to support the ground forces of the expeditionary corps under Lord Gort (Lysanders, Blenheims, and Hurricanes).

themselves. In encounters with the new Bf 109E, the Morane 406 and the Curtiss H-75 had been distinctly outclassed, the latter less so, however. For this reason, as early as December 1939, General d'Harcourt called for bringing into service a fighter plane with better performance. But neither the Dewoitine 520, the Bloch 152, nor the VG 33 was yet available in large enough quantities or, as was the case for the latter, operational.

Several times, between November 1939 and May 1940, the Air Force was alerted and informed of a possible enemy offensive. Thus in January 1940, following a chance landing on Belgian territory of a German liaison plane carrying plans for invasion of that country, the whole G.I.A.B.S.E. prepared to move to the Northeastern Front at twelve hours' notice. Finally, on May 7, the intelligence gathered gave reason to fear an imminent action against Belgium and the Netherlands. The next day the G.Q.G.A. called upon the fighter forces and the air base defenses to prepare for any eventuality.

The French Air Force, its planes, its doctrines, and its organization were about to face the test of reality.

Losses of the French Air Force during the "Phony War"

	Airplanes Destroyed	Airplanes Damaged
1939		
September	26	6
October	8	2
November	13	–
December	2	–
1940		
January	2	1
February	–	1
March	5	7
April	7	1

Total: 63 planes lost and 18 damaged. Through the action of the French Air Force the German Luftwaffe lost 80 planes and had 34 probable losses.

A Fairey Battle of the Advanced Air Striking Force. These planes flew sacrifice missions in the attack on the bridges of the Albert Canal and on the German pontoons thrown across the Meuse in the vicinity of Sedan.

The French Air Force on September 3, 1939

Unit	Plane Type	Stationed at:	Attached to:
Pursuit			
GC I/1[1]	Dewoitine 510	Chantilly (Oise)	Fighter Grouping 21
GC II/1	Dewoitine 510	Buc (Seine-et-Oise)	Fighter Grouping 21
GC I/2	Morane 406	Beauvais (Oise)	Fighter Grouping 21
GC II/2	Morane 406	Clermont-les-Fermes (Aisne)	Fighter Grouping 21
GC III/2	Morane 406	Cambrai (Nord)	Fighter Grouping 21
GC III/6	Morane 406	Villacoublay (Seine-et-Oise)	Fighter Grouping 21
GC I/3	Morane 406	Velaine-en-Haye (Meurthe-et-Moselle)	Fighter Grouping 22
GC II/4	Curtiss H-75	Xaffevillers (Vosges)	Fighter Grouping 22
GC II/5	Curtiss H-75	Toul (Meurthe-et-Moselle)	Fighter Grouping 22
GC II/7	Morane 406	Luxeuil (Haute-Saône)	Fighter Grouping 22
GC I/4	Curtiss H-75	Wez-Thuisy (Marne)	Fighter Grouping 23
GC I/5	Curtiss H-75	Suippes (Marne)	Fighter Grouping 23
GC II/6	Morane 406	Anglure-Vouarces (Marne)	Fighter Grouping 23
GC II/3	Morane 406	Fayence (Var)	Fighter Grouping South
GC III/3	Morane 406	Salon (Bouches-du-Rhône)	Fighter Grouping South
GC III/7	Morane 406	Ambérieu (Ain)	Fighter Grouping North
GC I/8	Dewoitine 510	Hyères (Var)	Fighter Grouping South
GC III/8	Potez 631	Marignane (Bouches-du-Rhône)	Fighter Grouping South
GC II/13	Potez 631	Plessis-Belleville (Oise)	Mixed Night Fighter Grouping No. 1
GC I/13	Potez 631	Meaux (Seine-et-Marne)	Mixed Night Fighter Grouping No. 2
ERC 1/561[2]	Nieuport 62 & Dewoitine 501	Rouen (Seine-Inférieure)	Fighter Grouping 21
ERC 2/561	Nieuport 62 & Dewoitine 501	Rouen (Seine-Inférieure)	Fighter Grouping 21
ERC 3/561	Nieuport 62 & Spad 510	Saint-Inglevert (Pas-de-Calais)	Fighter Grouping 21
ERC 4/561	Nieuport 62 & Spad 510	Villacoublay (Seine-et-Oise)	Fighter Grouping 21
Flight 562	Dewoitine 501	Lyons-Bron (Rhône)	Fighter Grouping North
Air School Patrol	Morane 406 & Morane 225	Salon-de-Provence (Bouches-du-Rhône)	Fighter Grouping North
5th Autonomous Group	Dewoitine 510	Sidi-Ahmed (Tunisia)	Tunisian FA North[3]

[1] GC: Groupe de Chasse; Fighter Group
[2] ERC: Equipe de Réparation de Corps d'Armée; Army Corps Maintenance Section
[3] FA: Force Aérienne; Air Force

The French Air Force on September 3, 1939; continued

Unit	Plane Type	Stationed at:	Attached to:
GC I/6	Morane 406	Biskra (Algeria)	5th Air Army
GC I/7	Morane 406	Biskra (Algeria)	5th Air Army
ERC 571	Dewoitine 501	Algiers (Algeria)	5th Air Army
ERC 572	Nieuport 62	Oran (Algeria)	5th Air Army
ERC 573	Spad 510	Rabat (Morocco)	5th Air Army
ERC 574		Tunis (Tunisia)	5th Air Army
Bombing			
GB I/11[1]	Bloch 210	Istres (Bouches-du-Rhône)	11th Squadron
GB II/11	Bloch 210	Istres (Bouches-du-Rhône)	11th Squadron
GB I/12	Bloch 210	Auzainviliers (Vosges)	12th Squadron
GB II/12	Bloch 210	Damblain (Vosges)	12th Squadron
GB I/15	Farman 222	Avord (Cher)	15th Squadron
GB II/15	Farman 222	Avord (Cher)	15th Squadron
GB I/21	Bloch 210	Laon (Aisne)	21st Squadron
GB II/21	Bloch 210	Athies (Aisne)	21st Squadron
GB I/23	Bloch 210	Istres (Bouches-du-Rhône)	23rd Squadron
GB II/23	Bloch 210	Istres (Bouches-du-Rhône)	23rd Squadron
GB I/31	Bloch 200	Connantre (Marne)	31st Squadron
GB II/31	Bloch 200	Marigny-le-Grand (Marne)	31st Squadron
GB I/32	Bloch 200	Dijon (Côte d'Or)	32nd Squadron
GB II/32	Bloch 200	Chissey (Jura)	32nd Squadron
GB I/34	Amiot 143	Abbeville (Somme)	34th Squadron
GB II/34	Amiot 143	Poix (Somme)	34th Squadron
GB II/35	Amiot 143	Lyons-Bron (Rhône)	35th Squadron
GB I/51	Bloch 210	La Perthe (Aube)	51st Squadron
GB II/51	Bloch 210	Troyes (Aube)	51st Squadron
GB I/54	Mureaux 115 & Potez 633	Mons en Chaussée Péronne (Somme)	54th Squadron
GB II/54	Potez 540	Montdidier (Somme)	54th Squadron
GB I/19	Bloch 210	Kalaa-Djerda (Tunisia)	Tunisian FA South
GB II/19	Bloch 210	Kalaa-Djerda (Tunisia)	Tunisian FA South
GB I/25	Bloch 200	Sidi-Ahmed (Tunisia)	Aeronautics of the 4th Maritime Region
GB II/25	LeO 257 A	Bizerte (Tunisia)	
GB I/38	Amiot 143	Sétif (Algeria)	Tunisian FA North
GB II/38	Amiot 143	Sétif (Algeria)	Tunisian FA North
GB II/61	Bloch 200	Biskra (Algeria)	Tunisian FA North
GB I/62	LeO 206	Meknes (Morocco)	FA of Morocco
GB II/62	LeO 206	Meknes (Morocco)	FA of Morocco
GB I/63	Amiot 143	Sétif (Algeria)	Tunisian FA North
GB II/63	Potez 540	Marrakech (Morocco)	FA of Morocco
GB I/39	Bloch 200	Rayack (Levant)	Air Command Levant

[1] GB: Groupe de Bombardement; Bomber Group

The French Air Force on September 3, 1939; continued

Unit	Plane Type	Stationed at:	Attached to:
Reconnaissance			
GR I/22[1]	Bloch 131	Chatel-Chehery (Ardennes)	FA 102 (IInd Army)
GR II/22	Bloch 131	Etain (Meuse)	FA 103 (IIIrd Army)
GR I/33	Potez 637	Saint-Dizier (Haute-Marne)	G.Q.G.A.[2]
GR II/33	Potez 637	Soissons (Aisne)	G.Q.G.A.
GR I/35	Bloch 131	Courlaoux (Jura)	FA 7 (VIIth Army)
GR I/36	Potez 540	Vitry-en-Artois (Pas-de-Calais)	FA 101 (Ist Army)
GR II/36	Potez 540	La Malmaison (Aisne)	FA 109 (9th Army)
GR I/52	Potez 637	Chaumont (Haute-Marne)	1st Air Army
GR II/52	Potez 637	Herbeviller (Meurthe-et-Moselle)	FA 105 (Vth Army)
GR I/55	Bloch 131	Orange (Vaucluse)	FA 106 (VIth Army)
GR II/55	Bloch 131	Lure (Haute-Saône)	FA 108 (VIIIth Army)
14th GR	Bloch 131	Martigny (Vosges)	FA 104 (IVth Army)
GR I/61	Bloch 131	Biskra (Algeria)	5th Air Army
GR II/39	Potez 39	Damas	Air Command Levant
Observation			
GAO 501[3]	Mureaux 115	Lille (Nord)	FA 101 (Ist Army)
GAO 502	Mureaux 115	Attigny (Ardennes)	FA 109 (IXth Army)
GAO 503	Mureaux 115	Rouen (Seine-Inférieure)	Activated after September 3, 1939
GAO 504	Potez 39 & Le0 C 30	Chartres (Eure-et-Loir)	Activated after September 3, 1939
GAO 505	Potez 39 & 25	Epernay (Marne)	FA of 5th C.A.[4]
GAO I/506	Mureaux 117 & Potez 540	Conflans (Meurthe-et-Moselle)	FA 105 (Vth Army)
GAO 2/506	Mureaux 117	Buzy (Meuse)	FA 103 (IIIrd Army)
GAO 507	Mureaux 115	Chalon (Saône-et-Loire)	Reserved element
GAO 1/508	Breguet 27	Sarrebourg (Moselle)	FA 105 (Vth Army)
GAO 2/508	Breguet 27 & Potez 25	Dijon (Côte d'Or)	Activated after September 3, 1939
GAO 509	Breguet 27	Tours (Indre-et-Loire)	Activated after September 3, 1939
GAO 510	Potez 39 & 25	Rennes (Ille-et-Vilaine)	Interior
GAO 511	Potez 39	Nantes (Loire-Inférieure)	Activated after September 3, 1939
GAO 512	Potez 39 & 25	Limoges (Haute-Vienne)	Activated after September 3, 1939
GAO 513	Potez 39 & 25	Montbéliard (Doubs)	FA 108 (VIIIth Army)
GAO 1/514	Mureaux 117	Tallard (Hautes-Alpes)	FA 106 (VIth Army)

[1] GR: Groupe de Reconnaissance; Reconnaissance Group
[2] G.Q.G.A.: Grand Quartier Général Aérien; General Headquarters, Air
[3] GAO: Groupe d'Observation; Observation Group
[4] C.A.: Corps d'Armée; Army Corps

The French Air Force on September 3, 1939; continued

Unit	Plane Type	Stationed at:	Attached to:
GAO 2/514	Mureaux 117 & Le0 C 30	Challes-les-Eaux (Savoie)	FA 106 (VIth Army)
GAO 515	Mureaux 117	Avignon (Vaucluse)	FA 106 (VIth Army)
GAO 516	Breguet 27	Aix-le-Bourget (Savoie)	FA 106 (VIth Army)
GAO 517	Potez 39 & Le0 C 40	Toulouse (Haute-Garonne)	Activated after 3 September 1939
GAO 518	Breguet 27 & Potez 25	Bordeaux (Gironde)	Activated after 3 September 1939
GAO 1/520	Mureaux 115	Delme (Moselle)	FA 104 (IVth Army)
GAO 543	Breguet 27	Belfort	FA 108 (VIIIth Army)
GAO 544	Breguet 27	Bourges (Cher)	Reserved element
GAO 545	Breguet 27	Auxerre (Yonne)	Reserved element
GAO 546	Breguet 27 & Potez 25	Pau (Basses-Pyrénées)	Reserved element
GAO 547	Breguet 27 & Potez 25	La Malmaison (Aisne)	Reserved element
GAO 548	Mureaux 115	Fayence (Var)	FA 106 (VIth Army)
GAO 550	Breguet 27	Calvi (Corsica)	FA Corsica
GAO 1/551	Mureaux 115	Attigny (Ardennes)	FA 102 (IInd Army)
GAO 2/551	Mureaux 115	Villers (Aisne)	FA 109 (IXth Army)
GAO 3/551	Mureaux 117	Stenay (Meuse)	FA 102 (IInd Army)
GAO 4/551	Mureaux 117 & Le0 C 30	Clastres (Aisne)	FA 101 (Ist Army)
GAO 552	Mureaux 115, Le0 C 30, & Potez 540	Mourmelon (Marne)	FA 107 (VIIth Army)
GAO 553	Mureaux 115 & Potez 540	Sarrebourg (Moselle)	FA 105 (Vth Army)

Note: In North Africa there were 9 GAO's plus 6 flights. These units were equipped with Potez 25 TOE's. In the Middle East 2 observation flights were equipped with Potez 25 TOE's.

On May 10, 1940, the Air Force had only one group, the GC I/3, equipped with the excellent fighter plane, the Dewoitine 520. By June 25, 1940, 437 of these planes had been manufactured.

CHAPTER 11

The Battle of France

Although the French air forces were put on the alert on May 8, the German offensive came as a surprise. The reconnaissance missions undertaken during the night of May 9–10 between the Moselle and the Rhine and between the Saar and Bavaria had all turned out negative. At dawn on May 10 the Luftwaffe began the air battle, launching massive bomber and fighter formations against the French airfields.

At that moment the French Air Force had 2,176 planes at the front. (It had a total of 5,026, divided among France, North Africa, the Middle East, Indochina, and the other colonial territories.) Of the 2,176 planes present with the armies, only 1,368 counted as first-line planes, ready for action with a maximum delay of four hours; 717 others were unavailable, and fewer than 100 were in the depots. Facing 3,530 first-line German planes (1,210 fighters, 1,680 bombers, and 640 reconnaissance and observation planes), the French Air Force thus had only 637 fighters at its disposal (nearly half of its first-line complement) and 489 reconnaissance and observation planes. In addition, the Luftwaffe had succeeded in reducing its unavailable planes to 22 percent. The ratio of forces was, of course, less disproportionate because of the presence on the Continent of the British Air Forces in France (nearly 400 planes). It is true, however, that the majority of them were ground support planes or outdated light bombers (Fairey Battles).

Thus the French Air Force had to face the German Luftwaffe outnumbered two to five.

The Battle of the North

While their ground troops were penetrating into Belgium, Luxembourg, and the Netherlands, the Germans mounted air attacks on 47 airfields or landing areas of the French Air Force and succeeded in destroying about 60 planes of various types. The warning devices had been on for forty-eight hours, and as the runways had suffered relatively little damage, many fighter patrols were able to take off in time to intercept the enemy bombers and inflict losses on them.

As soon as the German offensive was reported, General Vuillemin, according to plan, turned over to General Tétu three straight reconnaissance groups, the whole of the daytime bomber force, the assault aviation groups and their Breguet 693's, and all the fighters available on the Northeastern Front except for the units reserved for defense of the Paris region. The commanding officer of the support air forces of the Northeast could then give the authorization to the Z.O.A.N. (Air Operations

Area North) to throw in its LeO 45's and its Breguet 693's. But the many shifts of units carried out during that first day of fighting did not allow the French bombers to be ready in time. On the other hand, the fighter force shot down 44 German planes with the loss of 24 of their own. The work it had accomplished was all the more remarkable in that the 360 sorties with which it was credited during that one day were the work of only 200 pilots. Finally, during the night, Farman 222's dropped several tons of bombs on the Luftwaffe airfields of Gladbach-Kheydt, Bonn-Hangelar, and Wittlich.

The reconnaissance missions ordered on the morning of May 11 revealed to the Allied general staffs that the Germans had crossed the Albert Canal west of Maestricht and were proceeding in the direction of Bilsen and Tongres, thus threatening the entire Belgian apparatus. The gravity of this situation led General Tétu to concentrate all the fighter cover he had on the First Army, which was advancing into Belgium, neglecting the Second and Ninth Armies, the pivots of the Dyle maneuver. Because the weakness of the resources available prevented French bombers from directly attacking the bridges over the Albert Canal, they were assigned the mission of attacking the enemy columns themselves. At 1600 hours General Georges, commander in chief of the Northeastern Front, asked General Tétu to make every attempt to slow down or destroy the German tanks, even if he found it necessary for that purpose to bomb towns or villages. The first action of French bombers in the battle took place at about 1800 hours, when 12 LeO 45's of Grouping 6 (GB I/12 and II/12), escorted by Morane 406's, attacked the approaches to three of the bridges and a column between Maestricht and Tongres. The arrival of German fighters put an end to the operation, in the course of which a single bomber was lost. All the rest, however, returned to their base more or less damaged. In addition, 4 Morane 406's were reported missing.

On September 12 General Tétu ordered the bombers to resume their actions of the day before. Sorely tried, Grouping 6 made it known that it was reorganizing and could not go into action before the end of the day. Thus in less than twenty-four hours the bomber force revealed its weaknesses and its inability to throw itself into massive, continuous attacks. At 1300 hours the Breguet 693's of Grouping 18 were thrown against the German tanks that were obstructing the roads from Tongres to Looz and from Tongres to Waremme. They suffered heavy losses (8 planes shot down out of 18). Grouping 6, for its part, did not appear over Tongres until 1830 hours and, in the face of sustained Flak fire, was able to do practically nothing. At the end of this third day of fighting, in the course of which French fighters had been credited with 35 combat victories, the mission of air support to the French armies that had entered Belgium came to an end. Between May 10 and 12 General Vuillemin had drawn from his reserves 5 fighter groups (GC I/3, I/8, II/8, I/1, and III/3) and 3 bomber groups (GB I/62, I/63, and I/31), which he had assigned, together with two maritime support groups, to General Tétu.

But the wear and tear on these units had been great, and in order to preserve in the fighter forces a certain part of their potential the commander in chief of the air forces was obliged to dismantle the defense of the Basse-Seine area by removing from it during the day of May 13 the GC II/10 and III/10, which he put at the disposal of the Z.O.A.N. In addition, GC I/6 was recalled from the southeast, while the fighter flights of the Paris region, two daytime bomber groups (I/62 and I/63), and Night Bomber Groupings 9 and 10 (I/34, II/34, and I/38) were subject to being used by General Tétu. It is true that the tank concentrations reported by the reconnaissance planes brought heavy threats to bear on a sector of the front between Dinant and Sedan. The taking of a bridgehead at Houx led General d'Astier de la Vigerie, commanding officer of the Z.O.A.N., to mount two bombing expeditions, the first with the LeO 45's of Grouping 6, the second, after nightfall, with several Amiot 143's, on the approaches to Marche, Ciney, and Dinant. The fact remains that by the evening of May 13 the Germans had seri-

Together with the Dewoitine 520, the Bloch 174 was one of the best French planes of 1940, but it was engaged too late and in too small quantities.

Reserved for the air defense of the lower Seine and the Paris region and for night fighting, the Potez 631's were in part engaged in the battle of 1940.

At the time of the declaration of war the Amiot 143 was completely outdated. It was, nevertheless, engaged in the daytime against the German bridgehead at Sedan on May 14. Groupings 9 and 10 suffered heavy losses there.

Although it required delicate handling, the Lioré-Olivier 451 was the best French medium bomber of 1940. It was poorly employed, however, and consequently suffered heavy losses.

ously weakened the line of resistance of General Corap's Ninth Army by establishing a whole series of bridgeheads on the other side of the Meuse. It was vital to recover them, and it was with that understanding that General Georges asked the air forces to act at dawn on May 14 against the enemy positions with all the means at their disposal. It was the planes of the Advanced Air Striking Force that showed up first over the bridges across the Meuse. German Flak, soon supported by fighter planes, subjected them to a veritable slaughter (32 planes destroyed out of 67). In the afternoon it was the turn of the French bombers to go into the attack, although their resources were very weak. Thirteen Amiot 143's, barely capable of carrying out night bombings, and 6 LeO 45's were sent into a real massacre over the suburbs of Bazeilles and the ravine of Givonne. Five of them remained there, and two others, badly damaged, were able to land within French lines. During the following night the Amiot 143's of Groupings 9 and 10 returned to Bazeilles, Sedan, and Givonne.

At the start of the next day, May 15, the Ninth Army's situation was critical, to say the least, and the French troops were beginning to flow back toward the west. At 0800 hours General Tétu received orders to give the First Army all possible support in the vicinity of Mézières. Two hours later the Z.O.A.N. was appealed to by the Ninth and then by the Second Army. The weak bomber resources at General Tétu's disposal were then dispersed and employed in small groups (during the afternoon 9 Breguet 693's and 6 LeO 45's supported the counterattack of the Second Army). These actions were unable to remedy the insufficiency of the defense on the ground, which led to a penetration of the front by the end of the day.

The next day, May 16, General Tétu found himself facing the possibility of a withdrawal of the bomber bases threatened by the German advance. Meanwhile, at 0830 hours, the LeO 45's of Grouping 6 had been engaged over the Montcornet area, where they returned toward 1300 hours. Half an hour later they were replaced by assault aviation, whose Breguet 693's surprised a tank column in the open. Of the 26 planes that had participated in these operations, 4 had been downed. The number of planes damaged prevented any other sorties.

On May 17, when the intelligence received clearly showed that the Germans were ignoring Paris and rushing toward the west, General Tétu, in agreement with General Vuillemin, reached the decision not to engage fighter planes any longer except to support the troops on the front line and to destroy enemy bombers. That was, in fact, the only solution capable of limiting the increasingly heavy losses the French fighter forces had been suffering in furnishing escorts to bombers engaged in attacking troops on the ground. General Vuillemin suggested not employing them except against short-range objectives. These arrangements made it possible to achieve a concentration of fighter forces that had not been possible since May 10. All bombing expeditions were suspended for May 17 to permit regrouping and replenishing the units. On May 16 and 17 General Tétu was granted appreciable reinforcements to feed the fighting (a Navy dive-bombing flight equipped with Chance Vought 156's, GB's I/11, I/21, II/21, I/23, and I/31, and GC II/9). The sending, on the same day, of armed fighters from the schools and of many instructors clearly shows the disturbing degree of attrition that had taken place in the fighter forces.

On May 18, in his General Order No. 1, General Tétu made official the position that he had adopted in consultation with General Vuillemin. That did not prevent 12 LeO 45's from attacking the German columns in the Avesnes-Landrecies area that afternoon and, meeting with very violent anti-aircraft fire, reaching their objective in disorder. Early in the evening, 4 of the 8 Breguet 693's of Grouping 18 that were operating in the same area were shot down.

On May 19, while the fighter forces of the Z.O.A.N. were supporting the 4th Armored Division in its counterattack on the Laon-Crécy-sur-Serre axis, Grouping 6 was surprised on the ground by German bombers at the moment of takeoff on its airfield at Persan-Beaumont. All the LeO 45's with which it was equipped were more or less damaged.

All day long on May 20 the Air Force was employed in covering the right wing of the French First Army, which, threatened with encirclement, was withdrawing toward the southwest with the hope of joining the Seventh Army, installed on the Somme. At 1100 hours the Breguet 693's of Grouping 18 threw themselves against some German tanks reported in the Cambrai-Saint Quentin breakthrough. Of the 14 planes engaged, 3 were shot down.

Between May 10 and June 25, 1940, 47 Breguet 693's, the only French assault bombers, were lost in operations. The plane was poorly adapted to the missions that the command had it carry out.

Bloch 152's in flight. On May 10, 1940, only five fighter groups were equipped with this plane, and three others were in the process of being equipped.

The Farman 222-2 served in GB I/15 and II/15 in 1940. It carried out many bombing missions over German territory and in the enemy's rear without suffering a single loss.

Despite its deficient armament and low speed, the Caudron-Renault 714 used by GC I/145, made up of Polish aviators, registered 12 confirmed victories from June 2 to 13, 1940.

On May 21, concerned about the German infiltrations south of the Somme, notably in the vicinity of Le Tréport, General Georges asked the commander of the ground support air forces of the Northeastern Front to use his fighter and bomber groups to protect the southern flank of Army Group North. But because of the distances, the Z.O.A.N., which had fallen back to the Paris region and the lower Seine, could no longer undertake such actions without running considerable risks. For this reason the French and the British agreed to entrust to the Bomber Command and the Air Component the covering of the French, Belgian, and British armies whose encirclement in Flanders was becoming imminent, while the Z.O.A.N., seconded by the Advanced Air Striking Force, took the responsibility for the sectors of the Somme and the Aisne.

On May 22 the first German bridgeheads were established on the south bank of the Somme, and the attacks of Groupings 1 and 18 hardly changed the situation. The next day, in a desperate attempt, Army Group North rushed south to emerge between Arras and Cambrai. Hampered by bad weather, the reconnaissance force could not make out the positions of the troops on the ground, so that bombing actions had very little effect. On the other hand, the fighters downed 10 German planes during the day, losing only two of their own.

On May 23 Army Group North was quite cut off from the main body of the French armies established along the Somme and the Aisne. Since May 10 the air force losses had been very great. From the first days of the fighting the attempt to replenish all the groups at their airfields had had to be given up. The hardest hit among them, particularly the observation groups, some of which had been destroyed on the ground, had to be merged. Thirteen others were simply withdrawn from the front. The impossibility of resupplying three fighter groups with Morane 406's forced the command to send them to the rear to be reequipped with Dewoitine 520's and Curtiss H-75's. As for the bombing section, a number of its formations were appropriated as quickly as possible by the Training Grouping Southeast and then thrown into the battle. Some of them even took up their old materiel again before going up toward the line of fire. On May 23 Grouping 6, in which personnel losses had reached 30 percent and materiel losses almost 75 percent, had to be sent back to the general reserve for replenishment.

In the area of operational employment, the fighter force, torn between covering the ground forces, defending territorial air space, and escorting bomber formations, was never able to muster sufficient concentrations to act effectively at given points on the field of battle. When it was relieved of bomber protection missions, it won unequivocal successes, and its pilots showed a real superiority over those of the Luftwaffe. The bomber force, for its part, because of its manpower shortage and the scattered engagement of its units, arriving in succession from the southeast of France, suffered heavy losses, and the sacrifices of its crews did not suffice to restore a compromised situation on the ground. Moreover, it was undeniably lacking in planes, or did not possess them in sufficient numbers, to attack the enemy ground units effectively. Still, the night bombing force carried out many destructive actions on German territory and in the enemy's rear, particularly on both road and rail lines of communication. It also took action against troop and tank concentrations north of the Somme.

The Battle of the Somme and the Aisne

From May 25 to June 5, the date of the German offensive on the Somme and on the Aisne, the French air forces continued their attacks on the enemy bridgeheads south of the Somme. They also occupied themselves with reconstituting their units, which were seriously worn down by two weeks of hard fighting. Leaving the job of covering the encircled armies to the RAF and to two French formations based in England (GC II/8 and GR I/14), General Vuillemin took advantage of the considerable lull in the ground fighting to restructure his air force organization. On May 27 he adapted the Z.O.A.N. to Army Group No. 3, and two days later he modified the zones of action and territorial limits of the Z.O.A.N. and Z.O.A.E. On May 31, in his Special Order No. 27, the commander in chief of the air forces, concerned about a probable extension of operations toward the east, that is, from the Aisne to the Swiss frontier, took under his direct orders all the reserved forces except for Assault Group 18, which he had turned over to General Tétu at the beginning of the fighting. He then divided the fighter forces between the two air operations areas of the Northeastern Front with the mission of providing protection of the territory and of the air deployment as well as support of the ground fighting and escort of bomber formations.

The bombers had been reconstituted into three air divisions, one for each of the two air operations areas and the third capable of acting, for the benefit of the Z.O.A.N., against distant objectives. Thus the French bombers were to be capable of supporting friendly ground forces, destroying the German air formations at their bases, and also operating against industrial targets. According to General Vuillemin's instructions, the Air Force comprised, as of June 2, an Air Operations Area North with a strength of 16 fighter groups (including the GC II/8, which had returned from Great Britain, and the recently created Polish GC I/145) and 14 bomber groups, as compared to 7 fighter groups and 12 bomber groups in Air Operations Area East. In addition, in the face of the threat of Italy's early intervention in the conflict, a fighter unit had been assigned to the Air Operations Area Alps, while the bomber groups of the training grouping of North Africa, whose materiel conversion was on the point of being completed, remained on the spot to cope with any eventuality. In fact, the special order of May 31 took away from the general in command of the ground support air forces of the northeast the greater part of the resources he had had until then at his disposal. It is therefore not surprising that when he learned of that document General Georges reacted strongly. Underscoring the difficulties encountered since May 10 in coordinating the action of the ground forces and of the air forces, the general commanding the armies of the Northeastern Front indicated that the reorganization undertaken by General Vuillemin, far from ironing out those difficulties, would do nothing but intensify them because of an excessive centralization of the air resources. For another thing, General Georges showed himself to be opposed to the reinforcement of the Z.O.A.E., which he said would only be necessary in case of German aggression against Switzerland, an eventuality that appeared to him to be very improbable. It would be better, he said, to lend as much air support as possible to the fighting on the ground, by placing all available formations at the disposal of the Z.O.A.N. to break up the German tank offensive and reduce the enemy bridgeheads south of the Somme. But General Vuillemin preferred to stick to the principles defined on May 31, limiting the support of the reserved air forces placed at General Tétu's disposal to the air operations area echelon and prohibiting their use at the level of the air forces integrated with the land armies.

But even though the Air Force high command, aware of the disastrous consequences of dispersing its resources, was working to regroup them, the Air Force still set objectives that exceeded its potential and were far from corresponding to its real situation. However, during the first ten days of June the situation of the air forces, rather paradoxically, might have seemed more favorable than on May 10. Over 1,000 planes (599 fighters, 309 bombers, and 116 reconnaissance planes) had been delivered to the units. This raised the strength to 2,348 (1,084 fighters, 519 bombers, and 745 reconnaissance planes), or 172 more than on the day of the German offensive in the west. In fact, while at first glance the Air Force seemed to have been reinforced, in reality it had not been. Quite the contrary. On June 1, in spite of the replenishments, of the 2,086 planes present on the first and second lines only 599 were fit for combat, and the rest, that is, 1,487, were incapable of getting off the ground (or an unavailability rate of 71%, counting the unusable airplanes stocked in the army depots).

Thus at the moment when the decisive battle was engaged the air forces were on the verge of asphyxia for lack of replacements. Over 60% of the fighters and bombers and 86% of the reconnaissance planes were grounded because of mechanical or technical problems or for lack of equipment or armament. Even before losing the air battle, the Air Force had lost the battle for replacements.

Since May 28 the general situation had not ceased to deteriorate. That day the Belgians had laid down their arms. Their defection led to the collapse of a large section of the front of the armies encircled in Flanders, obliging the Allied command to speed up the withdrawal toward the coasts of the Channel and the North Sea while at the same time increasing the tempo of the reembarkation at Dunkirk. On the other hand, air reconnaissances clearly showed that the Germans were massing considerable forces along the Somme and the Aisne and were preparing to attack toward the south. The Air Force did what it could to oppose the enemy concentrations. On May 31, 57 bombers belonging to Groupings 1, 2, 6, and 8 attacked several German tank columns around Amiens and Abbeville and in the Saint Quentin area. They suffered heavy losses (13 planes did not return).

Two days after the start of the battle, and the day after a raid on Lyons, the Luftwaffe decided to strike a big blow at the bases of the Paris region (Nangis, Etampes, Meaux, Le Bourget, Orly, Villacoublay, Saint Cyr, Issy-les-Moulineaux, Les Mureaux), certain aeronautics factories, and the morale of the population. As early as May 23 the French intelligence services had been informed of German preparations for the operation. Therefore, the commanding officer of the Z.O.A.N., who received confirmation of it on June 1, took all the measures necessary to oppose it. He entrusted the defense of the threatened area to General Pinsard's fighter Grouping 21 (GC I/1, II/1, I/3, III/7, and the night fighters of the Paris region), to which he added, on June 2, fighter Grouping 23. At 1300 hours on June 3 three expeditions of enemy bombers, or nearly 200 planes, escorted by more than

Together with the Amiot 351, the Amiot 354 served in the 21st and 34th Bomber Groupings. Only about 10 of these planes were engaged in the fighting.

150 Bf 109's and 110's, showed up on the Rheims-Nangis-Saint Quentin-Crépy-en-Valois and Dieppe-Beauvais axes. But the first alert, transmitted from the Eiffel Tower at 1315 hours, reached only a small number of units. The others were informed only by the falling of German bombs on their airfields. A great deal of disruption and disorganization ensued, and the French patrols generally took off on the initiative of their crews. The high-altitude patrols could not gain the prescribed altitude and were quickly covered by enemy fighters. Only the low-altitude patrols succeeded in attacking the enemy bombers, and, in fact, there were only individual combats, in which, among others, the Poles of Fighter Group I/145 took part. The losses inflicted on the Luftwaffe (4 Bf 109's, 2 Bf 110's, 1 Ju 88, 4 Do 17's, 1 He 111, and an unidentified plane) were very meager compensation for those suffered by the French groups, the heaviest since the beginning of the campaign: 10 fighter pilots in single-seaters and the crew of a multi-seated fighter killed and 8 wounded. The results of the bombing, however, were not in proportion to the forces engaged by the Germans. About 15 factories reported slight damage, 6 landing places were seriously damaged, and 6 planes were destroyed on the ground.

Two days later the German offensive on the Somme and the Aisne started.

On June 5 the two air operations areas corresponding to the Northeastern Front included the following units:

Z.O.A.N. (Air Operations Area North)

Pursuit: Grouping 21 (GC I/1, II/1, I/4, I/6, II/10, III/10, and I/145); Grouping 23 (GC III/1, I/3, II/3, III/3, II/4, III/7, I/8, and II/9).

Bombing: Made up of the First Air Division with Groupings 1 (GB I/62, II/62, I/63, and II/63), 2 (I/19, II/19, and II/61), 18 (I/54, II/54, I/51, II/51, and II/35), and 7 (I/11 and II/23).

Z.O.A.E. (Air Operations Area East)

Pursuit: Grouping 22 (GC I/2, II/2, III/2, I/5, II/6, and II/7).

Bombing: Sixth Air Division with Groupings 6 (GB I/12, II/12, I/31), 9 (I/34, II/34, I/21, II/21), 10 (I/38 and II/38), and 15 (I/15 and II/15).

As soon as he was notified of the enemy attack General Vuillemin turned over to General Tétu the reserved air forces of which he had taken control on May 31. At the same time, and in response to the creation in Champagne of an Army Group Center, he ordered the establishment as of June 8 of an Air Operations Area Center (Z.O.A.C.), to which he assigned Group I/52 and the Third Air Division, composed of three groupings, as well as the ground support air forces FA 102 and 104, belonging to the Second and Fourth Armies respectively. In view of the gravity of the situation, the fighter resources that should have been assigned to the Z.O.A.C. remained at the disposal of the Z.O.A.N., which was also reinforced by 4 fighter groups and the bomber Grouping No. 6 from the Z.O.A.E. Supported by two dozen Blenheims from the RAF, all the air units of the Z.O.A.N. were engaged to the limít in the ground battle, which quickly turned to the disadvantage of the French armies. During the single day of June 5, the assault grouping attacked the German tanks four times, while Groupings 1, 6, and 7 threw themselves into the attack on road intersections and the bridges over the Somme to contain the German divisions. It was of no avail, for by the end of the following day, June 6 (the day before, the Air Force had lost 11 bombers and 15 fighters), the front was on the point of being broken. On June 7 the Germans began to exploit their successes of the preceding two days in the direction of Rouen on the one hand and in the direction of Compiègne on the other. As is emphasized in a report on the campaign of France: "For aviation it was the moment to sacrifice everything; it was called upon to substitute for the missing reserves, for the faltering arms." And, indeed, fighter planes were seen using their guns to attack tanks, whose returning fire allowed not a single plane to return undamaged. The light bomber forces with their Breguet 693's and 695's made up to three sorties a day against enemy columns and against the bridges.

The first Glenn Martin 167 F's were bought in the United States in February 1939. The French Air Force received 166 of them.

The attrition of the units of the Z.O.A.N. was so great that on June 8 General Tétu gave orders to the Z.O.A.E. to place at the Z.O.A.N.'s disposal 50 percent of its resources in fighter planes. That day about forty Morane 406's, Bloch 152's, and Dewoitine 520's machine-gunned the German armored and motorized divisions on the roads of the Gournay-en-Bray–Forges-les-Eaux area.

On June 9, because of the expansion of operations on Army Group No. 4's front, General Vuillemin, conscious of the gravity of the circumstances, went to the headquarters of the ground support air forces and from there sent to the Z.O.A.C. all the bomber forces and 9 fighter groups of the Z.O.A.N., for one day only, as well as all the bomber groupings and two fighter groups of the Z.O.A.E. This meant that for the single day of June 9 the Z.O.A.C. had assigned to it practically all of the bomber forces and 50 percent of the fighter forces of the Northeastern Front.

It soon had to return a certain part to the Z.O.A.N., where, during the afternoon, the situation had suddenly deteriorated, and in whose sector the Germans had come within sight of Rouen. On the evening of June 9 the G.Q.G.A. left Saint-Jean-les-Deux Jumeaux, where it had been since September 1939, and installed itself at Bonny-sur-Loire, near Briare.

The Agony

From then on everything went very fast. Starting June 11—Italy had entered the war the day before—the Air Force showed more and more obvious signs of disorganization. Occupied with its retreat toward the south, the fighter aviation of the Z.O.A.N. could make only a very few sorties that day, while the assault aviation did not take action on the battlefield until very late in the evening. Moreover, the inadequacy of lookouts did not take care of getting fighter units into action, and the lack of electromagnetic means of detection made any attempt at concentration impossible.

On June 15, when the G.Q.G.A. was again obliged to move, this time from Bonny-sur-Loire to Châtel Guyon, the air forces of the Z.O.A.E. had to fall back toward the center of France, where the lack of airfields was assuming more and more catastrophic proportions. The day before (which was also the date of the fall of Paris) General Vuillemin had authorized the regrouping of the fighter units and the army and army corps air forces to the south of the Loire and in the Dijon area. The bomber force, for its part, was to be transferred to the bases of the Massif Central, the Limousin, and the Charente. To the airplanes of the schools and training centers, which were already saturating the few airfields available, were soon added hundreds of combat planes. Pressed by the advance of the enemy mechanized divisions, the Z.O.A.N. massed its four fighter groups on the airfields of Royan and Cazaux, its reconnaissance aviation and groups (except for the assault grouping, which was directed toward Cognac) at Perpignan, and its observation units at Pau and Saint Gemme. For its part, the Z.O.A.E. had to establish the GR I/22 and II/22, as well as the GAO II/508, I/555, I/518, I/506, and II/506, I/520, 512, and 533, and the GR II/36 at Montélimar. The GR I/33 and I/55 and GAO 513 and I/584 went to Feurs, while Fighter Grouping 22 established itself at Carcassonne with groups I/5, II/5, I/2, II/2, and II/7. As for the bombers, they were sent to Istres (Grouping 6), Oran (Grouping 15), and Avignon (Grouping 10). Finally, the Z.O.A.C. concentrated its units at Limoges (FA 104), Agen and Bergerac (Grouping 9 of bombers and GR I/52), and Ussel-Aulnat (Grouping 43). Thus certain airfields had up to 250 or 300 planes, and it goes without saying that any sizable German air action would have led to irreparable losses.

In order to avert such a catastrophe and to continue the struggle from the territories of the empire, outside of France, General Vuillemin decided to have the groups that were equipped with the most modern planes cross the Mediterranean, to the extent, of course, that the range of those planes would allow. On June 16 the commander in chief of the air forces turned over GC II/1 and II/6 to the Air Operations Area of the Alps and scheduled the transfer to North Africa of four other units (GC I/4 and II/4 of the Z.O.A.N. and GC II/3 and III/3 of the Z.O.A.C.), as well as Bomber Groupings 1 (4 groups of Glenn Martin 167's), 2 (3 groups of Douglas DB-7's), and 15 (2 groups of Farman 222's). The movement became more marked when General Vuillemin, desiring to keep on the front in France only 9 fighter groups (40% of the available resources) and 11 bomber groups (39% of the whole), resolved to send to North Africa all of the reserve echelons of the fighter units equipped with Dewoitine 520's and with Curtiss H-75's at the same time as Bomber Groupings 7, 9, and 11, the GAO's and GR's that were not indispensable to the conduct of operations, and GB I/25.

These departures obviously weakened the Air Force formations that remained in place, which then had to reduce their activity. Since communications were becoming ever more uncertain and made the functioning of the command difficult, the air operations areas were fused on June 19. The Z.O.A.C. and Z.O.A.N. took the name of Air Operations Area West (GC I/1, I/8, II/10, I/6, II/9, II/8, III/7, and III/10; Bomber Groupings 18/19, and the FA of the Fourth, Sixth, Seventh, and Tenth Armies of the Army of Paris), and the Z.O.A.E. and Z.O.A.A. took the name of Air Operations Area Alps (GC I/2, II/2, II/1, III/9, III/1, and II/6; Bomber Groupings 6 and 10, and the FA of the Second, Third, Fifth, and Eighth Armies and the Army of the Alps).

As for operations, because of the confusion of friendly and enemy units and the presence of columns of refugees on the roads the Air Force high command, as early as June 16, had to prohibit daytime bombing sorties over the immediate rear of the battlefield. Bombing actions were then limited to night raids against objectives clearly specified by the ground command. From that time, weakened by the sending of units to North Africa and hampered by the shortage of airfields and the impossibility of employing its bomber groups, the Air Force was barely able to provide a few fighter cover missions for the benefit of the ground forces. The armistice agreement signed with Germany on June 22 suspended the departures for North Africa. Three days later the fighting stopped.

Air Operations against Italy

On June 10, 1940, when Italy joined Germany, the Air Operations Area of the Alps had only one fighter grouping, No. 24, created on May 26, which was entrusted with a purely defensive mission. It was made up of three subgroupings distributed as follows: the Subgroup of the North, stationed in the Lyons area and consisting of Fighter Group III/3, Night Fighter Flight 5/13, and the mixed Polish flight; the Subgroup of the South, commanded by Captain Stehlin, with the GC III/6 (Dewoitine 520's) and the Polish flight of Montpellier; and Subgroup 44, at Toulon, with a navy flight and a flotilla of seaplanes.

Although in case of conflict with Italy the Air Force high command had envisaged assigning there two frontier groups equipped with LeO 45's, the Z.O.A.A. remained totally lacking in bomber forces. For a time the RAF dispatched two squadrons of heavy bombers there based at Istres and Salon, which, however, did not engage in any action. On the other hand, Grouping 24 was reinforced on June 5 by Fighter Group III/1, which had arrived to be converted to Dewoitine 520's, and by night fighter flights 1, 2, 3, and 4/13.

June 10 and 11 were calm, and the Italian air force did not appear. After a few planes of the Italian Regia Aeronautica flew over the Antibes and Saint Tropez sector, several bombers attempted to destroy the torpedo factory in the latter locality. The first encounter between the planes of the two camps took place the same day over Antibes. There the French Dewoitine 520's demonstrated their superiority, as they were to do throughout the rest of the brief campaign, and shot down three Italian Fiat BR-20's. That lesson did not dissuade the Italian twin-engined planes from showing up a few hours later over the airfields of Fayence and Cannes-Mandelieu and then dropping a few bombs, which had no great effect, on the port of Toulon.

During the following night the Air Force decided to reply to the Regia Aeronautica's incursions by sending a few bombers of the Eleventh Air Division over the Novo Ligure airfield and the

A Heinkel He 111 shot down during the "phony" war. From September 1939 to May 10, 1940, the Air Force destroyed 80 Luftwaffe planes, to which may be added 34 probable victories.

Vado Ligure fuel tanks. For the fighter forces the activity of June 14 was limited to providing cover for the navy cruisers charged with cannonading the ports of Genoa and Vado. The next day the Italians mounted a massive attack with about fifty fighters and bombers against the airfields of Saint Raphaël, Cuers, Hyères, and Le Luc. Intercepted by the Dewoitines of GC III/6, they suffered heavy losses. On this occasion Warrant Officer Le Gloan shot down five enemy planes (Fiat BR-20's and Fiat CR-42's) in less than half an hour, an extraordinary feat that won him his second lieutenant's bars, the Croix de Guerre with the palm, and the congratulations of René Fonck, the unrivaled ace of the First World War.

After further actions of the Eleventh Air Division against the cities of Imperia, Savone, and then Turin, the departure of GC III/6 for North Africa considerably reduced the defense of the seacoast towns. The Italians took advantage of this weakness to intensify the pressure by bombing on June 19 the landing places in Corsica (Calvi, Campo del Oro, Bergo, and Chisonaccia). These attacks were followed by others on Cannes, Saint Raphaël, and Marseilles (June 21). Armistice negotiations with Italy did not slow down the activity in the air. A massive French operation in reprisal, taking off from North Africa and planned for June 24, was canceled upon the signing of the armistice agreement.

On June 25, 1940, at 1900 hours, the G.Q.G.A. was dissolved—a symbolic event. It seemed at the time that until peace was concluded in the future the French Air Force was condemned to disappear.

The Results of the Fighting

At Riom many high-ranking French army officers expressed opinions of the air forces that were all the more unfavorable as they were concerned with masking their own service's deficiencies in the area of tanks and antitank guns, as well as in that of antiaircraft, for whose weakness they were in part to blame. General Gamelin, commander in chief of the Allied armies until his replacement by General Weygand, asserted that the Battle of the Meuse was lost, materially and morally, because of the inferiority of French aviation. Thus the Air Force was put in the position of the accused and at the same time that of the scapegoat for the defeat. Its detractors held, once and for all and as an accepted fact, that in 1940 the sky was empty.

But, as General Vuillemin wrote, the air force was employed "not under the conditions expected for its normal employment, but rather on sacrifice missions." In the first part of the fighting the French fighter force, in spite of the weakness of its numbers and the inappropriateness of its materiel (the Morane-Saulnier 406 was beginning to be outdated, and the new planes, such as the Bloch 152 and especially the Dewoitine 520, were making a very hesitant entry into service) and without any hope of ever attaining effective concentrations, was dispersed in providing cover for the ground forces, defending the territory, and escorting bomber formations. What was worse, starting with the offensive of the Somme it even had to try to retard the progress of the German columns by doing the work of antitank weapons and assault aviation. It was the latter that the general staff had chosen, abandoning dive-bombing. It would still have been necessary for the Air Force to possess large enough numbers of Breguet 693's and 695's. And the sacrifice missions mentioned by General Vuillemin? Striking examples can be found during the fighting on the Meuse, when the command engaged the Amiot 143's of Groupings 9 and 10 in an area bombardment in full daylight when it could very well have mounted the same operation at night. As for reconnaissance aviation, its outdated materiel did not enable it to hold its own with the German fighters and accomplish its task. The Bloch 174, an excellent plane, arrived in the units too late and in too few numbers. Finally, the dispersion of many fighter and reconnaissance groups in the ground support air forces served to weaken the Air Force and contributed to its inability to attain a concentration of its resources. But even if it had to compensate for the deficiencies in antiaircraft and antitank weapons, the Air Force nonetheless saw its traditional doctrine of employment break down at the same time as the ground defense system based on infantry-artillery cooperation did, under the blows of the German air force and mechanized forces.

The French Air Force also suffered from a quantitative inferiority. The accounts of the campaign of 1940 often dwell on the presence in the depots of new airplanes apparently not used in the fighting. This is a complex question involving the system of materiel supply and the delivery procedure instituted between the aeronautics industry and the Air Force. When it came off the assembly line, the plane destined for military aviation was received by the C.R.A.S. (Receiving Center for Production Planes) to be tested for flight fitness. At that stage the plane in question had no radio equipment or armament; the Air Force installed these in its arsenals. Then the plane was declared "fit for service" and ready to go to the fighting units. But in 1940 this procedure was less and less respected, for, because of the increase in production due to the increased orders from the Air Ministry, the storage capacities of the airplane factories were very overburdened. Thus, in order not to impair the functioning of their factories, the manufacturers delivered to the C.R.A.S. planes that were not finished and for the most part not capable of flying. As the C.R.A.S. tacitly accepted this, the Air Force found itself with a number of planes that, while taken into account, were not "fit for service." Teams sent by the aircraft manufacturers to Air Force depots and even to the units—for certain groups did receive planes that were not finished—had to finish the assembly. Thus, of the 852 airplanes accepted by the air forces from May 10 to June 5, 1940, 581 were actually sent to the flying units, but 271, or over 30%, remained unequipped at the depots. It must, therefore, be conceded that at the end of the first phase of the campaign the Air Force, weakened by very hard fighting—it had lost 787 planes (473 fighters, 120 bombers, and 194 reconnaissance or observation

A few of the 700 fighter pilots who stood the shock of the Luftwaffe. At the end of the campaign the French pilots were overworked and showed distressing signs of physical and nervous fatigue.

The Douglas DB-7 was bought in the United States and assembled in Morocco. A few participated in the fighting with the GB I/19, II/19, I/32, II/32, and I/61.

planes)—could not proceed to replacements with new planes, not because these did not exist (on the contrary, their numbers amply covered the needs), but because over 30% of the planes delivered to the combat forces were unfinished and could not get off the ground. The Luftwaffe, on the other hand, had no trouble in making replacements.

To remedy this grave situation the G.Q.G.A. and the Air Force general staff decided to create special officers, "expediters," accredited with the technical and industrial directorate and the directorate of military air materiel and intended to reduce the delays between a plane's coming out of the factory and its delivery to a unit as "fit for service." There were five of these special officers, each specializing in one manufacturer, whose role consisted in getting planes that lacked only unimportant accessories sent from the assembly lines to the flights. Many other measures were taken to accelerate the coming into service of modern materiel, such as setting up twelve annexes to the central armament workshop at Châteaudun, which made it possible to arm a great many more planes, adding to the test center personnel, increasing the number of ferry pilots, and, sometimes, sending personnel from the units that needed to be refitted back to the airfields of the factories in the rear (Dewoitine in Toulouse, Bloch in Châteauroux). Although some of these measures were effective, they were not sufficient.

However that may be, the losses that the French Air Force inflicted on the Luftwaffe were heavy. From May 10 to June 24 the French fighter forces succeeded in destroying in aerial combat 733 German planes, while the ground antiaircraft forces credited themselves with 120, or a total of 853 airplanes. While the Luftwaffe's losses on the ground from bombing are not known to us, the estimates of accidents, generally resulting from combat, approached 450. This means that the Luftwaffe lost about 1,300 airplanes of all categories due to the action of the French Air Force, or 36.9% of its first-line planes as of May 10.

On its side, the Air Force lost only 410 planes in aerial combat, which demonstrates the superiority of its fighter pilots over the Luftwaffe's. But it counted 202 airplanes destroyed on the ground by bombing and 230 others by accident, or a total of 852, that is, 62.28% of the first-line planes as of May 10, 1940.

Of the 2.7 million soldiers that France had in the armed services in 1940, 77,500 (officers, noncommissioned officers, and enlisted men) belonged to the Air Force. Of this total, only 3,600 were flying personnel, and it was these 3,600 men that bore the entire brunt of the battle in the air. Pursuit represented 14% of this strength (796 men, including 700 pilots), observation and reconnaissance 30%, and bombing 24%. The latter figure indicates the weakness of the air forces in the area of bombing, considering that the crew of a bomber is larger than that of a fighter or an observation or reconnaissance plane.

Losses of personnel were very large, if not enormous, in comparison with the relative brevity of the campaign. In fact, 40% of the flying officers in the armed forces were killed or wounded, against 20% of the noncommissioned officers and enlisted men. Overall, more than 500 pilots were put out of action.

Thus, weakened by its quantitative and technical inferiority, the Air Force, conceived in a defensive perspective, remained subordinate to the land army. Its role was to carry out, under the protection of a strong fighter force, strategic reconnaissance missions for the benefit of the high command and observation on the ground for the benefit of the big land units. In addition, the fighter force, assigned to numerous tasks, was never able to operate in effective concentrations that would have enabled it to compete with the Luftwaffe for mastery of the skies.

However, the one thousand planes that the German air forces had lost when facing the French Air Force were quite certainly felt by Germany as a handicap when it launched its air attacks against Great Britain.

The Order of Battle of the French Air Force (May 10, 1940)

Commander in chief of the air forces: General Vuillemin. Commander of the ground support air forces of the Northeast: General Tétu.

Air Operations Area North (Z.O.A.N.): General d'Astier de la Vigerie.

- Fighter Grouping 21: General Pinsard (GC I/1, II/1, II/10, III/10, and III/3)[1]
- Fighter Grouping 23: General Romatet (GC II/2, III/2, I/4, I/5, and I/6)
- Fighter Grouping 25: Colonel de Moussac (GC III/1 and II/8)
- Night fighter command of the Paris region: Lieutenant Colonel Dordilly (Mixed Night Fighter Groupings No. 1, 2, 3, and 5, consisting of Flights 1/13, 2/13, 3/13, and 4/13, all equipped with Potez 631's)
- First Air Division: General Escudier with Bomber Grouping No. 6 (GB I/12 and II/12), No. 9 (GB I/34 and II/34), and Assault Bomber Grouping No. 18 (GBA I/54, II/54, and II/35), and GR II/33
- Air Forces 107 (Seventh Army): Colonel Chambe (GC III/1, GR I/35, GAO 501, 516, and 552, and balloon battalions)
- Air Forces 101 (First Army): General Canonne (GC III/2, GR I/14, GAO 503, 504, 505, 545, and 4/551, and balloon battalions)
- Air Forces 109 (Ninth Army): General Augereau (GC II/2, GR II/52, GAO 502, 511, 544, 547, and 2/551, and balloon battalions)
- Air Forces 102 (Second Army): General Roques (GC I/5, GR II/22, GAO 507, 510, 518, and 520, and balloon battalions)

Air Operations Area East (Z.O.A.E.): General Bouscat.

- Fighter Grouping 22: Colonel Dumêmes (GC I/2, II/4, II/5, II/6, III/7, and I/8)
- Third Air Division: Lieutenant Colonel Valin with Bomber Grouping No. 10 (GB I/38 and II/38), Heavy Bomber Grouping No. 15 (GB I/15 and II/15), and GR I/52
- Air Forces 103 (Third Army): General de Boysson (GC II/5, GR I/22, GAO 1/506, 2/506, 2/508, 1/551, and 3/551, and balloon battalions)
- Air Forces 104 (Fourth Army): Colonel Tavéra (GC I/2, GR I/36, GAO 509, 1/520, and balloon battalions)
- Air Forces 105 (Fifth Army): General Cochet

Order of Battle of the Armée de l'Air 9 May 1940

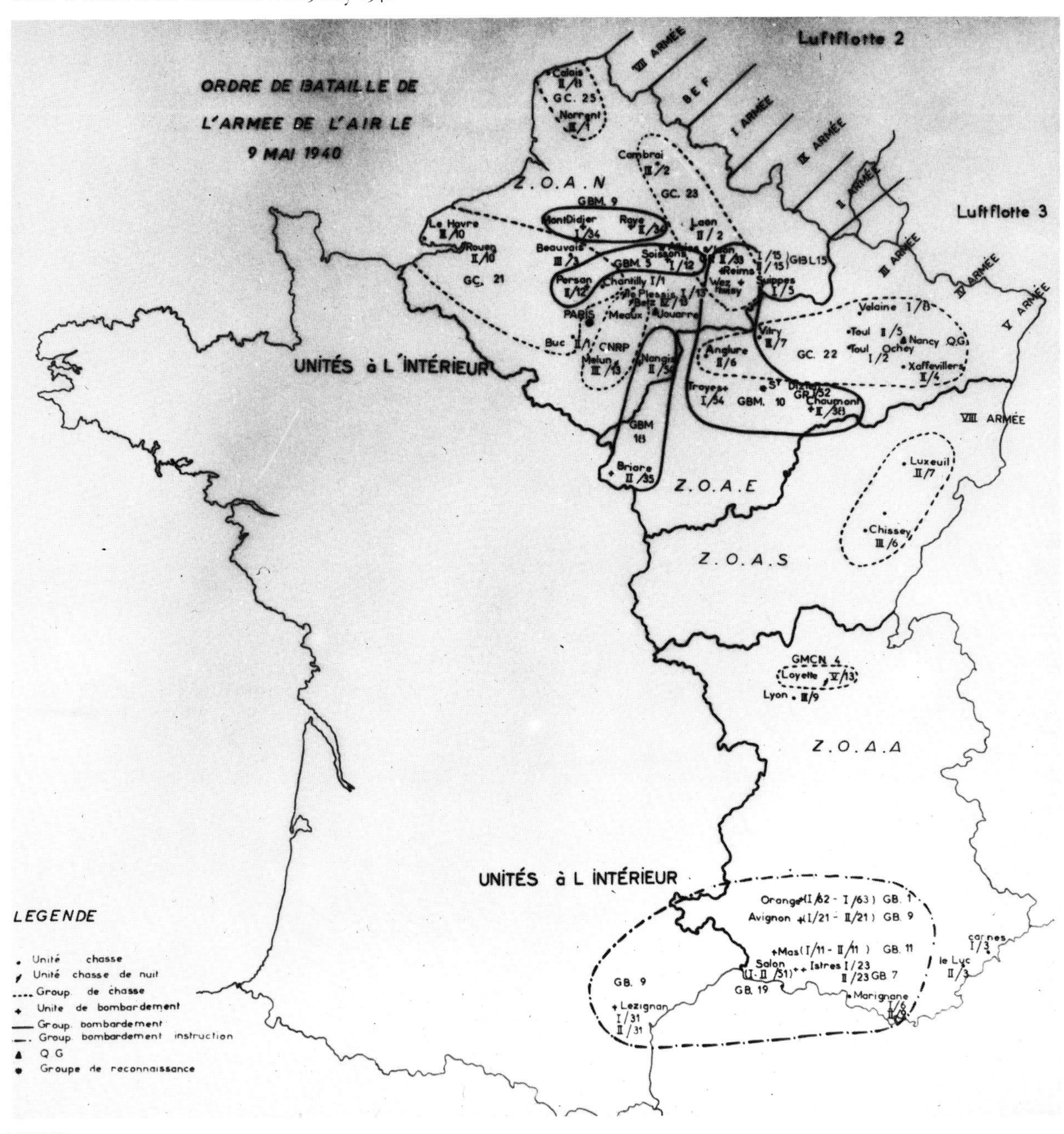

LEGEND

- Fighter unit
- Night fighter unit
- ---Fighter group
- —Bomber unit
- Bomber group
- —-Bomber training group
- Headquarters
- Reconnaissance group

Z.O.A.N. = Air Operations Area North
Z.O.A.S. = Air Operations Area South
Z.O.A.E. = Air Operations Area East
Z.O.A.A. = Air Operations Area of the Alps

(GC II/4, GR II/36, GAO 548, 1/508, 512, 517, and 553, and balloon battalions)

Air Operations Area South (Z.O.A.S.): General Odic.

- Fighter Grouping 24: Lieutenant Colonel Lamon (GC III/6 and II/7)
- Sixth Air Division: General Hebrard with the GR I/33
- Air Forces No. 38 (45th Army Corps): Major Toucanne (one balloon battalion)
- Air Forces No. 108 (Eighth Army): General de Saint-Ceran (GC II/7, GR I/55, GAO 543, 513, and 1/584, and balloon battalions)

Air Operations Area of the Alps (Z.O.A.A.): General Laurens.

- Fighter Groups I/3, II/3, I/6, II/9, and III/9
- Mixed Night Fighter Grouping No. 4: Lieutenant Colonel Giraud (Night Fighter Flight No. 5/13)
- Eleventh Air Division: General Gama's Bomber Aviation Training Grouping of the Southeast, with Light Bomber Grouping No. 1 (GB I/62 and I/63), Medium Bomber Grouping No. 7 (GB I/23 and II/23), Medium Bomber Grouping No. 11 (GB I/11 and II/11), and Assault Bomber Grouping No. 19 (GB I/51 and II/51), plus two groups detached from Bomber Grouping No. 6 (GB I/31 and II/31) and two from Bomber Grouping No. 9 (GB I/21 and II/21)
- Air Forces of the Army of the Alps: General Laurens (GR II/55, GAO 2/514, 582, 1/584, 548, 581, 1/589, and balloon battalions)

Airplanes Received by the French Air Force from September 3, 1939, to June 20, 1940

Date	Loire-Nieuport 41	Morane 406	Bloch 151, 152	Caudron 714	Dewoitine 520	Arsenal VG 33	Curtiss H-75	Potez 63-11	Bloch 174, 175	Glenn Martin 167	Douglas DB-7	LeO 45	Breguet 691 & derivatives	Amiot 351	Farman 223
1939															
Sept.	1	125	76	–	–	–	26	40	–	–	–	5	11	–	–
Oct.	–	110	87	–	–	–	1	78	–	–	–	11	9	–	–
Nov.	–	84	75	–	–	–	–	67	–	–	–	16	10	–	–
Dec.	–	69	46	–	–	–	1	63	1	–	–	13	10	5	–
1940															
Jan.	–	40	13	5	8	–	6	72	5	–	–	24	10	–	–
Feb.	–	37	–	4	23	–	–	55	22	8	–	25	4	12	–
March	–	25	72	22	1	–	–	131	3	32	8	46	23	4	–
April	–	7	2	13	33	–	–	92	11	69	17	42	19	16	–
May	–	10	69	9	142	–	60	72	7	60	20	116	65	19	8
June	–	–	53	3	95	5	25	42	12	20	19	52	24	5	–
Total	1	507	493	56	302	5	119	712	61	189	64	350	185	61	8

Total: 3,113 planes. Sept.: 284; Oct.: 296; Nov.: 252; Dec.: 208; Jan.: 183; Feb.: 190; Mar.: 367; Apr.: 321; May: 657; Jun.: 355.

CHAPTER III

The French Air Force under the Armistice

When the armistice between France and Germany was signed on June 22, 1940, in the village of Rethondes, General Bergeret, the Air Force representative to the French plenipotentiary, General Hunziger, had protested a few hours before against the humiliation that the German authorities wanted to inflict on the French pilots by forcing them to surrender their warplanes. He would have preferred to see them destroyed. It is true that the provisions of the armistice were particularly harsh with respect to the air forces. Article 4 specified that the French armed forces on land, on sea, and in the air were to be demobilized and disarmed within a period still to be determined. Article 5 emphasized that as a guarantee of the observance of the armistice all the airplanes and all war materiel that were on unoccupied territory at the time that the armistice came into force were subject to being turned over to the Axis forces. However, the Italians and the Germans intended to renounce this prerogative on the condition that all the planes in the French Air Force's possession be disarmed and placed in security under their control. Finally, the German army had prohibited any takeoffs from French territory and specified that in case of nonobservance of this requirement the Luftwaffe was authorized to intervene. In addition, the airfields and ground installations of military aviation on unoccupied territory were to be placed under the control of German-Italian commissions.

For the Air Force the armistice convention left no hope. The dissolution of the G.Q.G.A., of the major commands, and then of the units, scheduled for July 15, 1940, was to make way for a new organization sponsored by the German and Italian armistice commissions. Deprived of operational formations, the French air forces would consist of only a few permanent elements charged with insuring the smooth progress of demobilization. Later, at the time when peace was concluded with Germany, French military aviation would be reconstituted, but under such conditions as not to threaten the security of the Reich. The Germans consented to authorize the establishment of 42 groups and 10 flights, or 8 fighter groups, 8 bomber groups, and 8 reconnaissance groups in France proper, 5 bomber groups, 5 fighter groups, and 5 reconnaissance groups in North Africa, and 1 fighter group, 1 bomber group, and 1 reconnaissance group in the eastern Mediterranean.

But the Franco-British confrontation at Mers-el-Kebir in Algeria was to lead to a complete revision of the German-Italian plans.

Mers-el-Kebir

At the moment when the armistice came into force the greater part of French aviation, except for planes whose range did not allow them to cross the Mediterranean, was in North Africa. On June 27, 1940, 851 planes of all categories were crowding the airfields of Morocco, Algeria, and Tunisia:

Pursuit: 4 groups of Curtiss H-75's (102 airplanes), 5 groups of Dewoitine 520's (108 airplanes), 1 group of Dewoitine 510's (19 airplanes), and 3 groups of Morane-Saulnier 406's (49 airplanes), or a total of 13 groups and 278 fighters.

Bombing: 4 groups of Glenn Martin 167's (55), 5 groups of Douglas DB-7's (47), 5 groups of LeO 45's (41), 4 groups of Amiot 351's (41), 2 groups of Farman 222–223's (16), and 1 group of LeO H-257's (13), or a total of 211 bombers.

Reconnaissance: 2 groups of Potez 63-11's (13), 2 groups of Bloch 174's (17), and 1 group of Glenn Martin 167's (13), or 96 reconnaissance planes.

Observation: 18 groups of Potez 63-11's (54), 1 group of Bloch 175's (1), 1 group of LeO 45's (3), and 2 mixed groups (5 Potez 63-11's, 2 Mureaux 117's, 1 Potez 637).

Miscellaneous: 5 groups equipped with 14 Bloch 174's, 20 Potez 63-11's, 1 Glenn Martin, 1 Farman 222, and 5 Breguet 693's.

Though the number of groups appears large, these forces were actually all incomplete, lacking all or part of their components and short by a large number of mechanics and specialists. In addition, their deployment did not correspond to any tactical notion. Finally, it was impossible to make them operational quickly since, to avert the departure to British possessions of crews tempted by dissidence, the senior commanding general in North Africa had ordered all planes—even hospital planes—made incapable of flight (tanks drained, carburetors and magnetos removed). It was under these conditions that, immobilized and disarmed, the French Air Force would have to face up to the British aggression against the French fleet placed under the orders of Admiral Gensoul and moored in the roads of Mers-el-Kebir.

At 1030 hours on July 3 Admiral Gensoul notified Admiral Richard, the naval officer in command in Algiers, that an ultimatum had just been handed to him by Admiral Sommerville, chief of Force H, based at Gibraltar. At the same time he telephoned to Colonel Rougevin-Baville, commander of the base of Sénia, in Algeria, to ascertain the air resources that he might have at his disposal in case of an opening of hostilities. A little before 1100 hours General Pennès, senior air officer in North Africa, asked the air region of Algeria (General Bouscat) to alert all fighter or bomber groups in condition to fight. Early in the afternoon General Bouscat arrived in Oran to assume direction of the air operations, while several patrols belonging to GC II/3, III/3, I/5, and II/5 were already in the air. At 1745 hours Admiral Gensoul called for the immediate engagement of the fighters, and less than ten minutes after the first gun was fired by the English squadron, the French Curtiss H-75's appeared over Mers-el-Kebir. The first encounter with planes of the Royal Navy—Gladiators and Skuas—took place at 1820 hours and cost the British a plane. A few minutes later the Curtiss H-75's of GC II/5 shot down a Skua. During this first day of fighting, the bomber forces, slower to get into operation, had not taken action. However, General Pennès ordered them to be ready to be engaged the next day against any English vessels that might be sent to Casablanca, Tunis, or Bizerte, and at the same time recommended the rehabilitation of all the air units in North Africa. When informed of this initiative the next morning, the minister of air gave the senior air officer complete freedom to engage the air forces in cooperation with the navy. On July 4 five reconnaissance missions reported the return of Sommerville's fleet to Gibraltar, against which the naval air force launched two expeditions in reprisal, the first during the night and the second during the morning of July 5. On July 6, when the affair seemed entirely over, three British planes of their Fleet Air Arm made a torpedo attack on the stranded battleship *Dunkerque*. Unfavorable weather conditions and lack of air-to-ground communications pre-

The Dewoitine 520, along with the Curtiss H-75 and the Bloch 152, was one of the essential elements of the fighter groups of the Air Force under the armistice.

vented the fighter force from intercepting the assailants. Nevertheless, several aerial combats did occur over the naval base between 0700 and 0720 hours, in the course of which two Skuas were seriously damaged. On July 7 reconnaissances reported that the English fleet was leaving Gibraltar and heading eastward. Some bomber groups were immediately put on the alert at the Sénia and Saint-Denis-du-Sig bases. It was from the latter base that 9 LeO 45's took off on July 10 to bomb the vessels of the Royal Navy that were crossing the meridian of Oran 120 kilometers from the Algerian coast. Because of a navigational error the French bombers did not sight the British squadron and had to resign themselves to dropping their load of bombs in the sea. From July 3 to 10 the fighter forces had flown 180 sorties for the benefit of the navy and had succeeded in shooting down two British planes and damaging four others.

The British operation against Mers-el-Kebir saved the French Air Force from disappearing more or less completely. As early as July 3 the Italian armistice commission in Turin temporarily renounced the application of the provisions of the armistice, and, after having asked for a report on the affair, the German commission in Wiesbaden did the same. On July 4, in response to the maintenance of the Air Force's units, General Pujo, the minister of air, created an Inspectorate General of the Air Force, which he entrusted to General Vuillemin. Five days later the latter was instructed to take command of the air forces capable of being engaged against the British in France, Africa, and the eastern Mediterranean. But it was not until August 5 that the German high command decided exactly the size of the resources that it agreed to leave at the Air Force's disposal in order to resist a possible British aggression. These resources were as follows.

In France, Germany authorized the establishment of a general staff to coordinate the air and antiaircraft defense operations, but on a provisional basis, as well as air division and grouping commands; 6 groups of single-seated fighters (I/8, I/1, II/1, II/9, and III/9), 2 groups of multi-seated fighters (I/13 and II/13), 6 bomber groups (I/21, I/31, I/38, II/38, I/51, and I/54), and 3 reconnaissance groups (I/14, II/14, and II/22) made up the combat units of the Air Force with 289 planes (plus 44 in reserve). The antiaircraft forces had 50 guns, of 25, 75, and 90 millimeters.

North Africa, where 83 of the Air Force's 135

groups were stationed at the beginning of July 1940, was allotted 6 groups of single-seated fighters (I/3, II/3, I/5, II/5, III/6, and II/7), 9 bomber groups (I/11, I/19, I/23, II/23, I/25, I/32, II/32, and II/61), and 6 reconnaissance groups (I/22, II/33, I/36, I/52, II/52, and II/61).

In the eastern Mediterranean there were still a fighter group (I/7) and a bomber group (I/39), to which were added 1 flight (III/39), 1 reconnaissance group (II/39), and 6 flights of observation planes (Potez 25 TOE's).

The air commander in French West Africa controlled 1 fighter group (I/4), 1 fighter flight, 3 bomber groups (I/62, II/62, and I/63), and 3 reconnaissance flights. Equatorial Africa possessed a permanent detachment in Brazzaville and a mixed flight in Bangui, while Madagascar had only a single mixed flight in Ivato.

Finally, Indochina had a mixed group of 2 flights in Bach Maï, another mixed group of 2 flights in Tong, a mixed grouping in Tourane, a group in Bien Hoa, and a flight of Loire 130 seaplanes in Cat Laï, or about 100 airplanes, including Morane 406's, Potez 542's, and Farman 221's, as well as Potez 25 TOE's.

Having settled the question of the Air Force's future, the air minister could then speed up the demobilization operations, which until then had developed slowly because of the great uncertainty about the fate of the French air forces. At the same time, the release of the cadres was effected, pursuant to the restriction on personnel strength envisaged since the end of the 1939–1940 campaign. Composed of 8,892 officers and 157,280 noncommissioned officers and enlisted men on June 25, 1940, the Air Force had only 3,984 officers and 66,810 noncommissioned officers and enlisted men on August 20. Even these figures did not correspond to the quota fixed by the armistice commissions, and thus significant shortages showed up in September 1940 within the units in France, North Africa, and the eastern Mediterranean. The manpower crisis that began at that time was never, in fact, to be resolved. During the same period the territorial organization was established. The unoccupied zone had been divided, after some initial modifications, into two air regions, the First Air Region at Aix-en-Provence and the Second Air Region at Toulouse (August 20, 1940). On the other side of the Mediterranean, a Higher Air Command in North Africa was set up over three air commands in Algeria, Morocco, and Tunisia. The rest of the colonial territory was divided as follows: Air Commands in the eastern Mediterranean, French West Africa, French Equatorial Africa, the group of colonies in the Indian Ocean (Tananarive), and Indochina.

Dakar and Gibraltar

It was during this period that the events at Dakar took place. The big West African port had already, on July 7, 1940, undergone an attack by British torpedo planes which had concerned themselves with the battleship *Richelieu*. The authorities had reacted by dispatching the GC I/4 there, equipped with Curtiss H-75's. It is true that defense of French West Africa was provided at the time only by the completely outmoded Dewoitine 500's and 502's of Flight I/6. After Equatorial Africa went into the dissident camp, the Free French and the British resolved to topple French West Africa over into the Allied camp as well. A large fleet was assembled at Freetown, Sierra Leone (2 battleships, 1 aircraft carrier, 5 cruisers, 10 destroyers, 2 patrol boats, 3 dispatch boats, and 11 troop transports) and showed up before Dakar on September 23. Governor General de Boisson categorically refused the proposals of General Charles de Gaulle, who was present on the spot. The confrontation was inevitable, and hostilities began with a naval bombardment. In the air, the Curtiss H-75's of GC I/4 intercepted British planes that were dropping leaflets on the town and lost one of their own number. The next day, September 24, an expedition of 6 Swordfish was attacked and repulsed. Then, in the course of the same day, the Glenn Martin 167's of GB I/62 and II/62 attacked the English fleet and got a direct hit on a cruiser. On September 25 the

Curtisses succeeded in shooting down two seaplanes that were setting the range for the English vessels. But they mistook their objective and dropped bombs in the direction of two French cruisers, the *Georges Leygues* and the *Montcalm*, but failed to hit them. The French Air Force, which had destroyed five enemy planes and dropped 6 tons of bombs on the English fleet, had lost only a single Curtiss, with five other planes damaged. It had to remain on alert until the end of the first week of October, when all danger seemed to have been averted.

As soon as he was informed of the Dakar affair, General Bergeret (who had just replaced General Pujo as secretary of state for aviation), after consultation with the government, ordered the Air Force to mount an operation against Gibraltar in reprisal. By this action he meant to show that the Vichy régime not only was determined to defend the integrity of its colonial empire but also was capable of undertaking offensive actions. And so, on September 24, 1940, about sixty LeO 45's, Douglas DB-7's, and Glenn Martin 167's of GB I/23, I/19, II/23, II/61, I/32, and I/11, escorted by the

Only two bomber groups, GB I/54 and I/51, were equipped with Breguet 693's.

In 1942 French West Africa was defended by four bomber groups, three of which were equipped with Glenn Martin 167 F's: GB I/62, II/62, and I/63.

Dewoitine 520's and Curtiss H-75's of the GC II/3, I/5, and II/5, took off from their bases in North Africa to drop approximately forty tons of bombs on the British strategic base between 1300 and 1415 hours. Although the antiaircraft reacted vigorously, no French plane was shot down. A part of the arsenal and also a ship in the roads were hit. As no British fighter planes showed up on September 24, the responsible officers of the Air Force and the Aéronavale (which had engaged 19 of its planes in the raid) decided to renew their attack without having the fighter groups participate. On September 25, 80 bombers poured 56 tons of bombs on the port of Gibraltar. The British defense, this time on the alert, succeeded in shooting down a LeO 45 of the GB II/23 and damaging ten planes or so. On the whole the operation had been more symbolic than effective, for the Air Force succeeded in placing only 6 percent of its bombs on the target on the 24th and 19 percent on the 25th.

The Forgotten War

As for the integrity of the colonial empire, the French Air Force also had to defend it in Indochina, this time against Thailand (Siam), supported by the Japanese.

In 1940 its remoteness from France had caused Indochina to be totally spared by the war. After the defeat the Vichy régime had sent Vice-Admiral Decoux there with the title of governor general. But because of Japanese expansionism, heavy threats hung over Indochina, of which the Langson incident on September 22, 1940, was a precursor. That day the entry of a unit of the Japanese army into Indochinese territory led to a series of confused and violent conflicts. Alone of all the air forces present in the region, Flight 1/595, equipped with Potez 25 TOE's, engaged in the battle, flying a number of reconnaissance missions, in the course of which it threw itself against the Japanese fighters and lost one of its planes. For its part, Flight 2/41 made several sorties over the island of Hainan. The conflict was on the point of expanding when, on September 25, the Japanese gained a foothold at Haiphong. The crisis was choked off only because the French command had resolved to adopt a passive attitude toward the assailant. On November 30 the Japanese went back across the Tonkin border, and calm returned.

But, extinguished in one place, the fire spread elsewhere. Originally favorable to the Allied cause, Thailand, after the Franco-British defeat in Europe, had gone over to the camp of Japan and Germany and with the support of Tokyo was pursuing aims of hegemony on the Indochinese peninsula. As early as September 1940 it was claiming territories held by Laos and Cambodia. When Decoux refused to give it satisfaction, it stepped up the border incidents. By the end of 1940 open war appeared inevitable.

Against the one hundred planes of the French Air Force Thailand had at its disposal a heterogeneous assortment of 230 planes of all types and origins: Breguet XIV's, Spad 7's and 13's, Nieuport 15's and 29's, Heinkel He 43's, Bristol Bulldogs, Curtiss Hawk II's and III's, Vought Corsairs, Glenn Martin 139's, and Amagashi seaplanes. Its superiority in pilots—it had 500—was crushing. While Thailand was concentrating its forces, the French Air Force of Indochina was divided between the different theaters of operations where it might be led to act. The flight of Farman 221's, after having accomplished some transport missions, was held in general reserve. The Laos sector received the mixed air grouping (18 Potez 25 TOE's and Morane 406's), and the Cambodia sector had a regrouping of various formations comprising 6 Morane 406's, 3 Potez 542's, and 9 Loire 130's.

Hostilities began with Thailand's bombing of the town of Savannakhet on November 25, 1940. The Air Force could respond to this aggression only by organizing a few night air attacks, since the decrepitude of certain of its planes did not allow it to do more. The training of the French fighter pilots gave them the advantage in aerial combats. The reconnaissance and observation forces were capable of accomplishing their task without encountering excessive difficulties. But Japan, while theoretically

General Bergeret during an inspection in North Africa in November 1941. After being secretary of state for aviation under Marshal Pétain, General Bergeret went to North Africa in November 1942 and was a member of the imperial council under Darlan. The National Liberation Committee relieved him of his duties as commander of the air forces of French West Africa in 1943.

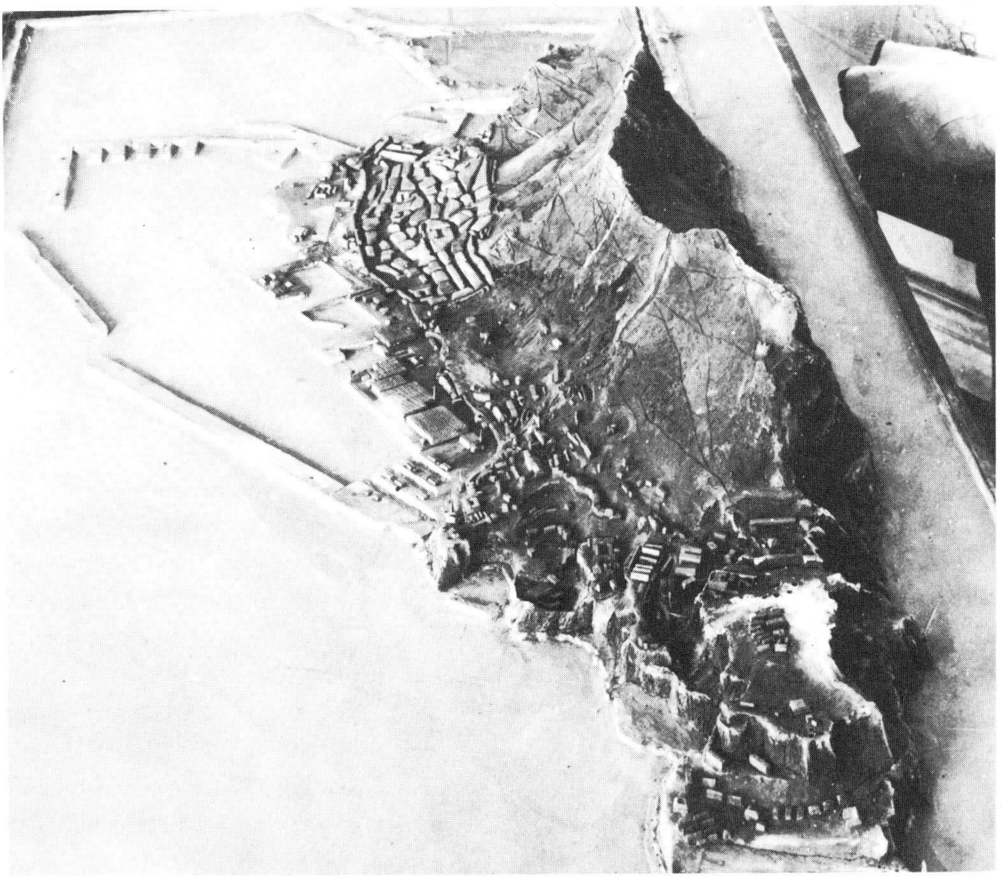

A model of the peninsula of Gibraltar prepared by GR I/22 for the bombings of September 1940.

neutral, did not refrain from sending modern air materiel to Thailand, and it even appears that many Japanese pilots fought in its units. This does not alter the fact that during the few weeks that the conflict lasted the French bombers dropped over 40 tons of bombs on objectives situated on Thailand's territory. At one time the French command envisaged a ground action toward Bangkok, but the Air Force's weakness dissuaded it from that. The war ended on January 28, 1941, after a Japanese offer of mediation, and a peace treaty was signed on February 7 in Tokyo. The French air forces had lost 1 Farman 221 and 2 Morane-Saulnier 406's, but had succeeded in destroying 20 enemy planes. A number of planes had been damaged or involved in accidents, but could be repaired and reconditioned.

The Syrian Affair

On May 27, 1941, when the Vichy régime signed the Paris protocols with Germany, Rashid Ali Pasha's pro-Nazi revolution in Iraq was already nearly two months old. It was on April 1, 1941, that the regent of the kingdom of Iraq was overthrown and the new régime, run by Ali Pasha, asked for German aid. The fear of being taken in the rear in the Middle East and the prospects of losing the rich petroleum deposits of Iraq pushed the British to act quickly in landing troops deep in the Persian Gulf. But the support that the Vichy government gave the Germans in this affair would inevitably lead them to intervene in the area. Even before the Paris agreements, 62 Luftwaffe planes transporting materiel bound for Iraq had already passed through airfields in Syria and Lebanon. Moreover, the protocols authorized Germany to use the military stores of the Middle East for the benefit of the insurgents directed by Rashid Ali Pasha.

As early as May 15, 1941, British airplanes had launched attacks on the Syrian and Lebanese airfields designed to destroy Luftwaffe planes that were making stopovers there. Palmyra, Rayack, Damascus, Baalbeck, Homs, Tripoli, and Beirut were involved. The frequency of the British aggressions led General Bergeret, secretary of state for aviation, to make a trip to the region to appraise the gravity of the situation and decide on the size of the reinforcements to be sent. And, in fact, the GC III/6 arrived from North Africa, not without having first obtained the agreement of the armistice commissions, and established itself at Rayack with its Dewoitine 520's. The Air Force of the Levant (Middle East) had great need of these modern planes. Commanded by General Jannekeyn, later secretary of state for aviation under the second Laval government, it had at its disposal a fighter group equipped with Morane 406's, the GC I/7, and a bomber group and a bomber flight (GB II/39 and Flight III/39) with Glenn Martin 167's and old Bloch 200's. The reconnaissance was reduced to one group (GR II/39) and one flight (GAO 583) equipped with Potez 63-11's. In addition, 5 flights of the Levant type provided surveillance of the territory with their Potez 25 TOE's (Flights 592, 593, 594, 595, and 596). The navy maintained a flight of Loire 130's at Tripoli. The total of all these units came to nearly 90 planes, most of which were not fit to engage in combat with the modern materiel that the RAF was in a position to bring into play.

After a renewal of their air attacks, toward the end of May, the British, supported by some Free French units, penetrated into Syria and Lebanon on June 8. The GC III/6 was surprised on the ground by the enemy Hurricanes and Curtiss P-40's, which, in several passes, burned up two Dewoitine 520's and damaged several others. From the very beginning of the fighting the French Air Force had to fight for the almost exclusive benefit of the ground forces. The bomber forces, acting without escort because there was little British fighter plane activity, attacked the enemy infantry columns and tanks along the Lebanese coast. Then it was thrown against the British fleet which was supporting with its cannon fire the advance of the Commonwealth troops on the coast in the region of Saïda. On June 9 two English vessels were hit.

The Potez 25 TOE's of the surveillance flights, incapable of taking part in daytime operations, had formed a night bomber grouping. During the first phase of the campaign, from June 8 to 15, the Air Force was able to achieve a certain air superiority, and the bombers were able to act without suffering very heavy losses. Moreover, besides the Potez 25 TOE's that General Jannekeyn had drawn from the storage depots, a fair number of reinforcements were sent to the eastern Mediterranean area. Using the Italian airfields and the German airstrips established in Greece to refuel, the Bomber Groups I/31 and I/14, equipped with LeO 45's, arrived in Syria on June 10 and 14. The Dewoitine 520's of the II/3 joined them there during the last week of the month. With the arrival of the LeO 45's of GB I/25 (June 17) and the Glenn Martin 167's of the 4th flotilla of the Aéronavale, the air forces of the Levant were putting on the line the most modern flying materiel that they possessed.

In spite of these reinforcements, the British took Damascus on June 21. In addition, after having crushed the Iraqi revolution, they mounted two attacks on the rear of the French army engaged in the fighting for the defense of southern Lebanon and the Damascus region, and threatened the Aleppo area, which was rich in airfields. To ward off the danger General Jannekeyn formed the GC I/7, II/3, and III/6 into a grouping of the north. The action conducted by this grouping did not prevent the enemy ground forces from surrounding Palmyra. In the last ten days of June the Air Force grew progressively weaker. Divided between ground attack missions and the fighting against enemy fighter planes, which, with the massive engagement of P-40's—superior to the Dewoitine 520—took control of the sky, the French fighter groups were decimated. They lost the superiority that they had temporarily achieved and were no longer capable of protecting the bombing expeditions. The capitulation of Palmyra opened the way to Homs and Aleppo for the British, and the Syrian campaign entered into its final phase.

The arrival in the Middle East on July 4 of the 12 Dewoitine 520's of Aéronavale Flight I AC hardly

After having commanded the French air forces in the Middle Eastern campaign, General Jannekeyn became secretary of state for aviation in April 1942 and held that post until 1943.

changed the balance of forces. On July 8 General Dentz, commanding the French troops in the Levant, asked for a temporary halt in the fighting. Six days later an armistice was concluded at Saint Jean d'Acre. In the interval the Air Force units had taken off one by one for France or North Africa.

In the course of the Syrian and Lebanese operations the Air Force had lost 179 of the 289 airplanes that it had thrown into battle. (This represents an overall total—losses in aerial combat, on the ground, and in accidents. The total British losses are not known.) The fighter groups, which had flown over 1,600 sorties, claimed 29 sure victories in aerial combat and 8 probable ones. The bombers had flown 859 sorties and reconnaissance, 583.

Aeronautical Collaboration

The war in the Middle East was an eye-opener for the French Air Force; it revealed its weakness and its inability to conduct defensive actions of long duration. This vulnerability was all the more disturbing since the air forces appeared as the only means of opposing an enemy quickly and well at a given point in the colonial territories. However, in the Syrian affair the Wiesbaden and Turin commissions, contrary to their custom, had shown themselves relatively flexible in giving the Air Force general staff a large amount of freedom of action and the possibility of shifting its formations as it wished, on the sole condition of notification. In fact, the causes of the reverses in the Middle East lay much deeper, and the real problems were connected with the very structures of the Air Force under the armistice.

Drawing its conclusions from the campaign in Syria and Lebanon, the command of the air forces noted that besides the below normal manpower within the groups, the limitation on the number of units imposed by the Axis countries from June to July 1940 on prevented the Air Force from showing real strength against any adversary.

It is true that the Germans and the Italians hampered the recruiting policy considerably and that, in any case, the attraction of the armed forces under the armistice was fairly weak. While the armistice commissions had authorized the reopening of the Air School at Salon and various other centers, they were still not inclined to permit very much development in the training and instruction of the personnel. Moreover, in the units themselves the hours of flying time and the fuel allocations were very limited.

Repairing and replacing airplanes was another important element in the weakness of the Air Force. The planes were wearing out at an extremely fast rate, and the shutting down of the aeronautics industry in June 1940 had interrupted all manufacturing of modern materiel. With the authorization of the control commissions, the formations could draw spare parts or even whole airplanes from the reserves in storage, but that practice was bound to have its own limits. Moreover, there was an urgent need for innovations since aeronautical technology was evolving very rapidly. The confrontations in Syria had shown the inferiority of the Dewoitine 520 to the P-40, and the high command had to admit that many types of planes no longer had any place within the flying units. The only solution would be to get the aeronautics industry under way again. An understanding with Germany on this matter might perhaps have given the Air Force the possibility of developing the Dewoitine 520 Z, a fighter plane of excellent quality. It was, therefore, military imperatives as much as political and economic ones that pushed the Vichy government into the path of aeronautical cooperation. The long, complex negotiations begun in the last months of 1940 in Paris and pursued in Wiesbaden resulted in the signing by General Bergeret and the German authorities, on July 28, 1941, of a joint program of aeronautical manufactures. The war in Syria had just ended barely two months earlier. The aeronautics industry of the free zone and of the occupied zone were to manufacture, for April 1943, 2,276 planes and 5,282 engines for Germany. France for its part would get 1,076 planes and 2,591 engines. Thus in 1943 the French Air Force was to have at its disposal 550 Dewoitine 520's, 225 LeO 45's, and 86 Bloch 175's.

Meanwhile, the officers in command of the air forces had asked the German authorities for expansion of their resources as well as complete freedom of action. They feared that the same sort of incidents that had taken place in the Middle East would be repeated in Madagascar or North Africa. Numerous air-sea incidents off Tunisia with the British posed heavy threats to that part of the empire, and the intelligence services reported that the British were on the point of taking action at Gabès, which they suspected of serving as a port of transit for supplies destined for Rommel's Afrika Korps.

In April 1942, on the eve of the operations in Madagascar, the Air Force had a little over 900 planes at its disposal, scattered over France and the empire, to resist any British aggressions.

Madagascar and North Africa

The forces in Madagascar were particularly weak. The large island in the Indian Ocean possessed only a single unit equipped with a few Morane 406's and Potez 63-11's, the mixed air group.

On the pretext of a possible Japanese invasion—it was the time when Japanese surface vessels and submarines were cruising in the Indian

Ocean—the British disembarked at Diégo-Suarez, in the northern part of the island, on May 5, 1942. The mixed air group had been alerted the day before. But the Diégo-Arrachart airfield was attacked from the air, and several planes were destroyed on the ground by the Grumman Martlets of the British Fleet Air Arm. First Lieutenant Rossigneux, head of the air detachment of that base, was shot down in his Potez 63-11 at the moment of takeoff. The French air forces then carried out a withdrawal toward the south, to Anivorane, where they joined the few planes available at Ivato. From there the Potez 63-11's tried to attack the British columns and suffered heavy losses. On May 7, in the course of an encounter with the Martlets, the Morane 406's were very roughly handled in an unequal combat in which Captain Léonetti, commanding officer of the mixed air group, was wounded and Captain Assolant was killed. Hostilities ceased when, on the same day, the British expeditionary force occupied Diégo-Suarez. The four Morane 406's and three Potez 63-11's that were left in the mixed air group settled in at Arivonimamo. It was there that the resumption of fighting surprised them on September 18, 1942, and, after successive retreats, they were destroyed one by one on the ground. The crews, formed into advanced patrols, then fought against the British ground troops. On November 6 the campaign ended.

North Africa's situation might appear more favored than Madagascar's since it was defended by

In February 1941 a compulsory national service of eight months was introduced. Men twenty years of age were required to serve in the Youth Workshops. In 1943 Jeunesse et Montagne *(Youth and Mountain) was combined with General de la Porte du Theil's* Chantiers de Jeunesse *(Youth Workshops). As early as 1943 the leaders of* Jeunesse et Montagne *were preparing to join the Resistance movement, and the following year, although this youth movement had been abolished, some organized units played an active part in the liberation of France.*

During the summer of 1940, in reaction to the dejection that resulted from the defeat, the Jeunesse et Montagne *movement was organized. Its founder was General d'Harcourt, and the idea of "putting the aviators on the mountain" derived from General Coche. The group was commanded by Jacques Faure, an alpine trooper and a former ski champion.*

400 planes. In Morocco, Algeria, and Tunisia the Air Force mustered 7 fighter groups, one of them with multi-seated fighters (4 of Dewoitine 520's, 2 of Curtiss H-75's, and 1 of Potez 631's), 9 bomber groups (5 of LeO 45's and 4 of Douglas DB-7's), and 4 reconnaissance groups (2 of Bloch 175's, 1 of Potez 63-11's, and 1 of LeO 45's). Be that as it may, those 20 formations were weakened by the lack of spare parts, and the quality of the personnel could not hope to compensate for the unreliability of the flying materiel.

The unusual movements of convoys reported by aerial reconnaissances from the beginning of November 1942 had pushed General Mendigal, senior air officer in North Africa, to put his units on alert. During the night of November 7–8 the danger became specific, and the "Célestin" and "Anatole" alerts, the former applying to Algeria and Tunisia and the latter to Morocco, came into force. At dawn on November 8, Casablanca, Rabat, Oran, and Algiers were cannonaded by Allied naval guns. Shortly afterwards American heavy pursuit planes attacked the air bases of the first three of these cities. In addition, troops that had already landed quickly threatened certain airfields. At Rabat the GC I/5 had to take off to avoid falling into American hands. The GC II/5, for its part, succeeded in shooting down 10 enemy planes, but at the price of 5 pilots killed and 4 wounded. At Oran, the GC III/3 succeeded in shooting down 17 Allied planes. On the other hand, the Americans got possession of all the planes of GC II/3 and III/6 that were present at the base of Algiers-Maison Blanche without firing a shot. The only offensive action mounted during the day consisted in a bombardment of the American landing forces by Douglas DB-7's and LeO 45's of the GB II/23 and I/32 escorted by 13 Curtiss H-75's of the GC I/5 and II/5. The balance drawn up on the evening of November 8 showed that the French had lost some 30 planes destroyed in aerial combat or on the ground. On November 9, although new attacks

A Bloch 147 with the colors of the French Air Force under the armistice: red and yellow horizontal bands on the engine cowling and tail fin.

A Potez 63-11 belonging to an observation flight from French West Africa, at Thiès, Senegal.

November 13, 1942: the remains, on the GR I/22's base at Rabat-Salé, Morocco, of the hard fighting that pitted the air forces of North Africa against the Allies during "Operation Torch."

were made against the Allied fleet, the Air Force's situation in Morocco was desperate. A number of planes had been destroyed on the ground, and on November 10 only some 60 planes (35 bombers and 25 fighters) could still go into action. The cessation of hostilities prevented them from hurling themselves once more against the American forces.

In the meantime important events were taking place in France. As soon as they were informed of the Allied landing, the Germans authorized the Vichy government to send reinforcements to North Africa and offered the support of the Luftwaffe. At 1300 hours, on that day, Admiral Darlan accepted the aid of the Axis but on the condition that the German and Italian planes operate from Sicily or Sardinia. One hour later the German armistice commission insisted on having the airfields of Tunisia made freely available to them, a demand that the Air Force satisfied a little later. Marshal Kesselring then sent about one hundred planes to Tunisia; they landed at El Aouin, which the French units, confined to strict neutrality, evacuated. About the same time General Jannekeyn, secretary of state for aviation, transmitted to the armistice commissions the list of air units that he felt it necessary to dispatch to North Africa in order to reinforce the defenses: from France, the GC I/1 (Dewoitine 520's) and the GB I/38 and II/38 (LeO 45's), and from French West Africa, still loyal to Vichy, the GB II/63 (Douglas DB-7's). But, in fact, the Germans' and the Italians' distrust prevented the transfer of any units. The only group that reached North Africa, the GC I/2 (Dewoitine 520's), had left before the Allied landing.

During the night of November 10–11, 1942, the Germans launched "Operation Anton," that is, the invasion of the unoccupied zone. Surprised in its barracks, the army of the armistice could not offer the slightest resistance. Moreover, General Jannekeyn had ordered the air formations not to budge. On November 27 the Germans and the Italians proclaimed the dissolution of the army of the armistice in its entirety. On December 12 the general staff of the French Air Force was abolished, giving way to a Directorate General of the Air Services, which was nothing but a sort of liquidating agency for it. In April 1943, after the demobilization or discharge of a large part of the personnel and the disappearance of the flying units, an air defense general staff was put in place, subordinate to a Secretariat General for Air Defense created the month before. Three inspectorates—antiaircraft and railroad antiaircraft, public air security, and passive defense—were attached to it. The first was to set up railroad antiaircraft sections, which were used against Allied airplanes, until its dissolution in February 1944.

The air force of North Africa, however, soon reinforced by that of West Africa, was preparing to fight, after rearmament, side by side with the British and the Americans. On November 13 and 14, 1942, on the occasion of a tour of inspection of the fighter groups of North Africa, General Mendigal had given that assurance to the pilots he had met.

Airframes and Engines Supplied to France and to Germany by the French Aeronautics Industry, 1940–1944

	Airframes		Engines		
Date	France	Germany	France	Germany	Remarks
1940–1941	76	925	255	1,927	The figures for engines are only for 1941.
1942	460	661	982	1,998	
1943	–	1,444	–	5,014	
1944	–	576	–	2,315	
Total	536	3,606	1,237	11,254	

Airframes: Arado 196's and 199's; Dornier 24's; Fieseler 156's; Fw 189's; Junkers 52's; Bf 108's; Siebel 204's; Bloch 175's; Caudron 445's; Dewoitine 520's; Laté 298's; LeO 45's; Loire 130's; Loire-Nieuport 40's; Morane 230's; Morane 406's; Potez 63's.
Engines: Renault 6 Q's; Argus 411's; Gnome and Rhône 14 N's, 14 M's, and 14 R's; BMW 132's; Hispano-Suiza 12 X's and 12 Y's.

CHAPTER IV

The Free French Air Forces

On June 23, 1940, in an official declaration announced by the BBC, the British government recognized the existence of a provisional national committee founded by a handful of political and military figures grouped around Charles de Gaulle, a then unknown general who had been acting undersecretary of state for national defense and war in the Paul Reynaud cabinet. Five days later de Gaulle assumed the status of head of the Free French, and on August 7 of that year an agreement concluded with the British sketched the juridical foundations of Free France and at the same time conjured up the notion of forming a force of volunteers to fight side by side with the forces of the British Empire against the Axis countries. Great Britain committed itself to supplying the Free French with financial and military resources in exchange for a promise of later reimbursement.

Since July 1 of the previous year the military forces of Free France, actually quite laughable, had begun to organize. In the army, navy, and air force, they represented a heterogeneous assemblage of fugitives from France, North Africa, and other parts of the colonial empire, repatriates from Norway, evacuees from Dunkirk, and even Frenchmen who, residing abroad, had spontaneously lined up on the side of dissidence, as Free France was called in Vichy, after having heard the news of the military disaster of May–June 1940. In fact, whatever the political or geographical horizons from which they came, these men were trying in their way to react against the defeat and the armistice that sanctioned it. Unlike the fighters from other countries occupied by Germany, for whom departure for Great Britain, where they found their governments in exile, might appear a logical and natural choice, the position of the French who constituted Free France was more delicate. Compared to the legal power established in Vichy by Marshal Pétain, de Gaulle represented both adventure and uncertainty. But, as one of them, François de Labouchère, pointed out, "The difficulty had come to be not doing one's duty but discerning it." Over 3,500 Frenchmen who served in the Free French Air Forces (FAFL) from 1940 to 1945 had been able to do just that.

The First Free French Air Forces

Some of these Frenchmen had resolved on their choice even before the signing and coming into

From July 1940 to July 1941 Admiral Muselier was the first commander of the Free French Air Forces, a position that he combined with that of commander of the Free French Naval Forces.

effect of the armistice. On June 15 Sergeant Demozay, destined to become the famous "Colonel Morlaix," left France in a British bomber that he had found abandoned on the Nantes airfield. On June 17, the day of the call for an armistice, 10 aviator officers and noncommissioned officers of the Mérignac base, among them the future Captain Charles, flew off in an RAF Handley Page. The next day, in three Simouns, 5 officers of the Royan pilot training school imitated them. On June 19 the flow seemed to expand with the departure from the port of Douarnenez of a lobster boat, the *Trébouliste*, carrying 108 trainees from pilot training school 23 at Morlaix led by First Lieutenant Pinot. Some asked to return to France when the cease-fire became effective, but most of them signed up in the FAFL. On June 20 Captain Goumin, accompanied by 18 officers and noncommissioned officers of the air training group of Saint Jean d'Angély, landed his Farman 222 at a British airfield. Thirty other aviators, some of them wearing the Polish uniform, took places on June 26 on the last ships leaving Port Vendres.

From North Africa 6 planes (3 Goélands and 3 Simouns) went to Gibraltar between June 26 and 28. Then on June 30, 2 Glenn Martin 167's arrived, one of which was shot down by Spanish antiaircraft fire. The four officers it was carrying were certainly the first of the FAFL to be killed. Another drama unfolded at Fez in Morocco when a Potez 540 carrying eight fugitives crashed at the end of the runway. Although the Mers-el-Kebir affair slowed down these escapes somewhat, it must be noted that from July 5 to August 23, 1940, 13 planes of all kinds, from liaison planes to bombers, deserted North Africa. Tunisia, too, furnished its batch of deserters with the flight on July 2 of 2 Glenn Martin 167's on board which were Captains Dodelier and Ritoux-Lachaud, both present at the creation, in Egypt, of Free French Flight 2.

But the basic recruiting of the FAFL was not limited to the home territory or to North Africa. From Djibouti in northeast Africa or from the Middle East (the example of Captain Tulasne, one of the flight commanders of the GC I/7, is the most famous), many pilots arrived in Aden or in Egypt. Others went from Madagascar to Portuguese East Africa. Finally, although engine trouble forced them to stop in Thailand, two French officers (Pouyade and Justin) succeeded in leaving Indochina and arriving in Singapore.

To these individual or group departures were added significant territorial adhesions. The New Hebrides, a Franco-British condominium, declared in favor of the dissident camp on July 20, 1940. But French Equatorial Africa's rallying to General de Gaulle on August 26 undoubtedly constituted the most important event for Free France in that gloomy period. The decisive action of Félix Eboué, the governor of Chad, and the decision of Colonel Marchand, René Pleven, and Colonel Leclerc gave the Free French their first major territorial seat. Moreover, it enabled certain aviators of the air forces of French West Africa to go over to de Gaulle, such as the Curtiss H-75 that escaped from Thiès.

It was from these elements, as they arrived, that the Free French Air Forces were organized on July 1, 1940. The command, curiously enough, was exercised by a sailor of uncompromising character, Admiral Muselier, who, by the way, gave them their emblem, the cross of Lorraine on a blue ground. Among the 500 aviators who went over to the Free French camp in this period (nearly 300 in Great Britain plus 100 in Egypt and another 100 in the territories of French Equatorial Africa) there was no high-ranking officer to take over as commander in chief of the FAFL. Therefore, General de Gaulle had decided to entrust to Admiral Muselier the combined responsibilities of the navy and the air force.

Although it is difficult to draw a portrait typical of the FAFL in the earliest period of its existence, it is still possible to reconstitute, at least in part, the personality of those who signed up in Great Britain and passed through Camp Odiham between June 1940 and July 1941. (Three-quarters of them had reached England in June or July 1940.) Officers represented 23% of the total number, noncommissioned officers 42%, and enlisted men 35%. Among the officers there were very few regulars. The breakdown by specialty favored pilots and student pilots (72%), then came observers (12%) and mechanics (4.5%), the rest being divided between radiomen and machine-gunners. Since the latter were scarce, the command had to draw on the Pacific battalion and train a certain number. The most remarkable fact was certainly the men's youth (the average age was twenty-three, with 90% being thirty or under), which was equaled only, for the most part, by their inexperience in the aviation field. Many of them were still in the middle of their apprenticeship at the time of the defeat and had to be trained in the British schools. Relations with the RAF became a little strained because of accidents attributable to the FAFL. But these trainees quickly familiarized themselves with the English methods and tactics and with the language as well. The dominant trait of all of these men was their impatience to get into combat, and the numerous letters that they addressed to the command for that purpose constitute an irrefutable proof of it.

The First Units

At the beginning of July 1940 the situation of the British was rather catastrophic for their leaders to concern themselves with organizing a Free French Air Force. At most they suggested to General de Gaulle that they incorporate the most experienced pilots into the RAF. Several Frenchmen did take part in the Battle of Britain, and in January 1941, 17 of them were serving in Squadrons 32, 73, 91, 92, 111, 132, 241, 242, 607, and 615 of the Fighter Command. But the head of Free France expected more of his allies. As General de Gaulle explains it in his memoirs: "While I naturally thought that in our forces anything that flew from the bases of Great Britain in planes furnished by the English should be part of the British air system, I wanted our airmen, too, to constitute a national force; that was not easy." But this construction of a special air force was, nevertheless, to pass through several successive stages. The French at the very beginning were obliged to accept integration of the groups or flights that they planned to form into the big British units.

The first creations of units took place in the Middle East on July 8, 1940, with the appearance of Free French Flights 1, 2, and 3. At the moment when the armistice went into effect Captain Jacquier, of GC I/7, left his unit, which was stationed in the Middle East, for Ismailia, Egypt, where he found a patrol of the same group placed at the disposal of the British before the cease-fire, which, under the orders of First Lieutenant Péronne, was getting ready to go to Syria. After a general discussion of events the two officers resolved to stay on the spot, and were thus the nucleus of the Free French Air Forces in Egypt. As there could be no question of their constituting a French command, with a dozen different types of planes, which, with no spare parts, would soon be unusable, they served in the RAF for the duration of the war. Nevertheless, they asked the British to authorize the organization of three units whose name would contain the word *France*. Hence the birth of the FFF (Free French Flights) 1, 2, and 3. The FFF 3 (composed of a Simoun 159 and a Bloch 81) made liaison flights, leaving from Heliopolis, between Egypt and Palestine until the middle of the following year, when it was dissolved and its members joined the French forces coming from Chad. The three Morane-Saulnier 406's and the 3 Potez 63-11's of FFF 2, commanded by Captain Jacquier, participated first of all in the air defense of Alexandria; then, because of the threats that hung over Haifa, they were based in Palestine from August 1940 to January 1941. By that date the French materiel was on its last legs. The RAF then provided the FFF 2 with a few Hurricanes, which, after a course of instruction at the transformation center in Ismailia, it used on interception missions over the Suez Canal. After a stay in Cyrenaica the unit took part, from Sidi Barrani, in the Battle of Crete, where it lost its commanding officer and in which its strength was decimated. This led to its dissolution in June 1941. As for FFF 1, equipped with two Glenn Martin 167's that came from Tunisia, it left for Aden on July 13, 1940, and was soon engaged on the East African Front. The first of its planes, in which Ritoux-Lachaud was flying, was shot down on September 8, and the second met the same fate on December 16. Thus that formation had a life as short as that of the two planes with which it was equipped.

England was another geographical center in which the air units of Free France developed. On August 1, 1940, at the Odiham base, Major de Marmier created the First Fighter Group, which also took the name "Jam," or "Menace," with some 20 planes divided into 4 flights: a fighter flight (2 Dewoitine 520's), a bomber flight (6 Bristol Blenheims furnished by the British), and two reconnaissance and liaison flights (Lucioles and Lysanders). During the same period an independent flight was also organized, which was nicknamed "Topic" and placed under the orders of Major Astier de Villatte with a complement of six Bristol Blenheims. According to agreements between the representatives of Free France and the British government, these two units were dispatched to Africa. There the First Fighter Group was to participate in "Operation Menace," that is, the attack against Dakar, while Topic went to the defense of Equatorial Africa. The operation against Dakar failed, and when General de Gaulle's emissaries arrived at the Ouakama base, on board Lucioles of the liaison flight of the First Fighter Group, they were made prisoners and immediately accused of high treason. Menace then left for Equatorial Africa, which had meanwhile become Free French Africa, where it rejoined Topic. In that region the fighting constantly confronted the Free French with the Vichy French in Gabon, and the authorities feared a return in force of troops loyal to Marshal Pétain from the territories of French West Africa.

The winning over of Equatorial Africa had been an important event, and the Free French were able to make use of the infrastructure of the country to augment the potential of their air forces. Created before the war to carry out liaison missions and give support to the ground troops in case of conflict with Italy, the permanent air force detachment of Chad brought to Free France 6 Potez 25–29 TOE's and Bloch 120 three-engined planes. It was in a plane of the latter type that General de Gaulle made a tour of these territories in mid-October 1940. The detachment was modernized the following month with the arrival of several Lysanders provided by the British. Late in August 1940 detachments of the same model were in Gabon and in the Middle Congo, under the orders of First Lieutenant Ezzano (Bloch 120's, Potez 25 TOE's), as well as in Cameroon with Captain Biarnais's Lysanders.

Finally, on September 29, 1940, the 1st Air Company, commanded by Major Bergé, made its appearance. It was to fight in Brittany and in Guyenne from March to April 1941 and later conduct commando raids in Crete, where its commanding officer was captured (in 1942), before being engaged in Libya.

The creation of all these units, however, was only the first stage toward the establishment of an organization specific to Free France. The next step was taken with the reorganization during the winter of 1940–1941, which resulted in the creation of Reserved Bomber Group No. 1, or GRB 1. Deprived of part of its planes and dispatched to Libya, Jam merged with the flight Topic and formed the first true bomber unit of the FAFL, then took the designation GRB 1. Placed under the orders of Major Astier de Villatte, this group consisted of 2 flights of 6 Blenheims each: the 1st under Captain Lager and the 2nd under Captain Saint-Péreuse. It took part, at the same time as the permanent detachment of Chad, in Colonel Leclerc's attack on the oasis of Kufra, on which it carried out three bombardments during the first few days of February 1941. Returned to Fort Lamy, the GRB 1 was split into two parts. One remained in Chad and the other was put on the road toward Abyssinia, where, integrated into Group 202 of the RAF, it carried out several bombing operations against the Italian troops from the base of Gondar-Asmara. It was later used to drop leaflets over French East Africa, then was sent to Damascus in August 1941, to become in September the Metz flight of the Lorraine group.

Meanwhile in January 1941 a Fighter Flight No. 1 had been created at Cairo. Formed from the fighter flight of the First Fighter Group, which had lost its Dewoitine 520's, it was incorporated into Squadron 73, with which it operated in Greece and in Cyrenaica. Withdrawn from the front in May 1941, it served as the nucleus of the Alsace fighter group.

One last unit, the Bomber Flight No. 2, was organized at Brazzaville in March 1941, in accordance with the agreements entered into in London between Lieutenant Colonel Pijeaud, who had

A Westland-Lysander of the Brittany group. The Rennes flight had 6 airplanes of this type.

replaced Captain Chevrier in the post of chief of the FAFL general staff, and Group Captain Collier. This flight, composed of crews that had come from Africa and from England, was intended to support the Free French ground units' action in Libya. It returned to Egypt in May 1941, took over Martin Marylands there, and came under the control of Squadron 39 of the RAF. Four months later, dissolved once again, it became the Nancy flight of the Lorraine group.

But after the fighting in Syria and the arrival in Great Britain of Lieutenant Colonel Martial Valin and his appointment to head the FAFL, the Free French Air Forces would experience a decisive evolution.

The Groups Named after French Provinces

When the war broke out in September 1939 Major Valin was in command of GR I/33. Two months later he went to the intelligence service of the First Air Army, and then in April 1940 was appointed to the French military mission in Brazil. It was in South America that he learned of the defeat at the same time that he learned of his promotion to the rank of lieutenant colonel. Asked several times by the Vichy authorities to continue as a French representative in Brazil, Valin had decided to join Free France and was preparing to leave for Great Britain. He was not able to do so until February 1941, and did not sail until April 9. The next day he affixed his signature to his engagement in the FAFL, of which he became chief of the general staff. In fact, General de Gaulle intended Valin for higher positions—as it turned out, the command of the FAFL—but first wanted him to learn all the ropes and make contact with his British counterparts with whom he would have to work. It was, therefore, not until July 1941 that, with the rank of colonel, he succeeded Admiral Muselier, who, for his part, retained his function with the navy. The next month Valin was raised to the rank of brigadier general. In September a Vichyist court sentenced him to death, revoked his French citizenship, and ordered the confiscation of his property. Finally, on September 24, 1941, after General

A Potez 29 TOE of the permanent air force detachment of Chad, over the Nile.

de Gaulle had created a National Committee, General Valin assumed the functions of National Commissioner for Air.

It was during Valin's brilliant ascent that fundamental changes had come about for Free France in general and for the FAFL in particular. On July 14, 1941, after a short but murderous campaign, the Vichyist forces of the states of the Middle East, led by General Dentz, had laid down their arms in accordance with an armistice signed at Saint Jean d'Acre. For Colonel Valin Syria and Lebanon's coming into the Free French camp represented the unexpected opportunity to have at last an infrastructure of airfields and bases of a different quality from those of Free French Africa, as well as the well-trained flying personnel and qualified mechanics of whom the FAFL was so much in need. In that respect the month of July 1941 was a turning point in the history of the air units of Free France. To win over the aviators of the French Air Force of the armistice Colonel Valin had accompanied General Catroux to Egypt even before the end of the Syrian campaign. The negotiations held with the Vichy representatives were disappointing, to say the least, inasmuch as barely ten percent of the personnel present in the Middle East had chosen the de Gaulle camp. However, the FAFL did have important bases and many specialists at its disposal. This explains why Syria constituted the primary geographical center for the birth of the first autonomous FAFL groups.

The establishment of such units met the wishes of General de Gaulle, who, soon after Valin's arrival as commander of the Free French Air Forces, had asked him to work in that direction. Valin had been struck by the existence of Czech and Polish air formations which operated autonomously within the big RAF commands, and applied himself to realizing the same organization on the French side. At that period individual and group escapes as well as the arrival in the units of pilots and other flying personnel trained in the British training centers had reinforced the manpower available for such an operation. In September 1941, at the time when the Alsace and Lorraine groups made their appearance, Colonel Valin had available 186 pilots (52 of them officers) and 17 officer navigators and bombardiers. Counting the other specialists, the flying personnel of the FAFL, including those integrated into the RAF, numbered 69 officers and 136 noncommissioned officers and enlisted men, or a total of 205. This was small in comparison to the 546 Czech fliers and the 1,813 Polish aviators, but it was still sufficient for the realization of Free France's plans. The establishment of autonomous groups could thus get under way. And, to remind the French under German occupation of the presence of some of their own men on the Allied side, Valin decided to give the groups the names of French provinces.

After having been in command of the FAFL from 1941 to 1943, General Valin became deputy chief of the general staff of the French Air Forces in 1943 while simultaneously commanding the French Air Forces in Great Britain. In 1946 he was named Air Force inspector general.

Meanwhile, the FAFL command had also been restructured. Colonel, later General, Valin was at the summit of the hierarchy and directed three theaters of operations: Great Britain, the Middle East, and Free French Africa. His powers were limited to control of the personnel, however, for the operational employment of the units and the logistics were provided by the British.

A Blenheim Mk IVL of the Lorraine group in Libya in 1942.

A Hurricane Mk II of the Alsace fighter group in Libya in 1942. The group remained there from April to August 1942 and then left for Great Britain, where it flew Spitfires.

Lieutenant Colonel Pijeaud, second chief of staff of the FAFL, took command of the Lorraine group in Libya in December 1941. He died the following month from wounds received in combat.

The first big FAFL formation originated on the air base at Rayack in Syria on September 1, 1941. This was the Alsace fighter group, which derived from the merger of the FFF 2 and Fighter Flight No. 1. Its first commanding officer was Major Tulasne, and its first planes were the GC I/7's Morane-Saulnier 406's seized by the British at the end of the campaign in the Middle East. Then the Alsace group received Hurricanes, with which it could be engaged in active operations. From April to August 1942 it participated in the fighting in Egypt and Libya from its base of Fuka. Withdrawn from the front and brought back up to strength, it was later assigned to the air defense of the city of Alexandria, which was undergoing attacks by Axis planes. The next September the group left for Cairo, and from there its pilots were sent to Great Britain. There they were retrained (in the Turnhouse area) in Spitfire V's and equipped with Spitfire IX's. After having adopted the designation of Squadron 341 of the RAF, the Alsace group made its first combat flights over France in 1943.

"Rather than leave our crews scattered in the RAF, I felt that it would be preferable to concentrate our efforts on forming a good unit that would show its French markings brilliantly in the Libyan campaign which was then imminent." Thus General Valin explains the formation of the Lorraine bomber group, which was organized on September 2, 1941, at the Damascus air base from Bomber Flight No. 2 and some of the crews of GRB No. 1. Its two flights were provided with Bristol Blenheim Mk IV's, with which they took part in the Libyan operations under the command of Lieutenant Colonel Corniglion-Molinier. The first mission was flown on November 21 with 5 planes. On November 28 the group registered its first losses with the disappearance of First Lieutenant de la Maisonneuve's crews. On December 13, abandoning his functions as chief of staff of the FAFL, Lieutenant Colonel Pijeaud arrived in Libya and replaced Lieutenant Colonel Corniglion-Molinier at the head of the Lorraine group. Pijeaud was to die under dramatic circumstances. Shot down, wounded, and made prisoner in the course of a bombing of Tobruk, he nevertheless succeeded in escaping. He then set out on a long walk in the desert and succeeded—how, no one knows—in reaching the British lines. He died in a hospital in January 1942. In him the FAFL lost one of their most representative figures. Major Pouliquen succeeded him on February 1, 1942, and led the Lorraine group in the actions of the Coastal Command during which an enemy submarine was destroyed. After an inspection by General Valin in the Middle East it was decided that the unit should depart for Great Britain. The crews embarked on the *Ordunia* and the *Empress of Canada* in October 1942. The voyage did not take place without incident: the second ship was torpedoed and sunk by a German submarine. Finally, the Lorraine group arrived in Glasgow in January 1943, came under the orders of Lieutenant Colonel de Rancourt, and received some Boston III A's. It flew its first combat sortie in Europe on June 12, 1943, after being given the designation of Squadron 342 of the RAF.

While the units in the Middle East were being organized, heated discussions were going on between navy men and aviators on the subject of the creation of the Ile-de-France group. The idea of forming an autonomous French fighter group dated back to early 1941, but the RAF had not shown much eagerness for the plan. If one adds to this the virulent polemic that developed on that subject between General Valin and Admiral Muselier, it is not surprising that it was not until October 1941 that the project took shape. The difference arose from the fact that the Ile-de-France group was to be composed of navy pilots and aviators, which explains why Muselier demanded its attachment to the Free French Naval Forces, while Valin called for its integration into the FAFL. Muselier then threatened to withdraw his pilots. But General de Gaulle settled the quarrel by deciding on the organization of the Ile-de-France group under the responsibility of the Free French Air Forces. Training began under the command of Squadron Leader Keith Lofts, and then in January 1942 the navy scored a point by getting the command of the new group entrusted to Lieutenant Commander de Scitivaux. Equipped with Spitfire V's, the Ile-de-France group carried out its first mission on April 10 in the sector of Cape Gris-Nez. It was on that occasion that Scitivaux was shot down and taken prisoner. The group also participated in the Dieppe raid (August 1942), during which operation it encountered the Luftwaffe's formidable Focke-Wulf Fw 190A's.

A French Fighter Group on the Eastern Front

Always driven by the understandable political desire to affirm wherever possible the French presence in the struggle on the side of the Allies, General de Gaulle envisaged early in 1942 the sending of a unit of the FAFL to the German-

After Major Tulasne's death in aerial combat, Major Pouyade took command of the Normandy fighter group and was replaced by Major Delfino in 1944.

Colonel de Marmier, after participating in the creation of the First Fighter Group in 1940, organized the military airlines that gave the FAFL considerable autonomy. He disappeared in the Mediterranean in December 1944.

Soviet front. The Soviet military attaché in London was informed of the wishes of the head of Free France early in February 1942, and on February 25 the general staff of the FAFL addressed a note on the subject to the Soviet military mission in Great Britain. The Soviet authorities replied that they would view the arrival of such a unit with favor and that they were giving careful study to the means involved. But, although they had given the project their approval in principle, the British reversed their decision and brought a great deal of pressure to bear on the leaders of Free France to renounce their intentions. General Valin was even summoned to the British secretary of state for war to be told that any insistence in this matter would lead to the pure and simple disappearance of the Free French Air Forces. Besides, the dealings with the Soviets were conducted through such complex channels that they were practically stopped. At one time the situation seemed so impossible of resolution that the FAFL chief of staff, weary of it, suggested to General de Gaulle that he give it up. He persisted, however, and he was right, for at the end of June Moscow finally approved the French proposals. On July 10 General Valin proceeded to organize, in the Middle East, Fighter Group No. 3, which was built around a nucleus consisting of officers from the Alsace group. It adopted the name Normandy in September 1942. As early as October 12 advance elements went to Teheran to prepare for the group's transit toward the Soviet Union, and the DC-3's carrying most of the personnel landed at the airfield near Teheran the very day after the signing in Moscow of the agreement authorizing the French presence. The French were then disembarked, on December 2, 1942, at the training center of Ivanovo, 250 kilometers northeast of the Soviet capital. The training started immediately on Yak 7's. Finally, in January 1943, the first combat planes arrived, Yak 1's, whose qualities delighted the aviators from Free France. On February 23 Major Pouliquen put the command of the Normandy group in the hands of Major Tulasne, and on March 22 the group's Yak 1's moved to a base close to the front, a few kilometers from Kaluga. The first encounter with the Germans took place on April 5, the first victory on the Normandy group's list. Reinforced by several Yak 9's, the group was thrown into the battle of Orel on July 5, 1943. It lost its commanding officer there on July 17 and was then sent to rest and await the Soviet autumn offensive.

New units were created in Africa as well. On January 1, 1942, the permanent air force detachment of Chad had given rise to the Brittany group (one flight, Rennes, of 6 Lysanders; another, Nantes, of 3 Glenn Martin 167's; and a liaison section), which, after accompanying General Leclerc in his offensive against the Italian posts of the Fezzan, joined hands with the British Eighth Army at Tripoli. Because of the decrepitude of its materiel, the group took no part in the Tunisian campaign. It had to wait until 1943 to be equipped by the Americans with B-26 Marauders.

Another unit, the Artois, was set up in Free French Africa on August 3, 1943. Its Lysanders and Avro Ansons were employed against the German submarines cruising in the Gulf of Guinea. The Picardy group, equipped with Blenheims and Potez 25 TOE's, took the responsibility for surveillance of the Middle East starting in June 1943. Finally, beginning in September 1941 Free France had at its disposal the military airlines (LAM) of Major, later Colonel, de Marmier, which gave them a certain independence of the Allies and which were destined to link the Middle East to Free French Africa and later to link Madagascar to Djibouti.

Thus in July 1943 at the time of the fusion with the air forces of Africa the FAFL had three fighter groups, two bomber groups, two coast defense groups, and a network of airlines. It was not much, to be sure, but the quality of the personnel made up for the small numbers, and the men who made up these units were the only ones who, from 1940 to 1942, symbolized the presence of the French Air Force on the side of the Allies.

CHAPTER V

The Rebirth of the French Air Force (1943–1945)

During the spring of 1942, although the possibility of a victorious return to France was still very remote, if not unforeseeable, General de Gaulle was already considering the introduction of a vast rearmament program applying to both the Free French Forces and to the units he planned to establish soon after the liberation of France. A plan worked out along these lines was submitted, in the form of proposals, to the representatives of the United States and Great Britain between July and September 1942. In taking the initiative the Free French desired above all to free themselves of the heavy restrictions which made it necessary for them, in everything that had to do with war materiel, to go through the channels of the British authorities, so that they could benefit directly from the advantages of the American Lend Lease Act. But the Roosevelt administration was reticent and ended up rejecting de Gaulle's proposals. It is true that the U.S. was already supplying enormous quantities of arms to China and the Soviet Union, but, most of all, Washington was hostile to de Gaulle and preferred General Henri Giraud to him, a man more capable, in the eyes of American political leaders, of rallying the whole of the French empire around himself.

All through the month of September 1942 fruitful meetings had taken place between several political and military figures in North Africa of the group of five and some of their transatlantic counterparts. These meetings had led the Americans to hope that their landing in Morocco and Algeria would encounter little resistance and that there was the prospect of a resumption of the fight against the Axis by the whole of French North Africa. These questions were raised anew on October 23, 1942, on the occasion of the secret interview at Cherchell in Algeria between General Clark and General Mast, Giraud's representative. A week later Robert Murphy, the American chargé d'affaires, reiterated Washington's promises to General Giraud and informed him of the application of Lend Lease for the benefit of the French army. Strong in these assurances, General Mast drew up a detailed rearmament plan known as the Mast Plan, which contemplated the creation of 8 infantry divisions, 2 armored divisions, and corresponding logistic and aerial support. Finding the project ambitious, the U.S. War Department declared in favor of giving the French the indispensable minimum. General H. H. Arnold, head of the U.S. Army Air Force, expressed a very lukewarm opinion on the air part of the program. He professed a certain distrust of French pilots, who had stubbornly resisted the attacks of the Allied air forces during "Operation Torch," and demanded proofs of their loyalty before any negotiations about supplying American planes. It was for that reason that he suggested having them first fight within squadrons of the USAAF before gradually putting them into wholly French units.

The French were not satisfied with that, however. As early as the middle of December General Giraud decided to modify the Mast Plan by giving it greater breadth and asking for the establishment of 8 infantry and 2 armored divisions.

Replenishment

In the revised Mast Plan the French gave the Americans to understand that they had enough flying personnel to operate an air fleet of 800 planes. But once again the Americans expressed their disapproval, explaining that because of the shortage of merchant vessels it was impossible to satisfy General Giraud's demands without seriously impeding the shipment of American reinforcements to the Mediterranean theater of operations. At the same time a French mission, which included General Béthouart and the civil commissioner Lemaigre-Dubreuil, left for the United States in order to establish the details of the rearmament of the French forces. Less than a month later the Anfa Conference somewhat relieved the uncertainties experienced by the Free French leaders. On the afternoon of January 19, 1943, General Giraud told the Americans and the British that he was ready to engage 300,000 men on their side. As for the air forces, he wanted them to comprise a thousand planes—500 fighters, 300 bombers, and 200 transport planes. The representatives of the USAAF and the RAF, General Arnold and Air Chief Marshal Portal, examined these figures and expressed the wish that the rearmed French air forces get into action as soon as possible side by side with the Allied air forces. Five days later the Allies promised General Giraud that they would equip the air force of Africa in accordance with French wishes.

The air force of Africa had urgent need of this new equipment. After the fighting that it had done from November 8 to 10 the air units of North Africa, equipped for the most part with outmoded planes, had strength only on paper. They still had nearly 250 planes (Dewoitine 520's and Curtiss H-75's for the fighter groups, LeO 45's and Douglas DB-7's for the bomber units, Bloch 174–175's for reconnaissance, and Amiot 143's and 354's and Potez 65's and 540's for transport), which there was no question of using for combat against their Luftwaffe counterparts but which might serve for training while they awaited conversion to American or British materiel. The fact remains that in spite of the fuel restrictions imposed by the German and Italian control commissions and the relatively reduced number of flight hours that had been granted them, the French pilots were of very high quality.

The conflicts with the Allies had barely ceased when, in his Directive No. 2 of November 21, 1942, General Giraud asked the responsible officers of the French Air Force to establish an air force employing the most modern airplanes and acting in close liaison with the ground forces. With this in mind General Mendigal, former senior air officer in North Africa and at that time commander in chief of the air forces in Africa, had planned, in an order of December 20, 1942, to mount an expeditionary air corps and to reorganize the Air Force. The reorganization was to take place in three stages: from November 15, 1942, to February 1, 1943—getting the units back in shape, continuing instruction with French materiel, beginning training with American materiel, perfecting the future organization, and incorporating and training the young recruits; from February 1 to April 1, 1943—realization of the new organization, instruction of the units in this new framework, disbanding of the units that had no further employment, and intensive operation of the schools; after April 1, 1943—possible engagement of the expeditionary air corps and functioning of the newly established organization.

Based on the mixed air groupings of which Lieutenant Colonel Gérardot had given an example in Tunisia, the expeditionary air corps consisted in an association of fighter, bomber, reconnaissance, and transport elements combined under a unified tactical command. It would employ three groupings each formed of three fighter groups, a dive-bombing group, a reconnaissance group, and a group of medium bombers. In addition, it included reserve elements consisting of a fighter group, three medium bomber groups, a battalion of parachutists, and an air command attached to the French armored corps. In this way the Air Force could have a large unit endowed with great fire power and adapted to modern warfare.

But the difficulties encountered by the high-ranking officers of the air forces, both in connection with materiel and personnel and in their relations with the Allies, rendered the creation of an expeditionary air corps improbable and then quite simply impossible. The mobilization carried out in North Africa and in French West Africa, a colony that had joined General Giraud, had brought the French Air Force human resources that were far from corresponding to what it had expected. Moreover, the training of the young recruits encountered such obstacles that practically nothing had been done before the establishment of a real plan for the rearmament of French aviation. In the area of materiel the situation was just as dramatic. Although General Béthouart had submitted the French aerial rearmament plan to General Arnold, the planes were delivered to the air forces of Africa in dribs and drabs. Thus, while the Americans had promised to supply, by the end of March 1943, 90 P-39 Airacobras, 67 A-35 bombers, and approximately 60 C-78 transports, only 30 P-39's had arrived in Africa by that time. Of course, the British had turned over to the French several Spitfires taken from their reserves in the Mediterranean

The P-39 Airacobras supplied to the French Air Force by the Americans carried out mainly Coastal Command missions in the Mediterranean and, in 1945, participated in the fighting in the Alps.

Accompanied by General Valin, General Bouscat visits some French pilots. He commanded the French Air Forces from July 1943 to May 1945 and was appointed Air Force inspector general and later chief of the Air Force general staff (March to September 1946).

theater of operations, but it was with the stipulation that they must not leave that theater.

In fact, the essential problem lay in the concept of the employment of the air forces. The difficulties that had arisen in connection with the Lafayette fighter group GC II/5 were a clear indication of that. This unit had been reequipped before any of the others because during the First World War many American aviators had fought in it. When the P-40's which the USAAF had supplied it were received and the GC II/5 was ready for action, the Americans opposed its being placed at the disposal of the French ground forces and demanded that the Lafayette group be transferred to their big air command. Although this arrangement took a valuable adjunct away from the French troops engaged in Tunisia, General Giraud found himself obliged to accept it. In any case, the Americans were pleased with the gesture, supplied 6 P-38 reconnaissance planes to the GR II/33, and authorized several bomber crews to get their training in B-25's, A-20's, or B-26's. Finally, the groups in the process of conversion to P-39's or A-35's were made acquainted with the American materiel. In reality, while the Allies conceived of the support of ground operations as a joint action carried on at the level of a big command and directed from end to end by one and the same chief, the French were inclined to disperse their resources (to the detriment of the principle of the concentration of forces) among the large units of the ground forces. During the talks of May 1943 certain Allied officials had given General Mendigal's chief of staff, General Montrelay, to understand that the rearming of the French Air Force was subordinated to the creation of an independent French air command. Satisfying the desiderata of the Americans and the British posed a double problem to the leaders of the French air forces: fighting against the French army for their independence and putting an early end to the organization of the expeditionary air corps already begun under the responsibility of General Gama.

For it was evident that the Allies could not tolerate the existence of such an organization, since they were interested only in the integration of the reequipped French units into their big air commands. It was General Bouscat that had to take on this double mission.

The Fusion

With the establishment of the Committee of National Liberation in Algiers on June 3, 1943, General Bouscat, who had been one of the chief figures in the contacts between de Gaulle and Giraud, took over as commander in chief of the Air Forces of Africa.

At that time the Tunisian campaign had just ended in an Allied success. Certain units of the French Air Force had participated in that campaign from its very beginning. The GR II/33, with its Bloch 174's, had accomplished many reconnaissance and dive-bombing missions. The GB I/25 and II/23 had been used to convoy from Morocco the munitions and materiel indispensable to the French troops fighting on the Tunisian front. They were then transferred to the North Tactical Air Force to make night bombing attacks on Rommel's retreating troops. Shortly before the capitulation of the German forces encircled at Cape Bon, the GC II/7, equipped with Spitfires, made its entry into operations. Finally, the Lafayette GC II/5, first in its P-40 Warhawks and then in its P-40 Tomahawks, had fought in the 33rd Fighter Group within the framework of the 12th Support Command, and then, attached to the Mediterranean Allied Coastal Command, it had undertaken Coastal Command actions, that is, providing cover for convoys in the Mediterranean and searching for crews that had fallen into the sea.

During this time General Bouscat was working on General Giraud, trying to obtain from him the independence of the air forces. On June 10, 1943, a meeting with Air Vice-Marshal Wingglesworth, assistant to Air Chief Marshal Tedder, had convinced him that there would be no massive rearmament before the establishment of a separate air command. He therefore asked the French Committee of National Liberation to confer on him the functions of commander in chief of the air forces simultaneously with the powers of secretary of state for aviation, insisting that it would be illusory to try to organize the participation of the French air forces in the fighting in any theater of operations within the framework of a single interallied command if the commander of the air forces was not responsible to the central French authorities or to such an agency constituted within the Committee of National Liberation to oversee the conduct of the war. The taking of such a position provoked a veritable outcry and an immediate reaction in army and navy circles, the tone of which was reminiscent of the debates over doctrine during the interwar period. But General Bouscat held firm and stuck to his demands. He knew that no other solution existed and that for the moment it was necessary to make concessions to the Allies. On June 30, 1943, he proclaimed the dissolution of the expeditionary air corps, a somewhat untimely idea in the context of 1943, and then introduced the final modifications into his draft plan for the reorganization of the French Air Force. On July 1 General Giraud gave his consent, except in regard to the transfer of the Aéronavale, the Naval Air Force, to the French Air Forces, and General Bouscat assumed the title of chief of the general staff of the French Air Forces and the functions of commander of aviation. The new organization was aimed at adapting the Air Force to combined operations with the army and navy within the framework of the Allied high command. It was based on the need to make better use of the territorial organization that existed in Africa and was aimed at placing at the disposal of the Allies, as they were provided with equipment, French units that were well trained and schooled and provided with the technical resources and services indispensable for participating in operations. In addition, it tended to avoid loss of contact with the units engaged in the big Allied commands. The French Air Force would thus comprise: a general staff, military and technical inspectorates, liaison detachments with the

Allied tactical commands and services, territorial command outfits, air formations, airborne infantry formations, air artillery units, schools for the training and advanced instruction of personnel, and ground units, depots, and services.

Besides the problem of controlling the units placed at the Allies' disposal, resolved by setting up liaison detachments, the formation of training centers was another outstanding feature of this organization. Those of North Africa, all in Morocco, were intended only for those who already had a certain amount of aeronautical experience: the school for practical training of flying personnel in Marrakech, created on January 1, 1943, the school for advanced pilot training in Casbah-Tadla, the school for firing and specialists' training in Agadir. The Air School in Morocco was also reopened.

In addition, the Americans opened wide the doors of their schools to uninitiated French personnel: Creek Field, Alabama, for student pilots and advanced pursuit; Turner Field, Georgia, for bombing; Tyndall Field, Florida, for machine-gunners; Lowry Field, Colorado, for armament technicians; and Scott Field, Illinois, for radiomen. After acquiring individual training in these schools, the men went to the practical schools in North Africa and then to the three Operational Training Units operating under the command of the North West African Training Command: American fighter planes in Berteaux, American bombers in Telergma, and English fighter planes in Sétif, Algeria.

All this, however, was only the first stage, for General Bouscat had provided that the Air Force should be allowed to develop and acquire increased independence of command each year. The authority of the Allies was necessary for this because of the special characteristics of the planes and the need to harmonize the tactical methods of employment. The evolution then took place by successive creations of larger and larger French commands, such as squadrons and brigades.

On July 3, two days after taking up his new duties, the chief of the general staff of the air forces addressed a veritable appeal for unity to all the air formations of North Africa, the Middle East, West Africa, Equatorial Africa, Djibouti, and Madagascar.

Henceforth the French Air Force is a homogeneous, coherent, indissoluble whole. May the unity of our thoughts and of our hearts deeply seal together the two blocs recently combined. May discipline, the supreme strength, harmoniously guide and unite, with a view toward a single effort, all our individualities and all our particularisms. May the wind that blows over the peaks where the life-giving military virtues blossom—duty, the spirit of sacrifice, love of country—sweep away the mediocrities, pettinesses, and impurities that remain.

Finally, the same day, in a general order to the FAFL, General Valin made the fusion official.

At the moment when I am leaving the command of the Free French Air Forces I should like to repeat a statement that I made on the London radio on April 10, 1941, addressing our comrades who were subject to the Vichy régime: "Having come here without personal ambition, I do not aspire to resume my place in the French Air Force until the day when it resumes the struggle." That day has arrived. Air Corps Commander Bouscat has just been appointed chief of staff of the French air forces. . . . Last May, leaving my own position out of consideration and faithful to my policy line, I had suggested to General de Gaulle, before his departure, the solution that I thought would best realize the unity of the Air Force. That solution has finally been adopted. . . . We shall now serve under the orders of a great leader and an aviator who has all his life given a thousand testimonies of his energy and spirit. I am convinced that you will serve under his orders with the same devotion and the same loyalty that you have always shown to me.

Plan VII

On July 13 General Bouscat announced to the Joint Rearmament Committee that his staff was putting the finishing touches on a rearmament plan. Three days later, after a meeting held in Algiers, the Permanent Military Committee recognized the necessity of presenting a detailed overall program in that area. On July 24 the chief of the general staff

From 1943 to 1945 the American training schools were opened to several thousand flying personnel of the reconstituted French Air Force. Here, a Boeing Stearman used for basic pilot training.

A North American NAA-57 of the advanced training school at Casbah-Tadla, Morocco. Besides being trained in North Africa, Air Force personnel were trained as pilots in the United States from 1943 on.

of the air forces decided on the dissolution of the air rearmament service, which was organized by General Mendigal in May 1943 and which had never been very effective. Four days earlier the draft of Plan VII, a name chosen to show the continuity with the plans carried out in 1940, had been completed. It set a strength of 20,520 military men, 6,500 civilians, and 5,000 women of the auxiliary services for the Air Force for July 1944. This personnel would operate 500 airplanes—8 fighter groups, 6 groups in the Coastal Command, 1 reconnaissance group, and 4 transport groups in the Mediterranean theater of operations, 4 fighter groups and 3 bomber groups in Great

Britain, and 2 fighter groups in the Soviet Union. The Americans had promised to provide the equipment for certain flying formations in North Africa (3 GC's, fighter groups, with P-39's, 6 GC's with P-47's, 6 GB's, bomber groups, with B-26 Marauders, 1 GR, reconnaissance group, with P-38's, 2 GT's, transport groups, with C-45's and C-47's), some antiaircraft units, and a regiment of parachutists. The British committed themselves to furnishing Spitfires for 6 fighter groups, Bostons for a bomber group, and Halifaxes for two other groups of the same type, as well as the materiel needed to reequip two regiments of FAFL parachutists. On August 8, 1943, at a meeting that took place in Algiers, Plan VII was submitted for the approval of the Allies. At that meeting Air Chief Marshal Tedder announced the creation of a joint Anglo-American commission, the Joint Air Commission, to take the matter of French aerial rearmament in hand. Headed by General Saville, it was established in Algiers on September 6 and quickly set out to establish a reequipment program based on Plan VII, the existence of which Bouscat had revealed. On September 29 Plan VII was definitively adopted, and on October 22 the Council of National Defense approved its contents.

The fact still remains that all was not well at that time in the French Air Force. The fusion of the air forces of Africa with the FAFL had given rise to a definite moral uneasiness, and the differences that had arisen in that connection between certain Free French aviators and those of the armed forces of the armistice forced General Bouscat to adopt stern measures to put an end to the crisis. On December 3, 1943, the chief of the general staff of the French Air Forces completely prohibited taking up "any subject of conversation that is political in character, any discussion bearing on the position of France before or after the Armistice, any political and military controversy, and in general any subject on which a stated point of view may lead to a contradiction."

Moreover, the realization of Plan VII was not effected without great difficulties. In September 1943 the Air Force marshaled only two groups of Spitfires (I/3 and II/7), three of P-39's (I/4, I/5, and III/6), and one, the II/5, equipped with P-40's. In the bomber section, GB I/25 and II/23 had just left for Great Britain for the purpose of obtaining Halifax heavy bombers before their integration into the Bomber Command. Four other formations were to get B-25's or B-26's. As for transport aviation, it would not receive its materiel until the end of the first half of 1944. There was only a single reconnaissance group, the II/33, equipped with six P-38's. In November, however, the situation had improved. Three fighter groups and a bomber group were operating from English bases; eight fighter groups and a reconnaissance group were fighting with the big Allied commands in the Mediterranean, chiefly on Coastal Command missions—on September 11 the year before, Pierre Le Gloan, of the Roussillon (GC III/6), died in a sortie of this type—and the Normandy fighter group was serving on the German-Soviet front. This represented nearly 250 planes. But, nevertheless, the Air Force was suffering from a personnel crisis (in November 1943 it had a strength of 34,302, including 1,778 flying officers and 1,205 nonflying officers, plus 4,487 flying noncommissioned officers and enlisted men and 26,852 nonflying ones) that could be solved only by recovering men from France proper—a rather remote prospect at the time—or by tapping certain units of the ground forces. This does not alter the fact that the organization had evolved, so that at the end of 1943 the air forces were subdivided as follows: a general staff and some directorates in Algiers and territorial commands with authority over all elements except the units engaged (command of the French air forces in Great Britain, air commands in Algeria, Tunisia, Morocco, Corsica, the Middle East, French West Africa, French Equatorial Africa, and East Africa). As early as November 14, 1943, the creation in Corsica of the 1st Fighter Squadron (GC II/7, Nice, I/3, Corsica, and I/7, Provence) marked a first step toward the establishment of major French operational commands. At about the same time the formations set up on the basis of the African forces obtained, after a lively

B-26 Marauders in action over Italy in 1944. These planes belong to the Brittany bomber group.

argument with General Valin, the right to bear names of French provinces, following the example of the FAFL groups.

The Return to France

In November 1943 General Bouscat, foreseeing an early return to the territory of France proper, had worked out, on the basis of information furnished by the Béthouart mission and within the limits set by the Committee of National Defense, a new rearmament program called Plan VIII. This plan was based essentially on the utilization of the manpower that would become available through the liberation of France. It was a logical sequel to Plan VII, and it was intended to give rise, between July 1, 1944, and April 1, 1946, to the creation of 123 air groups fit to participate in the continuation of the war in all foreign theaters of operations: 33 single-engined fighter groups of 25 planes each, 20 twin-engined fighter groups of 25 planes, 18 heavy bomber groups of 12 planes, 23 medium bomber groups of 13 planes, 11 reconnaissance groups of 13 planes, and 18 transport groups of 16 planes, with all the necessary services. At the completion of the plan the French Air Force would be capable of putting into action 1,325 fighters, 216 heavy bombers, 299 medium bombers, 288 transport planes, and 143 reconnaissance planes.

But it was still necessary to be able to set foot on the actual territory of France, an event in which the Air Force desired to play an effective part. General Valin had been carrying on negotiations along those lines with the British authorities since the beginning of 1944. He had obtained the participation in the landing operations of all the air forces based in Great Britain and of the two regiments of FAFL parachutists. Three fighter groups and one bomber group, the Lorraine, were thus assigned to the 2nd Tactical Air Force, while another fighter unit was attached to the Air Defence of Great Britain, constituting at the same time a potential reserve for employment in the Tactical Air Force. But the discussions had also borne upon the direct intervention of the French air command in the conduct of operations. On that point the Allies had turned obstinate and had replied that they would not make a decision until after the liberation of France.

On the eve of the landing the French air forces were divided between the British Isles and the Mediterranean theater of operations. In the former were the two FAFL groups Ile-de-France and Alsace for pursuit and Lorraine for bombing. In addition, two bomber groups from the air forces of Africa had arrived on the spot, been given Halifaxes, and then, renamed Guyenne (Squadron 347) and Tunisia (Squadron 346), had been transferred into the Bomber Command. In December 1943 the GC I/2 Storks (Squadron 329) landed in turn and were given Spitfire V's and then Spitfire IX's, and were followed in January 1944 by the II/2 Berry group (Squadron 345), which was also provided with Spitfires. The fighter groups stationed in Great Britain carried out missions of air defense of the territory and neutralization of the German pursuit and antiaircraft on the continent preparatory to the invasion. The Lorraine group sent its Bostons against the V-1 launching ramps and the lines of communication in the north of France and in Belgium.

In the Mediterranean, after the liberation of Corsica the organization of squadrons was continued and even accelerated. On January 1, 1944, the GC I/4, Navarre, I/5, Champagne, and III/6, Roussillon, had given birth to the 3rd Fighter Squadron, which, equipped with P-39 Airacobras, carried out Coastal Command operations. Three months later the GB I/22, Morocco, I/19, Gascony, and II/20, Brittany (FAFL) formed the 31st Bomber Squadron with B-26 Marauders, and on May 1, 1944, reequipped with P-47 Thunderbolts, the GC II/5, Lafayette, II/3, Dauphiné, and III/3, Ardennes, constituted a 4th Fighter Squadron destined for the Tactical Command (pursuit and bombing). Toward the end of 1943 the fighter groups Nice and Corsica together with the 1st flight of the reconnaissance group II/33 had flown numerous sorties over Italy. But just before the offensive against Rome the Air Force had at its disposal in Italy 11 formations of the 1st and 3rd

A crew from the Lorraine group in front of the Boston III's that the Free French unit received on its arrival in Great Britain early in 1943.

General de Gaulle reviewing the pilots of the Ile-de-France fighter group in Great Britain. This unit had the peculiarity of having in its ranks pilots from the French Air Force and from the Aéronavale (the Naval Air Service), hence the difficulties involved in its formation.

Fighter Squadrons and the 31st Bomber Squadron, whose role in breaking through the German front and in exploiting the success toward the Italian capital was not negligible.

Among the 11,000 Allied planes that covered the landing in Normandy on June 6, 1944, were those of the Lorraine and Berry groups. The former also hung a curtain of smoke along a beach on which the American troops were gaining a foothold. On June 13 the Spitfires of the Ile-de-France and Alsace groups landed for the first time on French soil. The Guyenne and Tunisia groups took action several times to destroy the German defenses around Caen and in the Falaise-Argentan pocket. On board their Typhoons the Free French pilots serving in the RAF were engaged against the armored divisions that were trying to cut the lines of the American 3rd Army in the Avranches area.

Over 5,000 Allied planes, including 250 French ones, provided continuous air support to "Operation Anvil-Dragon," which, launched on August 15, 1944, was aimed at the liberation of the south of France and joining hands with the troops coming from Normandy. Shortly after the landing in Provence the P-38 reconnaissance planes bearing French markings had made deep incursions over occupied territory. It was during one of these incursions, on July 31, 1944, that the aviator/writer Antoine de Saint-Exupéry disappeared, shot down by a Focke-Wulf 190. On August 15 the fighter-bombers of the 4th Squadron attacked the lines of communication of the Riviera, while the bomber groups assaulted the important bridge of Sisteron.

During the last months of 1944, when the French air groups were accompanying the Allied armies in their advance toward the frontiers of Germany, important changes were made in the Air Force's organization. In September the general staff had left Algiers to establish itself in Paris, where the following month an Air Ministry directed by Charles Tillon replaced the Air Commissariat that had been created in North Africa the preceding April. About the same time it was considered necessary to regroup the scattered French units. In July 1944 an agreement had been concluded with the Americans on the establishment of a French Tactical Air Command subordinate to an American Tactical Air Force. On September 1 a French

A P-38 Lightning of the Belfort reconnaissance group, II/33.

section of the 12th Tactical Air Command was set up. It did not direct any unit until the following November 15, when, after its transformation into a tactical command (French Forces of the Rhône and the Rhine), it received the 1st (Spitfire) and 4th (Thunderbolt) fighter squadrons as well as the tactical and strategic reconnaissance flights of the II/33. But while the command of the Air Forces of the Rhône and the Rhine left the American 12th Tactical Air Command on November 13, 1944, it was not until December 1 that it officially became the 1st French Air Corps (1st CAF).

At the beginning, and until the Pursuit and Air Defense Grouping (C.G.D.A.) came into action, the 1st CAF was dependent on the Americans for everything that had to do with communications. The part it played was no less important on that account, for it had to provide the French ground forces with all the air support that was necessary and at the same time carry out reconnaissance missions and provide escort for medium bomber expeditions (the 31st and 34th Squadrons, the latter created in Sardinia in September along with the GB I/32, Burgundy, II/63, Senegal, and II/52, Franche-Comté) mounted by the 1st Tactical Air Force (TAF).

On November 28, 1944, the air forces of the Atlantic were established. These forces, destined to deal with the German garrisons shut up in the French ports of the Atlantic coast, absorbed the many units formed with personnel from France proper at the time of its liberation: GB Dor, which became I/31, Aunis (Junkers 88's), GB I/34, Béarn (Douglas DB-7's), GC I/18, Vendée (Dewoitine 520's and Douglas A-24 Dauntlesses), GC II/18, Saintonge, derived from the group Doret (Dewoitine 520's), and GR III/33, Périgord (Fieseler Storchs). Finally, beginning in October 1944 and in spite of the opposition of the Americans, an air grouping of the Alps, equipped with Morane 500's, had been brought into action to support the French mountain troops. After having adopted the designation of aviation of the Alpine sector in November, it became GR I/35 and was attached to the 1st CAF.

Although the aeronautics industry had been dismantled by the occupying forces, those responsible for air policy decided during the first few weeks following the liberation to get it under way again. Their task would not be easy, however, since more than a third of the covered areas had been destroyed and the Germans had shipped nearly 30 percent of the machine tools to Germany. The labor force (40,000 persons) was not very large, either. Nevertheless, a plan called the 1944–1945 Plan was adopted, and the manufacturers received enormous orders: 4,926 planes and 8,828 engines. It was primarily a question of continuing the manufactures begun by the Germans (Ju 52's, Siebel 204's, Fieseler 156's, Do 24's, Bf 108's, Me 208's, and Fw 190's) and putting the emphasis on certain French models researched in secret under the occupation and promised at a certain time in the future (SO-161's, SO-94's, SO-30 R's, and Morane 472's). The fact remains that the relaunching of the aeronautics industry was laborious and that the job of getting the factories producing again dragged on for some time. At the end of the second half of 1944 only 95 planes and 53 engines had come off the assembly lines. But the recovery of thousands of machine tools in Germany and Austria dramatically improved the results for 1945, which exceeded the planners' expectations.

Victory

At the beginning of 1945 the French air forces were split up among five well-defined theaters of operations: 1) British and Canadian armies—Lorraine, Alsace, Berry, and Storks; 2) First French Army and American armies—General Gérardot's

M. Tillon, the minister of air, returns the colors of the Normandy-Niemen Regiment to its commanding officer, Lieutenant Colonel Delfino, in the courtyard of the Hôtel des Invalides, Paris, on June 21, 1945.

1st CAF (in which the GR I/33, Belfort, and II/33, Savoy, with P-51's, had been organized on January 1, 1945) and groups of medium bombers; 3) aviation of the Alps sector—GR I/35; 4) air forces of the Atlantic—GC I/18 and II/18, GB I/31 and I/34, and GR III/33; and 5) the German-Soviet front—the Normandy-Niemen regiment. In addition, the heavy bomber groups Tunisia and Guyenne were operating with the Bomber Command.

In February 1945, when the British launched their offensive toward the Rhine, the Lorraine, Berry, Storks, and Ile-de-France groups (the latter reequipped with Spitfire XVI's) made attacks on the enemy lines of communication in the midst of fearful antiaircraft barrages. The Ile-de-France and the Alsace groups then supported the troops who, after the annihilation of the town of Wesel on March 23 by a force of heavy bombers, crossed the Rhine. The Lorraine, equipped at the end of March with Mitchell B-25 twin-engined planes, flew its last sortie early in May.

In January the forces of the First Army were employed in Alsace in eliminating the Colmar pocket. The bomber groups participated in this operation engaging 66 Marauders on January 23. But the planes could not accomplish their mission because of the frost that interfered with the sights. Toward the end of the month the Tactical Command missions were intensified (248 sorties by the 3rd Squadron, 276 by the 4th). In the course of one of these missions Major Marin La Meslée met his death in a P-47. During this period the Flak was dangerous, for from January 19 to February 28, 7 fighter-bombers were shot down and 41 others were damaged by it. On the night of March 30–31, when the French First Army prepared to cross the Rhine, the 1st CAF lined up 98 P-47's, 40 Spitfires, and 11 Mustang P-51's (II/33) employed for tactical reconnaissance. The 11th Bomber Brigade (31st and 34th Squadrons) and the strategic reconnaissance group I/33, Belfort, were then operating at the army group level. The final offensive had been prepared for by air attacks intended to sweep from the sky the new German jet fighters, the Messerschmitt 262's, which were proving more and more aggressive. To avoid aerial combat with this adversary, which, to say the least, would have been dangerous, the air forces operated by sweeps over the enemy airfields. At the same time the fighter-bombers attacked the lines of communication in the aim of isolating the defenders of the front lines. Thus from March 15 to 25 the 1st TAF, to which the 1st CAF was subordinated, had flown 13,281 sorties, dropped 7,000 tons of bombs, and fired 1,000 rockets. From March 15 to 19 the French pilots had destroyed 2 airplanes, 30 locomotives, 486 railroad cars, 4 stations, 4 switchyards, a turntable, an electric power plant, a factory, and a gasholder and damaged thousands of railroad cars and automotive vehicles. At the time of the crossing of the Rhine the Spitfires of the 1st Squadron undertook the high-altitude cover, and the P-47's of the 4th Squadron provided close support for the ground units. The 3rd Squadron was assigned to provide a box barrage around the battlefield. The stubborn resistance of the German army obliged the P-47's of the Ardennes group to bomb certain sections of the city of Karlsruhe, which fell on April 4. The French B-26's were engaged before Schweinfurt to open the road to the ground troops. Then, beginning on April 16 the campaign entered its final phase. Driven from the sky or grounded for lack of fuel, the Luftwaffe made only timid appearances, and the German pilots generally avoided combat. A second fighter squadron, composed of the FAFL groups of Great Britain, came to reinforce the 1st CAF on April 24 and to provide the air support necessary for the liquidation of the pockets in the Black Forest. On May 5 at 1400 hours air actions were suspended. For the French pilots the war was over.

While the French First Army was breaking through into Germany the 5th Fighter Squadron (GC II/6, Travail, II/9, Auvergne, and I/9, Limousin), without the I/9, applied itself, together with the GR I/35, to furthering the advance of the French troops on the Alpine Front, created in March 1945. Beginning on April 9 the P-39's of GC II/6 and II/9 played an important part by destroy-

From the time of the liberation the FFI's (French Forces of the Interior) set up fighter units equipped with Dewoitine 520's abandoned by the Germans at Tarbes and at Toulouse. These planes formed the basis of the Saintonge and Vendée fighter groups.

A French Halifax over Paris. The heavy bomber groups Guyenne and Tunisia, which operated within the Bomber Command to the end of the war, were equipped with these four-engined planes.

A B-25 Mitchell of the Lorraine group, the unit which received the first planes of this type at the end of March 1945.

Integrated into the air forces of the Atlantic, the GB I/31, Aulis, formerly GB Dor, used Junkers Ju 88's taken from the Luftwaffe.

ing, sometimes in dive-bombing attacks, the enemy command posts and lines of communication.

It was also in April that the forces of the Atlantic took the offensive in their turn. Certain units, handicapped by overly worn-out materiel, had been reequipped with Spitfire V's. But for the most part the groups had kept their old planes. They were supported, however, by powerful formations of B-26 Marauders of the 42nd Wing and of B-17's and B-24's of the 8th Air Force based in Great Britain. Begun on April 14—in the meantime, the P-47's of the 3rd Squadron had arrived—the annihilation of the German garrison of Royan took four days. The crews of the GR III/33 put in up to ten hours of flying time a day, while those of the GC III/6 dropped 377 tons of bombs. Finally, on April 30 it was the turn of the island of Oléron.

Also in April the Normandy-Niemen regiment, stationed in East Prussia, carried out its last actions. The path traveled since the summer of 1943 had been a long one. In September of that year the Normandy had taken part in the offensive in the direction of Smolensk. Satisfied with the French pilots' comportment, the Soviets had then accepted the transformation of the group into a regiment and had even mentioned the possibility of setting up a second fighter regiment and a bomber regiment to constitute an air division to be called the France. In the meantime, the Americans, who, as was noted, undertook part of the rearming of the French Air Force, had expressed their opposition to sending any trained personnel to the Soviet Union. In spite of everything, the Normandy unit officially took the designation of a fighter regiment on January 1, 1944. Integrated into the 303rd Fighter Division of the Soviet First Air Army, it distinguished itself most especially in the fighting connected with the crossing of the Niemen, July 28 to August 5, 1944. Then, equipped with Yak 3's, the best fighter plane of the time, it arrived in East Prussia. It was there that on October 23, 1944, the French pilots learned that their unit had the right thereafter to add the title of the Niemen regiment to its original name. The taking of Königsberg and Pillau marked the end of operations for them. The 273 victories won by the pilots (Albert, Delfino, de la Poype, Littolf, André, Tulasne, Sauvage, Durand, Pouyade, and many others) had made it the top fighter unit of the French Air Force.

From June 1940 to May 1945, 1,000 of the Air Force's flying personnel had been killed and 500 wounded. French aviation claimed 675 enemy planes shot down, to which must be added 244 probables. The four fighter groups based in England (Alsace, Ile-de-France, Berry, and Storks) had flown 19,804 sorties and had 88 sure victories

General Corniglion-Molinier, who rallied Free France in 1941 and then commanded the Reserve Bomber Group No. 1, the groups Lorraine and Alsace, and the FAFL in the Middle East. He later directed the air forces of the Atlantic and was promoted to general at the time of the liberation. After the war he pursued a brilliant political career.

Marcel Albert, from the fighter group Ile-de-France, was among the first pilots assigned to the Normandy. He ended the war with the rank of captain and had 24 aerial victories, including 2 probable ones. This earned him the position of second-ranking French ace of World War II.

and 12 probables with a loss of 115 pilots (84 killed, 10 missing, 21 prisoners, and 2 wounded). Among the groups that came from North Africa, the Corsica flew 3,200 sorties, the Provence 3,000, the Nice 6,200, and the Navarre 4,000.

The bombers had dropped 16,000 tons of bombs in the course of 2,583 sorties for the heavy groups, 4,884 for the medium groups, and 3,059 for the Lorraine. But the sacrifices had been extremely heavy. The Guyenne and the Tunisia counted 175 killed, 35 missing, 41 prisoners, and 26 wounded. The Lorraine had 108 killed. As for medium bomber units, they had lost 100 killed, 34 missing, 8 prisoners, and 6 wounded.

The reconnaissance groups Belfort and Savoy had flown 2,305 missions, in the course of which 4 men had been killed, 2 were listed as missing, and 4 had fallen into the hands of the enemy.

In 1945 the knot had been tied, and it was a unified Air Force that had won the victory. No one could do it homage better than the man that had unified it in July 1943, General Bouscat: "If ever the term élite army has been deserved," he wrote, "it is to the Armée de l'Air that it must be applied. In the eyes of history it will remain the honor of French aviation. The efforts and the sacrifices have been crowned with success. It was thus with a certain pride that those who had lived through the winning of air zones North and East in North Africa could measure the distance traveled. The shame was wiped out. It was possible to come back into the ranks, the task accomplished, each one bearing in himself, with dignity, the finest recompense. Is it not the essential thing that, symbolically, the laurels shall bloom on the tombs of Mouchotte, Marin la Meslée, and Saint-Exupéry?" (René Bouscat, *De Gaulle–Giraud: Dossier d'une mission*, Flammarion, Paris, 1967, pp. 224–225).

After escaping from Syria in December 1940 Jean Tulasne commanded the fighter group Alsace. In September 1942 he was placed at the head of the Normandy. He died in aerial combat over the U.S.S.R., July 17, 1943.

A Yak 3 flown by Léon Ougloff on a free pursuit mission in the vicinity of Königsberg in 1945. The wing of Roger Sauvage's Yak 3 is visible in the foreground; he was one of the aces of the Normandy-Niemen.

French Units Activated in Africa, Reequipped in England, and Placed under British Tactical Command

Unit	Date of Engagement	Campaigns	Materiel
GB I/11	March 1943	Tunisia	A part of this unit engaged with the GB I/25
GB II/61	March 1943	Tunisia	3 planes detached to the GB I/25
GB I/25 Tunisia (RAF Squadron 347)	January 1943	Tunisia France Germany	Le0 45's, then Halifaxes
GB II/23 Guyenne (RAF Squadron 346)	January 1943	Tunisia France Germany	Le0 45's, then Halifaxes
GC I/2 Storks (RAF Squadron 329)	March 1944	Belgium Normandy Netherlands Germany	Spitfire V's, then Spitfire IX's
GC II/2 Berry (RAF Squadron 345)	April 1944	France Belgium Netherlands Germany	Spitfire IX's

Air Forces Activated in Africa, Reequipped in North Africa, and Placed under American Tactical Command

Unit	Date of Engagement	Campaigns	Materiel
2nd Flight of the GR II/33, which became GR II/33 Savoy	November 1942	Tunisia Italy Corsica France Germany	Bloch 174's, Spitfire IX's, P-51 Mustangs
1st Flight of the GR II/33, which became GR I/33 Belfort	November 1942	Tunisia Italy Corsica France Germany	Bloch 174's, P-38 Lightnings, and P-51's
GB I/22 Morocco	April 1943	Tunisia Italy France Germany Atlantic Pockets	Glenn Martin 167's B-26 Marauders
GB II/20 Brittany GB I/19 Gascony	June 1944	Italy France Germany Atlantic Pockets	See FAFL B-26 Marauders

Air Forces Activated in Africa, Reequipped in North Africa, and Placed under American Tactical Command; continued

Unit	Date of Engagement	Campaigns	Materiel
GB II/52 Franche-Comté	August 1944	Italy France Germany Atlantic Pockets	B-26 Marauders
GB I/32 Burgundy	September 1944	Italy France Germany Atlantic Pockets	B-26 Marauders
GB II/63 Senegal	September 1944	Italy France Germany Atlantic Pockets	B-26 Marauders
GC II/7 Nice (RAF Squadron 326)	May 1943	Tunisia Algeria Corsica Italy France Germany	Spitfire V's and IX's
GC I/7 Provence (RAF Squadron 328)	October 1943	Corsica Italy France Germany	Spitfire V's and IX's
GC I/3 Corsica (RAF Squadron 327)	August 1943	Corsica Italy France Germany	Spitfire V's and IX's
GC I/4 Navarre	September 1943	Italy France Germany Atlantic Pockets	P-39 Airacobras and P-47 Thunderbolts
GC III/6 Roussillon	August 1943	Italy France Germany Atlantic Pockets	P-39's and P-47's
GC II/5 Lafayette	January 1943	Tunisia Italy France Germany	P-40 Warhawks P-40 Tomahawks P-47's
GC III/3 Ardennes	February 1944	Palestine North Africa France Germany	P-39's and P-47's
GC II/3 Dauphiné	November 1943	North Africa Corsica Italy France Germany	P-39's and P-47's

Air Forces Activated in Africa, Reequipped in North Africa, and Placed under American Tactical Command; continued

Unit	Date of Engagement	Campaigns	Materiel
GC II/6 Travail	August 1944	Mediterranean Coasts Italy	P-39's
GC II/9 Auvergne	April 1945	Italy	P-39's
GC I/9 Limousin	April 1945	Algeria	P-39's
GT I/15 Touraine	December 1944	France Germany	C-47 Dakotas
GT II/15 Anjou	December 1942	Tunisia France	C-47's in 1945
GT III/15 Maine	April 1945	Germany	C-47's
GT I/34 Béarn	1944		C-47's
Flight I/56 Vaucluse	April 1944	France Greece Italy Balkans	Special missions

Air Forces Activated in France Proper

Unit	Date of Engagement	Campaigns	Materiel
GR III/33 Périgord	November 1944	Graves Royan La Rochelle Saint-Nazaire	Fieseler Storks
GB I/34 Béarn	August 1944		Formed in Africa as transport unit and converted to bomber group in France
GB I/31 Aunis, or Dor	October 1944	Royan Graves La Rochelle	Ju 88's
GC I/18 Vendée	August 1944	Lorient Saint-Nazaire Royan Graves	Dewoitine 520's and A-24's
GC I/18 Saintonge, formerly Doret	August 1944	La Rochelle Saint-Nazaire Lorient	Dewoitine 520's and Spitfires
Free group, Le Gaulois	September 1944	Royan La Rochelle	Unit of FFL infantrymen attached to the Armée de l'Air in November 1944

Special Topics, 1939–1945

AIRPLANE PURCHASES FROM THE UNITED STATES

During the years preceding the outbreak of the conflict the inability of the French aeronautics industry to satisfy the requirements of the Air Ministry and the Air Force led those responsible for the rearmament to apply to the transatlantic manufacturers of aviation materiel. (There were also contacts with Kolhooven in the Netherlands and Savoia-Marchetti in Italy.) After the policy of buying air materiel from the United States had been recommended by General Denain, it began to be applied somewhat in the summer of 1937, when Pierre Cot sent a mission to the United States to look over the engine industry. Late that same year Senator Amaury de la Grange, chairman of the Senate committee on aviation and a long-time friend of President Franklin D. Roosevelt, made the journey as well. He selected a certain number of planes suitable for consideration for French orders. However, it was necessary to await the arrival of Guy La Chambre in the Air Ministry in order to see the working out of a larger program. Since Plan V gave priority to enlarging the fighter forces, the French decided to acquire high-quality fighters first of all. In spite of virulent opposition, a contract for 100 Curtiss P-36's (Curtiss H-75's in an export version) was signed in May 1938.

After the Munich crisis, Prime Minister Daladier, concerned about the state of the Air Force, requested on December 9, 1938, the purchase of 1,000 airplanes from the United States. On December 15 La Chambre's technical adviser, M. Hoppenot, left France at the head of a mission that included Jean Monnet, the engineer General Mazer, Lieutenant Colonel Jacquin, and Captain Chemidlin. This time the emphasis was to be on reinforcing the French bomber forces, which at that time were in an alarming situation. Although a Neutrality Act had been passed, the French were able, thanks to the support of the Roosevelt administration, to make contact with many manufacturers. On February 6, 1939, 115 Glenn Martin 167 twin-engined bombers were ordered, followed a week later by 199 North American B.T. 9 trainers. On February 15, 100 Douglas DB-7's were purchased. Finally, March 1939 saw the acquisition of 100 new Glenn Martin 167's and 100 more P-36's. In addition, United Aircraft Corporation had committed itself to furnishing the French navy with 40 Chance Vought 156 dive-bombers.

At the time when France entered the war there were thus 785 planes and numerous engines and propellers that had been ordered from the American aeronautics industry. The first P-36's had been delivered starting in December 1938 after tests done in Buffalo, New York.

On September 3, 1939, Lieutenant Colonel Jacquin, accompanied by the aeronautics engineer Thouvenot, left for the United States with instructions to buy 3,300 airplanes. Once there he was informed of Guy La Chambre's decision to produce 2,200 training planes and all the engines available in North America. But the promulgation of the arms embargo considerably hampered the actions of the two Frenchmen; they could not act until the passage in November 1939 of the "Cash and Carry" law (France and Great Britain had to pay in cash). At that time France had ordered 2,065 airplanes and over 8,000 engines. Finally, the negotiations conducted by

René Pleven, who arrived in the U.S. in December 1939, resulted in the implementation of a joint Franco-British plan covering the delivery between October 1940 and October 1941 of 4,700 planes, 2,160 of them to go to France (plus 7,935 engines). Letters of engagement were also signed between May 9 and 18, 1940, dealing with procurement of Consolidated L.B.-30 Liberators, P-39's, P-40's, Glenn Martin 187 F's, and P-38's.

In fact, 980 airplanes (40 Vought 156's, 283 Glenn Martin 167's, 120 Douglas DB-7's, 316 Curtiss H-75's, and 341 North American B.T. 9's) arrived in France before the armistice, and 469 were taken into account by the Air Force. In July and August 1940 the Vichy régime succeeded in recovering 60 Glenn Martin 167's, 84 H-75's, and 49 B.T. 9's.

These French and British orders had important effects on the American aeronautics industry. They were the origin of its rise and gave it the initial impulse that carried it to the dizzying production levels of 1941–1945.

Beginning in 1938 France ordered several hundred Curtiss Hawk 75 A's and received 316 of them before the armistice in June 1940. Here, a preproduction plane evaluated by the French Air Force.

The first Douglas DB-7 delivered to France, shown here on the Inglewood airfield.

THE ROYAL AIR FORCE IN THE BATTLE OF FRANCE

From 1936 on the mounting perils and the ever more disturbing growth of the German air forces were the occasion of numerous contacts between the French Armée de l'Air and the British Royal Air Force aimed at the latter's participation in a possible battle on the Continent. While the first meetings proved disappointing, the development of the international situation compelled the French and the British to come to terms and make mutual concessions. Thus at the time of the Munich crisis the RAF was ready to dispatch from the other side of the Channel an advanced bombing force, the Advanced Air Striking Force (AASF), whose distribution over the French bases had been the subject of earlier studies. In March 1939 the annexation of Czechoslovakia led to the first meetings of general staffs, in London, from March 29 to April 4 and again from April 24 to May 5. The discussions concerned the employment of the British air forces sent to France, and it was on this occasion that real Franco-British strategic plans were worked out. Moreover, whereas they had until then opposed sending fighter units to the Continent—an essential problem for the French—the British now promised to study the transfer of four fighter squadrons, but only after the twenty-fifth day of hostilities. This was the most important concession made by the British during those discussions.

As early as September 2 the AASF sent its Battle squadrons across the Channel. On September 12, 160 planes of this type were ready to operate from their French bases. But none of the Blenheims promised by the British had arrived. This was all the more worrisome since the Battles were practically incapable of holding their own against the German fighters, as the first engagements demonstrated. On the other hand, the RAF detailed to the Air Component, that is, the air force that formed an organic part of the ground expeditionary force, four squadrons of Hurricanes, two of which were turned over to the AASF sometime later. In compensation, the Air Component had a right to two squadrons of Gladiators.

On May 10, 1940, the day of the German offensive in the west, the RAF mustered its Air Component in France, commanded by Air Vice-Marshal Blount (2 squadrons of Hurricanes, 2 of Gladiators, 4 squadrons of Blenheims, 5 squadrons of Lysanders, and 1 fast squadron of Dragons) and Air Vice-Marshal Playfair's AASF (2 squadrons of Hurricanes, 8 of Battles, and 2 of Blenheims). In addition, several formations based in Great Britain were capable of being thrown into the battle: 7 squadrons of Blenheims, 2 of Whitleys, and some strategic reconnaissance Spitfires.

On the afternoon of May 10 Air Marshal Barratt, commander of the British Air Forces in France (he was in command of the Air Component and the AASF) threw his Battles against the German columns crossing Luxembourg and lost 23 planes. The next day 7 other Battles were shot down, while all the Blenheims of Squadron 114 of the AASF, caught on the ground by German bombers, were destroyed. On May 12, 7 Blenheims of the AASF were intercepted and shot down. In two days of fighting Playfair had thus lost almost all of his medium bombers and had only his Battles to try to stop the German advance. He engaged them over the bridges of Maestricht and then, on May 14, over the pontoons at Sedan. That day 40 of the 64 British planes that showed up over the sector of the French Ninth Army were destroyed—the biggest losses registered by the RAF in operations of this type.

Severely beaten, the AASF found itself unable to mount other actions of any scope. The RAF then engaged, from England, the bombers of the 2nd Group. Beginning on May 19 and 20 most of the squadrons of the Air Component began to return to Great Britain. On June 4, 1940, after the evacuation of Dunkirk, the RAF had only 40 fighters and 90 bombers at its disposal in France. The commanding officer of the Fighter Command, Air Chief Marshal Dowding, had been so impressed by the personnel losses suffered in connection with "Operation Dynamo" that he decided not to let his precious fighters take part in the battle of the Somme and the Aisne. It seems that at that moment the British considered the Battle of France lost and were preparing to receive the shock of the Luftwaffe above their national territory. Nevertheless, a few fighter squadrons did take action intermittently from June 6 to 8, and on June 13, 48 Battles attacked enemy columns along the Seine and the Marne. Four days later—a symbolic act—Air Marshal Barratt left France. By June 18 there was not a single British plane left in France.

The losses suffered by the RAF in France are enough in themselves to demonstrate its effective participation in the battle of May–June 1940. Over 1,500 fliers were killed, wounded, or reported missing, and over 1,000 planes of all types were destroyed, including 299 for the AASF and 279 for the Air Component.

Max Guedj.

Jean Maridor.

THE FREE FRENCH PILOTS IN THE RAF

Although it is impossible to give their exact number, we should mention the presence in RAF squadrons of several FAFL, who were sometimes entrusted with command functions. There was notably Squadron Leader Ezzano, who commanded a unit equipped with Hawker Typhoons, Squadron 198. Colonel Livry-Level served in a squadron which, equipped with Mosquitos, contributed to opening a breach in the wall of the prison in Amiens on February 18, 1944 ("Operation Jericho"). René Mouchotte commanded a British squadron before disappearing in aerial combat in 1943 at the head of the Alsace group. Jean Maridor was killed in 1944 while attacking a V-1 that was headed for a hospital. As for Max Guedj, he specialized in the missions of the Coastal Command, became a wing commander, and received two Distinguished Flying Crosses and a Distinguished Service Order before dying on board a Mosquito on January 15, 1945, during a raid against German ships in Norway. Pierre Clostermann was appointed to command a British wing in 1945, and with 33 sure victories and 5 probables was the ranking French ace of the Second World War.

Pierre Clostermann.

René Mouchotte.

Paul Ezanno.

Colonel Livry-Level.

The First Units of the Free French Air Forces

Unit	Date of Creation	Date of Dissolution	Unit Commanders	Campaigns	Aircraft	Personnel Strength
Free French Flight No. 1	8 July 1940	End of 1940	Capt. Dodelier	Eritrea	2 Glenn Martin 167's	7
Free French Flight No. 2	8 July 1940	March 1941	Capt. Jacquier 1st Lt. Péronne	Libya & Palestine	2 Potez 63-11's 2 Morane 406's, then Hurricanes	13
Free French Flight No. 3	8 July 1940	End of 1940	1st Lt. Pompéi	Palestine Egypt	1 Simoun 158, 1 Bloch 81	4
1st Fighter Group	1 Aug. 1940	End of 1940	Maj. de Marmier	Dakar Gabon	2 Dewoitine 520's & 6 Blenheim 12's Lysanders	56
"Topic" flight	1 Aug. 1940	End of 1940	Maj. Astier de Villatte	French Eq. Africa	8 Blenheims	32
Permanent Detachment of the Air Forces of Chad	26 Aug. 1940	End of 1940	1st Lt. Noël	Kufra	1 Bloch 120 2 Potez 25 TOE's 3 Potez 29 TOE's 4 Lysanders	40
Detachment of Gabon and Middle Congo	29 Aug. 1940	End of 1940	1st Lt. Ezanno 1st Lt. Finance 1st Lt. Court 2nd Lt. Forestier 2nd Lt. Jourdain Capt. Kopp		Lysanders Potez 25 TOE's, Bloch 120's	25
Cameroon Detachment	27 Aug. 1940	2 Sept. 1941	Capt. Biarnais		Lysanders	
Reserved Bomber Group No. 1	24 Dec. 1940	2 Sept. 1941	Maj. Astier de Villatte	Kufra Eritrea Abyssinia	13 Blenheims	40
Fighter Flight No. 1	January 1941	May 1941	1st Lt. Denis	Egypt Greece Tobruk	Dewoitine 520's, then Hurricanes	6
Bomber Flight No. 2	Feb. 1941	2 Sept. 1941	Maj. Goumin Lt. Col. de Marmier	Crete Libya	Glenn Martin 167's	32

The Big Units of the Free French Air Forces, 1941–1945

Unit	Date of Creation	Date of Entry into Operations	Unit Commanders	Campaigns	Aircraft	Personnel Strength
Alsace Squadron 341 (Pursuit)	1 Sept. '41	2 Sept. '41	Maj. Tulasne Maj. Pouliquen Capt. Denis Maj. Mouchotte Maj. Dupérier Maj. Montet Capt. Andrieux	Palestine Libya Great Britain Occupied France	12 Moranes 18 Hurricanes Spitfire IX's 20 Spitfire XVI's	25 30 34
Ile-de-France Squadron 340 (Pursuit)	10 Nov. '41	10 Apr. '42	Squadron Leader Loft Capt. C. de Scitivaux Maj. Dupérier Maj. Shloesing Maj. Reilhac Maj. Fournier Maj. Massart 1st Lt. Hardi Maj. Aubertin	Great Britain & Occupied France	Spitfire V A's 18 Spitfire V B's Spitfire IX E's 20 Spitfire XVI's	25+ 32++ 30++
Normandy-Niemen (Pursuit)	1 Sept. '42	23 Mar. '43	Maj. Pouliquen Maj. Tulasne Lt. Col. Pouyade Maj. Delfino	Central Russia Minsk, Smolensk, Niemen, Tilsit, Königsberg	14 Yak 1's 12 Yak 9's 51 Yak 9's 39 Yak 9's	14 22 41 25
Lorraine Squadron 342 (Bombing)	2 Sept. '41	25 Oct. '41	Maj. Corniglion-Molinier Lt. Col. Pijeaud Capt. St.-Péreuse Lt. Col. de Rancourt Lt. Col. Fourquet Lt. Col. Soufflet Maj. Mentre	Libya Occupied France Germany	16 Blenheims 16 Bostons 18 Mitchells	61+ 87++ 110++

The Big Units of the Free French Air Forces, 1941–1945; continued

Unit	Date of Creation	Date of Entry into Operations	Unit Commanders	Campaigns	Aircraft	Personnel Strength
Bretagne (Bombing)	1 Jan. '42	1 Jan. '42	Maj. Noël Maj. St.-Péreuse Maj. de Maismont Capt. Lefevre Maj. Quenet Maj. Meyrand Maj. Ducray	Fezzan, Sardinia, Italy, South of France, Germany, pockets of the Atlantic	3 Glenn Martin 167's 6 Lysanders 5 Blenheims 2 Potez 540's and 2 Howards 18 Maurauders	24+ 100++
Artois (Coast Defense)	3 Aug. '42	3 Aug. '42	Maj. Bonnafe Maj. Kopp Maj. Morel	South Atlantic	6 Lysanders 7 Ansons	6+ 9++
Picardy (Coast Defense)	June 1943	1 July '43	Maj. Noël Maj. Allot	Syria	Blenheims Potez 25's Douglas A 24's Baltimores	10+ 32++
Military Air Lines (Transport)	Sept. 1941		Maj. de Marmier		6 Lockheeds	

\+ May 1942
\+ + May 1943

Major Collin.

Henri Romans-Petit.

THE FRENCH AIR FORCE AND THE RESISTANCE

It is obviously not within the scope of a book on the history of military aviation to discuss in any detail the Resistance movement in France from 1940 to 1944. Nevertheless, it is impossible to ignore the role that many aviators of all ranks played in that uprising of the French against the Nazi occupation.

Military aviators are found in the various organizations that arose, developed, and sometimes, unfortunately, disappeared between 1940 and 1944. They served as members of the information networks as radiomen, saboteurs of the "action" services, underground fighters. Many of them—tortured, shot, deported not to return—paid with their lives for their work in the service of their country.

One would like to mention all of them by name, the fighters in the shadows, heroes, martyrs even, but that is impossible. To symbolize them, let us recall just three of them.

Major Léon Faye, an active officer who graduated from Fontainebleau, who created the Alliance Network: arrested by the Gestapo on September 16, 1943, he was tortured, deported, and shot in January 1945 at Sonnenburg.

Colonel Henri Romans-Petit, an Air Force reserve officer, directed the famous underground of Ain, in which a number of former students of the Air School served.

Major Collin, from the military academy of Saint Cyr, former commanding officer of Group I/8, was arrested by the Germans in Montpellier on October 8, 1943, and shot in Lyons on February 21, 1944.

Léon Faye.

PART 5

Toward Revival

CHAPTER I

Reconstruction (1945–1958)

In August 1945, with the conflict terminated, the French Air Force could validly believe in its future. The war had proved the correctness of the views that the air command had never ceased to uphold from 1919 to 1939.

The air service, a revolutionary instrument, had played the leading role in all areas of the war. Many observers remembered the strategic bombings more than anything else, even though the results obtained in Europe had not measured up to the hopes entertained of them. Those results were judged only by the destruction wreaked on German industry, and it could be said that Germany still had considerable manufacturing potential in 1945. The decisive actions of the Allied heavy bombers in preparations for troop landings were forgotten.

Besides, the operations carried out in Europe seemed harmless compared to Hiroshima. The combination of the B-29 and the atomic bomb seemed to show that Douhet was right and to prove that from then on airplanes were capable of winning a war alone.

It is true that the atomic bomb opened a new era. Even though the bombing of Hiroshima had claimed fewer victims than the conventional bombings of Dresden or Tokyo, the results had been obtained in less than a minute and with a single plane.

The other lesson that was learned from the war in the air was the extraordinary potential of air action in support of ground troops. The Stukas of the 1940 campaign seemed ineffective when compared to the Typhoons and Thunderbolts of 1944 and 1945. From the time of the Normandy invasion they had prevented all daytime action on the part of the German army. They had even proved the possibilities offered by the ground-combat airplane by blocking the German armored counterattack against the flank of General Patton's troops at Avranches.

But it had been possible to carry out all these air operations—and this was less emphasized—because the air battle had been fought and won beforehand. That was, in fact, the fundamental lesson of the war, and Marshal Montgomery, as well as other great Allied commanders of ground troops for that matter, underscored it by stating forcefully that the acquisition of air superiority was the indispensable preliminary to the launching of any air or sea battle. One should note that such affirmations had already been made some thirty years earlier by the French G.H.Q. in drawing the lessons of Verdun and preparing to attack on the Somme.

All these convergent analyses could have made the Air Force hope that it would finally be given the place in the French military system that rightly belonged to it because of its future operational capacities.

That reflection, which was to emerge on the definition of a doctrine, was an essential factor in the foundations of the future development of the air forces; it was carried on as soon as the war ended. At the same time many other problems arose, connected with the demobilization and also with the weight of the preceding years, which had left their mark in several areas.

At the end of the war the problem that arose first of all was that of manpower. The problem was further complicated by the measures to be taken, parallel to demobilization, to recreate the unity of the French armed forces by amalgamating the different wartime contributions. The Air Force was not alone in experiencing that problem. While it was less acute for the navy, the army had to solve it under conditions rendered more difficult because of the large number of cases to be treated. The second task to be accomplished was to define and establish an organization which, while striving to stay within the legal framework, would take into account the lessons of the war and the operational demands imposed on the air formations.

This work of general reconstruction was complicated, of course, by the fact that it was necessary at the same time to carry out everyday tasks. These were made more onerous on the one hand by the events in Indochina and the need to reinforce the air resources of that territory and on the other by the obligation to develop and operate military air transport, which at the time was a vital need of the country, on a priority basis.

The "New" Debate on Doctrine

As we have already seen, from 1916 to 1940 a debate on doctrine had placed the air force in opposition to the other military services. That debate, resumed in North Africa in 1943, was not followed up at the time. The reequipped French air forces had been incorporated into the big American and English air units, which, as is well known, were not subordinated to the big ground units but simply juxtaposed, or "adapted."

It was reasonable to hope that since the lessons of the last war were obvious on that point, the angry quarrel carried on with the air forces in earlier years would finally cease. This was not the case. The conflict between the air and ground doctrines would reappear just as before in the discussions within the commission, headed by General Guyot, entrusted in the spring of 1946 with studying the plan for enlarging the Air Force at the National Defense General Staff level.

The army's position was presented very clearly by General Juin: "As a function of present needs, the missions to be demanded of our Air Force appear to have a priority orientation toward support of our active land and sea forces stationed all over French lands or in occupied territories, without ceasing, however, to maintain a nucleus suitable for strategic action."

The language used here is significant. In 1946 it was impossible to ignore strategic aviation, and so it was mentioned. But, in view of the restrictions applied, it was to be maintained only as a nucleus suited to making possible, in case of need, a hypothetical new start. Of the positions taken by the army general staff, this was doubtless the most reasonable. In 1946 France did not have the human, technical, and financial means that would make it possible to create a conventional strategic air force. In any case, such a force would rapidly become anachronistic. To be persuaded of this one need only remember that the current fleet of Mirage IV's has a capacity for instantaneous destruction fifty times as great as that of the RAF Bomber Command at the end of the Second World War.

What was more serious was that the acquisition of air superiority was considered only in case of a major conflict. Under that hypothesis the air battle

One of the P-51 Mustangs used by the French Air Force.

Marauders and P-47's on an airfield in North Africa in 1946.

A line-up of Yak 3's.

to win mastery of the sky would be fought by the Allied forces.

As in the past, the accent was put on support aviation, in which the airplane at "the corner of the woods," ready to come instantly to the support of the threatened battalion, company, or squad, replaced the mass of observation aircraft, the eyes of the infantry and artillery, that had been built up in 1939.

This surprising position, which evoked the anger of the aviators, whether of General Bouscat or of General Gérardot, who had a temper, had a number of explanations. The main reason, obviously, was that in a study preliminary to the allocation of resources among the armed services, it was necessary to adopt a doctrine that would enable the resources of one's own branch to increase, and that could be done only at the expense of the others. The second, and no doubt deeper, reason was that the military leaders of the ground forces in the Second World War had never been at a sufficiently high level of command to be familiar with the employment of the air forces. It must be remembered that the adaptation of the decisive air resources took place at the army group level. Certainly there were air resources placed at the disposal of the army, but that arrangement was temporary and revocable depending on the general air situation.

Never having had to understand aerial maneuver, which, by the way, was planned at the level of the theater of operations, the ground commanders saw in the action of the air forces only the operations carried out for the benefit of the ground units. The Stukas, which had so impressed them in 1940, had been replaced by fighter-bombers. Their effectiveness had increased, and that was exactly the weapon that suited the land army. To use that weapon well it was proper for all the forces to be placed under the orders of one and the same commander (who in the spirit of the time could only be a ground commander).

Moreover, since it was essentially a matter of an auxiliary service, aviation would link the stationing of its forces to that of the active ground forces. It was quite natural for the Air Force to answer, in the person of General Bouscat, that the priority given to air support appeared to it to be in complete contradiction of the lessons to be learned from the war.

He insisted on the fact that the first mission of the air forces was to win the freedom of aerial maneuver. The air battle preliminary to all other actions was to give mastery of the air. It did not appear reasonable to entrust to allies the burden of fighting the initial battle for France. What would happen to the French army if the aid it was counting on did not come—as the lessons of the past might cause it to fear—at the necessary moment?

Conscious of its weakness in materiel, the Air Force estimated that during an initial period the fighter-bombers could handle the two missions of support and of the fight for air superiority. Since at the beginning of a conflict the latter mission would have priority, the resources would be entirely at the disposal of the air commander.

Compromise solutions, along with the old ideas so often put forward in the past, were again proposed in the spirit of those envisaged between the wars.

Unfortunately, the Guyot commission filed conclusions on July 2, 1946, that gave the air forces the short end of the stick. In the state of the current resources there was no question of viewing, before 1950, the fight for air superiority as one of the missions of the Air Force.

Because aviation's resources were insufficient, its effort was to bear on fire support and reconnaissance missions adapted to the active ground forces, on transport aviation, and on overseas police and security actions. In equipment on the ground, priority would be given to air defense of the country itself, of French North Africa, and of the French West Africa–French North Africa axis.

Such conclusions were unacceptable to the Air Force and were challenged by General Bouscat. Many points had not been taken up by the commission (strategic aviation, aircraft), and, above all, as was emphasized in an internal note to the office of the engineering general staff, if the conclusions were adopted "we would be taking the path of a closer cooperation than ever with the land forces, which would be reminiscent of that army observation and fighter force created after the War of 1914–1918, which cost us 1940."

Since it was impossible to come to an understanding with the land army, the Air Force defined its own doctrine, aimed at drawing the lessons from the last war and adapting them to the foreseeable forms of future conflicts. The provisional order on the employment of the air forces, which was the result of studies done from April to November 1946 by a commission headed by General Gérardot, was issued early in 1947.

At the outset the order defined the characteristics of modern warfare and drew conclusions from them that were very different from those of the Guyot commission.

It would be too time-consuming to detail here all the points contained in that remarkable order, but it must be emphasized that it posed very controversial problems in new terms. The basis of the doctrine, of course, corresponded to what had already been said many times before.

The winning of air superiority was seen as the essential mission of the air forces. This would be accomplished by the destruction of the enemy's air potential in flight and on the ground. This air action needed free spaces and could not be confined within the narrow limits of the land armies. Ground support could not take place until after air superiority was secured. Finally, the employment of the air forces should give preference to independent missions planned at the highest level of military leadership and aimed at striking the enemy in its vital parts.

Just as there had been a great deal of debate on doctrines between the wars, there had also been a great deal of reflection on organization.

In this area, too, the problems were raised in the same terms as during the 1930s. The applicable law was still that of 1934, and it has been emphasized that its chief defect was that it did not provide continuity of command in the transition from peacetime to wartime. But the lessons of the war and the obvious potential of the air forces demanded more than ever before an absolute respect for continuity of organization.

The reorganization of the Air Force was rendered more delicate by the fact that while in 1944 the air regions had been reestablished, French aviation was still organized according to the criteria used by the Allies. Nevertheless, there was no major difficulty for the time being, since France had only one big air unit, the 1st Air Division, the units of which were stationed in Germany.

The return of certain units to France and the creation of new big commands—the D.A.T. (Territorial Antiaircraft Defense), the schools, and the G.M.M.T.A. (Military Air Transport Grouping)—posed the problem of relations between commands and air regions. Against their will the French had fallen back into a system close to that of 1936. This was not surprising since in 1946 the French organization was similar to those of the Allies, and they in turn, since they postdated the French organization, were derived from the same spirit.

The dilemma, and it remained one into 1960, was how to respect the law and at the same time preserve the effectiveness of the nation's air resources?

To get around the difficulty the idea was hit upon of combining under one and the same authority the regional command and the operational command. In 1947 the 3rd Air Regiment and the Air Schools Command were merged. Later the 1st Air Division and the 2nd Air Regiment were merged. These mergers, which were contrary to all reason, did not last and were quickly dissolved. The experiment was not continued, and the combining of the G.M.M.T.A. with the 2nd Air Regiment and the D.A.T. with the 4th Air Regiment, which had been envisaged, did not take place.

We shall see the evolution of this question later, but it is very important to dwell a bit on the D.A.T. and the G.M.M.T.A., which had been created under the stress of events.

For the D.A.T. it was necessary finally to do what it had been impossible to do before the war and place all of the responsibilities for air defense under one and the same authority. This was all the more necessary as it was urgent in that period of reconstruction to have a complete unity of doctrine for the establishment of the infrastructure on the ground, without which nothing could be done.

The other big command created under the pressure of circumstances was the G.M.M.T.A. Military air transport had not been developed in France as it had been in other countries. Between the wars several studies made on the subject had come to nothing because of the necessity of providing for the most immediate needs from 1936 on.

After the 1940 armistice three transport groups were activated in French North Africa, while transport activities developed under civilian cover. In Free France, Colonel de Marmier directed the military airlines. In May 1945 there were four transport groups—1/15, 2/15, 3/15, and 4/15—equipped with American airplanes and Junker 52's.

The government, confronting the problem of repatriating prisoners and deportees whose state of health did not allow repatriation by ground transport, put the problem to the minister of air, who decided to create an air grouping to carry out that mission and to place it under the command of Colonel Alias.

This grouping had permanently at its disposal the four transport groups of the Air Force and the transport flights of the Aéronavale.

For the transport missions it made use of the seven groups of Bomber Brigade No. 11, equipped with Marauders, and the two heavy bomber groups, equipped with Halifaxes. From June to August the G.M.M.T.A. carried out its mission, making 924 flights without any air mishaps.

During the same period the Marauders were converted into relatively comfortable transport planes, carrying out many repatriations from France to North Africa and vice versa.

Its mission accomplished, the G.M.M.T.A. should normally have been dissolved. But important new demands for air transport quickly arose in France and abroad, and the G.M.M.T.A. continued its illegal existence and prospered until it became the Military Air Transport Command in 1962.

Personnel Strength

A certain number of plans had been under study since 1943 for enlarging the Air Force, both at the time of the liberation of France and in the years that followed.

Plan VII, set up late in 1943, provided that personnel strength would rise from 30,000 in 1943 to 180,000 in 1945 and level off at 360,000 in 1946. This considerable increase was meant to take into account the normal increase in the size of the armed services. Whatever arguments could be advanced to support those figures, it was quite evident that the end of the war would inevitably lead to revising them sharply downward.

This was done as early as August 1944, although the plans still called for large numbers: a total of 109 groups in 1946, operated by 170,000 men. Of course, the concluding of peace greatly altered these plans. From 1946 on military needs yielded to civilian ones, priority being given to the reconstruction of the country after the devastation of the war years.

The Air Force, which numbered 145,000 men at the end of the war, had not only to stop increasing but also to reduce its strength. A new plan, on January 21, 1946, provided for a strength of 90,000, including 7,000 officers. This was still too many. After a new theoretical figure of 75,000 was put forward, the strength was reduced to 59,379 men. (This figure represents a basic establishment of 50,000, plus 4,812 men for Indochina, 2,518 for territorial antiaircraft defense, and 2,049 on detached service.)

These numbers would suffice in a pinch to fly the 27 existing groups for the time being, but they were definitely insufficient to establish and operate the indispensable means for operational work plus the technical maintenance of the air units.

In fact, as the personnel figures clearly show, after a sudden decline, with the low point in September 1946, the Air Force saw its strength stabilize at about 65,000 men before a definite rise which began in 1952.

To reach such low figures it was necessary to

take measures concerning the personnel. The first measures, which were the simplest to take, returned the draftees and reservists to civilian life. This was not enough, however. It was necessary to reduce the number of regulars, which ran in the opposite direction from what had been done in 1944 and posed many problems, including political ones.

From the time of the liberation it was mainly a question of reintegration and amalgamation. In August 1944 the active nucleus of the Air Force was relatively homogeneous, at least the combat portion. There had been certain differences between the Free French and the combatants from French North Africa, but they had faded out very quickly.

The personnel to be reintegrated came from different sources. The years spent in France from 1940 to 1944 had marked them deeply, and for that reason they had mentalities and reactions that were hard for their comrades, most of whom had lived through that period in North Africa, to understand. These mentalities and reactions also differed depending on whether the individual in question had or had not been active in the Resistance movement.

Even among the former members of the Resistance there were notable differences due to the diversity that was included in the very idea of the movement. There was also an additional difficulty in integrating the personnel who had won their ranks in that effort. Most of them were not flying personnel, and the regulations in force did not allow them to be reclassified legally in the existing regular organizations.

Obviously a certain political connotation was added to all this. The difficulties, which seemed considerable at the time, were in fact overcome relatively well.

In 1946 it remained to get the personnel that had just been integrated to leave the service. The law on dismissal of regular members of the armed forces and a sharp but temporary reduction of the age limits obtained the desired results.

For all that, the situation of the remaining personnel was extremely difficult in 1946 because of the low pay and the general hardships aggravated for the military by the frequent changes during that period of getting back to normal. It was not until 1948 and the adjustment of military pay to the salaries of the civil servants that there was a noticeable improvement in living conditions.

While personnel problems occupied an important place in the minds of Air Force leaders, materiel problems also had to be solved. To reequip the units with French materiel it was necessary to get the national aeronautics industry under way again.

As noted earlier, at the time of the liberation the aeronautics industry still had a certain production capacity. While the labor force was small—37,000 men in 1944—and the covered areas were only half what they had been in June 1940, the number of machine tools remained high. A production equal to about a third or a fourth of the June 1940 production could be reasonably counted on, so long as the industry was repairing or manufacturing the materiel of that period. Of course, adopting such a solution would inevitably lead France to increase its technological lag.

Another solution was available, namely, to enter resolutely into the engine race. This solution had the merit of leading to the production of planes that were cheap to manufacture and easy to operate.

It was, however, difficult to adopt, first, because it was necessary to take part as quickly as possible in the end of the conflict and, second, because urgent internal tasks required having a transport air fleet available quickly, part of which should be made in France.

The decisions made were aimed at preserving the potential of the country's aeronautics industry in order to increase it later. Most of the assembly lines abandoned by the enemy would be started up again, and production of the French planes made in 1940 would be resumed. Research done during the occupation would serve as a basis for future prototypes. For the immediate future the prototypes being completed would make it possible to bridge the gap.

The planes produced and the new orders are shown in the table, as well as the deliveries made by the end of 1945.

Orders Issued to the Aeronautics Industry after the Liberation and Deliveries to the End of 1945

Planes	Ordered	Delivered	Planes	Ordered	Delivered
Light Planes			Warplanes		
N. 1000	250	172	DO 24	40	28
N. 1100	205	0	VB 10	200	9
Stampe	1,400	51	B1 175	100	0
Morane 500	1,075	347	SO 1070	15	0
Morane 315	100	49	MS 472	1,000	0
Leopoldoff	4	0	S 10	80	0
Morane 230	100	0	Breguet 730	4	1
Poussin 123	47	0	*Total*	1,439	38
Total	3,181	619	Planes To Be Finished		
Light Twin-Engined Planes			PZ 6311	15	?
NC 701	390	47	JU 88	98	38
SO 90	25	0	Dewoitine 520	44	?
SO 91	200	0	Le0 451	48	?
C 449	385	39	JU 188	7	?
Transport Planes			He 177	3	?
SE 1010	20	0	FW 190	125	38
Bloch 161	125	5	*Total*	340	76
SO 30 R	20	0			
JU 52	390	181			
Laté 631	10	1			
SE 200	3	1			
Total	1,568	274			

It is immediately apparent that France had started on a path that, in the long run, would lead to its having only outdated combat materiel. Only the relatively rapid output of Ju 52's could enable it to equip an air transport service which had to undertake many tasks.

It is also apparent that in spite of the definite efforts made in fourteen months these manufactures were subject to considerable delays.

It was at that very moment that the financial situation led to a massive reduction in the orders issued in 1945. Since there was no wish to have the employees of the aeronautics firms bear the consequences, it was decided to use the manufacturing potential made available by the reduction in orders for other purposes. Starting in 1947, therefore, the aeronautics industry manufactured the most varied objects, from buses to refrigerators. Industry profits were low, of course, since the machine tools in the factories were not adapted to these new products.

From then on an overhaul was gradually effected, completed in 1949 by the law reorganizing the national companies. But apart from the manufactures, an extremely ambitious research program had been launched in 1946. Under this program research and development of the Espadon, the Grognard, the SO 4000, the NC 271, and the Cormorant were achieved. None of this research led to production runs, and the new prototype policy of the 1940s was subjected to criticism as sharp as that of the 1930s. But while these criticisms had some foundation, in view of the amounts that had been sunk into the research—there were 135 prototypes under study—it must be remembered that the failures experienced at that time led to the successes that were to come later.

French engineers, many of whom had been cut off for six years from the great advances made in the rest of the world, had gotten their hand in and had learned a great deal. Similarly, test centers—the Flight Test Center in Marignane, then in Brétigny in 1945, and the Military Air Experiment Center in Mont-de-Marsan—which had been started up again very soon after the liberation, were functioning perfectly, and the Test Flight and Inspection School for Flying Personnel (E.P.N.E.R.) was supplying specialists in flight tests.

In conclusion, France undoubtedly paid a high price for its adaptation to the new techniques, but it was to reap the benefits starting in 1950, when its aeronautics industry would turn out the materiel provided for in the program act which will be discussed later.

The years 1946–1947 marked a turning point for the French Air Force. Even though it continued to fly with the materiel of the last war, even though Indochina was taking up more and more of its resources, it was building for the future.

In spite of the trials that they had undergone and the daily difficulties that they were experiencing, the personnel continued to be very strongly motivated. They would demonstrate their operational capacities in Indochina, but as early as 1945 they showed, in air transport, what the country could expect of them. In 1946 the G.M.M.T.A. carried 200,000 persons, the civil airlines 300,000. The Air Force's youngest service was doing well indeed.

The peace following the Second World War was brief. It would soon become necessary to take part in the colonial wars in Indochina and, to a lesser extent, in Madagascar. However, no threat of war

An assembly line in 1945.

A Heinkel 274 at Orléans-Bricy in early 1946.

Work on an NC 701 Martinet in a hangar at Persan-Beaumont.

Preparing a Ju 52 for flight at Persan-Beaumont in 1953.

loomed up in 1947, and the accord signed with Great Britain at Dunkirk might appear to constitute sufficient protection against a possible aggressor, who still seemed most likely to be Germany.

Everything looked different after the "Prague coup" of February 1948. Europe saw a new danger rising up, that of aggression by a former ally, the Soviet Union.

This was no doubt what led to the signing in Brussels on March 17, 1948, of an assistance pact extending the Treaty of Dunkirk to Belgium, the Netherlands, and Luxembourg. The signing of the pact coincided with the Soviet Union's starting the Berlin blockade. The United States immediately began an airlift that was quite remarkable for the techniques employed and the amount of cargo transported. The French Air Force participated in the Berlin airlift for psychological and political reasons. It must be admitted that French participation proved rather troublesome for the organizers because of the slowness of the Ju 52's, their small capacity (1-1/2 tons), the language difficulty—the language used was English—and the inadequacy of French radio equipment.

This airlift, while technically perfect, was in reality only an epiphenomenon. Much more important was the Vandenberg resolution voted by the United States Senate, which authorized the president of the United States to sign security pacts outside the American hemisphere.

It was then possible to enter into negotiations, and they resulted in the signing of the North Atlantic Treaty in Washington on April 4, 1949. The treaty was followed by an assistance act promulgated on October 6, 1949, which provided for American assistance in Europe.

From then on French aviation was to consist of two wings: that placed at the disposal of NATO, the reequipping of which would benefit from American aid, and that which remained national, essentially for fighter aircraft, the D.A.T. (territorial air defense), which would be equipped with planes manufactured in France.

It does not fall within the scope of this book to develop the whole of French participation in the NATO forces, but merely to state that that participation was of considerable importance to the renovation of the French air forces. The agreements signed, put in concrete form by the aid received, imposed a framework of action that budgetary decisions could not ignore. Protected by NATO, the Air Force could thus develop without risk.

The phases of its development were set forth in various plans which, on the whole, were carried out. There is no question of citing all of them. From the signing of the Brussels Pact to 1955 there were seventeen of them, running from complete recasting to simple refitting.

Schools, 1949

B.E. 701 Salon	Air School	Toucan: 3 Anson: 31 Goéland: 1	P-47: 1 A.T.-6: 14	Penguin, Ramier: 1 Mo 315, Mo 250: 63
B.E. 702	Bombing Specialization	Martinet: 51	Penguin, Ramier: 1	
B.E. 703 Pau	On-Board Radiomen	Toucan: 8 Goéland: 1	Penguin, Ramier: 1	Misc.: 22
B.E. 704 Cognac	Single-Engine Conversion (Dissolved Dec. '49)	SIPA: 51 A.T.-6: 16	Penguin, Ramier: 71 Stampe: 16	Misc.: 58 Mo 315, Mo 250: 8
B.E. 705 Cazaux	Machine-Gunners, Navigators, Bombardiers	Anson: 31 Martinet: 11	Wellington: 35 Criquet: 2	Misc.: 40
C.I.E.T. Toulouse	Training Center for Transport Crews	Toucan: 13 Martinet: 17	Beechcraft: 9 C-47: 2	
B.E. 707 Marrakech	Service School for Flying Personnel	Goéland: 1 Cessna: 1	P-47: 11 Stampe: 29	
B.E. 708 Meknes	Fighter Pilots' Specialization	Goéland: 1 P-47: 13	Spit: 18 A-24: 27	P-39: 15 Misc.: 10
B.E. 724 Fez	Transmission School Base	Goéland: 2		

Schools, 1955

701 Salon	Air School	SIPA: 70 Mistral: 6	Flamant: 6	
702 Avord	Bombing Specialization	Flamant: 57		
707 Marrakech	Service School for Flying Personnel	T-6 D } 139 A.T.-16 }		
708 Meknes	Fighter Pilots' Specialization	T-33: 40 Vampire V: 96		
724 Fez	Transmission School Base	Toucan } 8 Dakota }	Misc.: 5	
C.I.E.T. Toulouse	Training Center for Transport Crews	Toucan } 20 Dakota }	Flamant: 21 Nord 2501: 3	Misc.: 14
C.B. 706 Cazaux	Firing and Bombing School	F-43: 12 B-26: 5	Misc.: 5	
C.I.P.N. Tours	Training Center for Flying Personnel	Meteor: 6 Flamant: 7		
Lahr	Blind Flying Training Flight	T-33: 15		
Rochefort	Helicopter Training Detachment	Sikorsky 551: 5		

Pursuit and Reconnaissance, 1949

Squadron	Groups	Base	Materiel
1st	1/1 Provence 2/1 Nice	Oran-la-Senia	35 Spitfire IX's (+ 8)
2nd	1/2 Stork 2/2 Alsace	Coblenz	35 P-47's (+8)
3rd	1/3 Navarre 2/3 Champagne	Gia Tam Nah Trang	35 Spitfire IX's (+ 8)
4th	1/4 Dauphiné 2/4 Lafayette	Friedrichshafen	35 P-47's (+ 8)
5th	1/5 Travail 2/5 Ile-de-France	Sidi Ahmed	35 P-63's (+ 8)
6th	1/6 Corsica 2/6 Normandy	Rabat-Salé	32 Mosquito VI's (+ 8) 2 Mosquito III's
33rd	1/33 Belfort 2/33	Fribourg	14 P-35's + 6 P-51's (+4 P-38's) 16 P-51's (+ 4 P-51's)
	1/37 Lorraine	Agadir	16 Mosquito XVI's

Pursuit and Reconnaissance, 1955

Squadron	Groups	Base	Materiel
1st	III/1 Argonne	Saint-Dizier	75 P-84's (+ 9)
	II/1 Morvan		
	I/1 Corsica		
2nd	I/2 Storks	Dijon	75 Hurricanes
	II/2 Côte-d'Or		
	III/2 Alsace		
3rd	I/3 Navarre	Rheims	75 P-84's (+ 9)
	II/3 Champagne		
	III/3 Ardennes		
4th	I/4 Dauphiné	Bremgarten	75 Hurricanes
	II/4 Lafayette		
	III/4 Flanders		
5th	II/5 Ile-de-France	Orange	48 Mistrals (+ 6)
	I/5 Vendée		
	III/5 Comtat Venaissin		
6th	II/6 Normandy-Niemen	Oran	32 Mistrals (+8)
	I/6 Oranie		
7th	II/7 Provence	Bizerte	32 Mistrals (+ 8)
	II/7 Nice		
8th	II/8 Languedoc	Rabat-Salé	32 Mistrals (+ 8)
	I/8 Maghreb		
9th	I/8 Limousin	Lahr	24 P-84's
	II/9 Auvergne		
10th	I/10 Valais	Creil	50 Mystère II's
	II/10 Seine		
	III/10 Paris		
11th	I/11 Roussillon	Luxeuil	75 P-84's (+ 9)
	II/11 Vosges		
	III/11 Jura		
12th	I/12 Cambrésis	Cambrai	50 Hurricanes, 25 Mystère II's
	II/12 Picardy		
13th	I/13 Artois	Lahr	75 miscellaneous planes
	II/13 Alps		
G.O. 2/21		Far East	20 F-8 F's
G.O. 1/22		Far East	20 F-8 F's
33rd	E.R. 1/33 Belfort	Cognac	54 P-84's (+ 14)
	E.R. 2/33 Savoy		
30th	1/3rd Loire	Tours	24 NF-11's
	2/3rd Camargue		
	3/3rd Lorraine		
E.L.R. 2/19		Far East	5 Invaders
E.R.O.M. 80		Far East	10 F-8 F's (+ 2)

Bombing and Transport, 1949

Formation		Stationing	Materiel
	1/21 Tunisia	Bordeaux	16 Halifaxes (+ 4)
	2/21 Guyenne		
G.T.L.[†]	1/60 G.L.A.M.*	Villacoublay	2 Goélands, 10 Beechcrafts, 11 Glenns, 7 Ramiers, 2 Penguins, 1 Stampe, 5 misc.
G.T.L.	2/60 G.A.E.L.		4 Le0 45's, 13 Goélands, 7 Penguins, 20 Martinets, 23 Ramiers, 2 Criquets
61st Squadron	1/61 Touraine	Le Bourget	16 C-47's (+ 4)
61st Squadron	2/61 Maine	Orléans-Bricy	16 Toucans (+ 4)
61st Squadron	3/61 Poitou	Chartres	16 Toucans (+ 4)
	1/62 Algeria	Alger	16 Toucans (+ 4)
	2/62 Franche-Comté	Blida	16 B-26's (+ 4), 10 A-24's
	1/63 Brittany	Thiès	16 Toucans (+ 4)
S./G.M.M.T.A.	1/64 Béarn	Batna	20 Toucans (+ 6)
S./G.M.M.T.A.	2/64 Anjou		18 C-47's (+ 4)

1955

Formation		Stationing	Materiel
	1/61 Touraine	Orleans	16 Nord 2501's
	2/61 Maine	Le Bourget	10 Languedocs (+ 1)
	3/61 Poitou	Orleans	16 Nord 2501's
T.L.A.	1/60 G.L.A.M.	Villacoublay	4 Flamants, 2 Bretagnes, 1 Skymaster, 6 Dakotas (+ 13 miscellaneous)
T.L.A.	2/60 G.A.E.L.	Villacoublay	2 Criquets, 8 Flamants, 41 Ramiers, 12 Martinets
	1/62 Algeria	Alger	25 Dakotas (+ 1)
	1/63 Brittany	Thiès	16 Dakotas (+ 1)
	2/63 Franche-Comté	Far East	25 Dakotas
	2/63 Senegal	Far East	25 Dakotas
	1/64 Béarn	Far East	25 Dakotas
	2/64 Anjou	Far East	20 Dakotas
91st Squadron	G.B. 1/19 Gascony	Far East	20 Invaders
91st Squadron	G.B. 1/25 Tunisia	Far East	20 Invaders

*Ministerial Air Liaison Group.
[†] Transport and Liaison Group.

Liaison and Overseas, 1949

Formation	Stationing	Materiel
S.L.A.[1] 41	Dijon	4 Goélands, 2 Ramiers, 1 Penguin
S.L.A. 43	Bordeaux	6 Goélands, 4 Ramiers, 2 Penguins, 10 Criquets
S.L.A. 44	Aix-les-Mille	3 Goélands, 1 Martinet, 4 Ramiers, 7 Criquets
S.L.A. 55	Baden	8 Goélands, 4 Ramiers, 7 Criquets, 1 B-17
S.L.A. 54	Lahr	3 Martinets, 2 Beechcrafts, 4 Ramiers, 1 Penguin, 3 Criquets, 1 Spitfire
S.L.A. 57	Innsbruck	4 Martinets, 3 Ramiers (1 miscellaneous)
S.L.A. 56 Vaucluse	Persan-Beaumont	5 Toucans, 2 Goélands, 3 Martinets, 1 Ramier, 1 Penguin (+ 9 miscellaneous)
G.L.A.[2] 45	Boufarik	5 LeO 45's, 1 Martinet, 1 Glenn, 8 Goélands, 8 Ramiers, 2 Criquets (+ 4 miscellaneous)
S.L.A. 46	Rabat-Ville	5 Goélands, 1 Glenn, 1 Penguin, 2 Martinets, 3 Ramiers, 2 Criquets
S.L.A. 47	Tunis	2 Goélands, 2 Ramiers, 4 Martinets, 2 Criquets, 1 Penguin
S.L.A. 48	Ouakam	3 Toucans, 2 Martinets, 3 Criquets, 2 Goélands, 4 Penguins
S.L.A. 49	Brazzaville	10 Toucans, 4 Martinets
S.L.A. 50	Ivato	6 Toucans, 3 Martinets, 1 Goéland, 1 Criquet
S.L.A. 51	Djibouti	3 Toucans, 4 Criquets
S.L.A. 52	Tan Son Nhut	1 Goéland, 2 Penguins, 5 Martinets, 5 Criquets
E.L.A.[3] 53	Bachmai	4 Goélands, 3 Stampes, 2 Penguins
Overseas Flights		
E.O.M.[4] 81 Mauritania	Bamako	8 Ansons (+ 5)
E.O.M. 82 Niger	Bamako	8 Ansons (+ 5)
E.O.M. 83 Béthune	Bangui	8 Martinets (+ 5)
E.O.M. 84 Arras	Pointe Noire	8 Martinets (+ 5)
E.O.M. 85 Madagascar	Ivato	8 Martinets (+ 3)

[1] S.L.A.: Secteur Liaison Air; Air Liaison Sector.
[2] G.L.A.: Groupe Liaison Air; Air Liaison Group.
[3] E.L.A.: Escale Liaison Air; Air Liaison Landing Place.
[4] E.O.M.: Escadrille d'Outre-Mer; Overseas Flight.

Liaison and Overseas, 1955

Formation	Stationing	Materiel
E.L.A.[1] 41	Dijon	1 Criquet, 5 Penguins, 4 Ramiers, 8 Martinets
E.L.A. 43	Bordeaux	3 Criquets, 2 Ramiers, 3 Martinets
E.L.A. 44	Aix-les-Mille	4 Criquets, 2 Ramiers, 7 Martinets (+ 2 miscellaneous)
E.L.A. 55	Lahr	3 Criquets, 4 Ramiers, 7 Martinets (+ 2 miscellaneous)
E.L.A. 56 Vaucluse	Persan-Beaumont	2 Martinets, 2 Dakotas, 9 Toucans (+ 5 miscellaneous)
G.L.A.[2] 45	Boufarik	4 Ramiers, 2 Toucans, 5 Martinets (+ 3 miscellaneous)
E.L.A. 46	Rabat-Ville	20 Ramiers, 6 Martinets (+ 3 miscellaneous)
E.L.A. 47	Tunis	2 Criquets, 5 Martinets, 5 Ramiers, 1 Toucan
G.L.A. 48	Dakar	4 Flamants, 2 Toucans (+ 4 miscellaneous)
G.L.A. 49	Brazzaville	1 Criquet, 8 Toucans, 2 Flamants
G.L.A. 50	Tananarive	8 Flamants, 6 Toucans
E.L.A. 57	Boufarik	10 helicopters
E.L.A. 57	Indochina	11 Criquets, 4 Penguins, 8 Martinets (+ 3 miscellaneous)
E.L.A. 54	Indochina	11 Criquets, 3 Penguins, 6 Martinets (+ 4 miscellaneous)
E.L.A. 1/65	Indochina	10 helicopters
E.L.A. 2/65	Indochina	12 helicopters
E.L.A. 51	Djibouti	3 Criquets, 3 Toucans
Overseas Flights		
E.O.M.[3] 81 Mauritania	Bamako	8 + 1 Flamant
E.O.M. 83 Béthune	Bangui	6 + 1 Flamant
E.O.M. 84 Arras	Pointe Noire	6 + 1 Flamant
E.O.M. 86 Hoggar	Blida	10 + 1 Flamant
E.O.M. 87 Tanezrouft	Blida	10 + 1 Flamant

[1] E.L.A.: Escale Liaison Aérienne; Air Liaison Landing Place.
[2] G.L.A.: Groupe Liaison Aérienne; Air Liaison Group.
[3] E.O.M.: Escadrille d'Outre-Mer; Overseas Flight.

The Stampe, an excellent training plane.

Morane 315's flying in formation in 1947.

An airplane little known in French aviation, the Barricuda, of the British Fleet Air Arm, specialized in torpedoeing and dive-bombing. It was used by the French Vaucluse air liaison flight from 1947 to 1956.

The first jet plane in service in the French Air Force, the Vampire.

The Ouragan (Hurricane), first of a long series.

These plans provided France, within the framework of mutual aid, with American planes, the F-84, F-86, and F-100, details of which are shown in the tables. They enabled the French to establish a remarkable operational infrastructure, financed in part by them, in part by Allied aid, and in part by the Allies themselves.

Besides these general plans established in an international framework, the nation was forced to plan its own efforts in order to attain the objectives necessary to its contribution to the common defense.

The most important plan of the period was indisputably the 5-year plan voted by the French Parliament on August 19, 1950. This was not an armament plan providing for production in all fields, but a program law permitting the expansion of the aeronautics industry. It provided program authorizations amounting to 217 billion francs—189 billion for the construction of 2,816 military

The Mystère IV A.

The SM B2.

A Vautour bomber.

F-84's in formation.

The reconnaissance version of the F-84.

The T-33.

The F-86 K Sabre.

The F-100, which was supplied to French units and was armed with the American atomic bomb, carried under double lock and key.

airplanes, 15 billion for military research, and 13 billion for civilian research.

Among the aircraft planned were the Ouragon (Hurricane), Vautour, Nord 2501, Fouga Magister, and Alouette helicopter, to which were added the jet planes Atar and Marbore.

It is, in fact, this 5-year plan that marks the renewal of the French aeronautics industry, with the Mystère IV, the Caravelle—which made its first flight in May 1955—and the Mirage I, which flew in June of the same year.

Another plan important for the Air Force was Plan VII, which embodied the decisions reached at the Lisbon conference, where the 92nd Session of the Atlantic Council was held in March 1952. This internal Air Force plan was an overall one covering all the steps to be taken to attain the objectives set. From then on all the resources of the Air Force increased regularly until 1960.

In fact, a large part of the resources employed were linked to the war in Algeria which developed from 1955 on. The strength, for example, varied depending on the number of conscripts kept on beyond the legal eighteen months of service. The units in France itself were also called on to deal with the situation in French North Africa.

In 1958, when General de Gaulle returned to power, defense policy took a very different orientation. This followed the end of the Algerian affair and France's withdrawal from the military organization of NATO.

It was during this period, which will be discussed later, that the Air Force assumed the appearance that it has today, but this would no doubt have been impossible without the decisions made under the Fourth Republic concerning nuclear arms.

After Russian atomic threats following the Suez expedition, Prime Minister Guy Mollet decided to orient the French military system toward the use of atomic energy. He increased the appropriations for nuclear research and launched research on an airplane capable of carrying a nuclear bomb beyond the iron curtain.

In spite of budget difficulties, major decisions were made in 1957 concerning the Mirage III, one hundred of which were ordered and whose derivative, the Mirage IV, was adopted as the first means of delivering a French atomic weapon.

To make possible the development of these planes as well as the development of a strategic ground-to-ground ballistic missile, the government was invited to present a 5-year aeronautical construction program.

The end of the Fourth Republic came before the draft of the law was presented, but from that moment the process was under way to provide France with a weapon capable of insuring its independence.

In service in the French Air Force in early 1961, the first Mirage III C's were received by Squadron 1/2, the Storks, and Squadron 3/2, the Alsace.

CHAPTER II

The French Air Force in Indochina (1945–1954)

When the war ended in Europe on May 8, 1945, the French presence in Indochina consisted only in the resistance of a few isolated posts on the borders of Cambodia and Laos. Since March 9, 1944, the Japanese had occupied the country, after a surprise attack in the course of which they had succeeded in capturing General Tavéra, the Air Force commander, and the greater part of the French garrisons.

At the time of the Japanese attack the French Air Force in Indochina, cut off from its sources of supply in materiel and spare parts, was no longer anything more than a patchwork force with no real effectiveness. With the dissolution of one unit after another, at the beginning of 1945 it had only a mixed air group under the command of Major Courthalac, consisting of Flight 1/CBS (Loire 130's) and the transport and bombing flight (Potez 542's and Potez 25 TOE's) and an air observation group which, commanded by Captain Postal, flew 19 Potez 25 TOE's, 3 Potez 542's, and 1 Potez 29 ambulance plane (Flights 1/595 and 1/42).

On March 9, 1945, the French defensive system evaporated under the blow dealt it by the Japanese army. In Cochin China in the south the Bien Hoa base was overwhelmed, while in Hanoi in the north the staff officers of the air command were captured at their residences. At the other bases the French blew up their fuel stocks and their planes, and only Flight 1/CBS, which had withdrawn to Dien Bien Phu, was able to carry out a few reconnaissances or machine-gun attacks against the Japanese columns for the benefit of General Alessandri. Rather than surrender, several officers organized detachments which disappeared into the jungle to go to unoccupied China or, in combination with French parachutists from the Indies, to continue the fight in Indochina (1st Lieutenant Chirent, Captain Mayaud, 1st Lieutenant Compain, Captain Horvatte, 1st Lieutenant Morlet, Captain Postal, Captain Descaves, etc.).

It was from China, moreover, that the first proposals came for reestablishing the French air forces in the Far East.

A Difficult Reestablishment

The French who had gone over into China were ready to place at the disposal of the Americans many pilots or observers who, because of their perfect familiarity with the Indochinese theater of operations, might become very valuable to them. And, in fact, the Americans made use of some of them, notably for observation missions on L-5's. The end of hostilities in Europe allowed the French to envisage, in the more or less immediate future, a return to Indochina and the reestablishment of an air force there. On May 17, 1945, General Sabattier, commander of the French troops in China, insisted on the reorganization of an Air Force command in Indochina. But at that time the situation of the Air Force did not permit sending to the Far East anything more than a few units equipped with C-47 Dakotas or P-47 Thunderbolts. Moreover, there was no question of sending any bombers at all, for the materiel of that category which the French had could not have been integrated into the B-24 Liberator and B-25 Mitchell units that the Americans were maintaining on the spot. However that may be, the creation of an Air Force command in Indochina was urgent both from considerations of prestige and in order to recover the great aerial infrastructure of the country. It was an established fact in August 1945, and Colonel Fay, Air Force attaché of the French mission to Admiral Mountbatten's Southeast Asia Command, took command of it.

Immediately, in anticipation of the organization of an expeditionary corps, the Air Force dispatched six C-47's and the Air Ministry scheduled the sending of transport and liaison sections (Ju 52's, Goélands, and Morane 500's) and of two groups of P-47's. But the idea of using P-47's in Indochina soon had to be abandoned. The United States, hostile to France's return to Saigon and Hanoi, would have refused to furnish the necessary spare parts. Moreover, the Thunderbolt, because of its weight and the length of runway necessary to operate it, could not have used any landing place in Indochina except Tan Son-Nhut, the Saigon airport. Early in September the Air Force general staff decided to form a complete squadron of Mosquitos (2 fighter-bomber groups and 1 reconnaissance group), which it proposed to engage in Southeast Asia. But in view of the enormous task facing the 6 Dakotas present at Jessore, in the Indies, the Air Ministry resolved to give priority to assigning 16 C-47's to the Indochinese theater of operations.

The fact remains that the allotment of air forces placed at Colonel Fay's disposal was far from corresponding to the real needs. The Air Force commander in Indochina would have needed many more transport planes, liaison planes, and fighter-bombers. For another thing, most of the airfields in Indochina, apart from the Tan Son-Nhut airport where RAF units were stationed, were occupied by thousands of Japanese military airmen. In October during a visit to Paris Colonel Fay had received many assurances concerning the equipping and reinforcement of the units that he commanded. He had been promised a transport group entirely equipped with Ju 52 Toucans, the GT 1/34, several Dakotas, and in particular a fighter group equipped with Spitfires that the British agreed to supply to the French. On November 15, 1945, after General Andrieu had been appointed Air Force commander in Indochina, Colonel Fay took charge of the units engaged. Early in the month, with all the Dakotas placed at his disposal he had formed a complete transport group, the Far East Frontier Group (Groupe de Marche d'Extrême-Orient/G.M.E.O.), which he had placed under the orders of Captain Grandvoynet. On November 26 Lieutenant Colonel Papin-Labazordière's 1st Fighter Squadron (GC I/7 and II/7) disembarked in Saigon. Since the Spitfire Mk IX's bought from the British were still not on hand, the Southeast Asia RAF turned over 8 Spitfire Mk VIII's to the French. In addition, several Ki-43 Oscars were taken from the Japanese and used for training the pilots of the I/7 at Phnom Penh.

In the operations that followed, in which several Catalinas from the Aéronavale took part, the transport air elements showed an astonishing faculty for adaptation to such diverse missions as the transport of VIP's (a C-47 took General Leclerc to Phnom Penh, where he brought about the reestablishment of diplomatic relations between France and Cambodia), logistic support of fighter groups, and even bombing (some C-47's were given bomb-dropping apparatus). Thus from September 1945 to February 1946 the Dakotas carried 8,000 passengers and 1,100 tons of freight, opening a series

Since allied materiel was not immediately available, the 1st Fighter Squadron had to use Japanese airplanes when it arrived in Indochina. Here, a Ki-43-IIB Oscar.

of airlines over Indochina, and dropped 15 tons of bombs. For their part, the fighter elements began on December 13, 1945, to operate with their Spitfire VIII's while awaiting the arrival of the Spitfire IX's. The latter were not ready until February 1946, but their entry into service reinforced the 1st Squadron's potential and made it possible to abandon the Japanese planes. They played a considerable part in operations by taking action in areas inaccessible to the ground troops and by making it possible to perfect tactical procedures used until the end of the Indochinese conflict. To reduce the delays in taking action on the ground, means of direct ground-to-air communication were developed and observation planes were assigned to guide the fighter planes to their objectives. Nevertheless, until its gradual replacement by the P-63 and later by the F6F and the F8F, the Spitfire remained poorly adapted to the Far Eastern theater of operations, essentially because of its short range (1-1/2 hours of flight, or 600 kilometers) and its inadequate radio equipment. On the other hand, it did not need very long runways, which was a very distinct advantage in view of the state of the infrastructure in Indochina.

The Insurrection

In April 1946 Colonel Fay's departure for France led to the fusion, under the orders of General Andrieu, of the Air Force command and the air forces engaged. At that time the Air Force had available: one fighter squadron, the 1st, divided between Tan Son-Nhut and Nha Trang; one subgrouping of transport aircraft, with the GT I/34 (Ju 52 Toucans) and the II/15, formerly the G.M.E.O. (C-47's); a section of liaison planes with Japanese craft and Morane 500's; and the support of a few units of the Aéronavale.

Arriving in Indochina in January 1947 with the Fighter Group I/3, Corsica, the Mosquitos were poorly adapted to the climate because of their wooden construction. Six months later their use had to be abandoned.

These forces had participated in the reconquest of Indochina, marked by the combined operation against Vientiane, in Laos, during which the Spitfires were engaged over 1,000 kilometers from their base, and the entry of French troops into Hanoi and Haiphong.

After the 1st Fighter Squadron was relieved by the 2nd (GC I/2 and III/2) in August 1946, the air forces of Indochina had to wait until the beginning of 1947 to receive a considerable reinforcement with the de Havilland Mosquito Mk VI's of the GC I/3, Corsica. Since October 30, 1946, the situation had seriously deteriorated, and on December 19 Ho Chi Minh had launched a general insurrection against the French. While the Mosquito made up for the Spitfire's shortcomings in range of action, it was very quickly found to be disappointing for many other reasons. It needed very long runways—which was why the GC I/3 was based at Tan Son-Nhut—and its wooden construction could not adapt itself to the climate. In addition, the lack of spare parts grounded many of the planes. For all these reasons the GC I/3 was withdrawn from operations in May 1947, five months after it went into action. Its replacement posed a number of problems that were insoluble at the time. The Air Force would have needed a colonial all-metal twin-engined plane capable of making ground attacks with bombs and machine guns and also carrying out observation missions. At one time the navy thought of the Bloch 175, but the idea was not followed up.

At about the same time, April 1947, General Bodet succeeded General Andrieu and proceeded to a reorganization of the Air Force. In July two tactical groupings were created and adapted to well-defined theaters of operations:

1) Tactical Grouping North (T.F.I.N.), attached to the command of the French troops of Northern Indochina, with the GC I/2, the GT Béarn, and a liaison section, plus an artillery observation air group (G.A.O.A.);

2) Tactical Grouping South (T.F.I.S.), adapted to the command of the French troops of Southern Indochina and directed by the Air Commander in the Far East himself, with a fighter group, the GT Anjou, part of the GT Béarn, Liaison Section No. 53, and the 1st and 2nd G.A.O.A.'s. Because of the size of the area that it had to cover, the T.F.I.S. was divided into two subgroupings, Cochin China and Annam.

Such an organization might seem to specialize the air forces in limited areas and, by dispersing them, reduce their effectiveness while also increasing their subordination to the ground command. Nevertheless, it was the only possible solution. Having no adversary in the air, the Air Force could do nothing but support the ground forces. However, with twenty-four hours' notice the command could concentrate all the transport aviation within one or the other of the tactical groupings.

In fact, up to that time, in spite of the presence of an Air Ministry representative in Hanoi, the tactical assignments had come down to the commanding officers of units (squadron, group, or detachment), who were themselves directly in contact with the ground units and at the same time base commanders. This decentralization and the creation of commands intended to coordinate all the air activities for the benefit of one or more defined territories signified an adaptation of the Air Force to the ground organization.

At that time, the middle of 1947, although the ground operations had slowed down somewhat, the air formations had not ceased to be engaged against the Viet Minh, whom they forced to dig in and among whom they generated a certain demoralization. That intensive engagement had entailed a rapid attrition of the materiel, and on the eve of the big confrontations of the fall of 1947 barely a score of Dakotas and Toucans of the transport subgroupings were in shape to fly. The relief of the 2nd Squadron by the 4th (GC I/4, Dauphiné, and II/4, Lafayette) brought new materiel to the fighter aviation, which was also in bad shape. During the first week of October 1947 the French offensive against the Viet Minh national redoubt of Haut-Tonkin was launched, supported by the GC I/4, some Morane 500 ambulance planes, two transport groups, and then, beginning on October 20, by the Dauntlesses and Catalinas of the Aéronavale. The breaking up of the Viet Minh formation in Haut-Tonkin made possible a better control of the frontier with China, and at the end of 1947 General Bodet regrouped the greater part of his units in Cochin China, organized a tactical subgrouping of South Annam, and prepared to proceed, in conjunction with the ground forces, to the pacification of those two regions. The operations began in February 1948 and assumed the form of a series of sudden, rapid, violent attacks, in which the airborne troops played an essential part.

The months of May and June were critical for the air forces of Indochina. The dissolution of the GT III/64, Tonkin, formed in October 1947, increased the burden on the transport forces. The C-47's needed important overhauls, while the Morane 500's had serious attrition problems. Finally, the Spitfires of the 4th Fighter Squadron were worn out. Of the 28 planes of that type at General Bodet's disposal, only 18 were in shape to take part in the operations in support of the ground forces. In September 1948 the arrival of the GC I/3, Navarre, of the 3rd Squadron distinctly

The Morane 500 Criquet, derived from the German Fieseler Storch, was one of the planes that adapted best to Indochina. It served in the air liaison squadrons and carried out evacuations of the sick and wounded.

Two Spitfire Mk IX's of the GC I/4 (4th Fighter Squadron). This plane did not need very long runways and was thus well suited for use in Indochina. However, its range of action was inadequate—a heavy handicap.

General Bodet, shown here in 1957, commanded the air forces in the Far East from April 1947 to March 1950.

improved the situation of the fighter element, which, in spite of the complaints of the command wanting to introduce a suitable colonial bomber in the Indochinese theater of operations, still had only the Spitfires. The Navarre group disembarked just in time to take part in two combined operations in Tonkin, "Ondine" and "Pegasus." At the beginning of 1949 it was joined by the other unit of the 3rd Squadron, GC II/3, Champagne.

The fighting of 1948 had confirmed the undeniable usefulness of fighter-bombers, which, in jungle operations, replaced artillery, which was difficult to use under such conditions. In addition, the March engagements had made use of the NC-701 Martinets, planes which had shown themselves to be first-class target finders and guides for the fighter units. Loaded with a heavy armament, they could even take part in supporting fire actions. The Air Command in the Far East did not think any the less of them because the few G.A.O.A.'s and Martinets that had been assigned to it were insufficient to mount an effective instruction force.

The Turning Point

At the beginning of 1949, faced with the evolution of the international situation and the necessity of replacing equipment which was no longer appropriate to the developing Indochinese conflict, General Bodet called for the modernization of the fighter units at his disposal with the introduction of the P-63 King Cobra. The turn of events in China, with the probable victory of the Communists, brought heavy threats to bear on Indochina itself. The responsible military officers feared that, once installed on the frontier of Tonkin (northern Vietnam), Mao Tse-tung's armies would actively support the Viet Minh or would give it considerable logistic support.

The Air Force was running into serious difficulties in another direction. The Spitfires were not capable of covering the Vietnamese border, from which danger might arise, and the Viet Minh antiaircraft was growing more and more destructive. In May 1949, 3 planes—1 Toucan and 2 Spitfires—were shot down and 25 others were hit. General Giap's Viet Minh troops were also adapting themselves to the air action and had learned how to disperse, camouflage themselves, and respect the strict rules of passive defense.

It was during the last half of the same year that the United States, concerned about the Communist advance in China, authorized the sending of P-63 King Cobras to Indochina. The first planes of this type arrived in the Far East toward the end of July 1949 aboard the aircraft carrier *Dixmude*. In the fall a whole squadron, the 5th (GC I/5, Vendée, II/5, Ile-de-France, and II/6, Normandy-Niemen), was ready to go into action. At the end of September the attack on fixed objectives, abandoned until then for lack of resources, could be resumed. During the same time the transport aviation was reinforced by a new group, the GT II/62, Franche-Comté, equipped with Toucans. Finally, with the creation of the EROM 80 at Bien Hoa on September 1, 1949, after the delivery of several NC-701's to the Air Command in the Far East, a specialized reconnaissance aviation made its appearance in Indochina.

At the beginning of 1950, when the Chinese Communists reached the Vietnamese border and decided to support Ho Chi Minh, the United States resolved to intensify its aid to France. In March 1950 General Hartemann, the new Air Commander in the Far East, met with representatives of the United States Army and informed them of his intention to organize an aerial battle fleet composed of four fighter groups equipped with jets, two bomber groups, and four transport groups. But the country's infrastructure hardly lent itself to the use of jet planes. And so the French got F6F Hellcats (2 cannon and 6 machine guns) and F8F Bearcats (four 12.7-mm machine guns or four 20-mm guns, rockets, napalm bombs or a load of conventional bombs). As for the bomber groups, they were to receive B-26 Invaders, which were especially well suited to the task that they would be entrusted with in Indochina (16 heavy machine guns and a range of 5½ hours of flight).

The first half of 1950 was also marked by the revamping of Tactical Groupings North and South and the appearance of the Tactical Air Groupings (G.A.T.A.C.) North, Center, and South, each adapted to an army operational staff. The term "adapted" did not indicate a subordination to the tactical ground commander, but rather direct contacts between the two staffs for a good functioning of air support. At that time the air forces were allocated as follows:

G.A.T.A.C. North: 2 groups of P-63's working as fighter-bombers; 2 groups of Ju 52's providing transport, parachuting, supply to isolated posts, and some bombing missions; 1 liaison flight, ELA 53, equipped with Martinets, Criquets, and Nord

A military review by General de Lattre, who arrived in Indochina in late 1950. In the background, the P-63's of the 5th Fighter Squadron.

The Junkers Ju 52 Toucan was an essential transport element in Indochina. Its hardiness made it very suitable for this theater of operations, and the crews, who at first had their doubts about it, very quickly came to appreciate it.

1000 Penguins; 1 observation and artillery ranging flight (3rd G.A.O.A.) with Morane 500's (command post at Hanoi);

G.A.T.A.C. Center: 1 group of Spitfire IX's (GC I/6, Corsica); the 1st G.A.O.A.; a few liaison planes (command post at Hué); and

G.A.T.A.C. South: 1 group of P-63's; 1 air liaison flight, ELA 52; the 2nd G.A.O.A.; the EROM 80; 1 detachment of Ju 52's (command post at Saigon).

In addition, a subgrouping of military air transport materiel controlled 3 transport groups (1 with C-47's and 2 with Ju 52's), two of which were at the disposal of the G.A.T.A.C. North.

At the end of October 1950 the first Hellcats brought by the aircraft carrier *Dixmude* arrived in Indochina. A little over two months later the arrival of General de Lattre de Tassigny at the head of the Far East expeditionary corps was aimed at reestablishing a general situation that was becoming more and more unfavorable to the French army. The Air Force was engaged in the Battle of Vinh Yen, on which, in the middle of January 1951, the future of all Tonkin was staked. Fighter aviation contributed to stopping the Viet Minh offensive against Hanoi, flying no fewer than 1,700 sorties, in the course of which it used napalm. The number of planes concentrated under the authority of the G.A.T.A.C. North at that time, 114 out of 147, is a good indication of the gravity of the threat that hung over the region.

In the meantime, the crews that had landed in Indochina at the beginning of 1951 had taken over the first B-26 Invaders allotted by the Americans and formed the bomber group GB I/19, Gascony. The event was of some consequence, representing a true rebirth of French bombing aviation, which had disappeared in 1945 and no longer existed except in the C.E.A.M. (Centre d'Expérimentation Aériennes Militaires/Military Air Experiment Center) in Mont-de-Marsan, where a sizable nucleus of former bombardiers was assigned. Based in Tourane, the Gascony group, which would later be joined by the GB I/25, Tunisia (March 1952), and the GB I/91, Burgundy (June 1954), was directly subordinate to the Air Command in the Far East, of which it constituted the general reserve. The first B-26's took part in the Battle of Mao Khé, engaged to safeguard Haiphong, and then in the Battle of the Day (May and June 1951). They gave very good results there both as assault planes and as bombers.

In November 1951 General de Lattre decided to take the initiative again, conducting two air-ground operations in the regions of Cho Bo and Hoa Binh, held by the Viet Minh. The Air Force therefore concentrated in Tonkin a large part of its forces (GC I/8, Saintonge, and I/9, Limousin, using Bearcats, GC III/6, using Bearcats and P-63's, a

A B-26 Invader from the Nha Trang air base. Until this powerfully armed, twin-engined plane was used, bombers had not participated in the conflict. The first B-26's went into action in February 1951 with the GB I/19, Gascony.

General Chassin succeeded General Hartemann at the head of the Far East Air Command after the latter's disappearance. Chassin remained in Indochina for two years, 1951 to 1953.

detachment of GB I/19, using B-26's, GT II/62, I/64, and II/64, plus one G.A.O.A.), which it launched in an attack which, although somewhat successful at the outset, rather quickly turned to the disadvantage of the French army. In the end the air forces had to cover the withdrawal of the ground forces toward the Red River delta. Under fighter protection, made necessary by the increase in Viet Minh antiaircraft fire, the transport groups were employed in an airlift operation that supplied the encircled Hoa Binh garrison.

Toward Dien Bien Phu

In April 1951 the tragic death of General Hartemann, killed when his B-26 had an accident over Cao Bang, had brought General Chassin, head of the 3rd Air Region, to the head of the Far East Air Command. Chassin, arguing from the results obtained by aviation in the operations of 1951, had sent word to France asking for an increase in his resources. But the Air Force was unable to extend itself any further and could maintain in Indochina only some 10,000 men, barely enough manpower to arm and engage 4 fighter groups, 3 transport groups, and 2 bomber groups. In the context of 1952 the 300 planes at the disposal of the air forces of the Far East did not represent a strength capable of controlling the whole of the theater of operations and opposing the Viet Minh initiatives while responding to the demands of the ground command. Nevertheless, in October 1952 when the Viet Minh set out for the attack on Nghialo, General Chassin was able to engage about a hundred fighters and twenty bombers guided by Criquets. The flares dropped over the battlefield at night by the Dakotas (Luciole missions) enabled the air forces to cover Nghialo continuously.

The F8F Bearcat, capable of carrying bombs, rockets, and napalm, was a formidable adversary of the Viet Minh in the last years of the conflict. Here, F8F's at Dien Bien Phu.

Parallel to this, in August 1952, the command mounted strategic bombing expeditions against the Viet Minh's lines of communication near the Chinese border. But until May 1954, when a bombing subgrouping was organized, the action of the B-26's nearly always took the form of close air support of ground troops.

In June 1953 General Lauzin succeeded General Chassin at the Far East Air Command. Two months earlier the Viet Minh pressure against Luang Prabang, the capital of Laos, had compelled the responsible officers of the Air Force in Indochina to create a sub-G.A.T.A.C. Laos, whose contribution to stopping the offensive of Giap's regiments was essential. For the transport element 1953 was the year of the airlifts, notably the evacuation of Na San by the C-47's (the Ju 52's had been gradually withdrawn from operations) of the GT II/62, I/64, and II/64. After its participation in "Operation Hirondelle" (a French offensive intended to seize the caves of Lang Son, where the Viet Minh were storing the materiel they received from China), the Air Force was engaged, within the framework of the actions conducted by General Navarre, the new commander in chief in the Far East, in "Operation Castor" (November 1953). This last operation was the taking of the village and valley of Dien Bien Phu. The place was invested by several battalions of parachutists supported by B-26's, Privateers, and Hellcats from the aircraft carrier *Arromanches*. An airfield was then established, on which the first C-47's landed on November 24.

Nevertheless, at the beginning of 1954 the situation in Indochina was not very good. The fighting that was going on more or less all over the country had compelled the Air Force to scatter its forces over some fifteen bases. Suddenly, on March 13, 1954, the Viet Minh divisions hurled themselves into the assault on Dien Bien Phu, and sixty-two hours later their artillery was able to fire on the airfield and destroy 11 airplanes and 2 helicopters there. Dien Bien Phu could not expect air support soon, except for what could be provided from bases within a few hundred kilometers of it. Two and a half fighter groups equipped with Bearcats, two bomber groups with B-26's, and 120 transport planes (100 Dakotas and 20 C-119 Boxcars sent by the United States) of the Air Force and the navy's Hellcats, Helldivers, and Privateers did what they could to delay the fall of the entrenched camp. The bombers and fighters poured tens of tons of bombs and a quantity of napalm on the enemy positions. But the Viet Minh antiaircraft, made up of 37-mm Soviet guns and 12.7-mm machine guns, was extremely dangerous, as is evidenced by the 62 aircraft lost in the battle. On May 8, 1954, the airlift conducted by the transport groups had to stop as a result of the capitulation of Dien Bien Phu.

After its fall the regrouping of the Viet Minh units and their installation in fortified villages chosen as starting bases for their offensive against the Tonkin delta became the object of a bombing

Toward the end of the conflict, and especially during the Battle of Dien Bien Phu, the United States supplied many C-119 Boxcar transport planes to the French Air Force.

With bombs exploding near it, a C-47 Dakota taxis on the runway at Dien Bien Phu. This twin-engined American plane was the mainstay of the transport aviation in Indochina. Besides airborne operations, the opening and operation of the airlines, and supply missions, it even did bombing.

General Lauzin (right), photographed here in Marrakech, October 1958, was appointed Far East Air Commander in June 1953.

A B-26 Invader with its eight 12.7-millimeter nose machine guns visible.

plan and provided suitable targets for massive actions by the B-26's, formations of which sometimes ran as high as 24 planes. Transport, for its part, was enriched by a new group, the GT Senegal, formed in January 1954. Finally, at the time of the cease-fire of July 27, 1954, the GT Anjou was in the process of conversion to Nord 2501's, but that plane was never tried out in operations.

Nevertheless, the transport aviation took on the task of evacuating civilian and military refugees from the north by mounting a series of airlifts. In addition, it carried the international control commissions all over Indochina and continued to operate the internal airlines.

Balance Sheet for a Nine Years' War

Far from carrying out independent actions, in Indochina the Air Force was almost always an immediate auxiliary of the ground forces. This situation appears as a consequence of the conditions under which the Indochinese conflict developed, since it was, in fact, nothing other than a long and bitter guerilla war punctuated at long intervals by a more intensive military action which resulted from a change in the balance of the forces on the spot (the equipping and enhancing of the Viet Minh forces through the aid of the Chinese Communists) or from the implementation of a

French campaign plan designed to bring about decisive results.

Therefore, aviation, a weapon of mass destruction, was employed in a reduced manner, limited to direct or indirect support actions, machine-gun attacks on the ground against a hidden enemy, or simple troop transport operations. The formula of the single command adopted in this theater of operations was not unconnected with that state of affairs. Apart from operations based on air transport, no common action offering possibilities of joint operations was considered. The air forces became a contributory arm called upon to serve rather than aid the ground forces. The organization of the latter, their deployment, and their equipment had a prime influence on the employment of the air forces.

One may wonder whether fighter aviation had any place in Indochina. In fact, most of the time it acted to give urgently needed aid to the ground forces. An assault air force equipped with tough, armored, two-seated twin-engined planes would no doubt have been more useful.

As for bombers, they were used in small groups. It is true that the enemy's potential supply source was inaccessible since it was situated in a foreign country, China. Moreover, the Viet Minh industrial and economic system was not very vulnerable because of its dispersion and dilution. The only action capable of reducing the enemy strength would have been the interception of supplies coming from China. But that was beyond the Air Force's capabilities. Transport aviation, however, had a principal role. Without it no airborne opera-

In 1950 the helicopter was introduced into the Indochinese theater of operations, where it effected the evacuation of the sick and wounded, picked up escaped prisoners of war and pilots who had been shot down, and flew combat missions with the liaison flights.

tion would have been possible nor any airlift. In addition, it supplied isolated posts and even big cities, such as Hanoi, where it averted famine in early 1947. It also established internal airlines which were soon found to be indispensable and profitable, and even compensated for nearly six years for the lack of an aerial bombing force. Reconnaissance aviation made use of such diverse craft as the Martinet, the R-F8F Bearcat, and the RB-26. But in the Far East, in spite of the services it rendered, it was defeated both by the enormous size of its field of action and by the difficulties of reconnaissance in the Indochinese terrain. Finally, the liaison flights, equipped with Martinets, Penguins, Criquets, and Beavers, were the jacks-of-all-trades in Indochina. However, they never received the means necessary to carry out the missions that the command demanded of them.

The Air Force used the helicopter for the first time in its history during the war in Indochina, starting in April 1950. It carried out evacuations of the wounded, until then entrusted to Morane 500's, and picked up fallen crews and escapees. Forty-two helicopters served in the Indochinese theater of operations (Hiller UH-12A's, H-23A's, H-23B's, and Sikorsky S-51's and S-55's). They effected over 10,000 evacuations and recovered 38 pilots and 80 escapees from 1950 to 1954.

CHAPTER III

The French Air Force in the War in Algeria (1954–1962)

The Adaptation of Operational Structures to the Army's Organization

As early as the end of 1954 the expansion of the Algerian insurrection launched on November 1 of that year had compelled the Air Force to reinforce the elements that it maintained there. At the same time the air forces had had to adapt themselves to the peculiar style of warfare involved in the operations to maintain order that were conducted by the army. This resulted in the adoption of very specific operational structures as well as the use of materiel which answered the needs of that theater of operations.

From the opening of hostilities to the cease-fire the Air Force in Algeria concentrated almost exclusively on support of the land and sea forces in the form of combined operations by reconnaissance, fire, and transport. To achieve this it had to model its operational structures on the organization of the army and at the same time develop its traditional means of action by building up a considerable light aviation and a fleet of helicopters.

The first of these objectives was pursued by the organization, starting early in 1956, of the G.A.T.A.C.'s (tactical air groupings), which permitted a certain decentralization of responsibilities and a greater rapidity of action. The G.A.T.A.C. No. 1 was associated with the command of the military region of Constantine, the G.A.T.A.C. No. 2 with that of Oran, and the G.A.T.A.C. No. 3 with that of Algiers. Each of these tactical air groupings had Air command posts (P.A.C.'s) adapted to operational sectors, which functioned effectively thanks to a solid network of signals based on radio and Hertzian cables from light and heavy support forces stationed on a tight gridwork of airfields. This organization thus resulted in a "continuous combined control of operations" between the Air Force and the army within operational command posts. These command posts exercised their authority over geographically and hence militarily homogeneous regions, for the sectors or zones of territorial responsibility based on the administrative boundaries of Algeria had no logical demarcation from the operational point of view. Moreover, the joint operations rooms provided the possibility of a complete check on the air and ground activities under way. This air-ground policy resulted in a previously unknown development of communications networks and in the creation of delegations of authority to officers who acted literally as inspectors of operations. The extension of such assignments to the army proved as indispensable as it was in the Air Force.

Early in 1959 the Air Force perfected the instrument that it had forged at the whim of circumstances during the preceding four years in order to give it the maximum effectiveness at the minimum cost. In accordance with the practice adopted in France proper, the fusion of the air defense zone (Z.D.A.) with the air region enabled the 5th Air Region to equip itself with proper means of checking on the whole of the operations. In this way the command was able to readapt the means necessary to operations that were under way, whether they were connected with maintaining order or with air defense in the strict sense. At the same time the G.A.T.A.C.'s received complete control of the light aviation flights stationed in their territory, which had formerly been run administratively and directed from the point of view of operational training by a regional entity called a light aviation grouping. The Challe plan, which was the basis of this

The AD-4 Skyraider single-engined assault fighter, shipborne or not, was engaged in Algeria within the general framework of modernization of the flying materiel in the three squadrons integrated into the 20th Pursuit Squadron.

A North American T-6 on patrol in Algeria. From the beginning of the conflict these training planes were armed and carried out fire-support missions.

In Algeria the helicopter proved to be a combat tool remarkably well adapted to the nature of the terrain and the mobility of the enemy. Here, a light Alouette II helicopter.

reform, also involved the provisional establishment of detachments in the zone where the commander in chief decided, with his reserves, to bring the greatest effort to bear. The air forces, thus closely linked with the conception and execution of the missions required by this plan, had to follow the rhythm imposed, just as the army did. However, setting up short-lived multiple elements by a staff such as that of the 5th Air Region could not insure the necessary flexibility. Thus arose the idea of decentralizing this responsibility by entrusting it, in each of the territories of the G.A.T.A.C.'s, to the commanding officer of a large base capable of quickly putting into action the logistic support corresponding to the shifting of helicopters, air command post antennas, air commandos, or detachments of light planes. Hence the appearance of the territorial support brigades (B.T.S.'s) directly responsible to the air region but expected to provide for the needs of a G.A.T.A.C.: the B.T.S. of Telergma for the G.A.T.A.C. No. 1, of Oran for No. 2, and of Blida for No. 3.

Thus the Air Force had provided itself with structures that enabled it to act quickly and effectively in support of the ground forces against a mobile enemy familiar with the terrain on which it was fighting.

Air Force Missions

At the beginning of the conflict the air forces were divided among four major types of missions: intelligence/reconnaissance, fire support, transport, and special missions. Later, in liaison with the army, they had to insure the impermeability of the barriers set up along the Tunisian and Moroccan frontiers after the independence of those two countries, which the National Liberation Front used as starting bases for its incursions into Algerian territory.

1) Intelligence: The Air Force's activity in this area gave rise to two kinds of missions, aerial observation and aerial reconnaissance.

Aerial observation, that is, the execution at short range, directly for the benefit of the ground units engaged, of all aerial intelligence missions by continuous air cover and immediate diffusion of

Sipa S 12's, planes which served with the Sipa 11 in the Light Aircraft and Support Flights (EALA's) from 1956 on. They were the "maids of all work" of the Algerian war.

intelligence, included sector surveillance missions aimed at the security of a formation, all the more indispensable since the ground units posted for the protection of sensitive points or of streams of traffic were very often isolated and since the terrain and the relative weakness of these units prohibited taking all the security measures desirable in the face of a scattered, camouflaged, and sporadically aggressive enemy; combat support missions designed for surveillance of the enemy's movements and activity; and fire control missions consisting in increasing the effect of aerial or surface fire by ranging, marking, or guiding.

Aerial reconnaissance, participation in the search for information in sensitive zones and diffusion of this information, included both visual and photographic reconnaissance missions and missions covering particular points.

2) Fire support: This included armed reconnaissance missions in the course of which a plane traversed a definite zone or itinerary and attacked the objectives that it discovered itself (this procedure was generally not very effective against a mobile enemy experienced in the art of camouflage); missions of accompanying and protecting troops, combined with observation missions, in the course of which the plane attacked objectives that it discovered or that were pointed out to it by the troops on the ground; missions attacking preplanned objectives, consisting in the destruction of objectives discovered by aerial intelligence or reported by agents (fortified douars—villages—or fortified mechtas, caves, wooded areas); and missions attacking special objectives, that is, support given at a request for aid sent by a unit in difficulty on the ground.

3) Transport support: This included missions of air transport of units or of personnel from one airfield to another (transport of a logistic nature between France and Algeria or convoying of units from one zone to another within the operational framework); transport of personnel or materiel by helicopter; supply by air; assault transport operations by airplane or helicopter; medical evacuations

An observation, liaison, and medical evacuation vehicle, the Max Holste 1521 Broussard was a plane particularly well adapted to the Algerian theater of operations.

In August 1960 the North American T-28 Fennec began replacing the T-6 in Algeria. About a hundred planes of this type were engaged in operations.

After first being used in the Indochinese conflict, the Noratlases served in the transport units stationed in Algeria: the 1/62, Algeria, the 2/62, Anjou, and the 3/62, Sahara.

(EVASAN); and liaison missions for the authorities in case of urgency or of a breakdown of the specialized land or sea channels.

4) Special missions, including:

Command in flight: flying army command post or combined army-air authority entrusted with the execution of a specific operation; flying air command post entrusted with throwing Air Force resources into a specified zone; guidance of an operation by marking objectives by means of smoke bombs, by observation of the attacks and transmission of corresponding corrections, or by photographic verification of results;

Radio relay: any plane that heard a call without an answer served, as far as possible, as a relay radio;

"Luciole" missions, which consisted in providing illumination of a reduced area during a limited time at the request of troops on the ground.

Other special missions included dropping leaflets, the protection of crops, the interception of doubtful planes, and interceptions intended to prevent violations of the frontier.

Resources and Materiel

The nature of the war waged in Algeria compelled the Air Force to develop a large support force of light aircraft as well as a fleet of helicopters. It should be noted that the heterogeneity of the materiel placed at the disposal of the units posed, throughout the conflict, important technical and logistical problems which led the command to attempt a simplification of the stock of aircraft.

For lack of sufficient resources the Air Force, from the beginning of the conflict, had to engage training planes armed with light machine guns. However, in June 1955 four flights of light airplanes (ELA 71 to 74), equipped with Morane 500's, were formed. They were reorganized in March 1956 to form a Grouping of Light Support Aircraft (G.A.L.A.) comprising 3 flights of Morane 733's, supplemented by a training flight. Another grouping of flights of light support airplanes (E.A.L.A.) was established in Morocco with 4 units of T-6's, parallel to the organization of 3 flights of Sipa 111's and 112's which did not belong to any grouping. The multiplicity of training units then led the command to create a single center (in June 1956) which, located in Reghaia until its dissolution in December 1956, was called the Training Center for Crews of Light Planes in North Africa (C.I.E.A.L.). Finally, to determine the needs of the light support aviation an antenna from the Military Air Experiment Center (C.E.A.M.) was sent to Telergma. It would be used for numerous tests there on Morane 733's and Max-Holste 1521 Broussards. In 1957 the E.A.L.A.'s were renamed liaison and observation flights (E.L.O.'s), and the Morane 500, which was at the end of its service days, was gradually replaced by the Broussard aircraft. In the meantime, the light support aviation had made considerable strides. By virtue of the formula of sponsorship, the fighter squadrons furnished it with many pilots trained in the United States within the NATO framework. (By 1960 the attrition of the T-6's forced the command to bring into action the T-28 Fennec, about a hundred of which served in Algeria.)

From the beginning of the rebellion the reservist training centers (C.E.R.'s) of North Africa were engaged in maintaining order and executing missions that would normally have devolved upon the light aircraft. In 1956 the extension of the conflict obliged the Air Force to call for a certain number of volunteer reservists, who filled the C.E.R.'s, whose regular personnel was also increased. On March 1, 1957, the two C.E.R.'s in Algeria were converted into reserve light support flights (E.R.A.L.A.'s), which ceased in February 1962.

In addition to the importance of light support aircraft, the war in Algeria revealed the full significance of the action of the helicopter. It was so important that certain officials even envisaged, on the eve of the 1960s, making it, within an air armament simplified to the maximum, the essential element of intervention. In fact, in Algeria the helicopter performed multiple functions, from carrying airborne assault troops to cannonading particular objectives, as well as reconnaissance and medical evacuation missions. In addition, it provided in the pacified regions of the country the omnipresence of the administration and the police. The Bell 47, the H-19, and most especially the H-34, sometimes armed with a 20-millimeter port gun, particularly distinguished themselves in the operations to maintain order.

The Algerian war thus displayed the advantages of massive employment of light support aviation in antiguerilla actions and at the same time the remarkable adaptation of the Air Force to a very specific theater of operations and to an enemy that was always on the move and that knew how to take full advantage of the terrain. There were, however, some disadvantages: the dispersion of the units entailed heavy costs in both technical personnel and in equipment.

CHAPTER IV

The French Air Force in the Suez Expedition (October–November 1956)

Unimportant as it may seem, the Air Force's participation in the Suez expedition ("Operation Musketeer Revised") was, nevertheless, spectacular. In fact, it took place at two levels: first, the units engaged within the framework of the Allied air forces, and, second, those which, under the Israeli flag, provided the defense of the nerve centers and cities of the Hebrew state. The former consisted of the 36 F-84 F Thunderstreaks belonging to groups 1/3 and 3/3 of the 3rd Fighter Squadron (based at Akrotiri on the island of Cyprus), the 15 F-84 F Thunderflashes of reconnaissance squadron 4/33, and the Noratlases and C-47 Dakotas of the transport formations 1/61, 3/61, and 2/63 stationed at Tymbou. The latter consisted of 18 Mystère IV's turned over to Israel during the last week of October, 18 F-84 F's which landed at Lydda at the end of October, and the Noratlases of the 64th Squadron, at Haifa. Thus General Brohon, who, under the command of Air Marshal Barnett, directed the French air forces in Cyprus and, unofficially, in Israel, had a little under 150 aircraft out of the 600 (including Aéronavale craft) that France and Great Britain were prepared to launch against Egypt. To oppose these, Egypt had about a hundred Meteors and Vampires but also some very modern Soviet planes such as the MiG-15 (120 planes) and fifty Il-28's.

The employment of the air forces had given rise to many discussions between the French and the British. The former wanted an air action limited to the Egyptian airfields, accompanied by airborne troops who in four days would assure the Allies of control of the Suez Canal. The latter felt, on the other hand, that after annihilating the Egyptian air force the Franco-British air forces should, before any land or airborne action, bring about a total paralysis of Egypt. This "aeropsychological" phase had the major shortcoming, as the French strategists emphasized, of allowing too long a time to elapse between the preliminary air attack and the landing of the ground forces. Moreover, it was unlikely that it would end in a popular revolution against Gamal Abdel Nasser. Events would prove the French views correct, and the "aeropsychological" phase was a more or less complete failure.

The Air Battle

Although the French Air Force officially entered the conflict on November 1, 1956, it was actually

An RF-84 of the 33rd Reconnaissance Squadron in Cyprus.

An F-84 F Thunderstreak of the 3rd Fighter Squadron being resupplied with munitions at the Akrotiri base in Cyprus.

on October 31 that it first pitted itself against the Egyptian army. That day the F-84 F's from Lydda attacked a brigade of heavy tanks that were blocking the Israeli advance in the central Sinai and destroyed 38 of them. During the night the RF-84 F's of the 4/33 reported that the modern planes of the Egyptian air forces were being dispersed. Nasser himself had been behind this action. Thus 20 MiG-15's and about 20 Il-28's went to Syria and Saudi Arabia, while 24 Il-28's regrouped at the Luxor airfield.

At dawn on November 1, 40 F-84 F's of the 3rd Fighter Squadron, armed with rockets and having a range of ninety minutes' flight, opened the air battle at the same time as the planes of the RAF and the British Fleet Air Arm. At the end of the day the Egyptian air force was largely neutralized, and the few airplanes that had succeeded in getting into the air had been swept from the sky. During the night the Bomber Command returned to the charge, bombing 4 enemy airfields. Finally, on the afternoon of November 2, the Franco-British commanders could consider the Egyptian air forces practically annihilated. The concentration of the enemy bases in the Suez Canal region and in the vicinity of Cairo had considerably facilitated the Allies' task. As in a ballet regulated to the smallest detail, the French and British fighter-bombers had appeared every quarter hour or even every ten minutes over their objectives, and they had prevented any attempt by the enemy to take off.

Once the air battle had been won, the Allied air forces occupied themselves with preparing the ground for the airborne and amphibian troops. Tank concentrations, barracks, roads, coastal batteries, and antiaircraft positions situated around drop zones were the object of powerful attacks. Also, since the 24 Il-28 bombers at Luxor might constitute a serious threat to the transport fleet for landing operations, the Canberras and Valiants of the Bomber Command tried two nights in a row to destroy them on the ground, but without success. It was necessary to call upon 18 French F-84 F's to accomplish that mission.

Apart from the antiaircraft fire, which grew stronger day by day and damaged several F-84's, the Allied aviation retained mastery of the skies throughout the remainder of the battle. It accompanied the Nord 2501's which dropped French parachutists of the 10th Division on the junction-canal on the morning of October 5 and at Port Fuad that afternoon. On that occasion it operated in cooperation with support control officers parachuted at the same time as the assault troops, destroyed several antiaircraft nests, and blocked the tank counterattacks. On October 6, while the amphibian forces were getting a foothold, the Allied air forces supplied the airborne troops' bridgeheads. During the following night the cease-fire went into effect and put an end to the operation. In the fighting the Air Force had lost only a single plane, an F-84 F that its pilot had had to abandon because of the failure of one of its jets while it was over the Sinai desert.

The Suez expedition brilliantly confirmed the validity of the concept of the preliminary air battle. And it is almost certain that, if it had not been annihilated on its air bases, the Egyptian air force could have hampered the airborne and amphibian phase of the expedition, just as it would have prevented the Allied planes from giving the ground troops all the desired support. In 1967 the Israelis had not forgotten the lessons of this campaign when they surprised the Egyptian air forces on the ground and were able to launch a lightning campaign, on the ground, which took them in six days to the banks of the Suez Canal.

CHAPTER V

The Air Force in the Nuclear Age (1958–1980)

The return to power of General Charles de Gaulle was to bring about, at the end of the Algerian war, a profound change in the orientation of the French nation's defense. That change, the principles of which were defined by the edict of January 1959, provoked a considerable change in the military structures.

The successive reorganizations of the Armed Forces Ministry would make it possible to manufacture and utilize better the military instrument that corresponded to the armed services' new missions. The Air Force, which would be the first to bring nuclear arms into play, finally defined the structures adapted to its operational and technical needs. It gradually took on a new appearance.

The creation in 1958 of the Armed Forces Ministry was accompanied by abolition of the offices of the secretaries of state, who were replaced by deputy ministers for Air, Land, and Navy. This step strengthened the powers of the minister but preserved the specificity of the Department of Air. In 1961 a new organization came into existence.

The deputy ministers for the three armed forces were phased out in their turn. Each chief of staff (Air, Land, Navy) was invested with powers of command in relation to the directorates which provided the maintenance and provisioning of his branch (with the exception, however, of the personnel directorates, which would not be subordinated to them until 1973). Immediately under the minister were a secretary general for administration and a deputy minister for armaments and, beginning in 1962, a chief of staff of the armed forces. In 1958 there was a general staff of the armed forces, replaced in 1961 by an interservice general staff with less extensive powers than the general staff of the armed forces of 1962.

These structures, shown in the table, and the functions of the principal officials as well, have changed little from 1962 to the present.

In 1960 the Air Force adopted an organization which included both specialized operational commands and air regions. This was slightly modified in 1964 when the management of all the common resources was entrusted to the regions, the operational commands retaining the specialized resources.

In the same period Order 1257 was issued, giving the air bases their present structure except for a few details. The new model air base, which was the result of many studies and experiments conducted in the 1950s, became the keystone of the total edifice of the Air Force. It was Order 1257 that established the unity of management exercised by the base commander over units subordinate to either a region or to various big commands. As an example, reproduced here is the organizational chart of Air Base 107, Villacoublay, in 1968.

These new Air Force structures were aimed at effectiveness; they were also especially economical. This desire for economy was of major importance between 1964 and 1968, when the Air Force was seeing its personnel strength decrease and its missions increase with the establishment of strategic forces of the first and second generations.

The missions assigned to the Air Force obviously flow from the general missions assigned to the armed forces. These have evolved very little since 1962, although the conditions of their execution have been marked by France's withdrawal from the military organization of NATO.

The missions of the armed forces are currently aimed at insuring the nation's independence; providing for the defense of the territory and its approaches, in cooperation with allies or alone; and protecting distant territories and meeting external obligations. Today's Air Force participates actively in these general missions.

It brings into play two components of the strategic nuclear force, the Mirage IV and the ground-to-ground strategic missiles. Within the tactical air force it has the combat aircraft Mirage III E and Jaguar, equipped with tactical atomic weapons.

Air defense, inseparable from the nuclear forces to which it gives a high level of protection, also participates in the mission of defense of the territory. For that purpose it continuously surveys the national air space by means of a completely automated radar network.

Finally, the capacity for external action is pro-

The Mirage III E began to reach the units in January 1964. The Air Ministry signed several contracts for the acquisition of 340 planes of this type.

vided by both the Jaguar planes, which can be refueled in flight, and by military air transport, mostly equipped with Transalls.

The French Air Force today, while profoundly different from what it was from 1947 to 1958, still owes a great deal to the efforts made in that period to modernize it. These include technical efforts to relaunch and develop an aeronautics industry, which, after a difficult start, has become one of the finest in the world. The work done to develop planes that can stand comparison with those of other countries—the Mirage, the Concorde, and the Airbus, to mention only the most famous—has been supplemented by the work accomplished in related or complementary fields, such as engines and telecommunications. Also included are efforts to create the operational and logistic infrastructures indispensable to the employment of modern aerial materiel, to study and define an organization at last adapted to the potential offered by the air service, and to shape, train, and perfect the personnel on whom the quality of the French armed forces primarily rests (this point must be insisted upon). Since the liberation the Air Force has done a great amount of work in the area of education, which has provided the country with talented specialists, particularly in the leading industries. Finally, one must note the efforts made to bring administrative and management resources up to the level of operational achievements.

All of these efforts were to be carried out from 1960 on at the financial pace determined by the military planning bills, the first two of which covered 1960–1964 and 1965–1970 respectively. At the close of the fourth consecutive planning bill's term it is no exaggeration to say that these efforts have produced positive results.

Through the various changes that it has known the Air Force of the 1980s is the direct heir of that of the 1950s. It is also the heir of that military aviation of the first years of the twentieth century which bequeathed to it the traditions that it proudly maintains.

Organization of the Armed Forces in 1960

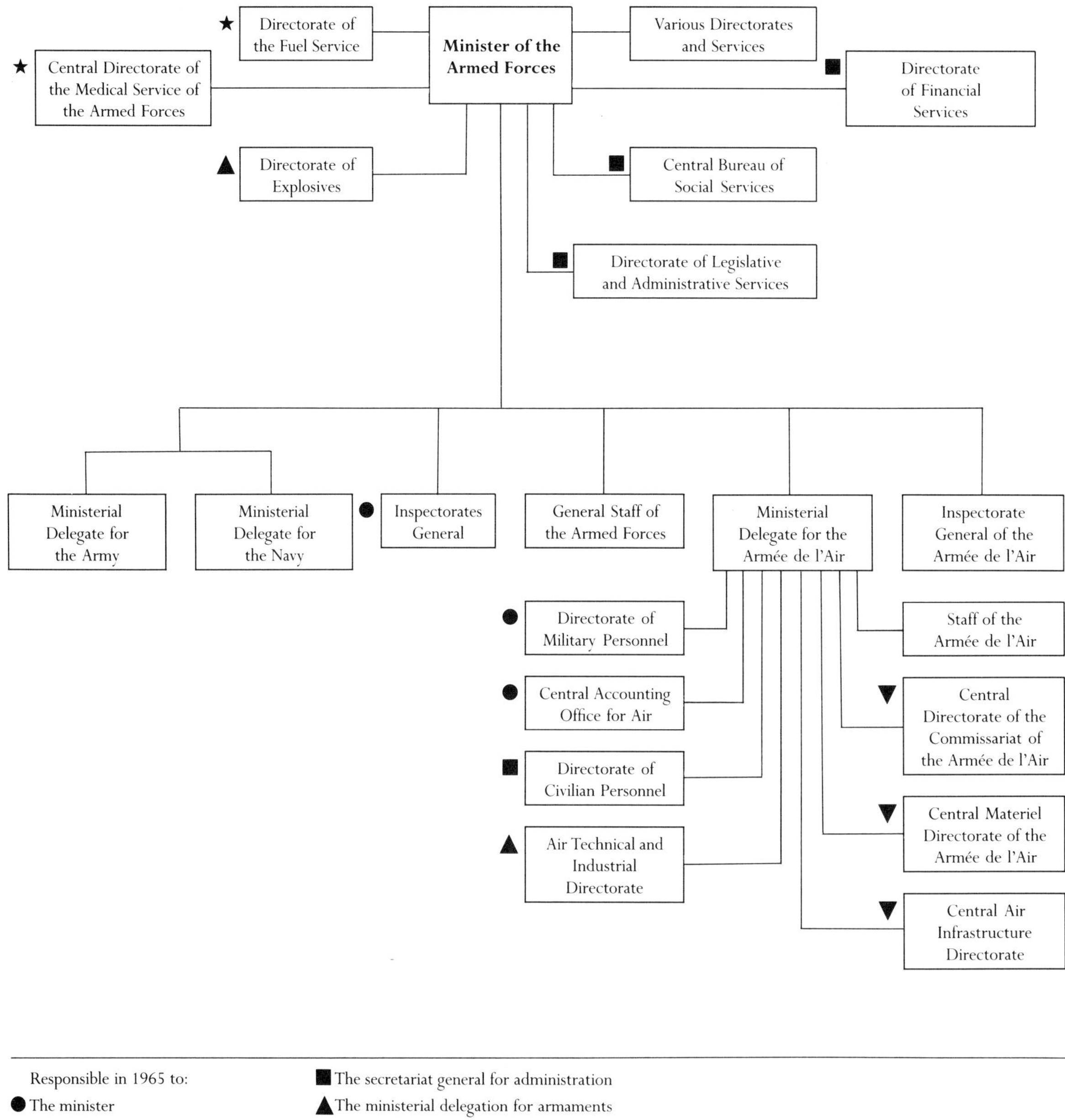

Responsible in 1965 to:

● The minister
★ The general staff of the armed forces
■ The secretariat general for administration
▲ The ministerial delegation for armaments
▼ The Air general staff

Organization of the Armed Forces in 1965

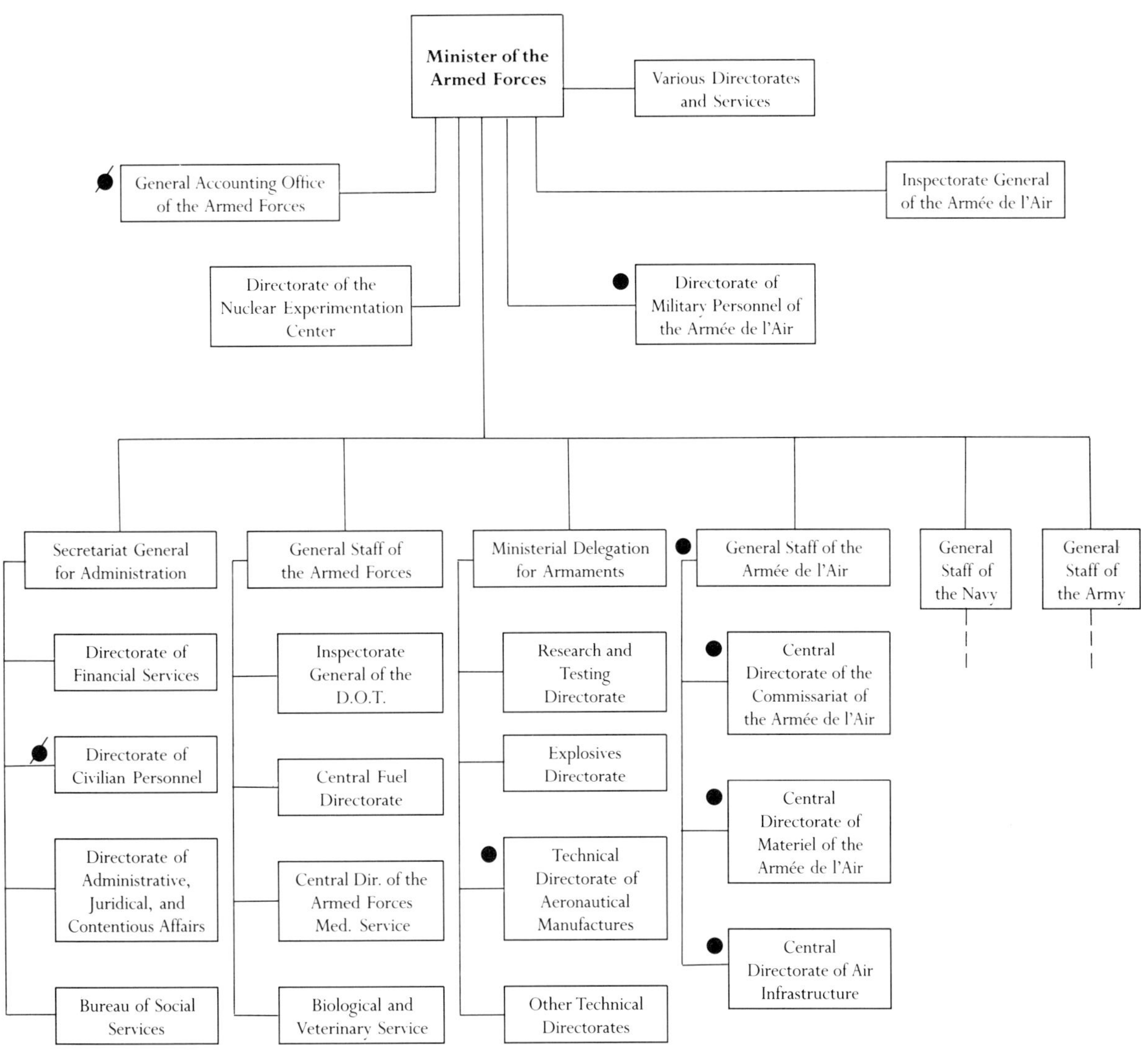

●, ⌀ Directorates which were formerly subordinated wholly (●) or in part (⌀) to the ministerial delegate for Air.

Organization of Air Base 107, Villacoublay, in 1968

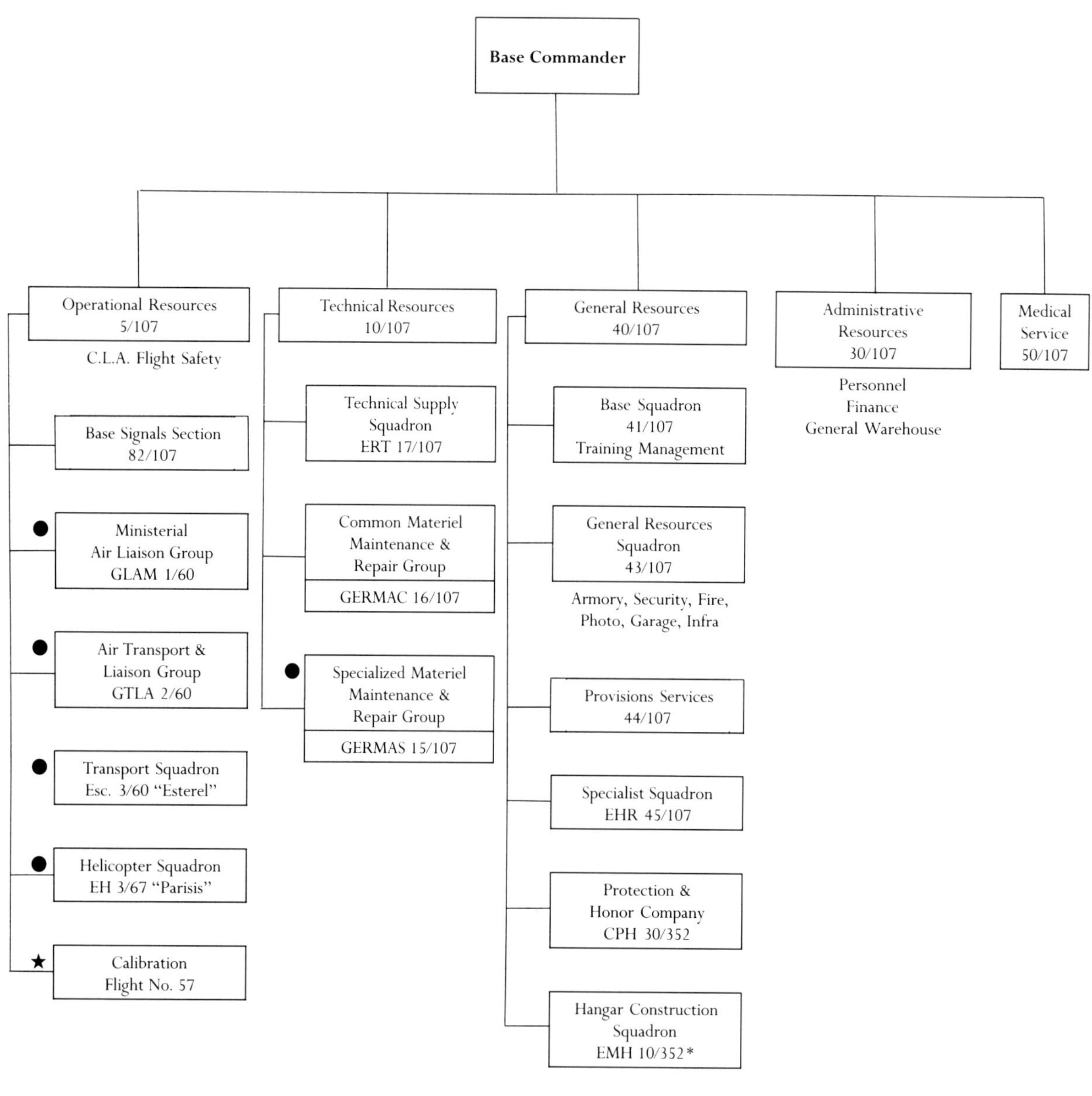

● Units of the Air Transport Command (COTAM)
★ Trans units
All other units are regional units
* Attached directly to the 2nd Region for employment

Chart of the General Organization of the Armée de l'Air at Present

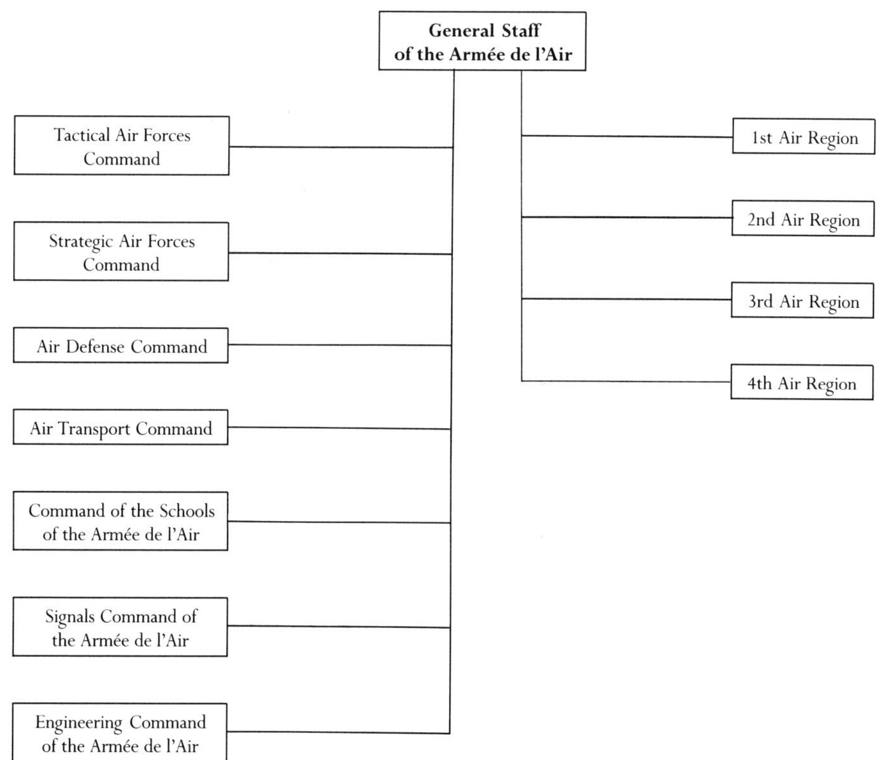

Distribution of Aircraft by Mode of Propulsion

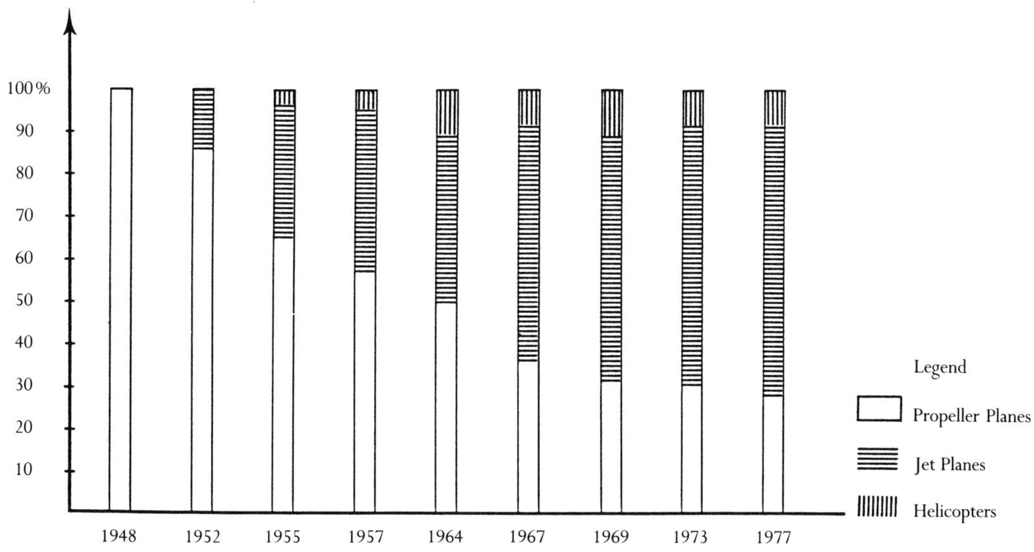

Personnel Strength of the Air Force, 1945–1973

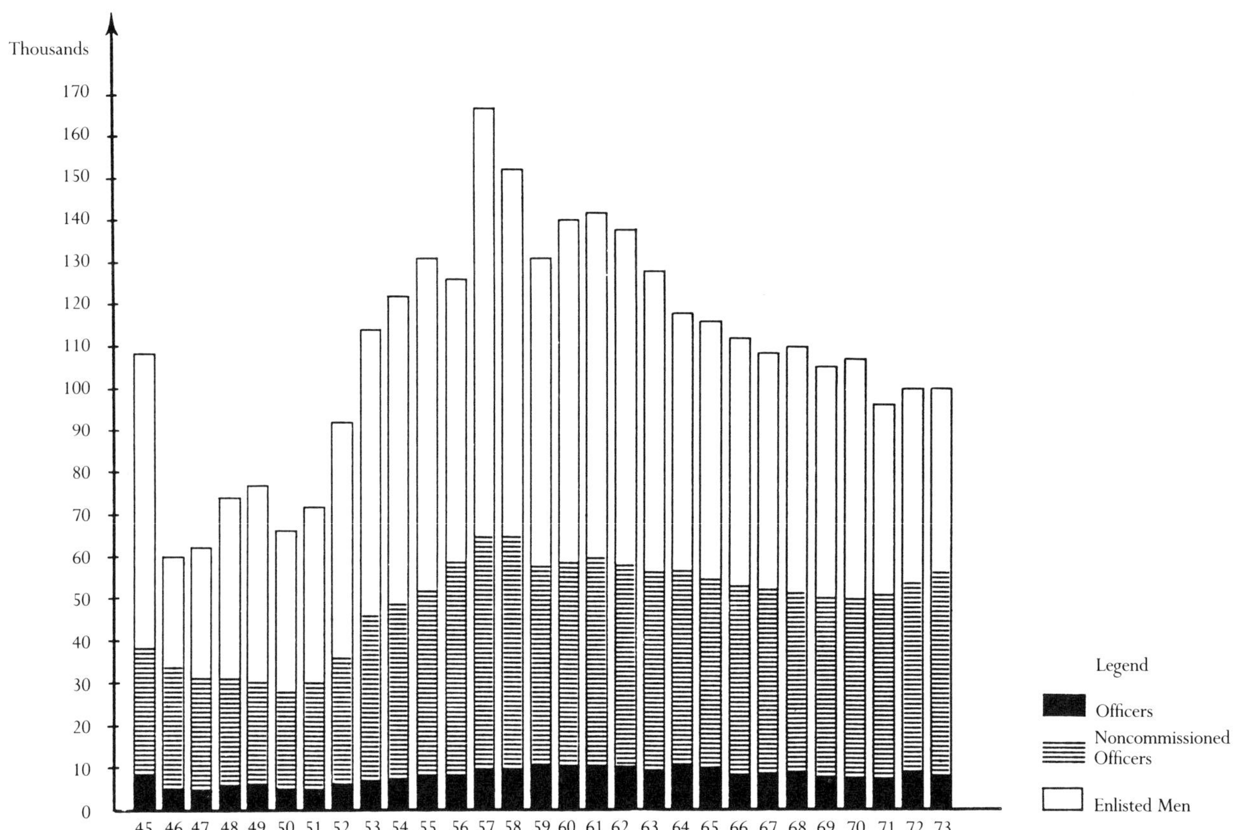

Distribution of the Aircraft in Service in the French Air Force by Country of Origin

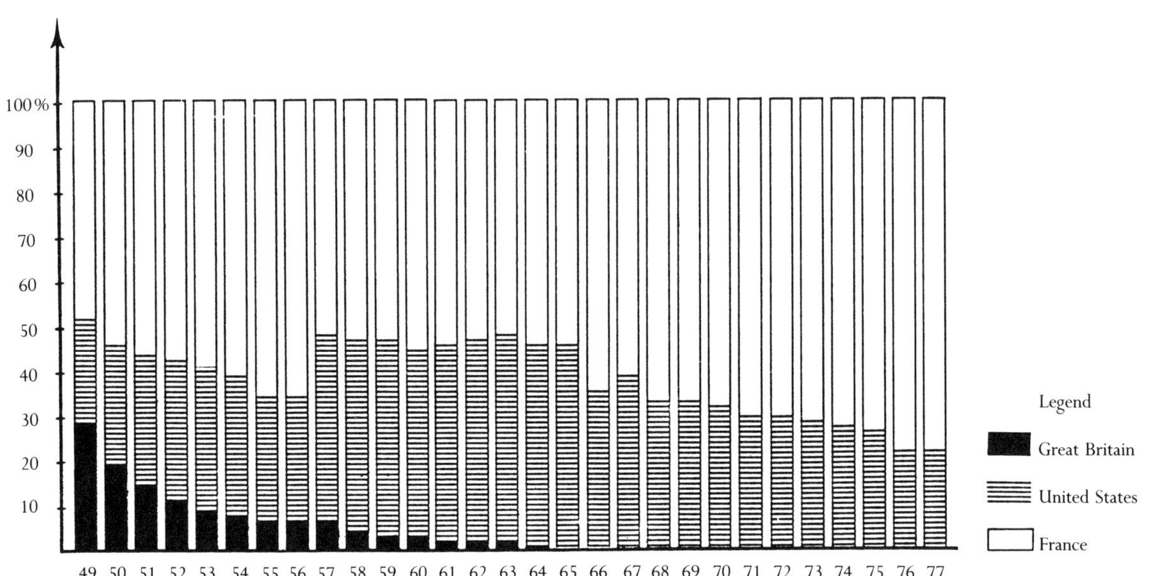

Chiefs of the General Staff and, Later, Chiefs of Staff of the Armée de l'Air since May 8, 1945

Name	Rank	Period	Title
Valin, Martial	Air Lt. General	31 Oct. '44–27 Feb. '46	Chief of the General Staff of the Armée de l'Air
Bouscat, René	Air General	28 Feb. '46–6 Sept. '46	Chief of the General Staff of the Armée de l'Air
Gerardot, Paul	Air Major General	7 Sept. '46–14 Feb. '47	Chief of the General Staff of the Armée de l'Air
Piollet, Jean-Ludy	Air Major General	15 Feb. '47–13 Jan. '48	Chief of the General Staff of the Armée de l'Air
Lecheres, Charles	Air Lt. General, later Air General	1 Feb. '48–19 Aug. '53	Chief of the General Staff of the Armée de l'Air
Fay, Pierre	Air General	20 Aug. '53–21 March '55	Chief of Staff of the Armée de l'Air
Bailly, Paul	Air Lt. General, later Air General	22 March '55–16 March '58	Chief of Staff of the Armée de l'Air
Gelee, Max	Air General	17 March '58–30 Sept. '58	Chief of Staff of the Armée de l'Air
Jouhaud, Edmond	Air General	1 Oct. '58–14 March '60	Chief of Staff of the Armée de l'Air
Stehlin, Paul	Air General	15 March '60–30 Sept. '63	Chief of Staff of the Armée de l'Air
Martin, André	Air General	1 Oct. '63–26 Feb. '67	Chief of Staff of the Armée de l'Air
Maurin, Philippe	Air General	27 Feb. '67–12 Dec. '69	Chief of Staff of the Armée de l'Air
Gauthier, Gabriel	Air General	13 Dec. '69–11 Dec. '72	Chief of Staff of the Armée de l'Air
Grigaut, Claude	Air General	12 Dec. '72–23 June '76	Chief of Staff of the Armée de l'Air
Saint-Cricq, Maurice	Air General	24 June '76–15 July '79	Chief of Staff of the Armée de l'Air
Fleury, Guy	Air General	16 July '79–	Chief of Staff of the Armée de l'Air

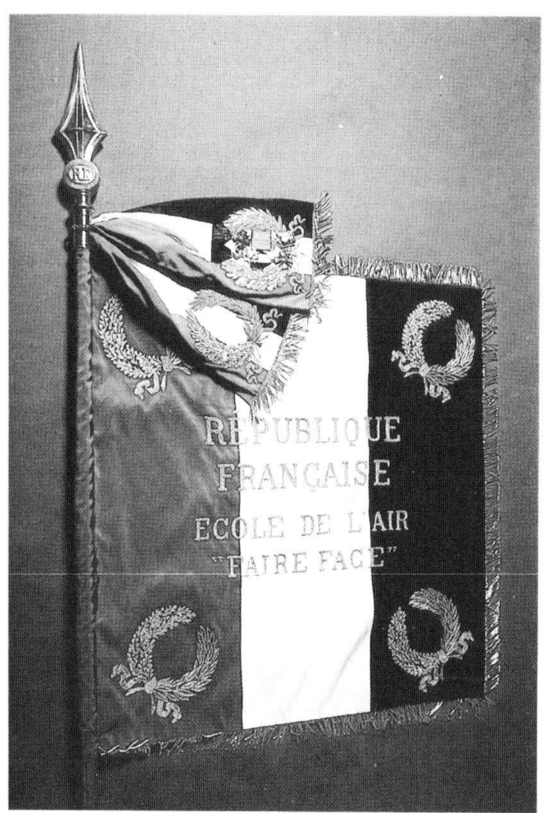

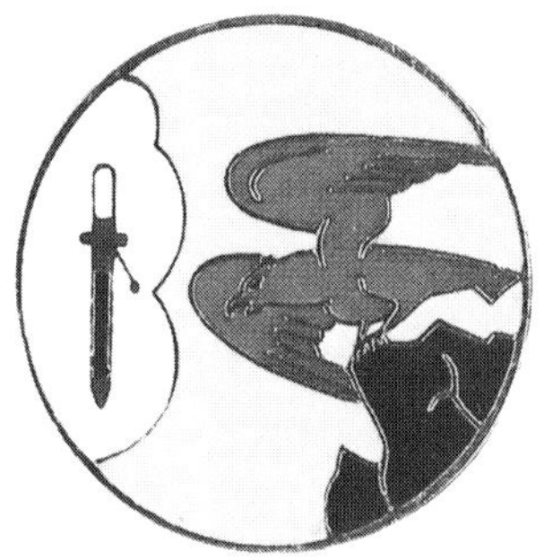

Air School Banners and Insignias.

Special Topics

THE AIR SCHOOL

The necessity of creating an Air School—a major military school on the same level as the Ecole Polytechnique, Saint Cyr, and the Naval School—was apparent from the birth of the Air Force.

Decided on by a decree of 1933, it became a reality in October 1935 when the fifty-two students of its first class entered the school, which was installed in the Petites-Ecuries at Versailles.

The school was headed by a prestigious aviator and World War I hero, General Houdemon, who had been seriously wounded in the line of duty.

The first class, creating traditions, adopted as the school song "Les Rapaces" (Birds of Prey), the song of a 1914 flight, as well as the school's insignia, a griffon vulture offering his young an officer's sword. This first class was called the "Guynemer" class.

The "chicks" of the next class, the "Captain Astier de Villatte" class, were the first to be put into fancy uniform and the last to reside at Versailles, at least before the war.

The third class assembled at Salon-de-Provence, where the "Piège" (Trap) would remain thereafter. It took the name "Mézergues."

The fourth class, called "Mailloux," organized in July 1939 the last peacetime air festival, the great "Zef" (Zephyr, or West Wind), which is still famous at Salon.

The war had already begun when the fifth class entered the school at Bordeaux, where the "Piège" had been moved because of fear of the Italians. Their instruction was brief. The class took the name of the second former student of the school to die on the field of battle, "Pinczon du Sel" (the first was Lieutenant Baize).

These first five classes were followed by many others. Those of the war years experienced different fates and a variety of stationings.

After the liberation the school was installed in the young ladies' college of Bouffémont, and then in the Petites-Ecuries again for a short time. At the end of October 1946 everyone was finally back at Salon in the sunshine of Provence. It was at Salon that the president of France, Vincent Auriol, presented the school with the cross of the Legion of Honor on April 14, 1947. As the first official celebration after the return of peace, it attracted many former students who wanted to celebrate their school as worthily as had been done at the "Grand Zef" of 1939.

The school is now definitively established at Salon, and the name of that town in Provence designates the Air School just as Saint Cyr designates the Special Military School. Class follows class, choosing names from among those of the heroes of French military aviation.

The school accepts students from foreign air forces, notably those of the French-speaking countries of Africa. It trains officers in a variety of specialties. Mechanics have had the benefit of direct recruiting since 1930, flying personnel since 1935.

In 1953 student judge advocates of the air force were included, as well as base personnel. Since 1973 the Air School has admitted "chicks" of the female sex.

Former students observe these transformations with calm and with pride. It matters little whether in the course of the years instruction at the school has put the emphasis in turn on the education of the officer, the training of the aviator, or the preparation of the engineer. The results are there, and the balance sheet that can be drawn up fifty years after the "Guynemer" class entered the school proves the quality of the "Piège."

The flag of the Air School (left) and of the Military Air School.

THE MILITARY AIR SCHOOL

In 1920 the first class of noncommissioned officers, cadet aeronautics officers, showed up at the Military Administration School in Vincennes. There were five of them. Other classes were admitted in 1921 to the schools in Fontainebleau, Saint Maixent, Saumur, and Versailles.

Beginning in 1922 two schools provided officers for Aeronautics: the school in Vincennes for accountants and for materiel inspectors (mechanics) and the school of engineering in Versailles for flying personnel.

In 1925 the School of Military and Applied Aeronautics was installed in the Petites-Ecuries in Versailles, which once housed the innnumerable horses, majestic carriages, and sedan chairs of the Sun King, Louis XIV.

The school replaced the Center of Aeronautical Studies which had been created in 1921 (and installed in the Petites-Ecuries in 1924) in order to improve the general tactical and technical instruction of the Aeronautics officers and to disseminate instruction relating to the technique and methods of employment of aviation among the officers of the other services and of the general staff.

The mission of the school was to train active and reserve cadet officers and to give second lieutenants leaving the major schools and entering aviation a complete course of instruction in that branch of the armed forces.

Thus began the assembling of cadet officers in a special Aeronautics school where flying personnel and inspectors of materiel were trained. Airplane flights were done at Villacoublay and the balloon ascensions at Mortemets, near the Swiss ornamental lake.

It should be noted that the 1926 class of materiel inspector cadet officers, commissioned on October 1, 1927, was the first to wear the emblem V (AR).

As of October 1, 1929, the Military Aeronautics School was made responsible for training all the E.O.A.'s (Air cadet officers) of the Air Force, including the future accounting officers and line officers previously trained at the school in Vincennes.

Upon the arrival in Versailles on October 1, 1935, of the first class of cadet officers of the corps of air officers coming from direct recruiting, the School of Military and Applied Aeronautics was transformed into the Air School. The order of May 28, 1935, relating to the provisional organization of an Air School in Versailles further specified that it was to provide training for the different corps of noncommissioned officers, cadet officers of the Air Force admitted to the competition of officers of the corps.

The idea of a Military Air School, which derives from an order of 1930, disappeared. In fact, this school existed under that name, as is known from the official documents. Thus an organizational order of 1952 specifies that the "Ecole des E.O.A." (Air Cadet Officers' School) is placed under the command of the general commanding the Air School.

The recruiting of officers from the E.O.A., interrupted in 1940, was resumed in 1942. From 1942 to 1944 the Military Air School recruited its cadets in France, French North Africa, and Indochina. The division of officers of the administrative services was installed in Toulouse, France, and Rabat, Morocco, during that period. Since 1945 it has been located in Salon-de-Provence.

The creation of the base officers' corps and of the Air Supply Corps School led in 1955 to the end of the recruitment of officers for the administrative services.

From 1922 to 1978 fifty-eight classes had gone through the Military Air School. Since 1945 those classes have borne the names of deceased officers, thus recalling to the young officers the memory of their honored predecessors.

THREE PRESIDENTIAL PLANES USED BY THE MINISTERIAL AIR LIAISON GROUP (G. L. A. M.)

The DC-4, number F-RAFA.

The Caravelle in which General de Gaulle often traveled.

The last of the "presidential" planes, the Falcon 50, number F-RAFI.

Valérie André.

Maryse Bastié.

Maryse Hilsz.

WOMEN IN THE FRENCH AIR FORCE

The idea of using female volunteers in military aviation is an old one. Even before the First World War Marthe Richard, a licensed pilot, proposed to General Hirschauer the creation of a female flight. He refused, however, saying that the plan was contrary to the Hague Convention of 1907.

Marie Marvingt and Hélène Dutrieu's idea of an ambulance transport aviation service met the same fate. In 1939 Madeleine Charmaux also took up the idea of a women's air auxiliary for medical and postal transport, but without success.

However, on September 1, 1939, Maryse Hilsz, Maryse Bastié, Claire Roman, and Paulette Bray-Bouquet were pressed into service to do convoy work.

The Resistance and the FAFL were to mark the real entry of French women into armed action. In the Resistance women participated in many networks. Among those of the aeronautical branch were Maryse Bastié, Suzanne Melk, and Suzanne Jannin.

After Simone Mathieu had created the women volunteers of the FFL, a special aviation status was defined on December 20, 1941, in London by Lieutenant Colonel Pigeaud, chief of staff of the FAFL. Second Lieutenant Ria Hackin, the first woman of the air forces to die in service, in the Atlantic, received the Cross of the Liberation posthumously.

The Women's Air Forces, made official on June 27, 1944, had 6,000 volunteers at the end of that year. Among them was the famous actress Josephine Baker, who served as a second lieutenant.

At the beginning of 1945 there was a pilot training course organized at the Châteauroux base with Tiger Moths and A-24's, but it was not repeated. At about the same time the mission of repatriation of prisoners and deportees entrusted to the military air transport led to a demand for the services of volunteer nurses. This became the point of departure for the recruiting of the famous "I.P.S.A.," Air First-Aid Nurse Pilots. Given a civilian charter in October 1946, they were later to furnish the basis of the Women's Air Convoy Corps created in 1951.

Moreover, several women pilots served as officers. Two of them, Maryse Hilsz and Maryse Bastié, died as pilots in the line of duty, the first aboard a Siebel in 1946 and the second aboard a Nord 2501 in 1954.

The situation of women personnel was better defined by the charter of October 15, 1951, which created the general service organization and that of the women's air convoy service.

Recruited under special conditions to serve in Indochina, women pilots like Valérie André and Suzanne Jannin carried out extremely daring medical evacuations. Valérie André, airplane and helicopter pilot and physician, has had a brilliant career, which she is still pursuing and which in 1976 made her the first French woman to be promoted to the rank of general.

In 1973 the new charter, the work of Defense Minister Michel Debré, adopted rules for women personnel analogous to those decreed in the charters for airmen. Since then, as the juridical distinction between male and female personnel has been practically abolished, women have access to the normal corps of officers and noncommissioned officers.

However, a maximum quota of 15 percent of the total of the corps is set for the recruitment of women officers, who have access by the traditional routes—competitions and rank—to the base officers' corps and the officer mechanics' corps.

In 1978 there were 149 women officers and 3,500 noncommissioned officers serving in the French Air Force.

PROTOTYPES

SO 6020 Espadon.

SE 212-01 Durandal.

Nord 1405 Gerfaut-II.

SE 2410 Grognard.

SE 5000 Baroudeur.

Leduc 022.

Breguet 1001 Taon.

Nord 1500 Griffon.

SO 9000 Trident.

a.

b.

c.

d.

e.

f.

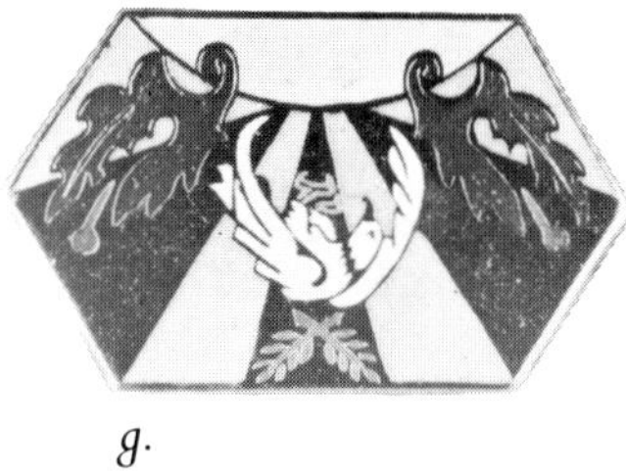

g.

h.

i.

j.

k.

a. Regional Establishment of the Air Commissariat (ERCA) 782, Evreux.
b. ERCA 781, Rheims.
c. ERCA 784, Portes-lès-Valence.
d. ERCA 783, Toulouse-l'Hers.
e. Subsidiary Regional Establishment of the Air Commissariat (ERACA) 02/781, Dole-Ville.
f. Territorial Air Administrative Center (CATA) 852, Tours.
g. CATA 854, Aix-en-Provence.
h. Administrative Service of the Air Commissariat (SACA) 00/875, Paris.
i. CATA 851, Metz.
j. CATA 853, Bordeaux.
k. Materiel Research and Procurement Service of the Air Commissariat (SETAMCA) 00/796, Brétigny.

THE AIR COMMISSARIAT

From the very beginning of the Air Force the need was felt to have an entity responsible for the administrative supervision provided for in the law of 1882. The draft of the law of 1934 defining the Air Force's organic charter provided for the creation of the specialized corps of air commissioners. For reasons of economy this was rejected by the French Parliament, however.

It was, therefore, necessary to have recourse to the intendance, which placed an intendant, as technical adviser, with each air region commander and then on the general staff. This solution was not satisfactory, and so on December 28, 1940, twelve positions of air intendant were created by the finance act.

The act of February 17, 1942, created the corps of air commissioner/paymasters. These were provided with a charter of authorities and responsibilities analogous to those of the intendants. They were recruited by a competition open to Air Force captains from the other areas of specialization. Those who were selected pursued two years of studies at the Intendance School (Ecole Supérieur de l'Intendance).

The organization of the Air Intendance had already taken shape around the territorial structure defined by the law of 1934. In 1941 the services were organized on the same principles in France and in North Africa. After 1942 the directorates situated in France experienced many changes of fortune, especially the one in the North zone, and it was quite naturally the "North African" segment that reorganized the service in Paris after the liberation.

The central service then was called the Directorate of Intendance and Administration of the Air Force, and it was not until 1947 that the official designation became Directorate of the Commissariat of the Air Force. At the same time the Technical Inspectorate of the Air Commissariat was also established. Thus, apart from the central depots, the Air Commissariat consisted only of the regional directorates. The regional directors had under their direct orders: 1) the Intendances of the Air Bases, which would become the Commissariats of the Air Bases, and 2) the regional clothing stocks. It is not possible to describe here in detail the entire range of the service, which spread from Germany via the overseas territories to Indochina.

The general revival of the Air Force after 1950 suddenly posed the problem of recruitment for the corps of commissioner/paymasters. The number of men in the corps had to be increased, for apart from administrative officers few captains took the examination for the Intendance School.

The idea that prevailed was to leave the commissioners with the authorities and responsibilities of intendants while providing them with a charter similar to that of the navy commissioners. This was done by a decree of April 28, 1953, and the first class of cadet air commissioners entered the Air School at Salon in October of the same year. The new name for the officers was better chosen; the term "paymaster" was dropped.

One should note in passing that at the time it was issued the decree was attacked before the Council of State by Lieutenant Colonel Roynette of the corps of air administrative officers and was then annulled as ultra vires (that is, going beyond legal authority) on October 16, 1959.

The law of July 30, 1960, put things back as they were, and, since it was retroactive to April 1953, the work accomplished and the situation of the personnel did not suffer from the High Assembly's decree.

As the corps evolved its functions were modified in the successive Air Force reorganizations.

The Territorial Air Administrative Centers (C.A.T.A.) had been created in 1951 under the authority of the commissioners of the bases in the aim of relieving the line officers of their administrative tasks.

More significant changes came with the establishment of the big functional commands, which set up a vertical structure not provided by the law of 1934. Decisions made in 1964 limited the administrative weight of this creation. Since the big commands had no services at their disposal, the air commissioner assigned to them was given the functions of a technical adviser. The commanders of regions, of course, being responsible for the combined logistics, continued as in the past to have on their staffs a director of the Air Commissariat.

The important modification of the commissariat came in 1972, when the administrative direction of the air bases was entrusted to the air commissioners as deputies, for that purpose, to the commanding officers of the bases. The pretext seized upon was that of getting operating budgets started, but beyond that it was an attempt to improve the administrative service and to draw the flying personnel and the commissioners closer together. In that sense the reform was in the same line as the adoption of direct recruiting or the terms served by the young commissioners, from 1956 on, in the flying units.

As the commissioners were designated to head the administration of the bases the C.B.A.'s were gradually phased out.

Today the Air Commissariat has reached full maturity. Its functions are defined by a decree of February 15, 1980. It is commissioned to: provide for the needs of the personnel; insure that the regulations concerning the operating budget are applied; work out the administrative regulations; exercise administrative supervision; advise the command in its area of competence; and participate in various administrative acts.

The central director, responsible to the minister for the administration and management of the entire service and placed under the authority of the chief of the Air Force general staff, has at his disposal for the exercise of these functions: the inspector of the Air Commissariat; the network of commissioners—directors of the commissariat of the air regions, technical advisers of the big commands, and the chief of the administrative resources of the air bases; a central establishment, the Materiel Research and Procurement Service of the Air Commissariat (S.E.T.A.M.C.A.) in Brétigny; external entities subordinate to the central directorate—an administrative service of the Air Commissariat (S.A.C.A.) in Paris, four regional establishments of the Air Commissariat (E.R.C.A.), plus one subsidiary establishment, and entities dependent on the regional directors (four territorial administrative centers of the Air Commissariat, C.A.T.A.).

THE PATROLS

The patrol of Etampes.

Major Gauthier's patrol, using Vampires.

The patrol of France today.

The first patrol of France, under Major de Lachenal, in F-84's.

A little-known patrol, the Guimauve Patrol, taking off in Nord 2501's. Patrol maintained by the crews of the C.I.E.T. (Training Center for Transport Crews).

The Franco-British antiradar missile, Matra A.S. 37 Martel, with which Mirage III E's and Jaguars are equipped at all times.

Jaguars.

Insignia of the staff of the Tactical Air Force and 1st Air Region, Metz-Frescaty.

THE TACTICAL AIR FORCE

Heir of the 1st Air Division and the 1st C.A.T.A.C., the Tactical Air Force Command, merged with the command of the 1st Air Region, is stationed at Metz-Frescaty.

The Mission

"Adapted" to the First Army and accordingly ready to support ground operations, the Tactical Air Force (F.A.Tac.) may also be called upon to participate in multinational operations designed to maintain free access to Berlin, mount an overseas expeditionary force, or be engaged in the face of any threat posed on any of the French frontiers or seacoasts.

The Combat Resources

6 fighter squadrons:
2nd Squadron, at Dijon
3rd Squadron, at Nancy-Ochey
4th Squadron, at Luxeuil
7th Squadron, at Saint Dizier
11th Squadron, at Toul
13th Squadron, at Colmar
1 reconnaissance squadron (E.R.):
33rd E.R., at Strasbourg

Either 8 groups of Mirage III E-B-BE's, 8 groups of Jaguars, and 2 groups of Mirage 5 F's
Or 3 groups of Mirage III R's and RD's

These planes are equipped with A.S. 37 antiradar missiles, A.S. 30 air-to-ground rockets, or "Magic" air-to-air rockets. They can be equipped with the A.N. 52 tactical atomic weapon.

Supplementary Aerial Resources

A prediction and radar instruction center (C.P.I.R.) equipped with Mystère XX's
A blind flight training center (C.E.V.S.V.) with T 33's
A liaison group equipped with M.S. 760 Parises, Nord 262's, and Broussards
A helicopter group equipped with Alouette II's and III's
An electronic flight equipped with Nord 2501's

Command and Control Resources

The F.A.Tac. has at its disposal for carrying out its missions a mobile tactical control system which supplements with a set of mobile radar and signal units the stationary air defense system, with which it is continuously connected, an air support operation center, advanced guidance posts, and advanced tactical air command posts.

Insignia of the Strategic Air Forces.

The S.S.B.S. missile S.3 in its silo.

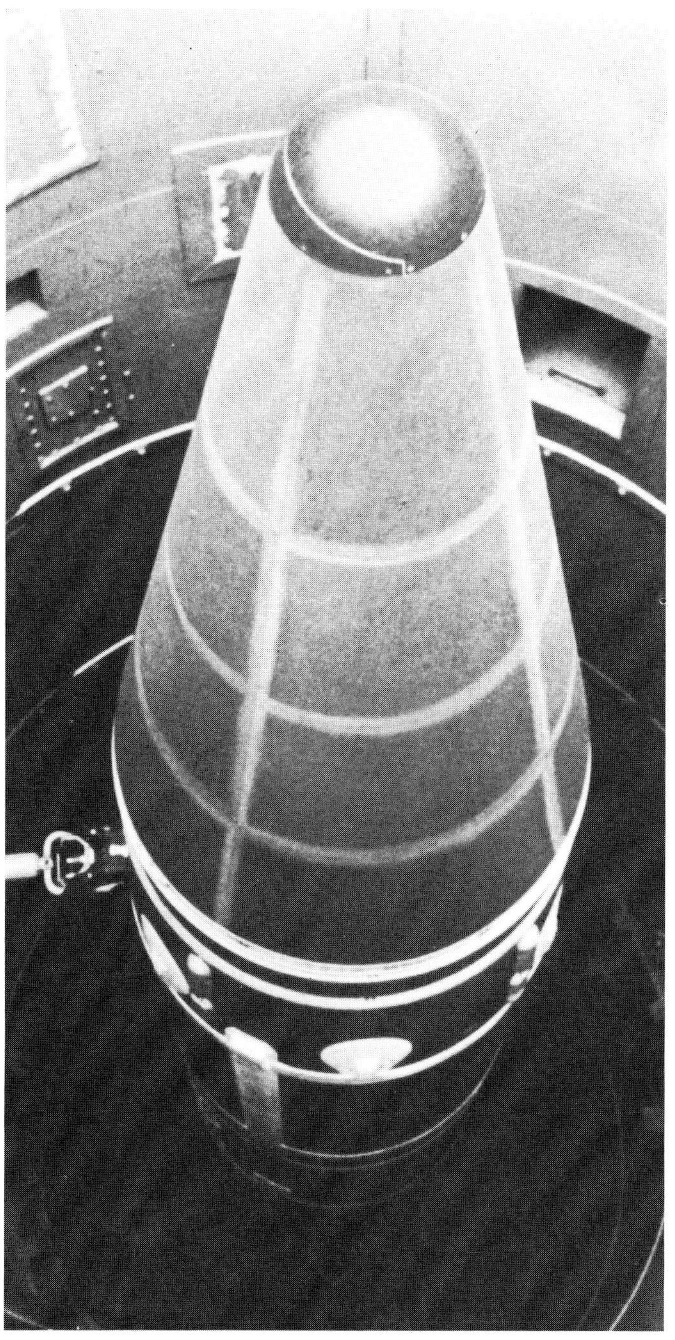

THE STRATEGIC AIR FORCES

In order to base its defense on nuclear deterrence France has acquired a set of strategic forces comprising submarines armed with sea-to-ground rockets, Mirage IV's, and strategic ground-to-ground rockets. The first of these components comes under the responsibility of the Navy; the Strategic Air Command, however, directs the other two.

Created in 1964, the Strategic Air Forces (F.A.S.) were first given, in October of that year, the Mirage IV's and their complement, the Boeing C-135 refueling planes. In 1971 the first Strategic Missile Grouping (G.M.S.) became operational at the base of Saint Christol.

The Mission

The general in command of the F.A.S. is responsible for maintaining the forces under his command in condition so that they can be readied for action at any moment in accordance with the government's orders. For this task of maintenance he is under the orders of the Air Force chief of staff; for the employment of his forces he is directly responsible to the head of state, the president of France. The commanding general of the F.A.S. would thus receive from the president orders to "assume a posture of readiness" and, if the circumstances demanded it, the order to engage his forces.

The Means

The F.A.S. comprise a staff and a technical directorate, two operations centers (the CO.F.A.S.), combat units, training units, and maintenance organizations.

The Operations Centers

CO.F.A.S. 1 is located at Taverny; CO.F.A.S. 2, ready to relieve the first, is at Lyon-Mont-Verdun. Controlling all of the strategic air forces, these two operations centers have especially reliable ground-to-ground and ground-air-ground transmitter systems. They are responsible for transmitting to the planes and missiles any engagement orders issued by the president of France.

The Air Resources

The units comprise bombing squadrons equipped with Mirage IV's and squadrons of Boeing C-135 F's for refueling in flight. Part of these resources is on continuous alert. With the adapted technique, functioning twenty-four hours a day, the force has an availability rate close to 90 percent.

The S.S.B.S. Weapons System

The S.S.B.S. missiles are based on the plateau of Albion in the Haute-Provence region in the south of France. There are 18 missiles buried in silos within a radius of 30 kilometers around Saint Christol. These missiles can carry a 150-kiloton nuclear charge—megaton warheads were recently installed—to a distance of 3,000 kilometers.

Here again, continuity is required, and the S.S.B.S.'s are subject to the following alerts: Condition Blue—possible firing of the 18 missiles within a time span of less than five minutes (this is the normal and regular state) and Condition Red—possible firing of the 18 missiles in less than one minute.

A recently created force, the Strategic Air Force is of considerable importance. It can have total effectiveness, however, only as long as the other means at the disposal of the Air Force are maintained at a very high operational level.

A Mirage IV being refueled by a Boeing C-135.

The Mirage F 1, equipped with Matra Super 530 rockets.

AIR DEFENSE

The lack of a coherent organization for the Air Defense of the Territory (D.A.T.) was painfully felt before the Second World War. As early as 1944 a D.A.T. command was created, and the Air Defense Command of today is derived directly from it.

The Mission

It is the mission of Air Defense to: keep watch over the French sky at all times to detect and identify any aerial movement and, if necessary, to evaluate the threat that it represents; give the alarm; challenge any unknown or hostile planes and have them identify themselves; and destroy hostile airplanes.

In addition, Air Defense controls military air traffic in close collaboration with the civil control centers; flies missions of in-flight assistance to aircraft of all kinds in difficulties; and flies search and salvage missions for crashed or missing planes.

The Means: Detection

To carry out its detection mission Air Defense has a radar network which makes possible the complete and continuous coverage of the territory up to an altitude of 50,000 meters.

Among the principal radars used are: 23-centimeter radars, which give an air space situation on a horizontal plane; Satrap radars, gradually coming into service, which take altitude measurements; and Palmier G radars, which measure direction, distance, and altitude and which resist electronic jamming.

The data obtained by radar are transmitted to the Air Defense Operations Center (C.O.D.A.) at Taverny. Supplemented with data furnished by neighboring and allied countries, they give the C.O.D.A. an instantaneous visualization of the air situation up to more than 1,000 kilometers from French borders.

To analyze the situation and make the decisions demanded by them it is necessary to be informed very quickly. Since manual systems are no longer adequate for this, the Air Defense has a System of Processing and Presentation of Air Defense Data (S.T.R.I.D.A.).

The Means: Intervention

The means for taking action are primarily airplanes, essentially Mirage F 1's, although one squadron is still equipped with Mirage III C's. These planes are armed with Magic ground-to-ground missiles for short range or Matra Super 530's for long range. These air resources, if the situation should require it, can be reinforced with Mirage III E's from the F.A.Tac. or with Crusaders from the Aéronavale.

Radar.

In addition, the Air Defense coordinates the action of the planes and the antiaircraft artillery belonging to the Army. This artillery consists of 30 and 40 Bofors light artillery, Hawk missiles, and Crotale missiles. Finally, beginning in 1978, 20-millimeter double-barreled guns have been coming back into service.

Operational Organization

The general commanding the Air Defense directs the complete accomplishment of the mission through the C.O.D.A.

French territory is divided into Air Defense Zones (Z.A.D.) adapted to the regions. The general commanding a zone, operationally associated with the general commanding an air region, is directly subordinate to the general commanding Air Defense.

In each Air Defense zone there is a Zone Operational Center (C.O.Z.) linked to the C.O.D.A. responsible (under the authority of the general commanding the Z.A.D.) for the decisions on engagement and for the conduct of the air battle in the zone.

The Transall.

MILITARY AIR TRANSPORT

Although a great deal of thought had been given in the past to the possibilities offered by military air transport, it was the Second World War that provided concrete proof of its effectiveness.

Military transport groups were created in French North Africa, while the Free French Air Forces started up the military airlines. An urgent need to develop these facilities arose in 1945.

The C-47 Dakota and Ju 52 transport planes, to which the Halifax and B-26 Marauder bombers were added, were combined in a provisional grouping, the G.M.M.T.A. (Grouping of Military Air Transport Facilities) to carry out an urgent mission of repatriation of prisoners and deportees. The G.M.M.T.A. not only outlasted the mission for which it had been created but also prospered. Without a break it participated in the Far Eastern and Algerian operations and also provided numerous military transports. It was dissolved in 1963 and became at that time the Military Air Transport Command (CO.T.A.M.).

The Mission

The mission of this command is to train its crews for air transports and parachute operations under wartime conditions and to provide the occasional or regular military transports needed in peacetime.

Many remarkable missions have been accomplished in recent years, such as the technical assistance to the polar expeditions in Greenland and Spitsbergen in 1977 and the tactical transport at Kolwezi in 1978.

To accomplish these missions the CO.T.A.M. has:

1) Four transport squadrons: the 63rd, at Toulouse, the 64th, at Evreux, the 65th, at Villacoublay, and the 61st, at Orleans.

2) Two units of a special type: the Ministerial Air Liaison Group (G.L.A.M.), at Villacoublay, specializing in the transport of members of the government, and the Esterel transport group, at Villacoublay, equipped with DC 8's.

3) Five liaison groups or mixed groups (liaison transport): the mixed air group Vaucluse, at Evreux, the liaison group Médoc, at Bordeaux, the liaison group Mistral, at Aix-les-Milles, the liaison and salvage group of Solenzara, and the liaison group Verdun, at Metz.

4) Five helicopter squadrons (E.H.): E.H. Parisis, at Villacoublay, Pyrenees, at Cazaux, Alpilles, at Istres, Valmy, at Metz, and Durance, at Apt.

5) Six overseas transport squadrons (E.T.O.M.) and two transport detachments: E.T.O.M. Ouessant, at Dakar, Ouessant, at Saint-Denis-de-la-Réunion, Ouessant, at Djibouti, Maine, at Faaa, Maine, at Cayenne, and Maine, at Nouméa.

6) The transport detachments at Abidjan and Libreville.

To these are added the center for training transport crews, at Toulouse, and the center for training helicopter crews, at Chambéry.

The CO.T.A.M. uses:

For transport: DC 8's, Caravelles, C 160 Transalls, and Nord 2501 Noratlases.

For liaison: Nord 262 Frigates, M.S. 760 Parises, M.H. 1521 Broussards, and Twin Otters.

Helicopters: S.A. 330 Pumas, Alouette III's, and Alouette II's.

With 4,000 persons, a third of them flying personnel, and a stock of 400 planes and helicopters, the CO.T.A.M. travels 100,000 flight hours a year, transports over 500,000 passengers and over 20,000 tons of freight, and drops over 300,000 parachutists and 3,000 tons of materiel.

Insignia of the Air Force School.

The Alpha Jet.

AIR FORCE SCHOOLS

In the interwar period the need to have schools capable of furnishing the necessary specialists in all fields of military aviation was not always adequately perceived. The first training plan worthy of the name was decided upon and decreed in 1938 thanks to the energetic efforts of General Vuillemin.

As early as 1945 the Air Force was aware that the quality of its personnel was the indispensable basis for realizing an air force of high quality. At that time several schools were reopened or created, some of which are still training Air Force personnel.

The direction of these schools, entrusted in turn to a command, a region, and then to the 5th Bureau of the staff, has been exercised since 1963 by a big specialized command, the Command of Air Force Schools (C.E.A.A.).

Apart from the Air School and the Military Air School, which do not come under the C.E.A.A. except for basic pilot training, the Air Force schools annually train 1,600 officers, including 1,300 reserve officers, 200 pilots and navigators, and 3,000 nonflying technicians. They also provide retraining for 4,000 noncommissioned officers every year.

There are about fifty specialties covered in the schools. The personnel trained, the duration of the training, and the level of the studies vary considerably from one specialty to another, and this explains the complexity of the problems to be solved. Programs of study are divided among 16 different schools or training centers, organizing 200 curricula and giving over 2,000 different courses.

For the flying personnel, the noncommissioned officer candidates, after taking tests at the Air Force Selection Center, are assigned to the Beginning School for Flying Personnel at Aulnat, where they are subject to a preliminary selection on C.A.P. 10 and are then given military training.

Upon completion of the program at Aulnat they are trained as pilots with Fouga Magisters at Cognac. Then, depending on their specialty, they are sent to Tours (for combat pilots) or to Avord (for future transport pilots). Navigators are trained at Toulouse before practicing on Transalls or Mirage IV's.

When they leave Tours, after having flown T 33's and Alpha Jets, the fighter pilots finish their training at Cazaux with Mystère IV's while learning to shoot.

Two paths are open to the nonflying personnel: that of the Air Force Technical Training School (E.E.T.A.A.) at Saintes, for boys of fifteen to sixteen years of age, and that of the Beginning Noncommissioned Officer Training School (E.F.I.S.O.) at Nîmes, which can be entered at the age of seventeen. In these basic schools the future noncommissioned officers are oriented toward the specialty corresponding to their choice and their capabilities.

Depending on these specialties they are trained at the Air Force Technical School at Rochefort, the Training Grouping at Evreux, or at the training centers in Chambéry, Dijon, Bordeaux, Cazaux, and Apt.

Beyond this initial training the C.E.A.A. provides advanced training for noncommissioned officer specialists in courses designed to give them the knowledge needed to serve as higher specialists or masters.

Finally, the School Command trains the instructors that work in the various centers.

This major activity of the Air Force plays a certain economic role in the country, which benefits from the training given to specialists who, at the end of their enlistment period, provide valuable, high-quality personnel for French industry.

Signals insignia.

SIGNALS

The importance of signals went unrecognized for a long time. The military aeronautics signals, and later the signals troops and services command, created in 1939, nevertheless tried to provide aviation with the networks that it needed.

Since the end of the Second World War the Air Force has realized that its effectiveness depends on the quality of its communications. The Air Signals Command was created in 1946 and the Air Telecommunications Exploitation Service in 1958.

In 1963, at the same time as the other big Air Force commands, the Air Force Signals Command (C.T.A.A.) was established. This command provides ground-to-ground communications over great distances via Hertzian cables or radio. On the other hand, air-to-ground, ground-to-air, and sometimes specific ground-to-ground communications of the big consumer commands belong solely to them.

The C.T.A.A. is responsible for the establishment, maintenance, and maneuver of the infrastructure signals networks of the Air Force. It has the following specialized units: Hertzian cable squads (E.C.H.) responsible for the Air 70 network; automatic telegraphic relay centers (C.R.A.T.), which operate the automatic digital data relays (R.A.I.D.); signals centers; installation and repair units; an electronics squad entrusted with protection of the networks; and a calibration flight for radio and electric aids.

A Hertzian wave terminal.

THE AIR ENGINEERS

The Air Engineering Corps began with a first organization set up in 1937 for the benefit of the Air Force with the "Air chief engineers" of the army engineering corps.

As early as 1939 the Air Force organized, parallel to this, "airfield companies" made up essentially of reservist public works specialists. It thus acquired the first organized units specialized in air infrastructure and under the Air Force's authority.

After the armistice in 1940 these units were dissolved. The Allied landing in North Africa led the Supreme Air Command to reconstitute them. They were in Corsica at the time of the liberation of that island, where they made a brilliant debut on the Ghisonaccia airfield.

Equipped with combat vehicles, the two companies that were activated (the 71st and 72nd) completed the airfield on the date required in view of the operations in Italy. In June 1944 in Oujda, Morocco, the 71st Air Engineering Battalion received modern equipment under the Lend Lease Act.

Within the 9th Engineer Command this battalion built, among others, a runway and its appurtenances at Dole-Tavaux and a runway at Colmar. In Germany it participated in the reconditioning and extension of a number of other runways.

Dissolved in 1946, the Air Engineering Corps was reestablished in 1949 in a very original form. In order to organize the units quickly it appealed to the army, which had personnel already trained in this area. For its part, the Air Force called upon its contingents of draftees for the enlisted men needed and assumed responsibility for the whole budget.

A joint decree of the Ministries of Air and War of January 13, 1950, made the creation of the new Air Engineering Corps official.

At present the Air Engineering Command has a strength of 2,300 persons and a stock of about 1,400 vehicles or machines. Its peacetime organization comprises: the Air Engineering Command, a staff whose central echelon is NEDEX (detonation of unexploded shells), and a technical directorate; and operational units, which include the 15th Air Engineering Regiment, at Toul, made up of a regimental staff and five companies (one C.C.S. company, one support company, one training company, and two works companies); the 25th Air Engineering Regiment, at Compiègne, with an identical structure; the 45th Reinforced Air Engineering Company, at Istres; and a Specialized Instruction Center (C.I.S.G.A.), an autonomous unit attached to the 15th Air Engineering Regiment.

Conclusion

The use of the air in war seems to have been presaged at the time of the French Revolution by the balloon used at Fleurus. In fact, military aerostation developed from 1877 on, but the year that became the point of departure for French military aviation was a much later one—1909, the date of the creation of the Permanent Aeronautics Inspectorate.

Since then military aeronautics has undergone an extraordinary development. In order to put the actual conditions of this development into context it is necessary to bear in mind a number of facts that clarify the difficulties with which its evolution has been surrounded.

First of all, one finds that the history of this military aviation has been written in less than eighty years. It is young, very young, in comparison with the other branches of the armed forces.

The second observation is that since its beginnings French military aviation has been at war most of the time. The only periods of relative peace that it has known were from 1909 to 1914, from 1934 to 1939, and from 1961 to the present. The wars that it has had to wage have marked its development in very different ways. The First World War revealed the importance of air action and saw the launching of the techniques and tactics that were to be used later on, as well as the birth of the new service's traditions—moral forces without which it would have had no future at all.

The colonial wars, both those of the interwar period and those of Indochina, Madagascar, and Algeria, sometimes give a false image of the employment of aviation, which was enough to influence certain judgments concerning the utilization of planes in the European theater of operations.

The Second World War confirmed the lessons of the first. In it aviation demonstrated, in addition to its potential for conducting independent actions, its capabilities for engaging and winning the preliminary air battle which would then enable it to provide the other armed services with its powerful contribution to victories on land and sea.

Unfortunately, in spite of the bravery of the crews, who in May and June 1940 provided the proof of what they could have done with materiel that was adequate in both quantity and quality, France experienced one of the most dismal defeats in its history. French aviation continued or resumed the fight on the side of the Allies, and that gave it a moral, intellectual, and technical capital that was of great assistance in carrying out its renewal in the 1950s and in later years as well.

Confronted with wars, aviation is also faced with an acceleration of technical advances. In no other area has this acceleration been so overwhelming. It suffices to compare an airplane of 1910 with its successor of 1980. The fragile early machine of wood and cloth with a maximum speed of barely 90 kilometers per hour contrasts sharply with the metal jet plane of today, whose speed far exceeds twice the speed of sound.

The aviator is marked by this technological progress. This may perhaps explain, at least to a certain extent, those debates on doctrine that have arisen ever since the birth of aeronautics. They could not, of course, take place today in the nuclear age, when the different branches of the armed forces are perfectly conscious of their roles in the nation's defense.

Within these armed forces the French Air Force is now conceded to be a major component of national defense. The aeronautics industry, thanks to the effort made after the liberation, has become the third most important in the world and produces materiel that can bear comparison in every respect with that used by the air forces of other nations.

The officer schools provide French aviation with leaders of very high quality. The effort made for the training of personnel places at its disposal highly qualified technicians, who are appreciated as such by the whole country.

The air units, serviced by experienced professionals, are trained solely with a view toward their engagement in operations. This ability to measure up in peacetime to actual wartime conditions is undoubtedly one of the factors that differs most from the situation of the interwar period.

High-quality materiel and a clear consciousness of the mission imposed on it have developed an excellent state of mind and fine morale in today's Air Force. Proud of its past, it also has confidence in its future.

It is not the task of the historian to predict that future. On this point he can do no better than to quote the words of one of the Air Force chiefs of staff.

Continuous availability, instantaneous power, and mobility seem today to be the principal qualities of the armed forces. Guarantors of the safety of the major instruments of deterrence and relying on the threat of resort to nuclear arms in the European theater, safeguarding the national sovereignty on its territory and in its maritime and air spaces, they must also constitute the means of limited external actions whose effectiveness will depend on the speed as well as on the force of such intervention.

The air arm exhibits precisely the characteristics needed for those actions. The organization of the air forces into specialized operational commands supported by a well-adapted territorial organization and their time-honored aptitude for continuous alert make them able to go into action on very short notice.

The instrument that is represented by the Air Force has the qualities of flexibility and adaptation needed to cope with its missions of today and of tomorrow.

Index

References to illustrations are in boldface type.